THE ECONOMICS OF ENVIRONMENT AND DEVELOPMENT

Dedication

To Jo, with love and thanks

The Economics of Environment and Development

Selected Essays

Edward B. Barbier

Reader, Environment Department, University of York, UK

Edward Elgar

Cheltenham, UK • Northampton, MA, USA

Published by
Edward Elgar Publishing Limited
8 Lansdown Place
Cheltenham
Glos GL50 2HU
UK

Edward Elgar Publishing, Inc.
6 Market Street
Northampton
Massachusetts 01060
USA

A catalogue record for this book is available from the British Library

Library of Congress Cataloguing in Publication Data
Barbier, Edward, 1957–
The economics of environment and development: selected essays/ Edward B. Barbier.
Includes bibliographical references.
1. Sustainable development—Developing countries. 2. Economic development—Environmental aspects. I. Title.
HC59.72.E5B367 1998
333.7—dc21 97–33566
CIP

ISBN 1 85898 685 0

Printed and bound in Great Britain by Bookcraft (Bath) Ltd.

Contents

Figures

Tables

Acknowledgements

The publishers wish to thank the following who have kindly given permission for the use of copyright material.

Blackwell Publishers for articles: 'The linkages between the timber trade and tropical deforestation – Indonesia' with N. Bockstael, J.C. Burgess and I. Strand in *World Economy*, **18** (3), 1995, pp. 411–42; 'Economic aspects of tropical deforestation in Southeast Asia' in *Global Ecology and Biogeography Letters*, **3**, 1995, pp. 1–20.

Cambridge University Press for articles 'Economic Analysis of Deforestation in Mexico' with J.C. Burgess in *Environment and Development Economics*, **1** (2), 1996, pp. 203–40; 'Wildlife, biodiversity and trade' with C.-E. Schultz in *Environment and Development Economics*, 1997.

Earthscan Publications for article: 'Economics for the wilds' in T. Swanson and E. Barbier (eds), *Economics for the Wilds: Wildlife, Wildlands, Diversity and Development*, 1992, pp. 15–33.

Elsevier Science Ltd for articles: 'Alternative approaches to economic–environmental interaction' in *Ecological Economics*, **2**, 1990, pp. 7–26; 'The conditions for achieving environmentally sustainable development' with A. Markandya in *European Economic Review*, **34**, 1990, pp. 659–69; 'Cash crops, food crops and agricultural sustainability: the case of Indonesia' in *World Development*, **17** (6), 1989 pp. 1378–87.

Environmental Conservation for article: 'The concept of sustainable economic development' in *Environmental Conservation*, **14** (2), 1987, pp. 101–110.

Island Press for the article: 'Natural capital and the economics of environment and development' in A.M. Jansson, M. Hammer, C. Folke and R. Costanza (eds), *Investing in Natural Capital*, 1994, pp. 290–322.

IUCN for article: 'An economic valuation of wetland benefits' with W.M. Adams and K. Kimmage in G.E. Hollis, W.M. Adams and M. Aminu-Kano (eds), *The Hadejeia-Nguru Wetlands: Environment, Economy and Sustainable Development of a Sahelian Floodplain Wetland*, 1993.

Kluwer Academic Publishers for articles: 'Rehabilitating gum arabic systems in Sudan: economic and environmental implications' in *Environmental and Resource Economics*, **2**, 1992, pp. 341–52; 'Capturing the pharmaceutical value of biodiversity in a developing country' with B.A. Aylward in *Environmental and Resource Economics*, **8** (2), 1996, pp. 157–91; 'Trade, tropical deforestation and policy interventions' with M. Rauscher in *Environmental and Resource Economics*, **4**, 1994, pp. 75–90.

Pion Limited, London for article: 'Environmental sustainability and cost–benefit analysis' with A. Markandya and D.W. Pearce in *Environment and Planning A*, **22**, 1990, pp. 1259–66.

Sage Publications, inc./Corwin Press, inc. for ' Elephant ivory and tropical timber: the role of trade interventions in sustainable management' in *Journal of Environment and Development*, **4** (2), 1995, pp. 1–32.

UN FAO for article: 'Trade in timber-based forest products and the implications of the Uruguay Round' *Unasylva*, **46** (183), 1995, pp. 3–10.

The University of Wisconsin Press for article: 'The farm-level economics of soil conservation: the uplands of Java' in *Land Economics*, **66** (2), 1990, pp. 199–211.

Preface

Introduction

Fifteen years ago the application of economics to the environmental problems of developing countries was virtually unheard of. In 1984, I was made painfully aware of this fact as a result of two incidents, both of which occurred while I was working that academic year as a temporary lecturer at the Geneva campus of an American college, Webster University of St Louis, Missouri. During this time I was also completing my PhD thesis, which among other things was exploring the role of environmental economics in economic development.

The first incident occurred when I was asked to give an economics lecture at another American university with a campus in Geneva. After the lecture, the director of that campus's economics programme asked me about the topic of my thesis. Upon hearing my interest in the economics of environment and development problems, the director remarked that in his opinion – which he considered to be the conventional view of the economics profession – not only was the topic too obscure for a PhD thesis but it was also largely irrelevant to economics.

The second incident occurred when I tried to sign on to a register of consultants for a well-known international non-governmental organization based in Geneva, which was working on conservation and development issues worldwide. When asked by the person in charge of the register to list my main area of expertise, I explained that I was an economist interested in the analysis of environmental problems of developing countries. The person replied that her organization did not need any consultant with that area of expertise. When I suggested sending in my curriculum vitae in the hope that the situation might change in the near future, she said not to bother as they did not include on their register any consultant without a PhD degree. Not surprisingly, some time later I found out this latter excuse to be untrue.

My main aim in recollecting these two incidents in this introduction is not to try and prove how wrong these two individuals were. Rather, I see these two events as important reminders – most of all to myself – of how much and how fast attitudes have changed in less than fifteen years. Today, the economics profession appears to have accepted that the application of economics to environment and development problems is a legitimate and important area of study. Perhaps the most tangible proof of this was the launching in September 1995 at the Royal Swedish Academy of Sciences of an academic journal, *Environment and Development Economics*, published by Cambridge University

Press. Equally, virtually every major bilateral and international donor agency in the world either has one or more full-time staff members engaged in the economic analysis of environmental problems in developing countries, or routinely contracts researchers and consultants to undertake such analysis. Many international non-governmental organizations (NGOs) and some NGOs within developing countries have also been sponsoring and conducting research into the economics of environment and development.

I have been extremely fortunate over the last fifteen years to find myself caught up in the rapid surge of research emanating from this new field. A large part of my good fortune stems from having worked, immediately upon completion of my PhD, at the International Institute for Environment and Development (IIED) over the period 1986–93. Founded by the economist Barbara Ward in the wake of the 1972 UN Conference on the Environment in Stockholm, IIED is an international nongovernmental research organization dedicated to the study of global environment and development problems. For me, being at IIED was the proverbial 'kid in a candy shop' cream come true.

Hired by Richard Sandbrook and Czech Conroy in early 1996, I initially worked with Czech on setting up an international conference on sustainable development and on the *World Resources Report*, which IIED produced jointly with the World Resources Institute and the UN Environmental Programme. At this time, Richard Sandbrook and IIED were assisting the Commission on Sustainable Development headed by the former Norwegian prime minister Gro Harlan Brundtland to conduct its global enquiry. Published in 1987, the now-famous Brundtland Report *Our Common Future* was responsible for bringing the concept of sustainable development to the world's attention. As a result of the report, economic policy makers and donor agencies globally began taking environment and development issues seriously, and were asking important policy questions concerning the practical implementation of sustainable development. Sensing this change, Richard Sandbrook encouraged me to set up a one-man Environmental Economics Programme at IIED to initiate policy-relevant economics research into environment and development issues. During this period Gordon Conway, who was setting up IIED's Sustainable Agricultural Programme, also asked me to work with him on integrating economic and ecological analysis in the study of the sustainability and development of agricultural systems, particularly in the marginal agricultural areas of the developing world.

Meanwhile, an important process was occurring in Washington, DC. Since the 1960s the World Bank has generally been viewed as the premier global agency concerned with economic development, and along with the International Monetary Fund, the Bank has generally led donor policy thinking on development. In the late 1980s an economist at the World Bank, Jerry Warford, among others became increasingly successful in convincing the Bank hierarchy that the economic analysis of environmental problems in developing countries should feature in Bank policy thinking. The so-called 'greening of the Bank' led to the establishment of the Environment Department and several environmental divisions within the regional departments of the World Bank, as well as the launching of several Bank country studies incorporating economic analysis of environmental and resource problems in developing countries. Other donor agencies were also 'greening'. Perhaps most notably and publicly was the US Agency for International Development in Washington, but also the major UK, Scandinavian, Canadian and West European bilateral donor agencies were developing key environment and development programmes with substantial impacts. Again, fortunately for me, the head of IIED's Washington office, David Runnalls, had been both following and encouraging the 'greening' of the North American donor agencies, and as a result, David got me involved early on in some of the environment and development economics studies launched by the World Bank and US AID.

Much of the initial policy research commissioned by Jerry Warford at the World Bank was also being conducted by David Pearce at University College London, who was based just around the corner from IIED at UCL's Economics Department. Another UCL economist, Anil Markandya, was also collaborating in much of the research. It became obvious that we would all benefit from pooling our 'London-based' research efforts collectively. With the enthusiastic support of Richard Sandbrook and Johan Holmberg of the Swedish International Development Authority, SIDA was persuaded to provide the initial seed money for the new venture. Thus in 1988 the IED–UCL London Environmental Economics Centre was created, with David Pearce as Director, Anil Markandya and myself as Associate Directors, and Joanne Burgess as the first researcher.

Over the next few years, the four of us at LEEC, plus others who joined us on some studies such as Tim Swanson, set about producing numerous books, journal articles and research reports concerned with the economic analysis of environmental problems in developing countries. Most of this research was concerned with applied policy analysis, concerned with sectoral, country and even global studies of key environment and development problems. However, no matter how much we tried to accomplish at LEEC there was always a demand for more; these were the days when the sudden surge in demand for economists working in our area far outstripped the available supply. Ironically, however, the most widely influential publication from this period was *Blueprint for a Green Economy*, which was a report commissioned by the UK Department of Environment on how Britain might implement sustainable development. Written essentially as a sideline to what we thought was our main area of research at LEEC, the phenomenal success of *Blueprint* was perhaps partly attributable to the rapidly expanding interest worldwide in all aspects of economic analysis of environmental policy and sustainable development, and not just for developing countries. A much more relevant – and still popular – book that we wrote based on our 'bread and butter' LEEC research of the time was *Sustainable Development: Economics and Environment in the Third World.*

In 1990 David Pearce left LEEC in order to devote his time fully as UCL's Director of the Centre for Social and Economic Research into the Global Environment. I agreed to become Director of LEEC, and Richard Sandbrook, Anil Markandya, Jo Burgess and I decided to return the Centre's focus exclusively to environment and development economics research. In this 'second phase' in LEEC's development, we tried to concentrate on more long-term applied economic studies of various key environmental problems in developing countries, both on our own at LEEC and in collaboration with other economics researchers worldwide. During this period, two additional researchers joined LEEC full time, Bruce Aylward and Josh Bishop. Both of them proved instrumental in the development of LEEC in its crucial second phase. Michael Collins also joined us in my last year as Director.

During LEEC's 'second phase', two events occurred which had an important influence on both developments at LEEC and my personal research interests. The first was the establishment of the *Agenda 21* of the 1992 UN Conference on Environment and Development, held in Rio de Janeiro, Brazil. Again, Richard Sandbrook and IIED had a vital role in shaping the development of the *Agenda*. There are certainly many important accomplishments to emerge from the Rio Conference. For me personally, however, the most significant was the endorsement by *Agenda 21* and the Rio Declaration of the need for environmental considerations to be integrated with economic development policy worldwide. The economic analysis of environment and development problems had finally received the full support of the international policy community, and this could be seen in tangible terms by the community's continued support for the type of research we were conducting at LEEC.

The second influential event took place well outside the public limelight. Over 1991–92 the Biodiversity Programme of the newly established Beijer International Institute of Ecological Economics of the Royal Swedish Academy of Sciences launched a series of meetings bringing economists and ecologists together to address both empirical and policy issues surrounding global biodiversity loss. The Director of Beijer, Karl-Göran Mäler, and the head of the Biodiversity Programme, Charles Perrings, were both interested in seeing whether the ecologists and economists gathered could improve upon inter-disciplinary theoretical and applied analysis of the main causes of biodiversity loss. To assist this latter aim, Karl-Göran and Charles asked Jo Burgess and me to collaborate with the Beijer Associate Director and ecologist, Carl Folke, in writing a book that presented in a more accessible style the insights from the various papers generated by the Biodiversity Programme. To do this, we attempted to synthesize from these papers the basis for a more integrated ecological–economic approach to the global biodiversity problem. The resulting book published in 1994, *Paradise Lost? The Ecological Economics of Biodiversity*, may not have achieved all of its ambitious objectives, but the process of collaborating on the book has certainly reinforced my belief that inter-disciplinary analysis may hold the key to better human understanding of some of the more complex and intractable environment and development problems facing the world today.

In 1993 Charles Perrings persuaded both Jo Burgess and me to join him in building a new department at the University of York, UK. The main aim of the Department of Environmental Economics and Environmental Management (EEEM) is to establish a staff of economists, ecologists and academics from related disciplines interested in both researching and teaching an inter-disciplinary approach to environmental problems. Over the past few years at EEEM, I have also continued to pursue my interest in environment and development economics, and I have been pleased that a number of graduate and undergraduate students have continued to find this topic of interest to their studies at EEEM as well. Hopefully, they and others interested in this field may find this collection of my essays to be a helpful introduction.

Outline of the book

I hope that the above, rather personal review of recent history will serve as a useful background in viewing the following chapters that are concerned with the economics of environment and development. I have grouped the chapters into four themes: Sustainable Development; Agriculture and Forests; Wetlands, Wildlands and Biodiversity; and Trade and Environment. Each of these themes represents a major area of my research interest, and together they cover broadly the range of topics that comprises the field of environment and development economics today.

Sustainable development

From my earliest days at IED and during the 'first phase' of the development of LEEC, I became interested in the concept of sustainable development especially what it implied practically for economic policy making in developing countries. David Pearce, Anil Markandya and I wrote a considerable amount on this topic, and much of this thinking is contained in the books we published at this time. However, we also produced a few papers on sustainable development as well, some of which are included here.

The first chapter under this theme, 'The concept of sustainable economic development', was written in my first year at IIED, when I was trying to understand both the economic and non-economic components of what the environment and development community was calling 'sustainable development'. I was particularly influenced in writing this piece by a meeting held at IIED in

September 1996, which is acknowledged at the end of the article. Given that I was attempting to integrate a concept of sustainable development across economic, biological and social perspectives, I deliberately chose to describe this concept qualitatively rather than to translate it into any precise, quantifiable measure for policy purposes. An additional aim of this little think-piece was to place the notion of sustainable development in the historical context of post-war development thinking. Although some of the latter remains in the published version, unfortunately a lot of this historical perspective was edited out.

'Alternative approaches to economic–environmental interaction' was originally contained in my PhD thesis, although it took me a long time to get around to publishing it. The chapter also summarizes parts of the book that is largely based on my PhD thesis, *Economics, Natural Resource Scarcity and Development: Conventional and Alternative Views*. As with the book, the main theme of the chapter is to demonstrate that the physical dependency of economic activity on the sustainability of crucial natural-resource systems and ecological functions could lead to important trade-offs between, on the one hand, the use of the environment by the economic process as a source of raw materials and a repository of waste, and on the other, the preservation of sustainability and environmental quality. 'Alternative' approaches in environmental economics are concerned with the economics of environmental degradation processes that typify such trade-offs, including land degradation, forest conversion and situations of ecological collapse threatening human livelihoods more generally. The general insights of the model of the paper are thus more widely applicable to any situation where economic activity leads to declining environmental quality and the loss of ecological functions – impacts which are often associated with many environmental problems in developing countries.

The next chapter, which is co-authored with Anil Markandya, 'The conditions for achieving environmentally sustainable development', was derived from an optimal control model that I developed originally in *Economics, Natural Resource Scarcity and Development*. Anil and I extended this model further in order to explore the long run conditions under which an economy might trade off environment and growth. One of the key features of this model that distinguishes it from other economic analyses of sustainability is the assumption that the economy needs to maintain some minimum or 'threshold' level of environmental quality in order to prevent ecological catastrophe (and thus economic collapse). Two interesting results emerge from this analysis. First, under certain conditions, such as a low initial endowment of environmental capital and a high discount rate, it may be optimal for a country to choose an 'unsustainable' growth path, that is, one that leads to ecological collapse in the long run. Second, the higher the discount rate, the closer the economy moves to the critical threshold value for collapse. The implications are that, for a less developed economy with a poor environmental endowment, to choose a higher discount rate and thus a growth path that yields more consumption and utility in the present may also mean a path that is irreversibly unsustainable in the long run.

Along with David Pearce, Anil Markandya and I also wrote a more 'micro-economic' paper on sustainability, 'Environmental sustainability and cost-benefit analysis'. Here, we were concerned with how to incorporate sustainability concerns into a 'cost–benefit analysis' rule for project appraisal. One criterion might be a *strong sustainability* rule, in which a portfolio of projects ensures that there is no net physical environmental degradation. A second criterion might be a *weak sustainability* rule, in which the value of the environmental damages of some of the projects in the portfolio are compensated by the value of the environmental benefits of other projects. In both instances, we demonstrate that the rules could be satisfied by the inclusion of one or more 'shadow' projects in the portfolio that fulfils the specific criteria for each rule.

The final chapter included under this theme, 'Natural capital and the economics of environment and development', actually began as a retrospective piece written in 1991 for the UN Commission on Sustainable Development as part of their process of developing *Agenda 21* for the 1992 Rio Conference. The later version of the chapter that appears here was published together with other plenary session papers presented at the 1992 International Society for Ecological Economics meeting in Stockholm. As the title of the chapter indicates, I was already suggesting that a sufficient body of work on the economic analysis of environmental problems in developing countries exists to justify the emergence of a new sub-discipline, which I called (no surprise) the 'economics of environment and development'. In the chapter, I not only review this body of work but also argue why developing countries should be concerned with the efficient and sustainable management of their 'natural capital' to achieve long-term economic development alms.

Agriculture and forests

The essays under this theme are concerned mainly with the topics of land degradation and tropical deforestation. In developing countries, these two processes can be related. Many erosive or 'marginal' farm lands in developing countries were once forest lands that have since been converted to agriculture. Equally, many poor rural households will abandon degraded marginal land in search of new land in frontier forest areas. Throughout the developing world, land use decisions by rural households are the key to many critical environment and development problems. The following essays focus both on the underlying causes of land degradation and deforestation, as well as the critical land use decisions driving these processes.

'Cash crops, food crops and agricultural sustainability: the case of Indonesia' is based on studies that I conducted for the World Bank and USAID in the late

1980s on agricultural sustainability in Indonesia. The influence on my work from collaboration with Gordon Conway is apparent throughout this chapter. In particular, I found his approach to agricultural sustainability a useful concept for assessing agricultural–environmental linkages in Indonesia. Another major aim in writing this chapter was to dispel the prevalent myth of the time that food crops are always 'good' for the environment whereas cash crops are inherently 'bad'.

As a result of my early USAID and World Bank research in Indonesia I became interested in the incentives of upland farmers to control land degradation by investing in soil conservation. 'The farm-level economics of soil conservation: the uplands of Java' is based on my adaptation of a model originally developed by Ted McConnell of the University of Maryland, to make it more applicable to soil conservation decisions of a rural farming household in a developing country. The results derived from this model seemed generally to accord with much of the anecdotal and empirical evidence on farmer behaviour emerging from studies of upper watershed degradation in Java, including my own work.

During 1988–89 LEEC and IIED embarked on an ambitious and extremely interesting study on rehabilitating the Sudano–Sahel gum arabic belt, in collaboration with the Institute of Environmental Studies of Sudan. Sadly, the political situation in Sudan deteriorated fairly rapidly soon after our study was completed, and our recommendations were never adopted. As my chapter 'Rehabilitating gum arabic systems in Sudan: economic and environmental implications' attempts to show, the decline of the gum belt is a serious economic and environmental loss to Sudan, yet it would not be that difficult to reverse given the right government policies. Moreover, substantial gains from regenerating the gum belt would accrue to many poor farmers and labourers living and cultivating under extremely difficult conditions in the semi-arid regions of Sudan. Finally, once again I would like to acknowledge my appreciation to Mohammed El-Serafy, who provided me with invaluable field knowledge and survey data to conduct my analysis of the various gum arabic systems.

I was asked to write 'Economic aspects of tropical deforestation in Southeast Asia' for a workshop held at the School of Oriental and African Studies, University of London. At the time, I was grateful for the opportunity to reflect upon the various economic forces influencing deforestation in the region, as well as to synthesize and summarize the empirical and policy conclusions emerging from different country studies. Having worked extensively in Southeast Asia on tropical forest related problems, I had noted that across the region similar economic incentives were driving deforestation. The main purpose of the chapter is to discuss these common incentives and their implications for policy.

The last major project that Jo Burgess and I undertook with colleagues at LEEC was an economic analysis of deforestation in Mexico, which was produced for the World Bank and the Government of Mexico. 'Economic analysis of deforestation in Mexico' is based on this work, and attempts an empirical analysis of the causes of cropland expansion and livestock growth as a proxy for deforestation across Mexico. The estimated effects are linked to studies of the economy-wide effects for Mexico of the North American Free Trade Agreement in order to determine the possible implications of NAFTA for deforestation as well. The resulting analysis owes a debt of gratitude to Luis Constantino of the World Bank, who initially commissioned the study and who provided invaluable advice and support throughout.

'Economic analysis of tropical forest land use options' had a long gestation period in the early 1990s. Its roots lie in theoretical work I developed originally as part of a LEEC study for the UK Overseas Development Administration as well as theoretical and empirical work that Jo Burgess undertook as part of her PhD thesis. However, our main interest in writing the chapter was out of concern that to date many empirical analyses of tropical deforestation (including our own) were rather *ad hoc* and generally lack any theoretical foundation. Drawing on yet another basic model constructed by Ted McConnell – this time on urban–agricultural land use decisions – this paper develops a theoretical analysis of agricultural-forest land use decisions at the stand and forest level as the basis for deriving an expression for the demand for forest land conversion. We then estimate this equation for 53 tropical countries in order to test the relative influences of the demand for forest conversion suggested by the theoretical model.

'The role of smallholder producer prices in land degradation: the case of Malawi' is based on analysis that I conducted for a larger World Bank study of smallholder land degradation in Malawi. The latter study was undertaken with Jo Burgess in 1990. Although it appeared as a LEEC discussion paper, I never got around to publishing it. I have decided to include it for the first time in this volume as it fits in well with the other chapters under the Agriculture and Forests theme. Using an analysis similar to the farm-level soil erosion model I developed for Java (see above), this chapter explores the influence of changes in relative crop prices on the soil conservation decisions of poor rural smallholders in Malawi. As the chapter notes, over many years the Government of Malawi would set agricultural prices on a crop-by-crop basis, with frequent and large fluctuations in relative prices from year to year. As a consequence, small farmers are unable to gauge the comparative returns to farming systems that incorporate less erosive crops, and thus are discouraged from investing in such systems. I am particularly grateful to Rick Scobey, who not only was an excellent mission leader but also provided extremely helpful advice for this analysis based on his long-term experience in Malawi.

Between 1993–96 I served on the Programme Committee of the Economy and Environment Programme of Southeast Asia, which is an initiative of Canada's International Development Research Center based in Singapore. The Director of EEPSEA, David Glover, asked me to write and present a paper at an EEPSEA workshop in May 1996. The main purpose of 'The economics of soil erosion: theory, methodology and examples' was to overview the theory and application of the economics of soil erosion in the Southeast Asian context. The chapter examines what is known about the economic incentives influencing rural farmers' decisions to invest in soil erosion, and then discusses the appropriate methodology for assessing the on-site and off-site costs of erosion by referring to specific studies from Southeast Asia.

Wetlands, wildlands and biodiversity

One of the critical environmental and development issues facing developing countries is how to manage their remaining 'wild' or natural habitat areas. The extreme environmentalist or 'deep green' view that these areas should be preserved at all costs is simply not realistic, given the pressures of poverty and population growth in developing countries that make some conversion for the sake of economic development inevitable. On the other hand, excessive loss of wetlands, wildlands and biodiversity is currently occurring in many developing regions because the full economic and ecological values of these areas are often neither properly assessed nor considered relevant to economic development decisions. Determining the optimal use and management of natural areas in development decisions is the main focus of the chapters included under the wetlands, wildlands and biodiversity theme.

I have included 'Economics for the wilds' as the first chapter because it provides a general overview of the economic issues involved in reconciling conservation and development issues in developing countries. It was written as an introductory chapter in a book devoted to this theme, *Economics for the Wilds: Wildlife, Wildlands, Diversity and Development*, which I co-edited with Tim Swanson. I hope it also serves as a good introduction here as well.

In 1991 I worked with two geographers from the University of Cambridge, Bill Adams and Kevin Kimmage, to attempt to assess the agricultural, fuelwood and fishing benefits of a natural floodplain system in the semi-arid Hadejia-Jama'are River Basin of Northern Nigeria. The study was conducted for the World Conservation Union (IUCN), who support the Hadejia Nguru Wetland Conservation Project based in the floodplain. Hydrologists working in the region, notably Ted Hollis of UCL and his then PhD student Julian Thompson, had called attention to the threat of major upstream irrigation projects and dams diverting substantial water from the Hadejia and Jama'are rivers and thus permanently disrupting the natural flood regimes of the regime. As our study 'An economic valuation of wetland benefits' shows, the potential losses to rural households dependent on the floodplain could be substantial. Thanks to Henry Thompson and others at HNWCP, our study was widely disseminated among local and federal government officials responsible for water management in Northern Nigeria, and the result has been a rethinking of policy to consider 'regulated' flood releases from upstream water projects and dams to save the floodplain – a strategy supported by the hydrological models of Ted Hollis and Julian Thompson. Sadly, Ted Hollis died suddenly in late 1996; all of us who have worked on the floodplain management problem in Northern Nigeria and in Africa generally have lost a great ally and friend.

Having worked on tropical wetland management problems throughout the developing world, I thought it was important to write a chapter that summarized the key economic aspects of the problem. The result is 'Valuing environmental functions: tropical wetlands'. The chapter has two aims. The first is to argue that a key feature of many tropical wetlands is that they often contain important ecological functions that support and protect economic activity. Examples include coastal mangroves serving as a habitat and breeding ground for marine fisheries, flood control by riverine wetlands, and groundwater recharge by natural floodplains. However, because the economic benefits arising from many of these wetland ecological 'services' are essentially 'intangible' and generally not reflected in market prices, development decisions that exploit or convert tropical wetlands often ignore such benefits. Thus the second aim of the paper is to argue that analyzing and valuing tropical wetland functions may be critical to improved management of tropical wetlands and the economic services they provide. A promising valuation methodology appears to be the 'production function' approach, which has been pioneered by Karl-Göran Mäler among others.

During 1991–93 LEEC was asked by the Swedish International Development Authority to conduct an economic analysis of the pharmaceutical prospecting activities of Costa Rica's National Biodiversity Institute (INBio), to which SIDA was providing assistance. This turned out to be a critical point to be conducting such a study, as INBio had just concluded its infamous contract deal with the pharmaceutical multinational Merck in order to provide biotic samples from prospecting in Costa Rica's tropical forest conservation areas. The study was led by Bruce Aylward, with my support and that of INBio, the Tropical Science Center of Costa Rica and other Costa Rican researchers. Once the study was completed, Bruce and I wrote 'Capturing the pharmaceutical value of biodiversity in a developing country' in order to summarize some of the key lessons we had learned. An important conclusion of the chapter is to point out that, although pharmaceutical prospecting offers the potential for substantial financial rewards if successful, the economic gains from prospecting alone are generally not aufficient to cover all the costs associated with establishing and managing a protected area in a developing country.

Trade and environment

Whether international trade rules and agreements or domestic environmental management concerns should take precedence is an issue that the world community has been grappling with for some time now. Trade and environment conflicts became an important focus in the build up to the conclusion of the General Agreement on Tariffs and Trade Uruguay Round in 1994, and the recently established World Trade Organization is attempting to establish new rules to resolve such conflicts. I first became involved in this area of research as a result of LEEC's 1987–89 study on the economics of the trade in African elephant ivory. I have continued to explore trade and environment issues since then, particularly examining the role of developing countries managing and exploiting key natural resource assets that also have global non-consumptive values, for example, biodiversity, ecotourism and preservation values. The following chapters explore this theme.

'Elephant ivory and tropical timber: the role of trade interventions in sustainable management' was my attempt to summarize the policy analysis and results of two major LEEC studies. The first was the above-mentioned study of the ivory trade. The second was the economic analysis conducted over 1991–93 for the International Tropical Timber Organization on the linkages between the global trade in forest products and the incentives for more sustainable management of tropical forests supplying this trade. As the chapter emphasizes, both studies show that long-term sustainable management of these two key resources – African elephants and tropical production forests – can be best served by appropriate domestic management policies supported by carefully designed incentive mechanisms generated by international trade. Thus under certain conditions, trade can actually act as an incentive for sustainable resource management, whereas trade bans, prohibitive taxes and quotas can often be counterproductive over the long term.

While leading the LEEC study for ITTO on the tropical timber trade, I wanted to explore a number of critical theoretical issues linking the trade to timber exploitation in a tropical forest country. At the Beijer Biodiversity Programme in 1991, I met Michael Rauscher (then of the University of Kiel now of the University of Rostock, Germany) who was also interested in examining these issues. Thanks to the encouragement and financial support provided by Karl-Göran Mäler, Michael and I were able to write 'Trade, tropical deforestation and policy interventions'. The theoretical results of the chapter show that interventions in the tropical timber trade (that is, taxes and quantitative restrictions by importing countries) are a second-best way of encouraging a tropical forest country to reduce deforestation in the long run; however, transfers from the rest of the world to the country can lead to more forest conservation.

Another analysis that I wanted to conduct for the ITTO study was an empirical investigation of the effects of various trade and domestic policy scenarios on deforestation on a major tropical forest exporting country. Thanks to an FAO–Government of Indonesia study on the timber markets and forest resources of Indonesia which generated much data, this country was selected. At an

International Society for Ecological Economics workshop held in Mexico in 1991, Jo Burgess and I met with Nancy Bockstael and Ivar Strand of the University of Maryland, who became interested in the modelling aspects of our analysis. Nancy and Ivar spent a short while with us at LEEC to further work on this problem, and as a consequence, the four of us wrote 'The linkages between the timber trade and tropical deforestation – Indonesia'.

An important consultant for LEEC on the ITTO study was Jim Bourke of the Forest Products Division of FAO. Soon after I moved to the EEEM Department in 1993, I was persuaded by Jim to conduct an analysis for FAO examining the likely impacts of the Uruguay Round Agreement on the trade in forest products. The study consisted of both a quantitative analysis of the gains in the global forest products trade from tariff reductions agreed at the Round and an assessment of the likely 'new' trade barriers that could affect the trade. The latter include important domestic environmental and trade restrictions in both importing and exporting countries. The results of the FAO study were summarized in 'Trade in timber-based forest products and the implications of the Uruguay Round'.

During my first year at the EEEM Department we also had as visiting professor Carl-Erik Schulz of the University of Tromsö, Norway. Carl-Erik and I discovered that we had a mutual concern that most renewable resource management models were based on bioeconomic models more suited to fisheries management than the management of terrestrial natural habitats in developing countries where land conversion is a major threat. This led us to collaborate on 'Wildlife, biodiversity and trade'. Adapting a model originally developed by Scott Barett for optimal management of conservation reserves, the chapter shows that the inclusion of the opportunity costs of holding onto land as natural habitat in a developing country leads to a different long run level of biological resource exploitation and stock than a more conventional bioeconomic model that ignores these costs. However, the inclusion of the opportunity costs of habitat preservation still do not affect the general results of the earlier analysis that I conducted with Michael Rauscher (see above); namely, that trade interventions are still a second-best means of encouraging a developing country to conserve more of a biological resource.

Acknowledgements
I would first of all like to thank all of the individuals who co-authored some of the chapters that appear in this volume. I have gained immensely from collaborating with them, and we also had much fun in the process. I am lucky to have made many good friends through this collaboration as well.

I would also like to express my gratitude to all of the other individuals mentioned in this preface, who have been so influential and helpful in the ways I have tried to describe. However, this list is woefully short; there are many more individuals who have also provided me with much assistance over the period in which these essays were written. My apologies for any neglectful omissions.

Finally, I would like to offer my collective thanks to everyone at IIED, LEEC and the EEEM Department, University of York for being such inspiring colleagues. However, I cannot finish this preface without signalling out one individual – Richard Sandbrook – whose general leadership at IED and support for my work over the years have been invaluable to me. As I pointed out at the beginning of this preface, when no one else was bothered about the application of economics to environment and development problems, Richard not only perceived that this was a necessary field to foster but he also then proceeded to persuade much of the world's development policy makers that their backing for such an approach is essential to global progress. Perhaps some day the world may acknowledge this and many other of Richard's achievements in establishing global interest in environment and development issues.

Ed Barbier
Environment Department
University of York

PART ONE

SUSTAINABLE DEVELOPMENT

1. The concept of sustainable economic development

Introduction

In recent years there has occurred a major revision in development thinking that is presenting a fundamental challenge to the conventional consensus on economic development. This new approach emphasizes meeting the basic needs of the poor, advocates cultural sensitivity, and encourages 'grassroots' participation in the development process. More crucially, it stresses that 'real' improvement cannot occur in Third World countries or anywhere else unless the strategies which are being formulated and implemented are environmentally sustainable. As a result, there is a growing 'recognition that the overall goals of environment and development are not in conflict but are indeed the same, namely the improvement of the human quality of life or welfare for present and future generations' (Bartelmus, 1986, pp. 13–4).

However, the concept of sustainable economic development is a difficult one to grasp analytically. Given that one is attempting to describe the environmental, economic, and social features of an ongoing process, the difficulty lies in arriving at a universally acceptable definition that is also analytically precise. More often than not, precision is sacrificed for acceptability. For example, the *World Conservation Strategy* (IUCN, 1980) emphasizes 'the maintenance of essential ecological processes and life-support systems, the preservation of genetic diversity, and the sustainable utilization of species and ecosystems', with the overall aim of achieving 'sustainable development through the conservation of living resources'. While lauding the general underlying message, sympathetic economists have none the less been critical of the definition and objectives outlined in the *World Conservation Strategy* for being too imprecise to be operational, for failing to perceive crucial issues of trade-offs among economic and conservation goals, and for ignoring valuation problems (Tisdell, 1983; Pearce, 1985).

While it may be extremely difficult, if not impossible, to define sustainable development in any analytically rigorous way, there is still a need to describe its characteristics and to distinguish it from other concepts of development. To do this is the aim of the following chapter, which attempts to refine and substantiate the concept of sustainable economic development. Stressing the unique environmental, economic, and social, features of sustainability, is the first step towards an interpretation that is sufficiently rigorous to provide the useful tools needed for practical analysis and policymaking. This chapter limits itself to discussing the concept of sustainable economic development as applied to the Third World.

Development and economic development

As, over the years, economic policy goals have changed, concepts of economic development have also been modified. The current consensus in non-Marxist thought defines economic development as the 'process whereby the real per capita income of a country increases over a long period of time – subject to the stipulations that the number below an "absolute poverty line" does not increase, and that the distribution of income does not become more unequal' (Meier, 1976, p. 6). This consensus ascribes the following characteristic features to economic development:

1. It is only one part of the total development of society, and can be distinguished and analysed separately;
2. Its quantitative dimension is associated with economic accumulation, or growth in real per caput output;
3. Its qualitative dimension is associated with technological and institutional change, or 'innovation' broadly defined; and
4. It should ideally be measurable, that is, economic development is associated with direct and readily measurable economic gain.

The 'total development of society' involves not only changes in economic activity but also political, social, and cultural, transformations. In assessing the 'total development of society', economics tends to focus primarily on economic changes and thus isolates economic development from 'total' development. The general consensus remains that 'it is conventional to begin with an increase in per capita real income as the best available overall index of economic development' (Meier, 1976, p. 8).

However, although per caput growth is considered the crucial indicator of economic development, the conventional consensus also accepts that there are important qualitative dimensions to development that distinguish it from economic growth. That is, 'economic *development* implies not only more output but also different kinds of output than were previously produced, as well as changes in the technical and institutional arrangements by which output is produced and distributed' (Herrick and Kindleberger, 1983, p. 21). In addition to the invention and diffusion of new technology, these 'innovations' would include changes in organization, government policy, patterns of ownership, human skills and tasks, and consumer tastes and preferences.

In its efforts to establish empirical validity and conceptual concreteness, economics has been keen to translate any notion of 'economic improvement' into a variable to be measured and compared. Thus if increases in aggregate real per caput income are considered 'the best available overall index of economic development', any relatively poor nation exhibiting both absolute and relative increases in real income must by definition be developing successfully. Moreover, quantitative indicators of economic development can be disaggregated and aggregated to any level. For example, the same criteria of relatively and absolutely increasing real per caput income can be applied to a relatively poor region, community, or income group, within a country.

The above-cited four features represent only the basic consensus, as the concept of economic development and its relationship to overall development have been constantly redefined throughout the post-war (World War II) era. As this 'semantic history' has been carefully reviewed elsewhere (Arndt, 1981; Meier, 1984), it will not be discussed further here.

The meaning of sustainable economic development

The 1970s saw the emergence of a major revision in development thinking that presents a fundamental challenge to the conventional consensus on economic development. In common with the call for a 'basic needs strategy' (ILO, 1976; Streeten *et al.*, 1981; Stewart, 1985), this revision emphasizes improving the basic needs of the poor. However, the sustainable development approach additionally argues that 'real' improvement cannot occur in Third World countries unless the strategies which are being formulated and implemented are environmentally sustainable over the long term, are consistent with social values and institutions, and encourage 'grassroots' participation in the development process. Thus it is argued that 'there will be no sustained development or meaningful growth without a clear commitment at the same time to preserve the environment and promote the rational use of resources' (Tolba, 1984). Similarly, to be socially and culturally sustainable, 'development must be gauged by the values [which] a society itself, or some member thereof, deems to be requisite for its health and welfare' (Goulet, 1971, p. 333).

The 1972 United Nations Conference on the Human Environment, held in Stockholm, is usually credited with popularizing the concept of sustainable development, although Caldwell (1984) suggests that the origins of the term probably lie in the Paris 'Biosphere Conference' and the Washington, DC conference on the Ecological Aspects of International Development, which were both held in 1968. In general, the concern has been that 'few if any countries take adequate account of environmental considerations when making policy or planning development. Few allocate or regulate uses of their living resources so as to ensure that they are environmentally appropriate and sustainable. Many lack either the financial or technical resources, or the political will, or adequate legislative, institutional, or public, support for conservation (or any combination of these) to carry out fully the conservation measures required' (IUCN, 1980, para. 8.8).

The result of those lacunae is that, at the level of project planning and design, unwanted environmental impacts have arisen from inadequate attention having been paid to environmental consequences, and from the lack of knowledge and information necessary to predict them; other causes have included ignorance of cost-effective preventive or mitigating measures, and failure to consider alternative project designs or locations (Lee, 1985).

Perhaps the most important contribution of sustainable development approaches is the recognition of a fundamental process of 'cumulative causation' (Myrdal, 1968) in situations of poverty, environmental degradation, and under-development:

> Poor people in their struggle to survive are driven to doing environmental damage with long-term losses. Their herds overgraze; their shortening fallows on steep slopes and fragile soils induce erosion; their need for off-season incomes drives them to cut and sell firewood and to make and sell charcoal; they are forced to cultivate and degrade marginal and unstable land. Putting people first, and enabling them to meet their needs, can be, then, to reduce these pressures, to reduce degradation, and to maintain potentials for sustainable agriculture and sustainable development at higher levels of productivity. And this in turn means that more people in future can have adequate, secure, and decent, levels of living. (Chambers, 1986b, p. 7)

Although rapid population growth and uneven distribution in some areas undoubtedly complicates natural resource management, it is also true that 'population pressures on resources usually reflect an extremely skewed distribution of resources. When farmers encroach on tropical forests or cultivate erodible hillsides, population pressure is blamed, but the pressure typically stems from the concentration of land in large holdings' (Repetto, 1986c, p. 45). Nor can the vagaries of climate be solely blamed for the environmental degradation occurring even in ecologically fragile regions. For example, a World Bank (1985) study concludes that drought by itself does not pose a threat to the long-term sustainability of rural production systems in the West African Sahelian and Sudanian zones, but accelerates the negative consequence of resource abuse enforced by poverty:

> The spread of rainfed, extensive agriculture into forest, bush and pasture areas reduces total forage available to transhumant livestock, particularly when, as now, mixed farmers increasingly collect and stock crop residues to carry their own animals through the dry season period. When drought strikes, transhumant pastoralists do what they can to save herds. Lacking alternative forms of forage, they try to increase their animals' intake of browse. They vigorously lop trees already weakened by lack of soil moisture. Many trees die as a result of this abuse. Pressure then intensifies on the remaining woodstock during the next drought. Clearing fields for animal traction or machine cultivation may disrupt existing soil fertilization cycles based on nutrients that in-field trees return to

the soil surface in the form of humus. If these organic nutrients are not replaced by organic and/or chemical fertilizers, crop yields decline. Stripping trees from fields also reduces the windbreak effect that even an open canopy can provide, and increases wind erosion. When fields are fallowed, in those systems where man/land ratios still permit it, natural regeneration occurs much more slowly. In the meantime, soils may suffer both wind and water erosion. (World Bank, 1985, p. 7)

Thus the basic premise of sustainable economic development is that 'many environmental problems in developing countries originate from the lack of development, that is from the struggle to overcome extreme conditions of poverty' (Bartelmus, 1986, p. 18). Poor people often have no choice but to opt for immediate economic benefit at the expense of the long-run sustainability of their livelihoods For example, one of the consequences of deforestation and the depletion of fuel-wood supplies is that it forces poor households to divert dung for use as fuel rather than for fertilizer. The 'present value' of the dung as fuel is higher than its value as a soil nutrient, but 'the context is one where there is no choice anyway since there are neither fuel nor fertilizer substitutes to which households can gain access' (Pearce, 1986, pp. 5–6). The result, however, is most certainly a decline in soil fertility, low levels of productivity, and loss of future economic welfare.

The primary concern of sustainable economic development, therefore, is ensuring that the poor have access to sustainable and secure livelihoods. At the national level, this calls for policies, regulations, and incentives, to induce economic behaviour that is 'environmentally rational' (Lee and Goodland, 1986). As will be discussed below, this 'macro' approach to sustainable development has been endorsed by the World Commission on Environment and Development and is currently being explored within the World Bank and the Asian Development Bank (Asian Development Bank, 1986; Conable, 1986; Warford, 1986). However, macroeconomic or 'top-down' approaches are not sufficient; ultimately, the focus must be on 'the needs and priorities of poor people as they perceive them'(Chambers, 1986a). As emphasized by a recent submission to the World Commission, 'satisfaction of basic human needs – food, clean water, fresh air, fuel, shelter, health-care education, and employment – is essential to sustainable development'(Global Tomorrow Coalition, 1985, p. 5).

In addition, for economic development to be truly 'sustainable' requires 'tailoring the design and implementation of projects to the needs and capabilities of people who are supposed to benefit from them' (Uphoff, 1985, p. 359). As a recent review of development projects has shown, not only does 'attention to issues of sociocultural compatibility ... pay off in economic terms – among others, in economic rates of return twice as high as those of the socially insensitive and inappropriate projects', but it also lays to rest 'the fallacy of overinnovation and of a socially insensitive development strategy that justifies change in terms of abstract goals rather than in terms of locally perceived needs' (Kottak, 1985).

Any attempt to reduce environmental degradation will be counterproductive if there is failure to respect the needs and encourage the participation of those social groups which are most affected by any change. For example, World Bank-financed social forestry programmes in India have failed in the past to have an impact on the landless, small and marginal farm households that are most responsible for deforestation. This was because of a limited commitment to serving community needs, the lack of involvement of poor women (who collect fuel-wood and fodder), and the distrust of social forestry programmes by the landless (Centre for Science and Environment, 1985, pp. 56–7).

To summarize, in contrast to the conventional consensus on economic development, the following revised criteria underline sustainable economic development:

1. It is indistinguishable from the total development of society and cannot effectively be analysed separately, as 'sustainability' depends on the interaction of economic changes with social, cultural, and ecological transformations;
2. Its quantitative dimension is associated with increases in the material means available to those living, or destined to live, in absolute poverty, so as to provide for adequate physical and social well-being and security against becoming poorer;
3. Its qualitative dimension is multifaceted, and is associated with ensuring the long-term ecological, social, and cultural, potential for supporting economic activity and structural change; and
4. It is not easily subject to measurement; the quantitative and qualitative dimensions are mutually reinforcing and inseparable, and thus cannot be fully captured by any concept of direct and measurable economic gain.

Sustainable economic development is therefore directly concerned with increasing the material standard of living of the poor at the 'grassroots' level, which can be quantitatively measured in terms of increased food, real income, educational services, health-care, sanitation and water supply, emergency stocks of food and cash, and so on, and only indirectly concerned with economic growth at the aggregate, commonly national, level. In general terms, the primary objective is reducing the absolute poverty of the world's poor through providing lasting and secure livelihoods that minimize resource depletion, environmental degradation, cultural disruption, and social instability.

Towards an analytical method

Because the criteria underlying sustainable economic development differ so markedly from the conventional economic consensus, there is really a need for a completely new analytical approach in that regard. Unfortunately, a rigorous exploration of such a new methodology has yet to be attempted. At best, this chapter can only suggest some of the basic steps required in formulating such an approach.

There are many obstacles to overcome. For one, the conceptual complexity of sustainable economic development makes precise measurement of its 'success' through quantitative indicators extremely difficult. The quantitative dimensions of sustainability (for example, increases in food, real income, life expectancy, and so on) can perhaps be captured by some 'basic needs' or 'physical quality of life' index. However, the more qualitative dimensions (for example, cultural diversity, social cohesion and stability, improvements in environmental quality, greater self-esteem, and so on) are virtually impossible to quantify.

In addition, not all the quantitative and qualitative aspects of sustainable economic development can be maximized simultaneously in all situations. This suggests that any development effort must surmount a continuous and dynamic configuration of trade-offs, such as between increased productivity and environmental degradation, or improving the status of women and preserving traditional values, or introducing new techniques and relying on traditional skills. Assessing the appropriate choice in the face of these trade-offs will require knowledge of the benefits and costs involved in alternative decisions.

Given that many of the qualitative dimensions of various trade-offs cannot be quantitatively measured, precise analysis of all benefits and costs cannot be assured. Moreover, the dynamic nature of development, and the diverse social, economic and ecological conditions in which it must be pursued, mean that the various trade-offs involved are constantly changing over time. This makes continuous assessment of benefits and costs even more crucial. One basic analytical approach is to view this process as an interaction among three systems: the biological (and other resource) system (BS), the economic system (ES), and the social system (SS).

Each system has its own unique set of human-ascribed goals:

Biological system goals:
- genetic diversity
- resilience
- biological productivity

Economic system goals:
- satisfying basic needs (reducing poverty)
- equity-enhancing
- increasing useful goods and services

Social system goals:
- cultural diversity
- institutional sustainability
- social justice
- participation

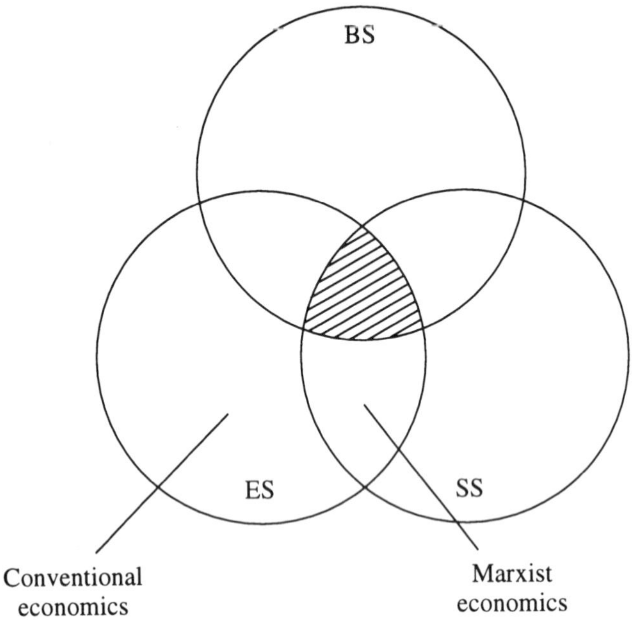

Note: *Sustainable economic development maximizes the goals across the biological and resource system (BS), the economic system (ES), and the social system (SS), as illustrated by the shaded area. In contrast, conventional development approaches maximize only ES goals, and Marxist economics maximizes only ES and SS goals.*

Figure 1.1 Sustainable vs. conventional development

The general objective of sustainable economic development, then, is to maximize the goals across all these systems through an adaptive process of trade-offs, as illustrated by the shaded area in Figure 1.1. In contrast, the current conventional consensus on economic development attempts to maximize only economic system goals, and Marxist economics maximize only ES and SS goals.

Sustainable development involves a *process of trade-offs* among the various goals of these three systems; as noted above, it is not possible to maximize all these objectives all the time. For example, as the economic process of production and consumption is dependent on resource use, increasing even useful goods and services may conflict with ensuring the maximum productivity and genetic diversity of the biological and resource system. There may also be conflict among intra-system goals. For instance, in some rural communities institutional sustainability could mean reinforcing societal norms that inhibit women's economic independence and limit their social participation. This may conflict with rural women organizing themselves to secure increased social justice, participation, and access to land, credit, skills, and so on (Muntemba, 1985). Given these potential trade-offs among goals, a choice must be made as to which objectives should receive priority, and thus greater weight, in the development strategy.

This process of trade-offs among goals must also be *adaptive*, for as individual preferences, social norms, ecological conditions, and so on, change over time, so must the relative weights attached to the various goals. Thus, for example, after social norms have adjusted to allow women greater economic independence and increased social participation, perhaps there will be less conflict generated by pursuing institutional sustainability (for example, in terms of the process of community decision-making, social organization of production activities, and so on).

As economic, social and ecological conditions also vary in different locations and situations, priorities among goals should also differ. For instance, in the West African Sahelian and Sudanian zones, biological and resource productivity and resilience are clearly a high priority (World Bank, 1985). For agro-ecosystems in the critical uplands of East Java, the trend of increasing absentee land-ownership raises the additional issue of equity in land tenure. This may indirectly affect sustainability through its impact on the incentives for soil conservation (KEPAS, 1985).

Finally, interactions among BS, ES and SS goals (Figure 1.1) change as the scale or hierarchy of the systems is extended from the local to the regional, and thence to the national and even global, level. As 'systems theory holds that the behaviour of higher systems in such a hierarchy is not readily discovered simply from a study of lower systems, and *vice versa*' (Conway, 1987), the choice of sustainable development goals to be pursued at, say, the national level, may differ from those advocated at the local level.

Sustainable economic development applied

The next stage in making the concept of sustainable economic development operational would be to develop the tools necessary to analyse the trade-offs among the systems, and to apply these tools to interacting systems at different levels of scale (hierarchy), over various timescales and locations, and under markedly different economic, social, and ecological, conditions. However, before this next stage can be adequately tackled, two additional issues concerning the applicability of the concept of sustainable economic development need to be clarified: first, is the concept only relevant to agriculture, including forestry and rangeland and wildlife management, or can it also be made applicable to all forms of economic and social activity, including industrial and human settlements? Second, does sustainability in agriculture require the returning of all organic matter to the soil and thus support a subsistence rather than a surplus-producing system? The latter question will be addressed first:

'In agricultural development, ecosystems are transformed into hybrid agro-ecosystems for the purpose of food or fibre production' (Conway, 1985, p. 34). While agricultural sustainability requires the organic material of the soil to be replenished, this criterion can be met in a number of ways by both subsistence and surplus agricultural systems. For example, there exist many 'naturally subsidized solar-powered ecosystems', such as tidal estuaries and river deltas, where biomass productivity is greatly enhanced by the flowing of water that assists the importation of organic matter and nutrients from other regions (Odum, 1975, pp. 17–18). Many important agro-ecosystems (for example, delta-based agricultural systems) have traditionally tapped these regions to produce a surplus without much loss of sustainability – precisely because the natural now of organic material into the system continues to maintain the latter's fertility. In fact, many agro-ecosystems are not 'closed' with respect to material cycling but are interdependent on one another and on other natural ecosystems for a continuous inflow of organic material and nutrients to maintain soil quality (for example, natural soil and nutrient runoff from the highland, fertilizing lowland agricultural areas). In these instances '100 per cent recycling of organic materials' is not necessary to avoid long-term soil degradation; instead, what is required are agricultural techniques and practices that do not degrade soil quality and ecological functions at a rate faster than the natural cycles and flows can 'repair' the damage.

Moreover, in many instances of sustainable rural or agricultural 'development', one is talking about transforming a system that was previously unsustainable into one that is at least relatively sustainable. A good example is a World Neighbors project in Honduras (Bunch, 1987). At a cost of $13 per person the Guinope Integrated Development Program has transformed a previously unsustainable smallholder agro-ecosystem through appropriate agricultural technology, training, and erosion control – including intercropping of 'green manure' crops with the traditional corn or sorghum – into a surplus-producing system with yield increases of over 300 per cent and a marketable surplus of vegetables. Even in drought-prone Africa, there are numerous successes in improving agricultural sustainability – ranging from the large-scale Kenyan Soil and Water Conservation Programme to the Yatenga Water Harvesting Project in Burkina Faso (Harrison. 1987).

Finally, if maintaining the nutrient levels and organic material of soil is a necessary condition for agricultural sustainability, there should be no fundamental problems in maintaining an agro-ecosystem by 'some increase of external inputs' provided those inputs are ecologically benign or even beneficial (for example, organic fertilizers, appropriate biotechnology, integrated pest management, and so on). If the acquisition of those additional inputs actually improves soil quality sufficiently to raise productivity, then farmers may be better off with them than they were formerly. For example, a Lutheran World Relief project in Niger will have built an estimated 3200 wells by the end of 1987. At an estimated cost of US $400 each, these wells have not only increased subsistence food output from project gardens but have also yielded a marketable surplus of between US $400 and $2000 per hectare. This has allowed gardeners to pay back the costs of the wells – to purchase seed, fertilizer, and other inputs and to acquire valuable marketing skills (Cottingham, 1987).

Although it is clearly much easier to conceive of the sustainability of agricultural, forestry, rangeland and wildlife systems than of economic development, the concept of sustainable development should also be applicable to all forms of economic and social activity, including industry and human settlements. This can best be explained with reference to the various definitions of sustainability in the literature. As the previous discussion makes clear, in the case of agriculture, or agro-ecosystems, application of the concept is self-evident, as one is talking about systems that are directly dependent on environmental resources and essential ecological functions for 'sustainability'. This is particularly true if we take Gordon Conway's (1987) more technical definition of agricultural sustainability as 'the ability of a system to maintain its productivity when subject to stress or shock', where the stress is 'a regular, sometimes continuous, relatively small and predictable disturbance, for example the effect of growing soil salinity or indebtedness', and the shock is 'an irregular, infrequent, relatively large and unpredictable disturbance, such as is caused by a rare drought or flood or a new pest'.

As noted above, unchecked resource abuse within an agro-ecosystem, whether the result of inappropriate use of petrochemicals and fertilizers, overcropping of erodible soils, poor drainage, and so on, can affect overall agro-ecosystem sustainability by increasing either stress, shock, or both. The key is to reduce the resource degradation, and therefore the disturbances associated with it, to a level where the natural processes and function of the agro-ecosystem can counteract them and thus preserve overall sustainability.

Of course the crucial element in all this is that the productivity of the agro-ecosystem is essential to human livelihoods; hence one is really talking about 'sustainable livelihoods' as defined by Chambers (1986b) as 'a level of wealth and of stocks and flows of food and cash which provide for physical and social well-being and security against becoming poorer'. Moreover, one of the priorities of sustainable development must be to 'balance' the need for poor people to gain better livelihoods than formerly, with the needs of future generations. Thus, in rural settings where livelihoods are dependent on the productivity of agro-ecosystems and its equitable distribution, one is back to Conway's view of agricultural sustainability as maintaining 'productivity when subject to stress or shock'.

Alternatively, one could take Goodland and Ledec's (1986) even broader definition of sustainable development as 'a pattern of social and structural economic transformations (i.e. "development") which optimizes the economic and other societal benefits available in the present without jeopardizing the likely potential for similar benefits in the future'. Then one can clearly consider as sustainable development any economic activity that raises social welfare with the maximum amount of resource conservation and the minimum amount of environmental degradation allowable within given economic, social, and technical, constraints. In this sense, industry and human settlements are subject to the criteria of sustainable development.

In the case of industry, for example, it is precisely because industrial activity involves some resource use and some waste generation, that it is necessary to find a pattern of activity that is more resource- and waste-minimizing than maximizing.

Absolute sustainability may not be physically possible for any particular pattern of industrial development, but one must still find a pattern that is relatively more sustainable than are others. In other words, because industry is dependent on raw material and energy inputs from the primary sector (agriculture, forestry, fishing, mining, and quarrying, and so on), and the prospect of 100 per cent recycling of waste residuals is still a technical impossibility, it is essential to ensure that the resulting impacts on the environment and its resources are as minimal as possible. As a result – depending on economic and technical feasibility – some of the 'sustainability' criteria that are applicable to industrial activity could include increased recycling, minimal use of non-renewable resources, exploiting renewable resources at a rate less than their natural rate of 'ecologically safe' regeneration, reducing waste-generation levels to well within the assimilative capacity of the environment, and ensuring maximum resource-use efficiency within industrial processes.

Finally, because some form of industry and manufacturing capacity is essential to tackling the mass poverty in Third World countries, emphasizing a 'sustainable' pattern of industrial development is practically as important as emphasizing sustainable agricultural development. Moreover, there are important social criteria that must also be included in sustainable industrial development if we are also to talk about its providing 'sustainable livelihoods'. These criteria are best enunciated by the population affected by industrial development; but, at the very least, they should include providing secure employment and favourable indirect and induced employment effects, the use of technology that is appropriate to the level of skills and knowledge of its local labour force together with introducing new skills which can be easily assimilated through training, and a minimal displacement of traditional economic activities on which livelihoods currently depend. These are similar to the economic and social criteria that should be inherent in sustainable agricultural development, and are broadly consistent with the ES and SS goals discussed previously.

The case of micro-hydrosystems' manufacture and use in Nepal, funded and run by United Mission Nepal, is a good illustration of sustainable industrial development (Hislop, 1987). Hand-processing of rice, with traditional wooden water-mills, produced low yields and kept women working for 18 hours a day in some seasons. Nepal then began manufacturing its own modern cross-flow turbines and accessories for small hydroelectric schemes for about 400 mills scattered across remote villages and run by small entrepreneurs. The turbine-powered mills give better yields and do the work in 15 minutes at the cost of a small percentage of the produce. This frees women's labour for other essential tasks, and with a power output of around 1–7 horsepower the modern turbines make possible a wide range of new activities on top of the traditional rice-milling – including power generation and hence electric cooking which saves fuel-wood.

Another industrial development project that has had a similar benefit in terms of saving scarce wood supplies is the Kenya Improved Charcoal Stove Programme (Opale, 1987). A whole industry has now emerged around the production of an improved stove design. The efficiency improvements of the new ceramic jiko stove, of up to 30 per cent for charcoal burning, means that the stove pays for itself after 2 or 3 months. By the end of 1985, 180000 stoves had been sold. This has created a substantial increase in trade for local tinsmiths, potters, and small-scale urban industries producing ceramic liners.

With regard to human settlements, particularly in urban areas, there is a similar case to be made for sustainable settlement development. As Hardoy and Satterthwaite (1984, p. 329) conclude, 'in most cities lack of land-use control and lack of legal alternatives to unauthorised settlements creates a haphazard, sprawling pattern and a density of development too dispersed to allow for cost-effective infrastructure and service provision. It also promotes illegal housing developments on dangerous land-sites, unnecessary sprawl over prime agricultural land, and the destruction or degradation of the natural landscape with little or no provision for public space.' Moreover, 'The housing environments of lower-income groups in Third World cities are among the most degraded and dangerous living environments that exist', and are characterized by 'a lack of readily-available drinking-water, sewage connections (or other systems to dispose of human wastes), garbage collection, and basic measures to prevent disease and provide primary health-care' as well as by 'crowded, cramped conditions, which mean that communicable diseases such as TB flourish – usually aided by low resistance among the inhabitants due to malnutrition' (ibid., pp. 318–19).

There is grave need, therefore, for appropriate human settlements projects to tackle those problems and thus minimize the environmental degradation and vicious poverty trap suffered by the residents. One interesting example is the Orangi Pilot Project (OPP) in Karachi, Pakistan (Hasan, 1987). Orangi Township is the largest squatter colony in Karachi, with 700000 people on 5000 acres (2025 ha) of land. People have built their own dwellings, and have indicated that their most pressing need is a single, low-cost form of sanitation for the disposal of excreta and wastewater. Participating residents agreed to form local 'lane' organizations to contribute funds and organize work detail. After five years, 1571 'lane' organizations had built their sewage systems, serving approximately 200000 people, at a cost of $1.7 million (all but $100000 funded by residents). Equivalent work would have cost government agencies $8.5 million. Moreover, the enthusiasm and public learning generated by the OPP has sponsored additional follow-on programmes in housing, women's welfare, and women's work, initiated by the 'lane' organizations.

Economics revisited

As the above discussion indicates, there are certain development projects and programmes that reflect the principles of sustainable economic development. However, there is yet to be a systematic application of these principles in development policymaking and strategies as a whole. Part of the problem is that the leading policymaking institutions, such as the World Bank, are only just beginning to emphasize the need to incorporate environmental considerations in their development strategies (Conable, 1986; Runnalls, 1986). On the other hand, as the previous sections make clear, the concept of sustainable economic development needs to be made more concise, systematic and rigorous before it can be usefully applied in policymaking and planning.

A further problem is that most proponents of sustainable development usually advocate 'grassroots' or 'bottom-up' approaches to development planning, whereas conventional policymaking has consistently been 'top-down' in approach – beginning at the international or national level and filtering down to the regional and local levels. This explains why the conventional economic consensus on development, with its emphasis on economic growth and national economic performance, is more suited to 'top-down' than to 'bottom-up' development.

Nevertheless, the growing recognition that environmental considerations must be incorporated into development strategies is having some influence on policymaking and planning. This influence is beginning to be felt in economics, which is the discipline best able to analyse trade-offs among environmental costs and benefits. There are essentially four different developments in economics, particularly in the sub-discipline of environmental and resource economics, concerned with deriving policy recommendation from the issue of environmental sustainability. These areas can be referred to as cost-benefit analysis', 'resource accounting', 'macroeconomic policymaking', and 'sustainability-applied research'.

As was pointed out by the authors of the classic UNIDO *Guidelines*, the main rationale for conducting social cost–benefit analysis is to subject project choice to a consistent set of general objectives of national policy' (UNIDO, 1972). As perceptions of national policy objectives in Third World countries have changed, for example emphasizing the need for scarce foreign exchange and equitable income distribution, project appraisal and planning have been expanded to reflect the new objectives (Little and Mirlees, 1974; Squire and Tak, 1975). Consequently, the recent emphasis on the role of environmental quality and the long-run productivity of natural resource systems in sustaining economic development, has led to further extensions of social cost–benefit analysis to include environmental impacts (Dixon and Hutschmidt, 1986; Dixon *et al.*, 1986). That is, in contrast to traditional project evaluation which considers only the direct project benefits and costs, 'the expanded approach includes the external and environmental improvement benefits (*plus* the benefits from environmental protection), as well as the costs of external and/or environmental damages and of environmental control measures' (Dixon and Hufschmidt, 1986, p. 7). The basic methodology is first to identify and measure the environmental effects, and then, secondly, to translate them into monetary terms for inclusion in the formal project analysis.

However, extending cost–benefit analysis to incorporate the environmental impacts of projects encounters a number of problems. First, physical estimation of environmental effects is often difficult. Second, as most environmental resources are non-marketed common-property 'goods', economic valuation of their services is not straightforward. Third, little consensus exists regarding methods for monetary valuation of 'intangible environmental goods, such as the need to preserve unknown species for their intrinsic value (Goodland and Ledec, 1986).

Finally, as this expanded approach inevitably raises issues of intertemporal choice, the interest rate chosen to discount the future may determine whether environmental degradation is 'optimal'. It is often stressed that the appropriate discount rate should emerge from the project appraisal process (UNIDO, 1972). In practice, imperfect capital markets, inconsistent data on the productivity of capital, and large variances in domestic borrowing for investment, makes it difficult to establish an economic accounting rate of interest for Third World countries (Phillips, 1986). Furthermore, in many examples of poverty-induced environmental degradation, the sacrifice of long-term sustainability for immediate economic returns implies a high discount rate. This behaviour, however, is itself 'the result of the resource degradation process which compels actions to be taken which imply high discount rates' (Pearce, 1986, p. 13). In other words, the high apparent discount rates are a reflection of the constraints imposed by environmental degradation rather than the desired social choice.

In contrast to social cost–benefit analysis, resource accounting involves adjusting national income accounts to register both the direct costs inflicted by environmental degradation and the 'depreciation' of natural capital to allow for losses in future production potential (Environmental Accounting Workshop, 1985; Repetto, 1986b). Although the national accounts record the income earned from harvesting resource stocks (for example, fish catch, timber, meat, and so on), the loss of future income through declining resource stocks and deteriorating environmental quality is excluded. By allowing for such 'depreciations' in the natural capital stock, the net contributions of resource degradation to national income are much lower, and more accurately reflect the impact on economic welfare. For example, depreciation of the forest stock in Indonesia due to deforestation and timber extraction was estimated to cost around $3.6 thousand million in 1982, or approximately 4 per cent of GNP (Repetto, 1986b).

Because resource accounting uses the existing system of national accounts, it appeals to economic policymakers. Nonetheless, there are a number of limitations on its application. For one, measuring the stock of economic capital and its rate of depreciation in Third World countries is in itself a complicated task. Given the difficulties in quantifying and monetizing environmental goods, extending depreciation accounting to the stock of natural capital would prove even more difficult. Moreover some natural resources, such as the forest timber and fish stocks of a country, may be readily counted as discrete units, whereas others, such as soils and watersheds, are not easily measurable 'stocks' as such. Finally, accounting for the depreciation of natural resource stocks does not include all the externality, or 'off-site', environmental quality effects. For example, the total environmental costs of deforestation and timber extraction should include the economic costs of soil erosion, siltation of waterways, flooding and climatic impacts. Thus the direct depreciation loss of S3.6 thousand million for deforestation in Indonesia must be an underestimation of the total environmental costs of forest depletion.

A more comprehensive economic approach to the problems of environment and development is the integration of environmental and natural resource management directly into macroeconomic policy This is proposed in two ways: '(a) through the design of investment programs supporting environmental and natural resource objectives, and (b) through promotion of economic, social, and institutional, policies and incentives that influence the environmentally related behaviour of government agencies, major resource users, and countless small-scale resource-using activities, which occur throughout a nation's economy' (Warford, 1986). The appeal of such an approach is that it would rely on traditional economic tools and concepts, such as marginal opportunity cost, to measure the total environmental cost borne by society of depleting a natural resource (Pearce, 1986; Warford, 1986). Moreover, some existing economic policies such as irrigation subsidies, fiscal and financial inducements for livestock rearing, and agricultural export taxation, not only encourage environmental degradation but may also be economically inefficient (Repetto,

1986a). Correcting these policies offers the opportunity to pursue both environmental and developmental goals.

Designing macroeconomic policies and incentives for natural resource management may in the long run provide the best potential for initiating policies based on the concept of sustainable economic development. At present, however, this approach has yet to be developed sufficiently for implementation as a source of concise policy guidelines for Third World countries. Along with cost–benefit analysis and resource accounting, this approach faces the difficulty of quantifying and monetizing environmental impacts. There also need to be clearly defined priorities and mechanisms built into macroeconomic policies when the goals of development and environment are not mutually compatible. For example, exploitation of wilderness forest-lands may cause irreversible environmental damage over time; on the other hand, the scarce foreign exchange earnings generated by timber and mineral exports are an immediate benefit.

Similarly, the abolition of taxes on agricultural exports may mean higher incomes for cash-crop producers, but the rise in producer prices may encourage the extension of cultivation onto 'marginal' land. Finally, macroeconomic policies are by definition top-down in implementation. Although some degree of flexibility is necessary to allow for regional variations in economic and environmental conditions, such an approach cannot be ideal for encouraging grassroots participation in decision-making. Thus, it is essential that macroeconomic policies for natural resource management be supplemented by projects at the regional and local levels that have sustainability as their primary objective.

Projects and sectoral policies for sustainable economic development are therefore a natural complement to any macroeconomic environment and development initiative. This in turn requires appropriate applied analysis of the sustainability of development projects and policies at the local, regional, and sectoral, levels. For example, as discussed above, Conway (1985 and 1987) has developed an approach for assessing the sustainability of agro-ecosystems. Similarly, there is a growing interest in reviews of policies affecting the sustainable development of forest lands, such as the review recently conducted in Indonesia (Government of Indonesia and IIED, 1985).

Until very recently, the issue of sustainability has been largely ignored in conventional economic analysis. As discussed above, the traditional approach to cost–benefit analysis maximizes discounted net income flows. Unless the sustainability of the economic activity generating income is explicitly included as a welfare objective, it may be optimal 'to drive or exploit a system so that it is not longer sustainable' (Tisdell, 1986, p. 10). This is another argument in favour of extending cost–benefit analysis to include the external environmental impacts of projects. As Pearce (1985, p. 21) has argued, however, even if the external environmental costs imposed by resource depletion are estimated, 'there is nothing in the conventional concept of an external cost to account for the decay of ecological processes themselves', and as a result, 'in the absence of perfect information about both perfect and instantaneous response to ecological disequilibrium, the system can be unsustainable'. In other words, because the soil erosion, increased flooding and sedimentation accompanying deforestation also affect other economic activities, those impacts will be counted as external costs; however, any decline in the resilience of the forest system and its ecological functions resulting from further stress, is not strictly an economic 'externality'.

Thus if the sustainability of the ecological processes underlying economic activity is recognized to have value, then sustainability must explicitly be included as one of the objectives to be pursued by development planners and policymakers. As has been stressed throughout this paper, the pursuit of sustainability in turn may require balancing several goals that are spread over three systems – economic, social, and biological and so on. As not all of these objectives can be simultaneously maximized, the possible trade-offs for different activities and conditions need to be analysed. Making explicit the types of trade-offs involved is a vital function that economics can provide in applied sustainability research.

Summary

Increasing recognition that the overall goals of environmental conservation and economic development are not conflicting but can be mutually reinforcing, has prompted calls for 'environmentally sustainable' economic development. Although there are difficulties in defining sustainable development in an analytically rigorous way, there is still a need to evolve a concept of sustainability that both distinguishes it from other post-war meanings of development and is useful for practical analysis and policymaking.

Economic development is conventionally defined as the 'process whereby the real per capita income of a country increase over a long period of time – subject to the stipulations that the number below an "absolute poverty line" does not increase, and that the distribution of income does not become more unequal' (Meier, 1976, p. 6). This consensus has underlined most post-war interpretations of development, with perhaps the exception of the 'basic needs' approach, which places priority on *improving* the living conditions of the absolute poor.

Sustainable economic development additionally argues that 'real' improvements cannot occur unless the strategies which are being formulated and implemented are ecologically sustainable over the long term, are consistent with social values and institutions, and encourage 'grassroots' participation in the development process. As the primary objective is to provide lasting and secure livelihoods that minimize resource depletion, environmental degradation, cultural disruption, and social instability, this process can be viewed as an interaction among three systems: the biological and resource system, the economic system, and the social system. The general objective is to maximize the goals across all these systems through a dynamic and adaptive process of trade-offs.

To be truly useful as a concept of economic development, 'sustainability' must be applicable to all forms of economic and social activity, ranging from agriculture and forestry to industry and human settlements. Policy recommendations are emerging in four areas: 'cost–benefit analysis', 'resource accounting', 'macroeconomic policymaking', and 'sustainability–applied research'. The next stage must be to develop the analytical tools which are necessary to apply the concept of sustainable economic development to various economic–environmental systems.

Acknowledgements

I would like to thank Czech Conroy, Gordon Conway, Richard Sandbrook, and Robin Sharp, all of IIED, and anonymous referees, for useful comments on an earlier version of this chapter. The chapter has also benefited from a discussion on sustainable development that was held on 29 September 1986 at IIED, London, England. Besides the author, participants included Czech Conroy, Gordon Conway, Paul Harrison, Gerald Leach, Jules Pretty, and Richard Sandbrook. Comments, by David Hall and David Pearce, on discussion notes prepared for that meeting by the author, Paul Harrison, and Gerald Leach, were also helpful, as were the notes themselves.

References

Arndt, H.W. (1981), 'Economic development: a semantic history'. *Economic Development and Cultural Change*, **29** (3), 457–66.

Asian Development Bank (1986), *Environmental Planning and Management*, Regional Symposium on Environmental and Natural Resources Planning, Manila, Philippines, 19–21 February.

Bartelmus, Peter (1986), *Environment and Development*, London: Allen & Unwin.

Bunch, Roland (1987), *Case Study of Guinope Integrated Development Program*, paper presented at IIED's Conference on Sustainable Development, London, 28–30 April. London: IIED. Mimeo.

Caldwell, Lynton K. (1984), 'Political aspects of ecologically sustainable development', *Environmental Conservation*, **11** (4), 299–308.

Centre for Science and Environment (1985), *The State of India's Environment 1984–85: The Second Citizen's Report*, New Delhi: Centre for Science and Environment.

Cernea, Michael M. (ed.) (1985), *Putting People First: Sociological Variables in Rural Development*, New York: Oxford University Press for the World Bank.

Chambers, Robert (1986a), *Poverty in India: Concepts, Research and Reality: an Exploration*, University of Sussex, Brighton: Institute of Development Studies.

Chambers, Robert (1986b), *Sustainable Livelihoods: An Opportunity for the World Commission on Environment and Development*, University of Sussex, Brighton: Institute of Development Studies.

Conable, Barber B. (1986), *Address to the Board of Governors of the World Bank and the International Finance Corporation*, Washington, DC, 30 September, Washington, DC: World Bank.

Conway, Gordon R. (1985), 'Agroecosystem analysis', *Agricultural Administration*, **20**, 31–55.
Conway, Gordon R. (1987), 'The properties of agroecosystems', *Agricultural Systems*, **24** (2): 95–117.
Cottingham, Robert (1987), *Dry-season Gardening Projects, Niger, West Africa*, paper presented at IIED's Conference on Sustainable Development, London, 28–30 April, London: IIED. Mimeo.
Dixon, John A. and Maynard Hufschmidt (eds) (1986), *Economic Valuation Techniques for the Environment*, Baltimore, MD: Johns Hopkins University Press.
Dixon, John A., Richard A. Carpenter, Louise A. Fallon, Paul B. Sherman and Supachit Manopimoke (1986), *Economic Analysis of the Environmental Impacts of Development Projects*, Manila: Asian Development Bank.
Environmental Accounting Workshop (1985), *Environmental Accounting: A Report with Specific Recommendations*, Washington, DC: World Bank.
Global Tomorrow Coalition (1985), *Sustainable Development and How to Achieve It*, paper prepared by Non-governmental Organizations for submission to the World Commission on Environment and Development, 5 May, Washington, DC.
Goodland, Robert and George Ledec (1986), *Neoclassical Economics and Principles of Sustainable Development*, Office of Environmental and Scientific Affairs, Washington, DC: World Bank.
Goulet, Denis (1971), *The Cruel Choice: A New Concept in the Theory of Development*, New York: Atheneum.
Government of Indonesia and IIED (1985), *Forest Policies in Indonesia: The Sustainable Development of Forest Lands*, vols I–IV, Jakarta: Government of Indonesia.
Hardoy, Jorge E. and David Satterthwaite (1984), 'Third World Cities and the Environment of Poverty', *Geoforum*, **15** (3), 307–33.
Harrison, Paul (1987), *The Greening of Africa: Breaking Through the Battle for Land and Food*, London: Paladin.
Hasan, Arif (1987), *The Low-cost Sanitation Programme of the Orangi Pilot Project: Six Questions*, paper presented at IIED's Conference on Sustainable Development, London, 28–30 April, London: IIED. Mimeo.
Herrick, Bruce and Charles P. Kindleberger (1983), *Economic Development*, 4th edn, Tokyo: McGraw-Hill.
Hislop, Drummond (1987), *Micro-hydro Programme in Nepal – A Case Study*, paper presented at IIED's Conference on Sustainable Development, London, 28–30 April, London: IIED. Mimeo.
ILO (1976), *Employment, Growth and Basic Needs, A One World Problem*, Geneva: ILO.
IUCN (1980), *World Conservation Strategy: Living Resource Conservation for Sustainable Development*, Gland: IUCN–UNEP–WWF.
KEPAS (1985), *The Critical Uplands of Eastern Java: An Agro-ecosystem Analysis*, Kelompok Penelitian Agro-Ekosistem, Indonesia: Agency for Agricultural Research.
Kottak, Conrad P. (1985), *When People Don't Come First: Some Sociological Lessons*, pp. 325–6 in Cernea (q.v.).
Lee, James A. (1985), *The Environment, Public Health and Human Ecology: Considerations for Economic Development*, Baltimore, MD: The Johns Hopkins University Press for The World Bank.
Lee, James A. and Robert Goodland (1986), 'Economic development and the environment', *Finance and Development*, **23** (4), 36–9.
Little, I.M.D. and J.A. Mirlees (1974), *Project Appraisal and Planning for Developing Countries*, London: Heinemann.
Meier, Gerald M. (1976), *Leading Issues in Economic Development*, 3rd edn, New York: Oxford University Press.
Meier, Gerald M. (1984), *Emerging From Poverty: The Economics That Really Matters*, New York: Oxford University Press.
Muntemba, Shimwaayi (1985), *Rural Development and Women: Lessons from the Field*, Geneva: ILO.
Myrdal, Gunnar (1968), *Asian Drama: An Inquiry into the Poverty of Nations*, 3 vols, New York: Pantheon.
Odum, Eugene P. (1975), *Ecology*, 2nd edn, London: Holt Rinehard and Winston.

Opale, Monica (1987), *The Introduction of the Kenya Jiko Stove. A KENGO Experience*, paper presented at IIED's Conference of Sustainable Development, London, 28–30 April, London: IIED. Mimeo.

Pearce, David W. (1985), *Sustainable Futures: Economics and the Environment*. Inaugural Lecture, University College, London, 5 December, London: University College.

Pearce, David W. (1986), *The Sustainable Use of Natural Resources in Developing Countries*. Discussion Paper 86–15. Dept of Economics, University College. London. Mimeo.

Phillips, David A. (1986), 'Pitfalls in estimating social discount rates: a case study', *Project Appraisal*, **1** (1), 15–20.

Repetto, Robert (1986a), *Economic Policy Reforms for Natural Resource Conservation*, Washington, DC: World Resources Institute.

Repetto, Robert (1986b), *Natural Resource Accounting in a Resource Based Economy: An Indonesian Case Study*, Washington, DC: World Resources Institute.

Repetto, Robert (1986c), *World Enough and Time: Successful Strategies for Resource Management*, New Haven, CT: Yale University Press for World Resources Institute.

Runnalls, David (1986), 'Factors influencing environmental policies in international development agencies', pp. 185–229 in Asian Development Bank (q.v.).

Squire, Lyn and Herman G. van der Tak (1975), *Economic Analysis of Projects*, Baltimore, MD: Johns Hopkins University Press.

Stewart, Frances (1985), *Planning To Meet Basic Needs*, London: Macmillan.

Streeten, Paul, Shahid Javed Burki, Mahbub Ul Haq, N. Hicks and Frances Stewart (1981), *First Things First: Meeting Basic Needs in Developing Countries*, New York: Oxford University Press for The World Bank.

Tisdell, Clement A. (1983), 'An economist's critique of the World Conservation Strategy with examples from the Australian experience', *Environmental Conservation*, **10** (1), 43–52.

Tisdell, Clement A. (1986), *Sustainable Development: Conflicting Approaches of Ecologists and Economists, and Implications for LDCs*, New South Wales, Economics Department, University of Newcastle.

Tolba, Mostafa K., quoted in Margaret R. Biswas and Asit K. Biswas (1984), 'Complementarity between environmental and development processes', *Environmental Conservation*, **11** (1), 39.

Uphoff, Norman (1985), 'Fitting Projects to People', pp. 359–95 in Cernea (q.v.).

UNIDO (1972), *Guidelines for Project Evaluation*, New York: United Nations.

Warford, Jeremy J. (1986), *Natural Resource Management and Economic Development*, Projects Policy Department, Washington, DC: World Bank.

World Bank (1985), *Desertification in the Sahelian and Sudanian Zones of West Africa*, Washington, DC: World Bank.

2. Alternative approaches to economic–environmental interactions*

Abstract

The key questions raised by recent developments in resource and environmental economics have been what useful economic functions does the environment provide and how are these functions affected by the process of economic–environmental interaction? This chapter distinguishes between two different formal approaches to answering these questions: the more conventional approach which is concerned with the optimal allocation of economically valuable exhaustible resources and an alternative analysis that considers the trade-off between, on the one hand, environmental quality, and on the other, resource depletion and waste generation by the economic process. To illustrate and extend the latter approach, a model is constructed to show how this trade-off might lead to continuously declining environmental quality and a future ecological constraint. Society must therefore optimally allocate output between consumption and services to improve the environment and choose between increased capital accumulation and environmental degradation. Although strict application of such a model may be limited, it has wider implications for the role of technological change and the value of the environment in any system experiencing deteriorating environmental quality.

Introduction

Economic analysis of resource and environmental problems has been extensively developed in recent years. To distinguish its general approach from those of other scientific disciplines, this analysis has relied on one guiding principle, that is 'that the satisfaction of any value requires the use of scarce productive services of some type, and we must necessarily have some way to allocate them' (Herfindahl, 1974a, p. 5). The crucial questions that environmental and resource economists have been asking, therefore, are what useful economic functions does the environment provide and how are these functions affected by the process of economic–environmental interaction?

This chapter distinguishes between two different formal approaches to answering these questions: the more conventional approach which is concerned with the optimal allocation of economically valuable exhaustible resources[1] and an alternative analysis that considers the trade-off between, on the one hand, environmental quality and, on the other, resource depletion and waste generation by the economic process. To illustrate and extend the latter approach, a model of economic–environmental interaction is constructed to show how this trade-off might lead to continuously declining environmental quality and a future ecological constraint.

Although strict application of such a model may be limited, it has wider implications for the role of technological innovations and the value of the environment in any system experiencing deteriorating environmental quality. The concerns, and indeed some of the propositions suggested in this model, are not new. It builds on earlier attempts to integrate environmental dimensions into growth models, and the experiences learned from incorporating ideas from thermodynamics and ecology into economics. The model of this chapter therefore demonstrates the physical dependency of economic activity on the sustainability of crucial natural resource systems and ecological functions, and indicates the economic costs, or trade-offs, resulting from the failure to preserve sustainability and environmental quality. The objective is 'sustainable' growth and development, and it mirrors the increasing concern over new – possibly irreversible – environmental dangers, such as the greenhouse effect, ozone-layer depletion, land degradation, deforestation, and so forth, rather than reiterating the previous concern with material and energy shortages *per se*. In short, the alternative approach is more applicable to the emerging problems of *environmental degradation*, which require a different method of analysis than the conventional problem of *depletion of a specific resource stock*.

Conventional approaches

Following the classic work by Hotelling (1931), the conventional economic approach is to treat natural resources as comparable to other assets of wealth in the economy worth 'holding' in the present. Consequently, the conventional definition of natural resources is usually limited to those environmental resources providing economically valuable productive services in the economic system, meaning that only one function of the natural environment – as supplier of the raw material and energy inputs to the economic process – is considered relevant to the phenomenon of natural-resource scarcity. Since they are valuable commodities traded in markets, as these resources become increasingly scarce, their prices will rise relative to those of other goods.

What makes certain material and energy-yielding natural resources worth holding compared to other assets, therefore, is the expected threat of future scarcity from over-exploitation and depletion. Hence the conventional economic approach is to ask what is the optimal rate of extraction or depletion of these economically valuable resources. Ideally, for any particular resource, this will depend on its relative scarcity, and thus (shadow) price, over time compared to other assets (both 'natural' and economic), which in turn should depend on the availability of substitutes, technological innovation, economies of scale, market imperfections, the pattern of property rights and whether the resource is 'renewable'.

The general convention is to 'call extractive resources renewable or non-renewable depending on whether they exhibit economically significant rates of regeneration' (Fisher and Peterson, 1977, p. 681). In the case of strictly 'non-renewable' resources, it may be optimal to deplete the resource completely if the availability of future technologies and perfect substitutes mean that exploitation of the resource is no longer 'essential' for future production (Dasgupta and Heal, 1974, 1979; Solow, 1974b; Stiglitz, 1974; Kamien and Schwartz, 1978; Dasgupta and Stiglitz, 1981). That is, because the future scarcity of the resource has been mitigated, the resource is not worth holding compared to other income-earning assets, and the optimal choice may be to exhaust the resource quickly and invest in these other assets. Even in the case of renewable resources, such as a forest valued for its timber, exhaustion may be optimal if the resource is growing at a slow rate, harvesting costs are low and its value appreciates more slowly than the market rate of interest (Clark, 1976; V.L. Smith, 1977).

Thus the conventional approach to natural resource scarcity usually engenders optimism, that is, 'there seems to be little reason to worry about the exhaustion of resources which the market already treats as economic goods' (Nordhaus and Tobin, 1977, p. 402; see also Barnett and Morse, 1963; Beckerman, 1974; Solow, 1974a). For those resources of the environment used as basic material and energy inputs, market forces should dictate the optimal rate of exploitation automatically and effectively.[2]

Alternative approaches

An alternative approach to resource and environmental problems is to recognize that there is not just one but three important functions performed by scarce environmental resources: first, as emphasized by conventional approaches, the environment provides useful material and energy inputs for the economic process; second, the environment assimilates the waste by-products generated by this process; and third, the natural environment provides certain utility-yielding services, or ecological functions, that are essential for supporting the economic system and human welfare.[3] The latter range from recreational, health, cultural, educational, scientific and aesthetic services to the maintenance of essential climatic and ecological cycles and functions (Freeman, 1979; Pearsall, 1984; Barbier, 1989a).

Together, these three economic functions of the environment underline the physical dependency of the economic process and human welfare on ecological stability and the sufficiency of potentially scarce environmental resources. The fundamental scarcity problem, therefore, is that as the environment is increasingly being exploited for one set or uses, say, to provide new sources of raw material and energy inputs and to assimilate additional waste, the quality of the environment may deteriorate over time. The consequence is an increasing 'relative' scarcity of essential environmental services and ecological functions (Barbier, 1989a). In other words, if 'the environment is regarded as a scarce resource', then the 'deterioration of the environment is also an economic problem' (Hueting, 1980, pp. 1, 3).

Such an approach may lead to applying different criteria for the economic exploitation of environmental resources. For example, where conventional criteria might justify the cutting down of a forest, alternative criteria might justify preservation if the expected loss of value resulting from the decline in genetic diversity, soil quality, ecological stability, natural beauty, and so on were considered too high (Krutilla and Fisher, 1985). In other words, only by looking at the *total economic value* provided by *all* the functions of an environmental asset, is it possible to weigh the environmental benefits of preservation foregone against the net benefits of development (Pearce, Barbier and Markandya, 1990).

There are a growing number of studies emphasizing the environmental costs of economic activity, such as 'the transformation and loss of whole environments as would result, for example, from clear cutting a redwood forest, or developing a hydroelectric project in the Grand Canyon' (Fisher, Krutilla and Cicchetti, 1972, p. 605; see also Arrow and Fisher, 1974; Krutilla and Fisher, 1985; Miller and Menz, 1979; Turner, 1988; Southgate, 1989). Thus Krutilla and Fisher (1985) demonstrate that irreversible conversion of natural areas in fixed supply may have a high opportunity cost by foreclosing the future option of deriving environmental services from these areas. Other studies have stressed the essential utility-yielding role of natural ecosystems and their environmental functions (Freeman, 1979; Hueting, 1980; Farnworth et al., 1981; Pearsall, 1984; Farber and Costanza, 1987; Turner, 1988; Barbier, 1989a; Barbier and Markandya, 1989). The conventional approach to optimal resource depletion has also been broadened to incorporate the conditions that allow the preservation of natural environments containing resources used as productive inputs (Krautkraemer, 1985; Southgate, 1989), or to embrace an integrated approach to a variety of resource allocation problems (Dasgupta, 1982; V.K. Smith and Krutilla, 1979). In addition, analysis of optimal choice over time among consumption, accumulation and environmental quality has been the focus of a number of studies (Vousden, 1973; Maler, 1974; Becker, 1982; Barbier, 1989a; Barbier and Markandya, 1989). On still a broader front, Norgaard (1984, 1985) discusses the 'coevolutionary development' of ongoing feedback and interaction between social and ecological systems, whereby the feedback mechanisms previously maintaining the ecosystem are assumed by or shifted to the social system.

The model of this chapter follows, and hopefully clarifies, these approaches by addressing a situation where economic–environmental interaction not only leads to increasing 'relative' scarcity of utility-yielding environmental services, but as environmental quality declines, there is also the possibility of widespread ecological disruption and disturbances. That is, in the long run, an absolute ecological constraint may arise because the increasing environmental degradation inflicted by the economic process irrevocably disrupts natural ecosystems, permanently impairing essential environmental functions on which economic activity and human welfare depend (Daly, 1979; Barbier, 1989a).

Such a model may be appropriate in cases where cumulative resource depletion and waste generation by the economic process lead to severe ecological disruption and the collapse of human livelihoods. For example, with continuous tropical deforestation, there may be adverse local and interregional ecological disturbances that radically alter rainfall patterns, climate and species diversity. The result may be a catastrophic decline in the ability of the forest area and neighbouring regions to support dependent economic systems and human populations (Myers, 1984; Sioli, 1985; Southgate, 1989). Similarly, climatic changes resulting from excess emission of greenhouse gases from industrial activity may significantly affect agricultural productivity and thus the ability of some regions of the world to feed their populations (Oram, 1985; Barbier, 1989b). Intensive agricultural production on marginal lands can lead to accelerating problems of soil erosion, watershed degradation and even desertification (American Farmland Trust, 1984; Barbier, 1988; Nelson, 1988; Southgate, 1988). Long-term combustion of fossil fuels emitting SO_x and NO_x pollution may increase 'acid rain' to levels intolerable for forest and freshwater ecosystems, thus destabilizing livelihoods dependent on fishing and forestry activities (WRI/IIED, 1986, ch. 10).

A model of economic–environmental interaction

The following model analyses the prospect of irreversible damage to the natural environment arising from resource depletion and waste generation; the outcome is a steady decline in environmental quality leading to potential long-run disruptions to important ecological systems and functions. In order to capture these 'relative' and 'absolute' scarcity impacts of increasing environmental degradation over time, several assumptions are adopted.

First, to indicate the dependency of human welfare on essential environmental services and ecological functions, a stock variable representing environmental quality, X_t,[4] is included along with consumption, C_t, as arguments in the social welfare function, U:

$$U = U\,(C_t, X_t) \tag{2.1}$$

with $U_c(C_t) > 0$, $U_{cc}(C_t) < 0$, $U_x(X_t) > 0$, $U_{xx}(X_t) < 0$. Equation (2.1) indicates that at any time t social welfare is a concave, increasing function of consumption and environmental quality. To simplify analysis, the welfare function is additively separable, that is,

$$U_{cx} = U_{xc} = 0$$

Second, it is assumed that at any time t any output, Q_t, produced by the economic system that is not used for consumption, for providing environmental improvement services, V_t, or for replacing depreciated capital, wK_t, leads to a net accumulation in the capital stock, $K_t - K_{t-1}$:

$$K_t - K_{t-1} = Q_t - (C_t + V_t) - wK_t \tag{2.2}$$

Capital depreciates at the constant rate w. Environmental improvement services can be divided between those that directly improve environmental quality through, say, conservation practices, resource management, pollution clean-ups and so on, and those that indirectly improve X_t by increasing recycling and abatement of waste residual otherwise emitted into the environment.

Third, following the 'relative' scarcity argument of the 'alternative' approach, it is assumed that at any time t as the economic process extracts resources, R_t, from the environment and generates (net) waste, N_t, increasing environmental degradation, $S_t - S_{t-1}$, occurs and, as a result, environmental quality declines:

$$S_t - S_{t-1} = f(R_t, N_t) \tag{2.3}$$

$$X_t = X(S_t, V_t) \tag{2.4}$$

$$X_t < X_{t-1} \tag{2.5}$$

with $f_r(R_t) > 0$, $f_n(N_t) > 0$, $X_s(S_t) < 0$ and $X_v(V_t) > 0$. Equation (2.4) shows that environmental quality is a decreasing function of environmental degradation, S_t, and an increasing function of environmental improvement services, V_t. A crucial assumption is that, since $S_t - S_{t-1} > 0$ throughout any time period t, then X_t must also be declining (conditions (2.3) and (2.5)). That is, environmental degradation occurs each period because the economic process must require some resource inputs, R_t, for production and generate some net waste, N_t. However, to suggest that the result is lower environmental quality each period implies that: (a) the level of environmental improvement services, V_t, is insufficient to counteract the increased environmental degradation, and (b) ecosystems are unable to 'repair' the resulting damage to crucial functions, cycles and resources through converting the energy flow from the sun or utilizing any inputs of material and energy from neighbouring ecosystems. These are clearly strong assumptions that may not hold for all economic–environmental systems.[5]

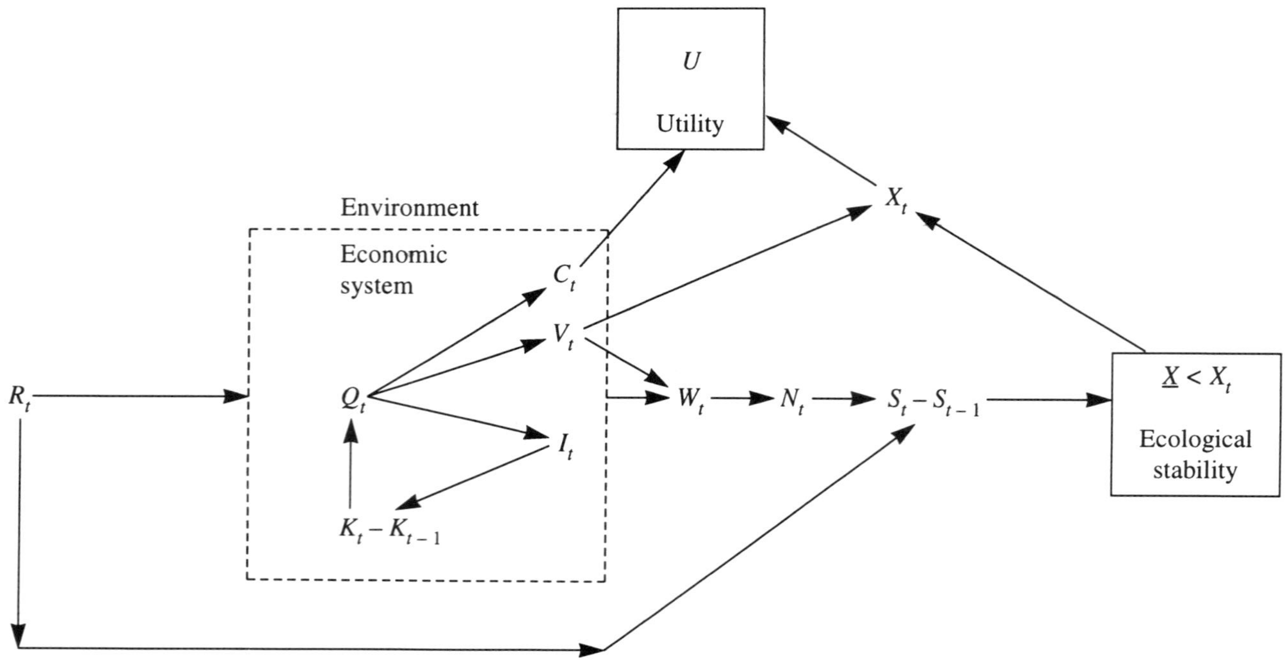

Figure 2.1 *Flow diagram of economic–environmental interaction*

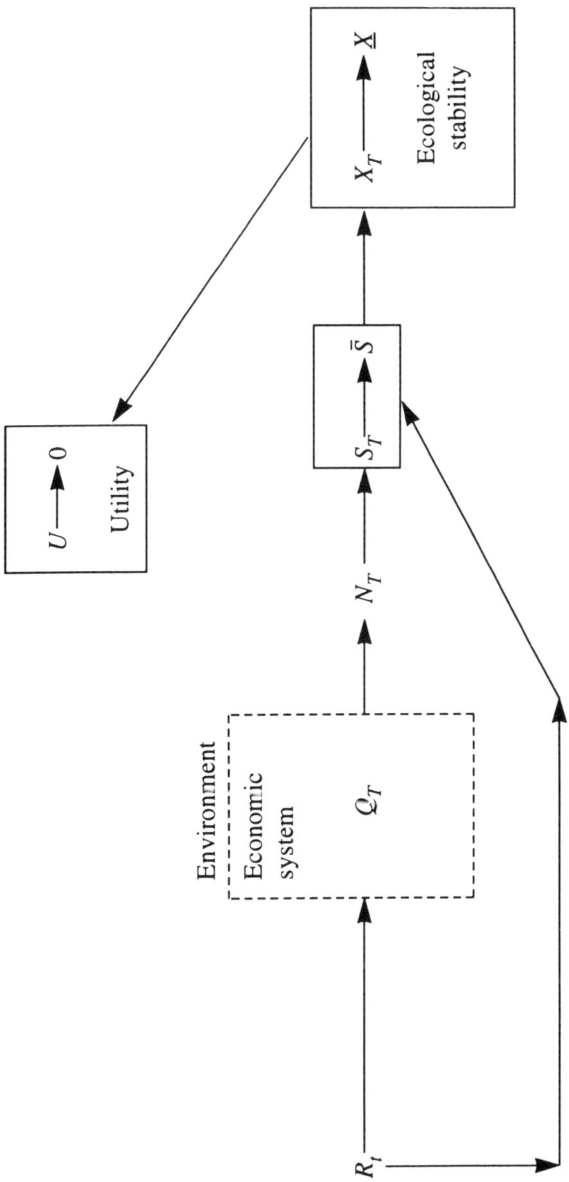

Figure 2.2 Long-run ecological constraint

Fourth, in order to incorporate the ‘absolute’ ecological constraint discussed above, the life of the economic–environmental system is assumed to be finite, where terminal time T is that period at the end of which environmental degradation reaches some maximum level, $\overline{S}$, driving environmental quality to some minimum level, X, and thus irrevocably destabilizing the entire economic–environmental system. This constraint on the system can be summarized as:

$$t_0 \leq t < T, \quad \underline{X} < X_t \quad \text{and} \quad U = U(C_t, X_t) \qquad (2.6)$$
$$\lim_{t \to T} t, \quad \lim_{S_t \to \overline{S}} X(S_t), \quad \text{and} \quad \lim U \to 0$$

The size of the population and its growth often impact on the environment. However, in this approach this affect has been left out of consideration. Assuming population growth is constant, the remaining functional relationships of the model can be simplified to:

$$Q_t = Q(K_t) \text{ with } Q_k(K_t) > 0 \text{ and } Q_{kk}(K_t) < 0^6 \qquad (2.7)$$

$$R_t = R(Q_t) \text{ with } R_q(Q_t) > 0 \qquad (2.8)$$

$$N_t = W(Q_t) - B\,(V_t) \qquad (2.9)$$

with $B_v(V_t) > 0$, $B_{vv}(V_t) < 0$ and $W_q(Q_t) > 0$. That is, production is a function of the capital stock; resource use and waste generation, W_t, are functions of total output; and net waste generation is W_t less any recycling, B_t.

Finally, the initial and terminal conditions of the model are respectively:

$$K_0 = \underline{K}, \quad S_0 = \underline{S} \qquad (2.10)$$

$$K_T \geq \overline{K} \geq 0, \quad S_T \geq \overline{S} \qquad (2.11)$$

The functional relationships of the model for period $t_0 \leq t \leq T$ are summarized in Figure 2.1, and the operation of the absolute constraint in period T is shown in Figure 2.2.

Optimal allocation over time

Thus the planning problem suggested by the model is how best to allocate economic and environmental resources over time given the current ‘relative’ scarcity problem of declining environmental quality and the threat of a future ecological constraint on the entire system. A dynamic discrete time optimization problem can be constructed from the model with the aid of a few substitutions.

Substituting (2.7)–(2.9) into (2.3) yields:

$$S_t - S_{t-1} = f(R(Q(K_t)), W(Q(K_t)) - B(V_t)) = g(K_t, V_t) \tag{2.12}$$

with $g_k(K_t) > 0$ and $g_v(V_t) < 0$. That is, as capital accumulation leads to production growth and – in the absence of technological change – more resource throughput, whereas environmental improvement services reduce waste through recycling, then environmental degradation is essentially an increasing function of K_t and a decreasing function of V_t at time t.

Expressions (2.12) and (2.4) can be substituted for X_t in the social welfare function (2.1), which is now summed over the finite planning period $[t, T]$ and discounted at the rate $0 < r < 1$:

$$U = \sum_{t=1}^{T} \frac{1}{(1+r)^{t-1}} U\left(C_t, X\left(S_{t-1} + g\left(K_t, V_t\right), V_t\right)\right) \tag{2.13}$$

A Lagrangean function, L^*, can now be formed from (2.13), (2.2), (2.10) and (2.11):

$$\begin{aligned} L^* = & \sum_{t=1}^{T} \frac{1}{(1+r)^{t-1}} U\left(C_t, X\left(S_{t-1} + g\left(K_t, V_t\right), V_t\right)\right) \\ & + \sum_{t=1}^{T} p_t\left(K_{t-1} + Q_t\left(K_t\right) - \left(C_t + V_t\right) - wK_t - K_t\right) \\ & + p_0\left(\underline{K} - K_0\right) + p_{T+1}\left(K_T - \overline{K}\right) + u\left(\underline{S} - S_0\right) + a\left(S_T - \overline{S}\right) \end{aligned} \tag{2.14}$$

The Lagrangean multiplier p_t can be interpreted as the utility value of an additional unit of capital, that is, the social value of capital accumulation that becomes available in period t. Similarly, the multiplier u represents the social value of an increase in the initial level of environmental degradation, S_0, whereas a indicates the social value of a 'relaxation' in the binding terminal constraint, as represented by an increase in $\overline{S}$.

Thus the dynamic optimization problem is to maximize (2.14) by optimal choice of C_t, V_t and K_t. Assuming C_t, V_t, K_t and $S_t > 0$, the first-order conditions are:

$$\frac{\mathrm{d}L^*}{\mathrm{d}C_t} = \frac{1}{(1+r)^{t-1}} U_c\left(C_t\right) - p_t = 0 \quad t = 1, \ldots, T \tag{2.15}$$

$$\frac{dL^*}{dV_t} = \frac{1}{(1+r)^{t-1}} U_x(X_t)\big(X_s(S_t)g_v(V_t) + X_v(V_t)\big) = 0 \qquad t = 1,\ldots, T \tag{2.16}$$

$$\frac{dL^*}{dK_t} = \frac{1}{(1+r)^{t-1}} U_x(X_t)X_s(S_t)g_k(K_t) + p_{t+1} - p_t + p_t\big(Q_k(K_t) - w\big) = 0 \quad t = 1,\ldots, T \tag{2.17}$$

$$\frac{dL^*}{dK_0} = p_1 - p_0 = 0 \tag{2.18}$$

$$\frac{dL^*}{dS_0} = U_x(X_1)X_s(S_1)\big(1 + g(K_1, V_1)\big) - u = 0 \tag{2.19}$$

$$\frac{dL^*}{dS_T} = \frac{1}{(1+r)^{T-1}} U_x(X_T)X_s(S_T) + a = 0 \tag{2.20}$$

As specified, the complexity of the model prevents characterization of a final solution to these equations. Interpretation of these conditions, however, does provide some useful insights into society's allocative choices when faced with the unique 'relative' and 'absolute' scarcity constraints of the model. For example, condition (2.15) can be substituted into condition (2.16) to yield:

$$\frac{U_c(C_t)}{U_x(X_t)} = X_s(S_t)g_v(V_t) + X_v(V_t) \qquad t = 1,\ldots, T \tag{2.21}$$

This suggests that the marginal rate of substitution of X_t for C_t is equated in each period with the impacts on the environment of a marginal increase in environmental improvement services. These services either protect the environment directly, $X_v(V_t)$, or indirectly by recycling waste and thus reducing some of the negative impact of the economic process on the environment, $X_x(S_t)\ g_v(V_t)$. Thus condition (2.21) defines the optimal trade-off between increased consumption and provision of services to improve the environment. That is, at any time $t = 1, \ldots, T$ any allocation of output between C_t and V_t must obey this rule.

Condition (2.17) can be rearranged as:

$$p_{t+1} - p_t = p_t\left(Q_k(K_t) - w\right) + \frac{1}{(1+r)^{t-1}} U_x(X_t) X_s(S_t) g_k(K_t) \quad t = 1, \ldots, T \qquad (2.22)$$

which indicates that the social value of capital is changing in each period according to the benefits of marginal capital productivity net of depreciation, $p_t(Q_k(K_t) - w)$, less the discounted marginal damage of the environmental degradation accompanying this increased productivity, $U_x(X_t)\ X_s(S_t)\ g_k(K_t)$. Capital accumulation that is not replacing depreciated stock leads to increased output and thus socially valuable consumption and environmental improvement services. At the same time, however, the increased output requires a greater use of resources by the economic system, which in turn increases environmental degradation. The former can be considered the benefits of capital accumulation and the latter the costs. If in any period the costs exceed the benefits of capital accumulation, then its social value will decline. If the costs equal the benefits, the value remains constant, that is,

$$\text{if } p_t\left(Q_k(K_t) - w\right) = \frac{1}{(1+r)^{t-1}} U_x(X_t) X_s(S_t) g_k(K_t)$$

$$\text{then } p_{t+1} - p_t = 0 \quad t = 1, \ldots, T \qquad (2.23)$$

Expressions (2.22) and (2.23), therefore, are the rule governing the optimal rate of capital accumulation, and thus growth, in the economy.

Condition (2.18) states that the social value of additional capital in the first planning period and the period before are equal; that is, the social value of capital is unchanged up to the first period. Condition (2.19) shows that the negative social value of a decline in the initial state of the environment must be equal to the marginal damage of an increase in environmental degradation in the first period. Any such increase in S_0 must be a social cost, for it both lowers initial environmental quality, X_1, and it brings the system that much closer to the level of environmental degradation that causes its 'collapse', $\bar{S}$. In contrast, an increase in $\bar{S}$ would prolong the life of the economic–environmental system and is therefore beneficial to society. From condition (2.20), this benefit is equivalent to the marginal utility of a decrease in environmental degradation in the last period.

To summarize, this model has derived the optimal conditions for allocating economic and environmental resources in an interdependent economic–environmental system where any resource depletion and waste generation by the economic process leads to deteriorating environmental quality and an eventual ecological collapse. As the model has stressed that the state, or quality, of the environment is an essential determinant of social welfare, environmental improvement services are recognized as a socially valuable component of economic output, and in every period, society must optimally allocate output between consumption and services to improve the environment. Although the key to expanding output is capital accumulation, the cost of capital accumulation and production growth is increased environmental degradation. If this cost exceeds the benefits of economic expansion, then the social value of capital accumulation and thus growth declines. Under certain conditions determining the social welfare function, for example, individuals giving more weight to environmental quality than consumption in their utility considerations, society may opt for slower or for even no production growth and to allocate an increasing share of output to environmental improvement services. Such allocative choices are clearly consistent with a preference for ecological preservation over increased aggregate consumption, a preference that is perhaps spurred by apprehension over the type of future 'absolute' ecological constraint included in this model.

Thus the quantitative results of the model clearly depend on: (a) the relative preferences of individuals, (b) the development of technology, and (c) the resilience and regenerative capacity of ecosystems and life-support functions. It is to these wider issues that the chapter now turns.

Wider implications: technology, tastes and time

As noted in section one, conventional approaches to natural resource scarcity often indicate that technological innovation, substitution and improvements in resource management can be mitigating factors in overcoming increasing relative scarcity. The crucial question is whether the type of scarcity effects envisioned by the above model can also be mitigated by technological innovations and proper environmental management. The answer must be yes, albeit with some qualifications. One key is, of course, slowing down the rate of environmental degradation to a level low enough that there is little appreciable or significant deterioration in vital ecological functions or natural resource systems. As suggested by equation (2.3) of the model, this invariably calls for innovations that can slow down the rate of resource throughput in the economy by reducing the inflows of material and energy required from the environment and the outflows of waste. There are essentially two broad types of resource-saving innovations that can be applied to economic activity:

1. Resource-saving innovations in the process of production:
   (a) *factor-substitution*, for example, labour-power for energy, resource-saving capital for energy and materials;
   (b) *reuse of scrap and waste materials*, that is, improvements in recovery and recycling producer and consumer waste;

   (c) *increased efficiency of resource conversion and utilization*, that is, obtaining the maximum amount of end-use energy and material for production of final goods and services from the primary inflows of resources into the economic system.
2. Other resource-saving innovations:
   (a) *improved organizational techniques*, that is, better organization of production, distribution and consumption activities to reduce resource inefficiencies and resource use;
   (b) *changes in the composition of output*, for example, from non-durables to durables, from resource-using goods to services, and so on;
   (c) *changes in product quality and/or design*, for example, reducing sizes and weights of vehicles, eliminating 'built-in-obsolescence', re-designing throwaway packages and containers, improving energy-efficiency in appliances, etc.

The technology necessary to achieve these resource-saving innovations may already exist, or is easily achievable, in the advanced industrialized countries. As a recent report from the US Office for Technical Assessment (OTA, 1988) has indicated, thanks to the revolution in information technology, resource savings of 40-60 per cent of current use could be *feasible* in the near future for the United States *without* any sacrifice in economic growth. However, as Page (1977) has emphasized, what is technologically feasible in terms of resource saving may not actually be realized unless some conservation criterion, such as keeping the resource base intact for future generations, is accepted as a valid macroeconomic policy goal. Perhaps the recent policy debate over the use of a 'carbon tax' to reduce emissions, encourage resource-saving innovations and thus mitigate any possible CO_2-induced 'global warming' is one indication that policymakers are increasingly taking into account long-term considerations of future economic security and welfare.

As implied by equation (2.4), better techniques of environmental improvement and management could also mitigate any decline in environmental quality. The quality of the environment will generally be improved by a variety of innovations ranging from improvements in resource, land and water management to developments in ecologically appropriate planning of tourist facilities, conservation areas and environmental policies to the dissemination of new conservation skills and training. Particularly in the case of agricultural systems, where 'ecosystems are transformed into hybrid agroecosystems for the purpose of food or fibre production' (Conway, 1985, p. 34), the result may also be a direct increase in production. For example, in the Sahel small farmers struggle to produce a predominantly millet-based cropping system under conditions of drought, high temperature and marginal soil fertility. Through the introduction of improved multi-cropping techniques, new drought and pest-resistant varieties of cowpeas and no-tillage mulching, water run-off and soil erosion were reduced and yields increased (IITA, 1985, pp. 22–6). Similar examples from around the world show how improved land-management techniques and cropping systems – accompanied by appropriate economic policies, incentives and investment strategies – can overcome land and watershed degradation (American Farmland Trust, 1984; Barbier, 1988; Nelson, 1988; Southgate, 1988).

Despite optimism that the combination of resource-saving and environmental management techniques could indefinitely postpone the type of binding ecological constraint suggested by condition (2.6), there a number of reasons why such innovations may not be 'automatically' or 'effectively' implemented in response to declining environmental quality.

First, in the conventional case of increasing scarcity of raw materials, the existence of identifiable markets for these resources means that the price system can automatically respond to this increasing scarcity and thus induce the appropriate innovative responses. However, many environmental resources exist outside the economic system as integral components of complex resource and ecological systems, and are thus nonmarketed common property resources. Although 'markets indirectly and other institutions directly influence the allocation of these resources' for use as resource inputs and waste assimilation as opposed to preservation, 'unfortunately none of these can be relied upon to provide the information on the marginal valuations of the resources involved in these allocations' (Smith and Krutilla, 1979, p. 281). As Pearce (1985, p. 21) has argued, even if external environmental costs imposed by resource depletion are estimated, 'there is nothing in the conventional concept of an external costs to account for the decay of ecological processes themselves', and as a result, 'in the absence of perfect information and both perfect and instantaneous response to ecological disequilibrium, the system can be unsustainable'. Without a mechanism for conveying this information, the appropriate technological response to environmental degradation is not assured.

Furthermore, the appropriateness and effectiveness of technological innovation in halting environmental deterioration depend on a clear understanding of the ecological impacts of pollution and resource depletion. However, changes in the state of the environment and its resources usually involve substantial qualitative changes and interactions. The aggregate effects on ecological functions and systems may in some cases be an unusual capacity for resilience and regenerative capacity, whereas in others, a tendency towards rapidly reinforcing disturbance and disruption (Conway, 1985). Because such changes are rarely stable, frequently irreversible and often cumulative and discontinuous, environmental systems almost never 'settle' to an equilibrium state in response to perturbations and disturbances. Even in the relatively simple case of a constant input of pollution into a stream ecosystem, the environmental system may or may not reach an equilibrium condition for years, as the pollutant may differentially affect the survival rate and perhaps even the course of evolution of species in the stream. In the case of multiple pollutants, the combined changes rarely equal the sum of the separate effects (Norgaard, 1985, p. 384).

In addition, there may be physical limits on the extent to which resource-saving innovations can reduce resource throughput in the economic process. It may be possible, as noted above, to reduce current US resource use by 40–60 per cent and still have reasonable economic growth, but any further reductions may not be feasible under even the most optimistic technological assumptions. As argued by Daly (1977, 1979) and Georgescu-Roegen (1971, 1979), the source of these restrictions stem from the first and second laws of thermodynamics as analogously applied to the economic process:

1. from the first law, as material and energy can neither be created nor destroyed, production and consumption must require some inputs of material and energy from the environment and generate some waste.
2. from the second law, as material and energy used in transformation must irrevocably dissipate or decay, some degradation of material and energy from a useful to a useless state by the economic process is inevitable and irreversible.

In other words, resource-saving innovations may minimize, but they cannot eliminate, resource throughput in the economic process. Given uncertainty over ecological processes and environmental change, even the minimum resource-throughput level required to sustain an economic process may continue to damage the environment, particularly if it has been subject to stress from past resource-using technologies for a significant period of time, or if the regenerative capacity/resilience of affected ecosystems is low. Many current environmental problems, such as the global greenhouse effect, land degradation in resource-poor areas, deforestation and so forth, contain elements of this problem.

Finally, just as conditions (2.21)–(2.23) indicate that optimal allocation of output between consumption, environmental improvement services and investment is influenced by the relative preferences of consumption to environmental quality and changes in the social value of capital, choices of resource-saving and environmental management innovations over other possible technological 'mixes' will be dictated by individuals' tastes and preferences. The classic problem here, of course, is that choice of innovations today will affect both future consumption and environmental quality, yet there is no method available to measure the intensity of future preferences and the preferences of future generations. For example, very little of the yield-enhancing technical progress in US agriculture over the postwar period was induced by concern about the cumulative effects of soil erosion, and has thus contributed to the current problems of soil degradation on erodible croplands, which is now an urgent and pressing concern (Crosson and Stout, 1983). In assessing both future and present reactions to environmental degradation, the crucial problem remains that 'the level of the shadow price of environmental functions is largely indeterminate because insufficient information is available on the preferences for environmental functions' (Hueting, 1980, p.141).

In sum, resource-saving technological and environmental management innovations should in principle be capable of overcoming the type of scarcity effects depicted by the model of this chapter. However, because the main indicator of these scarcity effects – the relative decline in the quality of the environment and ecological functions – occurs largely outside the institutional mechanisms of the economic system, and at best, is only indirectly and partially captured by the market through impacts on productivity, human health, resource management costs, and so on, the appropriate innovative responses may not be automatically forthcoming. Moreover, given the complexity of ecological relationships, their often unstable responses to stresses and shocks, the uncertainty over future and even current preferences for environmental functions and resources, and the physical limits to resource-saving techniques, the effectiveness of innovations in ameliorating environmental deterioration may be constrained. If this is the case, then the trade-off between consumption and environmental improvement services, and between more production growth and increased environmental preservation, suggested by conditions (2.21)–(2.23) may be unavoidable.

Summary and conclusion

The model of this chapter has confirmed the general conclusion of many alternative approaches to natural resource scarcity that if individuals express preferences for essential environmental resources and functions which are perceived to be deteriorating over time, then it may be optimal to consider trade-offs between consumption and services to improve the environment and between more resource-using growth and environmental preservation. With its strong assumption of increasing environmental degradation leading to ecological collapse, the model may be strictly applicable to only a limited number of economic–environmental systems. Its general insights, however, are more widely applicable to any situation where economic activity leads to declining environmental quality and loss of ecological functions. To borrow Hueting's (1980) phrase, this is the 'new scarcity' that is affecting all global systems, including the advanced industrialized economies. Given the uncertainties surrounding appropriate and effective innovative responses, there must be concern that 'we could get into serious difficulty simply because of inability to cope in time with ... deterioration in the quality of the environment' (Herfindahl, 1974b, pp. 272–3). As 'no one model provides the means for understanding how the ends of both economic growth and ecological sustainability might be achieved' (Norgaard, 1985, p. 388), further developments in both the conventional and alternative approaches described in this chapter are necessary for improving our understanding of the complex interaction between economic and environmental systems.

Acknowledgements

I am indebted to my fellow participants at the 13th Annual Convention of The Eastern Economics Association (5–7 March 1987, Washington, DC) for comments. I would also like to thank Robert Costanza, Partha Dasgupta, Roefie Hueting, David Pearce, Henry Peskin, Somnath Sen, Ron Smith and Dennis Snower for their suggestions and comments. Any errors in thinking or exposition are. of course, my own.

Notes

* Based on a paper presented at the 13th Annual Convention of the Eastern Economic Association, Washington, DC, 5–7 March 1987.

1. According to Dasgupta and Heal (1979, p. 3), 'a resource is exhaustible if it is possible to find a pattern of use which makes its supply dwindle to zero'.
2. As Dasgupta and Heal (1979, pp. 5–7) point out, however, although in theory 'capital-resource substitution may be sufficient to overcome the "drag" imposed by an essential and exhaustible resource', in practice this requires 'a complete set of forward markets', a condition which 'is certainly not met' in actual market systems, and 'as a consequence resource markets may be unstable, and will almost certainly display "market bias", in the sense of depleting the resource at a rate different from an optimal rate'. Quite clearly. the problem is 'uncertainty about future resource stocks and about future technology'.
3. d'Arge (1972) provides an alternative classification of these functions into four categories: '(a) source of raw materials; (b) space for waste accumulation and storage; (c) assimilation-regenerative capability for chemically or biologically active wastes; and (d) determinant of health and life style, and of aesthetic satisfactions'.
4. Following Becker (1982) and Mäler (1974), it is assumed that environmental quality is measured by a stock of environmental goods that yield a flow of services proportional to that stock in each time period. However, Becker (1982) defines this stock variable as 'the differences between the level of pollution for which life ceases and the current level of pollution'. Similarly, Mäler (1974) in his intertemporal models considers that only the quality and flow of waste residuals and recycling have an impact on environmental quality. Here, it is assumed that environmental quality may be effected not only by (net) waste generation but also by resource depletion and services to improve the environment, such as conservation and resource management. For a given type of ecosystem with its associated energy flow, a measure of environmental quality may include, in addition to Becker's definition. the ecosystem's biomass (that is, the volume or weight of total living material found above or below ground) plus some measure of the distribution of nutrients and other materials between the biotic (living) and abiotic (nonliving) components of the ecosystem. Such a measure is discussed in more detail in Barbier (1986, ch. 8), and is more consistent with this model's broader concept of deteriorating environmental quality, or environmental degradation, which 'comprises not just the loss of environmental quality that impinges on the senses, but also the damage to the natural purification and regenerative processes of the environment itself' (Pearce, 1985, p. 21).
5. In fact, it may be possible to make this condition explicit by constructing an index of environmental degradation that is proportional to some measure of R_t and N_t (Barbier, 1986, ch. 8).
6. Note that, as discussed above and indicated in Figure 2.1, some beneficial services of the environment, such as maintenance of soil, air and water quality or of climatic stability, directly

aid economic production. This would suggest that environmental quality, X_t, should also be included in the production function for economic output, Q_t. Recent discussions of the 'sustainability' of production in the Third World imply this relationship (Conway, 1985; Pearce, Barbier and Markandya, 1990). However, to simplify analysis in this model, the more traditional production function for the economy is employed. Instead, the stream of benefits provided by environmental quality to production activities are included as part of the overall contribution of X_t to welfare. Hence, X_t in equation (1) can be interpreted as representing both the direct utility-yielding impacts of environmental quality on individuals and the indirect impacts on overall social welfare through assisting production and other intermediate economic activities. This in any case may be a more appropriate way of accounting for these latter services, as their benefits are often 'externalities' to private production and consumption allocation decisions.

References

American Farmland Trust (1984), *Soil conservation in America: What do we have to lose?*, Washington, DC.

Arrow, K.J. and A.C. Fisher (1974), 'Environmental preservation, uncertainty, and irreversibility', *Quarterly Journal of Economics*, **88**, 312–19.

Barbier, E.B. (1986), *Alternative economic approaches to natural resource scarcity*, PhD thesis, Economics Department, Birkbeck College, University of London.

Barbier, E.B. (1988) *The economics of farm-level adoption of soil conservation measures in the uplands of Java*. Environment Department Working Paper 11, Washington, DC: World Bank.

Barbier, E.B. (1989a), *Economics, natural resource scarcity and development: Conventional and alternative views*, London: Earthscan Publications.

Barbier, E.B. (1989b), 'The global greenhouse effect: economic impacts and policy considerations', *Natural Resources Forum*, **1**, 20–32.

Barbier, E.B. and A. Markandya (1989), *The conditions for achieving environmentally sustainable development*, LEEC Paper 89–01, IIED/UCL London Environmental Economics Centre.

Barnett, H.J. and C. Morse (1963), *Scarcity and Economic Growth: The Economics of Natural Resource Availability*, Baltimore, MD: Johns Hopkins University Press.

Becker, R.A. (1982), 'Intergenerational equity: the capital–environment trade-off', *Journal of Environmental Economies and Management*, **9**, 165–85.

Beckerman, W. (1974), *In Defence of Economic Growth*, London: Cape.

Clark, C.W. (1976), *Mathematical Bioeconomics: The Optimal Management of Renewable Resources*, New York: Wiley.

Conway, G.R. (1985), 'Agroecosystem analysis', *Agricultural Administration*, **20**, 31–55.

Crosson, P.R. and A.T. Stout (1983), *Productivity Effects of Cropland Erosion in the United States*, Baltimore, MD: Johns Hopkins University Press.

Daly, H.E. (1977), *Steady-state Economics*, San Francisco, CA: Freeman.

Daly, H.E. (1979), 'Entropy, growth and the political economy of scarcity', in V.K. Smith (ed.), *Scarcity and Growth Reconsidered*, Baltimore, MD: Johns Hopkins University Press, pp. 67–85.

d'Arge, R.C. (1972), 'Economic growth and the natural environment', in A.K. Kneese and B.T. Bower (eds), *Environmental Quality Analysis: Theory and Method in the Social Sciences*, Baltimore, MD: Johns Hopkins University Press, pp. 1–25.

Dasgupta, P.S. (1982), *The Control of Resources*, Oxford: Basil Blackwell.

Dasgupta, P.S. and G. Heal (1974), 'The optimal depletion of exhaustible resources', in *Review of Economic Studies Symposium, Economics of Exhaustible Resources*, pp. 3–28.

Dasgupta, P.S. and G. Heal (1979), *Economic Theory and Exhaustible Resources*, Cambridge: Cambridge University Press.

Dasgupta, P.S. and J.E. Stiglitz (1981), 'Resource depletion under technical uncertainty', *Econometrica*, **49**, 85–104.

Farber, S. and R. Costanza (1987), 'The economic value of wetland systems', *Journal of Environmental Management*, **24**, 41–51.

Farnworth, E.G., T.H. Tidrick, C.F. Jordan and W.M. Smathers Jr. (1981), 'The value of natural ecosystems; an economic and ecological framework', *Environmental Conservation*, **8**, 275–82.

Fisher, A.C. and F.M. Peterson (1977), 'The exploitation of extractive resources, a survey', *The Economic Journal*, **87**, 681–721.

Fisher, A.C., J.V. Krutilla and C.J. Cicchetti (1972), 'The economics of environmental preservation, a theoretical and empirical analysis', *American Economic Review*, **62**, 605–19.

Freeman, A.M. III (1979), *The Benefits of Environmental Improvement*, Baltimore, MD: Johns Hopkins University Press.

Georgescu-Roegen, N. (1971), *The Entropy Law and the Economic Process*, Cambridge, MA: Harvard University Press.

Georgescu-Roegen, N. (1979), 'Energy analysis and economic valuation', *Southern Economic Journal*, **45**, 1023–58.

Herfindahl, O.C. (1974a), 'Is resource economics unorthodox?', in D.B. Brooks (ed.), *Resource Economics: The Selected Works of Orris C. Herfindahl*, Baltimore, MD: Johns Hopkins University Press, pp. 3–6.

Herfindahl, O.C. (1974b), 'Effects of resource depletion and economic growth on the quality of life', in D.B. Brooks (ed.), *Resource Economics: The Selected Works of Orris C. Herfindahl*, Baltimore, MD: Johns Hopkins University Press, pp. 255–73.

Hotelling, H. (1931), 'The economics of exhaustible resources', *Journal of Political Economy*, **39**, 137–75.

Hueting, R. (1980), *New Scarcity and Economic Growth: More Welfare Through Less Production?*, Amsterdam: North-Holland.

IITA (1985), *Research Highlights for 1984*, Ibadan, Nigeria: International Institute of Tropical Agriculture.

Kamien, M.I. and N.L. Schwartz (1978), 'Optimal exhaustible resource depletion with endogenous technical change', *Review of Economic Studies*, **45**, 179–96.

Krautkraemer, J.A. (1985), 'Optimal growth, resource amenities and the preservation of natural environments', *Review of Economic Studies*, **52**, 153–70.

Krutilla, J.V. and A.C. Fisher (1985), *The Economics of Natural Environments: Studies in the Valuation of Commodity and Amenity Resources* (2nd edn), Baltimore, MD: Johns Hopkins University Press.

Mäler, K.G. (1974), *Environmental Economics: A Theoretical Inquiry*, Baltimore, MD: Johns Hopkins University Press.

Miller, J.R. and F.C. Menz (1979), 'Some economic considerations for wildlife preservation', *Southern Economic Journal*, **45**, 718–29.

Myers, N. (1984), *The Primary Source: Tropical Rain Forests and Our Future*, New York: Norton.

Nelson, R. (1988), *Dryland management: the 'desertification' problem*, Environment Department Working Paper 8, Washington, DC: World Bank.

Nordhaus, W.D. and J. Tobin (1977), 'Growth and natural resources', in R. Dorfman and N.S. Dorfman (eds), *Economics of the Environment* (2nd edn), New York: Norton, pp. 179–88.

Norgaard, R. (1984), 'Coevolutionary development potential', *Land Economics*, **60**, 161–73.

Norgaard, R. (1985), 'Environmental economics: an evolutionary critique and a plea for pluralism', *Journal of Environmental Economics and Management*, **12**, 382–94.

Oram, P.A. (1985), 'Sensitivity of agricultural production to climatic change', *Climate Change*, **7**, 129–52.

OTA (1988), *Technology and the American Economic Transition*, Washington, DC: Office for Technical Assessment.

Page, T. (1977), *Conservation and Economic Efficiency: An Approach to Materials Policy*, Baltimore, MD: Johns Hopkins University Press.

Pearce, D.W. (1985), *Sustainable futures: economics and the environment*, Inaugural lecture, London: University College. Mimeo.

Pearce, D.W., E.B. Barbier and A.M. Markandya (1990), *Sustainable Development: Economics and Environment in the Third World*, Aldershot, UK and Brookfield, US: Edward Elgar.

Pearsall, S.H., III (1984), 'In absentia benefits of nature preserves: a review', *Environmental Conservation*, **11**, 3–10.

Sioli, H. (1985), 'The effects of deforestation in Amazonia', *Geographical Journal*, **151**, 197–203.
Smith, V.K. and J.V. Krutilla (1979), 'Summary and research issues', in V.K. Smith (ed.), *Scarcity and Growth Reconsidered*, Baltimore, MD: Johns Hopkins University Press, pp. 276–90.
Smith, V.L. (1977), 'Control theory applied to natural and environmental resources: an exposition', *Journal of Environmental Economics and Management*, **4**, 1–24.
Solow, R.M. (1974a), 'The economics of resources or the resources of economics', *Papers and Proceedings American Economic Review*, **64**, 1–14.
Solow, R.M. (1974b), 'Intergenerational equity and exhaustible resources', *Review of Economic Studies Symposium, Economics of Exhaustible Resources*, 123–37.
Southgate, D. (1988), *The economics of land degradation in the third world*, Environmental Department Working Paper 2, Washington, DC: World Bank.
Southgate, D. (1989), *Efficient management of biologically diverse tropical forests*, LEEC Paper 89-03, IIED/UCL London Environmental Economics Centre.
Stiglitz, J.E. (1974), 'Growth with exhaustible natural resources; efficient and optimal growth paths', *Review of Economic Studies Symposium Economics of Exhaustible Resources*, 123–37.
Turner, R.K. (1988), 'Wetland conservation: economics and ethics', in D. Collard, D.W. Pearce and D. Ulph (eds), *Economics, Growth and Sustainable Environments: Essays in Memory of Richard Lecomber*, London: Macmillan, pp. 121–59.
Vousden, N. (1973), 'Basic theoretical issues of resource depletion', *Journal of Economic Theory*, **6**, 126–43.
WRI and IIED (World Resources Institute and International Institute for Environment and Development) (1986), *World Resources 1986*, New York: Basic Books.

3. The conditions for achieving environmentally sustainable development

with A. Markandya

1. Introduction

A review of the literature on 'sustainable' development suggests that two interpretations of that concept have emerged: a wider concept concerned with sustainable economic, ecological *and* social development, and a more narrowly defined concept largely concerned with 'environmentally sustainable development', that is, with optimal resource and environmental management over time.[1] This chapter is interested in the 'narrower' interpretation – the relationship between environmental quality and sustainable economic activity. The latter is interpreted as that level of economic activity which leaves the environmental quality level intact, with the policy objective corresponding to this notion being the maximization of net benefits of economic development, subject to maintaining the services and quality of natural resources over time.

The term 'natural resources' is used broadly. It includes *renewable* resources, such as water, terrestrial and aquatic biomass; *non-renewable* resources, such as land in general, minerals, metals and fossil fuels; and *semi-renewable* resources, such as soil quality, the assimilative capacity of the environment and ecological life support systems. Consequently, maintaining the services of a natural capital stock does not necessarily imply maintaining this physical stock of composite resources intact, which in any case, may not be desirable or feasible for non-renewables. On the other hand, keeping the level of *environmental quality* intact implies caution in assuming that an irreversible loss of the natural capital stock is justified if it results in the formation of more man-made capital. Some of the functions of the environment are not replicable by reproducible capital, such as complex life support systems, biological diversity, aesthetic functions, micro-climatic conditions and so forth. Others might be substituted but not without unacceptable cost. In addition, degradation of one or more parts of a resource system beyond some threshold level may lead to a breakdown in the integrity of the whole system, dramatically affecting recovery rates and resilience of the system. The total costs of the system breakdown may exceed the value of the activity causing the initial degradation.[2]

The conditions governing the optimal trade-off between environmental quality and consumption over time have been analysed in various models of economic–environmental interaction (see Barbier, 1987a; Becker, 1982; Maler, 1974; Vousden, 1973). Although these models assume some form of environmental degradation process, and thus implicitly assume transgression of biophysical constraints by the economic system, no attempt is made to examine explicitly how an economy might respond to the limits imposed by these constraints and hence to identify the conditions for optimal sustainable economic growth. In the next section, a simple model is developed to characterize the conditions necessary to maintain the environmental sustainability of an economic system over time.

2. A model of environmentally sustainable economic activity

The following model will be used to analyse optimal growth paths for an economy faced with the choice of operating under the three long-term biophysical constraints: harvesting of renewable resources within their natural and managed rates of regeneration; extracting exhaustible resources at the rate at which renewables can be substituted for them (which over the long run implies a zero rate of exhaustion of the 'composite' resource), and emitting wastes within the assimilative capacity of the environment.

The key to the following model is a particular definition of environmental degradation. At any time t, the rate of degradation $\dot{S}$ is a function of: (i) the flow of waste (W) in excess of the amount assimilated by the environment (A); and (ii) the flow of renewable resources harvested from the environment (R) in excess of the (managed or natural) biological productivity of these resources (G), plus the flow of exhaustible resources extracted from the environment (E). Mathematically, this may be written as

$$\dot{S} = f([W - A], [(R - G) + E]). \quad (3.1)$$

The following assumptions are made about (3.1):

1. It is a differentiable, increasing function of its arguments. As the net waste level increases and as the excess rate of harvesting increases, so does the level of environmental degradation.
2. It is a convex function of its arguments.
3. A sufficient condition for zero degradation is $W = A$ and $(R + E) = G$.[3]

Having defined the level of environmental degradation as a function of net waste generation and net resources consumed, we now wish to link it to the level of economic activity (consumption) and the 'stock' of environmental assets available. We label each of these respectively as C and X, and postulate the following functions with the following properties.[4]

$$W = W(C),\ W'(C) > 0,\ W''(C) > 0, \tag{3.2}$$

$$R = R(C),\ R'(C) > 0,\ R''(C) > 0, \tag{3.3}$$

$$E = E(C),\ E'(C) > 0,\ E''(C) > 0, \tag{3.4}$$

$$A = A(X),\ A'(X) > 0,\ A''(X) < 0, \tag{3.5}$$

$$G = G(X),\ G'(X) > 0,\ G''(X) < 0. \tag{3.6}$$

In other words W, R and E are increasing convex functions of C, and A and G are increasing concave functions of X. The concept of environmental quality adopted by this model is fairly broad and essentially synonymous with the entire stock of environmental goods. The assumption that W, R and E are all increasing functions of economic activity are well known results stemming from material-balance models (see, for example, d'Arge and Kogiku, 1973; Kneese, Ayres and d'Arge, 1970; Maler, 1974; Victor 1972). In addition, the assumption of the convexity of waste generation, $W(C)$, and the concavity of assimilative capacity, $A(X)$, is consistent with the models developed by Forster, which examined optimal economic growth under one set of these biophysical constraints, namely that waste levels should not exceed the assimilative capacity of the environment. (Forster, 1973, 1975 and 1977). Similarly, standard models of renewable resource harvesting assume concave growth functions, $G(X)$, and convex harvesting rates, $R(C)$ (see, for example, Clark, 1976; Dasgupta, 1982).

Substituting (3.2)–(3.6) into (3.1) yields an equation in which dS/dt is a function of C and X. Since A and G are concave functions, it follows that $-A$ and $-G$ are convex. In addition we wish to impose a minimum value on X, which we define as the minimum environmental stock that provides a viable base for sustained economic activity. Hence dS/dt, which is an increasing convex function of its original arguments, $[W - A]$ and $[(R - G) + E]$, will also be a convex function in its transformed state, as a function of C and X, for X greater than $\underline{X}$. This can be written as

$$\begin{aligned} \dot{S} &= h(C, X), & X &\geq \underline{X}, \\ \dot{S} &\gg 0, & X &< \underline{X}, \end{aligned} \tag{3.7}$$

where $h_c > 0$, $h_{cc} > 0$, $h_x < 0$ and $h_{xx} > 0$ and $h_{cc}h_{xx} - h_{xc}^2 > 0$. Finally, a link can be established between $\dot{S}$, the rate of environmental degradation, and $\dot{X}$, the rate at which environmental quality is changing. Clearly, the basic relationship is an inverse one: as the degradation increases so the environmental stock declines. Assuming both are measured in comparable units, we can represent this by

$$\dot{X} = -a\dot{S}, \tag{3.8}$$

$$\dot{X} = -ah(C, X), \qquad X \geq X, \tag{3.9}$$

$$\dot{X} << 0, \qquad X < \underline{X},$$

where a is a constant scalar.

3. Optimal sustainable economic growth

Using the above model, it is now possible to explore the conditions for environmentally sustainable growth. For example, it is assumed that social welfare at any point in time is measured by a strictly concave utility function U of current C and the current stock of X:

$$U = U(C, X), \tag{3.10}$$

with $U_c > 0$, $U_{cc} < 0$, $U_x > 0$, $U_{xx} < 0$, $U_{cx} = 0$, $\lim_{c \to 0} U_c = \infty$, and $\lim_{x \to 0} U_x = \infty$.

Equations (3.1) and (3.7) were deliberately constructed to reflect the sustainability criteria of observing the biophysical constraints. That is, a minimum condition for an economic growth path to be sustainable over the long run is $W = A$, $R + E = G$, which ensures that no environmental degradation will occur, that is, $\dot{S} = 0$. Thus one possible choice open to society is to plan for a growth path that in the long run produces zero environmental degradation.

Conditions (3.8) and (3.9) also indicate, however, that as long as some (net) environmental degradation is continuing to occur, environmental quality will decline. Equation (3.9) suggests that there is a lower limit to environmental quality. As noted above, if X is driven below $\underline{X}$, environmental degradation will have destroyed the natural clean-up and regenerative processes in the environment. This is tantamount to an environmental 'collapse', and economic growth leading to such a collapse can be said to be environmentally 'unsustainable'. Nevertheless, there may be conditions under which society may have no choice but opt for an unsustainable growth path.

However, in general, there will also be conditions leading society to a sustainable growth path. The pursuit of sustainability inevitably involves some intertemporal trade-offs between levels of consumption and environmental quality. From the convexity of the C–X locus in equation (3.7) it follows that, as society sacrifices consumption now, so the improvements in the environment get smaller and smaller. On the other hand, the value of that sacrifice increases because of a diminishing marginal rate of substitution between consumption and environmental goods (that is, the convexity of the indifference curve). Presumably then there will be a point where the two would balance out. In the long-run equilibrium, the utility value of a unit of consumption sacrificed today should equal the discounted present value of the higher consumption *and* environmental quality afforded in perpetuity to future generations. The higher the discount rate, the less the latter would be and so the equilibrium would be at a lower point on the C–X curve. This is because the benefits of a unit of consumption in terms of the higher X value it permits fall as C falls.

We therefore examine further the optimal conditions leading to sustainable versus unsustainable economic growth. Given a positive rate of time preference, r, the planning problem is to find solutions which will

$$\max \int_0^{\infty} e^{-rt} U(C, X) \mathrm{d}t \tag{3.11}$$

subject to $\dot{X} = -ah(C, X)$, $X(t=0) = X_0$, $X(t=\infty)$ free, $X \geq \underline{X}$. Given the continuous function $P(t)$, the Hamilton of the problem is

$$H = e^{-rt}\{U(C, X) + P[-ah(C, X)]\}. \tag{3.12}$$

From the first order conditions for an interior solution we can express C as a function of P and X where

$$\frac{\mathrm{d}C}{\mathrm{d}P} = \frac{ah_c}{U_{cc} - Pah_{cc}} < 0, \tag{3.13}$$

and

$$\frac{\mathrm{d}C}{\mathrm{d}X} = \frac{Pah_{cx}}{U_{cc} - Pah_{cc}} > 0, \tag{3.14}$$

if $h_{cx} < 0$. As will be discussed below, the latter is important with respect to the comparative static analysis of the equilibrium. Furthermore it can be shown that the behaviour of the system from any initial point, (X_0, P_0), is governed by

$$\dot{P} \gtreqless 0 \quad \text{as} \quad [r + ah_x]\, P \gtreqless U_x, \tag{3.15}$$

$$\dot{X} \gtreqless 0 \quad \text{as} \quad -ah(C, X) \gtreqless 0. \tag{3.16}$$

The slopes of the stationary loci satisfying (3.15) and (3.16) with equality are given by

$$\left.\frac{\mathrm{d}P}{\mathrm{d}X}\right|_{\dot{P}=0} = \frac{U_{xx} - Pah_{xx} - Pah_{xc}\mathrm{d}C/\mathrm{d}X}{\left[r + ah_x\right] + ah_{xc}\mathrm{d}C/\mathrm{d}P}, \tag{3.17}$$

and

$$\left.\frac{\mathrm{d}P}{\mathrm{d}X}\right|_{\dot{X}=0} = -\frac{\left[h_x + h_c\mathrm{d}C/\mathrm{d}X\right]}{h_c\mathrm{d}C/\mathrm{d}P}, \tag{3.18}$$

which cannot be definitely signed. If $h_x \rightarrow -\infty$ as $X \rightarrow \underline{X}^+$, as seems very plausible, the configuration of the phase diagrams satisfying (3.15)–(3.18) will look as shown in Figure 3.1. This yields a stable and an unstable solution. (X_2^*, P_2^*) is a stable equilibrium, whereas (X_1^*, P_1^*) is unstable. If $X_0 > X_1^*$, then the optimal policy is to select P_0 so as to place the economy on a growth path that ends at the stable equilibrium (X_2^*, P_2^*). This represents an environmentally 'sustainable' growth, given the assumption that if $\dot{X} = 0$ and $X > \underline{X}$, then biophysical constraints are being observed. If $X_0 = X_1^*$, then it is optimal to remain at X_1^* forever. If $X_0 < X_1^*$, then the growth path of the economy could lead to $\underline{X}$. However, this growth path is unsustainable, for at $\underline{X}$, the assimilative and regenerative capacity of the environment will have been destroyed, and the economy will be forced to consume existing internal resource stocks. Eventually, the latter will be consumed and the economy will collapse. Thus X_1^* can be considered the *minimum* initial level of environmental quality required to ensure a sustainable growth path.

Thus with a low initial level of environmental quality, environmentally unsustainable economic growth may be an optimal strategy. Since the benefits of increased consumption occur in the present whereas environmental degradation and collapse is a future problem, this strategy is made optimal by a high rate of discount on future utility. Consequently, both the initial level of environmental quality as well as the rate of social discount are significant factors in determining the optimal choice between sustainable and unsustainable growth as one would expect.

These intuitive results have been shown to be correct if the relationship between the rate of environmental degradation, consumption and the stock of environmental assets takes a particular form. We have assumed, as seems normal, that other things being equal the rate of degradation increases as the level of consumption increases and as the stock of environmental assets declines. In addition, however, we are required to assume that the increase in the rate of degradation as consumption increases is higher with smaller environmental stocks than with larger ones. This is the economic/ecological interpretation of the

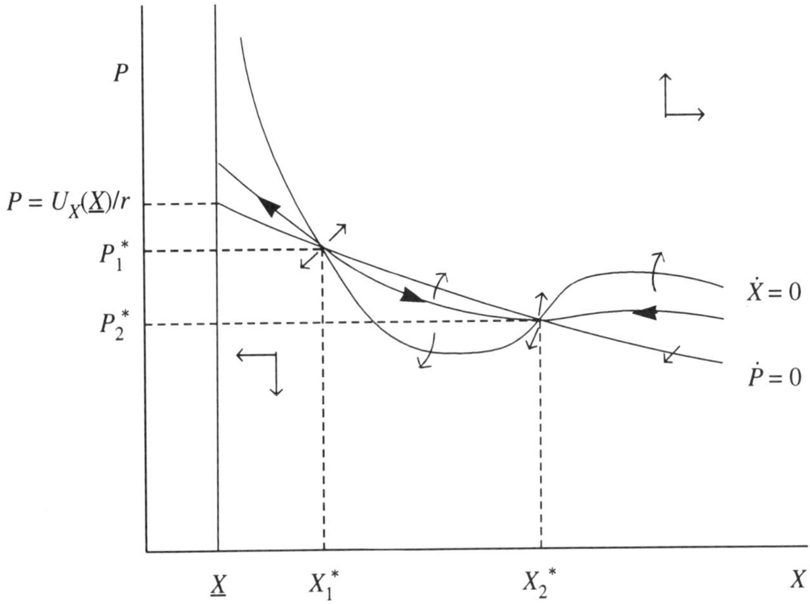

Figure 3.1 Dual equilibria solution to phase diagram

requirement that $h_{cx} < 0$. Note that the latter is a sufficient condition for the stable equilibrium to occur with a larger environmental stock at a lower discount rate, and for the unstable equilibrium to occur at a smaller environmental stock in the same circumstances.

For example, it is apparent from (3.15) that an increase in the discount rate would have the effect of shifting down the $\dot{P} = 0$ curve. As shown in Figure 3.2, the end result may be a unique equilibrium, but one that is stable only if $X_0 \geq X_3^*$. However, if $X_0 < X_3^*$, it may be optimal to choose an unsustainable growth path; that is, one that heads towards $\underline{X}$. Note that, as $X_3^* > X_1^*$, an economy with an increased discount rate requires a higher minimum initial level of environmental quality to avoid a growth path that might be environmentally unsustainable.

In contrast, lower discount rates would shift the $\dot{P} = 0$ curve up, requiring a lower minimum initial level of environmental quality to ensure sustainable growth (that is, $X_5^* < X_1^*$).

These results appear to confirm the conclusions discussed above of the role of discount rates in determining the sustainability of the economic process.

It can be confirmed that the minimum bound on the social rate of time preference, r, is not independent of the historically given level of environmental quality, X_0. Note that in (3.15), for $\dot{P} = 0$ it is a requirement that $r > -ah_x$. Given

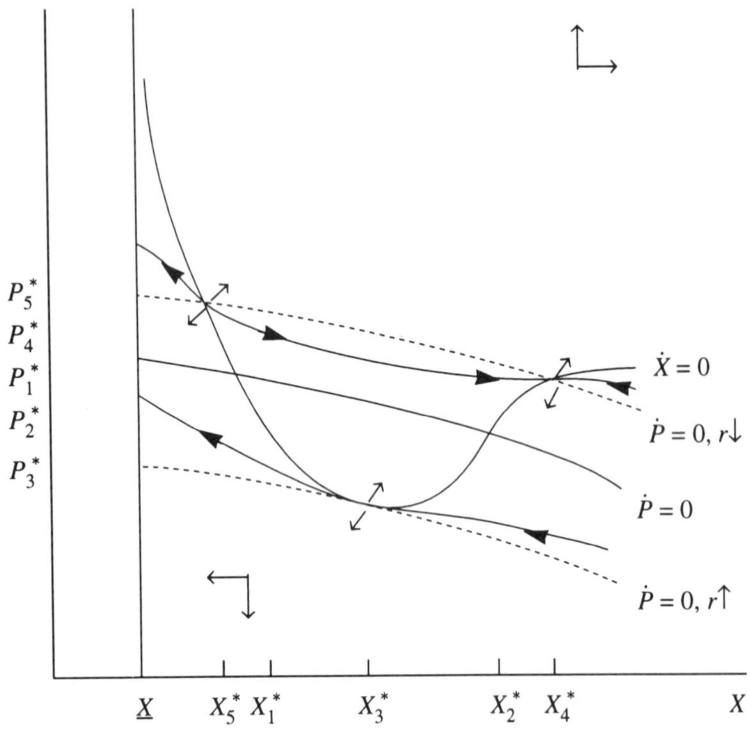

Figure 3.2 The effects of changes in r

the properties of $h(C, X)$ outlined in (3.7), a lower initial X will cause $-ah_x$ to rise, thus requiring a higher r to keep $\dot{P} = 0$. Conversely, a higher X_0 will have a lower rate of discount.

4. Conclusion

The results of the above model indicate that both the initial level of environmental quality as well as the rate of time preference are significant factors in determining the optimal choice between sustainable and unsustainable growth. For example, if technical condition $h_{cx} < 0$ is satisfied, with a low initial level of environment quality and a high rate of social discount, environmentally unsustainable economic growth may be an optimal strategy as the benefits of increased consumption occur in the present whereas environmental degradation and collapse is a future problem. Moreover, the initial level of environmental quality influences choices of discount rates, so that a historically lower initial level of environmental quality leads to a high rate of discount and vice versa.

In other words, a low initial level of environmental quality forces resource users to discount the future heavily. That is, poor people faced with marginal environmental conditions have no choice but to opt for immediate economic benefits at the expense of the long-run sustainability of their livelihoods. This particularly holds for the marginal lands of the Third World, which are areas characterized not only by lower quality and productivity but also by their greater instability, especially as regards to micro-climatic, agroecological and soil conditions (see, for example, Barbier, 1988; Conway and Barbier, 1988). Thus if economic development is to offer the resource-poor the opportunity of sustainable and secure livelihoods, then sustainable resource management must become a primary development goal.

For example, one of the consequences of deforestation and the depletion of fuelwood supplies is that it forces poor households to divert dung for use as fuel rather than for fertilizer. The 'present value' of the dung as fuel is higher than its value as a soil nutrient, but 'the context is one where there is no choice anyway since there are neither fuel nor fertilizer substitutes to which households can gain access'. This behaviour, therefore, is itself 'the result of the resource degradation process which compels actions to be taken which imply high discount rates' (Pearce, 1988). In other words, the high apparent discount rates are a reflection of the constraints imposed by environmental degradation rather than the desired social choice.

The above analysis also has implications for the incorporation of environmental impacts into cost–benefit analysis of development projects. As this expanded approach inevitably raises issues of intertemporal choice, the interest rate chosen to discount the future may determine whether environmental degradation is 'optimal' – as demonstrated formally in the model of this paper. But it does not necessarily follow that manipulating the discount rate is the best approach to incorporating concerns for environmental sustainability in the project analysis.

For example, it is often stressed that the appropriate discount rate should emerge from the project appraisal process (see UNIDO, 1972). In practice, imperfect capital markets, inconsistent data on the productivity of capital and large variances in domestic borrowing for investment make it difficult to establish an economic accounting rate of interest for developing countries (Phillips, 1986).

Introducing environmental considerations further complicates the picture. As Markandya and Pearce observe, natural resources are more likely to be over-exploited at high discount rates than at low ones, whereas low discount rates discriminate against projects with an environmental dimension that have a long gestation period (Markandya and Pearce, 1988). Given the additional problems posed by environmental risk and irreversible impacts, these authors conclude that it is generally preferable to adjust the project costs and benefit values and adopt additional sustainability criteria than to adjust the discount rate.

Alternatively, one could require as a planning criterion that the environmental damages inflicted by a given portfolio of projects must be compensated by the net environmental benefits generated by an additional set of projects (Pearce, Barbier and Markandya, 1988).

Thus the fact that the choice of discount rate is not independent of the historically given level of environmental quality – that is, that the resource degradation process may compel actions that imply high discount rates – does not necessarily mean that choosing a low level of discount rate will automatically make development projects more 'sustainable'.

Notes

1. For further discussion of the different economic interpretations of sustainable development, see Barbier (1987b, 1989) and Pearce, Barbier and Markandya (1990). The following paper and model is based on Barbier and Markandya (1989), which provides more details on the analysis and underlying assumptions. An earlier version of the model appeared in Barbier (1989, ch. 10).
2. Examples where this may be the case include extensive deforestation of tropical forests, such as is occurring in Amazonia, upper watershed degration through inappropriate upland farming and even the global warming induced by greenhouse gases. For further discussion of the economic aspects of these 'system breakdowns' see Barbier (1989).
3. As W is total waste from the economic process and thus comprises waste from exhaustible resource extraction, from renewable resource harvesting and production and consumption, it may appear that equation (3.1) is double counting. But equation (3.1) is not accounting for the flow of material through the economic system but for the total impact on the environment, that is, the 'composite' resource base, of the waste generation and resource depletion created by the economic system. For example, a forest might be depleted faster than its rate of regeneration, whereas the total waste generated by the harvesting plus production and consumption of the wood products may not exceed the assimilative capacity of the environment. Looking at the total impact on the environment of this economic activity therefore requires accounting for both the impact of the total waste generation – which is negligible in this example – and the impact of the harvesting – which is significant.
4. Following Becker (1982) and Mäler (1974), it is assumed that environmental quality – our X variable – is measured by a stock of environmental goods that yield a flow of services proportional to that stock in each time period. However, Becker defines this stock variable as 'the differences between the level of pollution for which life ceases and the current level of pollution'. Similarly, Maler considers only the quality and flow of waste residuals and recycling to have an impact on environmental quality in his intertemporal models. Here it is assumed that environmental quality may be affected not only by net waste generation but also by net resource depletion, as both of these may contribute to environmental degradation if biophysical limits are exceeded (see equation (3.1)). This implies a fairly broad, but perhaps more realistic, concept of the 'stock' of environmental assets. For a given type of ecosystem with its associated energy now, a measure of environmental quality may include, in addition to Becker's definition, the ecosystem's biomass, that is, the volume or weight of total living material found above or below ground, plus some measure of the distribution of nutrients and other materials between the biotic (living) and abiotic (nonliving) components of the ecosystem.

References

Barbier, E.B. (1987), 'The concept of sustainable economic development', *Environmental Conservation*, **14**, 101–10.

Barbier, E.B. (1988), *Sustainable agriculture and the resource poor: Policy issues and options*, LEEC Paper 88–02, London Environmental Economics Centre.

Barbier, E.B. (1989), *Economics, natural resources scarcity and development: Conventional and alternative views*, London: Earthscan Publications.

Barbier, E.B. (1990), 'Alternative approaches to economic–environmental interactions', *Ecological Economics*, **2**, 7–26.

Barbier, E.B. and A. Markandya (1989), *The conditions for achieving environmentally sustainable development*, LEEC Paper 89–01, London Environmental Economics Centre.

Becker, R.A. (1982), 'Intergenerational equity: The capital–environment trade-off', *Journal of Environmental Economics and Management*, **9**, 165–85.

Clark, C.W. (1976), *Mathematical bioeconomics: The optimal management of renewable resources*, New York: John Wiley.

Conway, G.R. and E.B. Barbier (1988), 'After the green revolution: Sustainable and equitable agricultural development', *Futures*, **20**, 651–70.

d'Arge, R.C. and K.C. Kogiku (1973), 'Economic growth and the environment', *Review of Economic Studies*, **40**, 61–78.

Dasgupta, P. (1982), *The control of resources*, Oxford: Basil Blackwell.

Forster, B.A. (1973), 'Optimal consumption planning in a polluted environment', *Economic Record*, **49**, 534–45.

Forster, B.A. (1975), 'Optimal pollution control with a nonconstant exponential rate of decay', *Journal of Environmental Economics and Management*, **2**, 1–6.

Forster, B.A. (1977), 'Consumption–pollution trade-offs', in J.D. Pritchard and S.J. Turnovsky (eds), *Applications of control theory to economic analysis*, Amsterdam: North-Holland.

Kneese, A.V., R.U. Ayres and R.C. d'Arge (1970), *Economics and the environment: A material balances approach*, Baltimore, MD: Johns Hopkins University Press.

Mäler, K.-G. (1974), *Environmental economics: A theoretical inquiry*, Baltimore, MD: Johns Hopkins University Press.

Markandya, A. and D.W. Pearce (1988), *Environmental considerations and the choice of discount rate*, Environment Department Working Paper no. 3, Washington, DC: World Bank.

Pearce, D.W. (1988), 'The economics of natural resource degradation in developing countries', in R. Kerry Turner, (ed.), *Sustainable environmental management: Principles and practices*, London: Bellhaven Press and Boulder, CO: Westview Press.

Pearce, D.W., E.B. Barbier and A. Markandya (1988), *Sustainable development and cost–benefit analysis*, LEEC Paper 88–03, London Environmental Economics Centre.

Pearce, D.W., E.B. Barbier and A. Markandya (1990), *Sustainable development; Economics and environment in the third world*, Aldershot, UK and Brookfield, US: Edward Elgar.

Phillips, D.A. (1986), 'Pitfalls in estimating social discount rates: A case study', *Project Appraisal*, **1**, 15–20.

UNIDO (1972), *Guidelines for project evaluation*, New York: United Nations.

Victor, P.A. (1972), *Pollution: Economics and the environment*, London: Allen & Unwin.

Vousden, N. (1973), 'Basic theoretical issues of resource depletion', *Journal of Economic Theory*, **6**, 126–43.

4. Environmental sustainability and cost–benefit analysis

with A. Markandya and D.W. Pearce

Abstract

Efforts to 'operationalize' a concept of sustainability into appraisal methods for practical decisionmaking have been few and generally unpersuasive. In this chapter it is argued that this need not be the case if a set of environmentally compensating, or 'shadow', projects within an overall portfolio are used to ensure a sustainability objective of setting a constraint on the depletion and degradation of the stock of natural capital. This can be achieved through both a 'weak' and a 'strong' sustainability criterion. In both cases the resulting optimum differs from the efficient optimum of the conventional cost–benefit criterion, but the basic cost–benefit model remains intact.

1. Introduction

The extent to which cost–benefit analysis (CBA) can adequately account for environmental concerns is the subject of an extensive and controversial literature. Views range from the belief that it is a 'matter of time' before CBA succeeds in valuing the most significant environmental effects, to those that deny a pervasive role for the monetary evaluation of environmental gains and losses (Sagoff, 1988). An additional concern arises with respect to the distribution of gains and losses over time. It is widely thought that conventional procedures for discounting discriminate against future generations by (a) rapidly depleting exhaustible resources, (b) 'shifting the burden' of distant costs (for example, nuclear waste disposal) to future generations, and (c) not sanctioning investments with benefits that are subject to long gestation periods (for instance forestry).

In this chapter we suggest a way of accommodating these concerns without entering the controversial area of the discount rate but with a full assault on the valuation problem.

CBA embodies intuitive rationality in that any course of action is judged acceptable if it confers a net advantage, that is, if 'benefits' outweigh 'costs'. What constitutes a gain or loss depends on the objective function chosen. Most CBA operates with a function based on economic efficiency, that is, any increase in total net benefits is desirable irrespective of the distribution of these benefits or the impact of the action on the noneconomic objectives. But this is only *one* objective function. It is widely used because economic efficiency is embodied in the very structure of the welfare economics developed over the last century. CBA is essentially the operational version of welfare economics. In principle, however, any other objective function can be chosen, or, more profitably, a *set* of objectives can be chosen.

Common parlance has it that CBA in which more than one objective is used is termed 'extended' CBA. Such terminology is neutral if the idea is to compare multiobjective CBA with the 'norm', that is, CBA based on economic efficiency alone. It is a misleading terminology if it is meant to imply that the basic structure of CBA is somehow overturned by the inclusion of other objectives.[1] One such additional objective that is often put forth is the notion that investment should be 'environmentally sustainable'; that is, it must ensure nondepreciation of the stock of natural environmental assets. In this chapter we argue (a) that sustainability does have an economic interpretation, (b) that integrating the sustainability objective into CBA can be shown to leave the basic structure of CBA intact, but (c) that the resulting modifications to the basic theorems are of interest, and, we suggest, of importance.

2. The sustainability criterion

'Sustainable development' is a somewhat vague term popularized in the Brundtland report (WCED, 1987) but earlier espoused in the World Conservation Strategy (IUCN, 1980). It is typically taken to mean that the wellbeing of the current generation should not be advanced at the expense of future generations. *Within* a generation, sustainability also implies particular concern for the most disadvantaged in society. An economic interpretation of sustainable development is possible and focuses on the traditional concerns of economic efficiency and an equitable distribution of income. This interpretation involves the following sequence: (a) in order to ensure that future generations are not disadvantaged by the present generation, actual compensation of future generations by the present generation is required. This is a departure from the conventional hypothetical compensation requirements of cost–benefit analysis; (b) the form in which compensation takes place is via a transfer of capital assets; and (c) this 'capital compensation' requires that no less than the current capital stock, in terms of its value, be passed on to future generations. These requirements are spelled out in more detail in Maler (1989) and Warford and Pearce (1990).

The stock of capital may be interpreted as the combined total stock of man-made capital assets and environmental assets (soil, minerals, biomass, and so on), or, more narrowly, as the stock of environmental assets only ('natural capital'). The former interpretation (for example, see Repetto, 1986) is relevant to the Hartwick–Solow rule which shows that reinvestment of the total 'rent' from exhaustible resource exploitation will secure a constant stream of consumption over time, which is thus 'intergenerationally fair'. Solow (1986) demonstrates that such a fairness rule is formally equivalent to keeping the stock of all capital constant. Basically, if an exhaustible resource such as oil is depleted, the profits, or 'rent', from depletion should be reinvested in other forms of capital (machinery, roads, and so on) so as to compensate for the decline in natural assets. Failure to do this may be consistent with intergenerational *efficiency* but is not consistent with intergenerational *equity*.

The narrow definition of the resource base in terms of environmental assets only, does not dispute the importance of man-made capital in the sustainable development process, but emphasizes the *nonsubstitutability* of many natural-resource functions by man-made capital. Notable among these are the life-support functions of natural environments in terms of biogeochemical cycles. In the narrower definition, then, natural capital is 'special' and this accounts for the requirement that it should not be degraded (Pearce *et al.*, 1990). This suggests that sustainability can be introduced into CBA by setting a constraint on the depletion and degradation of the stock of natural capital.

'Constancy' of the natural capital stock can take on different meanings – interpretations in terms of constant *physical* capital stock and the constant *economic value* of that stock are common (Bishop, 1978; Page, 1977; Pearce *et al.*, 1988). In constructing a sustainability criterion for CBA, we can be more specific: essentially, the objective of economic efficiency is modified to mean that all projects yielding net benefits should be undertaken subject to the requirement that environmental damage (that is, natural capital depreciation) should be zero or negative. However, applied at the level of each project such a requirement would be stultifying. Few projects would be feasible. At the programme level, however, the interpretation is more interesting. It amounts to saying that, netted out across a set of projects (a programme), the *sum* of individual damages should be zero or negative. That is, if E_i is the damage done by the *i*th project, we require that

$$\sum_i E_i \le 0. \tag{4.1}$$

In such a formulation time is ignored. In the next section, we address the question directly and show that two formulations of the sustainability constraint emerge. Under weak sustainability it is the present value of $\Sigma_i E_i$, pv(ΣE_i), which is constrained to be nonpositive. Under strong sustainability ΣE_i is constrained to be nonpositive for each period of time.

As it is not feasible to set pv(E_i) or E_i to be zero or negative for each project, but it is feasible to set pv(ΣE_i) or ΣE_i to be nonpositive, the sustainability constraint amounts to including within any portfolio of investments one or more *shadow projects*, the aim of which is to compensate for the environmental damage from the other projects in the portfolio.[2]

$$\sum_t d_t\left[\sum_i \left(B_{it} - C_{it} - E_{it}\right)\right] > 0, \tag{4.2}$$

where B is nonenvironmental benefits, C is nonenvironmental costs, E is net environmental costs or benefits, t is time, and d_t is the discount factor.

The environmentally compensating project(s), j, would be chosen such that the inequality

$$\text{pv}\left(\sum_j A_j\right) \geq \text{pv}\left(\sum_i E_i\right) \tag{4.3}$$

applies for the weak sustainability criterion, and the inequality

$$\sum_j A_{jt} \geq \sum_i E_{it}, \quad \forall t \tag{4.4}$$

applies for the strong sustainability criterion, where the net environmental benefits of the jth project, $A_{j1}, A_{j2}, \ldots, A_{jT}$, compensate for the damage done by the other projects. For the compensating projects, then, the normal CBA decision rule does not apply, although we would wish to minimize the cost of achieving the sustainability criterion.

In the following section we develop this approach further in a formal analysis of sustainability and CBA.

3. Analysis of sustainability and cost–benefit analysis

The traditional criterion for project appraisal is that the discounted benefit of each project i should equal or exceed its costs; that is,

$$\sum_j d_t\left[B_{it} - C_{it}\right] \geq 0, \quad i = 1, \ldots, n. \tag{4.5}$$

where B_{it} is the benefits of the ith project in time period t, C_{it} is its costs in that time period, and d_t is the discount factor, equal to $1/(1 + r)^t$. We assume a finite time horizon $[0, T]$.

For a portfolio of projects, inequality (4.5) becomes

$$\sum_t d_t \left[\sum_i (B_{it} - C_{it}) \right] \geq 0. \tag{4.6}$$

As argued by Markandya and Pearce (1988a, 1988b), the 'correct' approach to 'internalizing' any environmental damage caused by a project might simply be to adjust net benefits, $B_{it} - C_{it}$, to include the costs of such damage. That is, if E_{it} is defined as the costs of environmental damage generated by the ith project at time period t, then inequalities (4.5) and (4.6) become, respectively:

$$\sum_t d_t [B_{it} - C_{it} - E_{it}] \geq 0, \quad i = 1, \ldots, n. \tag{4.7}$$

and

$$\sum_t d_t \left[\sum_i (B_{it} - C_{it} - E_{it}) \right] \geq 0. \tag{4.8}$$

Although criteria (4.7) and (4.8) are effective in 'internalizing' the environmental costs of projects in the appraisal process, they are insufficient for overall environmental 'sustainability'. For example, criteria (4.7) and (4.8) could hold, while at the same time in some time periods, the total environmental damage costs generated by the portfolio of n projects could be greater than zero, that is,

$$\sum_i E_{it} > 0, \quad \text{for some } t. \tag{4.9}$$

Thus, the portfolio as a whole is continuing to degrade the environment. Over the long run, the cumulative environmental degradation (for example, soil erosion, deforestation, waste accumulation) may severely degrade or deplete the resource base.[3]

Consequently, to ensure that a portfolio of projects does not undermine the sustainability of the resource, one must adopt an explicit constraint. As noted in the previous section, there are two possibilities – a 'weak' and a 'strong' sustainability condition. The weak sustainability condition is that the discounted present value of the environmental damage costs across all projects is nonpositive, whereas the strong sustainability criterion requires that the net environmental costs across all projects be nonpositive for each and every time period. These are represented mathematically in inequalities (4.11) and (4.12).

The planning criteria for each of the sustainability conditions can be expressed as follows. In addition to the portfolio of projects, $i = 1, ..., n$, there is a portfolio of environmentally mitigating, or shadow, projects, $j = 1, ..., m$. Each project j in this portfolio has associated with it a cost profile, $C_{j1}, C_{j2}, ..., C_{jT}$; a benefit profile, $B_{j1}, B_{j2}, ..., B_{jT}$; and a set of net environmental benefits, $A_{j1}, A_{j2}, ..., A_{jT}$. For the sustainability criterion to be met in an optimizing framework, the sum of the returns from *all* projects must be maximized, subject to the net environmental damages being nonpositive:

$$\underset{Q_{it}, Q_{jt}}{\text{maximize}} \sum_t d_t \left[\sum_i (B_{it} - C_{it} - E_{it}) \right] + \sum_t d_t \left[\sum_j (B_{jt} - C_{jt} - A_{jt}) \right], \qquad (4.10)$$

subject to the condition

$$\sum_t d_t \left(\sum_i E_{it} - \sum_j A_{jt} \right) \leq 0, \quad \text{for weak sustainability,} \qquad (4.11)$$

and

$$\left(\sum_i E_{it} - \sum_j A_{jt} \right) \leq 0, \quad \forall t, \text{ for strong sustainability,} \qquad (4.12)$$

where each ith and jth project is defined by its activity level, Q_{it} and Q_{jt}, respectively and the functions B_{it}, C_{it}, E_{it}, and A_{it} are differentiable in Q.[4] Assuming $Q_{it} > 0$, $Q_{jt} > 0$, and $P_t > 0$, for all i, j, and t, we can write the Kuhn–Tucker maximization conditions of the Lagrangean formed for the weak sustainability criterion (4.11) as

$$\sum_i \frac{1}{\mathrm{d}Q_{it}} (\mathrm{d}B_{it} - \mathrm{d}C_{it} - E_{it} - P_t \mathrm{d}E_{it}) = 0, \quad \forall t, \qquad (4.13)$$

and

$$\sum_j \frac{1}{\mathrm{d}Q_{jt}} (\mathrm{d}B_{jt} - \mathrm{d}C_{jt} + \mathrm{d}A_{jt} - P_t \mathrm{d}A_{jt}) = 0, \quad \forall t, \qquad (4.14)$$

P_t is the Lagrangean multiplier, the value of which will depend, in general, on all the Qs and d_t. It can be interpreted as the 'price' of the sustainability constraint. Its value is equal to the user cost of degrading the environment, or alternatively, the marginal net present value of all the projects from 'relaxing' the constraint.

As $(dB_{it} - dC_{it})/dQ_{it}$ is the marginal net benefit ($B_{it}^{\text{m.net}}$) of the ith project and dE_{it}/dQ_{it} is its marginal cost of environmental damage ($C_{it}^{\text{m.env}}$), inequality (4.12) can be rearranged as

$$\sum_i \frac{B_{it}^{\text{m.net}}}{C_{it}^{\text{m.env}}} = (1 + P_t), \quad \forall t. \tag{4.15}$$

Equation (4.15) expresses that the total net marginal benefits across the n projects should be equal to their total net marginal cost of environmental damage, *plus* a factor λ_t $(= P_t \Sigma_i C_{i,t}^{\text{m.env}})$ which represents a premium arising from the sustainability criterion. If there were no constraint, it would be rational to equate the net benefits of the portfolio to its environmental costs; that is, the optimal solution reduces to the standard efficiency CBA criterion (4.8). Figure 4.1(a) depicts this optimum for the portfolio, which occurs at total activity level Q_{nt}^*. However, if the factor P_t is positive, implying that the 'weak' sustainability criterion (4.11) is enforced, then a new curve in Figure 4.1(a) is drawn, which represents the environmental costs plus a 'sustainability' premium.[5] The new optimum, Q_{nt}^{**}, is to the left of the unconstrained one, Q_{nt}^*, implying a lower level of total activity.

Similarly, if we define $(dB_{jt} - dC_{jt})/dQ_{jt}$ as the marginal net benefits ($B_{jt}^{\text{m.net}}$) of the jth environmentally compensating project, and dA_{jt}/dQ_{jt} as its marginal environmental benefits ($B_{jt}^{\text{m.env}}$), equation (4.14) can be rewritten as

$$\sum_j \frac{-B_{jt}^{\text{m.net}}}{B_{jt}^{\text{m.env}}} = (1 + P_t), \quad \forall t. \tag{4.16}$$

Thus, as depicted in Figure 4.1(b), rule (4.16) indicates that sufficient environmentally compensating projects, j, should be chosen to ensure that their total (negative) marginal net benefits equal their total marginal environmental benefits plus a 'sustainability' premium λ_t $(= P_t \Sigma_i B_{jt}^{\text{m.env}})$. This premium is the social value of ensuring that the environmental improvements generated by the m projects compensate for the environmental damages inflicted by the other n projects in the combined portfolio ($m + n$ projects). As shown in Figure 4.1(b), when this constraint is binding, the total activity level of the environmentally

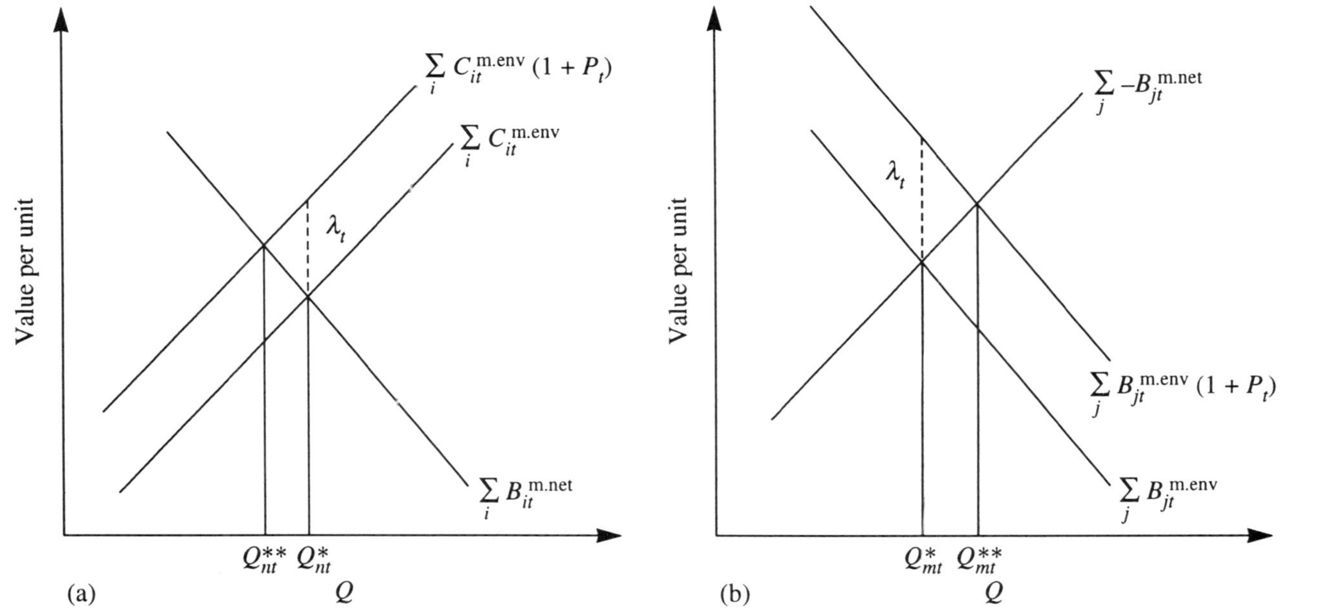

Figure 4.1 *The sustainability optimum for (a) environmentally depleting projects, and (b) environmentally compensating projects*

when this constraint is binding, the total activity level of the environmentally compensating projects (Q^{**}_{mt}) is higher than the unconstrained optimum (Q^{*}_{mt}).

Two points should be noted about the above analysis. First, when the premium λ_t is not positive, the returns to the m shadow projects are sufficient to net out all environmental damage, even though they are operating at their unconstrained maximizing levels. In that event there would be no need for these environmentally compensating projects to be justified as 'shadow projects' but as ones that were valid in their own right, as indicated by the CBA criterion (4.8). The second point is that when the sustainability premium is positive, the shadow projects individually may not satisfy the traditional appraisal criterion, as given in equation (4.5), or even the modified rule expressed in inequality (4.7). This is clear from equation (4.16). A shadow project could have a negative net present value, but its output of A_{jt} could be so great as to justify the project in terms of its contribution to fulfilling the sustainability constraint.

Under the strong sustainability criterion (4.12), it can easily be confirmed that the Kuhn–Tucker maximization conditions become

$$\sum_i \frac{B_{it}^{\text{m.net}}}{C_{it}^{\text{m.env}}} = \frac{d_t + P_t}{d_t} = 1 + P_t(1+r)^t, \quad \forall t, \tag{4.17}$$

and

$$\sum_j \frac{-B_{jt}^{\text{m.net}}}{B_{jt}^{\text{m.env}}} = \frac{d_t + P_t}{d_t} = 1 + P_t(1+r)^t, \quad \forall t, \tag{4.18}$$

(where r is the rate of discount) for Q_{it}, Q_{jt}, and P_t all greater than 0. Equations (4.17) and (4.18) are analogous to equations (4.15) and (4.16), respectively, but state that the sustainability premium grows exponentially with time. Equations (4.17) and (4.18), along with the constraint (4.12), are a system of equations that determine the values of $P_1, P_2, \ldots, P_T$; $Q_{i1}, Q_{i2}, \ldots, Q_{iT}$; and $Q_{j1}, Q_{j2}, \ldots, Q_{jT}$ for all i and j. In order to find out how the values of P_t change with d_t and how the sustainability premium changes with r, one has to carry out a full comparative statics exercise on this system of equations. Unfortunately, no general results appear to be available, and more structure would have to be put on the problem before results of this kind could be obtained.

4. Conclusion

The above analysis indicates that both a weak and a strong sustainability criterion can be easily incorporated into CBA through the use of 'environmentally compensating' projects. This is in contrast to a widely suggested alternative approach, in which the discount rate for environmentally beneficial projects is lowered relative to the rate for those that generate environmental damage (Kula, 1984, 1985). It is possible to show that adjusting the discount rates for some 'environmental risk premium' can produce similar results to those suggested here, but the adjustments are complex, and the actual determination of the risk premium for damaging projects (or the discount for beneficial projects) is liable to generate impossible informational demands (Markandya and Pearce, 1988a, 1988b). Yet another suggestion, that *all* projects should attract a lower discount rate can actually be counterproductive to the basic idea of maintaining natural capital stocks. This is because lower discount rates encourage a larger *total* of investment and this will 'drag' through the system more materials and energy and hence more waste (Markandya and Pearce, 1988a, 1988b).

There is therefore an attraction to using a procedure which avoids adjusting discount rates. The 'sustainability constraint' or 'compensating project' approach achieves this aim. It has a cost in that, in order to know if environmental assets are being 'held constant', it is necessary to value the assets. Elsewhere we have suggested that valuation procedures have advanced considerably in recent years and can be advanced much further (Barbier, 1988; Pearce and Markandya, 1989). We conclude that the 'compensating project' approach is more profitable as a way of modifying CBA practically. The burden then falls on the proper economic valuation of the environmental impacts, E_{it}.

Notes

1. Thus, it is sometimes suggested that incorporating a distributional objective into CBA leads to a fundamental modification. But this is not so. See Pearce (1986) and, for the context of developing countries, Little and Mirrlees (1974) and Dasgupta *et al.* (1972).
2. The idea of a shadow project is suggested by Klaassen and Botterweg (1976) in what appears to be a neglected paper.
3. The constraint here is formulated in value terms for environmental damage. This may not be the relevant concept if it is in fact the physical damage that one wants to restrict for each type of degradation. The analysis presented here can easily be extended to the case of several environmental constraints, but the only implication as far as this presentation is concerned is that the mathematics would become more complicated.
4. For expository purposes, it is assumed that Q varies freely from period to period, although this may not be likely. It is also assumed that the projects selected are fixed, that the functions $A(.)$ and $B(.)$ are concave, and that the functions $C(.)$ and $E(.)$ are convex.
5. On the idea of a sustainability premium, see Pearce (1988).

References

Barbier, E.B. (1988), 'Economic valuation of environmental impacts', *Project Appraisal*, **3**, 143–50.

Bishop, R. (1978), 'Endangered species and uncertainty: the economics of a safe minimum standard', *American Journal of Agricultural Economics*, **60**, 10–13.

Dasgupta, P.S., S. Marglin and A. Sen (1972), *Guidelines for Project Evaluation*, Vienna: United Nations Industrial Development Organization.

IUCN (1980), *World Conservation Strategy*, International Union for Conservation of Nature, 1196 Gland, Switzerland.

Klaassen, L. and T.H. Botterweg (1976), 'Project evaluation and intangible effects – a shadow project approach', in *Environmental Economics: Volume 1 – Theories*, ed. P. Nijkamp, Dordrecht: Martinus Nijhoff, pp. 33–50.

Kula, E. (1984), 'Derivation of social time preference rates for the United States and Canada', *Quarterly Journal of Economics*, **99**, 873–82.

Kula, E. (1985), 'An empirical investigation on the social time-preference rate for the United Kingdom', *Environment and Planning A*, **17**, 199–212.

Little, I.M.D. and J. Mirrlees (1974), *Project Appraisal and Planning for Developing Countries*, London: Heinemann.

Mäler, K.-G. (1989), 'Sustainable development', mimeograph, available from Economic Development Institute, World Bank, Washington, DC.

Markandya, A. and D.W. Pearce (1988a), 'Natural environments and the social rate of discount', *Project Appraisal*, **3**, 2–12.

Markandya, A, and D.W. Pearce (1988b), 'Environmental considerations and the choice of discount rate in developing countries', Working Paper 3, Environment Department, World Bank, Washington, DC.

Page, T. (1977), *Conservation and Economic Efficiency*, Baltimore, MD: Johns Hopkins University Press.

Pearce, D.W. (1986), *Cost Benefit Analysis*, London: Macmillan.

Pearce, D.W. (1988), 'Optimal prices for sustainable development', in *Economics, Growth and Sustainable Environments*, eds D. Collard, D.W. Pearce and D. Ulph, London: Macmillan, pp. 34–47.

Pearce, D.W. and A. Markandya (1989), *The Benefits of Environmental Policy, Monetary Valuation*, Paris: OECD.

Pearce, D.W. and J.J. Warford (1993), *World Without End: Economics, Environment and Sustainable Development*, Oxford: Oxford University Press.

Pearce, D.W., E.B. Barbier and A. Markandya (1988), *Sustainable Development and Cost Benefit Analysis*, LEEC paper 88–03, joint study by International Institute for Environment and Development and University College London; available from London Environmental Economics Centre (LEEC), 3 Endsleigh Street, London WClH 0DD.

Pearce, D.W., E.B. Barbier and A. Markandya (1990), *Sustainable Development: Economics and Environment in the Third World*, Aldershot: Edward Elgar.

Repetto, R. (1986), *World Enough and Time*, New Haven, CT: Yale University Press.

Sagoff, M. (1988), *The Economy of the Earth*, Cambridge: Cambridge University Press.

Solow, R. (1986), 'On the intergenerational allocation of natural resources', *Scandinavian Journal of Economics*, **88** (1), 141–9.

WCED (1987), *Our Common Future*, World Commission on Environment and Development, Oxford: Oxford University Press.

5. Natural capital and the economics of environment and development[1]

Abstract

In recent years economic analysis of the natural resource management and environmental problems of developing countries has increased considerably. This analysis treats the environment as an 'asset' or form of 'natural capital' that must be managed to sustain economic development. The crucial decision is how much to 'draw down' stocks of natural capital and to reinvest in other economic assets (that is, reproducible, man-made capital, foreign assets, and human resources), in order to meet both current and future economic demands. Thus the value of natural resources as economic assets in the development process depends on the present value of their economic welfare potential compared to those of other assets available to the developing economy. It follows that an 'optimal' strategy for a developing economy with sufficient natural resources would be to draw down its stock of natural capital to finance economic development by reinvesting the proceeds in other assets that are expected to yield a higher economic return. However, there are obvious problems in applying this strategy to developing countries. Major difficulties include (1) ecological limits on the substitutability for the environmental functions of natural capital with man-made capital, (2) some environmental values may not be known or reflected in the 'prices' of resources, (3) markets may be distorted, (4) resource extraction may be inefficient, and finally, (5) rents may not be reinvested in other assets but dissipated and dispersed The following chapter discusses these difficulties in more detail, drawing on empirical evidence from developing economies. The chapter concludes by suggesting that efficient and sustainable management of natural resources requires improved policies and accounting procedures to reflect the actual value of natural capital in the development process.

Introduction

As part of the *Agenda 21* preparations for the UN Conference on Environment and Development in June 1992, the UNCED Secretariat made the following statement:

> In the last two decades, there has been some progress through conventional economic policy applied in parallel with environmental policy. It is now clear that this is not enough, and that environment and development must be taken into account at each step of decision making and action in an integrated manner. (UNCED, 1992b)

A recent review of progress in economic research on natural resource degradation in developing countries in the 1980s has also shown important research initiatives in 'resource accounting' methods: (1) the impact of economic policies on the environment, particularly pricing policies for natural resource products and resource-based activities; (2) the effects of 'user incentives' such as common property rights, land tenure and distribution, intra-household division of labour, perceptions of risk, and degree of participation in deciding how individuals should manage the resources available to them; and (3) improvements in the methodology of economic valuation of environmental impacts through the appraisal of the benefits of environmental preservation and the costs of degradation (Barbier, 1991b).

In short, there is a rapidly emerging 'new' sub-discipline of *economics of environment and development*, and there is an even more rapidly expanding demand for policy analysis that applies environmental economics to development problems. In the near future, this analysis will be concerned with the following issues:

- proper economic valuation of natural resources,
- integration of environmental considerations into economic planning and policymaking
- economic incentives for sustainable resource management,
- the role of trade and international economic policies in resource management, and
- the relationship between poverty, population growth, and the environment.

An overriding feature of recent economic analysis in environment and development has been to treat the environment as an 'asset' or form of 'natural capital' that must be managed to sustain economic development. The crucial decision is how much to 'draw down' stocks of natural capital to reinvest in other economic assets (that is, reproducible, man-made capital, foreign assets, and human resources), in order to meet both current and future economic demands. This decision is of paramount importance to many low-income, developing countries, which are usually characterized as having an abundance of natural capital and too little human and man-made capital. Similarly, poor people within developing countries are considered to be overly dependent on natural resources and primary production, because of the lack of economic opportunities in other sectors of the economy and insufficient (man-made) capital formation.

The following chapter addresses the role of natural capital in the economics of environment and development. The first issue is, given the development priorities of the South, whether loss of natural capital is an economic problem for developing countries. The next two sections examine this issue in more detail by exploring the economic significance of natural capital depletion for development and the implications for resource-dependent, low-income economies in particular. A second issue is the relationship between natural capital and poverty – the existence of a poverty-environment 'trap'. The available evidence suggests that there are many misconceptions over this issue, which will be briefly discussed and, hopefully, clarified. Finally, the fundamental issue in the end to be addressed by policymakers is the design of appropriate economic incentives for efficient and sustainable natural resource management. Unfortunately, as presented in the conclusion of this discussion, these are often distorted in development by policy and market failures.

Is natural capital depletion an economic problem in developing countries?

To answer this question requires addressing two additional issues:

- are natural resources an efficient form of retaining 'wealth' for developing countries?
- are the opportunity costs of natural resource degradation for developing countries greater than the benefits gained?

Although apparently different, the questions are inherently related and represent two aspects of the same fundamental economic problem concerning natural capital depletion in developing countries.

Like other 'assets' in developing economies, environmental resources can be seen as a form of 'natural' capital. That is, they have the potential to contribute to the long-run economic productivity and welfare of developing countries. Thus the value of a natural resource as an economic asset depends on the present value of its income, or welfare, potential. However, in any growing economy there will be other assets or forms of wealth that yield income. Any decision to 'hang on' to natural capital, therefore, implies an opportunity cost by foregoing the chance to invest in alternative income-yielding assets, such as man-made 'reproducible' capital. If natural resources are to be an 'efficient' form of holding on to wealth, then they must yield a rate of return comparable to or greater than that of other forms of wealth. In other words, an 'optimal' strategy for a developing country would be to 'draw down' its stock of natural capital to finance economic development by reinvesting the proceeds in other assets that are expected to yield a higher economic return. Under such circumstances, natural resource depletion is not an economic problem but is economically justified; it should proceed up to the point where the comparative returns to 'holding on' to the remaining natural capital stock equal the returns to alternative investments in the economy. If the latter always exceeds the former, then in the long run even complete depletion of natural capital is economically 'optimal'. The only economic problem remaining is that this process of depletion of natural capital and its transformation into other economic assets is done in the most efficient manner possible.

The idea that economic wellbeing, or welfare, may not be affected and may even be enhanced if the rents derived from depleting natural capital such as tropical forests, wetlands, biodiversity, energy, minerals, and even soils, are reinvested in reproducible capital has been around for some time in economics literature. For example, what is now known as the 'Hartwick–Solow rule' states that reinvestment of the rents derived from the intertemporally efficient use of exhaustible natural resources are reinvested in reproducible and hence non-exhaustible, capital will secure a constant stream of consumption over time (Solow, 1974, 1986; Hartwick, 1977). Similarly, basic renewable resource economic theory suggests that, for slow-growing resources such as tropical forests, it may, under certain conditions, be more economically optimal to harvest the resource as quickly and efficiently as possible and reinvest the rents in other assets that increase much faster in value. Similarly, it the harvesting costs are low, or the value of a harvested unit is high, then the resource may also not be worth retaining today (Clark, 1976; Smith, 1977).

However, there are obvious limits to the applications of the above rules to the environment and development problems in the South. For example, the Hartwick–Solow rule assumes that there is sufficient substitutability between reproducible, man-made and natural capital over time, such that they effectively comprise a single 'homogeneous' stock. Moreover, the above rules assume that (1) all economic values are known and reflected in the 'prices' of resources, (2) markets are undistorted, (3) resource extraction is efficient, and (4) rents are reinvested in other assets in the economy. As a consequence, more recent theories now stress the limits to 'substitution' between many forms of natural and man-made capital, even for developing countries interested in 'drawing down' their natural capital stock in favour of investing in other forms of capital (Barbier, 1989a; Barbier and Markandya, 1990; Bojö, Mäler and Unema, 1990; Pearce, Barbier and Markandya, 1990). From an ecological standpoint, a major shortcoming is the failure to consider the economic consequences of the loss in 'resilience' – the ability of ecosystems to cope with random shocks and prolonged stress – that results from natural capital depletion (Common and Perrings, 1992; Conway, 1985; Conway and Barbier, 1990; Holling, 1973).

For example, certain functions of a tropical forest, such as its role in maintaining micro-climates, protecting watersheds, providing unique habitats, and supporting economic livelihoods of indigenous peoples, may be irretrievably lost when the forest is degraded or converted. Often the economic values of these and other functions of tropical forest are not properly accounted for in decisions concerning forest use. There is uncertainty over many of these values, such as the forest's role in maintaining biodiversity and global climate. Finally, there is little evidence to suggest that tropical forest resources are currently being exploited efficiently, nor that the rents earned from activities that degrade or convert the forests are being reinvested in more 'profitable' activities. Rather, market and policy failures are often rife, and economic rents tend to be dissipated and misused.[2]

In addition, the degradation of resources in many low-income countries is often occurring in 'fragile' environments – semi-arid rangelands, 'marginal' cropland, coastal ecosystems, converted forest soils. If resource degradation affects the 'resilience' of these environments to respond to further stresses (for example, soil erosion, devegetation) and random shocks (for example, drought, pest attacks), then the economic livelihoods of peoples dependent on these environments can be affected. If carrying capacities and ecological tolerance limits are transgressed, then collapse of these economic–environmental systems is a possibility (see Barbier, 1989a, 1990a; Conway and Barbier, 1990; Perrings, 1990; Scoones, 1993).

A further problem facing the conventional efficiency conditions driving the Hartwick–Solow rule is that it does not take into account the potential threat posed by population growth to the sustainability of economic development. The conventional rule suggests that for future generations to have the same aggregate level of real consumption expenditure as the present generation, the aggregate value of the capital stock must be maintained. However, in developing countries where populations are currently expanding rapidly, the concern should be with per capita rather than with aggregate real consumption expenditure. Thus maintaining the per capita value of natural assets should also be the relevant sustainability issue. Moreover, as per capita natural capital is 'depreciated' both by use and population growth in developing economies, more resources need to be devoted to the preservation of the asset base where population is growing than where it is not.[3]

In summary, although it is theoretically possible that the current rates of resource depletion in developing regions are economically 'optimal', it is unlikely. Too often, decisions concerning natural capital depletion and conversion are made without considering the opportunity cost of these decisions.[4] In short, we do not know whether it is worth 'holding on' to the natural capital as an economic asset because we do not know or bother to take into account the potential economic benefits that it yields. As a result, decisions will always be biased towards environmental degradation because the underlying assumption is that the foregone benefits provided by natural capital in developing countries are necessarily negligible. If this is not the case, as much evidence suggests, then current levels of resource depletion in developing countries may not be optimal but 'excessive'. Hence, depletion of natural capital may indeed be an economic problem for developing countries – a problem that stems not just from the inefficient transformation of natural capital into other forms of capital but also from its 'unsustainable' management for economic welfare.

Resource-dependent developing economies

So far it has been argued that if current development strategies are to be considered *sustainable*, then net depreciation of the natural asset base should be compensated by investment in renewable (human or physical) capital, and where this is not possible for some natural assets and ecological functions, then environmental degradation should be avoided. Moreover, if natural resource management for development is to be *efficient*, then the benefits of depleting natural capital and its transformation into other economic assets must exceed the costs.

Unfortunately, there is little evidence to suggest that current development strategies are either efficient or sustainable. One of the major reasons for this is the failure to appreciate the critical role of natural capital in economic development. Natural resource management is usually accorded a low priority on the development agenda, and even basic facts about the natural asset base are ignored. If governments of developing economies are to be convinced that sustainable and efficient management of their resource base is essential to economic development, then they must perceive the role of natural resources in supporting the economy as a whole.

Tables 5.1–5.8 indicate the high degree of *resource dependency* of many low- and lower-middle-income developing countries. Many of these economies are directly dependent on natural resource products for the overwhelming majority of their exports (Tables 5.1 and 5.2). In most cases, export earnings are dominated by one or two commodities. Resource dependency has been a feature of these economies over the past 25 years, and for most low-income countries, has remained a persistent feature since the mid-1960s. More lower-middle income economies have reduced their resource dependency with time, but this will clearly be a long-term process. Careful management of the natural resource base may be necessary to maintain the 'capital' required for this transition and to achieve long-term development goals. Running down the natural resource base today through inefficient and unsustainable exploitation could jeopardize development efforts by reducing future export earning potential, as well as needlessly wasting current earnings.

The failure to manage resources efficiently and sustainably also increases vulnerability to the economic stresses imposed by external debt. External debt as a percentage of the gross national product (GNP) and debt servicing as a proportion of GNP and exports have risen substantially in virtually all low- and lower-middle-income resource-dependent economies (see Tables 5 3 and 5.4). For these economies the ability to meet debt repayments and to induce further economic development will depend on the continued successful exploitation of their natural resource bases. Without sustainable management the debt burden may severely constrain development efforts.

Table 5.1 *Low-income economies with high export concentration in primary commodities*[a]

Contribution of primary commodities to total exports[b]		Export share in 1980/81	Export share in 1965	Main export commodities[b] 1		2	
over 90%					%		%
Uganda ($280)	100	100	100	Coffee	95.6	Tea	[c]0.3
Eq. Guinea ($410)	100	91	NA	Cocoa	34.4	Coffee	3.1
Sao Tome & Principle ($490)	99	100	NA	Cocoa	95.5	Copra	1.8
Ethiopia ($120)	99	99	99	Coffee	53.8	Hides	15.3
Rwanda ($320)	99	99	100	Coffee	75.5	Tea	[c]10.8
Yemen PDR ($430)	99	NA	94	NA		NA	
Zambia ($290)	98	99	100	Copper	83.0	Cobalt	5.4
Burkina Faso ($210)	98	85	95	Cotton	32.6	Livestock	[e]26.8
Nigeria ($290)	98	99	97	Petroleum	87.3	Cocoa	4.7
Liberia ($450)[c]	98	98	97	Iron Ore	63.4	Rubber	[e]16.1
Ghana ($400)	97	98	98	Cocoa	51.1	Gold	20.3
Mauritania ($480)	97	99	99	Fish	65.8	Iron Ore	33.3
Niger ($300)	96	98	95	NA		NA	
Somalia ($170)	95	99	86	Meat	39.7	Banana	34.5
Zaire ($170)	93	94	92	Copper	35.8	Coffee	[e]11.2
Sudan ($480)	93	99	99	Cotton	30.3	Livestock	24.4
Togo ($370)	92	85	97	Phosphate	36.2	Cotton	12.6
Comoros ($440)	[c]92	[e]86	NA	Cloves	41.7	Vanilla	[c]33.3
Laos PDR ($180)	90	[e]100	NA	Timber	51.7	Electricity	19.0
over 80%							
Chad ($160)	[c]89	[e]96	97	Cotton	69.4	Hides/Skins	[e]3.8
Myanmar ($210)[c]	89	[d]81	NA	Rice	32.7	Teak	[e]32.2
Guinea-Bissau ($190)	[c]87	[d]71	NA	Cashewnut	73.3	Groundnut	[c]16.7
Guyana ($420)	[c]87	NA	NA	NA		NA	
Madagascar ($190)	84	92	94	Coffee	26.6	Cloves	5.7
Malawi ($170)	83	93	99	Tobacco	62.8	Tea	10.3
Burundi ($240)	83	96	95	Coffee	82.6	Tea	5.0
Kenya ($370)	83	88	94	Coffee	26.2	Tea	[c]21.9
Tanzania ($160)	81	86	87	Coffee	31.4	Cotton	12.7
over 70%							
Maldives ($410)	[c]77	[e]70	NA	Fish	[c]57.1		
Benin ($390)	74	96	95	Cotton	13.4	Fuel	9.4
Indonesia ($440)	71	96	96	Petroleum	40.0	Rubber	5.0
Mali ($230)	70	83	97	Cotton	36.9	Livestock	29.0
over 60%							
C.A.R. ($380)	60	74	46	Diamonds	40.9	Coffee	18.9
over 50%							
Sri Lanka ($420)	57	79	99	Tea	25.9	Rubber	[c]7.0

Notes:
[a] Low-income economies are those with per capita incomes of $545 or less in 1988. US dollar figure 1980 at country listed indicates GNP per capita in 1988. [b] Contributions to the value of total merchandise exported in 1988, unless indicated. [c] 1987 value. [d] 1981–83 average value. [e] 1984 value.

Source: Based on various editions of the following World Bank documents: *World Development Report*; *Trends in Developing Countries*; *Commodity Trade and Price Trends*; *African Economic and Financial Data*.

Table 5.2 *Lower-middle-income economies with high export concentration in primary commodities*[a]

Contribution of primary commodities to total exports[b]		Export share in 1980/81	Export share in 1965	Main export commodities[b] 1		2	
over 90%					%		%
Bolivia ($570)	97	100	95	Gas	40.1	Tin	13.9
Papua N.G. ($810)	95	100	90	Gold	37.7	Copper	28.9
Ecuador ($1120)	93	93	98	Petroleum	44.8	Fish/Shrimp	19.0
over 80%							
Yemen A.R. ($640)	89	49	100	Oil	93.7		
Honduras ($860)	89	89	96	Bananas	39 0	Coffee	21.0
Congo ($910)	89	94	37	Oil	71.6	Timber	15.6
Cote d'Ivoire ($770)	88	90	95	Cocoa	25.7	Coffee	13.1
Cameroon ($1010)	88	97	94	Petroleum	48.9	Coffee	12.2
Paraguay ($1180)	88	NA	92	Cotton	10.3	Timber	2.5
Chile ($1510)	85	90	96	Copper	48.4	Agriculture	13.2
over 70%							
Panama ($2120)	79	91	98	Petroleum	31.7	Banana	[d]7.9
Peru ($1300)	78	83	99	Copper	12.9	Zinc	8.8
Senegal ($650)	75	81	97	Fish	26.9	Groundnut	14.8
Columbia ($1180)	75	72	93	Coffee	30.2	Oil	17.0
Syria ($1680)	75	NA	90				
Egypt ($660)	74	92	80	Oil	64.4	Cotton	6.5
Dominican Rep. ($720)	74	81	98	Nickel	31.2	Sugar	20.5
El Salvador ($940)	71	63	83	Coffee	60.6	Fish	[c]3.5
over 60%							
Guatemala ($900)	62	71	86	Coffee	34.8	Banana	7.6
Zimbabwe ($650)	60	63	85	Tobacco	21.5	Gold	13.1
Costa Rica ($1690)	60	68	84	Coffee	30.4	Banana	18.8
over 50%							
Malaysia ($1940)	55	80	94	Rubber	9.8	Palm Oil	8.4
Jordan ($1500)	53	57	89	Minerals	38.6	Food	10.2
Brazil (42160)	52	59	92	Soya	9.4	Coffee	6.8
Morocco ($830)	50	72	95	Ph. Acid	16.8	Phosphate	13.3

Notes:

[a] Lower-middle-income economies are those with per capita incomes of $2160 or less in 1988. US dollar figure at country listed indicates GNP per capita in 1988.

[b] Contributions to the value of total merchandise exported in 1988, unless indicated.

[c] 1987 value.

[d] 1984 value.

Source: Based on various editions of the following World Bank documents: *World Development Report*; *Trends in Developing Countries*; *Commodity Trade and Price Trends*; *African Economic and Financial Data*.

Table 5.3 *Debt and debt service ratios in resource-dependent low-income economies*[a]

	External total debt as percentage of GNP[b]		Debt service as percentage of:			
			GNP		Exports	
	1970	1988	1970	1988	1970	1988
over 90%						
Uganda (100)	7.3	34.3	0.5	1.0	2.9	14.0
Eq. Guinea (100)	[c]140.2	120.1	NA	NA	[c]6.0	28.5
Sao Tome & Pr. (99)	[d]54.3	146.0	NA	NA	[d]4.7	251.0
Ethiopia (99)	9.5	50.6	1.2	4.3	11.4	37.4
Rwanda (99)	0.9	25.5	0.2	0.7	1.5	9.6
Yemen PDR (99)	[d]85.3	199.4	NA	10.8	[d]5.1	46.5
Zambia (98)	37.5	116.7	4.6	4.9	8.0	14.2
Burkina Faso (98)	6.6	43.4	0.7	2.0	7.1	11.9
Nigeria (98)	4.3	102.5	0.7	7.0	7.1	25.7
Ghana (97)	22.9	44.6	1.2	4.0	5.5	20.6
Mauritania (97)	13.9	196.2	1.8	11.9	3.4	21.6
Niger (96)	5.0	66.0	0.4	5.6	4.0	32.6
Somalia (95)	24.4	185.2	0.3	0.4	2.1	4.9
Zaire(93)	9.1	118.0	1.1	2.8	4.4	6.9
Sudan (93)	14.8	74.6	1.7	0.6	10.6	9.5
Togo (92)	16.0	81.6	1.0	7.0	3.1	18.3
Comoros (92)	[c]94.3	[e]94.4	NA	NA	[d]1.9	[e]3.2
Lao PDR (90)	[c]50.2	153.5	NA	1.8	[c]112.6	143.5
over 80%						
Chad (89)	9.9	33.2	0.9	0.7	4.2	2.7
Myanmar (89)[c]	[d]25.3	[e]45.7	NA	NA	[d]20.3	[e]59.2
Guinea-Bissau (87)	[d]118.4	[e]271.0	NA	NA	[d]0.0	[e]92.0
Madagascar (84)	10.4	192.7	0.8	9.3	3.7	39.0
Malawi (83)	43.2	85.9	2.3	4.6	7.8	19.0
Burundi (83)	3.1	69.8	0.3	3.3	2.3	25.1
Kenya (83)	26.3	58.5	3.0	5.7	9.1	25.3
Tanzania (81)	20.7	140.1	1.6	3.0	6.3	17.8
over 70%						
Maldives (77)	[c]71.6	44.2	NA	NA	[c]16.9	[e]5.9
Benin (74)	15.1	49.3	0.7	1.0	2.5	5.4
Indonesia (71)	30.0	61.7	1.7	11.5	13.9	39.6
Mali (70)	71.4	100.8	0.2	2.5	1.4	14.2
over 60%						
C.A.R. (60)	13.5	53.3	1.7	1.1	5.1	5.9
over 50%						
Sri Lanka (57)	16.1	61.6	2.1	4.8	11.0	17.6

Notes:
[a] Percentage figure after each country listed indicates contribution of primary commodities to total exports. Low-income economies are those with GNP per capita of $545 of less in 1988. [b] Total debt includes public, publicity guaranteed and private nonguaranteed debt. [c] 1980 value. [d] 1984 value. [e] 1987 value.

Source: Based on World Bank, *World Development Report 1990* and World Bank, *Trends in Developing Economies 1989*.

Table 5.4 Debt and debt service ratios in resource-dependent lower-middle-income economies[a]

	External total debt as percentage of GNP[b]		Debt service as percentage of:			
			GNP		Exports	
	1970	1988	1970	1988	1970	1988
over 90%						
Bolivia (97)	49.3	114.9	2.5	5.6	12.6	32.9
Papua N.G. (95)	33.4	64.2	4.8	15.6	24.5	30.9
Ecuador (93)	14.8	94.2	2.2	5.7	14.0	21.4
over 80%						
Yemen A.R. (89)	[c]35.1	41.7	NA	3.4	[c]1.3	16.0
Honduras (89)	15.6	68.3	1.4	7.2	4.9	28.6
Congo (89)	46.5	205.0	3.4	13.1	11.5	28.7
Cote d'Ivoire (88)	19.5	135.1	3.1	12.4	7.5	31.9
Cameroon (88)	12.6	27.0	1.0	4.6	4.0	27.0
Paraguay(88)	19.2	36.4	1.8	5.0	11.8	24.6
Chile (85)	32.1	79.3	3.9	7.9	24.5	19.1
over 70%						
Panama (79)	19.5	81.2	3.1	0.2	7.7	0.2
Peru (78)	37.3	56.1	7.0	1.3	40.0	8.7
Senegal (75)	15.5	63.6	1.1	5.2	4.0	19.3
Columbia (75)	22.5	42.1	2.8	8.0	19.3	42.3
Syria (75)	10.8	25.0	1.7	2.6	11.3	21.1
Egypt (74)	22.5	126.7	4.8	4.4	38.0	16.6
Dominican Rep. (74)	23.9	77.3	2.7	5.8	15.3	14.4
El Salvador (71)	17.3	31.5	3.1	3.3	12.0	18.8
over 60%						
Guatemala (62)	6.5	28.3	1.6	4.5	8.2	27.2
Zimbabwe (60)	15.5	37.3	0.6	8.2	2.3	27.9
Costa Rica (60)	25.3	89.2	5.7	7.7	19.9	19.9
over 500%						
Malaysia (55)	10.8	56.3	2.0	16.5	4.5	22.3
Jordan (53)	22.9	94.0	0.9	19.6	3.6	31.9
Brazil (52)	12.2	29.6	1.6	4.5	21.8	42.0
Morocco (50)	18.6	89.8	1.7	6.5	9.2	25.1

Notes:

[a] Percentage figure after each country listed indicates contribution of primary commodities to total exports. Lower-middle-income economies are those with GNP per capita of $2160 or less in 1988.

[b] Total debt includes public, publicity guaranteed and private nonguaranteed debt.

[c] 1980 value.

Source: Based on World Bank, *World Development Report 1990* and World Bank, *Trends in Developing Economies 1989*.

Table 5.5 Land use changes in resource-dependent low-income economies, 1975–87[a]

	Total land area 1987 ('000 km²)	Land use ('000 km²) and % change since 1975–77							
		Cropland		Pasture		Forest		Other[b]	
		85–87	%	85–87	%	85–87	%	85–87	%
Uganda (100)	200	67	21.4	50	0.0	58	–7.9	25	–21.3
Eq. Guinea (100)	28	2	0.0	1	0.0	13	0.0	12	0.0
Ethiopia (99)	1101	139	1.4	451	–1.1	275	–3.5	236	5.9
Rwanda (99)	25	11	18.6	4	–27.3	5	–5.5	5	1.8
Yemen PDR (99)	333	1	9.2	91	0.0	15	–6.1	226	0.4
Zambia (98)	741	52	3.8	350	0.0	293	–3.0	46	18.3
Burkina Faso (98)	274	31	19.4	100	0.0	68	–8.1	75	1.3
Nigeria (98)	911	313	3.8	210	0.8	146	–17.0	243	7.5
Ghana (97)	230	29	5.5	34	–2.8	84	–7.7	84	8.4
Mauritania (97)	1025	2	0.0	393	0.0	150	–0.9	481	0.3
Niger (96)	1267	35	32.0	93	–8.4	25	–19.1	1113	0.5
Somalia (95)	627	9	3.0	239	0.0	89	–5.3	241	2.0
Zaire (93)	2268	66	8.2	92	0.0	1756	–1.9	353	8.7
Sudan (93)	2376	125	1.8	560	0.0	471	–6.2	1220	2.4
Togo (92)	54	14	1.0	2	0.0	14	–26.3	24	25.3
Lao PDR (90)	231	9	5.9	0	0.0	1	–11.1	6	6.7
Guinea-Bissau (87)	28	3	15.8	11	0.0	11	0.0	3	–11.9
Chad (89)	1259	32	4.0	450	0.0	131	–5.7	647	1.0
Madagascar (84)	582	31	8.5	340	0.0	149	–9.7	62	28.1
Malawi (83)	94	24	4.3	18	0.0	44	–13.2	8	272.2
Burundi (83)	26	13	5.3	9	6.3	1	9.6	3	–32.8
Kenya (83)	567	24	5.6	37	–1.0	37	–7.5	469	0.4
Tanzania (81)	886	52	2.9	350	0.0	425	–2.7	58	21.6
Benin (74)	111	18	3.3	4	0.0	37	–12.0	51	9.5
Indonesia (71)	1812	211	8.1	440	0.0	180	0.1	868	1.3
Mali (70)	1220	21	4.6	300	0.0	86	–4.5	814	0.4
C.A.R. (60)	623	20	5.1	30	0.0	358	–0.3	215	0.0
Sri Lanka (57)	65	19	–1.0	4	0.0	17	–2.2	24	2.5

Notes:

[a] Percentage figure after each country listed indicates contribution of primary commodities to total exports. Low-income economies are those with GNP per capita of $545 or less in 1988.

[b] Other land includes uncultivated land, grassland not used for pasture, built-on areas, wetlands and roads.

Source: World Resources Institutes/UNEP/UNDP, *World Resources 1990–91*.

Table 5.6. Land use changes in resource-dependent lower-middle-income economies, 1975–87[a]

	Total land area 1987 ('000 km^2)	Land use ('000 km^2) and % change since 1975–77							
		Cropland		Pasture		Forest		Other[b]	
		85–87	%	85–87	%	85–87	%	85–87	%
Bolivia (97)	1084	34	3.0	268	−1.2	558	−1.3	224	4.5
Papua N.G. (95)	453	385	8.9	1	−18.5	383	−0.5	65	3.0
Ecuador (93)	277	26	1.4	49	61.5	121	−19.6	81	14.9
Yemen A.R. (89)	195	14	0.3	70	0.0	16	0.0	95	0.0
Honduras (89)	112	18	5.9	25	8.3	36	−18.5	33	18.5
Congo (89)	342	7	2.7	100	0.0	212	−0.9	22	9.1
Cote d'Ivoire (88)	318	36	22.4	30	0.0	69	−42.1	183	31.2
Cameroon (88)	465	70	7.2	83	0.0	250	−4.2	63	11.2
Paraguay (88)	397	22	71.2	192	26.0	166	−20.4	18	−25.2
Chile (85)	749	56	4.0	119	1.7	87	0.0	487	−0.8
Panama (79)	76	6	4.5	13	8.3	40	−7.0	17	11.3
Peru (78)	1280	37	12.8	271	0.0	694	−3.5	278	8.1
Senegal (75)	193	52	0.6	57	0.0	59	−4.2	24	3.7
Columbia (75)	1039	53	3.2	398	7.3	515	−5.5	73	1.5
Syria (75)	184	56	1.3	83	−3.1	5	16.2	40	25.3
Egypt (74)	995	25	−7.5	0	0.0	0	0.0	970	0.2
Dominican Rep. (74)	48	15	13.2	21	0.0	6	−3.1	7	−18.9
El Salvador (71)	21	7	8.9	6	0.0	1	−35.4	6	−1.0
Guatemala (62)	108	18	10.2	14	7.9	41	−16.4	36	17.4
Zimbabwe (60)	387	28	9.1	49	0.0	199	0.0	111	−2.0
Costa Rica (60)	51	5	6.1	23	34.1	16	−22.9	6	−16.4
Malaysia (55)	329	44	3.1	NA	NA	152	−0.3	167	57.9
Jordan (53)	89	4	5.5	6	0.0	134	0.0	6	0.0
Brazil (52)	8457	767	22.7	1670	6.4	5604	−4.2	415	0.3
Morocco (50)	446	84	9.0	209	7.7	52	0.2	101	−17.9

Notes:

[a] Percentage figure after each country listed indicates contribution of primary commodities to total exports. Lower-middle-income economies are those with GNP per capita of $2160 or less in 1988.

[b] Other land includes uncultivated land, grassland not used for pasture, built-on areas, wetlands and roads.

Source: World Resources Institutes/UNEP/UNDP, *World Resources 1990–91*.

The resource base in poor resource-dependent economies is far from static. Although comparison of land classifications across countries is fraught with difficulties, the most notable change over the last 15 years in most economies is the decline in forest area and the increase in cropland (see Tables 5.5 and 5.6). Much of the forest land has presumably been lost to agricultural conversion, with fuelwood and fodder gathering a factor in some areas and depletion for timber operations important in major producing countries. Some empirical explorations of the causes of deforestation, particularly from frontier agriculture expansion, are discussed further.

Expansion of cropland clearly appears to follow the classic agricultural extensification pattern (see Tables 5.7 and 5.8). Particularly in low-income resource-dependent economies, low levels of fertilizer use and yield changes suggest very little agricultural intensification, with the notable exception of Indonesia, Sri Lanka, and to some extent, Kenya, Benin, Ghana, Nigeria, and Zambia. A worrying trend in some poor sub-Saharan economies is the fall in agricultural yields, particularly for cereals. Many other economies show substantial yield increases only because yields were abysmally low in the mid-1970s. Some economies that have increased agricultural intensification – for example Indonesia, Sri Lanka, and Kenya – also face rapid population growth and severe constraints on cropland availability, as indicated by extremely low levels of cropland per capita. In general, most of the low-income resource-dependent economies have long since extended cropland beyond their stock of favourable land with good chemical and physical properties for agriculture. Those countries that do still have 'excess' favourable land face difficulties in cultivating it, as much of this land occurs in areas with climates and growing seasons (for example, arid/semi-arid zones) that prevent or severely constrain rainfed cultivation.

Cropland use and productivity in resource-dependent lower middle income economies follow similar patterns as in the low-income economies (see Table 5.8). In general, fertilizer use and yields and yield changes appear higher in the lower-middle-income groups compared to the low-income economies, suggesting a slightly higher level of agricultural intensification. However, like the low-income countries, many lower-middle-income economies also display low cropland availability per capita and a low ratio of favourable to total cropland. Climatic conditions again limit cultivation of much of the 'excess' favourable land in the North African and Middle Eastern countries, whereas social, economic and climatic constraints on frontier agricultural expansion also limit exploitation of the additional favourable land available in the South American countries. Clearly, much cultivation of marginal – or ecologically fragile – land occurs in resource-dependent lower-middle-income economies.

Thus the continuing dependence of most of the world's poorest economies on their resource base should make environmental management a high priority as a development concern. This is particularly true given that past economic policies and investments have led to rapid changes – frequently with adverse economic consequences – in resource stocks and patterns of use. Demographic trends have often worsened the relationship between population and resource carrying capacity in many regions. Continuing agricultural extensification into marginal lands have increased the susceptibility of economic systems and livelihoods to environmental degradation.

Table 5.7. Cropland use and productivity in resource-dependent low-income economies[a]

	Cropland ha ('000 ha) 1987	Cropland ha per capita 1989	Fertilizer use (kg/ha) 85–87	% change[b]	% Yield changes 76–78 to 86–88 Cereals	Roots	Favourable land index[c]
Uganda (100)	6705	0.38	0	0	6	29	8.8
Eq Guinea (100)	230	0.53	0	0	NA	–12	9.1
Ethiopia (99)	13930	0.30	4	100	22	–9	[d]105.9
Rwanda (99)	1120	0.16	1	100	0	–12	8.1
Yemen PDR (99)	119	0.05	13	86	12	12	[d]2753.8
Zambia (98)	5208	0.64	16	33	19	3	11.4
Burkina Faso (98)	3140	0.36	5	67	34	18	[d]206.9
Nigeria (98)	31335	0.29	10	400	43	6	28.5
Ghana (97)	2870	0.20	10	150	12	6	9.7
Mauritania (97)	199	0.10	7	0	47	45	[d]14723.1
Niger (96)	3540	0.51	1	0	–2	–10	[d]1362.5
Somalia (95)	933	0.13	3	–25	76	–5	[d]366.2
Zaire (93)	6690	0.19	1	–50	15	8	18.2
Sudan (93)	12478	0.51	4	–33	–24	–24	[d]599.3
Togo (92)	1431	0.43	7	250	–1	–24	19.3
Lao PDR (90)	901	0.23	2	200	66	3	4.1
Guinea–Bissau (87)	335	0.35	1	0	42	14	0.0
Chad (89)	3205	0.58	2	0	20	25	[d]966.5
Madagascar (84)	3067	0.26	4	33	2	5	71.7
Malawi (83)	2377	0.29	17	70	–9	–28	46.2
Burundi (83)	1332	0.25	2	100	5	–4	5.0
Kenya (83)	2420	0.10	46	109	4	20	[d]252.4
Tanzania (81)	5230	0.20	9	50	34	–18	57.0
Benin (74)	1840	0.40	37	95	10	9	12.3
Indonesia (71)	21220	0.12	100	270	45	26	35.5
Mali (70)	2076	0.23	15	200	26	–3	[d]1674.0
C.A.R. (60)	2005	0.71	1	0	48	58	39.9
Sri Lanka (57)	1887	0.11	106	116	49	50	25.9

Notes:

[a] Percentage figure after each country listed indicates contribution of primary commodities to total exports. Low-income economies are those with GNP per capita of $545 or less in 1988.

[b] Percentage change in annual average fertilizer use since 1975/77.

[c] Index denotes (favourable land/total cropland)*100, where favourable land denotes land with good chemical and physical properties relevant for crop fertility and management, as defined by the fertility capability classification (FCC) system.

[d] Much of the favourable land in these countries occur in areas with climates and growing seasons (for example, arid/semi-arid zones).

Source: World Resources Institutes/UNEP/UNDP, *World Resources 1990–91*.

Table 5.8 Cropland use and productivity in resource-dependent lower-middle-income economies[a]

	Cropland ha ('000 ha) 1987	Cropland ha per capita 1989	Fertilizer use (kg/ha) 85–87	% change[b]	% Yield changes 76–78 to 86–88 Cereals	Roots	Favourable land index[c]
Bolivia (97)	3399	0.48	2	100	19	−12	254.3
Papua N.G. (95)	336	0.10	30	50	5	0	NA
Ecuador (93)	2646	0.25	34	8	7	−35	75.6
Yemen A.R. (89)	1360	0.18	13	86	2	46	[d]184.7
Honduras (89)	1785	0.36	19	36	54	121	35.2
Congo (89)	679	0.35	5	25	15	18	0.0
Cote d'Ivoire (88)	3640	0.30	9	−36	14	29	3.8
Cameroon (88)	6995	0.64	7	133	13	7	27.6
Paraguay (88)	2176	0.52	5	400	20	10	493.1
Chile (85)	5580	0.43	46	130	90	44	79.6
Panama (79)	575	0.24	58	35	30	10	28.0
Peru (78)	3725	0.17	43	13	30	15	362.1
Senegal (75)	5225	0.73	4	−56	15	8	59.7
Columbia (75)	5318	0.17	81	65	11	9	95.0
Syria (75)	5630	0.47	42	160	41	28	15.2
Egypt (74)	2560	0.05	347	85	18	31	[d]817.9
Dominican Rep. (74)	1474	0.21	47	−8	33	−1	30.8
El Salvador (71)	733	0.14	111	−26	11	39	34.5
Guatemala (62)	1865	0.21	62	24	20	43	25.1
Zimbabwe (60)	2759	0.29	56	8	−6	29	32.2
Costa Rica (60)	526	0.18	166	31	13	−11	16.0
Malaysia (55)	4380	0.26	154	126	2	6	6.5
Jordan (53)	414	0.10	34	113	126	39	[d]716.9
Brazil (52)	77500	0.53	49	20	32	5	29.2
Morocco (50)	8462	0.35	36	57	39	22	[d]107.1

Notes:

a Percentage figure after each country listed indicates contribution of primary commodities to total exports. Lower-middle-income economies are those with GNP per capita of $2160 or less in 1988.

b Percentage change in annual average fertilizer use since 1975/77.

c Index denotes (favourable land/total cropland) *100, where favourable land denotes land with good chemical and physical properties relevant for crop fertility and management, as defined by the fertility capability classification (FCC) system.

d Much of the favourable land in these countries occur in areas with climates and growing seasons (for example, arid/semi-arid zones) that prevent or severely constrain rainfed cultivation.

Source: World Resources Institutes/UNEP/UNDP, *World Resources 1990–91*.

As mentioned elsewhere, a reappraisal of demographic and agricultural policies to take into account (1) the new realities of resource-carrying capacity constraints and (2) the need to improve the potential of marginal lands while sustaining the productivity of high potential lands, is required (Conway and Barbier, 1990; Barbier, 1989b; FAO, 1990; Leonard *et al.*, 1989; Pearce, 1991; Pretty *et al.*, 1992; Repetto, 1987; Repetto and Holmes, 1983). With regard to population–environment linkages, one useful approach is to view the role of population growth in terms of increasing the 'scale' of human demands on limited natural systems (Foy and Daly, 1989). Another approach is to extend economic theories of household resource allocation to determine the extent to which increased family size is a cause and/or effect of environmental degradation (Dasgupta, 1992; Repetto and Holmes, 1983).

To summarize, this section has argued through the use of basic indicators that the natural asset base of the poorest, resource-dependent economies is being rapidly run down. Yet these economies remain in a fundamental state of 'under-development'. In short, development is essentially 'unsustainable' because net depreciation of the natural asset base (and any increase in population) is not being compensated by investment in renewable (human and physical) capital. Clearly, a higher priority should be placed on efficient and sustainable management of the natural resource to maintain the 'capital' required for this transition and to achieve long-term development goals. As will be discussed in the following section, rethinking from an economic perspective the relationship between poverty and environmental degradation in developing countries is also a necessary component of this new development thinking.

Poverty, environment, and degradation

If developing countries are not using their resources sustainably, then either resource users within these countries are not being confronted by the social opportunity cost of resource use, or they are constrained by limited asset holdings and/or income, or both. In the next section, the factors influencing inefficient resource use (that is, divergence between private and social opportunity cost) are explored. This section discusses how resource endowments – especially conditions of poverty – influence resource utilization.

A common assumption is that the effectiveness of public policies and economic incentives in controlling environmental degradation in developing economies is limited by the existence of a poverty-environment 'trap'. Given the presence of both high levels of poverty and environmental degradation in developing countries, it is tempting to conclude that poverty *causes* environmental degradation. However, poverty and environmental degradation may be positively correlated, but correlation does not imply causation. If anything, recent evidence suggests that poverty–environmental linkages cannot be reduced to simple unidimensional cause–effect relationships (Barbier, 1989b; Conway and Barbier, 1990; Dasgupta, 1992; Hardoy, Mitlin and Satterthwaite, 1992; Jagannathan, 1989; Pearce and Warford, 1993; Pretty *et al.*, 1992).

There are numerous complex factors that influence poor people's perceptions of the environment and their behaviour towards natural resource management. These range from the economic distortions arising from policy and market failures, to underlying labour and capital endowments and constraints (including pressures to increase family size), to access to alternative employment and income-earning opportunities, to institutional and legal factors such as tenure or access security, property rights, and delivery systems. Often what is perceived to be a *direct* link between poverty and environmental degradation proves to be an *indirect* link under careful analysis. Public policies and other factors often affect the incentive structures and redirect capital and labour flows between sectors and regions, with adverse consequences for the poor and their ability or willingness to manage resources sustainably (Jagannathan, 1989).

As poor people have little or no access to capital and must rely on family or low-skilled labour for earning income, it would make no economic sense for them to degrade any 'natural' capital at their disposal. Many studies have revealed that poor people and communities are often acutely aware of the essential role of natural resources in sustaining their livelihoods, and equally, of the costs and impacts of environmental degradation.[5] This would suggest that, *ceteris paribus*, there exist tremendous *incentives* for the poor to manage and sustain the stock of natural capital at their disposal in order to maintain or enhance both their immediate and future livelihood options. Where they choose to degrade their environment – and there may be rational grounds for doing so under certain circumstances – it is because changing economic and social conditions have altered the incentive structures of the poor, including perhaps their control over or access to essential resources.

Thus from an economic perspective, simply observing that poor people are 'driven' to degrade the environment – even when this appears to be the case – is not helpful. Designing appropriate policy responses to alleviate problems of poverty and environmental degradation, therefore, requires careful analysis of the *determinants* of individual behaviour. Such an analysis would clarify the factors leading them to degrade their environment, their responses to environmental degradation, and the incentives required to induce conservation.

Where further analysis reveals that poverty is not the direct 'cause' of environmental degradation, design of appropriate policy responses will nevertheless be affected by poverty's indirect role. The response of poor people and communities to incentives encouraging sustainable resource management may be affected by special factors influencing their behaviour, such as high rates of time preference induced by greater risk and uncertainty over livelihood security, labour, and capital constraints, insecure tenure over and access to resources, imperfect information and access to marketed inputs, and a variety of other conditions and constraints (Barbier, 1989b, 1990b; Binswanger, 1980, Pender and Walker, 1990).

Moreover, the poor are not a homogenous group. The work of Lipton (1983 and 1988) highlights how the 'ultra' or 'core' poor, marginally poor, and the non-poor in developing countries all differ in terms of demographic, nutritional, labour market and asset-holding characteristics.[6] A recent study in Malawi highlights how the marginally poor and the 'core' poor face different incentives and constraints in combating declining soil fertility and erosion, which is a serious problem afflicting smallholder agriculture (Barbier and Burgess, 1992b).

In Malawi, female-headed households constitute a large percentage (42 per cent) of the 'core-poor' households. They typically cultivate very small plots of land (< 0.5 ha) and are often marginalized onto the less fertile soils and steeper slopes (> 12 per cent). They are often unable to finance agricultural inputs such as fertilizer, to rotate annual crops, to use 'green manure' crops or to undertake soil conservation. As a result, poorer female-headed households generally face declining soil fertility and lower crop yields, further exacerbating their poverty and increasing their dependence upon the land. The special constraints and needs of poor female-headed households must be carefully considered when designing economic policies to alleviate poverty and control land degradation. Otherwise, an important subset of the rural population will not respond fully to policy measures and incentives to improve environmental management, and the problem of land degradation may continue unmitigated.

A worrying trend in developing economies is the concentration of the poorest groups in 'ecologically fragile' zones – areas where environmental degradation or severe environmental hazards constrain and even threaten economic welfare. As indicated by Leonard *et al.* (1989) around 470 million, or 60 per cent of the developing world's poorest people, live in rural or urban areas that can be classified as 'ecologically fragile'.[7] Around 370 million of the developing world's poorest people live in 'marginal' agricultural areas. These less favourable agricultural lands, with lower productivity potential, poorer soils and physical characteristics, and more variable and often inadequate rainfall, are easily prone to land degradation due to overcropping, poor farming practices and inadequate conservation measures.

The result is that the economic livelihoods and welfare of the poorest income groups in low potential areas are at greater risk from increasing environmental degradation. It is this risk, combined with the impact of public policies, institutions, and investments on the economic incentives that the poorest face that may have the most profound – and often perverse – effects on the willingness and ability of the poorest groups to counteract degradation.

Another major 'poverty reserve' in developing countries is peripheral urban areas, or 'squatter' settlements. Recent evidence from West Java and Nigeria confirms that the informal employment sector and settlements around urban and semi-urban settlements are often the preferred 'open access' resource for the poor (Jagannathan, 1989). Although precise estimates are scarce of how many of the 1.3 billion urban dwellers in developing countries live in 'squatter' settlements, it is common for between 30–60 per cent of the population in large cities to live either in illegal settlements or in tenements and cheap boarding houses. In smaller urban centres of fewer than 100000 inhabitants – which contain about three quarters of the developing world's urban population – the proportion of people living in illegal settlements may be smaller than in the large cities. However, the proportion living in areas with inadequate infrastructure or services may be as high or even higher in smaller compared to larger urban centres (Cairncross, Hardoy and Satterthwaite, 1990). As a consequence, the economic welfare of a substantial and growing number of the poorest urban dwellers is threatened by the environmental hazards and health risks posed by pollution, and inadequate housing, sanitation, water and other basic infrastructure services.[8]

The concentration of the poorest groups in developing countries in 'ecologically fragile' areas suggests that it is the welfare of the poorest in developing economies that is at the greatest risk from continued environmental degradation. As argued by Kates (1990), throughout the developing world the poor often suffer from three major processes of *environmental entitlement loss*:

1. the poor are *displaced* from their traditional entitlement to common resources by development activities or by the appropriation of their resources by richer claimants;
2. the remaining entitlements are *divided* and reduced by their need to share their resources with their children, or to sell off bits and pieces of their resources to cope with extreme losses (crop failure, illness, death), social obligations (marriages, celebrations) or subsistence; and
3. the resources of the poor are *degraded* through excessive use and by failure to restore or to improve their productivity and regeneration – a process made worse by the concentration of the poor into environments unable to sustain requisite levels of resource use.

As a result of these processes, the economic livelihoods of the poor become even more vulnerable to the risks posed by environmental degradation, and their ability and willingness to manage resources sustainably may become even more constrained.

Moreover, statistics indicate that the poorest groups in the relatively more affluent developing regions of Latin America and Asia are even more concentrated in ecologically fragile areas than the poorest groups in Africa (Leonard *et al.*, 1989). This would suggest that the problem does not easily disappear with economic growth and rising national income.

In short, whether poverty is directly or only indirectly the 'cause' of environmental degradation seems less relevant a concern when compared to the implications of pervasive environmental degradation for the livelihoods of the poor. This is the real 'poverty-environment' link that should be the focus of development efforts. If poverty alleviation is an ultimate aim of economic development, then efficient and sustainable environmental management is a necessary means for achieving this goal. Yet past economic policies and investments in developing countries have led to rapid changes in resource stocks and patterns of use – frequently with adverse economic consequences, particularly for the poor. It is to this issue that the next section now turns.

Public policies and natural resource management

Unsustainable and inefficient resource use in developing countries can often be attributed to individual resource users not facing the social opportunity costs of their actions. That is, the private costs of actions leading to environmental degradation do not reflect the full social costs of degradation, in terms of the foregone environmental values. This section summarizes the underlying causes, focusing particularly on the problem of inadequate government policies.

Much excessive degradation of the environment and natural resources in developing countries is thought to result from individuals in the marketplace and by governments not fully recognizing and integrating environmental values into decision-making processes. If markets fail to adequately reflect environmental values, *market failure* is said to exist. Typical examples include poorly defined or no property rights, the presence of externalities (for example, pollution or 'public goods'), imperfect market competition, and divergence between public and private rates of time preference. *Institutional failure*, such as lack of formal markets, poor information flows and inadequate regulatory bodies and government services, may also exacerbate these problems. In addition, where government decisions or policies do not fully reflect environmental values, there is *policy* or *government failure*. Throughout the developing world, the existence of poorly formulated input and output pricing policies, insecure land titling and registration, tax thresholds and rebates, cheap and restricted credit facilities, overvalued exchange rates, and other policy distortions, has exacerbated problems of natural resource management. By failing to make markets and private decision makers accountable for foregone environmental values, these policies may contribute to market failure. At worst, the direct private costs of resource-using activities are subsidized and/or distorted, thus encouraging unnecessary environmental degradation.

The result of market, policy, and institutional failures is a distortion in economic incentives. There are several reasons for this outcome.

First, the market mechanisms determining the 'prices' for natural resources and products derived from conversion of natural resource systems *do not automatically take into account wider environmental costs*, such as disruptions to ecological functions, assimilative capacity, amenity values, and other environmental impacts or foregone *option* and *existence values* – that is, the value of preserving certain natural environments, species, and resources today as an 'option' for future use or simply because their 'existence' is valued. Nor do market mechanisms account for any *user cost* – the cost of foregoing future direct or indirect use benefits from resource depletion or degradation today.

In addition, even the direct costs of harvesting resources or converting natural resource systems *are often subsidized and/or distorted by public policies*. As a result, individuals do not face even the full *private costs* of their own actions that degrade the environment. Unnecessary and excessive degradation ensues.

If public policies are to be redirected to achieve efficient and sustainable management of natural resources in developing countries, major changes are required. Economic valuation of the environmental impacts arising from market and policy failures is essential for determining the appropriate policy responses. Often, however, insufficient data and information exist to allow precise estimation of the economic costs arising from market and policy failures. In most cases, cost estimates as orders of magnitude and indicators of the direction of change are sufficient for policy analysis.[9]

However, with many natural resource problems in developing countries we are not even at this state of *optimal ignorance* to begin designing appropriate policy responses. In the face of such uncertainty we should be humble in our public policy prescriptions. Even the standard economic tool of 'improved pricing policy' should be invoked with caution. In most developing countries there is little empirical understanding of the linkages from price changes to short- and long-term supply and demand responses to natural resource impacts. The situation is complicated by the presence of underemployment, informal and incomplete markets, labour and capital constraints, and above all, the problem of widespread poverty. Thus we are often ignorant of the impact of public policies on the economic incentives faced by individual producers and households for managing natural resources, particularly in the case of the poorest groups who are on the 'margin' of the formal economic and social systems.

This problem occurs frequently in the economic analysis of *dryland degradation*. The term 'drylands' is usually applied to all arid and semi-arid zones, plus areas in the tropical sub-humid zone subject to the same degradation processes that occur on arid lands. Accounting for about one-third of global land and supporting a population of 850 million, the world's drylands are rapidly being degraded through population growth, over-grazing, cropping on marginal lands, inappropriate irrigation and devegetation. Yet these areas are being asked to support increasing numbers of the world's poorest people. The process of dryland degradation is often referred to as 'desertification', where the productive potential of the land is reduced to such an extent that it can neither be readily reversed by removing the cause nor easily reclaimed without substantial investment.

However, there are few economic studies of the costs of dryland degradation.[10] Even further behind – and more controversial – is the analysis of the effects of economic and resource management policies on dryland degradation in developing countries. This is often attributed to the superficial identification of the causes of desertification and to the frequently poor identification of the reasons behind the failures of dryland projects (Nelson, 1988). Although the majority of 'causes' are attributable to population growth and natural events, dryland degradation is also symptomatic of an agricultural development bias that distorts agricultural pricing, investment flows, research and development (R&D) and infrastructure towards more 'favoured' agricultural land and systems (Barbier, 1989b).

Where drylands 'development' is encouraged, it is usually through the introduction of large-scale commercial agricultural schemes that can conflict with more traditional farming and pastoral systems. Frequently, appraisal of the environmental impacts of these large-scale schemes has shown that the investments should be modified, and in some cases, should not proceed at all. For example, in the arid zone of northern Nigeria, upstream irrigation development investments on the Hadejia and Jama'are rivers and their tributaries threaten traditional floodplain agriculture and pastoralism downstream. The assumption behind these investments is that the benefits of the upstream irrigation developments far exceed the benefits of the floodplain system, which are routinely ignored in project analysis of these developments. However, a recent analysis of the net benefits of the Hadejia-Jama'are floodplain shows that benefits are considerable, particularly in comparison with one major irrigation project, the Kano River Project (Barbier, Adams and Kimmage, 1991). The results suggest that the opportunity cost of diverting water to upstream developments in order to preserve floodplain benefits could be high, and these costs must be considered carefully in any analysis of these developments.

The complexity of social, economic, and environmental relationships confronting dryland management is often formidable. A common misconception is that the extension of private property rights, commercial agriculture, and markets will 'automatically' solve dryland management problems in the long run. At the same time, not all dryland farmers and pastoralists, even in the most distant and resource-poor regions, are totally isolated from agricultural markets. Virtually all subsistence households require some regular market income for cash purchases of some agricultural inputs and basic necessities; many farmers and pastoralists provide important cash and export crops. As a result, alterations in market conditions – whether from changes in policies, climatic conditions, R&D innovations, or other factors – do have a significant impact on the livelihoods of rural groups in dryland areas. Understanding their responses to these changing market conditions is a crucial aspect of the dryland management problem.

In many instances, market responses are governed by the complex economic–environmental relationships found in dryland management systems, which can lead to unintended results. For example, the argument that higher slaughter prices in a dryland pastoral economy will, *ceteris paribus*, encourage higher rates of offtake, and so lower levels of grazing, has been questioned (Perrings, 1990). Higher slaughter prices can reduce both the real product cost of herd maintenance and the real product cost of carrying capacity, and these have opposite effects on grazing pressure. In situations where the cost of carrying capacity (a grazing fee) is zero, higher slaughter prices will not reduce rangeland degradation. Similarly, a study of Arabic gum production in the Sudan indicates that fluctuations in the real price of gum and its price relative to those of other agricultural crops have had important impacts on farmers, cropping patterns, diversification strategies and decisions to replant gum – with important consequences for the Sudan's gum belt (IIED/IES, 1990; Barbier, 1992a). Even though it is economically profitable *and* environmentally beneficial to grow gum, it is only when these economic incentives are properly dealt with by the government will rehabilitation of the important gum belt of the Sudan take place.

Soil erosion and land degradation are not confined just to drylands and other marginal lands; the problem is pervasive throughout all agricultural systems, degraded forest lands, public and privately owned lands, and large and small holdings in the Third World. Designing appropriate policy responses to control soil erosion and land degradation for all types of cropland in developing countries is again hampered by the data limitations and the lack of microeconomic analyses of farmers' responses to erosion and incentives to adopt conservation measures.

The limited evidence that does exist suggests that relationships – such as the effects of agricultural input and output pricing on farm-level erosion – are complex and difficult to substantiate.[11] Nevertheless, there are some indications that subsidies for non-labour inputs, notably inorganic fertilizers, can artificially reduce the costs of soil erosion to farmers and, on more resource-poor lands, substitute for manure, mulches, and nitrogen-fixing crops that might be more appropriate. On the other hand, the *inaccessibility* of inorganic fertilizers – for example, shortages caused by rationing cheap fertilizer imports – can actually lead to sub-optimal application and encourage farming practices that actually increase land degradation. Similarly, the relationship between erodibility and profitability of different cropping systems needs to be carefully analysed, particularly in relation to changing *relative prices* of different crops and changes in *real producer prices and incomes* over time. More complex incentive effects arise from the relationships between erosion and the availability of labour, off-farm employment, population pressure, tenure and access to frontier land, the development of post-harvesting capacity and other complementary infrastructure, and the availability of credit at affordable interest rates.[12]

A tentative conclusion is that there are often strong economic incentives determining farmers' decisions to invest in soil conservation. Farmers will generally not modify their land management practices and farming systems unless it is in their direct economic interest to do so. Such modifications are expensive and may involve risk. The risk may be further exacerbated by the price fluctuations for the various crops found in farming systems (Barbier, 1991c). Unless soil erosion is perceived to be a threat to farm profitability, or alternatively, unless changes in land management lead to at least some immediate economic gains, farmers will be less willing to bear these substantial costs. In addition, the more productive or profitable the land use, the more farmers will be able to maintain and invest in better land management and erosion control practices. Higher productivity and returns will also mean that farmers can afford to maintain terraces and other conservation structures and to continue with labour-intensive erosion control measures. On the other hand, poorer farmers dependent on low-return cropping systems, such as maize or cassava, may be aware that soil erosion is reducing productivity but may not be able to afford necessary conservation measures. At the other extreme, farmers with very profitable crops that are extremely erosive, such as temperate vegetables on steep upper volcanic slopes with deep topsoils, may not consider soil conservation measures if their returns do not appear to be affected by soil erosion losses. Unfortunately, we still do not sufficiently understand the economic and social factors determining these incentives for soil conservation in most developing regions.[13]

An equally important challenge for future economic analysis is to examine the causes of large-scale land use changes and resource degradation. Thus clearing forest land for agriculture is thought to be the major cause of tropical deforestation. A number of economic studies have been launched, particularly in Latin America, to analyse the main factors inducing people to settle in and to clear 'frontier' forest lands for agriculture.

For example, Binswanger (1989) and Mahar (1989) make the case for the role of subsidies and tax breaks, particularly for cattle ranching, in encouraging land clearing in the Brazilian Amazon. However, more recent analyses by Schneider *et al.* (1990) and Reis and Margulis (1990) emphasize the role of agricultural rents, population pressures and road building in encouraging small-scale frontier settlement. In the northern Brazilian Amazon, the total road network (paved and unpaved) increased from 6357 to 28431 km during 1975–88. A simple correlation between road density and the rate of deforestation shows that as road density increases, the rate of deforestation increases in larger proportions (Reis and Margulis, 1990). Schneider *et al.* (1990) argue that these factors encouraging frontier agriculture ('nutrient mining') far outweigh the more publicized impacts of fiscal incentives for cattle ranching. A statistical analysis by Southgate, Sierra and Brown (1989) of the causes of tropical deforestation in Ecuador indicates that colonists clear forest land not only in response to demographic pressure but also to 'capture' agricultural rents and to safeguard their tenuous legal hold on the land.

Although there are an increasing number of case studies examining the factors behind tropical deforestation and agricultural frontier expansion, there have been few attempts to explore these linkages through statistical analysis. One such analysis by Palo, Mery, and Salmi (1987) for 72 tropical forest countries identified a strong link between tropical deforestation and population density, population growth, and increased food production. A study by Capistrano (1990) and Capistrano and Kiker (1990) examined the influence of international and domestic macroeconomic factors on tropical deforestation.[14] The econometric analysis indicates the role of high agricultural export prices in inducing agricultural expansion and forest clearing, as well as the influence of domestic structural adjustment policies, such as exchange rate devaluation and increased debt-servicing ratios. Comparative analysis of 24 Latin American countries also highlights the strong but indirect relationship between population pressure and frontier expansion – increasing numbers of urban consumers raise the demand for domestic production and hence for agricultural land – and the countervailing role of increased agricultural productivity and yield growth in slowing agricultural expansion (Southgate, 1991). A statistical analysis by Burgess (1992) supports the hypothesis that population pressure and industrial roundwood production are positively associated with forest clearance in the tropics during the period 1980–85. Economic development, as represented by rising per capita GNP, and improvements in agricultural yields reduce forest clearing. However, the analysis also indicates that countries with relatively small forests to total area are depleting these forests at a high rate.

A recent study in Thailand highlights the complex linkages between agricultural crop prices, the relative returns from different crops, and the demand for land (Phantumvanit and Panayotou 1990). In Thailand, approximately 40 per cent of the increase in cultivated land in recent years can be attributed to converted forest land. The most important factors affecting the demand for cropland, and thus forest conversion, appear to be population growth followed by non-agricultural returns, although agricultural pricing also has a significant influence. Higher aggregate real prices may have a slightly positive influence on the demand for cropland, and thus increased forest clearing; however, this direct effect may be counteracted by the indirect impact of higher agricultural prices on raising the productivity of existing land and increasing the cultivation of previously idle land, thus reducing the demand for new land from forest clearing. Changes in relative prices also influence the demand for new cropland by affecting the relative profitability of land-saving as opposed to land-extensive cropping systems.[15]

The analysis of land clearing in Thailand also illustrates some of the potential linkages with agricultural input prices. For example, the relative returns to land-saving cropping systems can also be affected by the relative costs of inputs (for example, fertilizer, seed, credit, irrigation, and agrochemicals) where these differ between land-saving and land-extensive systems. More importantly, investments in land productivity will also be affected by the costs of these in puts. Thus the Thailand case study suggests that lower input prices generally would reduce the demand for new cropland and forest conversion both directly and indirectly by making previously idle land more attractive to cultivate. Changes in relative input prices could also make a difference on agricultural extensification by affecting the relative returns to land-saving cropping systems.

Clearly, both microeconomic analysis of individuals' behaviour and responses to environmental degradation, and macroeconomic analysis of the broader economic-environmental linkages affecting degradation will be required if coherent and effective public policies for natural resource management in developing countries are to be designed and implemented.

Conclusion

This chapter has sought to provide an overview of the role of natural capital in economic development. This role is the fundamental concern of a new discipline that has recently emerged and is growing rapidly – the economics of environment and development. As this discussion has highlighted, progress to date in this discipline has already produced one firm conclusion – efficient and sustainable management of natural resources requires improved policies and accounting procedures to reflect the actual value of natural capital in the development process. Further progress will require advances in the five areas described in the introduction.

However, in demonstrating the potential contribution of an economics of environment and development, this chapter has subsequently provided evidence that current rates of natural resource depletion are not promoting sustainable development, and the transformation of natural into human and/or physical capital does not appear to be efficient. Progress in this area will have to address two fundamental underlying causes: how current policy distortions and market failures allow resource users to avoid the social opportunity cost of environmental degradation and how environment-poverty linkages influence patterns of resource utilization.

Tackling these issues will be the key challenge facing the economics of environment and development for many years to come. What we perceive today to be the 'improved policies and accounting procedures' necessary for efficient and sustainable management of natural resources for development may not be what is required for tomorrow. This is particularly true given that economics must increasingly rely on improved ecological understanding of the basic environmental functions performed by natural and even human modified systems before we can appreciate the true contribution of these functions to development. An economics of environment and development must rest on sound ecological underpinnings to be meaningful in its policy prescriptions.

Although interest in these topics is finally growing, especially in light of the UN Conference on Environment and Development, what is needed most is 'political will'. Thus, in formulating a strategy for integrating environment and development at the policy, planning, and management levels, the UNCED concluded: 'The responsibility for bringing about changes lies with Governments in partnership with the private sector and local authorities, and in collaboration with national, regional, and international organizations, including in particular UNEP, UNDP, and the World Bank' (UNCED, 1992a). Ultimately, however, the clients of development are not policymakers or managers, but all people comprising present and future generations.

Notes

1. I am grateful to comments supplied by Charles Perrings, Stephen Viederman, and an anonymous referee.
2. For further discussion of these issues in relation to tropical deforestation, see Barbier (1992b).
3. I am grateful to Charles Perrings for drawing my attention to this point.
4. However, the methodology and its applications for incorporating environmental costs and benefits in investment and planning decisions in developing countries does exist, whether at the level of national accounts (for example, see Ahmad, El Serafy and Lutz, 1989; Repetto *et al.*, 1989; TSC/WRI, 1991), investment projects (Dixon *et al.*, 1988), or individual resource systems, such as tropical wetlands (Barbier, Adams and Kimmage, 1991; Barbier, 1993; Ruitenbeek, 1991), tropical forests (Barbier, 1991a, 1992b; Peters, Gentry and Mendelsohn, 1989; Ruitenbeek, 1989), drylands (Bojö, 1991; Dixon, James and Sherman, 1989, 1990), wildlands (Dixon and Sherman, 1990; Swanson and Barbier, 1992), agroforestry (Anderson, 1987; Barbier, 1992a), and watersheds (Easter, Dixon and Hufschmidt, 1986; Gregersen *et al.*, 1987).
5. For further discussion of the role of natural resources in the livelihood security of the poor, see Chambers (1987), Pretty *et al.* (1992), Richards (1985), and Wilson (1988).
6. The exact numbers and composition of poor and ultra-poor will obviously vary by country and region; however, as an approximate indication Lipton (1988) suggests that the ultra-poor can be defined as those at significant risk of income-induced caloric undernutrition and the poor as those with sufficiently low income to be at risk of hunger but not undernutrition, with the former usually falling in the bottom 10–20 per cent income category (for example, the 'poorest quintile').
7. The 'poorest people' are defined by Leonard *et al.* (1989) as the poorest 20 per cent of the population in developing countries. In commenting on the data presented by Leonard, Kates (1990) argues that it is too simplistic to equate all land of low agricultural potential and squatter settlements with 'areas of high ecologically vulnerability'. Thus 'while there is good reason to expect an increasing geographic segregation of the poor onto the threatened environments, both the purported distribution of the hungry and the actual state of environmental degradation needs to be examined much more carefully'.
8. Further examples of the impact of urban environmental problems and sub-standard living conditions on the welfare of the urban poor can be found in Hardoy and Satterthwaite (1989), Hardoy, Cairncross and Satterthwaite (1990), and Hardoy, Mitlin and Satterthwaite (1992).
9. See, for example, the case studies in Pearce, Barbier and Markandya (1990) and the discussion of tax and regulation policies in developing countries in Anderson (1990).
10. For recent examples of such studies, see Bishop and Allen (1989), Bishop (1990), and Lallement (1990).
11. See Barbier and Burgess (1992a) for a recent review.

12. For relevant case studies see Barbier (1989a, ch. 7); Barbier (1990b); Barbier and Burgess (1992b); Bojö (1991); Mortimore (1989); Phantumvanit and Panayotou (1990); and Southgate, Sierra and Brown (1989).
13. For recent reviews, see Barbier and Bishop (1993), Barbier and Burgess (1992a), and Southgate (1988).
14. Capistrano (1990) and Capistrano and Kiker (1990) use changes in timber production forest area as a proxy for total deforestation. Thus their analytical results are more relevant to the deforestation of tropical timber production forests than to overall tropical deforestation. For an in-depth review of the impact of logging relative to other factors influencing tropical deforestation, see Amelung and Diehl (1992), Barbier *et al.* (1993), and Burgess (1992).
15. The authors also examined the effects of relative price changes on land productivity and the cultivation of previously idle land, but found this relationship more difficult to estimate in such an aggregate analysis.

References

Ahmad, Y., S. El Serafy and E. Lutz (1989), *Environmental Accounting for Sustainable Development*, paper presented at a UNEP–World Bank Symposium, Washington, DC: The World Bank.

Amelung, T. and M. Diehl (1992), *Deforestation of Tropical Rain Forests: Economic Causes and Impact on Development*, Kiel, Germany: Institute of World Economics.

Anderson, D. (1987), *The Economics of Afforestation*, Baltimore: Johns Hopkins University Press.

Anderson, D. (1990), *Environmental Policy and the Public Revenue in Developing Countries*, Environment Working Paper No. 36, Washington, DC: The World Bank.

Barbier, E.B. (1989a), *Economics, Natural-Resource Scarcity and Development: Conventional and Alternative Views*, London: Earthscan.

Barbier, E.B. (1989b), 'Sustainable agriculture on marginal land: a policy framework', *Environment*, **31** (9), 12–17

Barbier, E.B. (1990a), 'Alternative approaches to economic–environmental interactions', *Ecological Economics*, **2**, 7–26.

Barbier, E.B. (1990b), 'The farm-level economics of soil erosion: the uplands of Java', *Land Economics*, **66** (9), 199–211.

Barbier, E.B. (1991a), *The Economic Value of Ecosystems, 2: Tropical Forests*, LEEC Gatekeeper GK 91–01. London: London Environmental Economics Centre.

Barbier, E.B. (1991b), 'Natural resource degradation: policy, economics and management', in *Development Research: The Environmental Challenge*, J.T. Winpenny (ed.), London: Overseas Development Institute.

Barbier, E.B. (1991c), *The Role of Smallholder Producer Prices in Land Degradation: The Case of Malawi*, LEEC Discussion Paper DP 91–05, London: London Environmental Economics Centre.

Barbier, E.B. (1992a), 'Rehabilitating gum arabic systems in Sudan: economic and environmental implications', *Environmental and Resource Economics*, **2**, 19–36.

Barbier, E.B. (1992b), 'Tropical deforestation', in T.M. Swanson and E.B. Barbier (eds), *Economics for the Wilds: Wildlife, Wildlands Diversity and Development*, London: Earthscan.

Barbier, E.B. (1993), 'Valuing tropical wetland benefits: economic methodologies and applications', *Geographic Journal*, Part I (59), 22–32.

Barbier, E.B. and J.C. Burgess (1992a), *Agricultural Pricing and Environmental Degradation*, Policy Research Papers, World Development Report, Washington, DC: The World Bank.

Barbier, E.B. and J.C. Burgess (1992b), *Malawi – Land Degradation in Agriculture*, Divisional Working Paper No. 1992-37, Washington, DC: The World Bank.

Barbier, E.B. and A. Markandya (1990), 'The conditions for achieving environmentally sustainable development', *European Economic Review*, **34**, 659–69.

Barber, E.B., W.M. Adams and K. Kimmage (1991), *Economic Valuation of Wetland Benefits: The Hadejia-Jama'are Floodplain, Nigeria*, LEEC Discussion Paper 91–02, London: London Environmental Economics Centre.

Barbier, E.B., J.C. Burgess, J.T. Bishop, B.A. Aylward and C. Bann (1993), *The Economic Linkages Between the International Trade in Topical Timber Products and the Sustainable*

Management of Tropical Forests, Final Report: ITTO Activity PCM(XI)/4, Yokohama: The International Tropical Timber Organization.

Barbier, E.B. and J.T. Bishop (1995), 'Economic values and incentives affecting soil and water conservation in developing countries', *Journal of Soil and Water Conservation*, **50** (2), 133–37.

Binswanger, H.P (1980), 'Attitudes toward risk: experimental measurement in rural India', *American Journal of Agricultural Economics*, **90**, 395–407.

Binswanger, H.P (1989), *Brazilian Policies that Encourage Deforestation in the Amazon*, Environment Department Working Paper No. 16, Washington, DC: The World Bank.

Bishop, J.T. (1990), *The Costs of Soil Erosion in Malawi*, Malawi Country Operations Division, Washington, DC: The World Bank.

Bishop, J.T. and J. Allen (1989), *The On-Site Costs of Soil Erosion in Mali*, Environment Department Working Paper No. 21, Washington, DC: The World Bank.

Bojö, J. (1991), *The Economics of Land Degradation: Theory and Applications to Lesotho*, The Economic Research Institute, Stockholm: Stockholm School of Economics.

Bojö, J., K.-G. Mäler and L. Unemo (1990), *Environment and Development: An Economic Approach*, Dordrecht: Kluwer.

Burgess, J.C. (1992), *Economic Analysis of the Causes of Tropical Deforestation*, LEEC Discussion Paper DP92–03, London: The London Environmental Economics Centre.

Cairncross, S., J.E. Hardoy and D. Satterthwaite (1990), The urban context', in J.E. Hardoy, S. Cairncross and D. Satterthwaite (eds.), *The Poor Die Young: Housing and Health in Third World Cities*, London: Earthscan.

Capistrano, A.D. (1990), *Macroeconomic Influences on Tropical Forest Depletion: A Cross-Country Analysis*, Ph.D. dissertation, Food and Resource Economics Dept. Miami: University of Florida.

Capistrano, A.D. and C.F. Kiker (1990), *Global Economic Influences on Tropical Closed Broadleaved Forest Depletion, 1967–85*, Mimeo, Food and Resource Economics Dept, Miami: University of Florida.

Chambers, R. (1987), *Sustainable Livelihoods, Environment and Development: Putting Poor Rural People First*, Discussion Paper 240, Institute of Development Studies, Brighton: University of Sussex.

Clark, C. (1976), *Mathematical Bioeconomics: The Optimal Management of Renewable Resources*, New York: Wiley.

Common, M. and C. Perrings (1992), 'Towards an ecological economics of sustainability', *Ecological Economics*, **6**, 7–34.

Conway, G.R. (1985), 'Agroecosystem analysis', *Agricultural Administration*, **20**, 3–55.

Conway, G.R. and E.B. Barbier (1990), *After the Green Revolution: Sustainable Agriculture for Development*, London: Earthscan.

Dasgupta, P.S. (1992), 'Population, resources and poverty', *Ambio*, **21** (1), 95–101.

Dixon, J.A. and P.B. Sherman (1990), *Economics of Protected Areas: Benefits and Costs*, London: Island Press; Earthscan.

Dixon, J.A., R.A Carpenter, L.A. Fallon, P.B. Sherman and S. Manipomoke (1988), *Economic Analysis of the Environmental Impacts of Development Projects*, London: Earthscan.

Dixon, J.A., D. James, and P.B. Sherman (1989), *The Economics of Dryland Management*, London Earthscan.

Easter, K.W., J.A. Dixon and M.M. Hufschmidt (1986), *Watershed Resources Management: An Integrated Framework with Studies from Asia and the Pacific*, Boulder, CO: Westview Press.

FAO (1990), 'Sustainable development and natural resource management', in: *The State of Food and Agriculture*, 1989, Part 3, Rome: FAO.

Foy, G. and H.E. Daly (1989), *Allocation Distribution and Scale as Determinants of Environmental Degradation: Case Studies of Haiti, El Salvador and Costa Rica*, Environment Department Working Paper No. 19, Washington, DC: The World Bank.

Gregersen, H.M., K.N. Brooks, J.A. Dixon and L.S. Hamilton (1987), *Guidelines for Economic Appraisal of Watershed Management Projects*, Rome, FAO.

Hardoy, J.E. and D. Satterthwaite (1989), *Squatter Citizen: Life in the Urban Third World*, London Earthscan.

Hardoy, J.E., S. Cairncross and D. Satterthwaite (eds) (1990), *The Poor Die Young: Housing and Health in Third World Cities*, London: Earthscan.

Hardoy, J.E., D Mitlin and D Satterthwaite (1992), 'The future city', in J. Holmberg (ed.), *Policies for a Small Planet*, London: Earthscan.

Hartwick, J.M. (1977), 'Intergenerational equity and the investing of rents from exhaustible resources', *American Economic Review*, **66**, 972–4.

Holling, C.S. (1973), 'Resilience and the stability of ecological systems', *Annual Review of Ecological Systems*, **4**, 1–24.

IIED/IES (1990), *Gum Arabic Rehabilitation Project in the Republic of Sudan: Stage I Report*, London: IIED.

Jagannathan, N.V. (1989), *Poverty, Public Policies and the Environment*, Environment Working Paper No. 24, Washington, DC: The World Bank.

Kates, R.W. (1990), *Hunger, Poverty and the Environment*, paper presented at the Distinguished Speaker Series, Center for Advanced Study of International Development, Michigan State University, Lansing, May 6.

Lallement, D. (1990), *Burkina Faso: Economic Issues in Renewable Natural Resource Management*, Agricultural Operations, Sahelian Department, Africa Region, Washington, DC: The World Bank.

Leonard, H.J., M. Yudelman, J.D. Stryker, J.O. Browder, A.J. De Boer, T. Campbell and A. Jolly (1989), *Environment and the Poor: Development Strategies for a Common Agenda*, New Brunswick: Transaction Books.

Lipton, M. (1983), *Labour and Poverty*, World Bank Staff Working Papers No. 616, Washington, DC: The World Bank.

Lipton, M. (1988), *The Poor and the Poorest: Some Interim Findings*, World Bank Discussion Paper No. 25. Washington, DC: The World Bank.

Mahar, D. (1989), *Government Policies and Deforestation in Brazil's Amazon Region*, Washington, DC: The World Bank.

Mortimore, M. (1989), *The Causes, Nature and Rate of Soil Degradation in the Northernmost States of Nigeria and an Assessment of the Role of Fertilizer in Counteracting the Processes of Degradation*, Environment Department Working Paper No. 17, Washington, DC: The World Bank.

Nelson, R. (1988), *Dryland Management: The Desertification Problem*, Environment Department Working Paper No. 8, Washington, DC: The World Bank.

Palo, M., G. Mery and J. Salmi (1987), 'Deforestation in the tropics: pilot scenarios based on quantitative analysis', in: *Deforestation or Development in the Third World*, M. Palo and J. Salmi (eds), Division of Social Economics of Forestry, Helsinki: Finnish Forestry Research.

Pearce, D.W. (1991), 'Population growth', in: D.W. Pearce (ed.), *Blueprint 2: The Greening of the World Economy*, London: Earthscan.

Pearce, D.W. and J.J. Warford (1992), *World Without End: Economics, Environment and Sustainable Development*, Oxford: Oxford University Press for The World Bank.

Pearce, D.W., E.B. Barbier and A. Markandya (1990), *Sustainable Development: Economics and Environment in the Third World*, London: Edward Elgar.

Pender, J.L. and T.S. Walker (1990), *Experimental Measures of Time Preference in Rural India*, Draft paper, Food Research Institute, Stanford: Stanford University and ICRISAT.

Perrings, C. (1990), *Stress, Shock and the Sustainability of Optimal Resource Utilization in a Stochastic Environment*, LEEC Discussion Paper DP90–04, London: London Environmental Economics Centre.

Peters, C., A. Gentry and R. Mendelsohn (1989), 'Valuation of an Amazonian rainforest', *Nature*, **339**, 655–56.

Phantumvanit, D. and T. Panayotou (1990), *Natural Resources for a Sustainable Future: Spreading the Benefits*, prepared for the 1990 TDRI End-Year Conference on Industrializing Thailand and its Impact on the Environment, Chon Buri, Thailand, December 8–9.

Pretty, J., I. Guijt, I. Scoones and J. Thompson (1992), 'Regenerating agriculture: the agroecology of low-external input and community-based development', in: J. Holmberg (ed.), *Policies for a Small Planet*, London: Earthscan.

Reis, E. and S. Margulis (1990), *Options for Slowing Amazon Jungle-Clearing*, paper presented at the Conference on Economic Policy Responses to Global Warming, Rome, September 5–7.

Repetto, R. (1987), 'Population, resources, environment: an uncertain future', *Population Bulletin*, **42** (2), special issue.
Repetto, R. and M. Gillis (eds) (1988), *Public Policies and the Misuse of Forest Resources*, Cambridge: Cambridge University Press.
Repetto, R. and T. Holmes (1983), 'The role of population in resource depletion in developing countries', *Population and Development Review*, **9** (4), 609–32.
Repetto, R., W.B. Magrath, M. Wells, C. Beer and F. Rossini (1989), *Wasting Assets: Natural Resources in the National Income Accounts*, Washington, DC: World Resources Institute.
Richards, P. (1985), *Indigenous Agricultural Revolution*, London: Hutchinson.
Ruitenbeek, H.J. (1989), *Social Cost-Benefit Analysis of the Korup Project, Cameroon*, prepared for the World Wide Fund for Nature and the Republic of Cameroon, London: World Wide Fund.
Ruitenbeek, H.J. (1991), *Mangrove Management: An Economic Analysis of Management Options with a Focus on Bintuni Bay, Irian Jaya*, prepared for EMDI/KLH, Jakarta, Indonesia.
Schneider, R., J. McKenna, C. Dejou, J. Butler and R. Barrows (1990), *Brazil: An Economic Analysis of Environmental Problems in the Amazon*, Washington, DC: The World Bank.
Scoones, I. (1993), 'Economic and Ecological Carrying Capacity: Applications to Pastoral Systems in Zimbabwe', in: E.B. Barbier (ed.), *Economics and Ecology: Contributions to Sustainable Development*, London: Chapman and Hall.
Smith, V.L. (1977), 'Control theory applied to natural and environmental resources: an exposition', *Journal of Environmental Economics and Management*, **4**, 1–24.
Solow, R.M. (1974), 'Intergenerational equity and exhaustible resources', *Review of Economic Studies, Symposium on the Economics of Exhaustible Resources*, 29–46.
Solow, R.M. (1986), 'On the Intertemporal Allocation of Natural Resources', *Scandinavian Journal of Economics*, **88** (1), 141–9.
Southgate, D. (1988), *The Economics of Land Degradation in the Third World*, Environment Department Working Paper No. 2, Washington, DC: The World Bank.
Southgate, D. (1991), *Tropical Deforestation and Agriculture Development in Latin America*, LEEC Discussion Paper 91–01. London: London Environmental Economics Centre.
Southgate, D., R. Sierra and L. Brown (1989), *The Causes of Tropical Deforestation in Ecuador: A Statistical Analysis*, LEEC Discussion Paper DP89–09. London: London Environmental Economics Centre.
Swanson, T.M. and E.B. Barbier (1992), *Economics for the Wilds: Wildlife, Wildlands, Diversity and Development*, London: Earthscan.
TSC/WRI (1991), *Accounts Overdue: Natural Resource Depreciation in Costa Rica*, Washington, DC: World Resources Institute.
UNCED Secretariat (1992a), 'Integrating environment and development in decision-making', Chapter 8 in *Agenda 21*, Part 1, New York: UNCED.
UNCED Secretariat (1992b), *Integration of Environment and Development in Decision Making*, Report to the Preparatory Committee for UNCED, New York: UNCED.
Wilson, K.B. (1988), *Indigenous Conservation in Zimbabwe: Soil Erosion, Land-use Planning, and Rural Life*, paper submitted to the Panel Session Conservation and Rural People, African Studies Association of UK Conference, September 14.

PART TWO

AGRICULTURE AND FORESTS

6. Cash crops, food crops, and sustainability: the case of Indonesia[1]

Summary
Recent evidence suggests that the main obstacle to sustainable agricultural development is the failure of any economic policy, whether promoting food crops or exports, to address adequately problems of natural resource management. Policies to achieve food self-sufficiency may therefore be neither inherently more nor inherently less environmentally sustainable than export-oriented agricultural development. Indonesia serves as a useful illustration, as the country's pursuit of both food self-sufficiency and export crop promotion strategies has encountered many problems of environmental and resource degradation. Overcoming these problems will require the explicit integration of natural resource management concerns within the economic policy framework for Indonesian agriculture.

1. Introduction

A frequently heard criticism of policies to promote export crop production in the Third World is that export-oriented agricultural development is less environmentally sustainable than food production for domestic consumption. There is also concern that cash crops are increasingly grown on the more fertile lands and are pushing food production, especially subsistence cultivation, on to marginal areas.

This chapter questions the assumption that policies to attain food self-sufficiency promote an inherently more sustainable pattern of agricultural development than do policies in support of production for export. Instead, it suggests that the main obstacle to sustainable agricultural development is the failure of any economic policy, whether promoting food crops or exports, to address adequately problems of natural resource management. The result is that the impacts of various agricultural investment programmes and incentive schemes on patterns of natural resource use are not properly monitored. As a consequence, agricultural programmes and incentives are not adjusted in response to resource degradation.

Indonesia serves as a useful illustration, as the country has been pursuing both food self-sufficiency and export crop promotion through primarily production-led policies. Recent evidence would suggest that the slow response to the problems of resource degradation encountered, and in some cases engendered, by these policies has raised questions as to the sustainability of this agricultural development effort. This view is increasingly being accepted by the Government of Indonesia (GOI), which is currently exploring ways to modify its policies.

This chapter is essentially divided into two parts. The first part provides an overview of the links between cash crops, food crops and agricultural sustainability in the Third World. Such an overview indicates that there is no general rule that sustainable agricultural development is better served by food crops than cash crops, even those that are predominantly exported. The second part discusses the experience of Indonesia to illustrate how problems of agricultural sustainability arise from the inadequate attention of agricultural policies to crucial natural resource management views.

2. Agricultural sustainability

As has been explored elsewhere, the concept of sustainable economic development is difficult to make analytically precise (see Barbier, 1987a). A typically broad definition is 'a pattern of social and structural economic transformations (that is, "development") which optimizes the economic and other societal benefits available in the present without jeopardizing the likely potential for similar benefits in the future' (Goodland and Ledec, 1986). In general, therefore, it could be argued that 'the structure of global agriculture is sustainable if both the real economic costs of production and the real environmental costs of production are expected to remain constant or to fall as production expands' (Douglas, Intro., 1984).

More analytically appropriate, however, may be Conway's approach of examining the issue of sustainability at the agroecosystem level, as through the process of agricultural development 'ecosystems are transformed into hybrid agro-ecosystems for the purpose of food or fibre production'. Consequently, agricultural sustainability can be defined as 'the ability of a system to maintain its productivity when subject to stress or shock', where the former is 'a regular, sometimes continuous, relatively small and predictable disturbance, for example the effect of growing soil salinity or indebtedness', and the latter is 'an irregular, infrequent, relatively large and unpredictable disturbance, such as is caused by a rare drought or flood or a new pest' (Conway, 1985, pp. 31–55; see also Conway, 1987). Thus unchecked resource abuse within an agroecosystem, whether the result of inappropriate use of agrochemicals and fertilizers, overcropping of erodible soils, poor drainage, and so on, can affect overall agroecosystem sustainability by increasing the susceptibility to stress, shock, or both. The key is reducing natural resource degradation, and the disturbance associated with it, to a level where the natural processes and functions of the agroecosystem can counteract them and thus preserve overall sustainability.

Hence, the failure to monitor the impacts of various agricultural investment programmes and incentive schemes on patterns of resource use within agroecosystems, and the failure to incorporate the environmental and externality costs as part of the total costs of expanding agricultural production, can lead to the adoption of inappropriate cropping systems and a less sustainable pattern of agricultural development. In other words, the true costs of agricultural policies are being underestimated. As the next two sections indicate, this problem is common to both export crop promotion policies and food self-sufficiency strategies.

3. Cash and food crop production in the third world

A major obstacle to analysing the sustainability of cash versus food crop production is that distinctions between cash crops and food crops are not clear cut. Often the terms 'cash crops' and 'export crops' are used synonymously. Strictly speaking, however, a cash crop may be sold at home or abroad and may be either a food or non-food commodity, whereas an export crop is a cash crop that is ultimately exported from the country producing it. The major non-food cash crops that are exported are cocoa, coffee, fibre crops, rubber, tea and tobacco. In contrast, the term 'food crop' usually refers to domestic production of basic staples (cereals, pulses, roots and tubers). Although these are the principal subsistence crops, they are also often marketed (as defined by von Braun and Kennedy, 1986, p. 1 and Table 1). For example, in Asia a sizeable proportion of rice and wheat, which are basic food staples, is sold for cash. Rice is a major export crop for Burma, China, Pakistan and Thailand. In Indonesia, the term 'estate crop' is preferred to distinguish cash crops primarily for export. Coconuts, however, are considered an estate crop, yet are almost entirely consumed domestically to provide cooking oil and are thus also classified as a 'food crop'.

Certainly the pattern of agricultural development, particularly the choice of crops, has been influenced by government agricultural policies and global trade and price trends. Many developing countries continue to promote industrialization at the expense of agricultural development through protecting domestic industries and overvaluing their exchange rates. The result is that the domestic prices of industrial import substitutes and nontradeable goods rise relative to the prices of agricultural products and exports. This effectively taxes agriculture and reduces its profitability (World Bank, 1986c, pp. 62–3). Within the agricultural sector, the distinguishing feature of government subsidies for the use of irrigation water, agricultural chemicals, and farm machinery is not that these subsidies are encouraging export crops at the expense of food crops, but that they promote a particular form of overall 'industrial' farming that is depleting natural resources and depositing residues and wastes as unwanted byproducts (Repetto, 1986, p. 59). In many developing countries, producers of export crops are being squeezed between government taxes on these crops to encourage domestic food production, raise revenues and promote processing by agroindustries, and the long-term decline in many commodity prices. In addition, protectionist policies in industrial countries are limiting Third World agricultural export earnings (World Bank, 1986c, pp. 64–6).

Nevertheless, it is often at the village level, in response to relative crop prices and import subsidies, where the final decision about the mix of crops to grow is taken. A farming family which produces its own subsistence takes decisions on the basis of how much land is needed to grow the food it requires, together with the mix of crops that it can sell to the market, whether export or local food crops, that are expected to yield the best possible return. In different regions and in different seasons various other resources, such as labour, water, and capital (including transportation and marketing facilities), may also be scarce. If cash cropping leads to greater income fluctuations, requires longer fallow or gestation periods, and substantially reduces soil fertility, farmers will assess these risks in deciding the optimal crop mix. Finally, choice of crops may depend on whether the men or the women of the households control cash or food income. In many cultures, men control cash income and women control food income, which may have a significant bearing on households' adoption and expansion of cash crops.[2]

The amount of land growing both export and food crops in developing market economies has increased in the last ten years due to the bringing into production of 'new' land. such as areas once under forest or previously considered marginal. The land under export crops expanded by 8.1 million hectares; land under basic food crops rose by 27.1 million hectares (Table 6.1). In Africa, the region most critically affected by food shortages, the land under food increased by 3.8 million hectares, whereas the land growing export crops hardly increased at all. In total, around 12 per cent of African crop land is growing export crops, a slightly lower proportion than for the developing world as a whole. As will be discussed below, in Indonesia expansion of both food and export crop production also requires increased use of marginal land.

A recent study has compared changes in the production of cash crops on arable land with changes in production of basic food staples in 78 developing countries (von Braun and Kennedy, 1986). Over the period 1968–82, only six countries showed an increase in the share of land used for cash cropping, while at the same time experiencing a decline in per capita food production. The majority of countries with positive growth in per capita production of basic staples have simultaneously expanded their area devoted to cash crops. In sub-Saharan Africa, constant or declining per capita food production has been associated with constant or declining shares of land allocated to cash crops (see Table 6.2). In general, countries tend to manage sufficient growth in both cash crops and staple food production or failed to achieve either. For example, as agricultural export earnings stagnated or declined in most of sub-Saharan Africa during 1970–82, countries in the region were unable to import sufficient agricultural inputs, spare parts, or raw materials, and consequently also experienced declines in per capita food production (Lele, 1985, pp. 167–9).

Table 6.1 Harvested areas under basic food and export crops (million hectares)

	All developing countries		Africa	
	1974–76 (average)	1984	1974–76 (average)	1984
Food:				
Cereals	301.9	322.2	69.7	70.9
Roots and tubers	20.7	23.1	11.2	13.0
Pulses	46.9	51.3	11.7	12.6
Total	369.4	396.5	92.6	96.4
Export:				
Cotton	20.2	20.7	4.0	3.9
Coffee	8.6	10.1	3.3	3.3
Cocoa	4.4	4.9	3.2	3.3
Tea	1.0	1.3	0.1	0.2
Tobacco	2.3	2.2	0.3	0.3
Sugar	11.4	15.0	0.5	0.6
Palm oil	3.9	4.8	0.7 (est)	0.9 (est)
Rubber	5.6	6.5	0.2 (est)	0.2 (est)
Total	57.4	65.5	12.3	12.7

Source: FAO (1985b) plus additional FAO figures.

Despite the aggregate evidence suggesting that expansion of cash cropping for export is not at the expense of staple food production in most developing countries, in some cases where planned expansion has taken place, encouraged by government policy and perhaps backed by foreign aid, it has occurred on fertile land that once grew food. When, for example, cocoa was introduced to the southern Volta region of Ghana, it was planted on the best land and food production moved to less fertile land (FAO, 1985a, p. 36). In Kenya, the government has been promoting sugar plantations for its own processing industries and fuel production. But it is the farmers in Kenya's traditional bread basket, the Western province, who have responded to government incentives and switched from growing sugar (Dinham and Hines, 1983, pp. 86–7). In the Cauca Valley of Colombia, large export crop estates employ permanent and contract labourers who also work their own subsistence farms on marginal lands. It is on these lands that the worst problems of environmental degradation, such as soil erosion and flooding, occur (Blaikie, 1985, pp. 123–4). In Southeast Mexico, there is concern that the planned introduction of techniques unsuitable to tropical lowlands to grow export crops may be displacing traditional maize cropping, maize–bean–squash mixed cropping, and homegarden systems that could instead be developed further as a more appropriate agricultural base (Gliessman, 1984, pp. 191–210).

Table 6.2 Changes in production of cash crops compared with changes in production of basic food staples, by region, 1968–82

Growth in share of cash crop area in total land use	Growth in per capita food production per year[a] Less than –1%	± 1%	More than +1%	Total
	(number of countries)			
Asia and Pacific				
Less than –1%	1	2	1	4
± 1%	3	3	5	11
More than + 1%	1	4	3	8
Total	5	9	9	23
Africa				
Less than –1%	5[b]	6[c]	1[d]	12
± 1%	7[e]	6[f]	1[g]	14
More than +1%	4[h]	3[i]	2[j]	9
Total	16	15	4	35
Latin America and Caribbean				
Less than –1%	1	0	1	2
± 1%	3	4	6	13
More than + 1%	1	2	2	5
Total	5	6	9	20
All countries				
Less than –1%	8	8	2	18
± 1%	13	12	13	38
More than 1%	6	9	7	22
Total	26	30	22	78

Notes:

[a] The rates of change are annual changes in estimated trend lines. Grains, pulses, root and tubers (in grain equivalents) are included.

[b] Chad, Mali, Mozambique, Togo and Uganda.

[c] Benin, Central African Republic, Congo, Nigeria, Sierra Leone and Burkina Faso.

[d] Niger.

[e] Angola, Ghana, Guinea, Kenya, Malawi, Morocco and Somalia.

[f] Burundi, Ethiopia, the Ivory Coast, Liberia, Senegal and Zaire.

[g] Tanzania.

[h] Egypt, Madagascar, Mauritania and Zambia.

[i] Cameroon, Rwanda and Zimbabwe.

[j] Sudan and Tunisia.

Source: von Braun and Kennedy (1986).

Thus agricultural output and pricing policies that do not take into account the possible environmental impacts and displacement effects of expanded production may lead to a less than optimal allocation of natural resources, including arable land. This is a common problem not only with policies to promote export crop production but equally with policies to achieve food self-sufficiency, as the next section illustrates with the production-led food policies of Indonesia.

Table 6.3 Comparison of harvested areas for some crops and their share in the total pesticide, herbicide and insecticide market

Crop	Harvested area (% 1979)	All pesticides (%)	Herbicides (%)	Insecticides (%)
Cotton	2.0	14.0	3.6	10.0[a]
Rice	11.0	10.3	3.7	4.4
Maize	9.0	15.5	11.3[b]	3.0
Soybean	4.0	9.0[c]	8.3[c]	1.1
Sorghum	4.0	1.4	1.0	0.4
Groundnuts	1.4	1.4	0.7	0.4
Wheat	18.0	6.0	4.2	0.6
Subtotal	50%	57%	33%	20%
World total (100%)	1326 320000 ha	US$9.7bn		

Notes:
[a] 70% of the cotton insecticide usage is in the developing world.
[b] 60% of the maize herbicide market is in the United States.
[c] 90% of the current market is in the United States, mainly herbicides.

Source: Balk and Koeman (1984).

The input requirements of various crops may also have important ecological impacts, particularly where appropriate use of these inputs is encouraged by government subsidies. Currently, about 25 per cent of world pesticide usage is in developing countries, mainly on cash crops (Balk and Koeman, 1984, pp. 18–19). The exception is rice, which as noted above, is an important staple and cash food crop in Asia. For example, in Indonesia 80 per cent of all subsidized sales of insecticides are used on rice crops. Herbicides are also increasingly used in rice production, especially in the outer islands where labour for weeding is scarce (Repetto, 1985, p. 20). About 70 per cent of the cotton insecticide usage is in the developing world, which reflects the fact that 70 per cent of cotton production is in the Third World. Although pesticides (almost entirely herbicides) are applied heavily to maize in the United States, virtually none are used on maize in developing countries (see Table 6.3). In the case of cotton, although some developing countries can achieve yields of over 1000 kilograms per hectare, this requires intensive cropping on large areas with extensive irrigation and chemical pest control (Goodland, Watson and Ledec, 1984, p. 65).

Pesticide and fertilizer imports for cash crops are often heavily subsidized by governments in developing countries. Where these crops are grown on large estates, the distribution of subsidies favours the large-scale farmers. Yet the side effects of pesticide use – poisoned farm workers, poisoned water supplies – and high levels of pesticide residue in food supplies adversely affect low-income households and the whole population. For example, in Honduras insecticide usage average about 3 kilograms per hectare, equal to the US rate. Insecticides are mainly used on large plantations producing export crops such as coffee, cotton, sugar, and bananas. The high pesticide subsidies mostly benefit these large growers, as distributors capture the subsidies intended for smaller growers (Repetto, 1985, p. 1).

Basic food staples may lag behind cash crops in applications of pesticides and fertilizers in developing countries, precisely because many subsistence farmers do not have the cash incomes to purchase these inputs. Even so, the input requirements of certain food crops, especially rice, are already causing environmental hazards. For example, the increasing severity of pest populations plagueing rice cultivation in Southeast Asia is producing pressure for more intensive, and subsidized, applications of pesticides. Spraying or dusting of rice is often needed at 10–14 day intervals, and since the new early maturing high yielding varieties can now be grown continuously on irrigated land, application rates of 10 to 20 times a year may become common. Similarly, because of the high rainfall in the tropics and the rapid growth of new leaves, cabbage requires pesticide application every three or four days (Conway, 1982, pp. 81–3. In Indonesia Malaysia and Thailand, fish stocks in irrigated rice paddies irrigation channels and ponds have been greatly reduced by pesticide poisoning (Repetto, 1986, p. 33).

Another major concern is the impact of various crops on erodible soils. Although some cash crops such as cotton, tobacco and groundnuts leave the land susceptible to soil erosion, oil palms, coffee and cocoa, with grasslands as ground cover, display rates of soil erosion two to three times less than typical erosion rates for staple root crops (for example, cassava and yams) or row crops (for example, maize, sorghum and millet, Repetto, 1986, p. 14). Thus government policies that encourage the production of food crops in areas that are ecologically less suitable may worsen erosion problems. For example, in Haiti pricing policies that have encouraged the growing of maize and sorghum in hilly areas at the expense of coffee and other tree crops have increased soil runoff and erosion

(World Bank, 1986c, p. 79). Similarly, throughout the Third World the planned extension of maize, sorghum and millet into dryland areas has tended to exacerbate problems of soil erosion and exhaustion (Goodland, Watson and Ledec, 1984, p. 16).

In many instances proper management techniques and agricultural practices can reduce environmental and soil erosion problems. For example, although cocoa exhausts the soil less than annual cropping, continual cultivation can result in gradual loss of organic matter and nutrients. When well managed, both coffee and tea are also capable of protecting the soil. As these trees are cultivated on sloping lands in high-rainfall areas, however, lack of soil conservation measures can lead to substantial soil erosion and runoff. The use of fuelwood to fire-cure tobacco in the Third World has led to the equivalent of about 1.2 million hectares of deforestation each year (Goodland, Watson and Ledec, 1984, pp. 35, 41, 56–7).

Reducing the undesirable environmental impacts of both food and cash crops may also require adopting appropriate intercropping techniques and agroforestry systems. For example, an appropriate ground cover of legumes, vines or grasses can reduce soil erosion and conserve organic matter in oil palm groves, as can intercropping with bananas, coffee, cocoa and other tree crops (Goodland, Watson and Ledec, 1984, p. 72). From 1969–71 to 1979–81, Rwanda increased yields of both root crops (13 per cent) and coffee (49 per cent) by intensifying farming through traditional multi-cropping and soil conservation techniques, such as heavy use of mulches on coffee groves, terracing on ridges, digging crop residues into cultivated fields, and mixing banana, coffee, and cassava with food crops to protect the soil against erosion (Harrison, 1987). In general, the risks of environmental damage appear to be much greater in mono-cropping either export crops (for example, cotton, sugar and tobacco) or food crops (for example, rice, maize, soybeans and cassava) than in multi-cropping. For example, in Rajasthan, India the establishment of a multi-purpose semi-pastoral system involving tree crops, forage crops and livestock produces higher expected net returns per hectare than the returns from cultivating annual crops alone. This system is also increasing soil fertility and quality of soil structure, controlling soil erosion, and improving wildlife habitats (Gupta, 1983, pp. 155–94).

The design of appropriate cropping and inter-cropping techniques, agroforestry systems and resource conservation measures requires a shift in agricultural policy emphasis from a crop-by-crop, production-led approach to a more general farming systems approach, where the choice of crops and production methods is more consistent with ecological conditions as well as the economic needs of farming households. As the next section indicates, such a change in approach has significant ramifications for both the objectives of agricultural policies and the institutional mechanisms and methods of implementation.

To summarize, the issue of whether agricultural sustainability in Third World countries is better served through a concentration on food as opposed to export crops is a complicated one. More often than not, however, it is not the choice of crop *per se* that causes problems of resource degradation and unsustainable cultivation practices, but the failure of agricultural policies to consider any of the implications for natural resource use. In addition, particularly for marginal lands. the choice of crop and fanning system must be suitable for the given agro-ecological conditions and economic needs of farming households; too often, production-led policies for both food and export crops are designed without sufficient knowledge of these conditions and their economic implications. The next section illustrates these points through discussing the case of Indonesia.

4. Agricultural policy in Indonesia

The overwhelming agricultural policy objective in Indonesia has been to increase production. More recently, the focus has been broadened slightly to the goal of increasing rural incomes through greater agricultural production and manipulation of prices. The issue of whether current patterns of resource use in some rural areas can sustain increased production, or whether current investment programmes and incentive schemes to boost production are contributing to problems of soil erosion, water scarcity, devegetation and deforestation, has not historically been a major policy concern.

Since 1967, the primary focus of agricultural policy has been self-sufficiency in rice, and in 1984 production for the first time exceeded domestic consumption. The accumulation of perishable stocks has recently prompted the Government of Indonesia (GOI) to reduce incentives for increased production. Coupled with the attacks of the brown planthopper pest (*wereng*), these measures significantly slowed down growth in rice output over 1985–86 (see Table 6.4). Since the late 1970s, however, a general economic objective has been to increase earnings from non-oil exports, of which agricultural commodities are the most significant (see Table 6.5). Thus despite unfavourable trends in world prices (except more recently for coffee), Indonesia has also expanded its main agricultural export crops of rubber, palm oil, coffee, tea, pepper and tobacco.

With the current emphasis on agricultural diversification, agricultural policy has been moving from a predominantly rice strategy to increasing production of major secondary food crops (for example, corn, cassava, soybeans, copra and sugar) and cash (estate) crops. The great hope is that the success in achieving rice self-sufficiency can be replicated with these other crops. Although in principle the extension of agricultural development efforts to formerly neglected rural areas – notably the rainfed uplands of Java – must be welcomed, there are significantly economic and environmental problems in applying a similar rice strategy approach to other crops.

Table 6.4 Indonesia: production of main agricultural crops (in million tons)[a]

	1982	1983	1984	1985	1986
1. Rice	22.8	24.0	25.9	26.5	26.7
b	(9.0)	(9.2)	(9.8)	(9.9)	(9.9)
2. Other main food crops	19.4	20.4	23.86	23.87	21.16[c]
Corn	3.2	5.1	5.3	4.3	5.4
b	(2.06)	(3.0)	(3.08)	(2.52)	
Cassava	13.0	12.1	14.2	14.1	12.7
b	(1.32)	(1.22)	(1.35)	(1.33)	
Soybeans	0.5	0.5	0.8	0.9	1.2
b	(0.61)	(0.64)	(0.86)	(0.88)	
Copra	1.61	1.61	1.75	1.8	1.86
Sugar	1.63	1.63	1.81	1.87	–
b	(0.25)	(0.35)	(0.36)	(0.38)	
3. Main export tree crops	2.16	2.41	2.52	2.73	2.94
Rubber	0.90	1.01	1.03	1.06	1.03
b	(2.48)	(2.58)	(2.61)	(2.66)	
d	(81.9)	(82.1)	(82.1)	(81.4)	
Palm oil	0.88	0.98	1.04	1.21	1.42
b	(0.33)	(0.41)	(0.44)	(0.47)	
d	(2.0)	(2.0)	(8.0)	(8.0)	
Coffee	0.28	0.31	0.32	0.34	0.35
b	(0.80)	(0.81)	(0.83)	(0.88)	
d	(94.5)	(94.2)	(94.3)	(94.5)	
Tea	0.09	0.11	0.13	0.13	0.14
b	(0.11)	(0.11)	(0.12)	(0.12)	
e	(17.8)	(20.8)	(21.3)	(22.0)	

Notes:

a Numbers may not add due to rounding.

b Harvested area, million ha.

c Excludes sugar.

d Smallholders' share of total harvested area.

e Smallholders' share of total output.

Source: International Monetary Fund and World Bank.

Table 6.5 Indonesia: non-oil liquefied natural gas (LNG) exports (in US$ millions)

	Fiscal year ending in March					
	1981	1982	1983	1984	1985	1986 estimated
Non-oil/LNG exports	4172	3929	5367	5907	6175	6610
Agriculture and forestry	2929	2723	3662	3663	3759	3951
Timber	952	899	1161	1167	1206	1376
Logs	504	310	267	135	2	1
Plywood	199	324	579	697	840	985
Sawn timber	244	256	302	320	346	370
Other	4	10	13	16	17	20
Rubber	770	615	984	856	709	610
Palm oil	79	103	92	95	170	115
Coffee	343	363	506	568	656	796
Tea	94	116	156	211	133	131
Tobacco	49	37	50	44	55	50
Pepper	49	41	58	66	82	105
Animal products	213	251	276	219	271	329
Shrimp	165	204	206	183	226	300
Tapioca	20	9	33	31	42	45
Other foodstuffs	71	50	101	98	121	110
Copra cakes	33	38	33	31	42	45
Hides	32	25	27	40	37	27
Rattan	85	82	87	96	80	70
Other	140	93	98	155	163	167
Minerals	757	676	800	775	800	753
Manufactured goods	334	530	905	1470	1617	1906
Unclassified	151	–	–	–	–	–

Source: International Monetary Fund.

For one, the financial costs of the rice strategy have been high. Rice self-sufficiency was attained through heavy support by government investment and subsidy programmes for irrigation, fertilizers, pesticides, higher yielding varieties (HYVs), credit and management. Over the period 1970–84. the area of HYVs has expanded from 0.8 to 6.8 million hectares, and on Java the average area planted with HYVs has reached 94 per cent; the irrigated area increased from 3.7 to 4.9 million hectares; and distribution of subsidized fertilizers from 0.2 to 4.1 million tons; and the distribution of subsidized pesticides from 1080 to 14210 tons. In 1986–87, the total cost of these input subsidies reached Rp 1.2 trillion (US$725 billion, World Bank, 1987a, pp. 97–9). These subsidies would have to be roughly doubled if the same support programmes were extended to other crops. As the total agricultural and irrigation development budget was only Rp 1.1 trillion (US$665 billion) in 1986–87, and is expected to fall by 15 per cent, in real terms in 1987–88 (Rucker, 1985, p. 49), such a strategy to achieve agricultural diversification is not financially realistic.

In addition, an important contribution to the rice strategy was the coordinated effort among different departments in providing the basic infrastructure necessary to increase production, that is, irrigation, roads, marketing mechanisms and processing facilities. A similar cooperative effort would be needed to meet the particular infrastructure needs of each of the secondary and estate crops. The recent budget restrictions coupled with the logistical problems of developing appropriate infrastructure for more geographically dispersed cropping systems are a major constraint on interdepartmental cooperation.

Finally, if diversification into secondary food crops and estate crops is meant to complement rather than displace rice production, then increased output of the former will mean intensifying production and extending the area cultivated of marginal lands. Rice production, which accounts for 69 per cent of the total area harvested under food crops, already occupies the most fertile lowland areas on Java, Bali, Southern Sulawesi and Southern Sumatra. In fact, as there has been little scope for increasing harvesting areas on Java, in recent years a quarter of the increased rice production has come from extending rice cultivation to marginal lands, in particular the tidal swamps of Sumatra and Kalimantan. In general, increased production of secondary and estate crops will also mean further development of marginal lands, which in addition to the Sumatran and Kalimantan swamplands (about 35 million hectares) include *alang-alang* grasslands (about 15 million hectares) and the 'critical' uplands, mostly on the inner islands of Java and Bali (about 10–40 million hectares), which are defined as lands suffering from severe degradation because of erosion (see Conway and McCauley, 1983; Conway, Manwan and McCauley, 1983, p. 392). Expansion of large-scale estate crop plantations will additionally require conversion of outer island forestlands, which also have poor quality soils. In addition. recent projections of Indonesia's rice needs suggest that, in order for self-sufficiency to be maintained over the long run, total wetland rice area must increase from 8.4 million hectares in 1986 to 10.3 million hectares by the year 2000. Wetland rice production, which accounts for 94 per cent of total rice supply, will therefore also require irrigated land 'extensification' on marginal lands outside of Java and Bali (Tabor, Altemeier, *et al.*, 1986, p. 12).

Much of the strategy to develop margin lands, both in terms of relieving population pressures on the inner island uplands and opening up outer island agricultural land, has in the past relied on Indonesia's transmigration programme.

In the third five year plan, Repelita III (1979–84), 365977 families were officially resettled and supported by the transmigration programme, although this figure also includes local people on the outer islands who were moved into transmigration projects and families that were resettled within the same province. An additional 169497 families were 'spontaneous' transmigrants, who moved with limited, or in most cases, no governmental assistance. This contrasts with the results of Repelita II (1974–79), which saw 55083 official and 7281 spontaneous transmigrant families resettled (Hardjono, 1986, p. 29). Since 1950, approximately 560000 official and at least 170000 spontaneous transmigration families have been moved. Nevertheless, the numbers of transmigrants moved from Java represent only 1.5 per cent of Java's current population, and of those officially resettled, 26 per cent were living in urban areas in 1980 and 50 per cent were working outside the agricultural sector, mainly in services (Repetto, 1983, p. 24).

The direct costs of resettlement in the official programme are high – approximately US$9000 per family. In addition. there are mounting economic and environmental problems in maintaining settlements. For example, because of poor soil quality and initial planning of settlement sites, much of the transmigrant agriculture will remain at subsistence level and may not be economically sustainable over the long run without additional government expenditures to improve infrastructure, introduce appropriate cash crops. provide access to markets, generate off-farm employment and improve land clearing and preparation practices. For example, a project on East Kalimantan financed by the German aid agency GTZ is spending an additional US$240/ha (excluding extension costs) just on developing more appropriate cropping systems. Given the high costs of resettlement, the reductions in the transmigration budget, the lack of support for the large spontaneous transmigration population, and above all, the failure to develop appropriate farming systems on marginal lands, the World Bank has recently recommended that the government abandon its target of officially settling 750000 families over 1984–89 and concentrate instead on improving site infrastructure, support for spontaneous transmigrants and farming systems and crop selection (World Bank, 1986b).

Despite these high costs of pursuing a production-led strategy of agricultural diversification, expansion of secondary foodcrops at affordable prices and estate crops is proceeding, often with little regard to natural resource management issues. The standard approach is to adopt area targets for selective crops, supplemented by price and input support incentives. For example, although corn and cassava production tend to suffer from substitution among food crops, in 1986 the government introduced price incentives for corn, which increased both the output and harvested area (see Table 6.4). Soybean production and harvested area is also expanding rapidly. due to a domestic price structure that is 60 per cent above world prices.

Among the estate crops, expansion of palm oil – half the output of which is exported – has been particularly encouraged, despite unfavourable world prices. Palm oil production occurs almost exclusively on large-scale private and public estates, which has facilitated the expansion programme. Over the 1985–95 period, the government is planning to expand palm oil plantations an additional 695 000 hectares on the outer islands (World Bank, 1986a). In contrast, smallholders account for almost all of the coconut production, and over 80 per cent of the rubber area is in smallholdings. This has hampered government efforts to raise productivity through more intensive use of fertilizers and HYVs (coconuts) and better management, tree selection and tapping techniques (rubber). Increases in the production of tea and coffee occurred mainly through yield and quality improvements.

As a means to increasing estate crops on the outer islands, and to facilitate marketing, processing and provision of inputs; the government is encouraging a system of nucleus estates. The idea is to group together smallholders on one plantation site, with each smallholder planting approximately 2 hectares with an estate crop and a remaining hectare with food crops or homegardens. The programme is being implemented, however, without adequate research into the suitability of soils, much of which is converted forestlands, and into problems of pest and disease attacks. Overfertilization is often a problem, as attempts are made to overcome poor soil quality and boost short-term yields. In addition, the system is intended to run under a cooperative management structure after five years. yet there is no history in Indonesia of such large-scale agricultural ventures being run cooperatively.

Input subsidies are also proceeding at a high rate. For example, in 1986–87 fertilizer subsidies to farmers reached Rp 365 billion (US$220.7 million), roughly 42 per cent of the agriculture and irrigation development budget, and an effective subsidy of about 38 per cent of the farmgate price (68 per cent of world prices). If support for fertilizer production and procurement is included, the fiscal cost may be as high as Rp 600 billion (US$362.8 million). As a result, consumption of fertilizer increased by 77 per cent (12.3 per cent per year) over 1980–85. The current rate of consumption, 75 kilograms per hectare of arable land, is much higher than in other Asian countries (for example, 32 kg in the Philippines and 24 kg in Thailand, World Bank, 1987a, pp. 101–2).The result is that the rice–fertilizer price ratio has now reached 1.5–2. Given that fertilizer comprises less than 10 per cent, of the production cost of rice, and that the largest production response is obtained at relatively low levels of application, such a high price ratio will tend to encourage inappropriate application and wastage, with little stimulation to rice output. For example, in some areas, applications of urea can reach 200–250 kg/ha. Pesticide subsidies in 1986–87 amounted to Rp 42 billion (US$25.4 million), yielding a farmgate price subsidy of more than 40 per cent.

This compares more favourably to the 1983–84 subsidy rate of around 80 per cent; however, as with fertilizers, support for production and procurement may mean an even higher fiscal cost (World Bank, 1987a, p. 103). Although the government has recently banned the use of 57 pesticides and is planning an integrated pest management programme with the World Bank and the Food and Agriculture Organization (FAO), the current subsidy levels will inevitably encourage inappropriate and excessive use. Moreover, although in its 1987–88 budget the government reduced the total subsidies for fertilizer and pesticides to Rp 204 billion (US$123.3 million), there has yet to be a corresponding increase in the prices of these inputs. Preliminary indications suggest that the costs of these subsidies are being shifted from the official budget to the operations of parastatal producers, who are financing the cost burden through additional borrowing.

Although public works schemes account for over 80 per cent of irrigation, the costs charged to farmers for irrigated water are minor. Most of the 5.2 million hectares of irrigated land in Indonesia is devoted to rice production; in the 1970s, about 16 per cent of the increased rice output was attributed to expansion and improvements in irrigation. For a medium-sized irrigation project, the average operation and maintenance (O & M) costs and annualized capital costs total about Rp 187 000 (US$115) per hectare, of which less than 13 per cent is covered by direct water charges and property taxes paid by farmers. This suggests an annual, government-financed subsidy of Rp 660 billion (US$440 million), spread over 4 million hectares. This level of subsidy is clearly causing a tremendous financial burden: even in 1985–86, before the latest budget cuts, total O & M spending fell to Rp 11 300 (US$10.17) per hectare, which is less than half the required level on average (World Bank, 1987a, pp. 104–5). Over the long run, failure to maintain the irrigation network will translate into losses of agricultural productivity, which will be exacerbated by any water scarcity problems caused by overuse.

Although most rural credit is now provided at market rates, agriculture does receive some subsidized liquidity credits. These amounted to about Rp 132 billion (US$119 million) in 1985–86. The bulk of this subsidy – larger than what the rest of agriculture receives – goes to sugar production, which accounts for only 3 per cent of the value of crop production (World Bank, 1987a, pp. 103–4).

5. Natural resource implications

In sum, such a production-led approach to agricultural diversification, focusing on area targets for specific crops and high input subsidies, presents two formidable natural resource management problems. First, in addition to imposing a potentially unsustainable financial burden on the government, the input subsidies for fertilizer, pesticides and irrigation in particular are imposing considerable external costs in terms of agricultural pollution and resource depletion. Some of these can be considered user costs – in terms of the losses in future agricultural productivity to the cultivator of pesticide resistance, misallocation of input investment on inappropriate use and any constraints imposed by future scarcity (for example, water). There are also, however, important 'pure' externality impacts of pesticide misuse, such as the effects on human health, fishing activities, and biological diversity. There are also problems of groundwater contamination and eutrophication of surface water from fertilizer runoff, and the diversion of scarce water supplies to irrigation from other valuable uses (for example, industrial purposes, fish ponds, potable water, and so on). Concern about these sort of environmental costs has surrounded rice production in Indonesia for some time. It is imperative, therefore, that as the government designs new programmes for agricultural diversification that these costs, represented in their full cross-sectoral impacts, are properly analyzed and incorporated as part of the total costs of any input subsidies.

For example, the cross-sectoral impacts of the GOI's pesticide subsidy are now well recognized (see Figure 6.1). As the recent Indonesian experience shows, just the user costs of inappropriate use and application can be quite high. Thus, in 1986–87 an estimated 50–60000 hectares of irrigated rice were lost to a new outbreak of brown planthopper. At prevailing world prices, the corresponding loss of 1 million tons of rice meant an estimated cost of US$180 million. In addition, however, 35 per cent of the total harvested rice area had to revert to the more resistant but less productive IR-36 variety. The resulting 10–15 per cent decline in yields meant another loss of about 1.2 million tons, or approximately US$120 million. In addition to these direct user costs, there are also the known but unquantified external costs to human health, fishing and other agricultural activities. Other input subsidization policies, such as for fertilizers and irrigation in agriculture and for credit in sugar and *tambak* expansion, also need to be examined for their cross-sectoral impacts.

Second, it is even questionable whether a production-led approach is suitable for the diversity of agroecological systems that characterize Indonesia's marginal lands, including converted forestlands. These lands consist of poor quality soils, with high levels of salinity, acidity and/or erodability. Favouring a mono-cropping pattern, or even attempting to replicate a multiple-cropping pattern that is successful, under totally different ecological conditions, may prove economically unfeasible. For example, although irrigated rice has had limited success on the better tidal swamplands of Southern Kalimantan, a coconut-based farming system supplemented by limited rice, livestock and fish pond production may be more successful and widely applicable (KEPAS, 1985b). Similarly, on the critical uplands of Java, the Citanduy, UACP and IBRD/FAO Solo projects have all used different combinations of agro-forestry and integrated farming

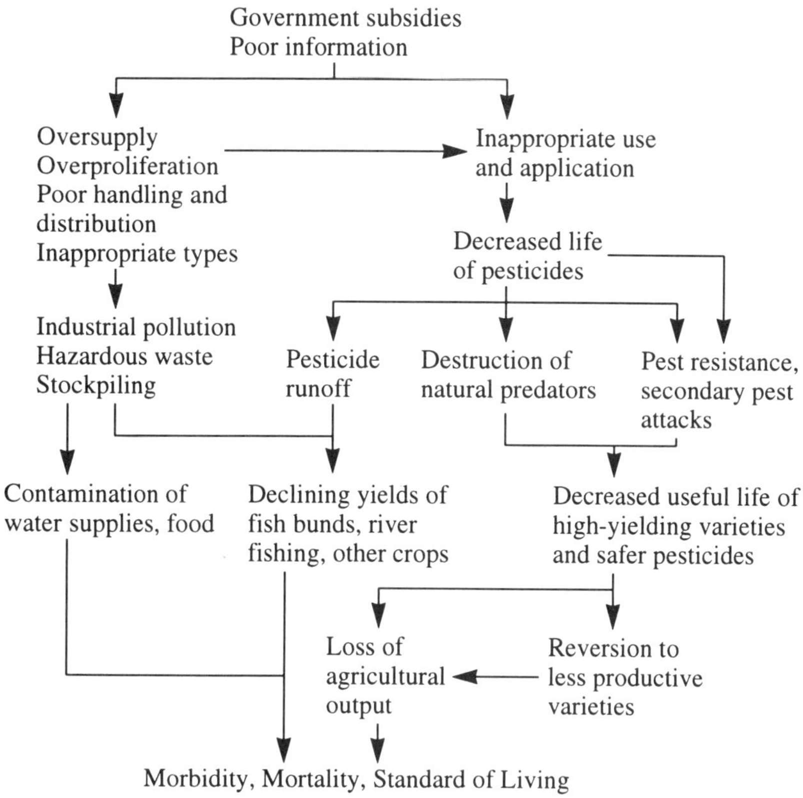

Figure 6.1 Subsidies and inappropriate use of pesticides

systems to combat severe soil erosion problems and raise economic returns. In contrast, in Kota Bangun, East Kalimantan, transmigrants are replicating the same soil erosion conditions as found on their native Java by converting upland forests to rainfed rice production. Due to the poor soil quality and the persistence of *alang-alang* infestation, the sustainability of these practices is even more limited than on the Javanese uplands. As discussed above, poor soil quality, disease and pest infestation may also prove a major constraint on monoculture estates placed on converted forestland.

Furthermore, existing secondary crop systems are extremely diverse. For example, a survey of the various cropping patterns in certain districts of East Java for soybeans, cassava, corn and peanuts revealed the following mixture of systems (Tabor, Adinugroho, *et al.*, 1986):

Jamber: (wetlands): paddy–soybean–paddy or soybean or tobacco.
Kediri: (wetlands): paddy–paddy–corn, paddy–corn/soybean, corn/soybean, corn–onion–corn–onion, sugarcane.
(drylands): corn–corn–fallow, cassava/corn, corn–onion, corn, sugarcane.
Tuban: (wetlands): paddy–peanuts, paddy–cassava/peanuts, paddy–paddy–peanuts.
(drylands): peanuts–peanuts–fallow, corn–peanuts–fallow, peanuts–peanuts/cassava, corn/peanuts–peanuts–fallow.
Malang: (drylands): corn–cassava, cassava–fallow, peanuts–cassava.

Some of these cropping systems may be appropriate for the given agro-ecological conditions of the region and the socio-economic needs of the households; others may not. The high rate of substitution among these crops, however, may mean that an arbitrary policy decision to target one or more for increased production may seriously dislocate any appropriate system that does exist. Instead, a more desirable approach in terms of improving incomes, employment and sustainability may be to adapt agricultural development strategies to fit the type of cropping systems already in existence.

Finally, failure to consider farming and cropping systems as the basis for agricultural development strategies means that many traditional agroforestry and homegarden systems are not being adequately developed. Support for these systems, however, would require a coordinated interdepartmental policy effort. Nevertheless, support for such an effort is crucial for stabilizing marginal lands, especially Indonesia's critical uplands.

Figure 6.2 illustrates the specific economic–environmental linkages associated with Indonesia's uplands erosion problems. As noted above, in Indonesia 36 watershed areas totalling 10.4 million hectares are classified as critical lands. On Java, the area of critical upland is increasing at the rate of 1–2 per cent per annum and now totals over 2 million hectares, approximately one-third of Java's cultivated uplands. With population densities in these areas averaging 700–900 people per square kilometre, with holdings averaging 0.4 hectares or less and 30 per cent of the population being landless, and with yields for upland rice and corn averaging 0.5–1.0 tons/ha, the general pattern is one of poor, predominantly subsistence households seeking to increase their immediate basic food requirements by using inappropriate cropping patterns that result in high soil erosion levels from their rainfed lands. In addition, significant erosion problems are caused by absentee and better-off owners cultivating highly profitable yet erodable crops, such as vegetables, on their steep lands, and by the failure to manage properly state-owned tree plantations, particularly the failure to prevent illegal fuelwood collection and agricultural conversion. Estimated sedimentation rates of rivers in Java from erosion vary from 10 to 40 tons per hectare per year.[3]

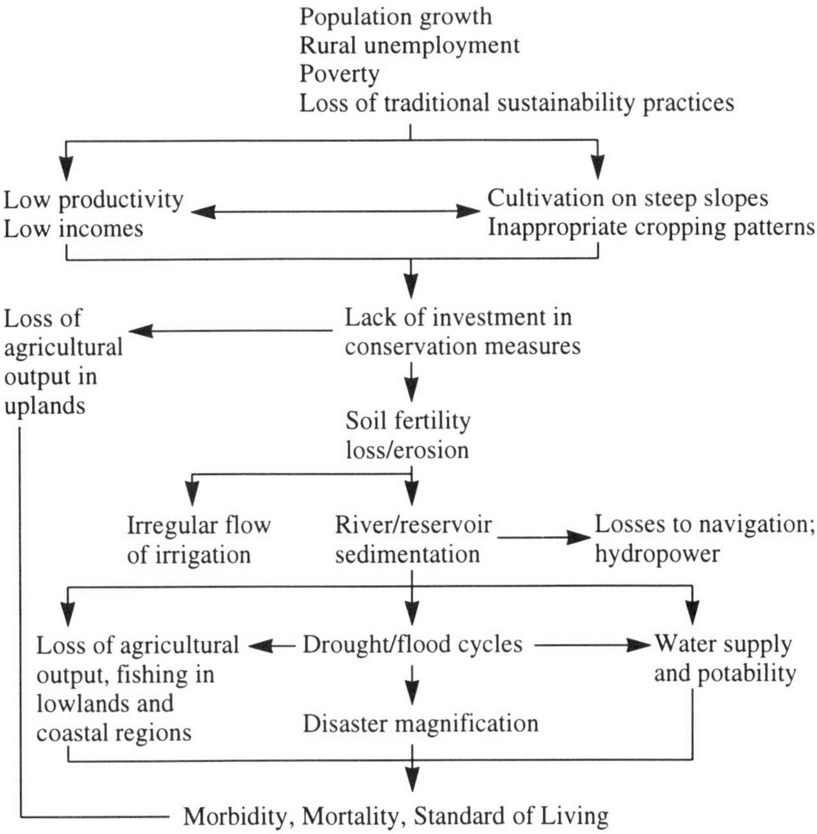

Figure 6.2 Uplands erosion problem

As Figure 6.2 shows, the direct user cost of upland erosion is the loss of agricultural output to upland farmers. Reliable estimates on the resulting loss of farmers' income are not available. Based on the government's Regreening programme (P3RPDAS), farmers' incomes could increase from Rp 64000 to Rp 320000 per hectare from soil conservation measures. Given an estimated 903092 hectares of critical upland farming area on Java, a rough estimate of the loss in farmers' incomes from the failure to control soil erosion is Rp 231.2 billion ($139.8 million) per year.[4] Although these user costs are significant, there may be even greater externality impacts of the disruption to water resources in the lowlands from erosion runoff and sedimentation. These latter costs would include the disruptions to irrigation, dams and water systems and supply; the losses to agriculture, aquaculture and fishing in the lowlands; the disruption to estuarian and coastal fisheries; the losses from diminished navigation and hydropower; and any magnification of natural disasters.

The uplands erosion problem, therefore, is part of the overall problem of water resources management. Any disruption to lowland water resources from upland erosion will inevitably induce greater costs in the allocation of Indonesia's already scarce water supplies. As Indonesia's population and economy continue to expand, water demands by the various competing uses – drinking water and other residential uses, irrigation, aquaculture, industrial processing, power generation, recreation, transportation and waste disposal – will also increase. For example, in the densely populated and fast-developing Jakarta–Puncak corridor, industrial and domestic demand for water in urban areas is anticipated to rise from 450 million cubic metres per year currently to around 2100 million cubic metres annually by the year 2000, and water for irrigation and agriculture will rise from 2800 to 4600 million cubic metres yearly. Overall demand for water is expected to double. This demand will have to be met by the surface water generated in West Java's water catchment areas and 3000 deep wells extracting 30 million cubic metres of groundwater each year. Already, there are water quality problems for the presence of nondegradable organic chemical compounds and heavy metals, agrochemicals, seawater infiltration and sewage in these water supplies (Environment, Resources and Management Consulting Group, 1983, sections 2.2.3, 2.3.1).

The need for agricultural diversification in Indonesia is self-evident. In addition to spreading further the potential employment and income gains of rural development, increased production of non-rice crops, for both import and domestic food requirements, offers more potential for post-harvesting domestic linkages with agricultural processing and export markets. This may be especially important for increasing on- and off-farm employment opportunities on Java. The sustainability of such an effort, however, depends crucially on a more flexible approach than current production-led policies. A more integrated farming or cropping-systems approach would require a greater investment in research, marketing infrastructure and extension. This could at least be partly financed by a reallocation of funds from the removal of pesticide subsidies, a gradual removal of fertilizer subsidies, an effective system of water changes (for example, increased taxes on irrigated lands) and the removal of credit subsidies to sugar cane. Where necessary, greater interdepartmental cooperation is required to ensure that the adequate infrastructure, marketing and processing facilities exist for such a systems-based approach. This is one of the successful lessons of the rice strategy that has yet to be incorporated in the agricultural diversification effort.[5]

6. Conclusion

The objective of this chapter has been to argue that production to achieve food self-sufficiency is neither inherently more nor inherently less environmentally sustainable than export-oriented agricultural development. Rather, the achievements of sustainable agricultural development requires the explicit integration of natural resource management concerns within the economic policy framework for agriculture.

Indonesia provides a good example, given its recent pursuit of both export crop promotion and food self-sufficiency policies. The failure to consider adequately the impacts of these policies on environmental degradation, and to modify incentive schemes and investment programmes accordingly, has presented many obstacles to sustainable agricultural development. It is worth noting, however, that more is known about these obstacles in Indonesia than in most Third World countries, precisely because the GOI is becoming increasingly aware of the importance of appropriate natural resource management policies. If Indonesia is successful in this task, then it could serve as a new model for other Third World countries seeking to develop their agricultural base without sacrificing long-run sustainability.

To summarize, if natural resource management policies for agriculture are to be effective in Indonesia – and in other developing countries – there are two overriding needs:

1. There is a need for substantive and extensive analysis of the natural resource implications of agricultural policies:
   - Given the increasing population pressure and economic demands on Indonesia's natural resource base, problems arising from environmental and natural resource degradation will continue to act as a constraint on the successful implementation of agricultural policies. Alternative policy options – including the pursuit of export crop production versus self-sufficiency strategies – need to be continually examined with explicit reference to these constraints.
   - Since overall agricultural policies determine and dictate the goals to be pursued at the project level, the success of agricultural development projects and programmes will also increasingly depend on the correct analysis of the natural resource management implications of agricultural policies. For Indonesia, this is particularly relevant for projects and programmes that aim to extend farming systems on to marginal lands.
2. At the more micro level, there is a need for further analysis of the economic costs of environmental impacts:
   - micro-level analysis of the natural resource allocation decisions at village or farmer level – and accompanying analysis of agroecological conditions – is essential to designing appropriate policies and investment programmes for natural resource management.
   - Such micro-level analysis is also important for monitoring the impacts of policy decisions and investment programmes at the village and household level. Although some of this information is sometimes

available from research stations, independent, project and provincial studies, it needs to be coordinated and reviewed consistently at the national level to be useful for national policy and investment decisions.

In general, the objective of sustainable agricultural development can only be attained if effective natural resource management is accepted as an overriding policy objective and economic strategy.

Notes

1. I am grateful to Gordon Conway and Jules Pretty for their comments. This work forms part of IIED's Sustainable Agriculture Programme, which is largely funded by USAID. Some of the research was conducted for *World Resources 1987* (published for IIED and World Resources Institute by Basic Books, New York, 1987) and for the USAID mission, Jakarta, Indonesia (see Barbier. 1987b).
2. Another concern is that to the extent that women's incomes decrease as cash cropping expands, family consumption and nutrition, particularly the nutritional status of children may decline. In general the nutritional status of preschool children may be better on farms including a mix of subsistence and cash crops than on mainly cash crop farms. See, for example, von Braun and Kennedy (1986), pp. 56–8.
3. See, for example, GOI/USAID, 1983; Carson and Utomo, 1986; KEPAS, 1985a; McCauley, 1985; Fagi and Mackie, 1987; World Bank, 1987b.
4. The P3RPDAS figures are from GOI/USAID (1983, p. 12); the figure for farming hectares is from Carson and Utomo (1986, p. 3).
5. This crucial aspect of diversification policy is emphasized by Hedley (1987).

References

Balk, I.F. and J.H. Koeman (1984), *Future Hazards from Pesticide Use*, Commission on Ecology Papers No. 6, Gland, Switzerland: International Union for Conservation of Nature.

Barbier, E.B. (1987a), 'The concept of sustainable economic development', *Environmental Conservation*, **14** (2) (Summer), 101–10.

Barbier, E.B. (1987b), 'Annex 1: Natural resources policy and economic framework', in J. Tarrant *et al.* (eds), *Natural Resources and Environmental Management in Indonesia*, Jakarta: USAID, October.

Blaikie. P. (1985), *The Political Economy of Soil Erosion in Developing Countries*, London: Longman.

Carson, B. and W.H. Utomo (1986), *Erosion and Sedimentation Processes in Java*, Jakarta: KEPAS and the Ford Foundation.

Conway, G.R. (1982), 'The future', in G.R. Conway (ed.), *Pesticide Resistance and World Food Production*, London: Imperial College, Centre for Environmental Technology.

Conway, G.R. (1985), 'Agroecosystem analysis', *Agricultural Administration*, **90**, 31–55.

Conway, G.R. (1987), 'The properties of agroecosystems', *Agricultural Systems*, **24** (2), 95–117.

Conway, G.R. and D.S. McCauley (1983), 'Intensifying tropical agriculture: the Indonesian experience', *Nature*, **302** (5906) (March), 288–9.

Conway, G.R., I. Manwan and D.S. McCauley (1983), 'The development of marginal lands in the tropics', *Nature*, **304** (4) (August), 392.

Dinham, B. and C. Hines (1983), *Agribusiness in Africa*, London: Earth Resources Research.

Douglas, G. (ed.) (1984), *Agricultural Sustainability in a Changing World Order*, Boulder, CO: Westview Press.

Environment, Resources and Management Consulting Group (1983), *Proposals for an Action Programme in the Jakarta–Puncak Corridor*, The Hague: 23 December.

FAO (1985a), *Women in Developing Agriculture*, Rome: FAO.

FAO (1985b), *Production Yearbook 1984*, Rome: FAO.

Fagi, A.M. and C. Mackie (1987), 'Watershed management in Upland Java: Past experiences and future directions', Paper presented at Soil and Water Conservation on Steep Lands, Soil Conservation Society of America, San Juan, Puerto Rico: 22–27 March.

Gliessman, S.R. (1984), 'Resource management in traditional tropical agroecosystems in Southeast Mexico', in G. Douglas (ed.), *Agricultural Sustainability in a Changing World Order*, Boulder, CO: Westview Press.

Goodland, R. and G. Ledec (1986), *Neoclassical economics and principles of sustainable development*, Office of Environmental and Scientific Affairs, Washington, DC: World Bank.

Goodland, R., C. Watson and G. Ledec (1984), *Environmental Management in Tropical Agriculture*, Boulder, CO: Westview Press.

Government of Indonesia/USAID (1983), *Composite Report of the Watershed Assessment Team*, 3 vols, Jakarta: USAID. May.

Gupta, T. (1983), 'The economics of tree crops on marginal agricultural lands with special reference to the hot arid region in Rajasthan, India', *The International Tree Crops Journal*, **2**, 155–94.

Hardjono, J. (1986), 'Transmigration: Looking to the future', *Bulletin of Indonesian Economic Studies*, **22** (2) (August), 28–53.

Harrison, P. (1987), *The Greening of Africa*, London: Paladin.

Hedley, D.D. (1987), 'Diversification: Concepts and directions in Indonesian agricultural policy', Paper presented at the Workshop on Soybean Research and Development in Indonesia, the CGPRI Centre, Bogor, Indonesia, 24–26 February.

KEPAS (1985a), *The Critical Uplands of Eastern Java: An Agroecosystem Analysis*, Jakarta: KEPAS, Agency for Agricultural Research and Development, January.

KEPAS (1985b), *Tidal Swamp Agro-Ecosystems of Southern Kalimantan*, Jakarta: KEPAS, Agency for Agricultural Research and Development.

Lele, U. (1985), 'Terms of trade, agricultural growth, and rural poverty in Africa', in J.W. Mellor and G.M Desai (eds), *Agricultural Change and Rural Poverty*, Baltimore, MD: Johns Hopkins University Press.

McCauley, D.S. (1985), 'Upland cultivation systems in densely populated watersheds of the humid tropics – opportunities and constraints relating to soil conservation: A case from Java', draft paper Honolulu: Environment and Policy Institute, East-West Center, August.

Repetto, R. (1983), *Specific incentives and disincentives for environmental and population policy*, Jakarta: Ministry for Population and Environment.

Repetto, R. (1985), *Paying the Price: Pesticide Subsidies in Developing Countries*, Research Report No. 2, Washington, DC: World Resources Institute, December.

Repetto, R. (1986), 'Economic policy reform for natural resource conservation', draft paper, Washington, DC: World Resources Institute, September.

Rucker, R.L. (1985), *A preliminary view of Indonesia's employment problem and some options for solving it*, Jakarta: USAID.

Tabor, S.R., B. Adinugroho, Suhartini, H. Nugroho and Mantau (1986), *An appraisal of the palawija crops marketing systems in East Java*, Directorate of Food Crop Economics, Jakarta: Department of Agriculture, 15 November.

Tabor, S.R., K. Altemeier, Nuryanto, Wardoyo and B. Adinugroho (1986), *Trends in agricultural supply and demand to the year 2000*, Working Paper No. 1, Supply and Demand Study, Food Crops Sector Model Sub-Study, Directorate of Food Crop Economics, Jakarta: Department of Agriculture, 15 December.

von Braun, J. and E. Kennedy (1986), *Commercialization of Subsistence Agriculture: Income and Nutritional Effects in Developing Countries*, Working Papers on Commercialization of Agriculture and Nutrition, No. 1, Washington, DC: International Food Policy Research Institute, April.

World Bank (1986a), *Indonesia Policy and Prospects for Non-Oil Exports: Annex 1*, Washington, DC: World Bank, 31 December.

World Bank (1986b), *Indonesia Transmigration Sector Review*, Washington, DC: World Bank, 24 October.

World Bank (1986c), *World Development Report 1986*, New York: Oxford University Press.

World Bank (1987a), 'Draft economic report on Indonesia – Chapter 5: Agricultural strategy', Jakarta: World Bank, 15 April.

World Bank (1987b), Indonesia – Java watersheds: Java uplands and watershed management', draft report, Washington, DC: World Bank, November.

7. The farm-level economics of soil conservation: the uplands of Java

1. Introduction

On the densely populated island of Java in Indonesia, the area of severely eroded upland is increasing at the rate of 1–2 per cent per annum and now totals around 2 million hectares (ha), approximately one third of Java's cultivated uplands. Average population density in these areas is 600–700 people per sq km, although it may fall to 400–550 per sq km in severely degraded upper watersheds. With holdings averaging 0.4 ha or less, with up to 20–25 per cent of the population being landless in some areas, and with yields for upland rice and corn averaging 0.9–2.5 tons/ha, the general pattern is one of poor, predominantly subsistence households seeking to increase their immediate basic food production by using cropping systems that result in high soil-erosion levels from their rainfed lands. In addition, significant erosion problems are caused by absentee and better-off farm owners cultivating highly profitable but erosive crops, such as vegetables, and by the failure to 'police' state-owned tree plantations properly, particularly in preventing illegal fuelwood collection and agricultural conversion (Barbier, 1987; Roche, 1987; World Bank, 1987b, 1988).

This chapter is concerned with the incentives for upland farmers on Java to adopt soil conservation packages as a means to control erosion and improve long-term land productivity and agricultural growth. The chapter reviews the soil conservation 'packages' currently offered to upland farmers and the factors influencing their adoption, as observed by existing farm-level studies.

The appendix contains a model characterizing this behaviour. As expected, farming households in Java are economically rational in their response to their environment, both physical and economic. Land tenure arrangements, soil characteristics, input and output prices, availability of off-farm employment, and discount rates all combine to influence acceptance or not of soil conservation. Government policies must take into account these variables if effective programmes are to be designed.

This chapter concentrates on the farmer s decision to invest in the control of soil loss and land degradation on privately owned and operated land in the Javan uplands. The additional erosion problems caused by the encroachment and conversion of 'open access' and publicly owned forest lands for fuelwood, fodder, and shifting cultivation are not examined, as these appear to be of less importance (Donner, 1987, pp. 67–8). Thus, the following analysis is generally applicable to land degradation problems arising from sedentary upland cultivation in developing regions rather than those arising from shifting cultivation and 'open access' degradation of forests (Lopez and Nicklitscheck 1988; Southgate and Pearce, 1987). This chapter also ignores the off-site impacts of upland soil erosion on Java, not because they are insignificant, but in order to concentrate on the upland farmer's decisions concerning soil conservation in the face of intertemporal depletion.[1]

2. Technical packages for upland soil conservation

The predominant technical approach for combating upper watershed degradation on privately owned land in Java has evolved from the FAO-funded Solo Watershed project (1972–78).

Bench terraces

In upper watershed areas of up to 50 per cent slopes, the basic approach involves subsidizing *bench terrace* construction through cash wages and/or agricultural inputs, either provided directly or on credit. After terraces are built, food crops are planted on the horizontal surface and grasses on the riser and lip to support livestock and to help control erosion. Farmers are also encouraged to adopt improved cropping patterns, which together with the introduction of new varieties, increased inputs (for example, fertilizer and pesticides), and better technical information are intended to improve the net returns from cultivation. For example, in the Citanduy II project in West Java, farmers were advised not to monocrop corn and cassava, and to switch to growing higher-valued crops. As a result, increased returns from terracing have been largely associated with changing crop patterns: cassava production fell from 42.4 to 12.4 per cent of the average value per plot, while rice production increased from 7.1 to 26.8 per cent and peanut production rose from 3.4 to 17.8 per cent (Saragih, Huszar and Cochrane, 1986).

The evolution in approach by these projects reflects the realization that the soil erosion and low productivity in upland areas result from farming and cultivation systems that meet households' immediate production needs, or increase short-run profits, but are inappropriate for the diverse topographic, soil and agro-ecological conditions found in these upper watersheds. For example, a study of bench terracing and related farming practices in the Citanduy basin revealed that model farms based on recent and pliocene volcanic soils have the lowest relative erodibility index and the highest net returns, whereas those located on the sedimentary derived (limestone) soils have low returns, and in some cases, actual losses. This is due not only to the generally lower fertility of the limestone soils but also to the greater labour involved in building and maintaining terraces and the higher rate of topsoil loss due to erosion (Kucera *et al.*, 1986).[2]

Table 7.1 Cost of bench terracing at various slopes, Java uplands[a]

Site	Slope (%)	Mandays per hectare (MD/ha)	Total cost (US$/ha, 1979 prices)	
1. *Labour requirements*			Opportunity cost of labor	
			Full	Half
Upper Solo	5–30	750	843	422
	30–50	1520	1830	915
Citanduy II	10–15	789	884	441
	45–50	1742	1957	979
Jogyakarta	10–20	845	950	475
	40–50	1833	2059	1030
2. *Material requirements*			Cost	
Citanduy II	NA	–	119	
Jogyakarta	25	–	112	
3. *Total* (1. + 2.)			Opportunity cost of labour	
			Full	Half
Citanduy 11	10–15	789	1003	560
	45–50	1742	2076	1098
Jogyakarta	10–20	845	1062	587
	40–50	1833	2171	1142
4. *Additional labour and material costs of livestock system*			Opportunity cost of labour	
			Full	Half
Citanduy II[b]	–	2–5	74–80	73–75

Notes:

[a] The additional costs to the farmer of periodic maintenance of terraces, waterways, and drop structures are not included.

[b] Assumes 20 per cent of a hectare consists of terrace risers and lips, and material costs of about $72/ha: A mature female sheep or goat costs about US$70.

Source: Bernstein and Sinaga (1983).

In spite of some input subsidies, the introduction of many soil conservation techniques onto upland farms may require a substantial investment of time and money by farmers (Table 7.1). It is generally assumed that the labour for constructing the terraces is provided by the farmer during the dry season. But the labour requirements often exceed the time he has available for terracing.[3] This may therefore mean additional cash expenditures on hired labour.

Thus, from the farmer's point of view the costs of terracing not only imply forgoing his own income-earning opportunities – either in off-farm employment during the dry season and/or less labour time devoted to crop and farm production – but also additional expenditures on material and possibly livestock costs.[4] This suggests that adoption of terracing-based technology for soil conservation may be limited to households with the cash available to hire additional labour, to those with more than one adult male member to supply labour, and wealthier households that can afford to forgo wage employment during the dry season.

For example, in Gubugklakah, East Java, only the relatively wealthy farmers who are engaged in profitable commercial apple production (approximately US$3–6000 per year profits – 1986 prices) are able to afford to construct extremely effective back sloping tied ridges capable of conserving topsoil and reducing erosion rates to less than 10 tons/ha (volcanic middle soils with a slope profile of 4 to 8 degrees) (Carson, 1987). Similarly, a survey of farmers who did not adopt bench-terracing technology in the Citanduy watershed of West Java revealed that 87 per cent of the respondents cited lack of money as the reason for not constructing terraces (Tampubolon and Saragih, 1986). This is attributed to a general shortage of rural credit at affordable interest rates in many upland areas (see Section 3).

Agroforestry

On slopes greater than 45–50 per cent, the recommended soil conservation strategy is for farmers to take land out of annual food crop production and adopt an agro-forestry-based system to produce tree crops for cash income (for example, clove, beverage crops, and citrus), fuelwood for home consumption and sale, fodder trees, and grass under the canopy for livestock. For upland farmers, however, there is an additional 'waiting' cost of three or more years to be borne between the initial year of land preparation and planting and the eventual maturing and harvesting of tree species. For example, although *Albizia falcata* is considered a relatively fast-growing tree with economic potential for fuelwood, sawn lumber, and supplementary dry-season forage, harvesting cannot begin before three years for fuelwood (five years for sawn logs), and it takes five years or more for cumulative returns to exceed the initial preparation and planting costs of around US$100/ha (1982 prices). Similarly, preparation and planting of *Glyricidia* requires 7.5 MD/ha and subsequently 3.5 MD/ha for maintenance, as well as a material cost of around US$45/ha (1982 prices).

Farmers, however, have to wait until the third year before making the first cut, and it is not until the fifth year that harvests reach their full economic potential (around US$300/ha/yr – 1982 prices) (Sumitro, 1983).

This suggests that adopting agroforestry systems may be extremely difficult for poorer farmers who are dependent on very small landholdings for food production and who have no alternative cropland or employment opportunities. On the other hand, farmers who are relatively well-off, who have sufficient lower-sloped cropland to grow food and/or who have access to off-farm employment opportunities may be able to afford the 'waiting cost' associated with agroforestry investments. Security of land tenure is an additional determinant as to whether upland farmers are willing to bear this 'waiting cost'.

3. Factors influencing farmers' decisions

Given that upland farmers face significant costs in adopting soil conservation measures and changes in farming systems, they are unlikely to make changes in their land management unless they can see an economic advantage in doing so. Higher productivity and returns will also mean that farmers can afford to

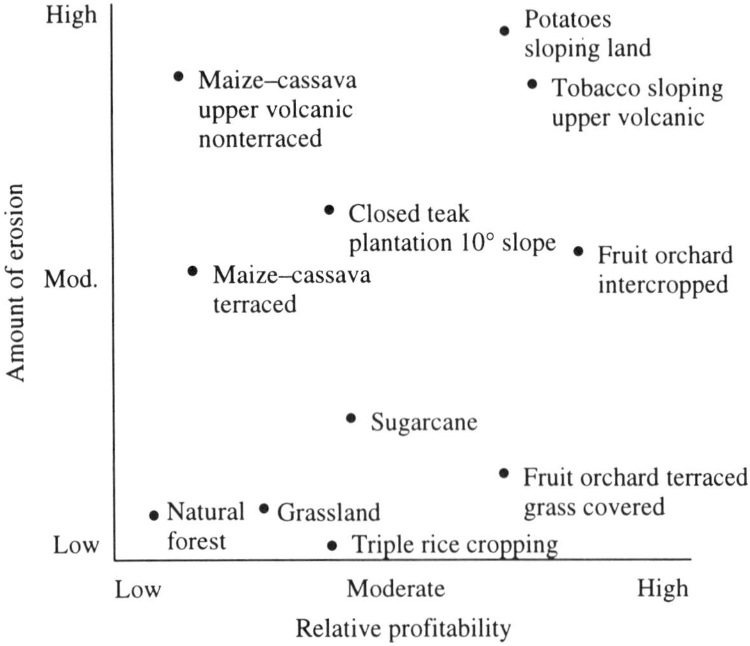

Source: Carson and Utomo (1986).

Figure 7.1 The relationship between relative profitability and amount of erosion of major crops, Java uplands

maintain terraces and other conservation structures and to continue with labour-intensive erosion control measures. On the other hand, poorer upland farmers dependent on low-return cropping systems, such as maize or cassava, may be aware that soil erosion is reducing productivity but may not be able to afford conservation measures. At the other extreme, farmers with very profitable crops that are highly erosive, such as temperate vegetables on steep upper volcanic slopes, may not consider soil conservation if their returns do not seem affected by soil erosion losses.

Thus, the relationship between the erodibility and profitability of different farming systems on different soils and slopes is an important determinant of whether upland farmers adopt a soil conservation strategy. In the appendix, a simple model is developed to show how farmers' acceptance of soil conservation measures is determined by the impact of soil erosion on profits. The model can also indicate how changes in input and output prices, the discount rate, soil characteristics, and population – including migration for off-farm employment – can influence the acceptance of soil conservation.

As shown for Java in Figure 7.1, the relationship between erodibility and profitability varies widely. Many profitable perennial crops – if accompanied by proper soil conservation measures – appear also to afford relatively better erosion control. On the other hand, high-valued vegetable and cash crops (for example, tobacco) cause substantial erosion on steep slopes. For annual crops such as maize and cassava, terracing can reduce erosion but without raising profitability substantially.

Poor quality soils

On poor quality, highly erodible soils the success of projects in encouraging farmers to adopt conservation packages is often determined by whether these packages allow farmers to shift to higher-valued crops. For example, in the Citanduy II project in West Java, it has been observed that, as one of the functions of terracing is to conserve soil moisture, such conservation measures have induced farmers to shift from low-value crops such as cassava to crops that earn three to five times more per kilogram. In addition, the mix of inputs (that is, labour and purchased inputs such as fertilizers, seeds, and pesticides) was observed to be sub-optimal before terracing, but after terracing approached the optimal mix (Saragih, Huszar and Cochrane, 1986). In recent times, however, this policy of discouraging the monocropping of cassava because of its deleterious impact on soil structure has been undermined by the quadrupling of cassava prices, which has been encouraged by the Government of Indonesia's current pricing, targeting, and export-promotion policies (World Bank, 1987b).

In Srigonco, East Java, the shallow limestone soils require an agroforestry approach to soil conservation based on introducing deep-rooted perennial, horticultural, and agroforestry species. Although the predominantly poor farmers with small land holdings are very much aware of the loss in productivity from soil erosion, many cannot afford the initial investment nor take on the extra risk needed to improve their existing cassava and cassava–maize farming systems. This attitude is often reinforced by lack of secure land tenure, and in some areas, a lack of interest in agriculture with increasing off-farm employment. For example, the badly managed, unterraced lands were invariably those not owned or controlled by the farmer but under a precarious lease system (*tanah marinir*). If profitability of maize and cassava drops too low, farmers will make the rational decision to leave the farm for urban areas, where labour has better returns than on the farm (Carson, 1987).

Highly productive soils

On the deep, highly productive volcanic soils of Java, soil productivity and its response to increased productive inputs are very high. Extremely deep topsoils also mean that it takes considerable time before soil erosion severely reduces soil productivity. Consequently, the long-run impact on productive topsoil depth may be negligible. As discussed above, such soils are considered ideal for growing high-valued horticultural crops, although there is increasing concern over the off-site impacts of the high erosion rates associated with their cultivation. Over the period 1976–86 in Java, the farmers' terms of trade for growing vegetables and their price relative to other crops have increased substantially, due to Government import controls and considerable demand in urban areas. As a result, upland vegetable farmers have little incentive to invest in conservation measures, and in fact, the production of vegetables in upland areas has expanded considerably. High, effective protection rates for fruit and other perennial crops encourage the switch to conservation methods based on agroforestry (Roche, 1987; World Bank, 1987b). For example, in Ngadas, East Java, because of deep volcanic topsoils, commercial vegetable farmers (mainly potato but also onions, garlic, and cabbages) do not appear to experience significant declines in yields despite average annual erosion rates of 150–200 tons/ha and the loss of 2 cm of soil each year. Soil conservation measures are therefore not perceived to be a high priority. Nevertheless, farmers rely on their land for all income and thus indicate a willingness to make land improvements if there is a demonstrable impact on productivity (Carson, 1987).

Input subsidies and credit

There is concern that the access to certain subsidized inputs by upland farmers might prove to be a disincentive to control the long-term productivity damage of soil erosion. This is particularly the case for fertilizers, the increased application of which may artificially boost yields in the short run on even severely degraded soils. With current subsidies for fertilizers in Indonesia estimated to be about 38 per cent of the farmgate price (World Bank, 1987a), upland farmers are encouraged to apply relatively cheap fertilizers to increase yields rather than consider more expensive but environmentally sound methods such as green manuring, mulching, and using compost to maintain soil fertility and stability. For example, in Ngadas, East Java, farmers are presently using over 1000 kg of subsidized chemical fertilizers per hectare to produce two 10-ton potato crops. These yields are less than one half of what could be attained with improved soil management techniques; as the farmers have only recently realized that the reduction in yields from soil erosion were not being offset by the massive fertilizer dosages, they are now increasing their use of organic fertilizers (Carson, 1987).

Similarly, in the Citanduy watershed of West Java, nearly two thirds of the supposed 'control group' outside of project areas and a significant number of non-subsidized farmers within these areas seem to be spontaneously adopting and adapting the bench-terracing based soil conservation packages. Although their use of non-labour inputs is less than project farmers who are subsidized for these inputs, these 'spontaneous' adaptors have nevertheless significantly increased their income and appear to have even outperformed the more recent model and expansion farmers (Tampubolon and Saragih, 1986). Thus, subsidies of conservation packages may not always be necessary if farmers can perceive an immediate economic gain from adopting these measures. Calculations of the net present value of the gains from terracing in the Citanduy II project suggest that, if terracing costs are around US$500 or less (1984/85 prices), farmers could be expected to adopt terracing without subsidies (Saragih, Huszar and Cochrane, 1986).

Higher lending rates also affect farmers' ability to invest in upland soil conservation measures.[5] For example, farm-level investment in upland soil conservation measures particularly requires medium- and long-term credit at affordable rates. Experience in the Citanduy II project in West Java indicates that returns from selected agroforestry and bench-terracing farm package investments are sufficient to pay loans at 24 per cent annual interest. Investments in terracing, however, require a medium-term loan for at least two years and a short-term loan for succeeding years. After nine years of investment in terracing and twelve years of investment in agroforestry, all loans could be repaid. Moreover, the increase in net benefits after ten years of investment supported by credit is three and four times greater, respectively, for terracing and agroforestry when compared to the net benefits of farms that do not adopt soil conservation measures (Tatuh, 1987). At present, neither the availability of rural credit nor its allocation is adequate in all of Indonesia, let alone in the uplands of Java. Despite an implicit agricultural credit subsidy of about US$80.3 million annually (1986/87 prices) that provides loans at 12 per cent a year, public liquidity credit is estimated to meet only 15 per cent of the demand for credit by farmers, and the other 85 per cent is obtained informally at an interest rate of around 60 per cent per annum. Indications are that small farmers in particular must rely on high cost, informal sources of funds (World Bank, 1987a). Such high interest rates are a disincentive to medium- and long-term investment by upland farmers in soil conservation measures and thus encourage a bias towards short-run production decisions that leave the soil vulnerable to erosion.

Other factors

Over the long term, the search for off-farm employment and permanent outmigration should be significant to upland degradation. For example, in Belik, East Java, a significant number of the village's permanent residents migrate seasonally to nearby towns to obtain work in cigarette factories, bakeries, and as construction workers, small traders, and domestic servants. For many families, this migration is quasi-permanent and only occasional return visits are made to Belik. If these demographic trends continue over the next ten to fifteen years, and assuming no acceleration in population growth, both the labour force and thus intensity of land use of Belik will decline.

As a result, there may be considerable potential for new perennial-based farming systems which have lower labour requirements than current food crop systems and generate less soil erosion (KEPAS, 1985, 95). The possibility of such trends has led some analysts to conclude that off-farm employment generated by urbanization on and off Java in Indonesia is potentially having a beneficial impact as an alternative to more intensive cultivation of fragile lands, and as a means for the rural poor to improve their incomes and living conditions (Williams, 1987). In the case of Java's uplands, there is insufficient data and analysis of the positive and negative impacts of trends in off-farm employment on land-use practices to test such a hypothesis.

There is also insufficient data and analysis of land tenureship in the Javan uplands and its impact on land management. The few village surveys conducted tend to confirm the general observation that farmers without security of tenure are interested in maximizing their short-term investment in seed, fertilizer, and labour for the crop that is in the ground. In most cases, the choice of farming systems is determined by – increasingly absentee – landowners, who are primarily concerned with immediate returns from the land. In both middle and upper volcanic areas on Java, share tenancy and absentee ownership are becoming more common with the increasing profitability of fruit crops, sugarcane, and vegetables (Roche, 1987). For example, in Sumberbrantas, East Java, families living outside the area own nearly half of the land, which tends to be leased out to local farmers for mainly potato growing. The major consequence is that there is relatively little interest shown by farmers in land conservation, and existing terrace management and elephant grass maintenance is inadequate. This lack of interest is reinforced by the high short-term profits associated with potato growing in the village (KEPAS, 1985, pp. 170, 176).

4. Conclusion

This paper has explored the incentives for upland farmers on Java to invest in soil conservation packages as an alternative to existing methods of cultivation that lead to considerable soil erosion. The evidence clearly demonstrates that without appropriate economic incentives upland farmers will not modify their land management practices and farming systems. In some cases, such as growing horticultural crops on deep volcanic soils in the steep uplands, there is little incentive as soil erosion appears to have negligible effects on farm profitability. Because of the high costs of bench terracing, especially in terms of labour, poorer farmers growing lower-valued crops may be reluctant to terrace – particularly on limestone-based soils where terracing is ineffective in improving returns. Other incentive effects can be traced directly to government policies, such as maintaining high relative prices for cassava and vegetables, high subsidies for fertilizers and the general poor availability of rural credit at affordable rates. More complex incentive effects arise from the relationship among the availability of off-farm employment, population pressure, security of tenure, and farming decisions.

More information and analysis of these different incentives is, of course, necessary. This paper nevertheless points to several factors that governments must take into account in designing effective programmes and policies to control upland soil erosion. At the programme and project level, there is a clear need to assess the economic profile of the target population, including continuous monitoring of the income, wealth, and employment status of households as well as changes in cropping systems, the use of inputs, and the returns to cultivation. This must be related to biophysical data indicating the effectiveness of different conservation packages in controlling erosion and boosting yields under different slope and soil characteristics. Continuous monitoring of, on the one hand, model farmers and subsidized adaptors, and on the other, a control group that could include 'spontaneous' adaptors may determine whether project-specific subsidization of inputs, including credit, is required to encourage acceptance of soil conservation packages.

Measures at the programme and project level must be complemented by appropriate pricing policies and investment strategies. A recent World Bank report has recommended a number of policy changes for Indonesia that might be effective in assisting the control of upland degradation on Java (World Bank, 1987b). These include, for example, ending subsidization and promotion of vegetable, cassava, and sugar production, as these are counter-productive in terms of promoting soil conservation. On the other hand, restrictive import controls for perennial fruits and animal products may be necessary in the medium term to encourage the spread of agroforestry and livestock-based systems in the uplands. And, as an investment strategy, extending fertilizer and input subsidies to the uplands may be less appropriate than more direct investments to build up the physical infrastructure of the uplands, such as rural transport, integration of markets, credit facilities, and post-harvesting technology and harvesting. Of particular importance is overcoming the bottlenecks in the production and dissemination of improved varieties of higher-valued crops (for example, dryland rice, soybeans, peanuts) more suitable to the varied upland agro-ecological conditions and in ensuring the availability of general rural credit at affordable interest rates.

Acknowlegements
A previous and longer draft of this chapter appeared in the World Bank's Environment Department Working Paper Series (Barbier, 1988). The author is indebted to Gloria Davis, John English, Ernst Lutz, William Magrath, Kenneth McConnell, David Pearce, Douglas Southgate, E. Zimmer-Vorhaus, and two anonymous reviewers for comments, as well as to his fellow participants in the 1987 World Bank study of upper watershed degradation on Java. The findings, interpretations, and conclusions expressed in this chapter are, however, entirely those of the author and should not be attributed in any manner to the World Bank, to its affiliated organizations, or to members of its Board of Executive Directors or to the countries they represent.

Appendix

A simple variant of the model developed by (McConnell, 1983) can be constructed to reflect the choices open to upland farmers on Java as to whether or not to adopt soil conservation packages.[6] It is assumed that only one crop is produced, or if there are multiple crops, their combined production can be explained by a single crop production function. This function is

$$q = f(z_1, x),\ f_1 > 0, f_{11} \leq 0, f_2 \geq 0, f_{22} \leq 0, f_{12} = f_{21} \geq 0, \qquad (7.1)$$

where $q(t)$ is output, $x(t)$ is soil depth, and z_1 (t) is a vector representing a conventional input package that includes productive inputs (including labour), crop varieties, and cropping patterns and techniques. An increase in z_1 leads to increased output, albeit at a declining rate. The depth of the soil, x, also has a beneficial effect on crop production. The positive cross partial derivative of f indicate that additional soil depth improves the crop productivity of the traditional input package, and an increase in these inputs adds to the beneficial effects of x on crop production.

However, the use of z_1 increases soil loss, and at an accelerating rate. Thus, the household has the choice of adopting an alternative input package, z_2, of appropriate soil conservation methods – such as the type described in Section 2 – that will conserve the soil. If h is defined as the change in soil depth, then

$$\dot{x} = h(z_1, z_2),\ h_1 \leq 0,\ h_{11} \leq 0,\ h_2 > 0,\ h_{22} \leq 0,\ h_{12} = h_{21} < 0. \qquad (7.2)$$

Let $p(t)$ be the price of the crop output. $f(z_1, x)$, normalized with respect to the price of any new crops associated with z_2, and $c_1(t)$ and $c_2(t)$ are the costs of the respective input packages.[7] The behaviour of the farming household in response to soil erosion is therefore determined by the impact of the soil on profits, over T years

$$PV = \int_0^{T\to\infty} e^{-rt}\left[pf(z_1, x) - c_1 z_1 - c_2 z_2\right]dt. \qquad (7.3)$$

where r is the farmer's discount rate.[8]

Thus, the upland farming household will maximize (7.3) through choice of z_1 and z_2, subject to (7.2) and the initial soil depth, $x(0) = x_0$.

Given the continuous function $u(t)$, the Hamiltonian of the problem yields the following first-order conditions

$$dH/dz_1 = pf_1 - c_1 + uh_1 = 0, \qquad (7.4)$$

$$dH/dz_2 = -c_2 + uh_2 = 0, \qquad (7.5)$$

$$\dot{u} = ru - dH/dx = ru - pf_2, \qquad (7.6)$$

$$\dot{x} = h(z_1, z_2), \qquad (7.7)$$

$$x(0) = x_0, \qquad (7.8)$$

and

$$\lim_{T\to\infty} u(T)x(T) = 0. \qquad (7.9)$$

Condition (7.4) indicates that, for conventional productive inputs, the value of the marginal product, pf_1, must be equal to the total costs. This includes not only the money costs of these inputs, c_1, but also their costs in terms of worsening soil erosion, uh_1. Condition (7.5) shows that the money costs of the soil conservation package must be equated with the additional value it generates by controlling soil erosion. The co-state variable, $u(t)$, can be interpreted as the true value, or shadow price, of soil. The implicit cost of soil loss, u, must therefore grow at the rate of discount less the soil's contribution to current profits, pf_2.

A comparative static analysis of the temporary equilibrium of the problem yields the following results

$$z_1 = z_1\left(\overset{-}{u}, \overset{+}{p}, \overset{-}{c_1}, \overset{+}{c_2}, \overset{+}{x}, \right), \tag{7.10}$$

$$z_2 = z_2\left(\overset{+}{u}, \overset{-}{p}, \overset{+}{c_1}, \overset{-}{c_2}, \overset{-}{x}, \right), \tag{7.11}$$

Thus, in the short run, an increase in the implicit cost of soil erosion and the costs of the traditional input package will favour the adoption of the soil conservation package over z_1. In contrast, an increase in the relative price of the traditional crop, in the costs of the soil conservation package or in the depth of the soil, will discourage the adoption of z_2 and favour the use of the traditional input package.

From (7.6) and (7.7) the long-run or steady-state equilibrium of the problem can be characterized by

$$A(u, x) = \dot{u} \gtreqless 0 \quad \text{if } ru \gtreqless pf_2(z_1(u, x), x), \tag{7.12}$$

$$B(u, x) = \dot{x} \gtreqless 0 \quad \text{if } h(z_1(u, x), z_2(u, x)) \gtreqless 0, \tag{7.13}$$

where in the steady state $\dot{u} = \dot{x} = 0$. The slopes of the stationary loci are given by

$$\left.\frac{du}{dx}\right|_{B=0} = -\frac{h_1 z_{1x} + h_2 z_{2x}}{h_1 z_{1u} + h_2 z_{2x}} > 0, \tag{7.14}$$

$$\left.\frac{du}{dx}\right|_{A=0} = -\frac{pf_{22} + pf_{21} z_{1x}}{r - pf_{21} z_{1u}} < 0, \tag{7.15}$$

if $f_{22} > f_{21} z_{1x}$. One such stable solution is depicted in Figure 7.2, with (u^*, x^*) representing the steady-state equilibrium of the system. Thus, the optimal policy of the farming household depends on whether the initial topsoil level is high ($x_0 > x^*$) or low ($x_0 < x^*$). If initial soil depth is extremely high – which seems to be the case in those areas of the Javan uplands with very deep volcanic soils – the optimal strategy for the farmer is to deplete the topsoil until the costs of soil erosion rise. It is only when the productivity impacts of soil erosion are

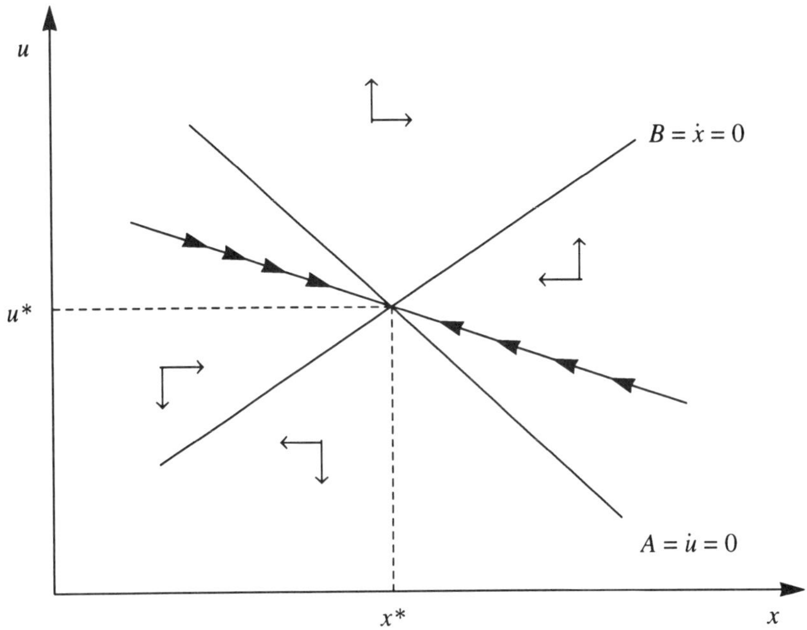

Figure 7.2 The phase diagram solution

significant that farmers will invest in a soil conservation package to halt erosion. In contrast, if initial soil depth is poor, the value of additional crop production associated with soil conservation exceeds its costs. The problem for most upland farmers on poor soils, however, is that the low productivity of these soils may mean they do not have sufficient capital to invest in conservation packages. Nor can they afford the additional risk involved in changing their farming methods and cropping systems.

Further insights into the economic incentives for upland farmers to invest in soil conservation can be gained through comparative static analysis of the model:

An increase in the discount rate, r, shifts down the $A = 0$ curve in the *ux* plane.[9] In the new long-term equilibrium both soil depth and its shadow price are lower. Thus, as the household becomes more myopic, it will tend to invest in traditional inputs to boost current productivity at the expense of conservation investments to halt soil erosion and improve future productivity. Eventually, however, the decline in the soil depth over time from this decision will mean lower productivity in the long run.

An increase in the relative price, p, of traditionally cultivated commodities causes both the $B = 0$ and the $A = 0$ curves to shift up, thus increasing the long-run value of soil depth. The change in the equilibrium level of soil depth will depend on whether the negative impact on soil erosion of an increase in p will exceed its positive impact on the current productivity of traditional production methods; that is,

$$dx^* \lesseqqgtr 0, \text{ if } h_1 z_{1p} + h_2 z_{2p} \gtreqqless f_2 + pf_{21} z_{1p}. \tag{7.16}$$

For example, on the poor quality, shallow limestone-based soils found in certain upland areas, the marginal productivity of the soil, f_2, is generally low and the boost to soil productivity of using additional productive inputs, f_{21}, is close to zero. On the other hand, the impacts of these inputs on soil degradation, h_1, are very substantial. As a result, condition (7.16) would suggest that the effect of an increase in p on these soils would be a drastic decline in soil depth over the long run.

An increase in the cost of the traditional input package, c_1, causes both the $A = 0$ and $B = 0$ curves to shift down, thus, reducing current traditional production and soil degradation and causing the long-run cost of soil degradation to fall. The final impact on soil erosion will depend on the effect on soil degradation relative to the effect on soil productivity

$$dx^* \gtreqqless 0 \quad \text{if } h_1 z_{1c1} + h_2 z_{2c1} \gtreqqless -pf_{21} z_{1c1}. \tag{7.17}$$

Thus, on poorer quality soils where the impact of increased productive inputs on soil productivity is negligible, that is, $f_{21} \to 0$, yet their impact on soil degradation, h_1, is high, one would expect an increase in c_1 to be an incentive for investments to control soil erosion over the long run.

An increase in the costs of soil conservation inputs, c_2, shifts up both the $A = 0$ and $B = 0$ curves, increasing the value of the soil over the long run. The final impact on soil erosion again depends on the relative impact on soil degradation compared to the impact on soil productivity; that is,

$$dx^* \lesseqqgtr 0 \quad \text{if } h_1 z_{1c2} + h_2 z_{2c2} \gtreqqless -pf_{21} z_{1c2}. \tag{7.18}$$

For most of the uplands on Java, one would expect conditions leading to a long-run increase in soil erosion ($dx^* < 0$). Thus, it is clear why most upland soil conservation projects have chosen to subsidize some of the inputs, particularly for farm labour, needed for conservation measures (see Section 2).[10]

Notes

1. Many studies emphasize the importance of off-site impacts of upland soil erosion in tropical and sub-tropical watersheds that result from siltation, water flow irregularities and agrochemical run-off (Easter, Dixon, and Hufschmidt, 1986; Gregerson *et al.*, 1986; Veloz *et al.*, 1985). A recent study for Java estimated the on-site crop productivity losses from man-made soil

erosion on upland farms to be around US$320 million annually, compared to the additional off-site sedimentation costs of US$25–90 million (Magrath and Arens, 1987).

2. In addition, bench terraces frequently collapse on limestone-based subsoils containing bentonite clay. During periods of peak rainfall, inappropriately bench-terraced fields can lose just as much, if not more, soil than adjacent fields cultivated using traditional methods (nearly similar to ridge terracing) (Fagi and Mackie, 1987).
3. Assuming a four-month dry season and a holding of 0.5 hectares (ha), a single farmer could provide a maximum of 100 mandays (MD) each dry season; however, this is far short of the terracing requirements of approximately 375 (low slope) to over 900 (steep slopes) MD/0.5 ha holding (Table 7.1). Alternatively, during a 100-working-day period, a farmer could only terrace 0.14 ha of low slope and 0.06 ha of steep slope (Bernsten and Sinaga, 1983).
4. One advantage of a livestock-based system is that owning small ruminants provides an opportunity for the household to use its own, often child, labour which has a low opportunity cost. Thus, by establishing grass intensively on terraces, households are able either to raise a greater number of animals with the same labour input or raise the same number of animals with perhaps only 20 per cent of the labour input required to feed small ruminants by cutting grass along roadways and on other public land (Bernsten and Sinaga, 1983) For example, preliminary evidence from the Kali Konto project in East Java indicates that, with terraces already established, a farming household can significantly raise productivity from animal husbandry with a relatively small additional investment in terms of labour and material costs (Dwiwarsito and de Graff, 1987).
5. See the analysis in the appendix and notes 8 and 9.
6. The full version of the model presented here can be found in Barbier (1988), which provides details on the underlying assumptions and analysis.
7. Where crop outputs or inputs are non-marketed, such as food produced for subsistence, in-kind inputs, labour exchange, and so on, $p(t)$, $c_1(t)$, and $c_2(t)$ represent the relevant shadow prices and costs, respectively.
8. Note that in his model, McConnell (1983) also includes a terminal resale value of the farm, $R(x)$, as part of the net value of the farm to be incorporated in the objective function. Thus, McConnell argues that a strong bequest motive or a smoothly functioning capital market induces the farmer to value $R(x)$ as part of his income stream. The capital markets in upland Java, however, do not operate 'smoothly', as evidenced by informal lending rates of around 60 per cent per annum (World Bank, 1987a). Similarly, with hereditary land rights and tenure arrangements, and with virtually all members of the household having a 'stake' in the current and future profitability of the land, the household may be more interested in the present value of the stream of profits in perpetuity rather than its resale value by a certain time T. This is the assumption underlying the model here.
9. A permanent increase in the discount rate, r, can be interpreted as an increase in the marginal opportunity cost of capital for farming households. An increase in r is therefore tantamount to a rise in the cost of credit available to the farmer for investment. However, there may be complicating factors caused by the absence of a credit market. For example, if farmers are unable to borrow, then there is no longer a relation between the rate of time preferences of farmers and their marginal value of capital, unless there is some sort of internal market for allocating funds within each farm household. I am grateful to Kenneth E. McConnell for pointing out this complication.
10. The original model (Barbier, 1988) also includes a comparative static analysis of the impact of population growth on the incentives for upland farming households to control soil degradation. The assumption is that changes in productive inputs, dz_1, and in conservation inputs, dz_2, represent changes in the input of labour in cultivation and soil conservation respectively. Alternatively, an explicit constraint on the supply of labour could be included in the model, some of which would be allocated to cultivation as opposed to conservation. This would yield the same results at the margin, but would show more explicitly the relative labour demands and costs of the two packages. Such an approach could be usefully extended to include the allocation of labour to off-farm employment.

References

Barbier, Edward B. (1987), 'Natural resources policy and economic framework'. in: James Tarrant *et al.* (eds), *Natural Resources and Environmental Management in Indonesia*, Annex 1. Jakarta: USAID.

Barbier, Edward B. (1988), *The Economics of Farm-Level Adoption of Soil Conservation Measures in the Uplands of Java*, Environment Department Working Paper No. 11, Washington, DC: World Bank.

Bernsten, R. and R. Sinaga (1983), 'Economics', Technical Appendix VI, Government of Indonesia/USAID, *Composite Report of the Watershed Assessment Team*, Jakarta: GOI/USAID.

Carson, Brian (1987), *A Comparison of Soil Conservation Strategies in Four Agroecological Zones in the Upland of East Java*, Malang: KEPAS.

Carson, Brian and Hadi Utomo (1986), *Erosion and Sedimentation Processes in Java*, Malang: KEPAS.

Donner, Wolf (1987), *Land Use and Environment in Indonesia*, London: C. Hurst & Co.

Dwiwarsito, Kurianto and Jan de Graaff (1987), *Economic Impact of Watershed Development Activities at the Village Level*, Malang: Kali Konto Project.

Easter, K. William, John A. Dixon and Maynard Hufschmidt (eds) (1986), *Watershed Resource Management: An Integrated Framework with Studies from Asia and the Pacific*, Boulder, CO: Westview Press.

Fagi, Achmad M. and Cynthia Mackie (1987), 'Watershed management in the uplands of Java: past experience and future directions', Paper presented at SCSA Conference on Soil and Water Conservation on Steep Lands, San Juan, Puerto Rico.

Gregersen, H.M., K.N. Brooks, John A. Dixon and Lawrence S. Hamilton (1986), *Guidelines for Economic Appraisal of Watershed Management Projects*, Rome: FAO.

KEPAS (1985), *The Critical Uplands of Eastern Java: An Agroecosystem Analysis*, Jakarta: KEPAS/AARD.

Kucera, Karl, *et al.* (1986), *Micro Model Farm Assessment of Land Resources*, Citanduy: Dept. of Forestry and USAID.

Lopez, Ramon and Mario Nicklitschek (1988), 'Notes for a research proposal on the interactions of natural resources and agricultural growth in sub-Saharan Africa: trade policy implications'. Draft proposal, World Bank, Washington, DC.

Magrath, William B. and Peter Arens (1987), 'The costs of soil erosion on Java – A natural resource accounting approach', Draft report, World Resources Institute, Washington, DC.

McConnell, Kenneth E. (1983), 'An economic model of soil conservation', *American Journal of Agricultural Economics*, **65** (February), 83–9.

Roche, Frederick C. (1987), 'Sustainable farm development in Java's critical lands: is a "Green Revolution" really necessary?', Department of Economics, Cornell University.

Saragih, Bugaran, Paul C. Huszar and Harold C. Cochrane (1986), *Model Farm Program Benefits: The Citanduy Watershed*, Jakarta: USAID.

Southgate, Douglas and David W. Pearce (1987), 'Natural resource degradation in developing countries: a causal analysis of agricultural colonisation', Discussion Paper 87–26, Department of Economics, University College, London.

Sumitro, Achmad (1983), 'Tree Crop Management', Technical Appendix V, Government of Indonesia/USAID, *Composite Report of the Watershed Assessment Team*, Vol. 3, Jakarta: USAID.

Tampubolon, S.M.H. and Bungaran Saragih (1986), 'Model farm upland farming technology in the Citanduy river basin: a state of the art', Draft report, USESE, Ciamis, Indonesia.

Tatuh, Jen (1987), 'Credits for soil conservation and dryland farming development in upper Citanduy watershed region', Draft report, USESE, Ciamis, Indonesia.

Veloz, Alberto, Douglas Southgate, F. Hitzhusen and Robert Macgregor (1985), 'The economics of erosion control in a subtropical watershed: a Dominican case', *Land Economics*, **61** (May), 145–55.

Williams, David (1987), 'Indonesia: investment strategies, management of natural resources, the urban sector', Draft paper, World Bank, Washington, DC.

World Bank (1987a), *Indonesia – Agricultural Incentive Policies: Issues and Options*, Vol. 1. Washington, DC: World Bank.

World Bank (1987b), *Indonesia – Java Watersheds: Java Uplands and Watershed Management*, Washington, DC: World Bank.

World Bank (1988), *Indonesia – Forests, Land and Water Issues in Sustainable Development*, Washington, DC: World Bank.

8. Rehabilitating gum arabic systems in Sudan: economic and environmental implications

Abstract
The economic and environmental benefits of gum arabic production in the Sudano – Sahelian zone appear attractive. However, the farm-level economics of gum arabic production is complex. and much more needs to be understood about the economic–environmental interactions determining farmers' gum cropping. The following chapter explores these issues in Sudan, through a crop profitability analysis of gum and other crops combined with financial and economic analyses of six representative gum arabic production systems. Although the returns from gum compare favourably with other crops in Sudan, essential investments by farmers in cultivating gum will depend on its real producer price being maintained and other incentives determining the relative profitability of gum.

1. Direct and indirect benefits of gum cultivation

Gum arabic, the gum produced by the *Acacia senegal* species of the Sahelian–Sudanian zone, is widely sought after in industrialized countries for use in confectionary and beverages, pharmaceutical, artistic materials, photography, lithography, printing and pesticides. It is produced mainly in Sudan, and is that country's second largest export, earning over US$65 million in 1987 (Bank of Sudan, 1988).[1]

Acacia senegal trees produce gum when they are 4–15 years old. Although there are large-scale private and public gum arabic plantations in the Eastern Provinces, most production occurs in the 'gum belt' proper of Central and Western Sudan, in sandy (*goz*) soils under water-scarce 'desert' conditions. In these areas, small farmers cultivate *A. senegal* in scattered gum gardens or as part of a 15–25 year 'bush-fallow' rotation with other crops Under these systems, *A. senegal* serves a variety of valuable economic and ecological functions in addition to gum production. These can be distinguished into *direct* (production) and *indirect* (environmental) benefits:

Direct benefits

- *fodder* for cattle, as well as sheep, goats and camels, who will also eat the pods of the tree;
- *fuelwood*, and in some instances, *charcoal*, from older trees (15 years or more) that no longer produce significant or good quality gum.

Indirect benefits

- *soil erosion/runoff reduction* – the deep tap root of the gum arabic tree and its extensive lateral root system means that it is the preferred species

in bush-fallow rotation and intercropping farming systems prevalent in the arid West of Sudan;
- *nitrogen fixation*, which encourages grassy growth for grazing of livestock, particularly of value to silvo-pastoral sedentary farming systems in Eastern Sudan and to some nomadic systems in the West;[2]
- *wind breaks* and *dune fixation*, reducing the risk of wind erosion;
- *desertification buffer* – as the tree can exist under extreme climatic conditions, easily tolerant of an annual average rainfall of less than 300 mm and of substantial rainfall and temperature variations, over wide stretches of the Northern Sudanian–Sahelian zone the presence of a gum arabic 'belt' helps to 'hold back' desertification.

The following chapter provides several different analyses of the economic benefits of gum arabic systems in Sudan. The next section briefly overviews previous financial and economic analyses of gum systems and points out the difficulties in analyzing the wider 'environmental' benefits of gum production. In Section 3, a crop profitability analysis of gum production for the whole of Sudan is conducted to indicate Sudanese farmers' comparative advantage in producing the crop. Such an analysis is important because, even if there are significant environmental advantages to growing the crop, it does not necessarily follow that farmers in Sudan find that they have a comparative advantage in cultivating gum relative to other crops. Sections 4 and 5 provide more in-depth financial and economic analyses of six representative gum arabic production systems from surveys conducted in different regions of Sudan. The analyses quantify the returns from the *direct production* benefits – gum, fuelwood and fodder – of growing *A. senegal*, plus the returns from cultivating other crops within the systems. In Section 6, the *indirect environmental* benefits of gum arabic trees are discussed but not quantified, although a distinction is made between benefits such as soil erosion/runoff reduction and nitrogen fixation, which are to some extent 'internalized' through maintaining or enhancing the yields of field crops within the system and more 'external' benefits such as dune fixation and large-scale desertification control. Section 7 concludes the chapter by summarizing the policy implications of the various analyses.

2. Previous analyses of gum systems

The total direct benefits to farmers of gum arabic planting can be significant. For example, based on a 16-year rotation, Pearce (1988) estimated the private, or financial, internal rate of return from gum, fuelwood and fodder production to be around 36 per cent.[3] For a typical bush-fallow system of Northern Kordofan province, consisting of gum trees rotated or intercropped with sesame, groundnuts, millet and sorghum, Sharawi (1986) calculated a positive financial net present value (NPV) for both gum arabic and fuelwood production alone for the entire system. The financial NPV for the bush-fallow system as a whole was Sudanese pounds 142.6 per feddan (1 feddan = 4200 m^2).

However, these favourable estimates of the financial returns from gum arabic offer no guarantee that the farmer will, in fact, undertake gum production. This decision will depend on what returns can be obtained from other crops and the time profile of these returns. Clearly the longer it takes to obtain the benefits, the less likely it is that a farmer, impatient for immediate returns, will be willing to undertake that activity, even if the future returns are high (Barbier, Markandya and Pearce, 1990). Many of the small farmers undertaking gum production in the gum belt are relatively poor and face significant opportunity costs of obtaining funds for investment. Their private rates of time preference, and therefore their private discount rates, are presumably very high. The tendency may be to prefer the immediate financial returns of annual cropping over the high cost of 'waiting' for the eventual gains from gum arabic production.

The potentially high financial rate of return to a gum-arabic based farming system coupled with its important environmental benefits would seem to imply that such a system would be ideal for combating desert encroachment and rehabilitating the gum belt. However, it does not necessarily follow that under conventional cost–benefit criteria, the NPV to a gum arabic planting project would be high or even positive, when the financial analysis is extended to an economic analysis.[4] Even for projects such as gum arabic rehabilitation where positive environmental benefits are known to be substantial, they may be difficult to value, and in any case, be offset by conventional discounting procedures, as these positive benefits are often more significant in long rather than short term (Barbier *et al*., 1990).

Sharawi (1986) uses an economic analysis to estimate the NPV of an 'ideal' rotation system for proposed gum arabic rehabilitation in Northern Kordofan. Each farmer is given a piece of land which totals 50 feddans (21 hectares) divided as follows:

10 feddans under agricultural crops
10 feddans under gum crop (age 16–20 years)
10 feddans under gum crop (age 11–15 years)
10 feddans under gum crop (age 6–10 years)
10 feddans under fallow (age 1–5 years).

In any one year, the farmer would have one plot of agricultural crops (for example, sesame, groundnuts, millet and sorghum), 3 plots producing gum and one plot under regeneration. Felling, yielding fuelwood, would be carried out every 5 years. The author compares the NPV from such a system of farming with that obtained from the typical bush-fallow system already in operation in Northern Kordofan. Also assessed was the NPV of a project to raise *A. senegal* in an irrigated scheme of 22 feddans (9.24 ha) in Rahad, Central Region. The NPVs of both the bush fallow and irrigated schemes were calculated with a shadow price of gum of 0.12 (assumes world demand for gum has a price elasticity of –1.13) and a shadow price of 1.0 (assumes the world demand for gum is perfectly elastic).[5] The analysis shows that (a) the improvement of the bush-fallow system in Northern Kordofan is marginal, depending critically on the shadow price of gum, and (b) the irrigation scheme in Rahad is economically not viable.

However, both these conclusions might not be correct if the environmental benefits associated with gum production were included. Since 'as far as N. Kordofan is concerned, agricultural production cannot be taken separately from the products of *A. senegal* since they are closely linked' (Sharawi, 1986, p. 125), the author assumes that the returns to crop production over the 20-year rotation period 'reflect' the indirect environmental benefits of gum arabic planting in terms of maintaining soil stability and fertility, water retention, dune stabilization and wind protection. Only the (considerable) social value of the gum belt as a buffer zone against desertification, and any 'external' impacts on neighbouring production systems of any other environmental benefits, cannot be captured.

However, there will always be some doubt as to how many of, or to what extent, these benefits are in fact 'internalized'. To demonstrate whether this is the case requires taking account of the differential yields of crops when calculating the NPVs of each system. As the accurate measurement of this differential is itself difficult, it is unlikely that the issue has been adequately dealt with in the analysis. A more direct approach would be to attempt to value each of the environmental benefits – soil stabilization, nitrogen fixation, dune fixation and anti-desertification – and then include them in the calculation of NPV. In an appraisal of rural afforestation in Northern Nigeria, Anderson (1987) demonstrates how this analysis can be conducted. Such an approach, however, is often hampered by the lack of reliable data (Barbier *et al.*, 1990). The difficulties in valuing the wider environmental benefits of gum arabic cultivation and the implications for economic analysis are discussed further in Section 6, below.

Another difficulty arises from comparing an 'ideal' with a 'typical' bush-fallow system. Such a comparison may be misleading, because cultivation systems in Sudan are extremely diverse and variable in gum production – and may even differ significantly within a gum belt region. Gum cultivation may not always be interspersed with crop production as part of a bush-fallow rotation system. A survey of three village areas in North-Central Kordofan region – El Khuwei, Mazroub-Tinna and Muglad – revealed that, although the majority of hashab owners adopt a shifting cultivation approach to gum production, with the trees dispersed among crops, many owners also have consolidated gum gardens that are cultivated independently of crops. Moreover, this pattern of gum production varied significantly from village to village. In El Khuwei 58.5 per cent of hashab owners had consolidated gum gardens, whereas in Mazroub-Tinna 35.3 per cent and in Muglad only 15.8 per cent had consolidated gardens (El Sammani, 1985, pp. 175–7). Thus in the financial and economic analyses presented in Sections 4 and 5, several types of systems rather than one single 'representative' gum system are appraised.

3. Crop profitability analysis

A crop profitability analysis comparing gum arabic to other major crops produced in Sudan is useful because:

- it indicates the profitability to the farmer of producing a particular crop if he or she were able to export it at the estimated world price, less the estimated marketing costs from Port Sudan to the farmer's region, and
- it can be used to calculate the domestic resource cost (DRC) of each crop, and thus Sudanese farmers' comparative advantage in producing the crop; for example, at a realistic exchange rate, a DRC ratio of less than 1 would suggest that such a comparative advantage exists for Sudan.[6]

A crop profitability analysis of the major crops in Northern Sudan has been conducted by Jansen (1989). Crops under irrigation in two areas of the Central Region, Gezira and Rahad, were analysed. as well as mechanized rainfed production of sesame, sorghum and sunflower in Gedaref, Kassala Province, traditional production of groundnuts, sesame and sorghum in Southern Darfur and traditional production of gum arabic near El Obeid, Kordofan. Two analyses for gum arabic and its major substitute crops were undertaken. One was based on an exchange rate of LS 6.5/US$ for revenue and LS 4.5/US$ for costs and is essentially a *financial* analysis of crop profitability. The other was based on an *economic* analysis, which adjusted the financial or market values to remove all taxes and subsidies and employed an estimated 'shadow' exchange rate of LS 9.0/US$. The DRC ratios generated by the analyses indicates that Sudan does have a strong comparative advantage in sesame, traditional groundnut and gum arabic cultivation, at either actual or shadow exchange rates. In contrast, there was no comparative advantage in growing sorghum on rainfed lands, and mechanized sunflower cultivation was only marginally efficient.

In 1989 the commercial, as opposed to the official, exchange rate for the Sudanese pound was LS 12.5/US$. Table 8.1 therefore re-calculates Jansen's crop profitability analysis taking into account the commercial exchange rate. In addition, Table 8.1 shows the *actual* farmgate profit received by farmers, rather than *border-equivalent* net returns. According to the analysis, only mechanized and traditionally cultivated sesame appears to yield a financial profit for farmers.[7] However, the DRC ratios show that Sudan has a comparative advantage

Table 8.1 *Relative crop profitability – Sudan. Gum arabic and major substitute crops, 1989–90 (actual exchange rate LS 12.5/$)*

	Sorghum		Groundnuts[a]	Sesame		Sunflower[b]	
	Mechanized Gedaref	Trad. So. Darfur	Trad. So. Darfur	Mechanized Gedaref	Trad. So. Darfur	Mechanized Gedaref	Gum Arabic El Obeid
Yield (KG/F)	360.00	180.00	161.00	150.00	80.00	300.00	20.00
Producer Price (LS/KG)	0.67[c]	0.67	1.11	4.00	3.30	1.46	9.46[d]
Output Value (LS/F)	240.00	120.00	179.29	600.00	264.00	436.76	189.19
Production Cost (LS/F)	430.36	257.44	356.76	356.56	159.07	839.75	297.62
Net Profit (LS/F)	−190.36	−137.44	−177.50	243.44	104.93	−402.98	−108.42
Border Price ($/KG)	0.12	0.12	0.33	0.49	0.49	0.21	2.80
Border Value ($/F)	41.40	20.70	53.13	73.50	39.20	63.00	56.00
Border Value (LS/F)	517.50	258.75	664.13	918.75	490.00	787.50	700.00
Production Cost (LS/F):	430.36	257.44	356.78	356.56	159.07	839.75	297.62
Traded inputs	227.69	39.06	124.94	175.58	29.67	559.31	7.08
Non-traded inputs[e]	202.67	218.39	231.84	180.97	129.41	280.44	290.53
Marketing Cost (LS/F):	67.37	115.68	184.88	190.79	127.48	175.32	72.17
Traded	55.10	76.85	61.96	33.62	39.79	63.08	3.37
Non-traded[e]	12.28	38.83	122.92	157.18	87.70	112.25	68.81
Total Cost (LS/F)	497.73	373.12	541.66	547.35	286.56	1015.07	369.79
Int'l Value Added (LS/F)	234.71	142.85	477.22	709.55	420.54	165.12	689.55
Domestic Resources (LS/F)	214.94	257.22	354.76	338.15	217.10	392.69	359.34
DRC Ratio[f]	0.92	1.80	0.74	0.48	0.52	2.38	0.52

Notes:
[a] Assumes entire groundnut crop is exported as Ashford nuts. [b] Assumes entire sunflower crop is exported as seeds. [c] Price of sorghum is LS60 per 90 kg sack (IES survey data). [d] Price of gum arabic LS425 per kantar (44.9 kg), El Obeid auction prices Feb. 1989. [e] Costs of non-traded items assumed to increase by 20% over 1988–89. [f] The DRC ratio is the ratio of domestic resource costs to International Value Added in Sudanese pounds. If less than 1 it indicates that Sudan has a comparative advantage in producing the crop.
LS = Sudanese pounds; KG = kilogram; F = feddan (1 feddan = 0.42 Hectares); $ = US Dollars.

Source: Calculated from data in Jansen (1989), unless otherwise indicated.

Table 8.2 Relative crop profitability – Sudan. Gum arabic and major substitute crops, 1989–90 (shadow exchange rate LS 21.5/$)

	Sorghum Mechanized Gedaref	Sorghum Trad. So. Darfur	Groundnuts[a] Trad. So. Darfur	Sesame Mechanized Gedaref	Sesame Trad. So. Darfur	Sunflower[b] Mechanized Gedaref	Gum Arabic El Obeid
Yield	360.00	180.00	1671.00	150.00	80.00	300.00	20.00
Producer Price (LS/KG)[c]	3.10	1.70	6.05	9.38	8.97	3.97	56.47
Output Value (LS/F)	1116.73	306.12	974.20	1406.37	717.92	1189.70	1129.41
Production Cost (LS/F)	611.23	248.32	667.19	466.82	153.73	754.31	225.34
Net Profit (LS/F)	505.51	57.81	307.01	939.55	564.20	435.39	904.06
Border Price ($/KG)	0.12	0.12	0.33	0.49	0.49	0.21	2.80
Border Value ($/F)	41.40	20.70	53.13	73.50	39.20	63.00	56.00
Border Value (LS/F)	890.10	445.05	1142.30	1580.25	842.80	1354.50	1204.00
Production Cost (LS/F):	611.23	248.32	667.19	466.82	153.73	754.31	225.34
Traded inputs	391.04	30.22	206.08	288.23	24.44	469.78	6.09
Non-traded inputs[d]	220.19	218.10	461.11	178.58	129.29	284.53	219.25
Marketing Cost (LS/F):	82.96	110.28	168.09	173.86	110.04	164.79	72.99
Traded	73.46	74.46	78.83	45.06	38.53	81.12	4.18
Non-traded[d]	9.50	35.82	89.26	128.80	71.51	83.66	68.81
Total Cost (LS/F)	694.19	358.60	835.28	640.67	263.76	919.10	298.33
Int'l Value Added (LS/F)	425.60	340.37	857.38	1246.96	779.83	803.59	1193.73
Domestic Resources (LS/F)	229.69	253.92	550.37	307.38	200.80	368.20	288.06
DRC Ratio[e]	0.54	0.75	0.64	0.25	0.26	0.46	0.24

Notes:
[a] Assumes entire groundnut crop is exported as Ashford nuts. [b] Assumes entire sunflower crop is exported as seeds. [c] Economic border-equivalent farmgate price. [d] Costs of non-traded items assumed to increase by 20% over 1988–89. [e] The DRC ratio is the ratio of domestic resource costs to International Value Added in Sudanese pounds. If less than 1 it indicates that Sudan has a comparative advantage in producing the crop.

Source: Calculated from data in Jansen (1989), unless otherwise indicated.

not only in rainfed sesame production but also in groundnut and gum arabic cultivation. Mechanized sorghum is only marginally efficient.

The shadow exchange rate for Sudan was also re-calculated. Using a conversion ratio of 1.72, this yields a rate of exchange of LS 21.5/US$.[8] Table 8.2 shows the result of applying this rate, as well as adjusted market (shadow) prices, to the crop profitability analysis. The net profit calculation is now in terms of border-equivalent farmgate prices. All crops are now economically profitable. The DRC ratios show that Sudan also has a comparative advantage in all crops. The relatively low DRC ratio for gum arabic indicates that Sudan can produce it efficiently compared to its rainfed substitute crops.

In sum, although Sudanese farmers can make losses on gum cultivation – at least in the case of the El Obeid example shown here – the crop is economically profitable and efficient for Sudan to produce. It also compares well against the returns to its major substitute crops. Of the rival crops, only sesame appears to make a profit for the farmer at actual prices, yet gum arabic is economically more profitable and efficient when full shadow prices are employed (Table 8.2). This would suggest that gum arabic production would greatly benefit from bringing actual farmgate prices more in line with border-equivalent prices, as well as further devaluing the exchange rate. This is not surprising, given that the output is totally exported, yet the overwhelming proportion of production costs is composed of non-traded inputs.

However, the drawback to a crop profitability analysis is that it only indicates comparative profitability on a single year's basis. No indication of the discounted returns over time is possible. In addition, the crops are analysed in isolation, whereas farmers actually cultivate multi-crop farming systems – and choose how much to grow of each crop on the basis of its relative profitability within the system. Thus an analysis of the returns to different farming systems over time is also required.

4. Financial analysis of cropping systems in Sudan

The following financial analysis is based on six different cropping systems surveyed by consultants in January–March 1989 as part of the Gum Arabic Rehabilitation Project (IIED and IES, 1990). They can be considered 'representative' systems containing gum arabic cultivation from the East and West Blue Nile Provinces, North and South Kordofan, and North and South Darfur. However, they are only single examples of the incredible diverse ways in which gum arabic is combined with other crops by farmers throughout the Gum Belt.

Discussion of each system and complete details on its financial analysis can be found in Barbier (1990). Table 8.3 summarizes the results for the six systems, which are distinguished by type of soil (clay or sandy) and size of holding (large or small). The distinction in soils is particularly important, for it affects gum arabic

Table 8.3 Summary of financial analyses of six cropping systems – Sudan (1988–89 market prices)

	Net present value (10%) per feddan[a]					
	A. Senegal[b]	Sorghum	Millet	Groundnut	Sesame	Total
Blue Nile (clay soil, largeholder)	334.41	588.85	232.80	–	–	1156.06
White Nile (sandy soil, smallholder, drought area, pest damage)	258.88	–1507.44	–1088.16	–231.16	19.92	–2547.96
North Kordofan (sandy soil, smallholder, drought area, bush fallow rotation)	56.32	–	–117.37	–	307.17	246.12
South Kordofan (clay soil, largeholder, water scarcity)	80.75	–585.94	–	601.34	1375.00	1471.15
North Darfur sandy soil, smallholder, drought area)	87.19	–	–407.94	–909.90	–	–1230.65
South Darfur (sandy soil, smallholder, drought area)	95.35	–1180.31	–403.65	–725.67	–	–2214.28
All systems (average)	152.15	–671.21	–356.86	–316.35	567.36	–519.93

Notes:
[a] 1 feddan = 0.42 hectares. [b] Total NPV from gum, fuelwood and fodder, except for Blue Nile and South Kordofan (gum only).

Source: Barbier (1990).

cultivation and uses considerably. For example, on clay soils gum arabic trees usually stop producing after their twelfth year and are generally not used for either fodder or fuelwood. In contrast, gum arabic can easily be grown on sandy soils in a sixteen-year rotation. In years 7–16 they also produce useful fodder, and at the end of the cycle (year 16) they are cut down for fuelwood.

As shown in Table 8.3, all six financial analyses indicate that the total benefits from gum cultivation are positive. That is, there are real financial benefits to farmers from growing gum in many diverse systems across the gum belt. Such a result is critically dependent on the real producer price of gum being maintained, however. For example, only when the government-determined floor price of gum arabic was raised to LS 400 per *kantar* (44.9 kg) in 1989 did gum producers find it remunerative to tap and pick their existing mature stands. As the above analysis of complete gum cycles shows, if the current price is maintained in real terms, it can be sufficient incentive for farmers actually to *re-establish* gum production in some drought-affected areas of the gum belt. Moreover, in the *goz* (sandy soil) systems, the fuelwood and fodder benefits of growing gum arabic trees are also significant. In the bush-fallow rotation system of North Kordofan, the financial NPV of gum production alone is actually negative, and it is the fuelwood and fodder benefits that make the total NPV from *A. senegal* cultivation positive.[9] In the South Darfur system, poor annual crop performance means that gum arabic cultivation is the only activity that has positive returns.

The above analysis also indicates that sesame production appears extremely profitable across the rainfed areas of Sudan, confirming the analysis of Tables 8.1 and 8.2. It may pose the most immediate threat to gum production, although it may be more variable to climatic and other environmental factors and thus be a more risky crop. For example, in the farming system at Tendelti, White Nile, sesame yields are poor due to the vagaries of climate and due to bird, camel and locust damage. The more steady income gum cultivation is necessary to offset these losses from sesame and other crop production. The analysis of the other cropping systems had insufficient data to take into account the possible impacts of environmental and climatic factors, which may be why the NPVs for sesame are generally so high. In addition, there can be indirect environment benefits of farmers intercropping sesame with gum. This is certainly the case of the North Kordofan bush-fallow rotation system, where rotation with hashab trees helps to maintain soil structure and water retention. Thus for a variety of reasons farmers may be reluctant to substitute sesame for gum cultivation in rainfed areas, even if the relative financial returns to sesame are attractive.

The returns to groundnut production appear more variable in the four systems containing the crop. On the sandy soils, the returns are surprisingly negative. This would suggest that groundnut production in these areas has become less of a threat to gum cultivation; in recent years as the price of gum has increased, groundnut prices have remained insufficiently remunerative for farmers in low-yielding areas. This again confirms the analysis of Tables 8.1 and 8.2. In contrast, as the analysis in South Kordofan shows, a largeholder on clay soils is capable of growing groundnuts very profitably, which explains the rapid expansion of groundnut (and sesame) production in these rainfed areas. In this system, gum yields are low due to the lack of water for the labour hired to tap and pick gum, which suggests that some gum arabic land may not be replanted after the cycle but converted to groundnut and sesame cultivation.

The poor returns to the food crops, millet and sorghum, both question the viability of these crops in rainfed areas and government policies to promote their cultivation. This conclusion particularly for traditional cultivation of sorghum is also highlighted by Tables 8.1 and 8.2. The smallholders on sandy soils are clearly growing these crops primarily to meet subsistence needs and to provide food to hired labour. These needs appear paramount, and the farmers may be willing to 'subsidize the losses made on these crops from their more profitable cash crops. Gum arabic appears to have an important function in this regard, particularly as its tapping and picking occurs after the normal cropping season and before the next planting of annual crops. Although the two food crops appear to fare better in the large-holding clay soil systems, the case of South Kordofan illustrated how declining yields over time, which can afflict mechanized sorghum growing and are expected to occur in this system, will seriously affect profitability.

5. Economic analysis of cropping systems in Sudan

An economic analysis of the six gum arabic cropping systems was also conducted through adjusting financial or market values and applying the border-equivalent farmgate prices. The NPVs per feddan for each of the six systems, calculated at a discount rate of 10 per cent, are summarized in Table 8.4.

The economic analysis generally confirms the short-run analysis of Table 8.3. All six systems are economically profitable if market values are adjusted and the shadow exchange rate of LS 21.5/$ is applied. All individual crops within these systems are also economically profitably, except for sorghum in Tendelti, White Nile. In all six systems, the foreign exchange component of costs is very low. Economic costs are therefore not significantly higher than actual costs for most crops. However, adjusting prices to their border-equivalent values leads to a major increase in revenues. The result is a substantial improvement in NPVs over the financial analysis.

The economic NPV for gum arabic is generally lower than that of other crops, except in the Tendelti system of the White Nile province where field crop damage occurs frequently. One reason for the relatively low returns for gum arabic is that, in most systems, there are initial losses made due to the need to establish gum gardens. At a positive discount rate, such as 10 per cent, these

Table 8.4 Summary of economic analyses of six cropping systems – Sudan (1988–89 border-equivalent farmgate and adjusted prices)

	Net present value (10%) per feddan[a]					
	A. Senegal[b]	Sorghum	Millet	Groundnut	Sesame	Total
Blue Nile (clay soil, largeholder)	2989.57	4606.83	2931.58	–	–	10 527.98
White Nile (sandy soil, smallholder, drought area, pest damage)	3923.82	–432.99	486.30	5 330.92	8 605.12	17 913.17
North Kordofan (sandy soil, smallholder, drought area, bush drought area, bush fallow rotation)	1471.36	–	2091.77	–	6 020.94	9 584.07
South Kordofan (clay soil, largeholder, water scarcity)	882.90	1644.44	–	13 109.44	13 776.95	24 913.82
North Darfur (sandy soil, smallholder, drought area)	1240.87	–	2363.89	9 687.69	–	13 292.45
South Darfur	1884.02	3830.80	3775.60	9 715.61	–	19 206.03
All systems (average)	2065.44	2412.27	2329.83	9 460.92	9 467.67	16 656.25

Notes:
[a] 1 feddan = 0.42 hectares. [b] Total NPV from gum, fuelwood and fodder, except for Blue and South Kordofan (gum only).

Source: Barbier (1990).

initial losses will inevitably carry more weight in the NPV calculation. Note also that the returns of the fuelwood and fodder benefits of hashab trees are relatively lower in the calculation of total *A. senegal* economic production benefits. This is inevitable when border-equivalent values are employed, given that gum arabic is a tradeable good whereas fuelwood and fodder are non-tradeable.

In the previous section it was noted that many farmers – particularly in traditional systems – grow millet and sorghum primarily to meet subsistence needs and to provide food for hired labour. The two crops are therefore often grown at a *financial* loss. However, as indicated in Table 8.4, the positive *economic* returns to sorghum and millet in virtually all systems suggest that this is not necessarily an inefficient approach. Only where food crops are subject to severe environmental and climatic stress (for example, Tendelti, White Nile), are they both unprofitable and uneconomical to grow in traditional systems. Although the economic returns from mechanized farming of the food crops appear to be generally higher than from the traditional systems, there are some exceptions (for example, South Darfur), and the performance of the mechanized and semi-mechanized schemes is conditional on the high yields being maintained. Thus the analysis is not conclusive on whether the mechanized systems yield higher economic returns from growing food crops than the traditional systems.

The analysis confirms that there are high economic returns for growing sesame and groundnuts on rainfed lands in Sudan. In the case of groundnuts, the high economic NPV across all systems contrasts with the *actual losses* being made in three of the four systems cultivating the crop (compare Tables 8.3 and 8.4). This would suggest that current government pricing and procurement policies for groundnuts may be severely distorting the incentives for farmers to cultivate the crop. There may be a possible trade-off here: to some extent, improved incentives for cultivating groundnuts may encourage dryland farmers to convert land previously under gum cultivation – with detrimental consequences in terms of land degradation. On the other hand, the higher the income from growing groundnuts may increase the economic opportunities of poor farmers and reduce overall pressure on marginal lands.

Sesame also yields high economic returns, as well as being financially profitable (Tables 8.3 and 8.4). This would suggest that distortions in the sesame market may be less severe than for groundnuts. However, not included in the analysis of groundnuts or sesame is the high risk factor associated with growing these crops from climatic and environmental variations.

In conclusion, the economic analysis of the six cropping systems would suggest that the economic returns from growing the cash crops sesame and groundnuts are substantially higher on a per feddan basis than for gum arabic or the food crops millet and sorghum. However, this does not necessarily imply that land under the food crops and *A. senegal* should be shifted to cultivate the cash crops. In the case of sorghum and millet, it is clear that in traditional systems cultivating some food crops may be a necessity. The economic analysis reveals that, even where this is not financially profitable, it can be economically efficient. In the mechanized and semi-mechanized systems, the cash crops may not be so amenable to mechanization as the food crops, especially sorghum. Thus whole-scale conversion of land under millet and sorghum to cultivating sesame and groundnuts may not always be possible.

It may not always be desirable or feasible to convert land under *A. senegal* to cultivating groundnuts or cash crops for several reasons.

First, some land under *A. senegal* may not be suitable for growing groundnuts and sesame, resulting in very low and fluctuating yields.

Second, in certain systems, it may be desirable or necessary to hold some land in fallow to maintain its productivity. Both the financial and economic analysis indicate that gum arabic is a profitable and economically efficient crop for this purpose.

Third, although the economic analysis includes the indirect production benefits of *A. senegal*, in terms of fuelwood and fodder, the lack of data prevented any direct valuation of other environmental benefits. In certain systems, particularly involving a closely integrated rotation system or intercropping, the benefits of hashab trees in terms of maintaining soil fertility and water retention do appear economically significant. These benefits may in fact be 'internalized' in terms of maintaining or enhancing the yields of the field crops within the systems. Similarly, the contribution of certain systems' gum gardens to the 'external' benefits of dune fixation and desertification control might also be significant.

Fourth, in some areas the cultivation of groundnuts and sesame might be extremely risky, with yields fluctuating under changing environmental and climatic conditions. Risk-averse farmers may therefore desire some of their land being held under gum cultivation, because the returns to gum – although lower than the maximum expected returns from the cash crops – may be less variable under stressful environmental and climatic conditions.

Finally, gum cultivation provides cash income to farmers outside of the growing season for cash crops. Thus unless the income from cash crops is substantial enough to meet household needs throughout the year, farmers may be reluctant to forego the off-season cash flow from gum cultivation. In the smallholder systems on sandy soils, the fodder and fuelwood provided by *A. senegal* – which would otherwise have to be purchased or collected elsewhere – may be important additional incentives to retain gum stands.

6. Extended economic analysis

The economic analysis of six cropping systems should be extended to include not only the direct production benefits of gum cultivation and of fuelwood and fodder but also the indirect environmental benefits of soil stabilization, water retention and nitrogen fixation, as well as the 'wider' external environmental benefits of dune fixation and anti-desertification.

As discussed previously, the indirect benefits of soil stabilization, water retention and nitrogen fixation may to some extent be 'internalized' in some systems through enhancing or maintaining the yields of field crops. The lack of agro-ecological and biophysical data has made it impossible to measure these indirect benefits or to determine the extent to which they have been 'internalized'. The general assumption would be that to the extent that these indirect benefits are significant, they would tend to be present more readily in those systems involving bush-fallow rotation or close intercropping of gum gardens with field crops. However, further research into these indirect environmental effects across different cropping systems is needed to verify their significance. For example, it is often stated that *A. senegal* has an important nitrogen-fixation effect, but this has never been proven to be scientifically conclusive.

Even less data and research is available on the 'wider' external environmental benefits of dune fixation and anti-desertification. Moreover, the contribution of a single cropping system to the overall external effect may not appear to be that significant, and in case, may be extremely difficult to measure. Further work is therefore required to determine the extent of these effects across systems.

Finally, the financial and economic analyses concentrated only on the cropping systems of the six households. Often, such as in South Darfur, livestock raising is an additionally important component of the overall farming system. In addition. off-farm employment opportunities, such as in Tendelti, White Nile, may provide significant support for the financial viability of the farming system and the household's livelihood. An extended analysis should therefore cover these important aspects of the farming systems as well.

7. Conclusion

Several conclusions emerge from the crop profitability, financial and economic analyses of gum arabic and other rainfed crops in Sudan.

Maintaining the real producer price for gum arabic is crucial to ensuring that farmers have appropriate incentives to rehabilitate and cultivate gum gardens as part of their cropping systems. It is both economically efficient and profitable for Sudan to cultivate gum, which compares favourably with other rainfed crops. Over the long run, maintaining the real producer price is essential for farmers to undertake the important investment decisions necessary to replant and rehabilitate stands; otherwise, other uses of the land, such as for groundnuts and sesame cultivation, may appear more attractive.

However, it is nonetheless important to consider *gum cultivation as part of an integrated cropping system* and not in isolation. As the analysis of the six systems show. across the gum belt gum arabic is one of several crops grown in farming systems. There may be several reasons, other than the direct financial returns, as to why farmers have included gum cultivation as part of their systems. These may range from the need for off-season income, more stable returns, the perception that hashab trees produce beneficial environmental impacts and the need for on-farm supplies of fuelwood and fodder. The total perceived benefits from *A. senegal* are therefore carefully weighed by the farmer against the expected returns and benefits from cash cropping, food cropping, and often from livestock raising and off-farm employment.

Thus, although the analysis suggests that, on the basis of comparative economic returns gum arabic cultivation may in some areas be under threat from groundnut and sesame cultivation, comparative returns may not be the only basis on which crop substitution is made in integrated farming systems. In any case, *maintaining the relative profitability of gum* to other crops should ensure sufficient incentives for farmers to include gum in their farming systems where it is appropriate.

Notes

1. *Acacia seyal*, also widely found in Sudan, produces a similar gum known locally as *talha*. The latter is inferior to gum arabic, however. For example, the market price for gum arabic at El Obeid, Sudan. in 1988/89 was around US$100–110, whereas the price for talha was about US$20–21.
2. It is not proven, however, whether nitrogen-fixation by gum arabic trees increases yields of rotated and intercropped annual crops, although many farmers do believe this to be the case.
3. In fact, the rate of return may be higher still, as Pearce (1988) believes the annual yield rate for fodder production of 11 kg per hectare might be an underestimate.
4. The standard distinction between a financial and an economic analysis is used here. A financial analysis determines the profitability, or returns, to a project or production system using actual market prices, whereas in an economic analysis net returns are determined by valuing all items in terms of their actual opportunity cost to society, or their 'shadow prices', which may differ from their market prices.
5. Gum arabic from Sudan is entirely exported and should therefore be valued at border prices. The conversion factor for adjusting the world price to obtain the shadow price is given by $(1-1/e)$, where e is the foreign elasticity of demand (Squire and van der Tak, 1975). If the demand for Sudanese gum were perfectly elastic on world markets – the assumption being that suppliers from Sudan do not affect world markets – then the conversion factor would therefore be 1. However, if one assumes a price elasticity of −1.13 – indicating that an increase in Sudanese production will raise export earnings – the appropriate conversion factor for the shadow price becomes 0.12. Recent econometric evidence (see IIED and IES, 1990, ch. 6) indicates that the own price elasticity of world demand for gum is considerably lower than one, both in the short and long run. This suggests that increased sales from Sudan actually reduce export earnings. The above formula therefore does not apply, and Sudanese gum should be valued at world prices.
6. The DRC ratio measures the domestic resource costs of earning a unit of foreign exchange. The standard calculation is the ratio of domestic resource costs (that is, domestic marketing costs plus costs of non-traded production inputs) to the international value added in Sudanese pounds (that is, border value of the output less the costs of traded inputs).
7. The loss made on gum arabic cultivation in El Obeid, North Kordofan seems surprising, given its general financial profitability over the long run (see Section 4). The estimates of the costs of non-traded inputs for gum arabic production provided by Jansen (1989) appear to be on the high side, particularly for family labour costs.
8. The standard conversion factor for calculating the shadow exchange rate is based on the formula used by Squire and van der Tak (1975):

$$\text{SCF} = \frac{M+X}{\left(M+T_M+X-T_X\right)},$$

where M = c.i.f. value of imports at current prices (LS 2296.6 million in 1987), X = f.o.b. value of exports (LS 384.9 million in 1987), T_M = net value of taxes on imports at current prices (LS 1027.5 million in international trade taxes plus LS 966.1 million in import duties in 1986/87) and T_X = net value of taxes on exports (LS 61.4 million in 1986/87). This leads to an SCF of 0.58, which implies a shadow exchange rate of 1.72.

9. For the North Kordofan bush-fallow rotation system, the financial NPV (10 per cent) for gum only was –33.61 per feddan, whereas the NPV for fuelwood and fodder was 89.93 per feddan. This indicates one of the advantages of the traditional rotation system in that trees can also he used continuously for fuelwood and fodder production. See Barbier (1990) for details.

References

Anderson, D. (1987), *The Economics of Afforestation*, Occasional Paper No. 1, Washington, DC: The World Bank.

Bank of Sudan (1988), *Bank of Sudan Twenty Eighth Annual Report 1987*, Khartoum: Bank of Sudan.

Barbier, E.B. (1990), *The Economics of Controlling Degradation: Rehabilitating Gum Arabic Systems in Sudan*, LEEC Discussion Paper 90–03, London: London Environmental Economics Centre.

Barbier, E.B., A. Markandya and D.W. Pearce (1990), 'Sustainable agricultural development and project appraisal', *European Review of Agricultural Economics*, **17**, 181–96.

International Institute for Environment and Development (IIED) and Institute for Environmental Studies (IES) (1990), *Gum Arabic Rehabilitation in the Republic of Sudan: Stage I Report*, London: IIED.

Jansen, D.J. (1989), *Crop Profitability Analysis for Sudan: 1984/85 – 1988/89*, Larkspur, CA: Development Technologies, Inc.

Pearce, D.W. (1988), 'Natural resource management and anti-desertification policy in the Sahel–Sudan zone: a case study of gum arabic', *Geojournal*, **17**, 349–55.

El Sammani, M.O. (ed.) (1985), *El Khuwei–Mazroub–Tinna Study Area North Central Kordofan and Messeriya Study Area Southern Kordofan: Final Report*, Khartoum: IES and USAID.

Sharawi, H.A. (1986), '*Acacia Senegal* in the gum belt of western Sudan: a cost–benefit analysis', MSc. Thesis, Department of Forestry, University College of North Wales, Bangor.

Squire, L. and H. van der Tak (1975), *Economic Analysis of Projects*, Baltimore, MD: Johns Hopkins University Press.

9. Economic aspects of tropical deforestation in Southeast Asia

Introduction

Along with Amazonia and Central Africa, Southeast Asia is one of the world's last great reserves of tropical moist forest (TMF). The region currently accounts for around 20 per cent of the world's tropical moist forest (see Table 9.1). The vast majority of Southeast Asia's tropical moist forests are concentrated in Indonesia, Papua New Guinea, Malaysia, the Philippines and Brunei. Indonesia alone accounts for over 50 per cent of the region's TMF and more than 10 per cent of the world's total.

However, the rate of deforestation in Southeast Asia, measured in terms of hectares (ha) lost per year, is fairly high – approximately 2 million ha annually – and the total area deforested is much higher than in Amazonia and Central Africa (see Table 9.1). Thus there is great concern that Southeast Asia may be depleting its forests rapidly, and to such an extent that it will soon resemble other regions (for example, West Africa) that once contained vast TMF areas but are now largely deforested.

The following chapter examines economic aspects of the problem of tropical deforestation in Southeast Asia, focusing mainly on the role of tropical timber production. The first issue to address is whether tropical deforestation in the region is at all an economic problem. It is also worth examining the extent to which timber production is a major cause of tropical deforestation in the region as well as the likely costs of such production. Crucial to the excessive depletion and conversion of tropical forests is market and policy failures in forestry and other sectors that distort economic incentives in favour of deforestation. The main focus of the chapter will be on the role of these distortions in affecting two of the principal factors, behind tropical deforestation in Southeast Asia – tropical timber extraction and the demand for agricultural land.

Is tropical deforestation an economic problem?

To answer this question requires addressing two additional issues:

- are tropical forests an efficient form of holding on to 'wealth'?
- are the opportunity costs of tropical deforestation greater than the benefits gained?

Table 9.1 Tropical deforestation in Southeast Asia and other regions[a]

	Total forest area (million ha)	Undisturbed operable forest (million ha)	Annual deforestation ('000 ha)	Total TMF area deforested (million ha)
Southeast Asia insular	167.3	72	1707	117
Indonesia	108.6		1315	
Papua New Guinea	33.5		22	
Malaysia[b]	18.4		255	
Philippines	6.5		110	
Brunei	0.3		5	
Southeast Asia Mainland[c]	39.3	18	346	NA
Myanmar	31.2		102	
Thailand	8.1		244	
Total Southeast Asia	206.6	90	2053	>117
Amazonia	613.6	453	4129	100
Central Africa	167.1	107	325	30
Other regions	58.4	<10	1900	177[d]
World total	1045.7	652	8480	424

Notes:

[a] Unless indicated, 1990 estimates based on R. Schmidt, 'Sustainable management of tropical moist forests', Presentation for ASEAN Sub-Regional Seminar, Indonesia, Forest Resources Division, Forestry Department. FAO, Rome, January 1990. Note that *tropical moist forests* are defined as broadleaf high closed tropical forests, including wetland and mangrove forests but excluding the deciduous dry forests of South Asia, sub-Saharan Africa and sub-tropical South America. In 1988, the FAO estimated the total area of all *tropical closed forests* (including deciduous dry forests) to be 1269.6 million ha.

[b] Includes forests from Peninsular Malaysia.

[c] End of 1980 revised estimates based on Forest Resources Division, Forestry Department, *An interim report on the state of forest resources in the developing countries*, FAO, Rome, 1988.

[d] May include estimates for Thailand and Myanmar.

NA: not applicable.

Although apparently different, the questions are inherently related and represent two aspects of the same fundamental economic problem concerning tropical deforestation.

Like most environmental 'assets', tropical forests can be seen as a form of 'natural' capital. That is, they have the potential to contribute to the long-run economic productivity and welfare of tropical forest countries. Thus the value of a tropical forest as an economic asset depends on the present value of its income, or welfare, potential. However, in any growing economy there will be other assets, or forms of wealth, that yield income. Any decision to 'hang on' to a tropical forest therefore implies an opportunity cost in terms of foregoing the chance to invest in alternative income-yielding assets, such as man-made 'reproducible' capital. If tropical forests are to be an 'efficient' form of holding on to wealth, then they must yield a rate of return that is comparable to or greater than that of other forms of wealth. In other words an 'optimal' strategy for a developing country would be to 'draw down' its stock of tropical forests to finance economic development by reinvesting the proceeds in other assets that are expected to yield a higher economic return. Under such circumstances, tropical deforestation is not an economic problem but is in fact economically justified; it should proceed up to the point where the comparative returns to 'holding on' to the remaining forest equals the returns to alternative investments in the economy. If the latter always exceeds the former, then even complete deforestation is economically 'optimal'.

The idea that economic wellbeing, or welfare, may not be affected and may even be enhanced if the rents derived from depleting natural resources, such as tropical forests, are reinvested in reproducible capital has been around for some time in the theoretical economics literature. For example, what is now known as the 'Hartwick–Solow rule' states that reinvestment of the rents derived from the inter-temporally efficient use of exhaustible natural resources are reinvested in reproducible, and hence non-exhaustible, capital will secure a constant stream of consumption over time (Solow, 1974, 1986; Hartwick, 1977). Similarly, basic renewable resource economic theory suggests that, for slow-growing resources such as tropical forests, it may under certain conditions be more economically optimal to harvest the resource as quickly and efficiently as possible and reinvest the rents in other assets whose value will increase much faster. Equally, if the harvesting costs are low, or the value of a harvested unit is high, then the resource may also not be worth holding on to today (Clark, 1976; Smith, 1977).

However, there are obvious limits to the applications of the above rules to reality. For example, the Hartwick–Solow rule assumes that there is sufficient substitutability between reproducible (man-made) and natural capital over time such that they effectively comprise a single 'homogeneous' stock. Moreover, the above rules assume that all economic values are known and reflected in the 'prices' of resources, markets are undistorted, resource extraction is efficient and rents are reinvested in other assets in the economy. As a consequence more recent theories now stress the limits to 'substitution' between many forms of natural and man-made capital, even for developing countries interested in 'drawing down' their natural capital stock in favour of investing in other forms of capital (Barbier, 1989; Pearce, Barbier and Markandya, 1990). In particular, certain functions of a tropical forest, such as its role in maintaining micro-climates, protecting watersheds, providing unique habitats and supporting economic livelihoods of indigenous peoples, may be irretrievably lost when the forest is degraded or converted. Often the economic values of these and other functions of tropical forest are not properly accounted for in decisions concerning forest use.

There can be a great deal of uncertainty over many of these values, such as the forest's role in maintaining biodiversity and global climate. Finally, as the rest of this chapter will demonstrate with examples from Southeast Asia, there is little evidence to suggest that tropical forest resources are currently being exploited efficiently, nor that the rents earned from activities that degrade or convert the forests are being reinvested in more 'profitable' activities. Rather, market and policy failures are often rife, and economic rents tend to be dissipated and misused.

Although it is theoretically possible that the current rates of tropical deforestation in Southeast Asia and other regions are economically 'optimal', it is unlikely that this is the case. Too often, decisions concerning tropical forest depletion and conversion are taken without considering the opportunity cost of these decisions. In short, we do not know whether it is worth 'holding on' to the tropical forest as an economic asset because we do not know or bother to take into account the potential economic benefits that it yields. As a result, decisions will always be biased towards converting or depleting the tropical forest because the underlying assumption is that foregone benefits of maintaining the forest are necessarily negligible. If this is the case, as much evidence suggests, then current levels of tropical deforestation may not be optimal but 'excessive', and hence tropical deforestation may indeed be an economic problem.

If tropical deforestation is an economic problem, it is because important values are lost, some perhaps irreversibly, when closed forests are 'opened up', degraded or cleared. Each choice or *land use option* for the forest – to leave it standing in its natural state, or to exploit it selectively, for example, for timber or 'minor' (that is, no-timber) products, or to clearcut it entirely so the land can be converted to another use, such as agriculture – has implications in terms of values gained and lost. The decision as to what land use option to pursue for a given tropical forest area, and ultimately whether current rates of deforestation are 'excessive', can only be made if these gains and losses are properly analysed and evaluated. This requires that *all the values* that are gained and lost with each land use option are carefully considered.

For example, preserving a tropical forest involves direct costs of preservation, in terms of setting up a protected area, paying forest guards and rangers to protect and maintain the area and perhaps the cost of establishing a 'buffer zone' for surrounding local communities. Development options, such as the use of the forest for commercial timber exploitation and of the converted forest land and resources for agriculture, mining and hydroelectricity, are sacrificed if preservation is chosen. These foregone development benefits are additional costs associated with the preservation option. Such costs are easily identifiable as they often comprise marketable outputs and income sacrificed (for example, timber revenue, agricultural income, mineral wealth, hydroelectricity). It is not surprising therefore that governments and donors usually consider the *total costs*

– the direct costs plus the foregone development benefits – of preservation in their choice of land use options for tropical forests.

But the same approach should be taken in evaluating development options of the forest. For example, if the forest is to be cleared for agriculture, not only should the direct costs of conversion (for example, clearing and burning the forest, establishing crops) be included as part of the costs of this land use option but so must the *foregone* values of the forest that has been converted. These may include both the loss of important *environmental functions* (for example, watershed protection, micro-climate maintenance) and *resources* (for example, commercial hardwoods, non-timber products, wildlife).

In other words, we must determine the *total economic value* (TEV), both marketed and non-marketed, that is being surrendered through modifications of the prevailing forest land use that any development option entails.[1] These values comprise direct and indirect *use* values, *option* values and existence values. Direct use values include timber and non-timber products and ecotourism. Indirect use values are essentially the ecological functions of tropical forests: their watershed protection, micro-climatic and material cycling functions. All these values may have an 'option value' component if we are interested in preserving them for future use. Finally, existence values are the values that people place on the forest 'in itself' and are unrelated to any use.

However, many of the component values in total economic value have no market – especially subsistence or underdeveloped non-timber products and the indirect use, option and existence values of forests. Choice of land use is therefore often *biased* in favour of land uses that do have marketed outputs, for example, development options such as ranching, timber exploitation, agriculture, mining, hydroelectricity. The result is too much conversion and overexploitation of forest and too little natural management of forest land.

The basic reason for the imbalance is that the non-market values of the natural/managed systems are not automatically reflected in the price of forested land. For example, the market value of land converted to agriculture fails to reflect the lost environmental benefits, such as watershed protection. If 'owners' (those with legal title and those who have acquired the land on a first-come basis) had to pay the full social cost of developing forested land, less land would be converted or over-exploited. Forested land is clearly *underpriced*. An important consequence is that once the land occupied has become sufficiently degraded and thus significantly less productive, the 'owners' have a strong incentive to abandon the land for new, virgin forested land which is 'cheap' to acquire and develop. The process repeats itself until it becomes difficult to get access to new forest lands, for example due to the lack of roads or waterways into a region.

Although it is clearly the responsibility of governments in ensuring that the total economic value of forest land lost through conversion and exploitation is accounted for as part of the costs of these development options, most evidence suggests that public policies are often at the core of the tropical deforestation problem.[2] Too often, the pricing and economic policies of countries with tropical forests distort the costs of deforestation, as follows.

- The 'prices' determined for tropical timber products or the products derived from converted forest land *do not incorporate the lost economic values* in terms of foregone timber rentals, foregone minor forest products and other direct uses (for example, tourism), disrupted forest protection and other ecological functions, and the loss of biological diversity, including any option or existence values.
- Even the direct costs of harvesting and converting tropical forests *are often subsidized and/or distorted*, thus encouraging needless destruction.

If proper economic valuation of forest losses takes place, the cost of forest conversion and degradation can often be high. For example, in Indonesia, the foregone cost in terms of timber rentals from converting primary and secondary forest land is in the order of US$625–750 million per annum. With logging damage and fire accounting for additional costs of US$70 million, this would represent losses of around US$800 million annually. The inclusion of foregone non-timber products, such as essential oils, honey, wildlife products, resins, bamboos, fruits and nuts, would raise this cost to US$1 billion per year. In addition, the loss of timber on sites used for development projects could be another US$40–100 million (Pearce *et al.*, 1990, ch. 5). The total cost of the depreciation of the forest stock would include not only the cost of conversion but also the cost of timber extraction and forest degradation. One study estimated this total cost for Indonesia to be around US$3.1 billion in 1982, or approximately 4 per cent of GDP. However, this estimate must be considered a lower bound, as it does not include the value of the loss of forest protection functions (for example, watershed protection, micro-climatic maintenance) and of biodiversity. The latter may particularly be important in terms of *option and existence values* – that is values reflecting a willingness to pay to see species conserved for future use or for their intrinsic worth – which could translate into future payments that the rest of the world might make to Indonesia to conserve forest lands. Similar arguments apply to the value of the forest as a *carbon store* (Pearce, 1990).

The potential economic losses in terms of non-timber products from deforestation may be particularly significant in Southeast Asia. In Indonesia, these products have a high commercial value; exports of non-timber products rose from US$17 million in 1973 to US$154 million in 1985, comprising 12 per cent of export earnings. Exports of rattan alone were US$80 million in 1985. However, the commercial potential of many non-timber products may be currently under-exploited. The foregone future value of these products may therefore be much higher than their value at present. Moreover, many of the important economic uses of non-timber products, for example, the use of 'wild' forest foods to supplement food security and meet subsistence needs, are non-market and thus are not often properly accounted for (Pearce *et al.*, 1990, ch. 5). Consequently, both the foregone commercial and non-market benefits of non-timber products must be incorporated into any assessment of the costs of deforestation.

Timber production, demand for land and tropical deforestation in Southeast Asia

In recent years it has become almost 'axiomatic' to state that the major 'cause' of tropical deforestation is the conversion of forests to agricultural land. Tropical timber production, although significant in large areas of 'production' forests, is considered to be a less significant factor in overall tropical deforestation.[3]

On available evidence, this basic 'axiom' broadly holds across the tropical forest regions of Southeast Asia. However, behind this axiom is a much more complicated story, which indicates a much more intricate relationship between tropical timber production and frontier agricultural land expansion in the region.

First, the production of tropical timber has largely two effects on the environment:

- *directly* through the removal of trees and other damage incurred to surrounding forest during timber extraction; and
- *indirectly* through opening up and improving access to the forests which then impacts on other socio-economic factors which may degrade the environment.

The direct effects of timber extraction have received most of the attention, and they include not only the decline in standing timber stocks but also the wider environmental effects of extraction. These external effects include the loss of other consumptive uses (for example, loss of non-timber products for subsistence and commercial value), of ecological functions (for example, watershed protection, carbon storage and micro-climatic role) and of other non-consumptive values (for example, ecotourism, genetic resources and existence values). More recently, some studies have begun examining the indirect role of timber production in 'opening up' previously inaccessible forest areas. This role may be more significant than previously thought, particularly if distinctions are made between outright tropical *deforestation* and the more prevalent problem of tropical forest *degradation*.

For example, a recent study by Amelung (1991) identifies the major shifts in land use changes and the causes of deforestation in tropical countries. Table 9.2 shows the percentage share of the various activities which cause outright deforestation. Deforestation here is taken to be fairly 'complete', a reduction in the crown cover to less than 10 per cent. The agricultural sector accounted for the largest share at over 80 per cent on average of total deforestation in all tropical forest countries. The direct impact of forest activities on deforestation is minimal (that is, less than 10 per cent of total deforestation). The result appears to hold even for Indonesia, which is one of the world's biggest tropical timber producers. This is partly because timber which is harvested by selective logging – which predominates in Indonesia as well as in most tropical timber producing countries – is not considered to contribute to deforestation given the 'strong' definition of deforestation used in this table.

Table 9.2 Sources of deforestation in tropical countries, 1981–88[a]

	Brazil	Indonesia[b]	Cameroon	All major tropical forest countries
Forestry	2[d]	9	0	2
				(10)[e]
Agriculture	89	80	100	(83)[f]
Shifting cultivators[c]	13	59	92	NA
	(23)	(67)	(95)	(47)
Permanent agriculture	76	21	8	36
pastures	40	0	0	17
permanent crops	4	2	5	3
arable land	32	19	3	16
Mining and related industries	<3	<0.3	0	NA
Hydroelectric production	4[b]	0	0	2[b]
Residual[g]	2	11	0	(13)[h]

Notes:

[a] Percentage shares in deforestation refer to averages for the respective period.

[b] Data refer to the 1980–90 period.

[c] Figures in parentheses show the results of the FAO for 1980. These data include also market-orientated farmers who produce cash and export crops and engage only partly in shifting cultivation.

[d] Deforestation due to logging is due to charcoal production.

[e] The figure in parentheses refers to the estimation of Enquete-Kommission zum Schutz der Erdatmosphäre, *Schutz der tropichen Wälder*. Deutscher Bundestag 11, Wahlperiode, Drucksache 11/7220, 24.05.1990, Bonn, 1990. The calculation includes only Indonesia and Brazil, since these countries account for the largest share in clear cutting by the forestry sector.

[f] This percentage rate is based on the assumption that the percentage share calculated for shifting cultivators can be taken as an average for the 1981–88 period.

[g] This includes other industries, housing, infrastructure services and fire loss.

[h] The residual has been calculated from the data in this column which includes data from different periods.

NA: not applicable.

However, Table 9.3 gives as an alternative to 'outright' deforestation two measures of forest degradation: biomass reduction and forest modification (Amelung, 1991). The role of the forestry sector in *biomass reduction* is much more significant than its role in deforestation as a whole, especially in Indonesia. However, agriculture continues to play the dominant role in forest degradation. In contrast, the forestry sector is almost completely responsible for converting virgin forests into productive closed forests or other forms of land use through *forest modification*. In short, Tables 9.2 and 9.3 provide some indication that timber extraction is largely responsible for opening up previously unexploited forest, which then enables other economic uses of the forest resources, such as agricultural cultivation, which lead to further forest degradation and outright deforestation. In other words, timber extraction and farm colonization are two sides of the *same* coin.

Table 9.3 Sectoral share in forest degradation and forest modification, 1981–85[a]

	Percentage share in biomass reduction (degradation)				Percentage share in forest modification			
Sector	Brazil	Indonesia	Cameroon	Total[b]	Brazil	Indonesia	Cameroon	Total[b]
Forestry	6	44	10	10	(100)[c]	(100)[c]	98	71
Agriculture[d]	85	49	90	76	0	0	2	26
Others[d]	9	7	0	13	0	0	0	4

Notes:

[a] For the definition of modification and biomass reduction (degradation) see FAO, *Tropical Forest Resources*, FAO Forestry Paper 30, Rome, 1982.

[b] Total refers to all major rain forest countries.

[c] Following FAO statistics, deforestation in virgin forests is 0, since clearing by agriculture and other sectors concentrates on disturbed forests. Even though some clearing occurs in virgin forests, there is reason to assume that the bulk of deforestation is due to forests that have been logged-over prior to the clearing of the respective areas.

[d] These figures have been derived from Table 9.2 and reflect averages for the 1981–88 period or, in the case of Indonesia, the 1980–90 period.

Source: Amelung (1991).

There is clearly some anecdotal evidence of this process at work in Southeast Asia. A recent review of timber management in the region concluded that the main factor hindering or preventing sustained-yield management of production forests is the illegal clearing of these forests, particularly logged-over areas (Burgess, 1989) The worst area affected is the Northeast of Thailand, but the problem is also very serious in the Philippines, Sarawak and Indonesia, and it could easily become serious in parts of Sabah. The provision of road access by logging roads is considered the major contributory factor to this problem.

The indirect role of tropical timber production in encouraging widespread deforestation may therefore be particularly prevalent in Southeast Asia. As harvesting tropical timber is extremely lucrative and can yield substantial short-term returns to loggers, there is already a significant incentive to open too much forest to exploitation. Thus, illegal logging of restricted areas, allowing production stands to be exploited either in excess of the sustainable cut or when it is silviculturally damaging to do so, over-issue of harvesting licences and contravention of concession agreements are all common practices that are difficult to control by under-staffed and 'politically influenced' forestry departments in the region (Burgess, 1989). The incentive for timber producers to engage in such practices is often reinforced by widespread public policy distortions (see below). If in addition logged-over concessions and 'opened' production forests are increasingly encroached for agricultural clearing, then there is even more pressure on loggers to over-cut existing stands as quickly as possible and to move on to other concessions further in the forest. Thus the process repeats itself, and tropical deforestation spreads and multiplies.

Acceleration of this process is likely given the trends in timber production in Southeast Asia. Table 9.4 provides an indication of the current state of forest land use, timber yield and forest products output of the major Southeast Asian tropical timber countries. With the exception of Sabah, Indonesia and probably Papua New Guinea, reserves of virgin forest are a relatively small proportion of total forest area. The majority of tropical forests have been allocated to conversion or permanent production forest (Table 9.4). However, a very large part of the production in the region in the past has come from the conversion forests, which are essentially clear-cut and turned over to agricultural purposes. Thus future supplies must depend on the permanent production forests (and any remaining virgin forest reserves allocated to them) – provided that these supplies can be maintained on a sustained basis. Although only a rough indicator of sustained yield potential versus current production from these forests, Table 9.5 does suggest some concern over management of the permanent production forests. For example, Sabah and Sarawak, and to a lesser extent Peninsular Malaysia, may be either still converting some forests to agriculture or overcutting the permanent forests substantially. Indonesia and the Philippines give the appearance of having some scope for expanding sustained production, but it is also likely that they have overestimated the extent of the production forest, under-reported current timber extraction (for example, there is substantial illegal felling), or both (Burgess, 1989). All in all, the current dominance of the major Southeast Asian tropical timber countries in the world production and trade of timber products that is indicated in Table 9.6 is likely to change rapidly in the near future. For example, several analysts predict a decline in the region's share of world production and trade, and some deterioration in the quality of hardwood timber produced from forests in the region (Arnold, 1991; Burgess, 1989; Sedjo and Lyon, 1990).

Table 9.4 Forest areas in major Southeast Asian tropical timber countries (km²)[a]

	Total land area	Total forest area	Permanent protection forest	Permanent production forest	Conversion production forest	Total production forest	Remaining virgin forest
Thailand	513 115	142 958	NA	NA	NA	NA	NA
Malaysia							
Peninsular	131 596	63 532	10 679	34 507	9 100	43 607	9 600
Sabah	73 711	44 869	6 000	29 984	4 080	34 064	7 815
Sarawak	123 253	94 384	24 200	32 400	37 784	70 184	50 387
Philippines	300 000	63 830	16 800	44 030	0	44 030	10 420
Papua New Guinea	468 860	359 900	NA	NA	NA	NA	NA
Indonesia	1 930 270	1 439 700	490 410	338 666	305 370	64 036	524 000
Total	3 540 805	2 209 173	548 089	479 587	356 334	835 921	602 222

Notes:
[a] Based on P.F. Burgess (1989).
NA: not applicable.

Table 9.5 Production and yield potential in major Southeast Asian tropical timber countries[a]

	Permanent production forest (million ha)	Sustained yield at 1.5 m^3 per year	Sustained yield at 2.0 m^3 per year	Annual timber harvest (m^3)
Malaysia				
Peninsular	2.85[b]	4 275 000	5 700 000	7 914 328
Sabah	3.00	4 500 000	6 000 000	11 739 262
Sarawak	3.24	4 860 000	6 480 000	11 470 000
Philippines	4.40	6 600 000	8 800 000	3 433 774
Indonesia	33.87	50 805 000	67 740 000	28 500 000
Total	47.36	71 040 000	94 720 000	63 057 364

Note:
[a] Based on P.F. Burgess (1989).
[b] The source does not explain the discrepancy between Table 9.4 and this table over the permanent production forest in Malaysia.

Of course, pressures to over-harvest forests for timber today will continue as long as 'opening up' forest areas leads to uncontrolled clearing for agriculture. A major factor in this process is the demand for agricultural land. Given the current economic and demographic situation in Southeast Asia, increasing demand for land in forest areas is inevitable.

For example, in Indonesia, dryland agricultural production in the Outer Islands that contain the country's tropical forests increased at around 3.6 per cent per annum in the 1970s and 80s. If expansion continues at the same annual rate, then the total area in agricultural production will be around 15.5 million ha by the end of the century. This implies an increase in the amount of new land to be brought into agricultural production of about 500 000 ha per annum, much of it through forest land conversion (Pearce *et al*., 1990, ch. 5). A major factor behind the rapid extensification of agriculture onto converted forest lands is their poor soil quality. Farmers on the Outer Islands require more land per family to earn the same income as in Java. For example, Sumatra as a whole requires 2.1 ha to produce the same value added as 1 ha on Java, Sulawesi 2.7 ha, Kalimantan 3.9, Maluku 10.7 and Irian Jaya 10.7 ha (Pearce *et al*., 1990. ch. 5).

More analysis needs to be conducted of the factors driving the demand for forest land for agriculture. A recent study in Thailand highlights the complex linkages between agricultural crop prices, the relative returns from different crops and the demand for land. In Thailand, approximately 40 per cent of the increase in cultivated land in recent years has been met by converted forest land. The most important factors affecting the demand for cropland, and thus forest conversion, appear to be population growth followed by non-agricultural returns, although agricultural pricing also has a significant influence (see Table 9.7). Higher aggregate real prices may have a slightly positive influence on the demand for

Table 9.6 *Production and trade of wood products in major Southeast Asian tropical timber countries*[a] *(1989 '000m³)*

	Products	Production	Imports	Exports	ADC[b]
Indonesia	Logs	23 684.0	0.0	0.0	23 684.0
	Sawnwood	10 546.0	0.0	2 692.0	7 854.0
	Plywood	8 500.0	0.0	8 040.0	460.0
	Veneer	53.9	0.0	29.0	24.9
Malaysia	Logs	38 900.0	10.0	21 100.0	17 810.0
	Sawnwood	7 660.0	197.0	5 134.0	2 723.0
	Plywood	1 001.0	15.0	915.0	101 0
	Veneer	445.0	5.3	248.7	201.6
Papua New Guinea	Logs	1 700.0	0.0	1 260.0	440.0
	Sawnwood	118.0	0.0	0.0	18.0
	Plywood	18.0	0.0	0.0	18.0
	Veneer	0.0	0.0	0.0	0.0
Philippines	Logs	2 773.0	393.5	6.0	3 160.5
	Sawnwood	975.0	12.0	438.1	548.9
	Plywood	341.0	3.0	130.9	213.1
	Veneer	75.0	0.0	53.1	21.9
Thailand	Logs	1 770.0	1135	0.0	2 905.0
	Sawnwood	1 160.0	744.0	30.0	1 874.0
	Plywood	185.0	4.0	35.0	154.0
	Veneer	60.0	2.0	5.0	57.0
Total Southeast Asia	Logs	68 827.0	1 538.0	22 366.0	47 999.5
	Sawnwood	20 459.0	953.0	8 297.1	13 114.9
	Plywood	10 045.0	22.0	9 120.9	946.1
	Veneer	633.9	7.3	335.8	305.4
Total ITTO producers[c]	Logs	126 967.0	2 536.7	25 749.2	103 754.5
	Sawnwood	48 846.0	1 083.5	9 518.1	40 411.4
	Plywood	12 115.6	59.2	9 565.2	2609.6
	Veneer	1 705.7	42.5	555.5	1192.7
Total World producers[d]	Logs	1 677 454.0	130 230.0	124 846.0	1 682 838.0
	Sawnwood	500 685.0	100 231.0	99 088.0	501 828.0
	Wood panels[e]	129 108.0	28 692.0	28 443.0	129 357.0

Notes:

[a] Based on International Tropical Timber Council, *Elements for the 1990 Annual Review and Assessment of the World Tropical Timber Situation*, Tenth Session, Quito, Ecuador, 29 May–6 June, 1991.

[b] ADC = Apparent domestic consumption.

[c] ITTO = International Tropical Timber Organization.

[d] All tropical and temperate timber producers, derived from FAO, *Forest Products Yearbook 1989*, Rome, 1991.

[e] Includes veneer sheets, plywood, particle board and fibreboard (compressed and non-compressed).

cropland, and thus increased forest clearing; however, this direct effect may be counteracted by the indirect impact of higher agricultural prices on raising the productivity of existing land and increasing the cultivation of previously idle land, thus reducing the demand for new land from forest clearing. Changes in relative prices also influence the demand for new cropland by affecting the relative profitability of land-saving as opposed to land-extensive cropping systems.[4]

Table 9.7 Thailand – the demand for agricultural land (cultivated), 1962–89

Explanatory variables	Coefficients[a] and *T*-statistics[b]
Real price of agricultural crops (lagged one year)	0.081 (2.00)
Agricultural population	1.337 (12.82)
Agricultural productivity (lagged one year)	–0.280 (–2.43)
Relative return to land from land-saving crops to land using crops	–0.155 (–3.95)
Relative return to labour from non-agriculture	–0.308 (–3.37)
Time dummy	–0.352 (–4.12)
AR(2)	0.437 (2.27)
R squared adjusted = 0.987	
Durbin–Watson = 2.00	
F-statistic = 330.00	
Degrees of freedom = 19.00	

Notes:

[a] Coefficients indicate the responsiveness of the dependent variable to changes in the explanatory variables; for example, a 10 per cent increase in aggregate real crops prices leads to an 0.8 per cent increase in the demand for land.

[b] *T*-statistics indicated in parentheses

Source: Phantumvanit and Panayotou (1990).

The analysis of land clearing in Thailand also illustrates some of the potential linkages with agricultural input prices. For example, in Table 9.7 the relative returns to land-saving cropping systems can also be affected by the relative costs of inputs (for example, fertilizer, seed, credit, irrigation, agrochemicals, and so on) where these differ between land-saving and land-extensive systems. More importantly, investments in land productivity will also be affected by the costs of these inputs. Thus the Thailand case study suggests that lower input prices generally (or crop price support policies) would reduce the demand for new cropland and forest conversion both directly and indirectly by making previously idle land more attractive to cultivate. Changes in relative input prices could also make a difference on agricultural extensification by affecting the relative returns to land-saving cropping systems.

Public policies and the forestry sector in Southeast Asia

As noted above, the links between public policies, the forestry sector and tropical deforestation are significant in Southeast Asia. However, it is often difficult to disentangle these linkages as they involve a complex array of domestic macroeconomic, sectoral and trade policies as they affect forestry (see Figure 9.1). The following section focuses on domestic policies, including economic policy, public investment and institutional arrangements. The next section will discuss the role of trade policies.

Domestic macro-economic policies, such as exchange rate devaluations and the level of debt servicing ratios, may impact on the timber trade and deforestation (Figure 9.1). An overvalued exchange rate acts as a subsidy to urban consumers on imported goods, while implicitly taxing timber exports produced domestically. Real currency devaluations, as frequently required by structural adjustment programmes for indebted developing countries, remove existing distortions and provide incentives for greater domestic production of exportables, including timber products. This is due to increasing international price competitiveness and increased domestic demand for home produced goods as imported substitutes become relatively more expensive. Both impacts can directly encourage deforestation through the expansion of wood production for the international and domestic markets. Increasing pressure to meet debt servicing payments may also contribute to deforestation if countries pursue short-term policies at the expense of long-term sustainable development. More generally, macroeconomic policies (for example, fiscal and monetary policy) can affect underlying demand and supply conditions, with knock-on effects in the forestry industry.

The impacts of macroeconomic policies on the forestry sector, and subsequently on deforestation, are difficult to analyse. Few, if any, economic studies have examined some of the above linkages with regard to Southeast Asia, and comparative studies involving all tropical forest countries often produce conflicting conclusions regarding macroeconomic influences on deforestation. For example, in a study of these linkages in tropical forest countries, Capistrano and Kiker (1990) found a negative correlation between debt–service ratios and deforestation. In contrast, Kahn and McDonald (1990) discovered a positive relationship between tropical deforestation and public external debt and annual

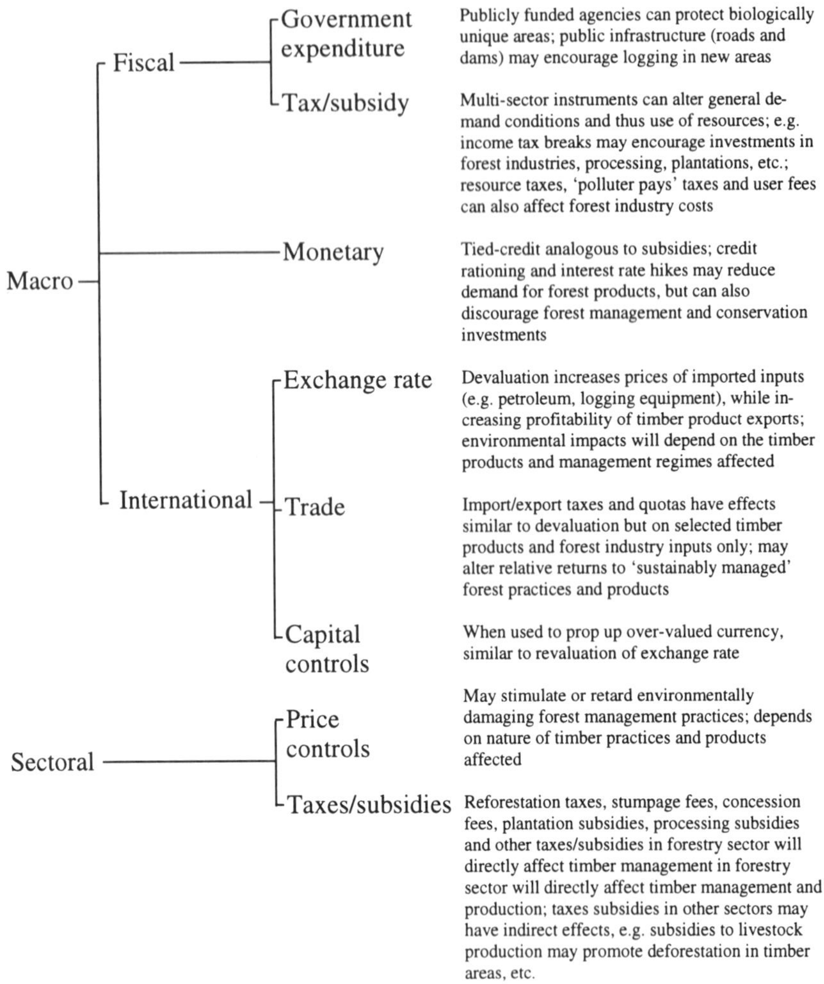

Source: Adapted from Bishop *et al.* (1991).

Figure 9.1 Economic policy and potential impacts on timber management

percentage changes in that debt. On the other hand the results by Capistrano and Kiker (1990) do show that the high availability of external funds in the early 1970s in tropical forest countries may have reduced the pressure on the use of domestic forest resources (for example, through the need for increased investments and production in forest extraction). Their study also indicates a high correlation between exchange rate devaluation and tropical deforestation.

Thus the indirect impact of debt on increased tropical timber extraction and deforestation, through the policy responses to correct or service the debt problem as implemented through structural adjustment programmes, may be significant.

Forest exploitation is directly affected by economic policies aimed specifically at the forestry sector, including domestic and trade instruments (for example, tax credits or subsidies for forest conversion, afforestation or for wood product exports). Forestry is also indirectly affected by economic policies which alter incentives and returns in downstream industries or related sectors, such as wood processing, construction and agriculture (Figure 9.1)

Public investment often has very direct effects on forest-based activities, particularly where transport infrastructure and public services are extended to previously inaccessible forested areas. Such investment may be considered an important subsidy to the logging and wood processing industry, by reducing the costs of gaining access to forest resources, and of bringing forest products to market. Public investment in remote forested areas also acts as an impetus to human population migration and agricultural expansion, frequently associated with forest clearing. The result may be conflicts over land use, or a misallocation of forest resources, as areas designated for timber exploitation are encroached upon by migrant farmers, ranchers, miners and others.

Institutional and legal arrangements governing land tenure and transactions can also have significant effects on forest land use. Formal property law and titling regulations in many developing countries, for example, often ensure that land clearing is the only means of securing claims to frontier forest landholdings. Important areas of old growth forest that could be exploited for commercial timber on a sustainable basis may be lost in this way.

Short concession periods for logging operations on public lands can reduce incentives for reforestation, while stumpage fees and licenses are frequently set at very low rates that fail to reflect the scarcity value of standing timber. Moreover, many governments are unable to manage effectively the public forest estate, resulting in illegal encroachment or logging. All of these factors reduce incentives for sustainable management of timber resources by private firms.

In sum, public policies can affect the incentives for timber forest management and its environmental impacts in a variety of ways. Designing policies to reduce these impacts and control excessive forest degradation is clearly complex and requires careful attention to harvesting incentives. As the following examples from Southeast Asia illustrate, many domestic policies do not even begin to approximate the appropriate incentives required to achieve a socially optimal level of timber harvesting. More often than not, pricing, investment and institutional policies for forestry actually work to *create* the conditions for short-term harvesting by private concessionaires, and in some instances, even *subsidize* private harvesting at inefficient levels.[5]

For example, in Malaysia and Indonesia, government policies to encourage the switching from the export of raw logs to processed timber products have led to substantial economic losses, the establishment of inefficient processing operations and accelerated deforestation (Repetto and Gillis, 1988). Throughout Southeast Asia the allocation of timber concession rights and leasing agreements on a short time scale, coupled with the lack of incentives for reforestation, have contributed to excessive and rapid depletion of timber forests. In the Philippines, the social gain from logging old-growth forest was found to be negative (around –US$130 to –US$1175 per hectare), once the social costs of timber stand replanting, the costs of depletion and the costs of off-site damages were included (Paris and Ruzicka, 1991).

Short-term concessions and poor regulatory frameworks coupled with inappropriate pricing policies often contribute to excessive rent-seeking behaviour in tropical timber production (Gillis, 1990). That is, concessionaires have an incentive to open up additional stands for harvesting in order to 'mine' timber for high short-term profits. Table 9.8 indicates government rent capture from tropical timber in three Southeast Asian countries. By not charging sufficient stumpage fees and taxes or by selling harvesting rights too cheaply, by and large most governments have allowed the resource rents to flow as excess profits to timber concessionaires and speculators, often through short-term harvesting operations.

Table 9.8 Tropical timber rent capture in Southeast Asia

	Potential rent from log harvest (1)	Actual rent from log harvest (2)	Official government rent capture (3)	3/2 (%)	3/1 (%)
Indonesia (1979–82)	4954	4409	1644	37.3	33.2
Sabah, Malaysia (1979–82)	2198	2094	1703	81.3	77.5
Philippines (1979–82)	1505	1033	171	16.5	11.4
Philippines (1987)	256	68	39	57.1	15.3

Note: All figures in US$ millions.

Sources: Repetto (1990) and Repetto and Gillis (1988).

For example, in the Philippines, if the government had been able to collect the full value of actual rents, its timber revenues would have exceeded US$250 million – nearly six times the US$39 million actually collected. Instead, excess profits of at least US$4500 per ha went to timber concessionaires, mill owners and timber traders (Repetto, 1990).[6] Although the total area of production forest in the Philippines is 4.4 million ha, the total area under timber concessions exceeds this at nearly 5.7 million ha – almost 90 per cent of the entire forest area. Concessions are awarded for 25 years but some for as little as 5 years, even though the minimum realistic telling cycle is 30 years and the rotation 60 years. Almost all the large logging companies have senior politicians on their boards and it is generally the politicians, not forestry officials, that ultimately determine concession policy and allocation (Burgess, 1989).

Public policies also have an important influence on the pattern of forest-based industrialization and its implications for long-term economic development and deforestation. Binkley and Vincent (1991) note that stumpage prices (that is, the prices of harvested logs at the stand) have a crucial role to play in the interrelated dynamics of timber reserve depletion and processing expansion, particularly in facilitating the transition of the forest sector from dependence on old-growth to secondary-growth forests and in coordinating processing capacity with timber stocks. Unfortunately, in most developing countries, stumpage prices tend to be administratively determined rather than set by the forces of supply and demand, thus understating stumpage values and failing to reflect increasing scarcity as old growth forests are depleted. A number of economic and environmental distortions result, as follows:

- old-growth forests are depleted too rapidly;
- forest land is inappropriately cleared for agriculture or other uses;
- inadequate and inappropriate investment is made in second-growth forests;
- inefficient processing facilities are installed;
- decisions on log and lumber trade policies and inefficient and encourage unsustainable management practices; and
- elaborate and counter-productive capital–export controls are needed to ensure that resource rents are not repatriated.

One of the case studies that Binkley and Vincent (1991) explore is logging in Peninsular Malaysia, which is mainly of old-growth tropical forests. In Malaysia, wood prices – timber charges, log prices and sawnwood prices – have been kept artificially low at every stage of forestry development, from log exporter to primary products to embryonic exporter of downstream products. The result has been the development of processing capacity that exceeds the forests' sustained yield capacity. In a contrasting case, in Chile the crucial policy issue has been how to build up an efficient industry based on the nation's increasing supply of timber from privately owned plantations (mainly of *Pinus radiata*). Initial success seems to have come from providing private investors with secure, long-term tenure for plantations. Another key policy has been to permit the export of logs, which forces domestic mills to pay world prices for sawlogs, pulpwood and woodchips and to be more efficient.

Timber trade policies and deforestation in Southeast Asia

As Southeast Asian tropical forest countries are major producers and exporters in the world market for forest products, the incentives for inefficient and unsustainable use of forest resources may not be linked to domestic public policies alone. They may also stem from distortions in global timber trade policies, such as protectionism or export subsidization and may affect forest resource use and related forest degradation. The following section explores some of these issues with regard to barriers to the trade in timber products faced by developing countries and particularly Southeast Asian producers, the use of timber export taxes and bans as a means of encouraging forest-based industrialization and the potential impacts on tropical deforestation of trade liberalization.

Bourke (1988) has conducted a study of the implications of timber trade barriers for developing countries. Although developing countries face on average, the lowest level of duties of all forest product exporters, there is the tendency for tariffs and the rates of protection imposed by importing countries to escalate; that is, they are lowest on unprocessed products and rise with increased processing. On the other hand, import tariff levels for wood products appear to be even higher in developing countries, and are also subject to escalation.

Nevertheless, the degree of tariff escalation between raw log and processed timber products has considerable implications for developing countries. The higher relative tariffs for processed products clearly restrict the ability of these countries to develop their own value-added processing capabilities. The traded products particularly affected by tariffs in developed country markets are plywood, some sizes and species of sawnwood, reconstituted panels and some wood manufactures. Some paper and paper products also display high tariff rates. For example, the cost advantage of plain plywood processing in Indonesia, Sabah, West Malaysia, the Philippines and Singapore over that in Japan ranged from 9 to 39 per cent in 1980; however, when the Japanese 20 per cent import duty was included, this cost advantage dropped significantly and was actually negative for Indonesia and Singapore (Bourke, 1988).[7] Many of these tariff barriers for timber products faced by developing countries are reinforced by additional non-tariff barriers, such as health, safety and technical standards, anti-dumping and countervailing duty investigations and import licensing schemes.

Unfortunately, it is extremely difficult to determine what the environmental effects of such trade barriers might be in developing countries. One argument is that, by deterring value-added processing by timber-producing countries, trade barriers are preventing efficient forest-based industrialization. World prices for raw logs are kept artificially low, further exacerbating the disparity between stumpage prices and the real economic scarcity value of logs. The result is that old growth forests are logged excessively, and the transition of the sector from dependence on old-growth to second-growth forests and in coordinating processing capacity with timber stocks is not made.[8]

However, there are complications with such an argument. As pointed out by Bourke (1988), although developing countries as a group have a comparative advantage in simply worked wood and wood manufactures, and possibly veneer and plywood, it is not certain that the timber-producing developing countries within this group would necessarily have the comparative advantage in producing all these products. For example, newly industrialized countries (NICs) that have no or negligible production forests but are major processors of timber from Southeast Asia, such as Taiwan, South Korea and Singapore, currently have a greater comparative advantage in more advanced processed products, such as plywood and veneer. Thus current import barriers may be discriminating more against the NICs rather than the Southeast Asian timber-producing countries. There may be a knock-on effect of discrimination against the NICs onto the timber-producing countries, but the magnitude of this impact is difficult to determine. The ultimate impacts on forest management and its environmental impacts of both the first-order and second-order effects of timber trade import barriers are therefore hard to discern. The situation is further complicated by the extensive use of non-tariff barriers to processed timber imports from timber developing countries. Bourke (1988) found substantial evidence that such barriers are restricting trade from the log producing countries. However, the effects of non-tariff barriers on trade flows is difficult enough to analyse, let alone the impacts on forest degradation.

In addition, the timber trade has been subject to severe distortions by export restrictions imposed by log-producing countries. One justification cited by timber-producing countries for imposing such export restrictions is that they compensate for the import barriers in developed economy markets by making the price of raw logs higher to the processors in the importing country while reducing the cost disadvantage faced by domestic processors within the timber-producing countries. Whatever the reasons for the export restrictions, they are an additional source of distortion in the timber trade, which make isolating the impacts of import barriers on trade flows and forest degradation more difficult.

Gillis (1990) has reviewed the role of the export taxes and bans in encouraging forest-based industrialization. Initially, the preference seems to have been for export taxes, through employing escalating rates. For most tropical forest countries, export tax rates on logs generally ranged between 10 and 20 per cent. Export taxes on sawn timber, veneer and plywood have been negligible. Where sawn timber exports were taxed, rates were typically half that of logs. This strategy proved only moderately successful in achieving the desired results; for example, although expanded processing capacity was established in Malaysia, the Philippines and Indonesia, it was achieved at high economic costs, both in terms of the direct costs of subsidization as well as the additional costs of wasteful and inefficient processing operations. In addition, as a long-term forest industrialization strategy, it may prove difficult to ensure export sales of processed products through denying processors in other countries access to logs (Bourke, 1988). Importers of Southeast Asian logs, such as Japan, have been known to substitute other raw materials (for example, cement, steel, plastics, fibreboard, and so on) for timber, and alternative sources of supply, such as sawlogs from temperate and other developing regions (Bourke, 1988).

In Indonesia, the *ad valorem* export tax on logs was doubled from 10 per cent to 20 per cent in 1978, while most sawnwood and all plywood were exempted. Beginning in 1980 controls on the export of logs were progressively enforced, until an outright ban was introduced in 1985 (Gillis, 1988). The export tax structure created effective rates of protection of 222 per cent for plywood manufacture, and the drop in export revenue to the government from diverting log exports was not compensated by any gain in value-added in sawmilling, resulting in a loss of US$15 per m^3 at world prices. The consequence has been the creation of inefficient processing operations and expanded capacity, with consequences for the rate of timber extraction and forest management. Gillis (1988) has estimated that over 1979–82, due to the inefficient processing operations resulting from this policy, over US$545 million in potential rents was lost to the Indonesian economy, or an average cost of US$136 million annually. Moreover, as the switch from log to processed exports occurred at a time when forest product prices were falling sharply in real terms, the cost to the economy in export earnings was high. Over 1981–84, the net loss in export earnings amounted to US$2.9–3.4 billion, or approximately US$725–850 million annually. Additional losses were also incurred through selling plywood below production cost, which amounted to US$956 million in 1981–84, or US$239 million annually (Fitzgerald, 1986).

Although the switch to value-added processing of timber initially slowed down the rate of timber extraction, the inefficiencies and rapidly expanding capacity of domestic processing may actually increase the rate of deforestation over the medium and long term.[9] For example, by the early 1980s, the major operational inefficiencies in domestic processing due to high rates of effective protection in Indonesia led to the lowest conversion rates in Asia. As a result, for every cubic metre of Indonesian plywood produced, 15 per cent more trees had to be cut relative to plymills elsewhere in Asia that would have processed Indonesian log exports (Gillis, 1988). Thus the protection given to Indonesian mills not only increased rather than reduced total log demand, but the gross operational inefficiencies also ensured that millions more logs may have been harvested than if a more efficient policy to boost domestic processing capabilities had been implemented.

More recent analysis of the impacts of the log export ban in Indonesia on the efficiency of timber processing industries confirms that the policy has not increased wood recoveries and thus reduced log consumption compared to pre-ban levels (Constantino, 1990). By depressing prices, the log export ban has led to the substitution of wood for other factor inputs, with substantial wood recovery losses in sawmilling and a slower growth in wood recovery than other factor productivities in plymilling. In both industries, wood consumption has been the main source of output growth over the 1975 to 1987 period, with efficiency gains contributing very little. However, the log export ban has not affected efficiency in the plywood industry so seriously, which could arise from the much newer capital vintages in plywood milling, its export orientation that requires higher production standards, and possibly its access to better quality logs.

Despite the problems with the export restriction policy, it is still being aggressively promoted by the government to encourage forest-based industrialization. In Indonesia, not only does the export log ban still remain in place, but in October 1989 export taxes on sawn timber were also increased substantially to prohibit exports and shift processing activities to plywood. A secondary objective of the policy is to eliminate the marginal mills, leaving only the competitive ones operational, thus improving overall industrial efficiency. The implications of the policy for wood recovery, log demand and thus tropical deforestation in Indonesia is less clear. However, a recent simulation analysis suggests that any gains in turns of reduced timber-related deforestation is more than offset by the economic losses incurred through discrimination against sawnwood exports and inefficient plywood processing (Barbier *et al.*, 1992).

Gillis (1990) has observed that the use of export tax structures to promote forest-based industrialization has become largely replaced by export bans in tropical forest countries, although export taxes are still being used in certain regions and for specific timber products. Table 9.9 summarizes some of these policies in developing countries.

As discussed above, many log-producing countries see the use of export taxes and bans as the means to compensate domestic processing industries for import barriers faced in developed economy markets. Bourke (1988) has argued that in the face of such barriers, log-producing countries can maintain some degree of cost-competitiveness by either (a) continuing with existing discriminatory policies against log exports in order to subsidize delivered log prices to domestic processors, or (b) improving the efficiency of processing operations, especially in plant capacity and conversion rates, in order to reduce costs. However, it is clear from the Indonesian case cited above that the use of export taxes and restrictions to encourage processing activities can undermine the efficiency of these activities, with counter-productive consequences for forest management and depletion. Such export trade policy distortions only serve to magnify the negative environmental impacts of domestic market and policy failures in producing countries.

Table 9.9 Export taxes and bans on tropical timber, Southeast Asia, 1989

Country	Tax rate/export policy	Remarks
Indonesia	20% *ad valorem* on logs	Tax imposed only on some logs in inaccessible regions. Log export ban since 1985 has made the tax irrelevant for other regions.
	Specific export taxes on sawn timber, ranging from US$250–2400 per m^3	Specific export taxes on sawn timber introduced in 1989; plywood exempt from all export taxes.
Malaysia		
Peninsular	Log export ban since 1971	
Sabah	No specific export tax or ban but see remarks	The Sabah timber royalty has a strong export tax feature: the royalty rate for log exports is almost 10 times the rate for logs used domestically.
Sarawak	15% *ad valorem* of f.o.b. log values	Tax applies to one hardwood species only.
Papua New Guinea	10% of f.o.b. log values	Tax reported to have been widely evaded through transfer pricing. Log export ban proposed
Philippines	Log exports restricted to 25% of annual allowable cut since 1979	Ostensibly to control deforestation.

Source: Gillis 1990).

On the other hand, very little evidence exists on the effects of timber trade liberalization – that is, the removal of either forest product import and/or export restrictions – on tropical deforestation. Theoretical arguments can be mustered to show that a timber-exporting country that has high environmental costs associated with its timber exploitation would actually gain from trade liberalization, only if it instigated some of the appropriate timber management and other policies necessary to 'internalize' the environmental costs of its forestry operations (Anderson, 1992). The failure to do so will certainly reduce the welfare gains from trade liberalization, and may mean that additional environmental costs from increased timber product exports through poor management and domestic policies, will not be compensated sufficiently by the increase in export earnings.

A study by Boyd, Hyde and Krutilla (1991) investigates some of the possible connections between broad trade liberalization, that is, the removal of export restrictions, across the major economic sectors, and tropical deforestation in the Philippines. Preliminary findings indicate that trade liberalization in the Philippines would increase deforestation, and that the effects through industrial logging would be particularly significant. Output and exports in the logging sector increase by 6.5 per cent and 28.5 per cent, respectively, while investment and employment in logging increase by 2.8 per cent and 13.0 per cent, respectively. The authors cite as the main reason that the wood-based manufacturing sector (as distinct from the rest of manufacturing) is highly export-orientated and receives no nominal tariff protection. However, as discussed above, the Philippines has a poor record of *domestic* policy failures affecting timber management and deforestation, including short-term concessions, poor regulatory frameworks and inappropriate pricing policies. For example, Boyd *et al.* (1991) believe the production restrictions and log export bans in the Philippines cited in Table 9.9, which are ostensibly to control deforestation, to be ineffectual. The authors argue that well-enforced restrictions would mitigate some of the logging impacts on deforestation associated with trade liberalization. Improvement in all aspects of forestry policy and timber management to control inefficiencies and environmental costs would clearly reduce these impacts further.

No comparable analysis has been made of the effects of removing timber trade import barriers on deforestation or forest degradation. However, an analysis of the estimated trade effects from a removal of the post-Tokyo round of tariffs on wood and wood products in ten major developed market economies has been conducted (Bourke, 1988). Tariff reduction can lead to *trade creation* by boosting demand through a lower import price. Tariff reduction can also produce *trade diversion*, if the price change causes the relative attractiveness of different timber imports to change, causing importers to switch part of their purchases to other suppliers. The analysis shows that tariff removals may create as much as US$150.6 million in new exports for developing countries – a 3.3 per cent increase – with trade diversion amounting to around US$1–3 million. Thus the additional trade created far outweighs any trade diversion. Almost all new trade that would be created for developing countries would involve the EEC, Japan and the United States. For developed market economies, trade creation totals about US$731.4 million, or an 8 per cent increase. Around US$11.8 million would be diverted, mainly in the EEC. Although for developed market economies as a whole the gains from additional trade creation exceed any diversion, Austria, Canada and Switzerland would benefit the most (Bourke, 1988).

In sum, although substantial trade creation could result from the removal of import trading barriers for timber products in developed market economies, it is unlikely that such a complete removal of tariffs would occur. The effects of a more gradual reduction are more difficult to predict. However, the impacts on forest resources and the environment are not easy to determine, and as discussed above, will involve important first- and second-order impacts.

Conclusion

This chapter has reviewed a number of key economic factors influencing tropical deforestation in Southeast Asia concentrating mainly on the role of timber production. Although timber extraction is not the major direct cause of deforestation in the region, the indirect impact of forest operations in 'opening up' the forest to subsequent agricultural conversion is a major problem in many areas. There is also genuine cause for concern over (1) the 'mining' of old growth forests in some regions of the world to service the trade, (2) the impacts of market, policy and trade distortions on the incentives for timber management and trade and (3) the consequent failure of many countries to make an efficient and sustainable transition from dependence on old-growth to second-growth forests and to match domestic processing capacity with the economic availability of timber stocks.

The crucial relationship – for all Southeast Asian countries – is the impact of forestry, agricultural and wider economic policies on the *incentives* for timber management at the stand, concession and processing levels and on the demand for forest land for conversion to agriculture. Efficient and sustainable timber management requires that proper economic signals be transmitted to timber operators, whether harvesting from private, public, plantation or old-growth forest stands, so that they may maximize the *long run* income generating potential of these forest assets and 'internalize' any environmental externalities associated with timber harvesting. Similarly, the demand for forest land must be met through minimizing excessive loss of forest land and the unnecessary creation of 'open access' conditions in frontier areas.

Without such policies, Southeast Asian countries will fail to manage the 'natural capital' inherent in their tropical forests in an efficient and sustainable manner. An economically valuable asset will be unnecessarily and too rapidly depleted, and any economic rents gained will be short term, inefficiently extracted, and most likely, sub-optimally invested.

Notes

1. For further details, see Barbier (1991) and Pearce (1990).
2. For recent comparative reviews of how public policies affect tropical deforestation, see Barbier (1991); Barbier *et al.* (1992); Binkley and Vincent (1991); Hyde and Newman (1991); Repetto (1990); Repetto and Gillis (1988).

3. For a recent review of the economic causes underlying tropical deforestation, as well as a statistical analysis of the relative role of timber production, see Burgess (1992).
4. The authors also examined the effects of relative price changes on land productivity and the cultivation of previously idle land but found this relationship more difficult to estimate in such an aggregate analysis.
5. For further examples and discussion across all tropical forest countries, see Barbier *et al.* (1992); Barbier *et al.* (1991); Gillis (1990); Hyde and Newman (1991): Pearce (1990); Repetto (1990) and Repetto and Gillis (1988).
6. As argued by Hyde and Sedjo (1991) and Paris and Ruzicka (1991), rent capture *per se* may not be as fundamental to an efficient outcome as ensuring proper 'internalizing' of the user costs of timber exploitation through appropriate contractual and concession terms. That is, even if government rent capture is low, it can still ensure through proper concession arrangements that the stand is harvested at the private long-run efficient level. However, in many countries poor rent capture and poor concession policies go hand in hand, combining to produce short-term and rent-seeking behaviour in concessionaires.
7. Bourke (1988) also points out that cost advantage in these cases does not necessarily imply comparative advantage. For example, in the comparison of plywood processing in the Southeast Asian developing countries as opposed to Japan, the primary cost advantage appears to be in the costs of logs, which were clearly affected by export controls and taxes in the developing countries that discriminate against the export of raw logs in order to encourage domestic processing. However, as discussed below, one reason why developing countries implement such restrictions may be to compensate their domestic processors for these import barriers they face in exporting to foreign markets.
8. For further discussion on this point see the previous section, and Binkley and Vincent (1991).
9. Barbier (1987) points out that much of the reported decline in log production over the initial period can be attributed to depressed world prices for all timber products, and therefore, is not necessarily attributable to less exploitation because of increased processing activities. There is also a discrepancy between officially reported harvesting levels and rates based on processing industry output.

References

Amelung, T. (1991), 'Tropical deforestation as an international problem', Paper presented at the Egon-Sohmen Foundation Conference Economic Evolution and Environmental Concerns, Linz, Austria, August 30–31.

Anderson, K. (1992), 'The standard welfare economics of policies affecting trade and the environment', in K. Anderson and R. Blackhurst (eds), *The greening of world trade issues*, ch. 2.

Arnold, M. (1991), *Forestry expansion: a study of technical, economic and ecological factors*, Oxford: Oxford Forestry Institute Paper No. 3.

Barbier, E.B. (1987), 'Natural resources policy and economic framework', in J. Tarrant *et al.* (eds), *Natural resources and environmental management in Indonesia*, Jakarta: USAID Annex.

Barbier, E.B. (1989), *Economics, natural resource scarcity and development: conventional and alternative views*, London: Earthscan Publications.

Barbier, E.B. (1991), 'Tropical deforestation', in D.W. Pearce (ed.), *Blueprint 2: greening the world economy*, ch. 8.

Barbier, E.B., J.C. Burgess and A. Markandya (1991), 'The economics of tropical deforestation', *AMBIO*, **20** (2), 55–8.

Barbier, E.B., B.A. Aylward, J.C. Burgess and J.T. Bishop (1992), *Timber trade, trade policies and environmental degradation*, LEEC Discussion Paper DP 92-01. London: London Environmental Economics Centre.

Binkley, C.S. and J.R. Vincent (1991), *Forest based industrialization. a dynamic perspective*, World Bank Forest Policy Issues Paper, Washington, DC: The World Bank.

Bishop, J., B. Aylward and E. Barbier (1991), 'Guidelines for applying environmental economics in developing countries', *LEEC Gatekeeper Series 91–102*, London: The London Environmental Economics Centre.

Bourke, I.J. (1988), *Trade in forest products: a study of the barriers faced by the developing countries*, FAO Forestry Paper 83, Rome: FAO.

Boyd, R., W.F. Hyde and K. Krutilla (1991), *Trade policy and environmental accounting: a case study of structural adjustment and deforestation in the Philippines*, Draft Paper, Economics Dept., Ohio University, Athens, Ohio.

Burgess, J. (1992), *Economics analysis of the causes of tropical deforestation*, LEEC Discussion Paper DP92–03. London: London Environmental Economics Centre.

Burgess, P.F. (1989), 'Asia', in D. Poore *et al.* (eds), *No timber without trees: sustainability in the tropical forest*, ch. 5.

Capistrano, A.D. and C.F. Kiker (1990), *Global economic influences on tropical closed broadleaved forest depletion, 1967–1985*, Food Resources Economics Department, University of Florida, USA.

Clark, C. (1976), *Mathematical bioeconomics: the optimal management of renewable resources*, New York: John Wiley.

Constantino, L.F. (1990), *On the efficiency of Indonesia's sawmilling and plymilling industries*, Directorate General of Forest Utilization, Jakarta: Ministry of Forestry, Government of Indonesia and FAO.

Fitzgerald, B. (1986), *An analysis of Indonesian trade policies: countertrade, downstream processing, import restrictions and the deletion program*, CPD Discussion Paper 1986–22, Washington, DC: World Bank,

Gillis, M. (1988), 'Indonesia: public policies, resource management, and the tropical forest', *Public policies and the misuse of forest resources*, Cambridge: Cambridge University Press, ch. 2, pp. 43–114.

Gillis, M. (1990), *Forest incentive policies*, Paper prepared for the World Bank Forest Policy Paper, Washington, DC: The World Bank.

Hartwick, J.M. (1977), 'Intergenerational equity and the investing of rents from exhaustible resources', *American Economic Review*, **66**, 972–4.

Hyde, W.F. and D.H. Newman (1991), *Forest economics in brief – with summary observations for policy analysis*, Draft Report, Agricultural and Rural Development, Washington, DC: The World Bank.

Hyde, W.F. and R.A. Sedjo (1991), 'Managing tropical forests: reflections on the rent distribution discussion', in W.F. Hyde and D.H. Newman (eds), *Forest economics in brief – with summary observations for policy analysis*, Appendix A, Draft Report, Agricultural and Rural Development, Washington, DC: The World Bank.

Kahn, J.R. and J.A. McDonald (1990), *Third world debt and tropical deforestation*, mimeo., Department of Economics, New York University, Binghampton, New York.

Paris, R. and I. Ruzicka (1991), *Barking up the wrong tree: the role of the rent appropriation in sustainable forest management*, Asian Development Bank Environment Office Occasional Paper No. 1.

Pearce, D.W. (1990), *An economic approach to saving the tropical forests*, LEEC Discussion Paper 90–06, London Environmental Economics Centre, UK.

Pearce, D.W., E.B. Barbier and A. Markandya (1990), *Sustainable development: economics and environment in the third world*, London: Edward Elgar and Earthscan.

Poore, D., P. Burgess, J. Palmer, S. Rietbergen and T. Synnott (1989), *No timber without trees: sustainability in the tropical forest*, London: Earthscan Publications Ltd.

Repetto, R. (1990), 'Macroeconomic policies and deforestation', Prepared for UNU/WIDER Project, *The Environment and Emerging Development Issues*.

Repetto, R. and M. Gillis (1988), *Public policies and the misuse of forest resources*, Cambridge: Cambridge University Press.

Sedjo, R.A. and K.S. Lyon (1990), *The long-term adequacy of world timber supply*, Washington, DC: Resources for the Future.

Smith, V.L. (1977), 'Control theory applied to natural and environmental resources: an exposition', *Journal of Environmental Economics and Management*, **4**, 1–24.

Solow, R.M (1974), 'Intergenerational Equity and exhaustible resources. Symposium on the Economics of Exhaustible Resources', *Review of Economic Studies*, 29–46.

Solow, R.M. (1986), 'On the intertemporal allocation of natural resources', *Scandinavian Journal of Economics*, **88** (1), 141–9.

10. Economic analysis of deforestation in Mexico*

with J.C. Burgess

Abstract

This chapter uses panel analyses to estimate relationships for agricultural planted area and beef cattle numbers at the state level in Mexico during the period 1970–85, in order to determine the main factors affecting forest land conversion. Of the key policy variables, maize and fertilizer prices appear to be the main influences on the expansion of planted area, whereas beef prices and credit disbursement influence cattle numbers. Population growth also affects both livestock and agricultural activities, and income per capita is positively correlated with cattle expansion. These estimated relationships are used to examine the effects both of agricultural and livestock sectoral policy changes and of trade liberalization in Mexico resulting from the North American Free Trade Agreement (NAFTA). To avoid any unintended impacts of NAFTA on deforestation, it may be necessary for Mexico to make complementary investments in land improvements, especially for existing cultivation on rainfed land.

1. Introduction

Mexico's total forest area is 49.6 million hectares, covering 25.3 per cent of total land. Of this, around 24.1 million hectares are temperate forests concentrated in the south and southeast, and 25.5 million hectares are temperate forests located in the mountains running through the country. Of this total forest area, 34 million hectares is classified as potential production forest, with the rest being conservation, steep or degraded forest. Approximately 70 per cent of the land is owned by *ejidos* (communal land owners), 25 per cent by individuals and 5 per cent by Amerindian communities (World Bank, 1989).

Current estimates of the rate of deforestation in Mexico range from 400 000 to 1 500 000 hectares per year. All estimates agree that there is much more deforestation in the tropical than in the temperate areas. For example, Masera *et al.* (1992) indicate that 46 per cent of all forest clearance occurs in the tropical deciduous forests and a further 29 per cent in the tropical evergreen forests. The dominant impact on forest conversion has been made by the rapid expansion of livestock production and the demand for pasture land, particularly in tropical areas. In addition, an increase in land under rainfed agricultural production has been achieved mainly through forest conversion. In some areas, poorly managed timber extraction and forest fires have led to degradation and loss of forests. Road-building and timber extraction may also be the principal cause of 'opening up' new areas of forest for encroachment by other activities (Barbier *et al.*, 1993).

In this chapter, we examine the extent to which government policies in the agricultural and livestock sectors have contributed to deforestation in Mexico. As previous studies of deforestation in tropical countries suggest that agricultural expansion and pasture formation are two major causes of forest conversion, we conduct a quantitative analysis of the underlying causes of deforestation in Mexico. Because of data limitations, however, the relationships influencing deforestation directly could not be examined. Instead, a more indirect approach is taken of using panel analyses to estimate relationships for agricultural planted area and beef cattle at the state level in Mexico over the 1970-85 period, which seem to be strongly correlated with loss of forest area. The results of the analysis of planted area and cattle expansion are then used to examine the likely implications for deforestation of specific government livestock and agricultural policy changes. Our policy analysis is combined with results from other studies to indicate the likely implications of the North American Free Trade Agreement (NAFTA) for deforestation in Mexico. Our chapter concludes by examining the need for additional investment programmes and policies to complement policy liberalization in order to reconcile economic development with improved incentives for forest management and limiting deforestation.

2. Government agricultural and livestock policies and deforestation

Policies in Mexico's livestock and agricultural sectors affect deforestation by influencing the incentives to convert forest land for these economic activities, rather than maintain the forest for timber production, harvesting of non-timber products, tourism, watershed protection and other uses. Thus the comparative returns gained from converting forests to agricultural and livestock production are a major factor determining deforestation. In addition, the decision to augment 'existing' agricultural and pasture lands with new 'frontier' lands is affected by the comparative gains from converting forest lands. Finally, the expansion of frontier agricultural production and related activities such as livestock-raising has its own dynamics of 'rent-seeking' behaviour.

Consequently, if agricultural and livestock policies in Mexico were designed with the implications for deforestation taken into account, then the following incentive issues should be addressed:

- the optimal allocation of forest land among competing economic uses
- the comparative returns to existing versus frontier agricultural livestock land

- the 'rent-seeking' motivation for frontier agricultural and livestock land expansion.

Although our main focus is on agricultural and livestock policies that affect deforestation in Mexico, it is important to note that they are only one of a variety of economic policies that can potentially influence forest conversion and degradation. In general, sectoral policies have the most immediate and visible impacts on deforestation, but many broader fiscal, monetary and international policies can also have important effects (Repetto, 1988).

The agriculture, livestock and trade sectors have been the target of extensive intervention by the Government of Mexico (GoM) over recent decades. Interventions have taken the form of price controls, guarantee prices, input subsidies, trade restrictions and subsidized imports. GoM parastatals have also developed an important role in marketing, storage and processing. In recent years, the GoM has undertaken reforms in the agricultural and livestock sectors that have aimed to reduce the role of government in marketing, storage and processing. The objectives of these reforms are to improve the efficiency and competitiveness of these sectors and reduce the heavy financial burden of extensive intervention.

An important economic objective of the Mexican government since 1950 has been to keep the price of key industrial inputs and basic foods low at the consumer level in order to encourage industrial growth and economic development. In addition, the GoM has attempted to maintain high producer prices to bolster production in the agriculture and livestock sectors, with the particular objective of achieving agricultural self-sufficiency in basic grains and cereals. These two conflicting objectives have resulted in a complex array of policy interventions in the agriculture and livestock sectors over the past thirty to forty years. The GoM's pricing policies have included:

- establishing guaranteed producer prices (with or without state purchasing activity)
- administering prices for products that are purchased by semi-government agencies
- direct subsidies to private and parastatal processors.

In recent years, all commodity guarantee prices, except for maize and beans, have been eliminated as part of the liberalization drive in preparation for NAFTA. However, the GoM's objective of maintaining low urban food prices has often overridden the objective of higher producer prices; as a result, farmgate prices were allowed to decline in the late 1980s, particularly in real terms in the interests of eliminating the consumer–producer price differential. For sorghum, soybeans, rice and wheat, agreement prices are now in place. Except for credit subsidies, all input subsidies have been eliminated. Over the period 1983–87, agricultural and livestock lending represented on average 57 per cent and 28 per cent respectively of total lending by the main financial institutions, although lending to these sectors appears to have declined more recently (Barbier *et al.*, 1993).

3. Other relevant analyses of deforestation in developing countries

Several previous studies of analyses of deforestation in developing countries are worth reviewing briefly. For our purposes, it is relevant to distinguish between those studies that analyse the *direct* impacts on deforestation of key socio-economic and policy variables and those that analyse the *indirect* impacts, for example through the influence of these variables on the demand for agricultural land which is considered to be the main source of deforestation. We discuss studies that analyse the direct impacts of deforestation first.

Although there is an increasing number of case studies examining the factors behind tropical deforestation and agricultural frontier expansion, there have been few attempts to explore these linkages through statistical analysis. Those that have been conducted are generally fairly aggregate and regressed on a cross-country level.[1] One such analysis by Palo *et al.* (1987) for 72 tropical forest countries identified a strong link between tropical deforestation and population density, population growth and increased food production. A study by Capistrano (1994) examined the influence of international and domestic macroeconomic factors on tropical deforestation.[2] The econometric analysis indicates the role of high agricultural export prices in inducing agricultural expansion and forest-clearing, as well as the influence of domestic structural adjustment policies, such as exchange rate devaluation and increased debt-servicing ratios. A more recent statistical analysis by Burgess (1993) of 53 tropical countries supports the hypothesis that population pressure and industrial roundwood production are positively associated with forest clearance in the tropics over the period 1980–85, although the former is much more significant in its impact. Economic development, as represented by rising per capita GNP, and improvements in agricultural yields reduce forest-clearing. However, the analysis also indicates that countries whose forests are small relative to total area are depleting these forests at a high rate.

In recent years, some important cross-sectional analyses of the causes of deforestation have been conducted for specific Latin American countries. For example, Reis and Margulis (1993) analyse the relationship between the spatial density of major economic activities and the share of deforested areas across 165 municipalities in the Brazilian Amazon. The model examines the densities of population, cattle, logging, crop area and roads as major factors in the deforestation process. The highest value of the elasticity of deforestation is 0.40 in relation to the density of crop areas, although elasticities for road density and population density are also relatively high. However, the elasticity of deforestation with respect to cattle density is less than one third of the value for crop area, and the coefficient on logging density is not statistically significant. With respect to cattle-raising, the authors argue that although one interpretation may be that its role in deforestation is grossly overstated, it is the process of cattle-raising following crop expansion that has made forest conversion irreversible in the Brazilian Amazon.[3]

Southgate *et al.* (1989) examine the causes of agricultural colonization and deforestation in eastern Ecuador in the early 1980s. They analyse the statistical significance of rural population pressure, local demand for agricultural commodities, infrastructure development and tenure security as factors explaining forest land clearing across twenty cantons. First, the area's agricultural labour force, a proxy for rural population pressure, is regressed against the factors thought to determine agricultural rents: urban population (increased demand), soil quality (productivity constraint) and roads (market accessibility and opening forest areas). Second, the extent of land clearing is regressed on the rural population pressure variable and an index of relative tenure security. The results of the analysis support the hypothesis that the incentive to capture agricultural rents is the main driving force behind forest conversion, and is further induced by tenure insecurity. The study emphasizes the role of population pressure in encouraging deforestation, directly through an increasing rural labour force and indirectly through rising urban food demand, but also emphasizes the role of misguided government policies regarding land tenure arrangements and extension of the road network into forested areas.

In Mexico, an attempt at a cross-sectional analysis of forest cover and agricultural intensity for 434 rural 'productive' units (for example, holding by *ejidatarios* and others) was conducted by Muñoz (1992). The basic source of land use data was the 1980 *Censo Agropecuario y Ejidal* (Rural Census). The independent variables explaining the changes in the percentage of land area per holding under forest or agriculture included climatic conditions, road density, population density, size of plot, type of property and measures of rural poverty. The results of the analysis indicate, as expected in a logit model, that explanatory variables have opposite effects on the two types of land use. Road and population density have an important influence on the probability of finding forest cover as opposed to agriculture on a plot, the size of the plot has a positive effect on forest cover but not on agricultural area; *ejidatarios* are more likely to have agriculture than forest cover on their plots; and in humid as opposed to dry regions the probability is higher of having forest rather than agricultural cover. Unfortunately, this promising analysis by Muñoz (1992) is marred by some significant flaws in the logit analysis, which cast doubt on some of the statistical results.[4]

As noted, the difficulty in obtaining data on forest cover or deforestation rates often leads to the analysis of deforestation indirectly through examining the factors explaining expansion of agriculture or other conversion activities. For example, many of the direct deforestation analyses have pointed to expansion of cropping and possibly livestock production as major factors underlying deforestation.

For example, a recent study in Thailand highlights the complex linkages between agricultural crop prices, the relative returns from different crops and the demand for land (Phantumvanit and Panayotou, 1990). In Thailand, approximately 40 per cent of the increase in cultivated land in recent years is accounted for by converted forest land. The statistical analysis indicates that the most important factors affecting the demand for cropland, and thus forest conversion, appear to be population growth followed by non-agricultural returns, although agricultural pricing also has a significant influence.[5] Higher aggregate real prices may have a slightly positive influence on the demand for cropland and thus increased forest clearing; however, this direct effect may be counteracted by the indirect impact of higher agricultural prices in raising the productivity of existing land and increasing the cultivation of previously idle land, thus reducing the demand for new land for forest-clearing. Changes in relative prices also influence the demand for new cropland by affecting the relative profitability of land-saving as opposed to land-extensive cropping systems. Finally, the relative returns to land-saving cropping systems can also be affected by the relative costs of inputs (for example, fertilizer, seed, credit, irrigation, agrochemicals) where these differ between land-saving and land-extensive systems. Presumably, then, the relative prices of crops to inputs would also affect the comparative returns of land-saving as opposed to land-extensive systems.

Comparative analysis of 24 Latin American countries also highlights the strong but indirect relationship between population pressure and frontier expansion and thus forest clearance – increasing numbers of urban consumers raise the demand for domestic production and hence for agricultural land – and the countervailing role of increased agricultural productivity and yield growth in slowing agricultural expansion (Southgate, 1991). An important addition of this analysis is the inclusion of a land constraint variable (for countries with a low potential agricultural land availability). Where there is little appropriate land available for conversion, the growth in arable land, and thereby forest clearance, is significantly reduced.

4. Policy analysis of the incentives to deforest in Mexico

The analyses of deforestation discussed in the previous section suggest that changes in government policies are likely to affect deforestation by influencing comparative economic returns to different economic activities on forest land and by affecting the comparative returns to these activities on existing as opposed to converted forest, or 'frontier' land. In addition, sectoral policies can stimulate or deter the rent-seeking motivation for continual frontier agricultural and livestock land expansion.

In practice, however, it is very difficult to determine the overall effects of policy changes on deforestation, as it is likely that a given policy change will have both positive and negative impacts on forest conversion and degradation. For example, in Mexico agricultural and livestock expansion are the activities thought to be most responsible for deforestation. As indicated above, the most powerful incentive effect of policy changes will be on the comparative returns of agricultural and livestock production. In the case of product and input price changes, the implications for returns and production can be very direct and immediate. By affecting the returns from agricultural and livestock activities, price changes influence the choice of crop and livestock inputs and outputs, production systems, land investments and the scale and extent of production. These production choices in turn determine the rate and scale of resource use, including forest land conversion, and investments in land improvements and management However, these latter implications are clearly second-order and indirect. Thus, although increasing agricultural and livestock prices may translate into higher returns from increased production, the resulting expansion of output does not necessarily lead to greater forest conversion; the way in which the extra cultivation is carried out is the key factor.[6]

In Mexico, an important consideration is that the expansion of planted agriculture and pasture land in recent years may have been achieved not only by the conversion of forest land but also by bringing previously unused or fallow land into cultivation. Almost one quarter of agricultural land is idle, perhaps proportionately more on larger farms. Any aggregate increase in production from improved returns to agriculture could come from either increased production on existing planted land, new production on previously fallow land or conversion of additional forest land to agriculture. The net effects on deforestation are not always readily apparent.

The situation is illustrated in Figure 10.1. Total agricultural land consists of existing agricultural land and any additional frontier agricultural land, if it is worth bring the latter into production through conversion of forest land. Thus the total land available for cultivation is OD + OG. However, not all of the convertible forest land, OG, may be worth cultivating. For example, if in the extreme case the returns to cultivating convertible forest land were zero, then existing agricultural land area OD would represent the total agricultural land in production. However, suppose, as actually shown in Figure 10.1, curve AH depicts the returns per hectare (ha) on existing agricultural land, and curve BG the returns that could be earned on convertible forest land if it were brought into production. Thus, area OC of existing land is under production, and the remaining CF ha of existing agricultural land is fallow. Additional agricultural production would therefore come from area CG of convertible forest land on the frontier. Note that

DF ha of fallow land would be idled because they are economically unproductive. However, CD ha would be idled because they could not compete with the returns from convertible forest land.

The impacts of agricultural frontier expansion on deforestation could be reduced by a policy that raises the returns on existing agricultural land so as to bring previously idle land into production as a substitute for additional production from convertible forest land. As shown in Figure 10.1, suppose that such a policy exists, for example, targeted land or irrigation improvements on existing agricultural land. Then the comparative returns on this land would increase, from AH to A'F. As a result, previously idled land becomes more attractive to cultivate, and the area of fallow land falls to EF. In addition, the comparative returns to convertible forest land are less attractive, and consequently the forest area that would be converted falls to EG ha.[7]

In practice, however, most agricultural and livestock policies are difficult to 'target' as depicted in Figure 10.1. Most sectoral policies in Mexico have had the overall objective of raising production of key agricultural and livestock products and are thus indiscriminate in terms of whether this increased production

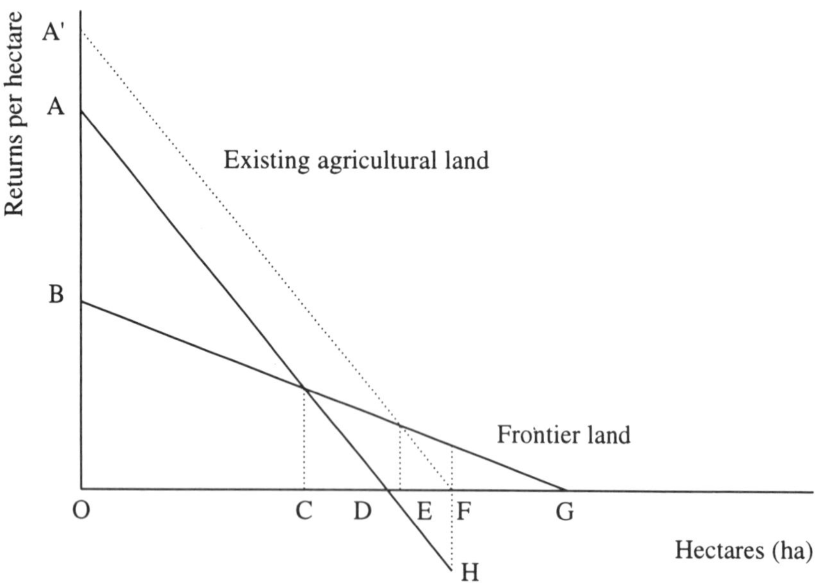

Note: As the returns to existing agricultural land increase (from AH to A'F), the amount of fallow land decreases (from CF to EF) and less land is exploited on the frontier (from CG to EG).

Figure 10.1 The comparative returns on existing and frontier land

comes from existing or frontier agricultural land. Although it is not shown in Figure 10.1, it is easy to indicate with this diagram that if the returns to both existing and convertible forest land increase (that is, curves AH and BG both shift out) then there will be little change in the amount of forest land converted to agriculture. In fact, as discussed throughout this chapter, many agricultural, livestock and other economic policies in Mexico may actually be encouraging deforestation by making the returns to frontier agriculture more attractive.

Policy analysis is further complicated by consideration of the comparative returns between agriculture and other forest land uses on the frontier. This situation is illustrated in Figure 10.2. For simplification, it is assumed that there are three competing uses of forest land: forestry, agricultural and livestock production. Forestry yields the highest returns (curve AE), but only on a limited amount of forest land. The amount of forest land retained for permanent wood production is OD ha. Where agriculture yields higher returns (curve BG), forest land is converted to agriculture. This amounts to DF ha. However, some

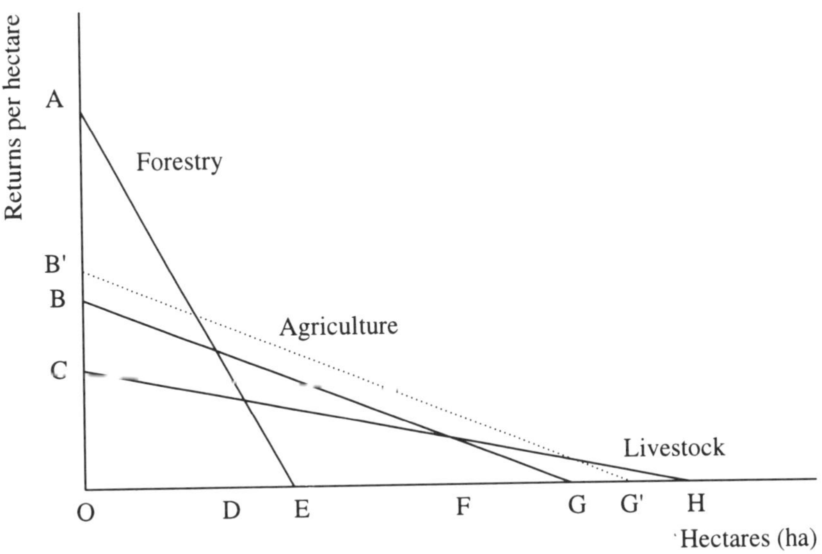

Note: An increase in the comparative returns to agriculture on forest lands (from BG to B'G') could lead to agricultural expansion at the expense of permanent forest production (OD decreases) and substitution from livestock to agricultural production on the frontier (FH decreases). The net effect on deforestation depends on the comparative returns to forestry and agriculture only.

Figure 10.2. The comparative returns to different forest land uses

forest land will yield higher returns under livestock production (curve CH), and thus FH ha of forests should be converted to pasture land.

An increase in the comparative returns to agriculture on forest lands (from BG to B'G') could lead to agricultural expansion at the expense of permanent forest production (OD decreases), and substitution of livestock by agricultural production on the frontier (FH decreases). The net effect on deforestation depends on the comparative returns to forestry and agriculture, and not on the substitution of agricultural for livestock production on frontier land. The latter effect is simply the substitution of one conversion activity for another. Moreover, there is an overall welfare gain as the returns to converted forest land in general are increased. If property rights are well defined, access to additional areas of unexploited forests is costly and the returns to the converted land can be maintained, then farmers may not have the incentive to expand frontier cultivation further through 'rent-seeking' behaviour. Finally, if as shown in Figure 10.2 the returns to forestry are fairly high on land allocated to permanent forest production, then very little net additional deforestation will occur through substituting agricultural for forestry activities. The increased agricultural activity would largely be confined to forest land demarcated for conversion anyway.[8]

Figure 10.2 again clearly represents an ideal situation. Forestry, agriculture and livestock production are being influenced by a variety of policies simultaneously. It is difficult to determine the implications for the comparative returns of the three frontier activities, let alone the net effects on forest land conversion. The conditions determining the extent to which these different forest land uses compete with each other also vary significantly across the different forest regions of Mexico. Finally, the basic legal and regulatory framework affecting forestry, agricultural and livestock production in Mexico is currently undergoing major revision, which could have important implications for rent-seeking motivation in frontier forest land exploitation.

The analysis of comparative returns indicated by Figures 10.1 and 10.2 formed the conceptual basis of our empirical analysis of the incentives to deforest in Mexico. Unfortunately, we were prevented from estimating the relationships represented in Figures 10.1 and 10.2 directly, by a number of limitations.

In Mexico, time series data on tropical forest area and conversion trends are not yet sufficiently disaggregated or complete to conduct a *direct* analysis of deforestation. Yet there is substantial evidence to suggest that forest clearance for agricultural and livestock production is prevalent throughout Mexico. However, data on total agricultural area and pastoral land are also insufficient and unreliable. In particular, it was impossible to disaggregate the data between existing and frontier livestock and agricultural activities, as suggested by Figure 10.1.

Nevertheless, it is possible to conduct an *indirect* analysis of the factors influencing forest conversion in Mexico, by focusing on the increases in agricultural planted area and beef cattle numbers disaggregated by state and over time. The key assumption is that increasing agricultural expansion and livestock grazing have been the principal *proximate* causes of deforestation in Mexico over the previous two and half decades, and the factors determining agricultural and livestock expansion are thus the *underlying* causes of forest conversion and degradation. Over the period 1970–91, as forest area has fallen, agricultural planted area and cattle numbers have increased, although the latter have started to decline in recent years.[9] This would again support the hypothesis that agricultural and livestock expansion are proximate factors influencing deforestation in Mexico. However, it is important to stress that this assumption remains a hypothesis, which cannot at this time be statistically proven. More importantly, the exact magnitudes of the relationships between increasing agricultural and livestock expansion and deforestation cannot be reliably estimated.

By taking this (untested) hypothesis as our starting point, it is possible to focus on the underlying causes of forest conversion by analysing the factors behind increases in agricultural planted area and beef cattle head in Mexico. With regard to the latter, assuming a zero rate of return to unconverted forest, Figure 10.2 suggests that not only will increasing returns to frontier agriculture lead to forest conversion but also, if agricultural and livestock production are competing activities on the frontier, then an increase in the returns from livestock production will negatively affect frontier agricultural land expansion. Equally, an increase in the returns from agriculture will reduce the demand for livestock expansion on the frontier. In the following analysis we were able to examine this hypothesis that agricultural and livestock production are competing activities on the frontier, by including livestock and maize prices in the regressions for planted agricultural area and beef cattle numbers respectively.

5. Analysis of planted agricultural area

There is strong evidence to suggest that the increase in land under agricultural production in Mexico over recent decades has been achieved mainly through the conversion of forests, particularly tropical forests. Moreover, a high proportion of agricultural land – almost one quarter – is idle or fallow. This would suggest that the planted area is expanded through bringing additional land into cultivation rather than utilizing the existing stock of arable land. The extent to which planted area increases in each state should therefore provide a good indicator of forest land conversion for agriculture.

The panel analysis of longitudinal data for planted agricultural area was conducted across the 31 states of Mexico plus the *Distrito Federal* (Federal District), over the 1970, 1980 and 1985 time periods. Several explanatory variables were examined, including real guaranteed maize prices, real fertilizer prices, income per capita, population levels, real rural wages and road density. In addition, real livestock prices were included, to determine the extent to which this variable influences the agricultural land expansion. Details of the relevant variables and sources are indicated in Table 10.1.

Table 10.1 Definition and sources of data for analysis of agriculture area planted and numbers of livestock

Variable	Definition and data sources
MAAP	Agriculture area planted (state level, '000 ha). Agricultural area planted data derived from SARH (1988).
MLH	Livestock head (state level, '000 head). Livestock numbers derived from SARH (1988) and INEGI (1992).
MGMFP	Ratio of guaranteed maize prices to fertilizer prices (national level, constant MEX$/ton). Maize and fertilizer price data derived from SARH (1988).
MLP	Real livestock prices (state level, constant MEX$/kg to constant MEX$). Livestock price data derived from SARH (1988) and Robles (1992).
MYC	Income per capita (state level, constant MEX$/population). Income data derived from SARH (1988). Population data derived from SARH (1988) and INEGI/SPP (nd).
MP	Population (state level, number). Population data derived from SARH (1988) and INEGI/SPP (nd).
MGMP	Real guaranteed maize prices (national level, constant MEX$/ton). Maize price data derived from SARH (1988).
MRD	Road density (state level, km/ha). Road and state area data derived from SARH (1988).
MC	Credit (state level, constant MEX$ mn). Credit represented by loans made by FIRA and BANRURAL; data derived from SARH (1988).

Discussion of the regression procedure, results and basic statistical diagnostic tests are included in the Appendix at the end of this chapter. A random-effects error component model utilizing feasible generalized least squares (FGLS) proved to be the preferred consistent and efficient estimator. The results of the FGLS regression for both 'with' and 'without' livestock prices are depicted in Table 10.9. Livestock prices prove to be highly insignificant in the regression. This suggests that the hypothesis that livestock prices should influence planted agricultural area is rejected by the model, and thus the FGLS regression version without livestock prices shown in Table 10.9a is preferred.

As Table 10.9a indicates, the only significant explanatory variables in the FGLS regression are relative maize/fertilizer prices and population. Real income per capita and road density are not significant. Table 10.2a summarizes the resulting elasticities for the two significant variables.

Table 10.2 Calculation of elasticities for planted agricultural area and beef cattle

a. Planted agricultural area ('000 ha)

Variable	Coefficient	Mean	Elasticity
MAAP		532.84	
MGMFP	167.49	1.0267	0.3227
MP	0.000077	1 986 278	0.2882

b. Beef cattle ('000 head)

Variable	Coefficient	Mean	Elasticity
MLH		958.05	
MLP	43.425	9.2548	0.4195
MP	0.000051	1 986 278	0.1062
MC	0.3765	347.06	0.1364
MYC	0.00865	10 280.77	0.0928

Note: For variable definitions, see Table 10.1.

Source: FGLS regressions in Appendix Tables 10.9a and 10.10a. Only the significant variables from these regressions are included.

Relative maize/fertilizer prices have the larger impact on agricultural planted area. A 1 per cent increase in this price ratio will lead to a 0.32 per cent change in planted area. As this is an output/input price ratio, it is an approximation of the returns to planting maize and related crops. In addition, any change in these returns would have an important influence on the allocation of forest land among competing uses, the comparative returns to existing versus frontier agricultural land, and the 'rent-seeking' motivation for frontier agricultural expansion. Thus, one would expect that an increase in the relative returns from maize would have an important influence on the total agricultural area planted across Mexico, and therefore possibly on forest clearance.

The other significant variable, population, should also be associated with increased planted agricultural area. There are essentially two reasons. First, a higher population could mean that the agricultural sector has to absorb more workers and subsistence farm families, thus putting more pressure on the land base, including forest. Second, higher populations create this pressure indirectly through demand for food, fuel, fodder and other consumptive goods. In our analysis, a 1 per cent increase in state populations leads to a 0.23 per cent rise in agricultural area planted.

A surprising result of the analysis is that road density is not significant, despite the fact that road-building in Latin America is generally considered to be associated with the opening up of forest area for agricultural expansion (Reis and Margulis, 1993; Mahar and Schneider, 1994). However, a distinction should be made between an increase in the *road network* as represented by the absolute number of road kilometres built, and *road density* as represented by the number of road kilometres built per square kilometre of total state area. Deforestation usually results from the extension of the road network into previously remote areas. Thus, as discovered by Southgate (1991), the absolute number of road kilometres built can be a significant factor in land-clearing. However, increasing road density at the state level may actually reflect rapid urbanization and modern-sector development. As argued above, this would reduce pressures on agricultural land expansion and forest-clearing. The inconclusiveness of our analysis may be due to a combination of these two effects.

To summarize, if increasing agricultural planted area is correlated with deforestation, then the results of our analysis reveal some important factors underlying forest conversion in Mexico. Increasing the relative returns to maize production, as reflected in the maize price ratio, leads to further pressure on the forest. Rising populations at the state level also have a positive impact on forest conversion. However, neither income per capita nor road density seems to affect significantly agricultural planted area. The hypothesis that livestock prices should influence planted agricultural area is also rejected by the model.

6. Analysis of beef cattle head

Beef cattle production is a highly land-extensive process. There are limits to the number of cattle that can be grazed on a given plot of pasture land before it is irrevocably degraded. Degradation of pasture land, in any case, can lead to the abandonment of that land in favour of new pasture formation. Moreover, legally each farmer is restricted to a maximum of 500 head of cattle (Maddison *et al.*, 1992). Consequently, an increasing number of cattle in a region or state is an indication that new farms and pastures are being established. Increases in the number of beef cattle per state are therefore a good approximation of the extent of pasture land expansion in Mexico.

Thus an additional panel analysis of longitudinal data for beef cattle numbers (that is, livestock head) was conducted across the 31 states of Mexico plus the Federal District, over the 1970,1980 and 1985 time periods. Several explanatory variables were examined, including real beef prices, income per capita, population levels, real rural wages, road density and real credit disbursement. Real guaranteed maize prices were also included, to determine how far the expansion in beef numbers is explained by this variable. Details of the relevant variables and sources are indicated in Table 10.1.

As discussed in the Appendix, the random-effects error component model utilizing FGLS again proved to be the preferred consistent and efficient estimator. The results of the FGLS regression both with and without maize prices are depicted in Table 10.10. Maize prices prove to be highly insignificant in the regression. This suggests that the hypothesis that maize prices influence livestock numbers is rejected by the model, and thus the FGLS regression version without maize price shown in Table 10.10a is preferred

Table 10.10a shows that livestock prices, population, credit and income per capita are all significant in explaining beef cattle demand. Road density is the only variable that is not significant. Table 10.2b summarizes the resulting elasticities.

Livestock prices have the largest impact on the number of beef cattle per state. As expected, the relationship is positive. A 1 per cent rise in these prices leads to a 0.42 per cent increase in the number of cattle. If it is assumed that increasing livestock prices are correlated with increasing returns to cattle-raising, then rising prices and thus greater returns lead to greater cattle herd expansion and conversion of forests through pasture formation.

An increase in real credit disbursement also leads to greater beef cattle numbers at the state level. Over the 1970–85 period, much credit was extended to the livestock sector, and these loans were heavily subsidized. Thus, one would expect that higher cattle numbers and pasture formation would result from an increase in credit disbursement. The analysis indicates that a 1 per cent rise in loans increases head of beef cattle by 0.14 per cent.

As in the case of planted agricultural area expansion, an increase in population at the state level is also a significant factor in determining greater cattle numbers. A 1 per cent rise in population causes cattle numbers to increase by 0.11 per cent. Like the growth in a planted area, a rise in population means more direct pressure on the land base, including the forest, through the establishment of new farms and ranching operations, and more indirect pressure through increased demand for beef and other livestock products.

Income per capita also appears to be positively correlated with greater livestock numbers over the 1970–85 period. A 1 per cent increase in per capita income at the state level leads to a 0.09 per cent increase in beef cattle. There may be two reasons for this positive relationship. Cattle-raising is generally a commercial activity that may be associated with a state's agricultural development from subsistence to commercial agricultural activities. In general, one would expect a state's average per capita income to increase with such agricultural developments. In addition, rising per capita income is associated with increasing demand for meat, which may be reflected in increased cattle numbers.

Finally, as in the case of planted agricultural area, a surprising outcome of the analysis of the demand for livestock head is that road density is not a significant variable. It is assumed that this is for the same reasons discussed above in Section 5.

To summarize, if increasing beef cattle numbers in Mexico are correlated with forest conversion to pasture, then several factors appear to play an important role. The most significant appears to be the returns to cattle operations, as reflected in the price of beef. Increasing credit disbursements, population levels and, to a lesser extent, rising income per capita are also important factors underlying forest conversion for cattle-raising. However, road density does not seem to be significant in affecting cattle numbers. The hypothesis that maize prices influence planted agricultural area is also rejected by the model. Together with the similar result for the effect of livestock prices on agricultural area planted, this suggests that over the 1970–85 period livestock production and agricultural expansion were not competing for land on the forest frontier in states across Mexico. Nevertheless, as the overall demand for land in Mexico can be expected to increase, especially with rising population, the result may be greater competition between livestock and agricultural activities for frontier land.

7. Analysis of specific agricultural and livestock policies

The major policies affecting Mexico's agricultural and livestock sectors are described in Section 2. In recent years, these policies have been undergoing major changes as part of the transition to a more outward development strategy and as the GoM has attempted to reduce government expenditures. Much of the economic reform in the direction of increased liberalization has been part of the transition to Mexico's participation in NAFTA. As a consequence, some sub-sectors in agriculture and livestock have been undergoing reduction in subsidies and other support programmes, in order to improve competitiveness.

As discussed above, analyzing the impacts of these sectoral policy changes on deforestation in Mexico poses many problems because of complex linkages. A further difficulty is that the process of internal economic reform and liberalization for many sub-sectors (for example, maize) in Mexico is slow and only just beginning. However, in the previous sections the analyses of the demand for agricultural land and cattle expansion indicated that certain policy variables may have important effects on forest conversion. We therefore analyse in this section the effect of policy changes on these variables, which are:

- maize and fertilizer prices as determinants of the returns to agriculture and thus expansion of planted area

- beef prices as a determinant of the returns to cattle-raising and thus expansion of livestock numbers
- rural credit disbursements as a determinant of the returns to cattle-raising.

We utilize the statistical analyses and results derived in Sections 5 and 6 as the starting point in examining these relationships.

Maize prices

Maize prices in Mexico are beginning to be liberalized as part of the drive towards Mexico's membership of NAFTA. Maize is a key agricultural sub-sector in Mexico since it is the main stable crop and its cultivation provides much rural employment. GoM maize policies have essentially maintained a divergence between producer and consumer prices, with the former generally above and the latter generally below the border-equivalent international price for maize. Given the strategic importance of the crop, efforts to liberalize the maize sub-sector are proceeding slowly.

In Section 8, we explore in more detail the implications of liberalization of the maize sub-sector for overall rural development and deforestation. As background to that discussion, we focus here on the potential effects of price changes for maize on the return to its cultivation and thus forest conversion. As discussed above, the latter impacts are the result of changing maize prices affecting the comparative returns to existing as opposed to 'frontier' agricultural land, the comparative returns to maize cultivation on forest land and the motivation for 'rent-seeking' through extending cultivation and forest conversion. Because maize accounts for over half the crop area harvested in Mexico, these effects of changing maize prices could be extremely important in determining forest conversion.

Unfortunately, the analysis of the expansion in planted agricultural area in Mexico over the period 1970–85 could not be disaggregated sufficiently to distinguish between new production on 'idle' land and new production on converted forest land (see Sections 4 and 5 and the Appendix). Rather, the analysis shows only the aggregate effect on planted area of increases in the maize/fertilizer price ratio. Not all of the increase in planted area would come from forest conversion, but without further information it is difficult to determine this proportion.

Table 10.2 indicates that an increase in the maize/fertilizer price ratio, our proxy for returns to agricultural and particularly annual crop production, has a strong and positive impact on the area of land planted in Mexico. In Table 10.3a, the elasticities estimated in our model are used to calculate the potential impact of various increases in maize prices on agricultural planted area, using 1990 values as the base case reference point.[10] For example, a 10 per cent decrease in maize prices would lead to a 3.23 per cent fall in area planted. Such 'instantaneous' effects, particularly for large price movements, represent approximate 'order-of-magnitude' indicators rather than predictors of actual responses [11]

Table 10.3 Effects of changes in key policy variables on planted agricultural area

a. Maize prices (nominal 1990 MEX$618,000/ton)

Effect on:	Base case value	Percentage change –10%	–50%	–70%
Real maize prices (MEX$ /ton)	3 471	–347	–1736	–2 430
Maize/fertilizer price ratio	1.31	–0.13	–0.66	–0.92
Planted area ('000 ha)	19 261	–622	–3108	–4351
(% change)		(–3.23%)	(–16.14%)	(–22.59%)

b. Fertilizer prices (nominal 1990 MEX$471,000/ton)

Effect on:	Base case value	Percentage change 10%	50%	70%
Real fertilizer prices (MEX$/ton)	2 645	265	1323	1852
Maize/fertilizer price ratio	1.31	–0.12	–0.44	–0.54
(% change)		(–9.09%)	(–33.33%)	(–41.18%)
Planted area ('000 ha)	19 261	–565	–2072	–2599
(% change)		(–2.93%)	(–10.76%)	(–13.29%)

Notes: All base case values are for 1990. Real values are in constant 1980 pesos (MEX$). Elasticity measures are derived from Table 10.2a.

Source: References in Table 10.1.

Due to the GoM policy of supporting the rural producer price well above the world price of maize, liberalization of the maize market would cause the price to fall considerably. For example, using 1989 values as their base case reference, Levy and van Wijnbergen (1992a) suggest that' 'instantaneous' liberalization would lead to a 50 per cent reduction in the rural producer price of maize (see also Section 8).

As indicated in Table 10.3a, such a large price response to 'instantaneous' liberalization would translate into a major impact on agricultural area planted (that is, a 16 per cent decline as an 'order of magnitude'). As discussed further in Section 8, the resulting impacts on the entire rural sector, particularly employment of subsistence and landless workers, would be severe. Moreover, a general fall in the price of maize would not conform to the 'ideal' policy described above, as it would affect indiscriminately the returns to agricultural production on both existing and frontier agricultural land. That is, there is little incentive for substituting previously idled land for converted forest land.

The effects of falling producer prices on the returns to maize cultivation and contraction of planted area will also be determined by the effects of other liberalization policies on the comparative returns to competing economic activities on forest land. Although our analyses suggest that competition between livestock and agricultural activities for converted forest land may not be that significant, this may not necessarily hold for large and very rapid relative price movements. For example, the forestry sector in Mexico has generally been much less protected than agriculture, particularly maize. As a consequence, liberalization of the maize market could conceivably reduce significantly the comparative returns of maize cultivation to permanent forestry operations on the frontier, and this might reduce deforestation. On the other hand, cattle-raising and beef production are also protected in Mexico. As discussed below, as this sector has also been liberalized recently, the resulting impacts on the comparative returns to maize and cattle-raising are less certain. It could be that when maize prices are eventually liberalized the returns to maize relative to cattle production fall. As a result, the decline in planted area on the forest land may be at the expense of expansion in cattle-grazing. Because one conversion activity is essentially being replaced by another, the net effects on deforestation are more marginal.

Finally, if displacement of rural workers and subsistence farmers does occur as a result of liberalization, there may be a 'second-order' effect on deforestation. Some of the displaced workers and farmers may migrate to the frontier and convert additional forest land. Increased rural unemployment could also reduce real wages, which may make employment of labour for forest conversion and agricultural expansion much less expensive.

On balance, it may be better for Mexico to forgo instantaneous liberalization of its maize market in favour of a more gradual liberalization coupled with a large-scale programme of land improvements for existing rainfed agricultural land. The programme could be targeted to benefit particularly smallholders and subsistence producers. It is urgently necessary to include in this investment programme improved research and extension support that will reach those subsistence and low-income rainfed farmers in states with high rates of deforestation. Research and extension could reduce deforestation through the combination of improving yields on existing agricultural land and disseminating knowledge of land-saving rather than land-using farming systems and techniques. In addition, it is important to coordinate the liberalization policy for maize with liberalization of other sectors that also affect forest land use. Such a strategy would conform more closely to the 'ideal' maize policy for controlling excessive forest conversion than would a policy of more rapid liberalization on its own.

Fertilizer prices

Over the period 1989–91 Mexico reduced substantially its fertilizer subsidies. For example, country-level real prices for urea, ammonium nitrate and ammonium sulphate increased by 58 per cent, 74 per cent and 60 per cent respectively. As a result, the price of fertilizer at the railhead and thus to farmers has also risen sharply. Fertilizer prices in Mexico may rise further in the near future, if they follow the generally upward recent trends in world prices. If the policy of maintaining a constant fertilizer price across the country is also abandoned, then fertilizer costs would most certainly rise for farmers in the more remote areas.

In our model, fertilizer price changes also affect expansion of planted area through the maize/fertilizer price ratio variable. Thus an increase in fertilizer prices would have similar impacts to the fall in the price of maize discussed above, mainly by reducing the returns to agricultural, particularly crop, production.

Table 10.3b indicates the effects of an increase in fertilizer prices on the maize/fertilizer price ratio and thus planted area. For example, a 10 per cent increase in fertilizer prices would lead to an 11 per cent decrease in agricultural area planted. As noted above, fertilizer prices increased by around 50–70 per cent in real terms over the period 1989–91 as a result of liberalization. Our model indicates that, other things being equal, such substantial price changes may have a dramatic impact in reducing planted area and thus deforestation.[12]

However, the actual implications of the recent rise in fertilizer prices on deforestation in Mexico are subject to the same considerations discussed above with regard to liberalization of the maize market. Much will depend on the impact of increased fertilizer prices on the comparative returns to maize and other frontier agriculture as opposed to other forest land use activities, particularly if liberalization brings large and very rapid relative price movements. In addition, as rising fertilizer prices may have reduced the returns to maize cultivation in the short term, any resulting loss of rural employment opportunities and fall in wages could lead to 'second-order' deforestation impacts through increased migration to the frontier and cheaper labour for conversion activities.

Finally, rising fertilizer prices also affect returns on both frontier and existing agricultural land. Although the more remote frontier areas have presumably experienced a greater increase because of increased transportation costs, the rapid and large rise in fertilizer prices will certainly have affected farmers on existing agricultural land as well. The burden may have fallen disproportionately on the poorer, mainly rainfed farmers, who may be discouraged from using fertilizer or reduce its use to suboptimal levels. Any resulting impact on yields and productivity would also have the detrimental effect of encouraging deforestation, since the alternative to increasing production through yield increases is to expand cultivated area. For example, in an analysis across 24 Latin American countries, Southgate (1991) found that increased agricultural productivity and yield growth lead to less agricultural expansion. Thus, if in the short run the recent steep rise in fertilizer prices has drastically curtailed yield and productivity growth in Mexican agriculture, then the results may be counterproductive for controlling forest conversion.

In sum, there were clearly strong reasons for eliminating fertilizer subsidies in Mexico, on fiscal and efficiency grounds alone. Liberalization may also have had a secondary impact in reducing pressure for deforestation by reducing the incentives for agricultural land expansion, although it is clearly a blunt and far from ideal policy tool for this purpose. Our main concern is that the policy may become counterproductive, particularly in the short term, by discouraging fertilizer use by farmers, especially poorer households and those with smallholdings. Any resulting reduction in aggregate productivity and yield growth in Mexican agriculture would encourage agricultural expansion and thus deforestation. Such second-order effects could be mitigated by a national programme of land improvement investments to maintain and enhance productivity. Smallholders and subsistence farmers should be targeted as the main beneficiaries of the investment programme.

Beef prices

Cattle-raising and beef production are generally less protected in Mexico than the maize market. Nevertheless, there have been substantial subsidies, particularly in terms of credit and feed prices (see below). However, the GoM curtailed substantially its support for the producer price of beef over the 1989–91 period, although the actual impact on real prices is less well documented.

Our analysis shows that the recent liberalization of beef prices may influence the expansion of cattle numbers substantially by affecting the returns to cattle operations, as reflected in the beef/labour price ratio (see Table 10.4a). According to our simulations, a 10 per cent decrease in prices would cause beef cattle numbers to fall by around 4 per cent. If real beef prices have fallen by around 50–70 per cent, then there may be an even more dramatic effect on cattle numbers. As discussed in Section 6, because there are limits on the amount of beef cattle held per farm, an increase in the number of farms and thus pasture area would be a likely outcome, unless there is sufficient investment in research and extension to improve productivity.

The analysis would therefore suggest that the recent reduction in beef prices may have reduced pressure on forest conversion to pasture. However, as discussed above, a crucial issue is how fast and to what degree liberalization has affected the comparative returns to cattle-raising as opposed to other activities at the forest frontier. To the extent that pasture area would decline at the expense of increased agricultural expansion, the net effects on forest conversion would be minimal.

Table 10.4 Effects of changes in key policy variables on beef cattle

a. Beef prices (nominal 1990 MEX$9,000/kg)

Effect on:	Base case value	Percentage change –10%	–50%	–70%
Real beef prices (MEX$/kg)	26	–3	–13	–19
Beef cattle ('000 ha)	32 054	–1345	–6723	–9413
(% change)		(–4.20%)	(–20.98%)	(–20.37%)

b. Credit disbursements (nominal 1990 MEX$21,389 billion)

Effect on:	Base case value	Percentage change –10%	–50%	–70%
Real credit disbursements (MEX$ billions)	120.13	–12.01	–60.07	–84.09
Beef cattle ('000 ha)	32.054	–437	–2186	–3061
(% change)		(–1.36%)	(–6.82%)	(–9.55%)

Notes: All base case values are for 1990. Real values are in constant 1980 pesos (MEX$). Elasticity measures are derived from Table 2b and Appendix.

Source: References in Table 10.1.

Credit

The livestock sector in Mexico, particularly cattle-raising, has benefited in the past from subsidized loans. In more recent years, the overall level of loans to both agricultural and livestock activities has declined substantially, mainly as a result of increasing fiscal constraints on the GoM. However, the precise level of credit subsidy for cattle-raising is very difficult to determine.

Our analysis has shown that credit disbursements in general are an important determinant of cattle expansion (see Table 10.4b). For example, a 10 per cent decrease in loans would lead to a 1.4 per cent fall in the number of beef cattle. Thus the elimination of all credit subsidies for pasture formation and cattle-raising should have a significant influence on the conversion of forest land for pasture. Whether overall deforestation is reduced would depend on whether cattle-raising on the frontier is replaced by agricultural activities or by other land uses, such as permanent forestry operations or ecotourism, that would not depend on whole-scale conversion.

The elimination of subsidies for cattle-raising could be an important policy for controlling conversion of forest for pasture. Studies in other countries have indicated the extent to which subsidized cattle ranching has contributed to deforestation, particularly in areas of concentrated development. For example, in Brazil subsidies accounting for 54 per cent of livestock project development costs made uneconomic operations profitable in financial terms for the private investor (Repetto, 1988; Mahar and Schneider, 1994). In Mexico, removal of all subsidies from cattle-raising and maintaining the price of beef on a par with world prices are essential to ensuring that the beef cattle sector not only is efficient but also minimizes unnecessary deforestation.

8. NAFTA and deforestation in Mexico

To analyse the implications of NAFTA for Mexico's shift in development strategy, Hinojosa-Ojeda and Robinson (1991) developed a three-country (Mexico, US and the rest of the world) multisectoral, computable general equilibrium (CGE) model. In addition to examining the removal of tariff and non-tariff barriers to Mexican and US trade, the authors explored several different growth, investment and migration scenarios. By combining some of the results of the CGE model with those from the analysis of agricultural and cattle expansion in Section 5, it is possible to obtain a broad indication of the deforestation impacts of Mexico's economic transition to liberalization. Tables 10.5 and 10.6 summarize the implications for planted area and cattle numbers of the seven different NAFTA scenarios.[13]

In general, the pursuit of an open development strategy (scenarios 4–6) combining high economic growth and liberalization appears to mitigate agricultural area and cattle expansion more than reliance on liberalization alone (scenarios 1–3). In scenarios 4–6, the impact of an increased labour force in stimulating growth in planted area and cattle numbers seems to be offset by higher real income per capita and rural wages in reducing agricultural and cattle expansion. In the liberalization and pro-competitive scenarios 1–3, the results are more mixed and uncertain. However, if Mexico undergoes a long transition to sustained economic growth and is subject to substantial return migration to rural areas (scenario 7), then the positive inducement to forest conversion from increases in the labour force and falling rural wages may outweigh the incentives to reduce agricultural and cattle expansion due to increasing real GDP per capita. Thus the ability of the Mexican economy and rural labour market to adapt to an open development strategy could be a key determinant of the overall impacts on deforestation.

In sum, if Mexico adopts an open development strategy of joining NAFTA while simultaneously pursuing vigorous economic development at home, then the increasing returns and output in agricultural and livestock production could translate into additional forest conversion. However, these impacts may be mitigated if the open development strategy is combined with the more specific agricultural and livestock sector policy reforms discussed in the previous section.

Table 10.5 Net deforestation effects of changes in labour force

Scenario	% change in labour force[a]	% change in planted areas[b]	% change in cattle numbers[b]
1. Tariff removal	–0.1	–0.03	–0.01
2. Liberalization	0.3	0.09	0.03
3. Pro-competitive	1.0	0.29	0.11
4. Mexican growth	0.1	0.03	0.01
5. Mex. transition	0.1	0.03	0.01
6. Growth & mig.	1.4	0.40	0.15
7. Trans. & mig.	5.0	1.44	0.53

Notes:
1. Remove all official tariffs.
2. Tariff removal plus removal of all quantity restrictions on imports.
3. Liberalization plus capital reallocation due to lower distortions in domestic capital markets in the USA and Mexico in light manufacturing, intermediates and consumer durables.
4. Pro-competitive liberalization plus increased aggregate capital stock in Mexico (7.6 per cent). No return migration.
5. Modified Mexican growth scenario, with half the increase in aggregate capital stock (3.8 per cent) plus increased foreign borrowing by Mexico. No return migration.
6. Mexican growth scenario plus return migration to Mexico.
7. Modified Mexican growth scenario plus return migration to Mexico.

Sources:
[a] Percentage change over 1988 base case values, from Hinojosa-Ojeda and Robinson (1991).
[b] See Table 10.2.

More detailed partial equilibrium analysis of the implications of NAFTA for the maize sub-sector in Mexico has been conducted (Levy and van Wijnbergen 1992a, b). However, this analysis also does not explicitly address the impacts on forest land conversion and degradation. Some possible effects of the different scenarios can nevertheless be inferred, which generally support the conclusions from our own policy analysis of agricultural expansion discussed in Section 7.

Maize accounts for over half the crop area harvested in Mexico and employs approximately one third of rural workers (World Bank, 1989). In 1989, out of a total production of 12.8 million tons, 8.8 million tons were produced by rainfed farmers, and rural own consumption accounted for 3.6 million tons. Thus, out of the estimated 2 250 000 maize producers in Mexico, at most 15 per cent of all producers are net sellers, comprising 250 000 large-scale producers on irrigated land and 80 000 rainfed farmers. This leaves approximately, 1 920 000 subsistence maize farmers on rainfed lands (Levy and van Wijnbergen, 1992a).

Table 10.6 Net deforestation effects on changes in real GDP

Scenario	% change in real GDP[a]	% change in real GDP per capital[b]	% change in cattle numbers[c]
1. Tariff removal	0.1	–1.7	–0.16
2. Liberalization	0.3	–1.5	–0.14
3. Pro-competitive	1.2	–0.6	–0.06
4. Mexican growth	6.4	4.6	0.43
5. Mex. transition	3.0	1.2	0.11
6. Growth & mig.	6.8	5.0	0.46
7. Trans. & mig.	4.5	2.7	0.25

Notes:

1. Remove all official tariffs.
2. Tariff removal plus removal of all quantity restrictions on imports.
3. Liberalization plus capital reallocation due to lower distortions in domestic capital markets in the USA and Mexico in light manufacturing, intermediates and consumer durables.
4. Pro-competitive liberalization plus increased aggregate capital stock in Mexico (7.6 per cent). No return migration.
5. Modified Mexican growth scenario, with half the increase in aggregate capital stock (3.8 per cent) plus increased foreign borrowing by Mexico. No return migration.
6. Mexican growth scenario plus return migration to Mexico.
7. Modified Mexican growth scenario plus return migration to Mexico.

Sources:

[a] Percentage change over 1988 base case values, from Hinojosa-Ojeda and Robinson (1991).
[b] Assumes annual average population growth of 1.8 per cent over 1989–2000.
[c] From Table 10.2.

To encourage domestic production, maize rural producer prices were heavily subsidized in Mexico. In 1989, the subsidy amounted to US$72.8 per ton, or 54 per cent of the world price (Levy and van Wijnbergen, 1992a). The net producer subsidy after rural consumption amounted to US$291.2 million, of which US$109.2 million (38 per cent) went to producers on irrigated lands and US$182 million (62 per cent) to rainfed farmers who were net sellers. In addition, subsidies to (mainly) urban consumers ensured that the consumer price of maize was well below the world price. This consumption subsidy amounted to US$50.37 per ton (37 per cent), or a total subsidy of US$327.40 million.

Levy and van Wijnbergen (1992a) conduct a comparative static analysis of the effects of complete liberalization of the maize market through Mexico joining NAFTA. They estimate that a move to free trade in maize would reduce the rural price of maize by approximately 50 per cent. The result would be a reduction in maize output from irrigated land of 0.97 million tons (from 1.5 million to 0.53 million tons) and of 4.5 million tons from rainfed land (from 8.8 million to 4.3 million tons). Approximately 3.21 million hectares of rainfed land and 0.32 million hectares of irrigated land would be taken out of maize production. As irrigated land would be switched to non-maize production (for example, vegetables) that is likely to be more labour-intensive, there may be a slight net employment gain. However, approximately half of the released rainfed land would be converted to pasture for grazing, with the remainder devoted to other grain crops or fallow. Unemployment on rainfed land may therefore increase by 145 000 workers, putting downward pressure on the rural wage rate.

On the positive side, the 3.75 million rural and mainly landless workers in Mexico would benefit as consumers from lower rural prices for maize. The 1.92 million subsistence producers on rainfed lands would gain or lose little. Levy and van Wijnbergen (1992a) estimate that the overall welfare benefits to the Mexican economy of moving to free trade would be US$154 million per year, with the reduction in rural price distortions accounting for US$122 million per year.

The implications of the scenario for deforestation in Mexico depend on a number of important factors. The fall in the rural producer price of maize ought to put less pressure on the demand for agricultural land, and thus for additional forest conversion. Section 7 discussed in some detail the implications of a large fall in maize producer prices as a result of liberalization. For example, in Table 10.3 a 10 per cent fall in maize prices would lead to a 3.2 per cent decrease in planted area; whereas the 50 per cent fall predicted by Levy and van Wijnbergen (1992a) would lead to a 16.1 per cent decrease, although as discussed in Section 7 any such large changes may not be realistic and should be viewed with caution. Nevertheless, one would expect a major reduction in the producer price of maize from liberalization to lead to a substantial contraction in production and thus planted area.

The key issue is what happens to the land currently under maize that is taken out of production. If, as Levy and van Wijnbergen (1992a) assume, one half of the released rainfed land is converted to pasture (1.6 million hectares), then the demand for additional forest land for pasture may also lessen, depending of course on the comparative returns of released maize and forest land for livestock grazing. On the other hand, if the 145 000 rural workers released by free trade in maize do not migrate to employment opportunities in the urban areas or the USA, then they may instead move to the forest frontier in Mexico as subsistence farmers.[14] In the extreme case, this could lead to the conversion of an additional 362 500 hectares of forest land – a more than 50 per cent increase in the current annual rate of deforestation of 668 000 hectares per year.[15] As discussed above and in Section 7, these 'second-order' deforestation effects through reduced rural employment opportunities could be significant and even outweigh the direct effects of the initial contraction in planted area.

A further partial equilibrium analysis of the impact of NAFTA on Mexico's maize sub-sector was also conducted (Levy and van Wijnbergen, 1992b). This more detailed analysis involved several scenarios concerning different intertemporal assumptions and effects. The implications for the value of rainfed and irrigated land under maize production were examined, along with the welfare and efficiency impacts. These effects are summarized in Tables 10.7 and 10.8.

Table 10.7 Effects of NAFTA on land values and holdings under maize, Mexico (million pesos per ha, 1989 values)

Scenario	Rainfed land	Irrigated land	Land holdings of subsistence and rainfed farmers	Land holdings of irrigated farmers
Base case	12.065	40.169	12.065	40.169
Case 1	9.231	40.800	9.231	40.800
Case 2	9.443	40.725	9.443	40.725
Case 3	9.180	40.668	11.499	40.668
Case 4	9.390	40.597	11.703	40.597
Case 5	9.608	42.175	12.030	42.175
Case 6	9.726	42.137	12.141	42.137

Notes:
Base case 1989 values as the reference case.
Case 1 Instantaneous liberalization of all maize prices in Mexico.
Case 2 Gradual liberalization, with maize prices in Mexico moving to world prices over next 5 years.
Case 3 As case 1, but 1.1 million ha of rainfed land are transformed to irrigation over next 5 years.
Case 4 As case 2, but 1.1 million ha of rainfed land are transformed to irrigation over next 5 years.
Case 5 As case 4, but US fruit and vegetable market is liberalized over next 5 years.
Case 6 US fruit and vegetable market is liberalized and 1.1 million ha of rainfed land are transformed to irrigation over next 5 years, but maize price liberalization in Mexico begins 1 year after irrigation programme starts.

Source: Levy and van Wijnbergen (1992b).

Instantaneous or even gradual liberalization on its own yields large efficiency gains for the Mexican economy, but the consequence is a large fall in land values for rainfed land to less than one quarter of those for irrigated land (see Table 10.7). Thus subsistence farmers, rainfed farmers who are net sellers, and landless rural workers would be made worse off by the contraction in maize production from rainfed land, the loss of its capital value and the subsequent displacement of rural workers. Although subsistence farmers benefit from lower consumer prices, they are doubly affected by the loss in value of their rainfed land and in employment opportunities as day labourers. The major concern is that lack of employment and income opportunities will induce rural workers and subsistence farmers to migrate towards frontier forest areas, or to convert remaining forest land available to them locally. These 'second-order' effects could outweigh the initial impacts of, say, a reduction in maize producer prices on planted agricultural area.

Table 10.8 Welfare and efficiency effects of maize liberalization, Mexico

Scenario	Subsistence farmer	Landless rural worker	Rainfed farmer	Irrigated farmer	Efficiency gains
Case 1	0.967	0.984	0.943	1.028	42.44
Case 2	0.971	0.985	0.949	1.024	23.17
Case 3	1.007	0.993	0.996	1.019	51.96
Case 4	1.011	0.995	1.001	1.015	49.57
Case 5	1.013	1.000	1.000	1.028	44.81
Case 6	1.015	1.001	1.003	1.025	43.18

Notes:

Base case	1989 values as the reference case.
Case 1	Instantaneous liberalization of all maize prices in Mexico.
Case 2	Gradual liberalization, with maize prices in Mexico moving to world prices over next 5 years.
Case 3	As case 1, but 1.1 million ha of rainfed land are transformed to irrigation over next 5 years.
Case 4	As case 2, but 1.1 million ha of rainfed land are transformed to irrigation over next 5 years.
Case 5	As case 4, but US fruit and vegetable market is liberalized over next 5 years.
Case 6	US fruit and vegetable market is liberalized and 1.1 million ha of rainfed land are transformed to irrigation over next 5 years, but maize price liberalization in Mexico begins 1 year after irrigation programme starts.
Welfare effects	Measured as a percentage of the base case.
Efficiency gains	Measured in 1989 US$ billion. In 1989, Mexico's GDP was US$ 207 billion.

Source: Levy and van Wijnbergen (1992b).

In comparison, a programme of investment in land improvements to increase the productivity of rainfed land could potentially mitigate the negative distributional implications of NAFTA on the maize sub-sector. Such a programme could involve investments not only in irrigation infrastructure for 1.1 million hectares of rainfed land but also in drainage, land levelling, ditch-clearing and soil conservation. The distributional impacts of maize liberalization in Mexico are particularly reduced if the land improvement programme is combined with greater access for Mexican farmers to the US fruit and vegetable market, and possibly if land improvement investments are initiated before liberalization. Consequently, expansion of rural farm employment opportunities on existing agricultural land, or off-farm employment opportunities generally, could be an important factor in mitigating deforestation. This suggests that a land improvement investment programme for existing rainfed farmers, particularly in states and regions prone to high deforestation rates, could provide indirect incentives for controlling deforestation by increasing the demand for rural labour.

The results of the analysis lead Levy and van Wijnbergen to conclude that Mexico would do better to forgo instantaneous liberalization of its maize market in favour of a more gradual liberalization coupled with a large-scale programme of investment in land improvements for rainfed agriculture. This conforms with our own conclusions in Section 7 from the policy analysis of the effects of maize and fertilizer prices on agricultural expansion. By increasing the value and returns of rainfed land through irrigation, the land investment programme would also enhance farmers' access to credit and encourage them to cultivate high value crops other than maize. Moreover, if targeted to farmers on existing rainfed land, the programme would possibly make it more attractive for farmers to bring their idle land into production, as depicted in Figure 10.1. That is, increasing the returns to existing rainfed farmland and transforming it into irrigation could reduce the incentives for farmers to 'abandon' their existing land to convert additional forest land. As irrigated land in Mexico is about 2.4 times more labour-intensive than rainfed land, the land improvement programme should also create a permanent demand for rural labour (Levy and van Wijnbergen, 1992b). Thus the possibility of displaced rural workers and subsistence farmers migrating to the forest frontier as a result of maize liberalization might be substantially reduced and possibly reversed.

Finally, it is worth commenting that although we have attempted to show the linkages between our analytical results and related general equilibrium studies of the impacts of NAFTA on the Mexican economy, the ability to use a partial analysis to predict economy-wide changes will clearly be limited. In particular, as the discussion in this section demonstrates, many crucial 'second-order' deforestation effects are beyond the predictive power of our analyses of the demand for agricultural land and livestock numbers. On the other hand, current CGE models that attempt to simulate the impacts of NAFTA on the Mexican economy usually exclude any likely deforestation effects.

The exception is a recent model by Boyd (1994). However, due to necessary aggregation, in this model deforestation is simulated by changes in fixed land demand and supply relationships in the overall forestry, livestock and agricultural sectors. Thus, as the author admits, there are limitations on the model's ability to forecast accurately deforestation effects. The results of the analysis suggest that agricultural and livestock production should be expected to increase as a result of NAFTA reforms, and there is likely to be an influx of unemployed workers displaced from industry (cross-border migration is not included in the analysis). The demand for land should increase and its price rise. The author suggests that these effects are likely to increase deforestation unless trade liberalization is implemented in conjunction with land reform. The goal of such land reform would be to absorb displaced workers onto improved existing agricultural and livestock land to prevent them from opening up frontier forest land.

9. Conclusions

Previous studies of deforestation suggest that agricultural land expansion and pasture formation are two major causes of forest conversion. Evidence presented in this chapter indicates that this is also the case for Mexico. The factors determining increases in the land under agricultural production and pasture would also be the underlying causes of deforestation.

However, unlike in some statistical analyses of deforestation, our analysis was unable to examine the relationships influencing deforestation directly. Instead, a more indirect approach was taken of using panel analyses to estimate relationships for agricultural planted area and beef cattle at the state level over the 1970–85 period. We believe that such an approach gives a strong indication of the factors underlying forest conversion, as increases in both land under agricultural production and beef cattle numbers seem to be correlated with loss of forest area.

In the case of increased planted area, increasing the relative returns to maize production as reflected in the maize price ratio leads to further pressure on the forest. Rising populations at the state level also have an impact on forest conversion. In the case of beef cattle numbers, the most significant influence appears to be the returns to cattle operations, as reflected in the price of beef. Increasing credit disbursements, population levels and, to a lesser extent, per capita income are also important factors underlying forest conversion for cattle-raising. Surprisingly, road density was not significant in either analysis. In addition, livestock prices did not influence the demand for agricultural land nor did maize price affect the demand for cattle. This suggests that, over the 1970–85 period at least, livestock production and agricultural expansion may not be competing for land on the forest frontier in states across Mexico. Nevertheless, as the overall demand for land can be expected to increase, especially with rising population, the result may be greater competition between livestock and agricultural activities for frontier land.

The agricultural land and cattle numbers analyses provide some indication of the key policy and socio-economic variables that may be influencing deforestation in Mexico. To utilize these results in policy analysis, we concentrated on the role of maize and fertilizer prices in affecting the returns to agriculture and thus the expansion of planted area; beef prices affecting the returns to cattle-raising and thus the expansion of cattle numbers; and credit disbursement affecting cattle operations.

Our general conclusion is that recent liberalization of the fertilizer market, which may soon be followed by removal of maize price subsidies, may have reduced incentives for expanding planted area and forest conversion. However, the failure to take into account the employment implications of 'fast-track' liberalization of the maize and fertilizer markets could translate into 'second-order' deforestation effects. The major concern is that lack of employment and income opportunities will induce rural workers and subsistence farmers to migrate towards frontier forest areas or convert remaining forest land available to them. These 'second-order' effects could outweigh the initial impacts of the reduction in the returns to maize production on planted agricultural area. Moreover, a rapid fall in the returns to maize cultivation could have tremendous welfare implications for low-income and subsistence rainfed farmers.

These second-order effects on deforestation may be counteracted somewhat if liberalization of the fertilizer and particularly maize markets is coupled with a large-scale programme for land improvements for existing rainfed agricultural land. Fiscal savings from the removal of subsidies could be redirected to finance these investments. The programme could be targeted to benefit particularly smallholders or subsistence producers. Such a programme has the additional benefit of providing alternative employment and income opportunities for landless and near-landless workers, thus reducing their incentive to encroach on forest land.

To improve its effectiveness in reducing deforestation, an investment programme in land improvement should include research and extension support for subsistence and low-income rainfed farmers in states with high rates of deforestation. Research and extension could reduce deforestation by both improving yields on existing agricultural land and disseminating knowledge of land-saving rather than land-using farming systems and techniques. In addition, it is important to coordinate the liberalization policy for maize with liberalization of other sectors that also affect forest land use. Such a strategy would conform more closely to the 'ideal' maize policy for controlling excessive forest conversion than a policy of more rapid liberalization on its own.

In the case of the cattle market, liberalization of beef prices may also reduce the pressure of pasture expansion on the forest. A crucial issue determining this outcome is still the comparative returns to cattle ranching as opposed to other frontier activities. Another factor is the extent to which the costs of production are still being subsidized through credit loans and other input subsidies. Thus a more important policy initiative would be the removal of these subsidies. In particular, the elimination of credit subsidies for cattle-raising ought to make this activity more efficient and reduce perverse incentives for deforestation.

The implications of NAFTA for deforestation in Mexico are difficult to discern. With the exception of a recent study by Boyd (1994) the impacts on forest conversion and degradation are generally ignored in CGE models of NAFTA's impacts on Mexico. Nevertheless, by combining the results from selected studies with those from our policy analysis, it is possible to identify some important relationships, which are to a large extent supported by the general results obtained by Boyd (1994).

The available evidence suggests that if NAFTA is used to complement additional internal economic reforms within Mexico, then this 'open development' strategy would lead to increased output and returns to Mexican agriculture. If forest conversion is to be minimized, then it is imperative that the more specific sectoral policy reforms discussed above, coupled with legal reforms, are implemented. First, pricing and other policies in the agricultural and livestock sector that artificially 'subsidize' the returns to conversion activities on forest land or the costs of conversion need to be reformed. Second, land tenure, forestry and environmental laws also need to be tightened to reduce the incentives for rent-seeking behaviour on the frontier or to improve the 'internalization' of any environmental impacts associated with forest conversion and degradation (Barbier *et al.*, 1993). Finally, specific investments for the agricultural and livestock sectors for improving productivity, infrastructure and research and extension must be targeted towards bringing existing idle arable land into production as well as improving productivity on land already under cultivation.

The specific example of maize liberalization illustrates the approach needed. Combining gradual liberalization with a major land improvement investment programme for existing rainfed agricultural land reduces the incentives for farmers to 'abandon' their existing land to convert additional forest land. However, the success of this programme in mitigating deforestation would depend critically on its being targeted to existing rain-fed land and not providing perverse incentives for farmers in frontier areas to convert forest areas rapidly to maize production in order to qualify for the investment programme. The programme would also create additional permanent rural demand, thus reducing any pressure on forest resources by displaced rural workers or subsistence farmers extending their planted area.

This chapter began by examining other studies of deforestation that are relevant to the factors influencing forest conversion in Mexico. We hope that the results of this policy analysis are in turn relevant to economic studies of the causes of deforestation in other developing countries. In particular, we believe that examining the extent to which changes in government policies are likely to influence deforestation through affecting the comparative economic returns to different conversion activities on forest land as well as the comparative returns to economic activities on existing as opposed to frontier land is important not only for Mexico and Latin America but for all tropical forest countries. As indicated, there were many limitations on our ability to conduct a full analysis of this problem. We hope that further studies will improve upon our policy analysis both for Mexico and for other countries.

Appendix

Description of the models for agricultural land and beef numbers
Given limitations on the data for deforestation in Mexico, planted agricultural area and beef cattle numbers were used as proxies for deforestation. These two indicators were then regressed on key policy and socio-economic variables to determine the significant factors in the deforestation process. The following describes briefly the data and analysis used in the two models.

Demand for agricultural land The panel analysis of longitudinal data for planted agricultural area was conducted across the 31 states of Mexico plus the *Distrito Federal* (Federal District), over the 1970, 1980 and 1985 time periods. Several explanatory variables were examined, including real guaranteed maize prices, real fertilizer prices, income per capita, population levels, real rural wages and road density. In addition, real livestock prices were included to determine the extent to which this variable influences the agricultural land expansion. Details of the relevant variables and source are given in Table 10.1.

In the original panel analysis of the demand for agricultural land, ordinary least-squares (OLS) regressions were employed (Barbier *et al.*, 1993). However, OLS provides consistent and efficient estimators of the coefficients of the explanatory variables only if any individual effects are constant over time and across all individual cross-sectional units (that is, the Mexican states including the Federal District). This is a fairly restrictive assumption that generally does not hold for panel analysis of longitudinal data (Hsiao, 1986; Greene, 1993; Baltagi, 1995). Instead, a common procedure is to test for the presence of individual effects in an OLS model in comparison to fixed- and random-effects versions of a (one-way) error component model. We used a least-squares dummy variable (LSDV) regression for the fixed-effects error component model, and a feasible generalized least-squares (FGLS) estimation for the random-effects version.

The LSDV approach requires the inclusion of dummy variables for each unit in the regression. We utilized the FGLS procedure suggested by Greene (1993), which follows the general approach adverted for random-effects models (Hsiao,

1986; Baltagi, 1995). This is a two-step procedure that involves deriving residual variance estimators from between-units (unit means) and within-units (LSDV) regressions, and using these estimators to derive θ for the following FGLS regression:

$$y_{it} - \theta\bar{y}_i = \alpha(1-\theta) + \beta'[x_{it} - \theta x_i] + u_{it} - \theta\bar{u} \quad i = 1, ..., N; t = 1, ..., T \quad (10.1)$$

where i denotes the individual cross-sectional units (that is, the states), t denotes time, α is a scalar, and β is the $K \times 1$ vector of coefficients on the K explanatory variables. It follows that y_{it}, x_{it} and u_{it} are the ith observations on the dependent variable, the K explanatory variables and the error term respectively, with $\bar{y}_i$, $\bar{x}_i$, and $\bar{u}$ being the respective unit means.[16]

Table 10.9 depicts the OLS, LSDV and FGLS regression results for planted agricultural area. Table 10.9a depicts the regression results without real livestock prices included as an explanatory variable; Table 10.9b shows the results with livestock prices. The coefficients of the relevant explanatory variables are depicted, with the absolute values of the t-test statistics indicated in parentheses below each coefficient.

An F-test for the null hypothesis of zero individual effects across states was performed. The hypothesis is soundly rejected in both versions of the regression, which suggests that the fixed-effects (LSDV) estimator is preferred to the OLS estimator. The Breusch–Pagan LM_1 test is also performed for the null hypothesis of zero random effects, which is distributed as χ_1^2. This null hypothesis is also rejected for both regressions, which suggests that the random-effects (FGLS) estimator is preferred to the OLS estimator. Finally, a Hausman test was performed with χ_K^2 degrees of freedom for the null hypothesis of no differences between the FGLS random-effects and the LSDV fixed-effects estimators. The statistic was significant at the 5 per cent level for the regression without livestock prices and at the 1 per cent level for the regression with livestock prices. Thus in both versions the null hypothesis can be rejected. The value of θ for the FGLS regressions, the F-test statistic, the Breusch-Pagan LM_1 statistic and the Hausman χ_K^2 statistic are indicated in Table 10.9.

The results of these diagnostic test results suggest that FGLS is the preferred estimator in both versions of the regression. In Table 10.9a the t-tests for the FGLS regression for planted agricultural area show that the only significant explanatory variables are relative maize/fertilizer prices and population. Real income per capita and road density are not significant. In Table 10.9b, t-tests for the FGLS regression indicate that only population is fully significant, as the two-tailed t-statistic for the coefficient on relative maize/fertilizer prices is no longer significant at the 5 per cent level. The other variables in the regression, including real livestock prices, are highly insignificant.[17] These results imply that the hypothesis that livestock prices should influence planted agricultural area is rejected by the model and that, of the two versions of the model, FGLS without livestock prices in Table 10.9a is the preferred estimator. Further discussion of the results of the model can be found in Section 4.

Table 10.9 Regression results for agricultural area planted (MAAP)

a. Without real livestock prices (N = 32, T = 3, K = 4)

	MGMFP	MP	MRD	MYC
OLS	342.18	0.000087†	–66.385*	–0.02073†
	(1.83)	(4.08)	(2.14)	(3.10)
LSDV	131.58	0.000070*	–0.472	0.00533
	(1.48)	(2.11)	(0.02)	(1.08)
FGLS	167.49*	0.000077†	–13.676	0.00087
	(1.86)	(3.13)	(0.52)	(0.18)

$\theta = 0.733226$.
$F_{N-1,\, NT-N-K} = 14.66$.†
Breusch–Pagan $LM_1(\chi_1^2) = 48.77$†.
Hausman $(\chi_K^2) = 10.88$*.
* Statistic significant at 5% level.
† Statistic significant at 1% level.

b. With real livestock prices (N = 32, T = 3, K = 5)

	MGMFP	MLP	MP	MRD	MYC
OLS	575.24†	–86.727	0.000085†	–82.271†	–0.02244*
	(2.53)	(1.76)	(4.06)	(2.58)	(2.35)
LSDV	112.13	6.866	0.0000740*	–0.258	0.00548
	(0.93)	(0.24)	(2.01)	(0.01)	(1.09)
FGLS	184.04	–4 543	0.000077†	–15.583	0.00029
	(1.86)	(0.16)	(3.00)	(0.58)	(0.06)

$\theta = 0.717463$.
$F_{N-1,\, NT-N-K} = 13\ 88$.†
Breusch–Pagan $LM_1(\chi_1^2) = 42.65$†.
Hausman $(\chi_K^2) = 29.57$†.
* Statistic significant at 5% level.
† Statistic significant at 1% level.

Notes: OLS = ordinary least squares; LSDV = least squares dummy variable; FGLS = feasible generalized least squares. For variable definitions, see Table 10.1.

Demand for beef cattle The panel analysis of longitudinal data for beef cattle numbers (that is, livestock head) was also conducted across the 31 states of

Mexico plus the Federal District, over the 1970, 1980 and 1985 time periods. Several explanatory variables were examined, including real beef prices, income per capita, population levels, real rural wages, road density and real credit disbursement. Real guaranteed maize prices were also included to determine the extent to which the expansion in beef numbers is explained by this variable. Details of the relevant variables and sources are given in Table 10.1. The same two-step procedure for panel analysis of longitudinal data described above for planted agricultural area was also employed to derive the estimators of livestock head.

Table 10.10 depicts the OLS, LSDV and FGLS regression results for cattle numbers. Table 10.10a depicts the regression results without real maize prices included as an explanatory variable; Table 10.10b shows the results with maize prices. As before, the coefficients of the relevant explanatory variables are depicted, with the absolute values of the *t*-test statistics indicated in parentheses below each coefficient. The value of θ for the FGLS regressions, the *F*-test statistic, the Breusch–Pagan LM_1 statistic and the Hausman χ_K^2 statistics are also indicated.

An *F*-test for the null hypothesis of zero individual effects across states was performed. The hypothesis is again soundly rejected in both versions of the regression, which suggests that the fixed-effects (LSDV) estimator is preferred to the OLS estimator. The Breusch–Pagan LM_1 test is also performed for the null hypothesis of zero random effects, which is distributed as χ_1^2. This null hypothesis is also rejected for both regressions, which suggests that the random effect (FGLS) estimator is preferred to the OLS estimator. Finally, a Hausman test was performed with χ_K^2 degrees of freedom for the null hypothesis of no difference between the FGLS random-effects and the LSDV fixed-effects estimators. However, for regressions both with and without maize prices this statistic proved not to be significant at the 5 per cent level. Thus in both versions of the regression for livestock numbers the null hypothesis of no difference between the FGLS and LSDV estimators can be rejected. Nevertheless, the highly significant Breusch–Pagan statistics suggest the presence of random effects; consequently, FGLS is still the preferred estimator in both versions of the regression.

In Table 10.10a the *t*-tests for the FGLS regression for livestock head show that livestock prices, population, credit and income per capita are all significant. Road density is the only variable that is not significant. In Table 10.10b, *t*-tests for the FGLS regression indicate that only population, credit and income per capita are significant. Real livestock and maize prices join road density in being highly insignificant.[18] These results imply that the hypothesis that maize prices should influence demand for beef cattle is rejected by the model and that, of the two versions of the model, FGLS without maize prices in Table 10.10a is the preferred estimator. Further discussions of the results of the model can be found in Section 4.

Table 10.10 Regression results for livestock head (MLH)

a. Without real guaranteed maize prices (N = 32, T = 3, K = 5)

	MLP	MP	MRD	MC	MYC
OLS	–26.712	0.000111†	–106.504*	0.9958†	–0.01303
	(0.40)	(3.12)	(2.17)	(6.23)	(1.19)
LSDV	41.328†	0.000037	–12.941	0.3573†	0.00923†
	(2.67)	(1.42)	(0.62)	(7.37)	(2.59)
FGLS	43.425†	0.000051*	–24.315	0.3765†	0.00865*
	(2.67)	(3.13)	(1.14)	(7.41)	(2.29)

$\theta = 0.886253$.
$F_{N-1,\,NT-N-K} = 82.05$.†
Breusch–Pagan $LM_1(\chi_1^2) = 884.22$†.
Hausman $(\chi_K^2) = 1.74$.
* Statistic significant at 5% level.
† Statistic significant at 1% level.

b. With real guaranteed maize prices (N = 32, T = 3, K = 6)

	MLP	MGMP	MP	MRD	MC	MYC
OLS	–79.948	–0.9132	0.000114†	–108.672*	0.9803†	–0.01292
	(0.84)	(0.79)	(3.18)	(2.20)	(6.07)	(1.18)
LSDV	18.005	–0.2776	0.000038	–5.086	0.3427†	0.00956†
	(0.61)	(0.92)	(1.43)	(0.23)	(6.72)	(2.65)
FGLS	24.620	–0.2266	0.000052*	–18.474	0.3652†	0.00888*
	(0.79)	(0.71)	(2.02)	(0.81)	(6.84)	(2.34)

$\theta = 0.886106$.
$F_{N-1,\,NT-N-K} = 81.29$.†
Breusch–Pagan $LM_1(\chi_1^2) = 855.99$†.
Hausman $(\chi_K^2) = 2.10$.
* Statistic significant at 5% level.
† Statistic significant at 1% level.

Notes: OLS = ordinary least squares; LSDV = least squares dummy variables; FGLS = feasible generalized least squares. For variable definition see Table 10.1.

Notes

* This chapter is based on a report prepared for the World Bank and the Government of Mexico (Barbier *et al.*, 1993). However, neither the World Bank nor the Government of Mexico nor

any individuals associated with these two institutions are responsible for the views and analysis contained in this paper. Any faults or errors lie with the authors alone. We would like to thank our co-authors on the original report, Michael Collins and Colleen Clancy, as well as Luis Constantino and Augusta Molnar and anonymous reviewers on behalf of the Government of Mexico and the World Bank. We are also grateful to two anonymous referees for their comments on behalf of *Environment and Development Economics*.

1. For a more detailed review of some of the following and other studies on the causes of deforestation, see Brown and Pearce (1994) and Burgess (1995).
2. Capistrano (1994) uses changes in timber production forest area as a proxy for total deforestation. Thus the analytical results are more relevant to the deforestation of tropical timber production forests than to overall tropical deforestation. For an in-depth review of the impact of logging relative to other factors influencing tropical deforestation, see Amelung and Diehl (1992), Burgess (1993, 1995) and Barbier *et al.* (1995a).
3. The results of the model may be affected, unfortunately, by collinearity problems between some independent variables, which the authors freely admit. See Reis and Guzmán (1994) for an updated analysis.
4. For example, the analysis uses three dummy variables and no constant regression. In addition, it is not clear whether the dependent variable for the percentage of land under forest area (FORS) is expressed as proportion or in logarithm form (for example, LN (FORS)). The latter is more appropriate for a logit analysis. However, of most concern is that each regression appears to include a constant equal to 1 as an explanatory variable. If this is the case, then the logit analysis is misrepresented. The resulting estimation is FORS or LN (FORS) = $\beta_0{}^*1 + \beta X$, where βX represents the other coefficients and respective explanatory variables of the regression. As a consequence, a near-singular matrix may be created by the regression, which would explain why all coefficients display confidence levels approaching unity. An alternative and more conventional specification of the logit regression would be LN (FORS) – LN(1 – FORS) = βX, with the constant generated by the regression as usual. For an application to tropical deforestation, see Barbier *et al.* (1995b).
5. Although the goodness of fit of the statistical results is impressive, they appear to be achieved through combining the log-linear model with the use of higher-order autogressive terms to correct for serial correlation, which generally tends to improve the explanatory power of such models. For a more recent analysis of the causes of deforestation in northeast Thailand see Panayotou and Sungsuwan (1994).
6. For further discussion and examples, see Barbier and Burgess (1992) and the case studies cited in the previous section. See also Section 5 for analysis of the factors determining the demand for agricultural land in Mexico.
7. Alternatively, correcting the market failures and policy distortions that effectively 'subsidize' the returns to convertible forest land and thus contribute to excessive deforestation would be represented by a decrease in the curve BG in Figure 10.1. This 'ideal' policy would also increase the comparative returns to existing agricultural land, thus leading to a substitution of idle for convertible forest land. However, as a maximum of CD hectares could be cultivated economically, production and efficiency losses would occur if the comparative returns to convertible forest land on the frontier fell sharply.
8. Although not shown in Figure 10.2, presumably some timber harvesting would also occur on forest land converted to agricultural and livestock production.
9. As the decline in more recent years is substantial and registered across all states, it could be due to calculation errors or statistical adjustments. However, this has proved difficult to verify. Any such adjustments or errors may have introduced an element of bias in the subsequent analysis of beef cattle head discussed below.
10. In Tables 10.3 and 10.4, because real values are expressed in constant 1980 prices, the unit of account is 'old' rather than 'new' pesos.
11. Moreover, as indicated in Table 10.2, these elasticities were calculated around the means of the panel data and small (per unit) effects. Applying these elasticities to much larger changes will invariably increase inaccuracy.
12. The simulated impacts on planted area for 50–70 per cent reductions in fertilizer prices in Table 10.3b must be viewed as approximate 'orders of magnitude'. First, as noted above, applying

elasticities calculated around the means of panel data and small (per unit) effects to much larger changes invariably increases inaccuracy. Second, such elasticities reflect 'instantaneous' changes. Although the fertilizer price rise in Mexico was fairly rapid, it did occur over a two-year period. Finally, liberalization in Mexico has been occurring across several sectors, which may make it difficult to distinguish the actual impacts on planted area of any single factor, such as rising fertilizer prices. Note that these same qualifications also apply to the simulations of beef prices and credit discussed below.

13. Table 10.5 assumes that increases in the labour force will have the same effect on planted area and cattle numbers as the explanatory variable for population in our analysis. In Mexico, the labour force, as defined by all individuals aged 15–64, comprises approximately 60 per cent of the total population.
14. However, in the future there may be limitations on large-scale migration to forest areas as most of this land is allocated to *ejidos*, which now have legal ownership rights. For further discussion, see Barbier *et al.* (1993).
15. The extreme scenario for deforestation assumes that the 145 000 displaced rural workers become subsistence maize producers on the frontier with an average holding size of 2.5 hectares. This scenario is clearly unlikely. However, it is worth noting that, assuming the same average holding, additional forest conversion of 100 000 hectares in Mexico would require only 40 000 displaced rural workers to move onto forest land.
16. From Greene (1993), $\theta = 1 - [(RVE_w)/(T * RVE_b)]^{1/2}$, where RVE_w is the residual variance estimator based on the within-units (LSDV) estimation and RVE_b is the residual variance estimator based on the between-units (unit means) estimation.
17. Both versions of the model were also run with real rural wages included, but this variable also proved to be insignificant. Moreover, its inclusion did not alter substantially the coefficients of the other variables nor did it affect their significance. Both an *F*-test and log-likelihood test on the null hypothesis that rural wages is a redundant variable were performed, but the tests were highly insignificant. Thus we omitted rural wages in both versions of the model in Table 10.9.
18. Both versions of the model were also run with real rural wages included, but incorporating this variable appeared to lead to severe problems of multicollinearity. In particular, rural wages seemed highly correlated with income per capita and livestock prices. Thus the inclusion of rural wages reduced substantially the significance of the latter two variables and distorted the regression generally. We therefore omitted rural wages in both versions of the model in Table 10.10.

References

Amelung, T. and M. Diehl (1992), *Deforestation of Tropical Rain Forests: Economic Causes and Impact on Development*, Kiel: Institute of World Economics.

Baltagi, B. (1995), *Econometric Analysis of Panel Data*, Chichester: John Wiley.

Barbier, E.B. and J.C. Burgess (1992), 'Agricultural pricing and environmental degradation', *Policy Research Working Paper* WPS 960, The World Bank, Washington, DC.

Barbier, E.B., J.C. Burgess, M. Collins and C. Clancy (1993), 'Mexico – forestry and conservation sector review sub-study of economic issues for implementation of the new forestry policy', Report prepared for the Latin American and the Caribbean Country Department, The World Bank, Washington, DC.

Barbier, E.B., J.C. Burgess, J.T. Bishop and B.A. Aylward (1995a), *The Economics of the Tropical Timber Trade*, London: Earthscan Publications.

Barbier, E.B., N. Bockstael, J.C. Burgess and I. Strand (1995b), 'The linkages between the timber trade and tropical deforestation', *The World Economy*, **18** (3), 411–42.

Boyd, R. (1994), 'NAFTA deforestation: a general equilibrium perspective', Paper presented at the Annual Meeting of the European Association of Environmental and Resource Economists, Dublin, 22-24 June.

Brown, K. and D.W. Pearce (eds) (1994), *The Causes of Tropical Deforestation*, London: University College London Press.

Burgess, J.C. (1993), 'Timber production, timber trade and tropical deforestation', *AMBIO*, **22**, 136–43.

Burgess, J.C. (1995), 'Biodiversity loss through tropical deforestation: the role of timber production and trade', in C.A. Perrings, K.-G. Mäler, C. Folke, C.S. Holling and B.-O. Jansson (eds), *Biodiversity Conservation*, Dordrecht: Kluwer Academic Publishers.

Capistrano, A.D. (1994), 'Tropical forest depletion and the changing macro-economy', in Brown and Pearce (eds), *The Causes of Tropical Deforestation*.

Greene, W.H. (1993), *Econometric Analysis*, 2nd edn, Englewood Cliffs, NJ: Prentice Hall.

Hinojosa-Ojeda, R. and S. Robinson (1991), 'Alternative scenarios of US–Mexico integration: a computable general equilibrium approach', Working Paper No. 609, Department of Agricultural and Resource Economics, University of California, Berkeley.

Hsiao, C. (1986), *Analysis of Panel Data*, Cambridge: Cambridge University Press.

INEGI (1992), *Estados unidos mexicanos resulta dos prelimin areas*, Mexico City: VII Censo Agropecuario, 1991.

INEGI/SPP (nd), *Sistema de cuentas nacionales de Mexico*, Mexico City: Estructura Economica Regional Produsto Interno Bruto por Entidad Federative.

Levy, S. and S. van Wijnbergen (1992a), 'Maize and the free trade agreement between Mexico and the United States', *The World Bank Economic Review*, **6** (3), 481–502.

Levy, S. and S. van Wijnbergen (1992b), 'Transition problems in economic reform: agriculture in the Mexico–US free trade agreement', *Policy Research Working Paper No. 967*, The World Bank, Washington, DC.

Maddison, A. *et al.* (1992), *The Political Economy of Poverty, Equity and Growth: Brazil and Mexico*, New York: Oxford University Press.

Mahar, D. and R. Schneider (1994), 'Incentives for tropical deforestation: some examples from Latin America', in Brown and Pearce (eds), *The Causes of Tropical Deforestation*.

Masera, O., M. Ordóñez and R. Dirzo (1992), *Carbon Emissions and Sequestration in the Forests: Case Studies from Seven Developing Countries: Volume 4 Mexico*, Washington, DC: Environmental Protection Agency.

Muñoz, Piña, C. (1992), 'Forest or no forest: a logit model of land use in Mexico', MSc dissertation, University College London.

Palo, M., G. Mery and J. Salmi (1987), 'Deforestation in the tropics: pilot scenarios based on quantitative analysis', in M. Palo and J. Salmi (eds), *Deforestation or Development in the Third World*, Helsinki: Division of Social Economics of Forestry, Finnish Forestry Research.

Panayotou, T. and S. Sungsuwan (1994), 'An econometric analysis of the causes of tropical deforestation: the case of Northeast Thailand', in Brown and Pearce (eds), *The Causes of Tropical Deforestation*.

Phantumvanit, D. and T. Panayotou (1990), 'Natural resources for a sustainable future: spreading the benefits', prepared for the 1990 TDRI End-Year Conference on Industrializing Thailand and its Impact on the Environment, Chon Buri, Thailand, 8–9 December.

Reis, E.J. and R. Guzmán (1994), 'An econometric model of Amazon deforestation', in Brown and Pearce (eds), *The Causes of Tropical Deforestation*.

Reis, E.J. and S. Margulis (1993), 'Options for slowing Amazon jungle clearing', in R. Dornbusch and J.M. Poterba (eds), *Global Warming: Economic Policy Responses*, Cambridge, MA: MIT Press.

Repetto, R. (1988), *The Forests for the Trees? Government Policies and the Misuse of Forest Resources*, Washington, DC: World Resources Institute.

Robles, R. (1992), 'La decade perdida de la agricultura Mexican', *El Cotidiano*, **50**, 169–85.

SARH (1988), *Estadisticas basics 1960–1986 para la planeqcion del desarollo rural integral, tomo 1*, Mexico City: Sector Agropeuario Forestal.

Southgate, D. (1991), 'Tropical deforestation and agricultural development in Latin America', *LEEC Discussion Paper* 91–01, London Environmental Economics Centre.

Southgate, D., R. Sierra and L. Brown (1989), 'The causes of tropical deforestation in Ecuador: a statistical analysis', *World Development*, **19** (9), 1145–51.

World Bank (1989), *Mexico – Agricultural Sector Report*, Washington, DC: The World Bank.

11. The economics of tropical forest land use options

with J.C. Burgess

Abstract
Tropical deforestation is generally characterized as conversion of forest land to alternative uses, notably agriculture. This would suggest the need for rational decision-making concerning the optimal allocation of tropical forest land between competing uses. The following chapter explores this problem by devising rules for determining optimal land use allocation between timber and agriculture at the stand and forest levels. A complementary intertemporal model for optimal allocation of forest land to agricultural conversion at the forest level is also developed and used to derive a demand relationship for agricultural conversion, which is then approximated through empirical estimation.

1. Introduction

Determining an appropriate allocation of land between alternative, competing uses is a fundamental problem that has posed complex questions in the past and continues to challenge us today. Economists have explored this resource allocation problem from the perspective of determining the *optimal allocation of land*. That is, as with other resources, land allocation is perceived to be optimal when the aggregate discounted social returns (that is, total net present benefits) from its alternative uses over time are maximized.

In the past few decades, increasing tropical deforestation has called attention to the problem of optimal allocation of forest land in developing countries. There are important reasons underlying this concern. First, empirical evidence indicates that the proximate cause of tropical deforestation is the conversion of forest land to an alternative use, principally agriculture. In addition, there is growing evidence that current patterns and rates of forest conversion and degradation in tropical countries may not be 'optimal' but excessive, resulting from widespread market and policy failures that foster distortionary incentives favouring deforestation.[1] In other words, conversion of tropical forests to alternative uses, such as agriculture, may not always be the most economically efficient land use option. Consequently, the concern that deforestation may mean wasted opportunities for economic development has led to increasing interest in rationalizing the decision-making process with respect to the allocation and use of tropical forest lands.

There are various ways to analyse the forest land allocation problem. Here we develop an optimization framework in order to provide some basic insights into the allocation of forest land between competing uses in the tropics. Similar approaches have been employed recently for specific aspects of the tropical deforestation problem. For example, Ehui, Hertel and Preckel (1990) construct a two-sector dynamic model for agriculture and forestry in a developing country, which is used by Ehui and Hertel (1989) to estimate the optimal steady-state forest stock in Côte d'Ivoire. López and Niklitschek (1991) model the role of natural biomass (vegetation cover) in tropical agricultural production, including the influence of property rights, which is then examined empirically by López (1995a, b) in Côte d'Ivoire and Ghana. Southgate (1990) uses a cost–benefit framework to examine the factors, including land security, that affect the decision of frontier farmers to abandon existing holdings and clear new land in the Amazon, which serves loosely as the basis for empirical estimation by Southgate, Sierra and Brown (1991) in Ecuador. Similarly, Mendelsohn (1994) shows the effects of property rights and land security on agricultural conversion of frontier forest land, which Deacon (1994) extends further to analyse the influence of government policies. The latter is the basis for the general empirical investigation by Deacon (1995) into the role of government instability and lack of accountability in tropical deforestation.[2]

While consistent with these approaches, we are concerned in this chapter with a more generalized framework as a basis for two types of empirical investigation: extending an appropriate 'cost–benefit rule' for allocating land at the stand level to the forest level, and developing a demand relationship for the optimal conversion of forest land that can be estimated at the country or regional level. Our main aim is to understand the key economic principles underlying the optimal allocation of tropical forest land to alternative uses as a starting point for empirical analysis of the general problem. We leave it to others to adapt and apply these principles to specific case studies and conditions in tropical forest countries. We focus on the social planner's perspective of the optimal allocation of tropical forest land between two competing uses – 'sustainable' forest management for timber harvesting and flow of environmental benefits, and conversion of forest land to agriculture for crop production. Given these competing uses, our starting point is the basic rule that forest land should be maintained under sustainable forestry so long as the net benefits from this land use option exceed those from conversion to agriculture. The implications of this rule at the stand and forest level are discussed as well as derived formally in the Appendix.

Although the analysis of stand and forest-level decisions to maintain or convert forest land is important, it is generally believed that the factors determining the overall demand for forest land conversion at the country or regional level are the key to tropical deforestation. Nevertheless, it is possible to show the linkage between the stand or forest level land allocation decisions and the aggregate demand for forest land conversion. To explore this relationship, we develop an inter-temporal model of the process of deforestation for determining the optimal allocation of forest land to agricultural conversion, given foregone forestry benefits including any environmental values. We also indicate the consistency between this approach and the allocation rule derived from the stand and forest-level analysis of tropical forest land use options. However, the main purpose of our deforestation model is to derive a demand relationship for agricultural land conversion, which is then approximated through an empirical analysis across tropical forest countries.

2. Allocation rules and the opportunity cost of forest land

Suppose that for a given stand of tropical forest land there are two competing land use options: 'sustainable' forest management for timber production and flow of environmental benefits, and conversion of forest land to agriculture for crop production. The net benefits from conversion of forest land to agriculture are derived from the production of agricultural goods on the newly converted forest land. It is assumed that these benefits are net of any disbenefits arising from land degradation and agricultural pollution (that is, soil erosion, chemical run-off, and so on) and include any one-off forest clearing costs and windfall timber benefits.[3] The net benefits from sustainable forest management are taken to include the periodic timber benefits and the flow environmental benefits of the forest, which may include important *environmental functions* (for example, watershed protection, micro-climate maintenance and carbon store), *resources* (for example, non-timber forest products, wildlife, forage) and *amenity services* (for example, recreation/tourism, scientific interest). Unfortunately, many of these environmental benefits have no market and thus are generally ignored in private and public land use decisions. However, the social opportunity cost of converting the forest land to agriculture ought to reflect both its value for marketed production (p) as well as non-marketed environmental net benefits (e).

For example, in order to determine whether agricultural (a) land use is preferred to forestry (f), the net benefits (B) of the two competing options need to be compared. As the opportunity costs of choosing option a is foregoing the net benefits of f, it is not sufficient for the net benefits of a to be positive. Thus if the total (discounted) net benefits of forest management are given by:

$$B^f = B^p + B^e \tag{11.1}$$

then this must exceed the foregone net (discounted) benefits of conversion to agriculture, B^a, if the latter is to be the preferred option. Hence:

$$B^a - [B^p + B^e] > 0 \tag{11.2}$$

Condition (11.2) is therefore the critical decision rule in deciding the best use of tropical forest land.[4] This is the basic cost–benefit rule for evaluating alternative tropical forest land use options that is the starting point for our analysis. Although we consider only two competing land use options – sustainable forestry and conversion to agriculture – this rule applies to any two or more competing forest land use options.

Given that most tropical forest land use options will have significant environmental impacts, taking these values into account is important. However, a recent review of case studies on the economic evaluation of forest land use options found only 55 studies that were strictly relevant (IIED, 1994).[5] The majority of these include some information on the economic costs and benefits of tropical forest land use options, but most of these simply present data on the net benefits of a single form of land use and do not attempt to analyse economic trade-offs among two or more land use options.

Nevertheless, there are a growing number of studies applying approaches similar to the cost–benefit rule advocated here to a range of competing forest land use options. For example, Peters, Gentry and Mendelsohn (1989) compare the net benefits of sustainable extraction of wild fruit and latex to the potential returns from conventional timber harvesting and ranching. They estimate fruit and latex yields based on measurement and inventory of trees on a one hectare plot. They use market prices to value the harvest and calculate net returns by deducting the estimated cost of harvest, using data on labour inputs, prevailing wage rates and transport costs. Similarly, Southgate (1992) compares three alternative timber plantation and agroforestry options. Using published data on physical inputs, rotation time and outputs obtained, plus price and wage information, he estimates net annualized returns for each land use option. These estimates are then compared to the 'price' at which farmers report that they would be willing to sell their land. The latter may be considered a rough proxy for the present value of private financial returns to the prevailing land use system of ranching and shifting agriculture. Finally, Ruitenbeek (1989) provides a comprehensive cost–benefit analysis of the Korup Project of rainforest conservation in Korup National Park, Cameroon. The total net benefits of the project yielded a net present value of £10.9 million. These include benefits from sustained forest use, agricultural production, tourism and biological diversity, as well as flood control, protection of fisheries and maintenance of soil fertility under natural forest vegetation. The analysis also estimated the opportunity costs of foregone earnings from clear-cutting timber in terms of lost stumpage value and the loss of subsistence production arising from the relocation of six villages. The total present value of these foregone uses amounted to £3.3 million, or less than a third of the estimated net project benefits. On the basis of this analysis, the Korup Project was considered beneficial to Cameroon.

Hartwick (1992) has shown that for a developing economy as a whole it is possible to derive a similar 'cost-benefit' rule to condition (11.2) for allocating forest land between competing uses. The optimal allocation of tropical forests between the two competing uses essentially determines the price of land. That is, land values are determined by discounted future rental values. These values are endogenously determined by the costs and benefits of forest clearance for agricultural production as opposed to maintenance of the forest for timber and environmental benefits. Hartwick (1992) has shown that land will be converted from forest to agriculture up to the point where the discounted future marginal rental value of land in agriculture (MB^a) equals the discounted future marginal rental value of land remaining forested (MB^f).

In the appendix to this chapter, we demonstrate formally how it is possible to utilize the stand-level rule for optimal allocation of tropical forest land uses to derive an equivalent rule at the forest or economy level and to link the stand and forest level decisions. The latter forest-level conditions not only are equivalent to Hartwick's rule but also underlie the basic conditions of the inter-temporal model of optimal conversion of forest land developed in the next section. Again, for simplicity we assume that the forest could be allocated between two competing land use options, agricultural production and 'sustainable' long-term forestry with environmental benefits. Denoting MB_j^f as the (discounted) marginal net benefits from allocating a unit of forest land to the jth timber stand and MB_m^a as the (discounted) marginal net benefits of allocating this land to the mth agricultural plot, the following allocation rules are derived in the Appendix:

$$MB_j^f = MB_j^p + MB_j^e = MB_m^a \qquad (11.3)$$

where MB_j^p and MB_j^e are the net (discounted) timber production and environmental benefits respectively of the jth timber stand. Condition (11.3) is the optimal rule for allocating tropical forest land to the competing uses of agriculture and sustainable timber production. Land should be allocated to any jth forestry stand until the marginal net timber and environmental benefits generated by the last unit equals its opportunity cost – the foregone marginal net benefits of instead employing this land under agricultural plot m. The comparison with equation (11.2) above is straightforward: it is optimal to continue allocating forest land to sustainable timber production as long as $MB_j^f > MB_m^a$. Alternatively, if $MB_j^f < MB_m^a$ then forest land should instead be converted to agriculture. Forest land will continue to be allocated in either of these ways until condition (11.3) holds.

To summarize, it is important in making forest land allocation decisions to include all the benefits and costs, including environmental values, associated with alternative uses. The failure to do so will result in a less than optimal allocation of land. In this section and in the Appendix, we have demonstrated theoretically how this rule can apply to both stand and forest level land use decisions. In the remainder of the chapter we build on this approach to develop a model of optimal agricultural land conversion, which in turn is used to specify a demand relationship for converted land that can be empirically estimated.

3. An inter-temporal model of optimal conversion of forest land

McConnell (1989) developed a model to explore the optimal allocation of land between agricultural land, park and public land, and urban land in the USA. This was later extended by López, Shah and Altobello (1994) to include environmental externalities. In this section we further adapt this approach to derive an inter-temporal process of tropical deforestation, emphasizing the optimal conversion of forest land to agriculture. It is possible to show that the conditions derived from this model are consistent with the stand and forest-level rules discussed in the previous section and derived formally in the appendix. However, the main objective of our deforestation model is to derive a demand relationship for agricultural land conversion, and following the approaches of McConnell (1989) and Lopez, Shah and Altobello (1994), introduce additional macroeconomic variables that may influence this demand. In Section 4 we demonstrate the extent to which this demand relationship can be empirically estimated across tropical forest countries.

Let, $t = 1, ..., T$ be the set of time periods of relevance for the dynamic forest land use allocation problem. We assume that $t = 1$ is the initial period and that $t = T$ represents the last (terminal) period. We also assume that the stock of forest land in the previous period determines the availability of forest land for current use. That is, forest land from the previous period (F_{t-1}) is either maintained as forest land in the current period (F_t) or is converted to agricultural land in the current period (A_t). Let x_t represent the net stock of forest land converted to agriculture. Therefore, the following equations define the change in forest and agricultural land respectively from period $t - 1$ to period t:

$$F_t - F_{t-1} = -x_t$$
$$A_t - A_{t-1} = x_t \qquad t = 1, \ldots, T. \tag{11.4}$$

That is, the accumulation of agricultural land, $A_t - A_{t-1}$, over any period t, is determined by deforestation in that period, $F_{t-1} - F_t$. As in the previous section, the total net benefits derived from leaving land under forest (B^f) consists of both net timber production benefits (B^p) and net environmental benefits (B^e).[6] Thus in any period t,

$$B^f = B^p + B^e \qquad t = 1, \ldots, T. \tag{11.5}$$

Net agricultural production benefits (B^a) are derived from conversion of the forest land to agricultural land for agricultural production, and depend on the value of agricultural goods produced minus the costs of production. Total net benefits (B) from allocation of forest land between maintaining the land as forest and converting the forest for agricultural land during any period t must therefore include timber, environmental and agricultural benefits:

$$B = B^p + B^e + B^a \qquad t = 1, \ldots, T. \tag{11.6}$$

The net benefits from maintaining land under forest (that is, B^p and B^e) in time t are assumed to be functions of the remaining stock of forest land, F_t and the flow of both production and environmental benefits from forest land are assumed to increase with additions to the stock of forest land, as confirmed by the analysis in the appendix. Net agricultural benefits, B^a, are also assumed to increase with forest land allocation – in this case A_t, or the stock of converted forest land. As forest and agricultural lands are productive inputs, the normal condition of diminishing marginal returns is assumed to hold. The above assumptions can be summarized as:

$$\begin{aligned} B^p &= B^p(F_t) \\ B^e &= B^e(F_t) \\ B^a &= B^a(A_t), \end{aligned} \tag{11.7}$$

where $B^p_F = \partial B^p/\partial F > 0$, $B^p_{FF} = \partial^2 B^p/\partial F^2 < 0$, $B^e_F = \partial B^e/\partial F > 0$, $B^e_{FF} = \partial^2 B^e/\partial F^2 < 0$, $B^a_A = \partial B^a/\partial A > 0$, and $B^a_{AA} = \partial^2 B^a/\partial A^2 < 0$.

In the previous section we argued that the land allocation decision would be influenced by whether environmental benefits are considered or not. Following the approach of Lopez, Shah and Altobello (1994), we can employ an indicator function (θ) to reflect whether environmental benefits are accounted for in forest land use decision making. Letting $\theta = 0$ implies that the forest land use decision is based on production decisions alone. This is socially optimally only if the net environmental benefits of forestry are zero. In contrast, letting $\theta = 1$ suggests that environmental benefits are present and need to be fully internalized into the optimal forest land use decision making process.

The following dynamic allocation problem can therefore be established in order to maximize total net benefits B through the choice of F_t, A_t and x_t from the perspective of a social planner:

$$\text{Max}_{F_t, A_t, x_t} \sum_{t=1}^{T} \left[B^p(F_t) + \theta B^e(F_t) + B^a(A_t) \right] \rho_{t-1} \tag{11.8}$$

subject to

$$F_t - F_{t-1} = -x_t$$
$$A_t - A_{t-1} = x_t$$

and

$$F_t > 0,\ A_t > 0,\ x_t > 0,\ F_0 = \bar{F},\ A_0 = \underline{A},\ A_T \geq \bar{A} \geq 0,$$

$$F_T \geq \underline{F}, \text{ where } B^p(\underline{F}) + \theta B^e(\underline{F}) = 0,\ \mathrm{Lim}_{F \to \underline{F}} \frac{\partial B^i(F)}{\partial F} \to \infty, i = p, e$$

$$\rho_{t-1} = \frac{1}{(1+\delta)^{t-1}}, \rho_0 = 1, \qquad t = 1, \ldots, T,$$

where ρ_{t-1} is the discount factor, and δ is the periodic discount rate. F_0 represents the initial forest stock, which prior to conversion to agriculture (and assuming no regrowth) is at its maximum. A_0 is the corresponding initial stock of agricultural land. As the stock of forest declines over time through conversion to agriculture the marginal production and environmental benefits derived from forest land rise to infinity. $F_T = \underline{F}$ represents the final stock of forest, which may have been reduced to zero if all forest land was converted to agricultural production, or may be greater than zero if some forest stock is left standing. When the forest stock reaches $\underline{F}$ the production and environmental benefits derived from forest land are assumed to be zero. The Lagrangian for this problem is:

$$\begin{aligned}
\mathcal{L} = & \sum_{t=1}^{T} \rho_{t-1}\left[B^p(F_t) + \theta B^e(F_t) + B^a(A_t)\right] \\
& + \sum_{t=1}^{T} \mu_t\left[F_{t-1} - F_t - x_t\right] + \mu_0\left[\bar{F} - F_0\right] + \mu_{T+1}\left[F_T - \underline{F}\right] \\
& + \sum_{t=1}^{T} \lambda_t\left[A_{t-1} - A_t + x_t\right] + \lambda_0\left[\underline{A} - A_0\right] + \lambda_{T+1}\left[A_T - \bar{A}\right], \qquad (11.9)
\end{aligned}$$

where μ_t is the shadow value of forest land maintained for sustainable timber production, and λ_t is the shadow value of converted forest land. Both multipliers are assumed to be in present value terms. The resulting first-order conditions for maximization are:

$$\partial\mathcal{L}/\partial F_t = \rho_{t-1}[B_F^p + \theta B_F^e] + \mu_{t+1} - \mu_t = 0, \qquad t = 1, \ldots, T-1 \quad (11.10)$$

$$\partial\mathcal{L}/\partial A_t = \rho_{t-1}[B_A^a] + \lambda_{t+1} - \lambda_t = 0, \qquad t = 1, \ldots, T-1 \quad (11.11)$$

$$\partial\mathcal{L}/\partial x_t = \lambda_t - \mu_t = 0, \qquad t = 1, \ldots, T \quad (11.12)$$

$$\partial\mathcal{L}/\partial \mu_t = F_{t-1} - F_t - x_t = 0, \qquad t = 1, \ldots, T \quad (11.13)$$

$$\partial\mathcal{L}/\partial \lambda_t = A_{t-1} - A_t + x_t = 0, \qquad t = 1, \ldots, T \quad (11.14)$$

$$\partial\mathcal{L}/\partial F_0 = \mu_1 - \mu_0 = 0, \quad (11.15)$$

$$\partial\mathcal{L}/\partial F_t = \rho_{T-1}[B_F^p + \theta B_F^e] - \mu_{T+1} - \mu_T = 0, \text{ and } \mu_{T+1}\,[F_T - \underline{F}] = 0 \quad (11.16)$$

$$\partial\mathcal{L}/\partial A_0 = \lambda_1 - \lambda_0 = 0 \quad (11.17)$$

$$\partial\mathcal{L}/\partial A_T = \rho_{T-1}[B_A^a] + \lambda_{T+1} - \lambda_T = 0, \text{ and } \lambda_{T+1}\,[A_T - \bar{A}] = 0. \quad (11.18)$$

Equations (11.15)–(11.18) are the initial and terminal boundary conditions for F_t and A_t, and equations (11.13) and (11.14) simply restate the difference equations (11.5). Assuming that environmental benefits are fully accounted for in forest land use decision making we can let $\theta = 1$. Equation (11.10) tells us that:

$$\partial\mathcal{L}/\partial F_t = \rho_{t-1}[B_F^p + B_F^e] - \mu_t + \mu_{t+1} = 0, \qquad t = 1, \ldots, T-1 \quad (11.10')$$

in any period t, the net present value marginal benefits of marginal net production and environmental forest benefits, $\rho_{t-1}[B_F^p + B_F^e]$, must equal the change in the shadow value of forest land $(\mu_t - \mu_{t+1})$. This represents the basic 'asset value' condition for forest land. That is, it is worth holding on to land as forest up to the point where the benefits of timber production and environmental benefits equal the change in the shadow value of forest land. Equation (11.11) yields a similar 'asset value' condition for land converted to agriculture, A_t; that is, agricultural conversion should take place up to the point where the discounted marginal benefits of agriculture ($\rho_{t-1}B^a_A$) equal the change in the shadow price of converted forest land ($\lambda_t - \lambda_{t+1}$).

However, from condition (11.12) it is clear that in each time period land should be allocated between forestry and agriculture up to the point where the shadow value of forest land for timber production, μ_t, equals the shadow value of converted agricultural land, λ_t. That is, optimal deforestation requires that μ_t, which is equivalent to the (discounted) marginal 'rental' value of forest land under timber production, must equal λ_t, which is the marginal 'rental' value of agricultural land converted from forest. Thus it follows from (11.12) that

$$\rho_{t-1}[B^p_F + B^e_F] = \mu_t - \mu_{t+1} = \lambda_t - \lambda_{t+1} = \rho_{t-1}[B^a_A] \qquad t = 1, \ldots, T-1 \quad (11.19)$$

or

$$B^p_F + B^e_F = B^a_A \qquad t = 1, \ldots, T-1.$$

Equation (11.19) represents the trade-off between forest land allocated to timber production and environmental benefits as opposed to agriculture.[7] Forest land is retained for timber production up to the point where the discounted marginal net benefits of timber production and environmental benefits, $\rho_{t-1}[B^p_F + B^e_F]$, equal the change in the shadow value of converted forest land, $\lambda_t - \lambda_{t+1}$. From equation (11.11) the change in this rental value or price of converted land must also equal to the discounted marginal net benefits of agriculture, $\rho_{t-1}[B^a_A]$. It therefore follows that the optimal allocation of forest land in any time period, t, requires that the marginal net benefits of timber production and environmental benefits from forested land, $B^p_F + B^e_F$, equal the marginal net benefits of agricultural production from converted land, B^a_A. Thus condition (11.19) is analogous to the forest level decision rule in equation (11.3) developed earlier.

Another useful interpretation of condition (11.19) is that the opportunity cost, or 'price', of converting an additional unit of forest land to agriculture in each time period is foregoing marginal timber production and environmental benefits that could have been obtained with that unit of land. Let v_t be defined as this price or opportunity cost of a unit of converted forest land in any time period, t. Thus (11.19) can now be represented as an inverse demand function for converted forest land:

$$v_t = B^a_A = D^{-1}_{At}(A_t), \quad t = 1, \ldots, T-1, \qquad (11.19')$$

where $v_t = B^p_F + B^e_F$. Alternatively, defining A^D_t as the quantity of converted forest land demanded:

$$A_t^D = D_{At}(v_t, P_t, Y_t, q_t), \qquad t = 1, \ldots, T-1 \qquad (11.20)$$

where $\partial A_t^D/\partial v_t < 0$, $\partial A_t^D/\partial P_t > 0$, $\partial A_t^D/\partial Y_t \gtreqless 0$ and $\partial A_t^D/\partial q_t < 0$. That is, the demand for converting forest land (A_t^D) in each time period is negatively related to its opportunity cost, or price, in terms of foregone timber production and environmental benefits from forest land. As the 'price' of conversion falls one would expect an increased demand for converting forest land to agriculture. This is represented by the downward sloping demand curve A_t^D depicted in Figure 11.1. Note that condition (11.19) also implies that under competitive market conditions the 'price' of converted forest land, v_t, should equal the change in the (current) rental value of agricultural land, $[\lambda_t - \lambda_{t+1}]/\rho_{t-1}$.

As indicated in equation (11.20) the demand for new agricultural land may also be influenced by additional exogenous macroeconomic variables, such as population, P_t, income, Y_t, and agricultural yields, q_t. This is confirmed by recent empirical studies of tropical deforestation.[8]

Increases in population in developing countries are expected to increase the demand for agricultural goods, and as a consequence, increase the demand for forest land conversion. However, the impact of rising incomes on the demand

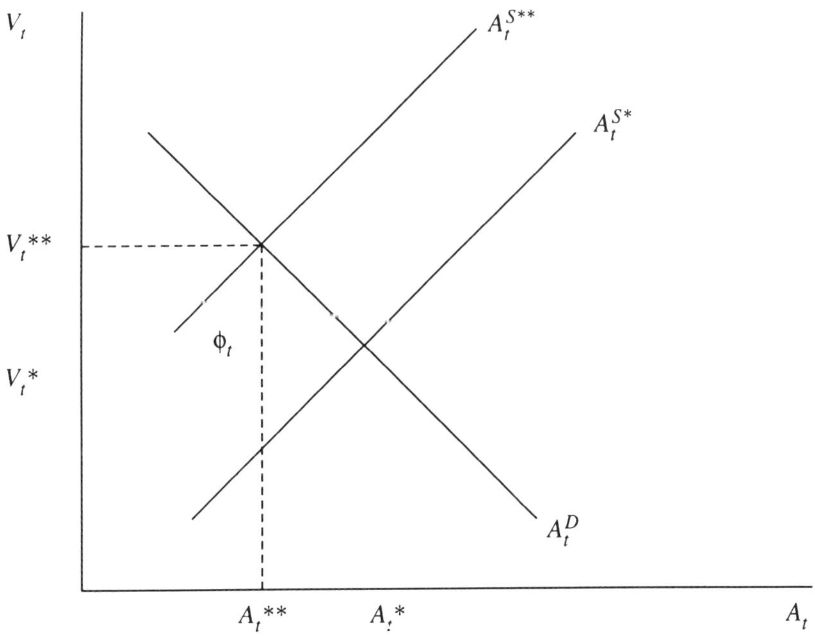

Figure 11.1 Optimal allocation of converted forest land

for agricultural land is less certain. Empirical evidence has provided conflicting results. On the one hand, an increase in income may be expected to increase the demand for agricultural products as a large proportion of the population in developing countries are 'poor' and experience calorie intakes well below the daily recommended rates. On the other hand, an increase in income may be associated with a reduction in the reliance on subsistence farming and primary production within a developing country, reflecting a shift towards manufacturing and service industries.[9] Finally, an increase in agricultural yields is generally expected to reduce the demand for new agricultural land, as yield increases imply more production from existing arable land.

The supply curve for converted forest land can be derived similarly from conditions (11.10) and (11.19). By substituting $F_t = F_{t-1} - [A_t - A_{t-1}]$ from (11.8) into the expression $v_t = B_F^p + B_F^e$ one obtains:

$$v_t = B_F^p\,(F_{t-1} - [A_t - A_{t-1}]) + B_F^e\,(F_{t-1} - [A_t - A_{t-1}]) \quad t = 1, \ldots, T-1. \quad (11.21)$$

Equation (11.21) indicates that to maintain an optimal allocation of forest land an increase in the 'price' of converted forest land, v_t, requires the marginal net benefits of timber production and environmental benefits to rise, that is, $\uparrow [\partial B^p/\partial F_t + \partial B^e/\partial F_t]$. From the second-order derivatives $B_{FF}^p = \partial^2 B^p/\partial F^2 < 0$ and $B_{FF}^e = \partial^2 B^e/\partial F^2 < 0$, we know that this in turn means a fall in F_t. This can only occur if less land is allocated to forestry and there is a corresponding rise in land converted to agriculture, A_t. Thus an increase in the price of converted forest land, v_t, must correspond to an increase in the supply of forest land converted to agriculture, A_t.[10] Consequently, (11.21) can be redefined as the inverted supply function of converted forest land:

$$v_t = S_{At}^{-1}(A_t), \qquad t = 1, \ldots, T-1, \qquad (11.21')$$

or, defining the supply of newly converted forest land as $A[St]$

$$A_t^S = S_{At}(v_t), \qquad t = 1, \ldots, T-1, \qquad (11.22)$$

where $\partial A_t^S/\partial v_t > 0$. Equation (11.22) is the supply function for converted forest land (A_t^S) in each time period, reflecting the limited availability of forest land for either agricultural conversion or maintenance as forest. Therefore, an increase in the supply of land for conversion to agriculture each period can only be achieved by bidding land away from forests at increasingly higher prices. As noted above, under competitive market conditions, the price of converted forest land will equal the change in the (current) rental value of agricultural land, $[\lambda_t - \lambda_{t+1}]/\rho_{t-1}$, and it will be optimal to allocate more forest land to agriculture if this market rate of return on agricultural land exceeds the rate of return on the remaining forested land, $[\mu_t - \mu_{t+1}]/\rho_{t-1}$. In Figure 11.1, the supply function is represented by the upward sloping marginal cost curve, A_t^S. Equations (11.20) and (11.22) can be solved to determine the market equilibrium value of forest land allocation, where the marginal benefits of converting forest land for agricultural production equals the marginal costs. In Figure 11.1, this is depicted where the demand and supply curves intersect at A_t^{**} quantity of converted forest land and price v_t^{**}.

The model can be adapted to take account of the failure to include environmental benefits in forest land use decision making by letting the indicator function $\theta = 0$. This implies that conditions (11.10) and (11.19) would now ignore environmental benefits:

$$\partial \mathcal{L}/\partial F_t = \rho_{t-1}[B_F^p] - \mu_t + \mu_{t+1} = 0, \qquad t = 1, \ldots, T-1 \qquad (11.10')$$

$$\rho_{t-1}\,[B_F^p] = \mu_t - \mu_{t+1} = \lambda_t - \lambda_{t+1} = \rho_{t-1}\,[B_A^a] \qquad t = 1, \ldots, T-1 \qquad (11.19'')$$

and

$$B_F^p = B_A^a \qquad t = 1, \ldots, T-1.$$

In each time period the present value of the marginal net timber production benefits, B_F^p, must equal the change in the shadow value of land between periods t and $t+1$ which in turn must equal the present value of the marginal net agricultural benefits, B_A^a. Therefore, at any time t land is allocated to forest up to the point where the marginal net timber production benefits of land retained as forest are just offset by the marginal net benefits of land converted to agriculture.[11] Once again, this is similar to our previous results – only now the opportunity costs to allocating land to agriculture in terms of foregone environmental benefits are not taken into account. Equation (11.19") also indicates that the exclusion of environmental benefits of tropical forests affects the forest land allocation problem by lowering the marginal costs of converting forest for agricultural production. This can be shown by using (11.19") to derive a new supply relationship for A_t. Let $v_t = B_F^p + B_F^e$ as before. If we now let $\partial B^e/\partial F_t = \phi_t$ represent the marginal environmental benefits of forest land, and substitute $F_t = F_{t-1} - [A_t - A_{t-1}]$ from (11.8), then we obtain:

$$v_t - \phi_t = B_F^p\,(F_{t-1} - [A_t - A_{t-1}]) \qquad t = 1, \ldots, T-1. \qquad (11.21')$$

Equation (11.21') essentially shows that if environmental benefits of sustainable forest management are not taken into account, then the price of agricultural land must now be high enough to cover only the foregone marginal timber benefits of forest land conversion. This means that in each time period the marginal costs associated with forest conversion fall for all levels of A_t. Therefore, the supply (or marginal cost) curve for forest conversion shifts to the right, resulting in lower prices for converted forest land but higher levels of deforestation, holding all other factors constant. As shown in Figure 11.1, the new equilibrium is at A_t^* quantity of converted forest land and price v_t^*. As before, under competitive market conditions one would expect v_t^* to equal the rate of return on land, $[\lambda_t - \lambda_{t+1}]/\rho_{t-1} = [\mu_t - \mu_{t+1}]/\rho_{t-1}$.

4. Empirical analysis of deforestation across the tropics

Using the demand for converting tropical forest for agricultural production from the previous section as the basis for our empirical analysis we can develop a testable model. The basic demand relationship is indicated by equation (11.20):

$$A^D_t = D_{At}(v_t, P_t, Y_t, q_t), \qquad t = 1, \ldots, T-1. \tag{11.20}$$

where $\partial A^D_t/\partial v_t < 0$, $\partial A^D_t/\partial P_t > 0$, $\partial A^D_t/\partial Y_t \gtreqless 0$ and $\partial A^D_t/\partial q_t < 0$. As the results of our theoretical model indicate, if rates of forest land conversion were socially optimal across the tropics, then agricultural land conversion should approximate some equilibrium level A_t^{**} at an equilibrium land price v_t^{**}. Thus under competitive market and socially optimal conditions the price variable in equation (11.20) should equal the market rate of return on agricultural land, which should in turn reflect foregone marginal timber production and environmental benefits resulting from forest conversion.

However, there are several important reasons to suggest that actual rates of forest conversion in tropical countries in recent years have been sub-optimal. First, the environmental costs of forest conversion are rarely estimated and have largely been ignored in most tropical forest land use decisions, yet it is believed that such costs can be significant (Burgess, 1993; IIED, 1994). If this is the case, then rates of agricultural conversion have exceeded the optimal level A_t^{**} predicted by our model. Second, very little of land under forestry has been harvested under sustainable forest management regimes in the tropics (Poore *et al.*, 1989). This would suggest that in making land use decisions, policy makers are either assuming that the long-term timber production benefits from sustainable forest management are low compared to alternative land use options, or are not taking these long-term timber benefits into account in land use decisions. In both cases, the perception is that the opportunity cost of converted forest land in terms of sustainable forestry is low or even zero. Finally, much timber production has been from land already earmarked for agricultural conversion (Poore *et al.*, 1989). Where this arises, the timber extraction is essentially a *complement* to agricultural production. This is, for all intents and purposes, they are joint products.

The combination of the above factors would suggest that 'excessive' tropical deforestation has been taking place due to the failure to take the full opportunity cost of forest conversion in terms of sustainable forest management into account, as well as relying on agricultural conversion forests for a significant proportion of tropical timber production. In any case, it appears that most tropical forest countries have been implementing agricultural conversion policies on the basis that the supply of converted forest land is much further to the right than A_t^S, in Figure 11.1.

The discrepancies between the optimal levels of forest conversion predicted by the theoretical model and actual conversion rates in the tropics would suggest that in many countries current levels of deforestation may bear little relationship to their opportunity cost in terms of foregone sustainable timber production and environmental benefits. In other words, empirical estimation of equation (11.20) based on actual forest conversion cannot reliably use v_t as the price determining the amount of land converted. Even if we did want to include these foregone benefits as our price variable, insufficient data exist across tropical countries to include them in our analysis. An alternative might be the actual price of converted forest land as an indicator of changes in rental value. However, data on land prices for converted forest land in tropical countries are also difficult to obtain, and the existence of imperfect land markets, tenure insecurity, land speculation and open access in 'frontier' forest regions are often cited as the reason why land values do not reflect the full opportunity cost of forest conversion (Barbier, 1993; Deacon, 1995; Mendelsohn, 1994; Schneider *et al.*, 1990; Southgate, Sierra and Brown, 1991).

Nevertheless, it is reasonable to presume that v_t, the price of converted forest land, is not zero in equation (11.20) for tropical forest countries. Moreover, it is clear from our theoretical model that even if environmental benefits of the forest are ignored, at the very least v_t should reflect foregone long-term sustainable timber production benefits. Ideally, this could be approximated by actual tropical timber stumpage values, but unfortunately the data for tropical countries do not exist or are poor approximations. An alternative may be to use border-equivalent export prices for wood production, but these may be misleading given that only around 11 per cent of roundwood production in developing countries is actually exported, and the widespread prevalence of bans and prohibitive taxes on logs has distorted export price data for many tropical countries. Despite this limitation, Cropper and Griffiths (1994) employed in their deforestation analysis international prices for forest products adjusted for the average mid-year exchange rates for each country as one possible proxy for v_t. In contrast, a more reliable 'proxy' measure of foregone production benefits for which data are readily available across tropical countries may be the level of industrial roundwood production, which could be expressed in per capita terms to indicate the relative importance of these benefits to the whole population.

However, with these measures it is not possible to distinguish between timber extraction that arises during forest conversion to agriculture from those benefits derived from the long-term sustainable management of forests for timber production.

We employ two alternative 'proxy' measures for v_t in demand equation (11.20). Following Cropper and Griffith's approach, we approximate v_t by using international roundwood export prices for the three main tropical forest regions (Latin America, Africa and Asia) adjusted by country exchange rates, which effectively become industrial roundwood export unit values expressed in terms of domestic currencies (FAO, 1994). As an alternative, we also use domestic per capita industrial roundwood production.

Empirical estimation of equation (11.20) is therefore based on an analysis of 53 tropical countries, examining the relationship between forest clearance and v_t (as approximated by our alternative 'proxy' variables of roundwood production per capita and adjusted roundwood export unit values) population density, income per capita, agricultural yield and income growth.[12] The most reliable data on changes in tropical forest area are currently derived from the global Forest Resource Assessment exercise conducted every ten years by the FAO and supplemented by interim assessments (FAO and UNEP, 1982; FAO, 1988, 1993; Schmidt, 1990). Unfortunately, changes in forest area in the 1990 Assessment for many tropical countries were estimated from population growth rates over the 1980–90 period, which according to some analysts makes it impossible to employ such data in an empirical analysis of deforestation if population or population density are considered to be important explanatory variables of changing forest cover (Cropper and Griffiths, 1994). However, FAO data on forest area (in '000 ha) for 1980 and 1985 can be used to estimate a five-yearly change in forest cover for tropical countries. The change in forest cover over 1980–85 was therefore the dependent variable for forest conversion used in our analysis.

However, it is possible to specify the dependent variable in two different ways, thus leading to two functional forms for equation (11.20) in our empirical analysis. First, the five-year change in forest cover can be represented by the logarithm of the forest area in 1985 minus the logarithm of the forest area in 1980. This leads to a semi-logarithmic specification of equation (11.20). Second, the change in forest cover can be represented by the ratio of forest area in 1985 to forest area in 1980. This leads to a linear specification of equation (11.20). In both versions, the explanatory variables are based on the initial period (1980) data.[13]

The data for industrial non-coniferous roundwood production are taken from FAO *Yearbook of Forest Products* (FAO, 1992b), and were expressed in per capita terms (m^3/total population) in the model. Real gross national product per capita in 1980 (in US$/1000) and population density in 1980 (people/1000 ha) are derived from World Bank (1992). The indicator for agricultural yield is approximated by cereal output per unit of cereal production area in 1980 (mt/ha) and is based on data from FAO (1992a). Finally, because deforestation rates have been lower in Latin America over the 1980–85 period than in other tropical regions, and production and exports of timber products have been generally less significant for Latin America, a dummy variable for Latin America is included in the model.

Table 11.1 Statistical analysis of forest clearance in tropical countries, 1980–85: semi-log regression[a]

Dependent variable: five-year change in closed forest area (log forest area 1985–log forest area 1980)

Explanatory variable	Estimated coefficients (*t*–statistic)	Estimated elasticities
constant	– 0.0958 (– 3.945)	
X1 Population density 1980	– 0.0524 (– 2.974)	– 0.0285
X2 Roundwood production per capita 1980	– 0.0772 (– 2.076)	– 0.0177
X3 Real GNP per capita 1980	0.0209 (1.9150)	0.0212
X4 Agricultural yield 1980	0.0381 (2.0693)	0.0574
X5 Dummy Latin America	– 0.0629 (– 2.2042)	– 0.0226

R^2:	0.227	*F*–Statistic:	2.76
S.E. of Regression:	0.080	No of observations:	53

Note: [a] As the dependent variable is negative, the positive coefficients for X3 and X4 indicate that forest conversion is decreasing with a unit change in these variables whereas the negative coefficients for X1, X2 and X5 indicate that forest conversion is increasing with a unit change in these variables.

The results of the model are displayed in Tables 11.1 and 11.2 for both the semi-log and linear regressions. Employing industrial roundwood export unit values expressed in terms of domestic currencies as a proxy for v_t proved to be highly insignificant in the regression, whereas employing industrial roundwood production proved significant.[14] Thus only the latter proxy variable for v_t is included in the regression results depicted in Tables 11.1 and 11.2. Both the semi-log and linear regressions yield similar elasticities for each of the explanatory variables, and both regressions are very similar in terms of overall explanatory power.

Table 11.2 Statistical analysis of forest clearance in tropical countries, 1980–85: linear regression[a]

Dependent variable: five-year change in closed forest area (forest area 1985–forest area 1980)

Explanatory variable	Estimated coefficients (*t*–statistic)	Estimated elasticities
constant	0.9122	
	(43.4299)	
X1 Population density 1980	–0.0468	–0.0298
	(–3.071)	
X2 Roundwood production per capita 1980	–0.0657	–0.0163
	(–2.041)	
X3 Real GNP per capita 1980	0.0188	0.0208
	(1.9858)	
X4 Agricultural yield 1980	0.0334	0.0547
	(2.0968)	
X5 Dummy Latin America	–0.0564	–0.0220
	(–2.2828)	

R^2:	0.239	*F*–Statistic:	2.96
S.E. of Regression:	0.069	No of observations:	53

Note: [a] As a fall in the dependent variable is associated with a greater change in closed forest area, the positive coefficients for X3 and X4 indicate that forest conversion is decreasing with a unit change in these variables whereas the negative coefficients for X1, X2 and X5 indicate that forest conversion is increasing with a unit change in these variables.

The regression results indicate that industrial roundwood production and population pressure are positively associated with forest clearance in the tropics for the 1980–85 period, that is, increasing levels of industrial roundwood production per capita and population density lead to higher rates of forest loss.[15] Combining the elasticities from both regression versions suggest that a 1 per cent increase in per capita roundwood production across tropical countries in 1980 increased the level of forest area converted over the 1980–85 period by around 0.016 per cent to 0.018 per cent. Similarly, a 1 per cent increase in population density led to a 0.028 per cent to 0.03 per cent rise in forest clearance.

In contrast, income per capita and agricultural yields are negatively associated with forest conversion, that is, improvements in overall economic development and agricultural performance appear to reduce the demand for more forest clearance. A 1 per cent increase in real GDP per capita across tropical forest countries in 1980 appears to have reduced the level of forest conversion by around 0.02 per cent to 0.021 per cent over the 1980–85 period. A 1 per cent increase in agricultural yields reduced deforestation by about 0.055 per cent to 0.057 per cent over this period.

With the exception of industrial roundwood production, all the estimated variables show the anticipated impacts on the demand for converted forest land as indicated by equation (11.20). Increased population density increases forest clearance, whereas rising income per capita and agricultural yields reduce the demand for converted land. However, despite being our 'proxy' for the opportunity costs of foregone production benefits from forestry, increasing industrial roundwood production is positively correlated with increasing forest conversion. There are two possible reasons for this result.

First, over the 1980–85 period much industrial non-coniferous roundwood production was being supplied from forests earmarked for conversion to agricultural, particularly in the major tropical timber producing countries (Barbier *et al.*, 1994; Poore *et al.*, 1989). For example, over 40 per cent of the total production forest area of 835 921 km^2 of South East Asia has been designated as conversion production forest, and during the 1970s and early 1980s much of this conversion forest area was clear cut for timber and converted to agriculture. Moreover, the data to distinguish between industrial roundwood production from permanent production forest as opposed to conversion forests in tropical countries over this period do not exist. As a result, the positive relationship between increasing log production and forest clearance estimated in our model is possibly reflecting the prevalent role of conversion forests in providing industrial roundwood across tropical countries over 1980–85.

Second, although timber production from permanent forests may not be the major direct source of tropical deforestation, there is ample evidence that forestry operations have led indirectly to deforestation through 'opening up' previously inaccessible forest regions to conversion activities, in particular agriculture (Amelung and Diehl, 1991). Part of the problem may have been that to date there has been very little sustainable management of production forests across tropical countries, which suggests that the long-term prospects of maintaining forest land in timber production have been ignored (Poore *et al.*, 1989). Certainly, forest regulations, concession terms and pricing policies in most tropical countries have worked against the control of timber-stand degradation, encroachment and premature abandonment (Barbier *et al.*, 1994; Hyde, Newman and Sedjo, 1991). Thus it is likely that during the 1980–85 period even roundwood production from permanent forests in tropical countries may have been correlated with forest land clearance.

The above caveats would suggest that a positive relationship between increasing industrial roundwood production in tropical forest countries during 1980–85 and forest clearance may be a valid empirical estimate. Over this period clearing forests for agriculture and timber production may well have been joint products on forest land, although perhaps inadvertently so for permanent production forests. However, this result also implies that if aggregate industrial roundwood production does reflect the foregone production benefits arising from forest clearance, and thus is a 'proxy' for the price of converted forest land in equation (11.20), then recent forest conversion in tropical countries may be far from optimal. Not only have foregone production and environmental benefits from sustainable forestry been ignored in tropical forest land use decisions but recent forestry practices and policies have directly and indirectly encouraged forest conversion. Of course, this result can only be confirmed by a more direct estimation of the relationship between the demand for converted forest land and the price or opportunity cost of conversion, in terms of foregone forest production and/or environmental benefits. Unfortunately, such an estimation will have to wait for better data to construct a more accurate indicator of v_t in equation (11.20).

5. Conclusion

This chapter has explored several approaches to the tropical forest land use decision. All approaches have attempted to illustrate the decision by focusing on the choice between, on the one hand, sustainable management of forests for timber production, and on the other, conversion to agriculture. The effects of including any net environmental benefits of land under forestry are also illustrated.

First, a basic cost–benefit rule for allocating forest land between two competing land use options – such as sustainable timber production and conversion to agriculture – was explored. This rule was also extended to include the net environmental benefits of forestry. In the Appendix we demonstrate more formally how it is possible to utilize the stand-level rule for optimal allocation of tropical forest land uses to derive an equivalent rule at the forest level. The aim of this first part of the chapter has been to show that the foregone timber production and, where relevant, environmental benefits of the forestry option must be incorporated as part of the opportunity costs of converting forest land to agriculture.

The second approach expanded the stand and forest-level approach to a more generalized inter-temporal forest land allocation problem for a tropical forest region or even a country. The demand for converted forest land was shown to vary inversely with the price, or change in rental value, of this land, which in turn was linked directly to the opportunity costs of foregone timber production and environmental benefits from sustainable forestry. The supply of converted forest land is, however, positively related to an increase in its rental value, as an increase land supplied for agricultural conversion can only be achieved by bidding land away from forests at increasingly higher prices. As shown in Figure 11.1, the supply and demand for converted forest land determines an optimal quantity of land converted and an equilibrium price. It was also demonstrated that the exclusion of environmental benefits in the opportunity cost of forest land conversion shifts the supply curve to the right, resulting in lower 'prices' for converted forest land but a higher optimal level of forest conversion.

The final approach was an empirical analysis across tropical countries of the demand equation for converted forest land derived from the inter-temporal model. However, the opportunity cost of foregone environmental benefits could not be included as part of the price of forest land conversion. In addition, lack of data meant that a proxy for this price variable had to be found for the estimation of the demand for converted forest land. Of the two alternative proxies, per capita industrial roundwood production proved to be significant in both versions of the regression. This variable was positively and not negatively correlated with forest clearance over 1980–85. This could nonetheless be expected given that during this period much timber production in tropical countries was actually from conversion forest land, and timber operations on permanent forest land may be indirectly responsible for subsequent land clearing. In contrast, the estimated coefficients for the other explanatory variables were entirely consistent with the theory underlying the demand for converted forest land. Increased population density increases forest clearance, whereas rising income per capita and agricultural yields reduce the demand for converted land.

In conclusion, the approaches developed in this chapter provide a foundation for the analysis of tropical forest land use decisions. Moreover, the theoretical approaches show explicitly the effects of incorporating environmental externalities, which is an important issue raised in the current literature on forest land use choices. In particular, the intertemporal model developed here furnishes a basis for empirical investigation of the hypothesis that deforestation has been excessive in many tropical countries because the potential rents that cleared land could have yielded as a site for long-term sustainable forestry have been neglected. Our empirical analysis provides some evidence supporting this hypothesis: the result that deforestation appears to be positively correlated with timber production indicates not only that foregone production and environmental benefits from sustainable forestry have been ignored in tropical forest land use decisions but also that recent forestry practices and policies may have encouraged even greater forest conversion.

Although our estimation of the demand for converted forest land across tropical countries yielded encouraging results, improving on this initial analysis will require both improved data on forest clearance as well as on the relevant indicator of the shadow value, or opportunity cost, of converted forest land. There may also be necessity to follow the approach of Deacon (1994) and expand the demand analysis to account for other factors, such as tenure insecurity and specific government policies, that may be important independent determinants of forest land conversion in many tropical countries.

Appendix: optimal land use at the stand and forest level

The following appendix indicates how optimal allocation of a forested stand between 'sustainable' forestry and agricultural land use options can be aggregated to derive similar rules for an entire forest comprising many stands. The latter forest-level conditions underlie the basic assumptions of the inter-temporal model of optimal conversion of forest land developed in Section 3 of the text.

Stand level

Assume that for a given tropical forest stand there are two competing land use options, agricultural production and 'sustainable' long-term forestry with natural regeneration. It therefore follows that to determine which of two competing land use options should be preferred, it should be sufficient simply to compare the discounted net benefits of the two options to see which yields a higher return. That is, defining $B^f = B^p$ as the net present value of forestry benefits over time and B^a the net present value of agricultural benefits, then forestry will be the preferred land use option of the stand if:

$$B^f = B^p > B^a. \tag{11.23}$$

Suppose that the forestry option consists of initial cutting of virgin forest followed by periodic harvesting of 'naturally' regenerated timber from a managed stand. If the logging operation is 'sustainable', then successive rotations could presumably be repeated indefinitely.[16] Consequently, the optimal management of the timber stand can be represented as a 'modified' Faustmann-type rotation problem.[17]

Let the amount of timber harvested per hectare, or timber value yield of the stand, be defined as:

$$H = H(T), \tag{11.24}$$

with T denoting time or age of the stand, and $H_T > 0$ for $a < T < b$ and $H_T(b) = 0$ over the relevant portion of the yield curve. Assume that the initial harvesting of timber from the virgin forest can be accomplished in the current time period,

$T = 0$. Let H_o be the timber harvested in this initial period. The net stumpage value of this timber, V_o, can be defined as:

$$V_o = (p^h - x^h)H_o, \tag{11.25}$$

where p^h is the stumpage price for the timber, and x^h is the total extraction cost. To simplify the analysis we assume that p^h and x^h are in constant real terms over time.[18]

After the first cutting operation of the virgin forest, the stand is then managed for successive rotational periods, T, with each rotation requiring an initial fixed investment, or cost, of silvicultural effort, E. The latter is typical of 'enrichment replanting' efforts in tropical forest stands logged 'sustainably' over successive rotations (Poore *et al.*, 1989). If r is the rate of discount (also representing the opportunity cost of capital) and p^h and x^h are in constant real terms over time, then the net present value of the operation over current and future rotations is defined through the optimal choice of stand age, T^*, as

$$\begin{aligned} B^f = B^p &= V_0 + \left[\left(p^h - x^h\right)H\left(T^*\right)e^{-rT^*} - E\right]\left(1 + e^{-rT^*} + e^{-2rT^*} + \ldots\right) \\ &= V_0 + \frac{\left[\left(p^h - x^h\right)H\left(T^*\right)e^{-rT^*} - E\right]}{\left(1 - e^{-rT^*}\right)} \end{aligned} \tag{11.26}$$

As demonstrated by Hartman (1976) and below, the basic Faustmann timber production model can be extended to include non-timber forest benefits. Condition (11.23) states that logging of the stand is the most highly valued use only if its net present value exceeds that of an alternative land use, in this case agricultural production. The latter derives from continuous cultivation of the land. Adapting an approach developed by Mendelsohn (1994), it is possible to represent the discounted stream of net agricultural benefits, B^a as

$$B^a = \int_0^\infty \left(p^q - x^q\right)Q_e^{*-(r+s)t}dt - S_o = \frac{\left(p^q - x^q\right)}{(r+s)}Q^* - S_0, \tag{11.27}$$

where p^q and x^q are agricultural output price and production costs respectively, which are assumed constant in real terms over time; Q^* is optimal agricultural yield or output per hectare; and S_0 represents initial establishment (that is, conversion) costs and benefits of forest land, in per hectare terms.[19] The parameter s represents exogenous physical productivity effects. That is, if s is positive in (11.27) it represents a net rate of decay in physical output over time, due to the general 'unsustainability' of agricultural production on poor quality converted forest soils; if s is negative then it represents net increases in productivity over time, presumably due to exogenous technological change.[20]

Consequently, for condition (11.23) to be fulfilled and sustainable timber management to be the preferred land use option for the stand

$$V_o = \frac{\left[\left(p^h - x^h\right)H\left(T^*\right)e^{-rT^*} - E\right]}{\left(1 - e^{-rT^*}\right)} > \frac{\left(p^q - x^q\right)}{(r+s)}Q^* - S_o. \qquad (11.23')$$

Forest level

By adapting the approach of Parades and Brodie (1989), it is possible to extend the above stand-level conditions to develop equivalent conditions at the forest level that hold for all timber stands and agricultural plots. If in addition it is assumed that forest land area is fixed, optimal rules for allocating this land between the agricultural and forestry options can be derived.

Assume that a tropical forest could be allocated to J stands for sustainable timber production, and let f_j be the total forest land area (in hectares) of stand j. Consequently, as before, after immediate harvesting of the virgin forest each stand j can be managed for successive rotational periods, T_j, with each rotation requiring an initial investment of silvicultural effort, E_j. Then (11.26) can be re-written for the jth stand as:

$$V_j^p = \left(p^h - x^h\right)H_{jo} + \frac{\left[\left(p^h - x^h\right)H_j\left(T_j\right)e^{-rT_j} - E_j\right]}{\left(1 - e^{-rT_j}\right)}, \qquad (11.28)$$

where V_j^p represents the net present value in per hectare terms of timber production from trees and land.[21]

As noted in the text, one of the advantages of allocating forest land to long-term sustainable timber production is that this land use option may also allow the provision of non-market environmental benefits. We now allow for this possibility in our forest-level analysis. Following Parades and Brodie (1989), if there is a flow of non-timber amenity and environmental services associated with stand j, then the flow of non-market benefits are likely to be proportional to the total area of the stand f_j. However, environmental services and amenities are also likely to be a function of stand age (Hartman, 1976; Bowes and Krutilla, 1985). Defining V_j^e as the net present value per hectare of environmental benefits from stand j

$$V_j^e = \int_0^{T_j} N_j(\tau)e^{-r\tau}d\tau\left(1+e^{-2rT_j}+e^{-3rT_j}+\ldots\right)+\int_0^{\infty} n_j e^{-rt}dt$$

$$= \frac{\int_0^{T_j} N_j(\tau)e^{-r\tau}d\tau}{\left(1-e^{-rT_j}\right)}+\frac{n_j}{r}, \qquad (11.29)$$

where $N_j(\tau)$ are the flow of non-market environmental benefits of stand j influenced by stand age, and n_j are the environmental benefits generated per hectare of stand area.[22]

It therefore follows from (11.28) and (11.29) that the total net benefits generated by all J stands of the forest for sustainable timber production and non-timber environmental benefits are

$$B^f = B^p + B^e = \sum_{j=1}^{J}\left(V_j^p + V_j^e\right)\cdot f_j, \qquad (11.30)$$

where the total net benefits of sustainable forestry B^f consist of both timber production net benefits B^p and environmental benefits B^e.

Similarly, the forest could also be divided into M plots for agriculture. Letting a_m denote the total area (in hectares) for plot m, then from (11.27) for the mth plot

$$V_m^a = \frac{\left(p^q - x^q\right)}{(r+s)}Q_m - S_{mo}, \qquad (11.31)$$

where V_m^a represents the net present value of agricultural production from plot m of converted forest land.[23]

It follows from (11.31) that the total net benefits from conversion and use of all M plots of forest land for agricultural production are

$$B^a = \sum_{m=1}^{M} V_m^a \cdot a_m, \qquad (11.32)$$

where B^a are the total net benefits of agricultural production from converted forest land.[24]

If total forest land is denoted by L, then from (11.30) and (11.32) the optimal allocation of tropical forest land to sustainable forestry and agricultural uses is determined by

$$B = B^f + B^a = \max_{\{T_j, f_j, a_m\}} \sum_{j=1}^{J} \left(V_j^p + V_j^e\right) \cdot f_j + \sum_{m=1}^{M} V_m^a \cdot a_m \qquad (11.33)$$

subject to

$$T_j > 0, f_j > 0, a_m > 0$$

$$\sum_{j=1}^{J} f_j + \sum_{m=1}^{M} a_m = L.$$

Defining λ as the shadow price of forest land, the Lagrangian of (11.33) is

$$\mathcal{L}\left(T_j, f_j, a_m, \lambda\right) = \sum_{j=1}^{J} \left(V_j^p + V_j^e\right) \cdot f_j + \sum_{m=1}^{M} V_m^a \cdot a_m - \lambda\left[\sum_{j=1}^{J} f_j + \sum_{m=1}^{M} a_m - L\right]. \qquad (11.34)$$

Three first-order conditions for maximization of (11.34) worth examining are

$$\partial \mathcal{L} / \partial T_j = \frac{\partial\left(V_j^p + V_j^e\right)}{\partial T_j} \cdot f_j = 0 \qquad \text{all } j \quad (11.35)$$

or $$\frac{\partial H_j}{\partial T_j} + \frac{N_j\left(T_j\right)}{\left(p^h - x^h\right)} = rH_j\left(T_j\right) + \frac{r}{\left(p^h - x^h\right)} \cdot \mathrm{Y}_j\left(T_j\right),$$

where $$\mathrm{Y}_j\left(T_j\right) = \frac{\left[\left(p^h - x^h\right)H_j\left(T_j\right)e^{-rT_j} - E_j\right] + \int_0^{T_j} N_j(\tau)e^{-r\tau}d\tau}{\left(1 - e^{-rT_j}\right)}$$

$$\frac{\partial \mathcal{L}}{\partial f_j} = \left(V_j^p + V_j^e\right) - \lambda = 0, \qquad \text{all } j \quad (11.36)$$

$$\frac{\partial \mathcal{L}}{\partial a_m} = V_m^a - \lambda = 0, \qquad \text{all } j \quad (11.37)$$

Equation (11.35) is essentially the standard Hartman–Faustmann condition for determining the optimal rotation for timber production and environmental benefits from the *j*th stand. That is, the optimal rotation should be at that age when the incremental timber yield and amenity values gained by delaying harvest must equal the opportunity cost of the delay in terms of holding on to trees and the land. Condition (11.36) determines the optimal allocation of forest land to sustainable timber production. It states that the *j*th stand will be allocated forest land until its opportunity cost (shadow price) equals the per hectare net present timber and environmental values of the stand. Similarly, condition (11.37) determines the optimal conversion of forest land to agriculture. It shows that the *m*th plot will also be allocated forest land until its opportunity cost equals the per hectare net present value of agricultural production from the plot.[25]

Denoting MB_j^f as the (discounted) marginal net benefits from allocating a unit of forest land to the *j*th timber stand and MB_m^a as the (discounted) marginal net benefits of allocating this land to the *m*th agricultural plot, then it follows from (11.36) and (11.37)

$$MB_j^f = MB_j^p + MB_j^e = MB_m^a \qquad (11.38)$$

where $MB_j^p = V_j^p$, $MB_j^e = V_j^e$ and $MB_m^a = V_m^a$ in this simple example.

Condition (11.38) is the optimal rule for allocating tropical forest land to the competing uses of agriculture and sustainable timber production. Land should be allocated to any *j*th forestry stand until the marginal net timber and environmental benefits generated by the last unit equals its opportunity cost – the foregone marginal net benefits of instead employing this land under agricultural plot *m*. The comparison with condition (11.23) is straightforward: it is optimal to continue allocating forest land to sustainable timber production as long as $MB_j^f > MB_m^a$. Alternatively, if $MB_j^f < MB_m^a$ then forest land should instead be converted to agriculture. Forest land will continue to be allocated in either of these ways until condition (11.38) holds.

Notes

1. For reviews of the empirical evidence, see Amelung and Diehl (1991); Barbier *et al.* (1994); Hyde, Newman and Sedjo (1991) and Repetto and Gillis (1988).
2. Some recent approaches have involved theoretical explorations without explicit empirical applications, whereas others are largely empirical investigations that are only implicitly based on an optimization framework. Interesting examples of the former include Barrett (1993), who models the optimal allocation of tropical forests between biodiversity 'preserves'

and agriculture, and Hartwick (1992), who explores optimal capital revaluations in the national accounts arising from changes in the value of land as it is converted from tropical forest to agriculture. Examples of purely applied analyses of relevance to this paper include Barbier and Burgess (1996), who estimate the demand for new cropland and pasture land in forested provinces of Mexico, Panayotou and Sungsuwan (1994), who analyse the demand for agricultural land expansion in Thailand, and Southgate (1991), who examines the demand for agricultural land across tropical forest countries of Latin America.

3. Note that B^a should also include any positive aesthetic and other non-market benefits of agricultural land, which may in some cases be significant (Lopez, Shah and Altobello, 1994). As stated in the text, B^a may include any forest clearance costs and windfall timber benefits, however see note 20.
4. For more discussion and examples of the application of this general rule to 'conservation, development and preservation options' for tropical forest land use, see Barbier (1992) and IIED (1994). Note that this rule is not limited just to tropical forest land use options but is applicable to competing uses of any resource or land use option. See, for example, the development of analogous rules for tropical wetlands by Barbier (1994).
5. In fact, given the paucity of studies on the economics of tropical forest land use options, the 55 case studies reviewed included a number of economic analyses of temperate forest land use options that were considered to provide important methodological insights.
6. To simplify notation, in what follows it the time subscript is suppressed for any benefit, B. Because we assume that remaining forest land is under 'sustainable' forest production, then as in the previous section, B^e is assumed to be positive. However, much tropical forest production across countries and regions does not appear to be sustainable currently (Poore *et al.*, 1989). The resulting environmental damages through forest degradation and biological modification, let alone outright deforestation through clear-cutting, may be significant (Amelung and Diehl, 1991). Thus our assumption that forest production is 'sustainable' is critical; if it were not, then B^e may prove to be negative.
7. Note that the terminal boundary conditions suggest that (11.19) also holds in period T provided that $F_T > \underline{F}$ and thus $\mu_{T+1} = 0$.
8. For example, see Allen and Barnes (1985); Barbier and Burgess (1996); Burgess (1993); Cropper and Griffiths (1994); Deacon (1994); Panayotou and Sungsuwan (1994) and Southgate (1991).
9. Environmental quality is also probably income-elastic in developing countries. Thus both any environmental damages associated with agricultural production and any amenity and non-market benefits should increase with a rise in income. The hypothesis that an increase in income may also be associated with an increase in the demand for environmental quality generally has been the basis for recent efforts to demonstrate an environmental 'Kuznets' curve. However, the results have been mixed, especially for tropical deforestation. For recent reviews see Cropper and Griffiths (1994) and Stern, Common and Barbier (1996).
10. From equation (11.19) we know that it will be optimal to continue allocating forest land to agriculture in time t until the marginal net benefits of agriculture equal that of timber production.
11. Note that the terminal boundary conditions again suggest that (11.19") also holds in period T provided that $F_T > \underline{F}$ and thus $\mu_{T+1} = 0$.
12. Tropical countries are taken to be those countries with the majority of their land mass lying between the tropics. This definition does not distinguish between moist and dry forests that lie between the tropics.
13. As a check on these two versions of the model, we also ran another linear specification of the regression equation using the percentage change in forest area (that is, the change in closed forest area from 1980 to 1985 divided by closed forest area in 1980) as an alternative dependent variable. This third regression yielded virtually the same results as shown in Table 11.2 for the linear regression with the ratio of 1980 to 1985 closed forest areas as the dependent variable. Thus it appears that using the latter ratio as the dependent variable is a good approximation of the half-decade rate of deforestation. It follows that the log of this ratio will also serve as a good approximation.

14. The *t*-statistics for industrial roundwood production export unit values were –0.5227 and –0.4756 in the semi-log and linear regressions respectively.
15. The model was also run using in turn total population, total rural population and rural population density as alternatives to overall population density. In both regressions total population and total rural population proved to be highly insignificant. Although rural population density was significant, inclusion of this alternative variable made real GNP per capita insignificant and reduced substantially the significance of industrial roundwood per capita in the linear regression, and reduced the significance of real GNP per capita in the semi-log regression. In neither version of the model was the overall explanatory power improved by the inclusion of rural population density as an alternative for overall population density.
16. See Poore *et al.* (1989) for detailed discussion of the technical requirements for sustainable forestry in tropical regions.
17. For applications of the Faustmann rule generally that are relevant to the following example, see Samuelson (1976), Hyde (1980), Johansson and Löfgren (1985) and Bowes and Krutilla (1985). For an application of the Faustmann rule to sequential harvesting a tropical forest stand, see Mendelsohn (1994). Unlike the following example, the latter does not consider initial harvesting of virgin forest area nor investments in silvicultural effort at the beginning of rotation periods, which is typical of enrichment replanting in logged tropical forest stands.
18. Although the stumpage price is not affected by the amount of timber harvested, extraction costs may vary with the location and accessibility of the stand. The result is that, although all timber faces the same market (stumpage) price, the *net* price can vary substantially from site to site. Thus logging forest stands that are inaccessible or face high harvesting costs would be uneconomic. See Hyde (1980) for further discussion of the economic implications, which are very relevant to tropical forestry. Our assumption of constant prices and costs, although a simplification, allows us nevertheless to focus on the key influence of land allocation between agricultural and timber production. For a stand-level analysis of changing stumpage prices and reforestation costs and their effects on switching between forestry and agriculture, see McConnell, Daberkow and Hardie (1983). For an aggregation to the forest level (but without the possibility of switching to agriculture) see Parades and Brodie (1989).
19. We assume here the typical case in developing countries, which is that farmers are not interested in or unable to capture any of the timber benefits from initially clearing the forest. For an alternative assumption, see Hartwick (1992).
20. For example, in his analysis Mendelsohn (1994) assumes s to be positive, for the reasons stated. Note that in (11.5) if $s < 0$ we additionally assume that $(r + s) > 0$.
21. If we assume that allocating more forest land to the stand has a positive 'scale' effect on timber yields including initial harvesting of the old growth trees, then $H_j = H_j(T_j, f_j)$, and increases in stand area will positively affect harvest yields albeit most likely at a diminishing rate, that is, $\partial H_j/\partial f_j > 0$ and $\partial^2 H_j/\partial f_j^2 < 0$. There is some evidence of this positive scale effect in tropical forestry (see Poore *et al.*, 1989).
22. Again, we could assume that some of the latter environmental benefits that may be influenced by stand area (for example, ecotourism, amenity values, wildlife and non-timber products), are subject to 'scale effects', that is, $n_j = n_j(f_j)$ with $n_j' > 0$ and $n_j'' < 0$.
23. As with the timber stand, we could also assume that allocating more forest land to the agricultural plot will have a positive scale effect on production yields, with $Q_m(a_m)$ and $Q_m' = dQ_m/da_m > 0$, $Q_m'' = d^2Q_m/da_m^2 < 0$. However the evidence for this scale effect in tropical developing county agriculture is less compelling.
24. As in the case of the intertemporal model of Section 3, any positive or negative externalities of agricultural production are ignored for simplicity sake. They could easily be included in this model.
25. Note that if the 'scale effects' discussed previously are present, then (11.36) would have to be adjusted for any additional timber yield and environmental benefits of a marginal increase in stand area. Similarly, (11.37) would have to be adjusted for any additional yield benefits of increased agricultural plot size.

References

Allen, J.C. and D.F. Barnes (1985), 'The causes of deforestation in developing countries', *Annals of the Association of American Geographers*, **75** (2), 163–84.

Amelung, T. and M. Diehl (1991), *Deforestation of Tropical Rainforests: Economic Causes and Impact on Development*, Tubingen, Mohr, Germany: Kieler Studien 241.

Barbier, E.B. (1992), 'Tropical forests', in T.M. Swanson and E.B. Barbier (eds), *Economics for the Wilds: Wildlife, Wildlands, Diversity and Development*, London: Earthscan Publications.

Barbier, E.B. (1993), 'Economic aspects of tropical deforestation in Southeast Asia', Southeast Asia Special Issue, *Global Ecology and Biogeography Letters*, **3**, 215–34.

Barbier, E.B. (1994), 'Valuing environmental functions: tropical wetlands', *Land Economics*, **70** (2), 155–73.

Barbier, E.B. and J.C. Burgess (1996), 'Economic analysis of deforestation in Mexico', *Environment and Development Economics*, **1** (2), 203–39.

Barbier, E.B., J.C. Burgess, J.T. Bishop and B.A. Aylward (1994), *The Economics of the Tropical Timber Trade*, London: Earthscan Publications.

Barrett, S. (1993), 'Deforestation, biological conservation, and the optimal provision of wildlife reserves', in E.B. Barbier (ed.), *Economics and Ecology: New Frontiers and Sustainable Development*, London: Chapman and Hall.

Bowes, M.D. and J.V. Krutilla (1985), 'Multiple use management of public forest lands', in A.V. Kneese and J.L. Sweeney (eds), *Handbook of Natural Resource and Energy Economics, Vol. II*, Amsterdam: North-Holland.

Burgess, J.C. (1993) 'Timber production, timber trade and tropical deforestation', *AMBIO*, **22** (2–3), 136–43.

Cropper, M. and C. Griffiths (1994), 'The interaction of population growth and environmental quality', *American Economic Review*, AEA Papers and Proceedings, **84** (2), 250–54.

Deacon, R.T. (1994), 'Deforestation and the rule of law in a cross-section of countries', *Land Economics*, **70** (4), 414–30.

Deacon, R.T. (1995), 'Assessing the relationship between government policy and deforestation', *Journal of Environmental Economics and Management*, **28**, 1–18.

Ehui, S.K. and Hertel, T.W. (1989), 'Deforestation and Agricultural Productivity in the Côte d'Ivoire', *American Journal of Agricultural Economics* **71**, 703–11.

Ehui, S.K., T.W. Hertel, and P.V. Preckel (1990), 'Forest resource depletion, soil dynamics, and agricultural development in the tropics', *Journal of Environmental Economics and Management*, **18** (2), 136–54.

Food and Agricultural Organization (FAO) (1988), *An Interim Report on the State of Forest Resources in Developing Countries*, Rome: FAO.

Food and Agricultural Organization (FAO) (1992a), *1991 Production Yearbook, Vol. 45*, Rome: FAO.

Food and Agricultural Organization (FAO) (1992b), *1990 Yearbook of Forest Products, 1978–1990*, Rome: FAO.

Food and Agricultural Organization (FAO) (1993), *Forest Resources Assessment 1990: Tropical Countries*, Rome: FAO.

Food and Agricultural Organization (FAO) (1994), *Forest Products Prices 1969–92*, FAO Forestry Paper 102, Rome: FAO.

Food and Agricultural Organization (FAO) and the United Nations Environment Programme (UNEP) (1982), *Tropical Forest Resources Assessment Project*, Rome: FAO.

Hartman, R. (1976), 'The harvesting decision when a standing forest has value', *Economic Inquiry*, **14**, 52–8.

Hartwick, J.M. (1992), 'Deforestation and national accounting', *Environmental and Resource Economics*, **2**, 513–21.

Hyde, W.F. (1980), *Timber Supply, Land Allocation and Economic Efficiency*, Baltimore, MD: Johns Hopkins University Press.

Hyde, W.F., D.H. Newman and R.A. Sedjo (1991), 'Forest economics and policy analysis: an overview', *World Bank Discussion Paper No. 134*, Washington, DC: The World Bank.

International Institute for Environment and Development (IIED) (1994), *The Economics of Tropical Forest Land Use Options: Methodology and Valuation Techniques*, Report prepared for the Natural Resources and Environment Department, UK Overseas Development Administration, London Environmental Economics Centre, London.

Johansson, P.-O. and K.-G. Löfgren (1985), *The Economics of Forestry and Natural Resources*, Oxford: Basil Blackwell.

López, R. and M. Niklitschek (1991), 'Dual economic growth in poor tropical areas', *Journal of Development Economics*, **36**, 189–211.

López, R. (1995a), 'Environmental externalities in traditional agriculture and the impacts of trade liberalization: the case of Ghana', Unpublished mimeo, Department of Agricultural and Natural Resource Economics, University of Maryland, College Park, Maryland.

López, R. (1995b), 'The tragedy of the commons in Côte d'Ivoire agriculture: empirical evidence and implications for evaluating trade policies', Unpublished mimeo, Department of Agricultural and Natural Resource Economics, University of Maryland, College Park, Maryland.

López, R.A., F.A. Shah and M.A. Altobello (1994), 'Amenity benefits and the optimal allocation of land', *Land Economics*, **70** (1), 53–62.

McConnell, K.E. (1989), 'The optimal quantity of land in agriculture', *Northeastern Journal of Agricultural and Resource Economics*, **18**, 63–72.

McConnell, K.E., J.N. Daberkow and I.W. Hardie (1983), 'Planning timber production with evolving prices and costs', *Land Economics*, **59** (3), 292–9.

Mendelsohn, R. (1994), 'Property rights and tropical deforestation', *Oxford Economic Papers*, **46**, 750–6.

Panayotou, T. and S. Sungsuwan (1994), 'An econometric analysis of the causes of tropical deforestation: the case of Northeast Thailand,' in K. Brown and D.W. Pearce (eds), *The Causes of Tropical Deforestation*, London: University College London Press.

Parades, G.L. and J.D. Brodie (1989), 'Land value and the linkage between stand and forest level analysis', *Land Economics*, **65** (2), 158–66.

Peters, C., A. Gentry and R. Mendelsohn (1989), 'Valuation of an amazonian rainforest', *Nature*, **339**, 655–6.

Poore, D., P. Burgess, J. Palmer, S. Rietbergen and T. Synnott (1989), *No Timber Without Trees*, London: Earthscan Publications.

Repetto, R. and M. Gillis (1988), *Public Policies and the Misuse of Forest Resources*, Cambridge: Cambridge University Press.

Ruitenbeek, H.J. (1989), *Social Cost–Benefit Analysis of the Korup Project, Cameroon*, Report prepared for the World Wide Fund for Nature (WWF) and the Republic of Cameroon, London: WWF.

Samuelson, P. (1976), 'Economics of forestry in an evolving society', *Economic Inquiry*, **14**, 466–92.

Schmidt, R. (1990), 'Sustainable management of tropical moist forests', ASEAN Sub-Regional Seminar, Indonesia.

Schneider, R., J. McKenna, C. Djou, J. Butler and J. Barrow (1990), *Brazil: An Economic Analysis of Environmental Problems in the Amazon*, Washington, DC: World Bank.

Southgate, D. (1990), 'The causes of land degradation along "spontaneously" expanding agricultural frontiers', *Land Economics*, **66** (1), 93–101.

Southgate, D. (1991), 'Tropical deforestation and agricultural development in Latin America', LEEC Discussion Paper 91–01, London Environmental Economics Centre, London.

Southgate, D. (1992), 'The economics of agricultural land clearing in Northwestern Ecuador', Unpublished mimeo, Instituto de Estrategias Agropecurias, Quito, Ecuador.

Southgate, D, R. Sierra and L. Brown (1991), 'The causes of tropical deforestation in Ecuador: a statistical analysis', *World Development*, **19** (9), 1145–51.

Stern, D., M. Common and E.B. Barbier (1996), 'Economic growth and environmental degradation: a critique of the environmental Kuznets curve', *World Development*, **24** (7), 1151–60.

World Bank (1992), *World Bank Tables*, Washington, DC: World Bank.

12. The role of smallholder producer prices in land degradation: the case of Malawi[1]

Introduction

The role of agricultural producer prices in influencing land degradation has been debated in recent years. One argument is that depressing agricultural prices reduces farm profitability and the incentives to improve land productivity through investments in soil conservation. On the other hand, increasing farm prices and land values is also thought to drive extensive cultivation of more 'fragile' lands (for reviews see Repetto, 1988 and Southgate, 1988). Empirically measuring these effects is extremely difficult.

Measurement of the *supply response* to agriculture producer price changes in developing countries has been frequently conducted over the years. Early studies in the 1950s and 1960s, first in developed economies and then extended to developing economies, indicated that on typical farms small changes in the relative prices of crops may make large changes in the cropping practices more profitable (Heady, 1955; Krishna 1963, 1967; Nerlove, 1956). These studies focused on changes in single-crop acreage as a proxy for supply responsiveness, and provided direct evidence of individual farmers' substituting among crops and adapting farming systems in response to relative price changes. The early analyses also noted that developing country farmers may respond to relative price changes by switching land and other resources between different individual crops but yet may be unable to increase (or decrease) aggregate output in response to overall rises in producer prices (Krishna, 1967).

More recent studies in sub-Saharan Africa confirm that the effect of changes in output prices on the aggregate level of production tends not to be substantial in many countries, but the responsiveness of *individual crops* to changes in *relative prices* is highly significant. Although individual crop supply elasticities vary between countries and between crops, elasticities of 0.5 or more were common (Bond, 1987; Fones-Sundell, 1987). The evidence again suggests that, as relative producer prices change, the increase in individual crop production is achieved at the expense of a reduction in substitute crops. However, in a critical review of agricultural supply response models in Sub-Saharan Africa, Ogbu and Gbetibouo (1990) argue that most models are deficient in the choice of relevant explanatory variables because either the structure of agricultural production in these countries is not properly modelled or the issues and constraints facing farmers is not known or over-simplified. Understanding the factors that explain the elasticities derived from empirical models is as important as the elasticities themselves.

Determining price and non-price supply responses for specific commodities is beyond the scope of this chapter. The concern here is less with measuring *the actual magnitude* of small farmer response to price incentives than in determining *how well* they respond. A crucial issue for land degradation is the extent to which price-induced substitution encourages farmers to move away from less-erosive crops and cropping systems to more erosive crops and systems. If changes in relative prices do influence farmers' choice of crops and land husbandry decisions – and this is an empirical question that still needs to be verified – how well do farmers respond to these price changes in making these investment decisions?

Evidence from Indonesia and Malawi suggests that under certain conditions, changes in relative producer prices can affect choice of crops and farming system, thus impacting on degradation (Barbier, 1989, 1990; Barbier and Burgess, 1992; Becker, 1990; Carson, 1987). The relationships governing farmer responses to relative crop prices are very complex, and depend on various factors such as household wealth and income, tenure security, attitudes to risk, access to off-farm employment, labour and capital constraints and intra-household allocation of labour. Nevertheless, the limited evidence does indicate that farmers will respond to higher relative prices for erosive crops by seeking short run economic rents from erosive crop cultivation at the expense of long-term land degradation. This result holds mainly for sedentary farmers cultivating rainfed plots in areas with predominantly 'closed' agricultural frontiers (that is, areas where agricultural extensification is reaching or has already reached its limits). In frontier agriculture, farmers will open up new areas to cultivation when the returns from the new land exceed those from existing land under cultivation (Southgate, 1990; Southgate and Pearce, 1988). Higher relative prices and returns to erosive crops will not only accelerate degradation on existing land but, as a consequence, will also induce a more rapid expansion into new areas and increased land clearance.

At the same time, fluctuations in relative prices can increase the uncertainty and risk borne by, in particular, small producers. Switching to and investing in new cropping systems and methods of cultivating involve high upfront costs and long payback periods for small farmers. Unless they can be assured that the relative prices and returns from the less-erosive systems will be sustained, these farmers may be less willing to invest in these new systems, or in incorporating less-erosive cropping patterns in their existing farming systems. Similarly, small producers may be less willing to invest some of the short-run profits from *erosive* cropping into expensive physical erosion control measures, such as bunds, contour ridging, bench terracing and so on, unless they can be sure that the high relative prices they receive for their crops today will also prevail in the future. Thus the *price risk* imposed by fluctuating relative prices may deter farmers from investing in land husbandry.

Insufficient attention has been given to date on the incentive effects of fluctuating relative prices for controlling land degradation. The following chapter explicitly examines this problem with the example of smallholder producer prices in Malawi. The chapter first develops a simple model illustrating the role of price fluctuations in land degradation, discusses its relevance to Malawi and analyses the available empirical evidence on relative price fluctuations of less-erosive and erosive crops.

Analytical framework

In analysing fluctuations in producer prices it is important to distinguish between that part of the variation that is predictable by producers and that which is not (Hazell, Jaramillo and Williamson, 1990). To the extent that producers can predict movements in prices, they will be able to adjust resources and cropping practices accordingly and perhaps avoid any sizeable investment losses. In contrast, unpredictable price changes represent a risk, especially to small producers in developing countries, who must essentially rely on self-insurance mechanisms and their own capital resources in the absence of futures, options or other insurance markets and little or no access to formal credit, especially for conservation investments. Thus a distinction should be made between *price risk*, the part of the total fluctuation in prices that could not have been predicted *ex ante* by small producers, and *price variability*, the simple variation of prices around a trend that is observed in a time series (Hazell, Jaramillo and Williamson, 1990). It is the effect of price risk arising from fluctuations in relative erosive to less-erosive crop prices in Malawi on smallholders' decisions to control land degradation that is the main focus of this chapter.

The importance of relative crop prices, and thus price risk, to the land management decisions of small producers can be reflected in a simple model.[2] It is assumed that the objective of the farmers is to maximize the net returns from production over time. The farmer has the choice between cultivating crops that result in soil erosion, that is, *erosive crops*, and crops that lead to some, but significantly less, erosion, that is, *less-erosive crops*. Holding input prices and quantities constant over time, net returns are determined by the prices and quantities of erosive and less-erosive crop cultivation and the costs of controlling land degradation.

Formally, the control problem, over an infinite horizon, is:

$$\max \Pi = f(x, y, z, t)$$
$$= \int_0^\infty e^{-\delta t}\{p^x x(z) + p^y y(z) - cg(z)\}dt, \qquad (12.1)$$

subject to

$$\dot{z} = g(z) - h(x, y),$$

with

$$h_x > h_y > 0, g'(z) > 0, g''(z) < 0, \tag{12.2}$$

$$x(t), y(t), z(t) \geq 0, \tag{12.3}$$

$$z(0) = z_0. \tag{12.4}$$

It is assumed that a small farmer maximizes the present value of his or her net returns from cultivation, Π, where δ is the farmer's rate of discount, $x(t)$ is the quantity of erosive crops and $y(t)$ less-erosive crops and p^x and p^y their respective prices.[3] In (12.1), both crops are assumed to be increasing, concave functions of topsoil depth, $z(t)$. The function $g(z)$ represents *erosion control effort*, which also depends on topsoil depth and is subject to constant costs, c. Thus, by choosing the choice of crops to maximize profits, the farmer also affects the rate of soil erosion and thus the amount of erosion control effort required.[4]

Constraint (12.2) indicates that changes in topsoil depth, $\dot{z} = dz/dt$, depends on erosion control effort, $g(z)$, less the relative impacts of the erosive and less-erosive crops, $h(x, y)$. Topsoil depth is either rising, stabilizing or falling depending upon whether degradation control effort is less than, equal to or greater than the erosion impacts of erosive and less-erosive crops. Increased cultivation of both erosive and less-erosive crops can increase land degradation, but as indicated above, less-erosive crops have the smaller impact, that is, $h_x > h_y$. At higher levels of topsoil depth, greater effort is required to control erosion, $g'(z)$, albeit at a declining rate, $g''(z) < 0$.[5] Constraint (12.3) is the standard set of non-negativity conditions. Constraint (12.4) defines the initial level of topsoil depth.

The current value Hamiltonian for the control problem (12.1)–(12.4) is:

$$H = p^x x(z) + p^y y(z) - cg(z) + \lambda[g(z) - h(x, y)], \tag{12.5}$$

where λ is the current value costate variable associated with the state equation (12.2). Assuming an interior solution, the first order conditions for maximizing (12.5) are:

$$H_x = p^x - \lambda h_x = 0, \tag{12.6}$$

$$H_y = p^y - \lambda h_y = 0, \tag{12.7}$$

$$-H_z = \dot{\lambda} - \delta\lambda = (p^x x_z + p^y y_z) + (c - \lambda)g_z + \lambda(h_x x_z + h_y y_z) \tag{12.8}$$

$$\lim_{t \to \infty}, e^{-\delta t}\lambda(t)z(t) = 0. \tag{12.9}$$

$$H_\lambda = \dot{z} = g(z) - h(x, y), \tag{12.10}$$

The costate variable, λ, can be interpreted as the implicit value, or shadow price, of the soil. If topsoil is depleted, λ represents the *user cost* of soil erosion, that is, the future returns forgone by a decision to deplete the soil faster today. Conditions (12.6) and (12.7) indicate that, along the optimal path, farmers should choose to cultivate each erosive and less-erosive crop to the point where the marginal returns from cultivation equal the marginal user costs of soil erosion, as determined by the kind of crop. Equation (12.8) indicates that relative returns to 'holding on' to the soil today as an economic asset. Finally, equation (12.9) is the transversality condition, and equation (12.10) repeats the state equation constraint (12.2).

By substituting equations (12.6) and (12.7) in (12.8) and re-arranging terms:

$$\dot{\lambda} = \delta\lambda - (\lambda - c)g_z. \tag{12.11}$$

Equation (12.11) indicates that the 'value' of holding on to soil today must rise at a rate equal to the total opportunity cost of conserving soil less the future returns from the soil. The cost of conserving soil includes an 'interest charge', δλ, as well as the cost of current soil conservation efforts, $cg'(z)$.[6] These costs essentially represent the 'depletion motive' for increasing soil erosion today. The future returns from topsoil are represented by $\lambda g'(z)$, which are the 'conservation' motive for maintaining topsoil.[7]

From equations (12.6) and (12.7):

$$\frac{p^x}{p^y} = \frac{h_x}{h_y} > 1, \tag{12.12}$$

Small farmers are essentially price takers. Equation (12.12) shows that farmers should adjust cultivation of erosive and less-erosive crops, and hence their relative impacts on the soil, in response to changes in their relative prices. However, erosive crops will have a greater impact on the soil, thus reducing its asset value in terms of future productive potential. From the farmer's perspective, it is always optimal that the price of erosive crops be higher than that of less-erosive crops.

Equation (12.11) can also be re-written to show how relative prices influence the depletion and conservation motives of farmers with respect to soil erosion. To facilitate notation, assume that the percentage rate of increase in soil erosion from cultivating additional erosive crops is constant, that is, $(dh_x/dt)/h_x, = a$. Using this expression and (12.12) in (12.11):

$$\frac{\dot{p}^x}{h_x} - \frac{ap^x}{h_x} = \delta \frac{p^y}{h_y} + cg'(z) - \frac{p^y}{h_y} g'(z)$$

$$\frac{\dot{p}^x}{p_y} = (a+\delta)\frac{p^x}{p^y} - \left[\frac{p^x}{p^y} - \frac{ch_x}{p^y}\right] g'(z). \qquad (12.13)$$

Equation (12.13) indicates how the 'depletion' and 'conservation' motive of farmers will change in response to price rises over time. If the price of erosive crops is increasing relative to less-erosive crops, then the depletion motive will outweigh the conservation motive; that is, the costs of conserving soil exceed the returns. The farmer would be expected to change cultivation of erosive and less-erosive crops, their impact on soil erosion and erosion control effort accordingly. If the relative price is falling, then the returns to conservation will exceed the costs. The farmer will have more incentive to conserve rather than deplete, and will change his farming system and practices to reflect this. Clearly, then, depending on the change in motives brought about by relative price movements, the farmer will adjust choice of crops, the rate of soil erosion and soil conservation effort.

The above model is obviously a simplification of the complex factors and choices determining a small farmer's decision to invest in soil conservation and less-erosive versus erosive crops. As argued by Ogbu and Gbetibouo (1990), both non-price and price factors must be taken into account in any modelling of agricultural supply responses of farmers in Sub-Saharan Africa. This is certainly the case when such responses are extended to take into account their impacts on land degradation, as a recent study in Malawi has shown (Barbier and Burgess, 1992).

However, the model does show that, to the extent that the general conditions suggested by the model hold, then the relative price of crops can have an important influence on land management decisions by small farmers. More importantly, farmers must be able to predict changes in relative prices in order to know what investment crop and land husbandry decisions to make. Clearly, relative crop prices are not the only factors affecting these decisions. Input prices, capital, labour and input constraints, access to information and technology, agroecological conditions among others will also be influential. By abstracting from these factors, the model is not trying to demonstrate the all-pervasive influence of prices; rather, it focuses on the role of relative prices to show the extent to which *price risk* can be an important factor in land management decisions. The following sections examine this influence empirically with the example of smallholder producers in Malawi.

Agriculture and smallholders in Malawi[8]

Although 4.3 million hectares (ha) of land in Malawi is classified as arable, only around 2.4 million ha is probably suitable for agriculture, most of which is already under cultivation. The 'dualism' of the agricultural sector is characterized by two distinct farming systems: the smallholder sub-sector, which accounts for about 80 per cent of food production and comprises around 90 per cent of the population, and the estate sub-sector, which accounts for 90 per cent of export earnings.

Approximately 1.6 million smallholder families cultivate up to 1.8 million ha under customary tenure. The principal crop is the staple food, maize, which is grown on 75 per cent of the cropped area, with other important crops being groundnuts, fire-cured tobacco, cassava, cotton, rice and various pulses, roots and tubers. Rapid population growth in Malawi of 3–4 per cent per annum has meant that approximately 30 000 new families must be absorbed on customary land each year. Given that less than 30 per cent of smallholders have access to fertilizer and the adoption rate for high yielding maize varieties is less than 10 per cent, average yields are very low – about 900 kg/ha for maize. This combination of population pressure on scarce land and low yields has led to depressed farm incomes, declining per capita smallholder food production, widespread household food insecurity and land degradation.[9]

Moreover, an important distinction in the smallholder sub-sector is between those households cultivating less than 1.0 ha – the minimum required for attaining sufficient household calorie requirements from their land – and those with larger holdings. Approximately 715 000 households fall into the former category, of which over 338 000 are 'core poor' households with less than 0.5 ha. Consequently, the majority of smallholders are food-deficit, low-income households, that spend almost half of their cash income on food and depend heavily on off-farm labour employment. These constraints are extremely binding on these poor households, particularly the poor female-headed households, and can severely hinder economic opportunities and improved land management.[10] It is only the households with relatively larger holdings that are self-sufficient in food production. Thus only about 20 per cent of smallholders in Malawi have access to credit and produce a marketable surplus – and these are generally farmers with holdings over 1.0 ha.[11]

Since 1979 Malawian agriculture has gone through a period of rapid macroeconomic adjustment, including extensive agricultural pricing and marketing reform for the smallholder sub-sector.[12] The objectives of the new pricing policy were to:

- stimulate increased smallholder export production by paying farmers prices closer to export parity;
- set a maize price that would achieve national maize self-sufficiency;
- leave only tobacco and cotton prices controlled, that is, as the government's Agricultural Development and Marketing Corporation (ADMARC) retains its legal monopoly over these two crops, the official prices paid by ADMARC are also the effective prices paid to smallholders; and
- ensure that for all other smallholder crops, including maize, the prices set by ADMARC represent a guaranteed minimum price as ADMARC is obliged to buy all quantities offered at that price.

To improve pricing policy, the Government of Malawi (GoM) has instituted an annual producer price analysis and review. As prices have to be announced before the planting season to be effective as incentives, they can often fail to match the eventual border prices prevailing at the end of the season given the frequent fluctuations in export prices. Nevertheless, since 1981 smallholder producer prices have generally been approaching border-price equivalents. In recent years, groundnut and cotton prices have even exceeded export-parity values. The exception is smallholder tobacco, which is being sold to ADMARC at prices significantly below local auction floor prices that are essentially equivalent to border values. In addition, some crops such as beans and pulses have been banned for export because of the uncertainty over sufficient supplies to meet domestic requirements and because market prices continue to exceed the floor prices set by ADMARC (Lele, 1989 and Christiansen and Southworth, 1988).

Although farmers may have been responding to changes in relative prices by shifting their cropping pattern, the impact of pricing policy on their aggregate response is less certain.[13] After growing at an annual average of approximately 4.9 per cent in real terms during the 1970s, agricultural growth slowed down to an average of 1.0 per cent in 1980–84, recovering only to an average of 2.5 per cent in 1985–88, still failing to keep pace with the population growth. In 1988–89 the total area sown to maize at 1.27 ha and production of 1.52 million tonnes – the highest levels on record – represented increases on the previous year of 4.9 per cent and 6.6 per cent respectively. Due to a drought in early 1990, maize production during 1989–90 was not expected to differ significantly from the previous year's production (Government of Malawi, 1990 and World Bank, 1989a).

However, what is of particular significance for land management and soil conservation is that the recent increases in agricultural output have been achieved by extensification of agriculture into marginal lands, rather than by improving the yields on existing cultivated land. The reasons for this are predominantly structural:

- rapid population growth and the corresponding fast decline in the land–man ratio has led to increased land pressure and the opening up of more marginal areas for cultivation;
- the pricing and marketing reforms have achieved little for the majority of smallholders cultivating less than 1.0 ha, mainly because the severity of the land constraint and low yields preclude production of net marketable services, thus limiting the main income benefits of these reforms to the relatively better-off producers;
- in fact, the food security of many food-deficit households may actually deteriorate as the price of maize and other food crops increases, thus limiting the ability of these households to diversify out of own-food production and to take risks;
- consequently, over the past five years there has been little change in the average yield for any of the main varietal maize groups – local, composite or hybrid – despite markedly higher rates of hybrid adoption and fertilizer use, and the low productivity of maize has in turn exacerbated the land constraint.[14]

The aggregate impacts of land degradation in Malawi may be highly significant. A recent study has shown that a conservative estimate of the on-site (user) costs of soil erosion in Malawi is around 4.8 per cent of national GDP (Bishop, 1990).

Analysis of price impacts on land degradation

Of particular concern is how smallholder producer pricing policy may have influenced these trends by changing the pattern of smallholder crop production and the relative returns to various crops, thus affecting the incentives for long-term land management. One concern is that recent swings in relative prices in Malawi may be making it difficult for smallholders to plan and develop viable land management and cropping systems to counteract erosion. This is particularly the case for the poorer smallholders who appear to rely on intercropping and relay cropping maize, groundnuts and pulses as a means to meeting nutritional needs, maintaining soil fertility and conserving soil. Alternatively, some 'progressive' farmers may abandon these mixed-cropping systems to plant the more erosive crops, such as maize, cotton and tobacco, in pure stands if there appear to be higher relative prices for these crops, but the uncertainty arising from the fluctuations in prices might prevent them from making land management investments (Barbier and Burgess, 1992).

Figure 12.1 shows the long-run price trends for pulses, groundnuts and maize in Malawi. Until the early 1980s, prices did not increase substantially. Prices for pulses and groundnuts began increasing in the early 1980s, and have risen rapidly. Maize prices were not increased significantly until after the 1986–87 season. Other key smallholder crops in Malawi are tobacco, cotton and cassava. Again, the prices of the cash crops cotton and tobacco did not increase substantially until the early 1980s, with tobacco prices rising dramatically in recent years (see Figure 12.2). Cassava prices have continued to remain low.

These trends in individual crop prices can be aggregated to derive price trends for the '*less erosive*' as opposed to the '*erosive*' crops.[15] As indicated in Figure 12.3, prices for both the major less-erosive crops – pulses and groundnuts and the major erosive crops – maize, cassava, cotton and tobacco – have been rising steadily at approximately the same rate of increase. Consequently, as shown in Figure 12.4, the less-erosive/erosive crop price index has not risen significantly from 1968–69 to 1989–90 or from 1979–80 to 1989–90. However, Figure 12.4 does indicate that this index has fluctuated considerably over both the longer and shorter time periods. Smallholders intending to invest in new cropping

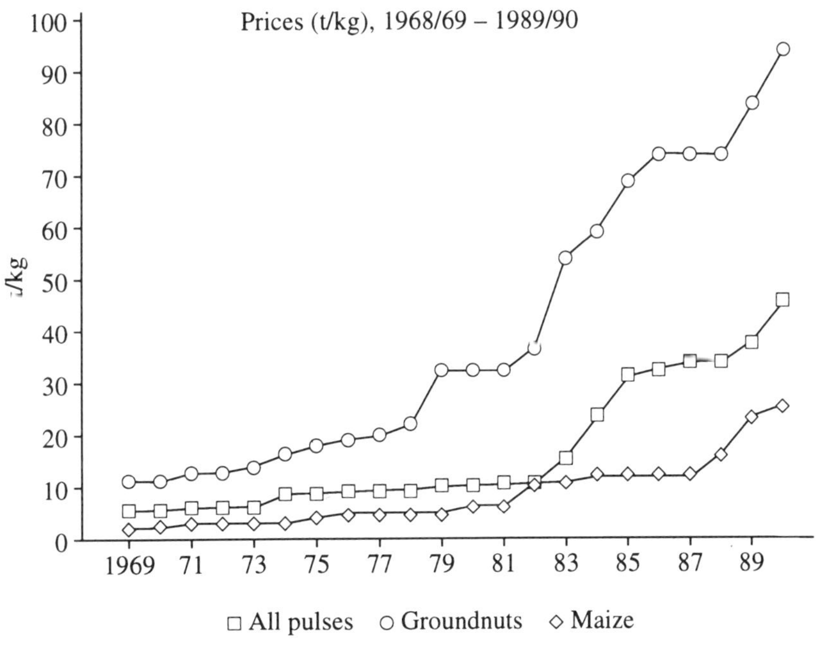

Figure 12.1 Pulses, groundnuts, maize

patterns and systems could therefore face substantial uncertainty and thus be less willing to undertake such investments. The implications for land management are:

- farmers who are not incorporating less-erosive crops in their cropping systems may be less willing to do so since the price fluctuations indicate a high risk of investment from crop season to season and small long-term gains; and
- farmers who already incorporate less-erosive crops may have less incentive to invest in improvements to these mixed cropping systems – again because of the investment risks from seasonal fluctuations in relative prices and apparently insignificant long-term gains.

The extent to which smallholders in Malawi can anticipate or 'predict' the relative price of less-erosive to erosive crops is based on past price levels and trends.[16] If farmers are to make significant land management investments in cropping patterns and systems, such as switching between erosive and less-erosive crops or substantially improving less-erosive cropping systems, then they would be interested in anticipating future relative price trends of less-erosive to erosive crops. Of particular interest is the extent to which past relative prices and

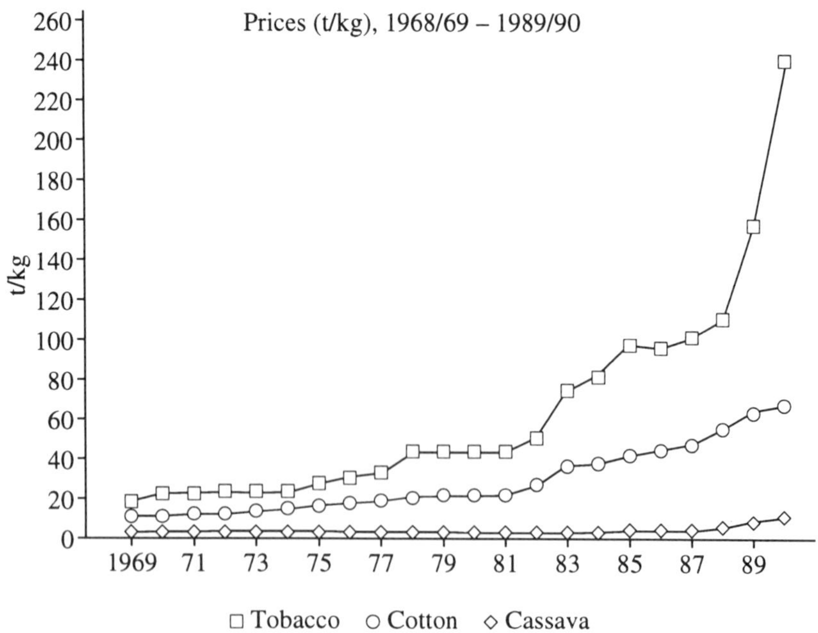

Figure 12.2 Tobacco, cotton, cassava

trends are an indicator of future prices, given that the past price levels and trends are probably all the information available to farmers for predicting future prices. If the relative price is highly unstable, then past prices will not be a good guide to the future, and the uncertainty surrounding farmers' investments is high; on the other hand, if the relative price is stable, then past prices could be highly predictive of future trends, and farmers would be less uncertain about the outcome of their investments.

An important issue is to determine the extent to which past price trends can be used to forecast future prices. The standard procedure would be to employ autoregressive and moving average (ARIMA) processes, without any other predictors, to our time series of relative less-erosive to erosive crop prices in Malawi. Various ARIMA representations were applied to this price series as well as to the prices of maize and groundnuts individually – the two major erosive and less-erosive crops respectively. For the latter prices, none of the ARIMA estimations yielded significant coefficients, either individually or jointly. Only one representation of the relative less-erosive to erosive price series displayed significant coefficients (ARIMA [2,1]), but this model also showed serial correlation and failed the maximum log-likelihood test, which would suggest a poor representation.[17]

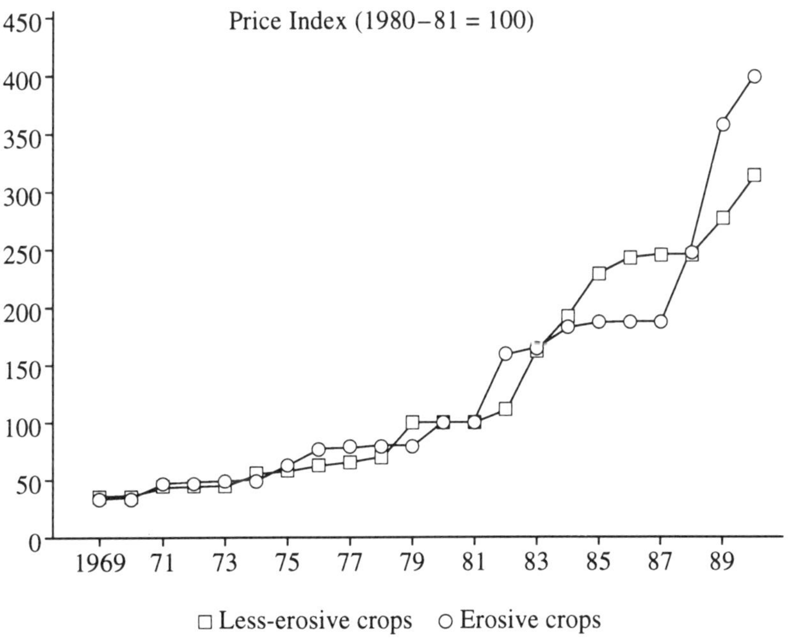

Figure 12.3 Price trends for less-erosive and erosive crops

As a consequence, it was hypothesized that all three price series display *random walk* characteristics. If this hypothesis is correct, then lagged prices would serve as the best predictions in the case of random walks. The presence of random walks also suggests that producer prices for less-erosive and erosive crops in Malawi are inherently unstable; that is, forecasting future prices is difficult because of abrupt and random changes in relative prices from year to year. As discussed above, the main cause of this instability – and hence unpredictability – in producer prices is most likely the frequent changes over the time period in government crop pricing policies.

Nevertheless, our theory suggests that smallholders do respond to relative price changes in controlling land degradation, including altering the choice of crops and pattern of cropping. On the other hand, unpredictable price changes represent a considerable price risk, which we defined as the part of the total fluctuation in prices that could not have been predicted *ex ante* by small producers. We therefore want to examine more specifically the extent to which these producers do face *price risk*.

Given that farmers in Malawi are most likely to base their expectations over future (that is, next year's) prices on a simple extrapolation of past price levels and trends, and given the hypothesized random walk properties of the price series,

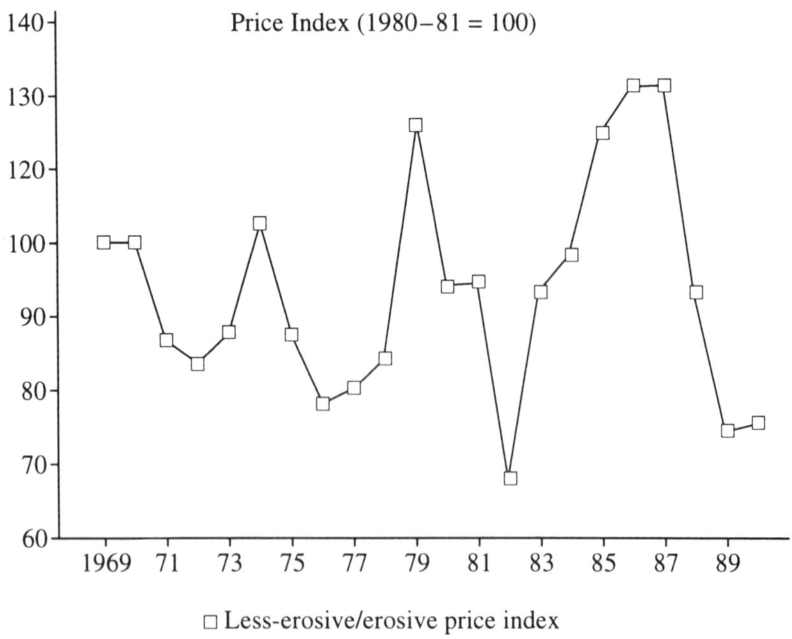

Figure 12.4 Less-erosive/erosive crops: price ratio

fitting an *autoregressive trend model* to the time series of relative less-erosive/erosive crop prices is the most straightforward method of testing the accuracy of such extrapolations. In short, a simple expectation–formulation process is assumed initially, where the change in price expectations by farmers in the current year is some proportion β of the error made in formulating expectations in the previous year.

The basic model is:

$$P^*_t = a + \beta P_{t-1}, \qquad (12.14)$$

where P^*_t = expected relative price of less-erosive to erosive crops in period t (the current year).

P_{t-1} = relative price of less-erosive to erosive crops in period $t-1$ (the previous year).

Additional past values of P (for example, for years $t-2$, $t-3$, and so on) may also be added. Unfortunately, doing this may also add to problems of *multi-collinearity* in any regression analysis, that is, high correlation between two or more independent variables. However, as the major use of the estimated relationship is to predict future levels of P and not to precisely estimate parameters *per se*, then the presence of any high multicollinearity is less serious a problem.

Several versions of the basic model (12.14) were estimated, including adding additional past values and incorporating changes in past values in semi-log versions of the basic model. The following were the best results:

$$\underset{}{P_t} = \underset{(3.96)}{4.118} + \underset{(2.35)}{0.441}\, P_{t-1} \underset{(-2.85)}{- 0.556} P_{t-3} \qquad (12.15)$$

period: 1972–90 $R^2 = 0.475$ adj $R^2 = 0.409$

S.E. = 0.524 $D-W = 1.77$ $F_{2,\,16} = 7.23$

$$LP_t = \underset{(38.64)}{1.289} + \underset{(2.78)}{0.134}DP_{t-1} + \underset{(2.48)}{0.138}DP_{t-2} \qquad (12.16)$$

period: 1972–90 $R^2 = 0.483$ adj $R^2 = 0.418$

S.E. = 0.140 $D-W = 1.98$ $F_{2,\,16} = 7.48$

where LP_t = natural log of P_t

DP_{t-1} = $P_{t-1} - P_{t-2}$, that is, difference between last year's price and the price prevailing the year before

DP_{t-2} = $P_{t-2} - P_{t-3}$, that is, difference between the price two years ago and the price prevailing the year before.

All estimated coefficients are significant at the 95 per cent confidence level or higher, with their *t*-statistics included in parentheses underneath. The more basic model (12.15) indicates that present relative less-erosive/erosive crop prices can be positively extrapolated from prices the year before, and given the price fluctuations, can be negatively extrapolated from prices three years ago. For example, on average the current relative price will be around 44 per cent of last year's price minus 56 per cent of the price three years ago. The semi-log model (12.16) shows how this year's prices might change in response to changes in price differentials in the past; that is, the coefficients indicate how a one unit change in past price differentials might be used to predict the percentage change in this year's prices. In this regression, the response is very low – only 0.13 per cent to a marginal change in past price differentials.

Unfortunately, however, the explanatory power of both models (12.15) and (12.16) is not very good, as indicated by their respective R^2 and adjusted R^2 values. This suggests that it is difficult to extrapolate future prices from past price levels alone. Moreover, even if equation (12.16) is accurate, it indicates that past price differentials are not a very good guide to future price changes.

Models (12.15) and (12.16) can also be modified to include a long-run price trend for less-erosive and erosive crops. The assumption would be that smallholders take into account not only more recent prices but also the long-run relative price trend for less-erosive and erosive crops. The long-run trend rates of growth for less-erosive crop prices, erosive crop prices and relative less-erosive/erosive crop prices were estimated directly from the price series data for 1968–69 to 1989–90 using an exponential growth function:

Less-erosive crops:	11.04 per cent per annum
Erosive crops:	11.18 per cent per annum
Less-erosive/erosive:	0.21 per cent per annum.

However, the estimated regressions for deriving trend rate of growth for the less-erosive/erosive price ratio was a very poor fit. This is not surprising, given the extreme fluctuation in this ratio as illustrated in Figure 12.4. Thus the trend rate of growth in the relative prices was derived indirectly from the difference between the rate of growth of less-erosive crop and erosive crop prices, that is, 0.14 per cent. Using this rate of growth, a long-run constant trend in the relative price was estimated, which was employed in the following regressions:

$$P_t = \underset{(-1.75)}{-29.531} + \underset{(1.51)}{0.285}P_{t-1} - \underset{(-3.69)}{0.757}P_{t-3} + \underset{(1.998)}{8.818}T \qquad (12.17)$$

period: 1972–90	$R^2 = 0.585$	adj $R^2 = 0.502$
S.E. = 0.481	$D - W = 1.84$	$F_{3,15} = 7.05$

$$LP_t = 0.135DP_{t-1} + 0.138DP_{t-2} + 0.325T \quad (12.18)$$
$$(2.94) \qquad (2.90) \qquad (40.73)$$

period: 1972–90 $R^2 = 0.502$ adj $R^2 = 0.439$
S.E. = 0.138 $D - W = 2.07$ $F_{2,\,16} = 8.05$

The interpretations of regressions (12.17) and (12.18) are similar to that of (12.15) and (12.16), although adding in the trend variable has changed the coefficients in regression (12.17) and a 33 per cent change in current prices in regression (12.18) is related to the long-run change in trend. However, the explanatory power of the regressions has improved only slightly, as indicated by the R^2 and adjusted R^2 values. Thus, even if smallholders were aware of both long-run relative price changes for less-erosive and erosive crops as well as past price levels, it would be difficult to extrapolate future prices with much accuracy. A large degree of uncertainty over future relative prices would remain. Thus, a great deal of *price risk* has existed with regard to relative erosive and less-erosive crop prices, which could have an important influence on the incentives for improved land management.

Gross margins and cropping pattern changes

Any significant impact of long-run price changes of erosive to less-erosive crops in Malawi should be reflected in changes in the returns and cropping patterns associated with each type of crop. The relative returns to different crops, in terms of gross margins and gross margins per standard man day (SMD), are given in Table 12.1. The relative returns of less-erosive to all erosive crops and of less-erosive to the high-value erosive crops (hybrid maize, cotton and tobacco) are displayed in Figures 12.5 and 12.6. Both the relative gross margins and the relative gross margins per SMD of less-erosive crops have clearly fluctuated over the 1980s, peaking in the mid-1980s and falling sharply in recent years. The fluctuation was mainly the result of rapid changes in the returns of groundnuts relative to maize, which has been influenced by policy reversals on the relative pricing of these two crops.[18] However, even when the relative returns to groundnuts were high, the gross margins of all less-erosive crops in aggregate remained below the aggregate returns to the high-value erosive crops. In terms of returns to labour, the gross margins per SMD of the less-erosive crops have always remained below those of the erosive crops.

Evidence on the change in cropping patterns in Malawi is sparse. Table 12.2 includes some trends, although the data must be treated with caution because of the possible inconsistencies relating to mixed stand and pure stand cropping as well as reliability of data and comparability across different surveys and national estimates. On the whole, although maize – particularly local varieties

Table 12.1 Malawi – estimated returns of crop production MK/ha, 1981/82–1989/90

A. Beans and groundnuts	1981/82	1982/83	1983/84	1984/85	1985/86	1986/87	1987/88	1988/89	1989/90
Beans									
Gross Margin (GM)[a]	33.91	–4.45	30.18	60.21	66.18	67.98	66.96	77.56	90.69
Gross Margin/SMD[b]	0.20	–0.03	0.18	0.35	0.39	0.40	0.39	0.45	0.53
All pulses									
Gross Margin (GM)[a]	30.86	–5.15	32.28	61.51	65.43	67.43	66.86	80.11	105.64
Gross Margin/SMD[b]	0.18	–0.03	0.19	0.36	0.38	0.39	0.39	0.47	0.62
Groundnuts (Chalimbana)									
Gross Margin (GM)[a]	90.79	171.31	202.62	236.20	250.11	251.22	238.42	230.96	222.35
Gross Margin/SMD[b]	0.80	1.50	1.78	2.07	2.19	2.20	2.09	2.03	1.95
Groundnuts (Manipintar)									
Gross Margin (GM)[a]	NA	NA	151.64	203.73	220.62	260.22	256.43	285.32	351.01
Gross Margin/SMD[b]	NA	NA	1.33	1.79	1.94	2.28	2.25	2.50	3.08
Less-erosive crops									
Gross Margin (GM)[a]	70.41	111.31	143.39	175.97	186.56	188.96	180.55	181.07	185.98
Gross Margin/SMD[b]	0.59	0.98	1.23	1.48	1.57	1.59	1.52	1.51	1.53

B. Maize	1981/82	1982/83	1983/84	1984/85	1985/86	1986/87	1987/88	1988/89	1989/90
Hybrid maize[c]									
Gross Margin (GM)[a]	211.37	193.15	214.78	196.46	174.02	166.83	253.15	414.45	350.89
Gross Margin/SMD[b]	2.12	1.93	2.15	1.96	1.74	1.67	2.53	4.14	3.51
Local maize[c]									
Gross Margin (GM)[a]	140.98	130.83	143.86	137.06	125.70	123.78	174.70	278.66	284.06
Gross Margin/SMD[b]	1.81	1.68	1.84	1.76	1.61	1.59	2.24	3.57	3.64
Local maize[d]									
Gross Margin (GM)[a]	86.10	86.10	94.70	94.70	94.70	94.70	128.65	187.00	201.50
Gross Margin/SMD[b]	1.65	1.65	1.81	1.81	1.81	1.81	2.46	3.58	3.86
All maize									
Gross Margin (GM)[a]	108.28	104.81	115.61	112.46	108.37	107.19	149.92	226.49	229.10
Gross Margin/SMD[b]	1.73	1.69	1.86	1.83	1.78	1.77	2.45	3.66	3.79

Table 12.1 continued

C. Tobacco, cotton and wheat	1981/82	1982/83	1983/84	1984/85	1985/86	1986/87	1987/88	1988/89	1989/90
Tobacco (NDDF)[e]									
Gross Margin (GM)[a]	264.54	390.92	491.72	530.50	511.16	533.16	542.36	798.61	1325.28
Gross Margin/SMD[b]	0.87	1.29	1.62	1.75	1.69	1.76	1.79	2.63	4.37
Tobacco (Sun/Air)[f]									
Gross Margin (GM)[a]	174.84	258.19	281.20	391.64	306.37	318.39	392.54	595.01	894.51
Gross Margin/SMD[b]	0.58	0.85	0.93	1.29	1.01	1.05	1.29	1.96	2.95
Cotton									
Gross Margin (GM)[a]	206.84	292.42	310.81	342.40	287.84	316.49	356.52	358.83	395.96
Gross Margin/SMD[b]	0.84	1.18	1.26	1.38	1.16	1.28	1.44	1.45	1.60
Wheat									
Gross Margin (GM)[a]	126.71	120.24	110.02	193.40	225.76	248.27	259.56	312.24	344.02
Gross Margin/SMD[b]	0.77	0.73	0.67	1.18	1.38	1.52	1.59	1.91	2.10
Erosive crops[g]									
Gross Margin (GM)[a]	112.29	112.34	124.22	122.52	117.02	116.82	159.15	235.84	244.85
Gross Margin/SMD[b]	1.69	1.67	1.84	1.82	1.77	1.76	2.42	3.59	3.74
High-value erosive crops[h]									
Gross Margin (GM)[a]	213.72	218.82	244.48	237.34	210.13	209.85	285.00	429.06	415.79
Gross Margin/SMD[b]	1.85	1.78	1.98	1.86	1.65	1.61	2.32	3.66	3.28

Less-erosive/erosive crops									
Gross Margin (GM)[a]	0.63	0.99	1.15	1.44	1.59	1.62	1.13	0.77	0.76
Gross Margin/SMD[b]	0.35	0.59	0.67	0.82	0.89	0.90	0.63	0.42	0.41
Less-erosive/high-value erosive crops									
Gross Margin (GM)[a]	0.33	0.51	0.59	0.74	0.89	0.90	0.63	0.42	0.45
Gross Margin/SMD[b]	0.32	0.55	0.62	0.80	0.95	0.99	0.65	0.41	0.47

Notes:
[a] Gross margin equals gross return minus total variable costs excluding labour.
[b] SMD = Standard Man Days per ha. These are calculated from the total man equivalent hours, divided by four. Man equivalent hours are used to account for the differences in age and sex composition of labour. The efficiency coefficients used are:

1 hour worked by a man = 1 man equivalent
1 hour worked by a woman = 0.7 man equivalent
1 hour worked by a child = 0.3 man equivalent

[c] With conventional fertilizer.
[d] Without any fertilizer.
[e] NDDF stands for Northern Division dark-fired tobacco.
[f] Sun/air refers to sun or air cured varieties of tobacco from the Southern Division.
[g] Erosive crops include all maize, NDDF and sun/air tobacco, cotton and wheat.
[h] High value erosive crops include hybrid maize, NDDF and sun/air tobacco and cotton.

Source: Barbier and Burgess (1992).

– continues to be the dominant crop, the hectarage under maize appears to have been generally lower in the late 1980s. However, there seems to be little change in the proportion of inter-cropped and pure stand maize cultivation. The survey results in Table 12.2A indicate that the area planted to pulses and groundnuts has increased in the 1980s, whilst the area planted to grains has remained fairly stable. Pure stand cultivation of groundnuts and some pulses are thought particularly to have increased (Kydd, 1989). This is not surprising, given the rapid rises in the prices of these crops since 1980–81 (see Figure 12.1). However the national estimates of crop hectarage indicate very little increase in the area planted to pulses and groundnuts (see Table 12.2B).

Table 12.2 Malawi – changes in smallholder cropping patterns

A. Malawi – surveys of cropping patterns in the smallholder sector, 1969/70–1987/88

Crops	Percentage of cultivated area[a]			
	1969/70[b]	1980/81[c]	1986/87[d]	1987/88[e]
Maize (pure stand)		57.7		55.4
Maize (interplanted)		15.1		14.6
Total Maize	78.4	72.8	66.7	70.0
Groundnuts	4.6	10.2	11.8	15.5
Pulses	4.8	0.5	7.9	8.6
Cassava	2.0	2.7	3.6	2.3
Potatoes	1.4	1.1	1.4	0.9
Sorghum	3.5	1.5	1.7	1.6
Millet		1.6	1.0	2.3
Rice		1.7	1.1	2.2
Cotton	2.9	2.9		6.4
Tobacco	5.3	2.9	2.2	3.1
Others		1.4	0.7	

Notes:

[a] Hectarages under mixed stands are included for each crop in the mixture, therefore the percentage totals for each crop are not additive. Not all crops grown are listed.

[b] National Sample Survey of Agriculture, 1968/69, (NSSA) a large scale sample survey.

[c] National Sample Survey of Agriculture, 1980/81, (NSSA).

[d] Taken from J. Kydd, 'Maize Research in Malawi: Lessons from Failure', *Journal of International Development*, Vol. 1, No. 1, January 1989, pp. 112–44, based on estimates made by the management of the Agricultural Development Divisions, informed by local sample surveys with uneven coverage.

[e] Annual Sample Survey of Agriculture, 1987/88.

Table 12.2 continued

B. Malawi – National smallholder hectarage estimates, 1982/83–1987/88

	1982/83		1983/84		1984/85		1985/86		1986/87		1987/88	
	('000 ha)	(%)	('000 ha)	(%)	('000 ha)	(%)	('000 ha)	(%)	('000 ha)	(%)	('000 ha)	(%)
Maize	1169.40	73.99	1182.60	70.21	1144.85	69.36	1193.28	67.96	1182.42	64.94	1215.23	66.82
- local			1067.53	63.38	1048.44	63.52	1104.58	62.91	1131.54	62.14	1137.64	62.56
- composite			26.07	1.55	21.48	1.30	20.10	1.14	13.78	0.76	18.70	1.03
- hybrid			89.01	5.28	74.94	4.54	68.59	3.91	37.10	2.04	58.89	3.24
Rice	20.31	1.28	21.92	1.30	20.81	1.26	22.87	1.30	19.08	1.05	21.24	1.17
Groundnuts	146.31	9.26	144.94	8.60	135.97	8.24	176.29	10.04	209.94	11.53	176.09	9.68
Tobacco	27.59	1.75	45.00	2.67	46.94	2.84	38.05	2.17	33.17	1.82	24.10	1.32
Cotton	32.60	2.06	51.06	3.03	60.82	3.68	51.91	2.96	34.50	1.89	43.65	2.40
Wheat	2.10	0.13	1.98	0.12	1.13	0.07	1.51	0.09	2.53	0.14	2.55	0.14
Sorghum	22.65	1.43	21.30	1.26	32.73	1.98	32.06	1.83	30.63	1.68	30.10	1.66
Millet	10.87	0.69	15.34	0.91	17.41	1.05	17.42	0.99	18.16	1.00	19.26	1.06
Pulses	82.93	5.25	91.32	5.42	79.97	4.85	113.66	6.47	152.08	8.35	157.40	8.66
Oil Beans[a]	3.30	0.21	3.00	0.18	3.00	0.18	2.30	0.13	2.00	0.11	4.45	0.24
Sunflower	3.06	0.19	3.07	0.18	3.51	0.21	4.08	0.23	2.55	0.14	2.96	0.16
Cassava	59.35	3.76	81.50	4.84	80.26	4.86	72.90	4.15	64.88	3.56	61.39	3.38
Potatoes			21.34	1.27	22.72	1.38	22.45	1.28	32.18	1.77	31.80	1.75
Cashew	0.05	0.00	0.01	0.00	0.01	0.00	6.55	0.37	24.03	1.32	27.30	1.50
Others[b]	0.03	0.00	0.05	0.00	0.46	0.03	0.48	0.03	12.75	0.70	1.05	0.06
TOTAL	1580.55		1684.43		1650.59		1755.81		1820.88		1818.58	

Notes:
[a] Oil beans include soya beans, ground beans and guar beans.
[b] Others include sesame, castor, coffee and chillies.

Source: Barbier and Burgess (1992)

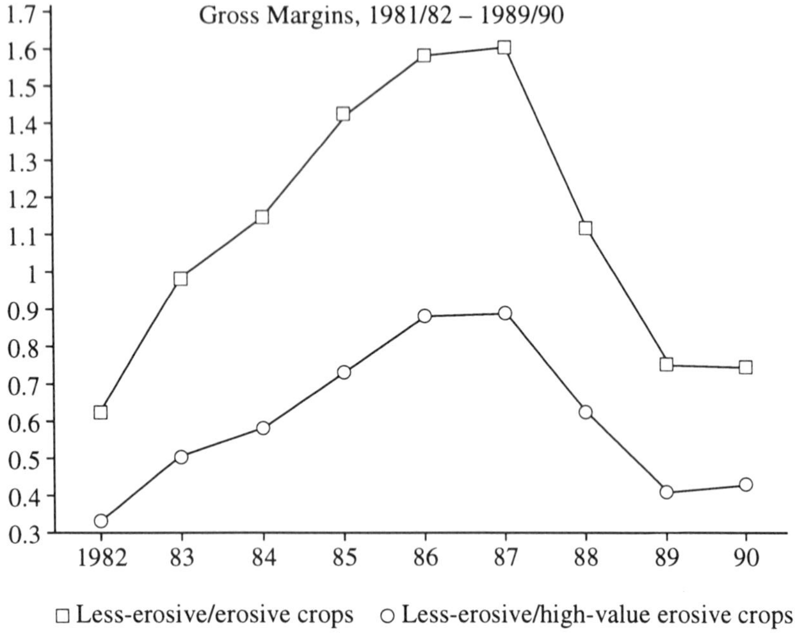

Figure 12.5 Less-erosive/erosive crops: gross margin ratio

Conclusion

This chapter has explored the role of relative producer prices in influencing soil conservation and land management decisions by small farmers in developing countries. The theoretical model developed has shown the potential of this problem, especially the susceptibility of farmers' land management decisions to price risk. An empirical analysis of the problem was conducted for the smallholder sector of Malawi, where price fluctuations have occurred in recent years.

The analysis shows that fluctuations in relative crop prices and returns may be exerting a significant impact on the incentives for smallholders to invest in improved cropping systems and land management by increasing the degree of price risk. The dynamics of price risk may produce the following effects:

- given the very small margins for risk among most smallholders and the widespread prevalence of household food insecurity, the uncertainty arising from fluctuating prices and returns is not conducive to improving farming systems, incorporating new crops or investing in substantial

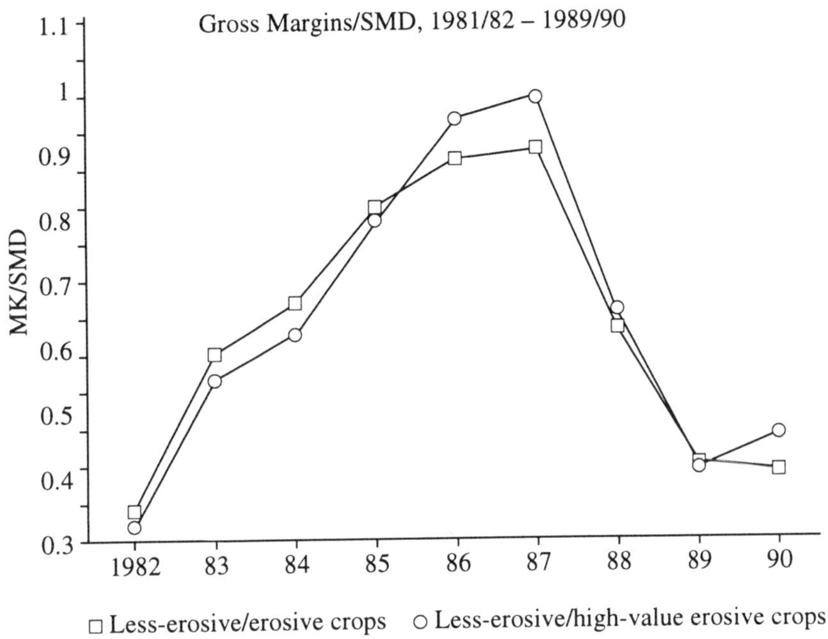

Figure 12.6 Less-erosive/erosive crops: gross margin/SMD ratio

improvements in existing cropping patterns, cultivation practices and conservation efforts;

- the relative poor returns of the less-erosive crops – groundnuts and-pulses – to the more erosive crops, particularly in terms of returns per labour, may be further constraining the income of those poorer households who continue to rely on intercropped systems, with consequences for both their food security and land management; and
- the asymmetrical impacts of pricing for most households – that is, that food-deficit households are likely to feel the impact of higher food prices as consumers rather than respond as producers to increase production – may have reinforced both the disincentive effect of price fluctuations on investment in improved farming systems and land management and the income constraints faced by poorer households.

Further, detailed analysis of these effects is required both in Malawi and other developing countries to improve understanding of the economic incentives, especially from relative price changes, on smallholder soil conservation and investment.

Notes

1. This paper is based on work conducted for the World Bank's Southern Africa Department and summarized in Barbier and Burgess (1992). I am grateful to Joanne Burgess, William Hyde and Richard Scobey for help and suggestions. An earlier version of this paper was also presented at the European Association of Environmental and Resource Economics Annual Meeting, Stockholm, 11–14 June 1991. The views expressed in this paper are those of the author alone, and cannot be attributed to the World Bank or to the above mentioned individuals.
2. The model used is adapted from Barbier (1990) and McConnell (1983).
3. In the model, time as a determinant of variables and functions has been omitted to simplify notation.
4. To simplify the model, erosion control effort is not a decision variable that the farmer controls directly. Rather, the farmer influences soil conservation effort indirectly by affecting the level of erosion. In practice one would expect the farmer to exercise more direct control over the soil conservation decision.
5. As in fishery models, *effort* can be thought of as some combination or *index* of the factor inputs required for soil conservation – capital, labour, materials, and so on. The assumption is that greater topsoil depth means more soil to protect from erosion.
6. If the private rate of discount reflects the opportunity cost of capital to the farmer, then the interest charge is essentially the income the farmer forgoes by not depleting the soil today and reinvesting in some other asset at the rate δ. The farmer's discount rate may also reflect his or her rate of time preference, which will be influenced by such factors as perceptions of risk and uncertainty, tenure insecurity and poverty. However, the social rate of discount will generally be lower than the private rate. For more on the factors influencing discounting in developing countries see Markandya and Pearce (1988), and for specific examples, Barbier (1990) and Pearce, Barbier and Markandya (1990).
7. See Vousden (1973). Ehui and Hertel (1989) develop a similar model for optimal deforestation and agricultural productivity in Côte d'Ivoire.
8. This section is based on Barbier and Burgess (1992) and the references cited therein.
9. For example, in 1986–87 average smallholder household income was only MK 382 (US$ 173), of which over 90 per cent was from on-farm activities, and over 55 per cent of households produced insufficient food for their needs (Government of Malawi, 1987).
10. Becker (1990) has developed a household model for analysing these constraints, especially for female labour, in Malawi. Barbier and Burgess (1992) provide more detail on how these constraints affect land management decisions, and the special implications for female-headed households, who comprise around 42 per cent of the 'core poor' households in Malawi.
11. For an excellent overview see Lele (1989), who aptly describes this condition as Malawi's 'dualism within dualism'. See also World Bank (1989b) on the food security and poverty conditions in Malawi.
12. For reviews, see Christiansen and Southworth (1988) and Lele (1989).
13. For example, using a microeconomic model of household choice to analyse supply response, Weaver (1989) found positive and significant own-price responses for rice, cassava and sorghum for smallholders in Malawi. For seed cotton and coffee, negative and significant own-price responses were found. Moreover, the model also estimated highly significant cross-price (relative) price effects. For example, an increase in the relative price of groundnut reduced sorghum production, while an increase in the relative price of cassava increased sorghum production. Similarly, groundnut and maize were found to be substitutes for cotton, whereas rice appeared to be a complement. However, Ogbu and Gbetibouo (1990) criticize Weaver's model for failing to distinguish between subsistence and commercial smallholders, as the authors believe that consumption, production and labour market decisions for these two classes of smallholders are different.
14. For more details, see Barbier and Burgess (1992), Christiansen and Southworth (1988), and World Bank (1989a).
15. Determining which crops are 'less-erosive' is of course difficult. All annual crop cultivation will produce some soil erosion, runoff and fertility declines. However, in making this distinction between erosive and less-erosive crops the relevant point is that, at least in the Malawi

context, some annual crops – for example, pulses and groundnuts – are considered to offer better ground cover, soil fertility maintenance and soil structure cohesion than do others – for example, maize, tobacco, cassava and cotton, thus reducing land degradation. Also, as noted above, it is not the crop *per se* which causes soil erosion but the method of cultivation and cropping pattern. Thus, for example, improper cultivation and cropping techniques of groundnuts and pulses can be associated with high rates of soil erosion. On the other hand, as indicated above, the latter two crops are also often intercropped by smallholders with each other and with maize and/or cassava, thus reducing the erosion of the entire cropping system.

16. As very little information exists on actual market prices in Malawi, the price series used in Figures 12.1–12.4 and in the following analysis are official prices. However, as the official prices are revised every year in light of market trends, these prices are thought to be sufficiently representative of prevailing price trends.
17. I am grateful to Fiammetta Cocuzza for research assistance in carrying out these ARIMA estimations. More details on these estimation results can be found in Cocuzza (1992).
18. See Christiansen and Kydd (1990).

References

Barbier, E.B. (1989), 'Cash crops, food crops and agricultural sustainability: the case of Indonesia', *World Development*, **17** (6), 879–95.

Barbier, E.B. (1990), 'The farm-level economics of soil conservation: the uplands of Java', *Land Economics*, **66** (2), 199–211.

Barbier, E.B. and J.C. Burgess (1992), *Malawi – Land Degradation in Agriculture*, Divisional Working Paper No. 1992–37, Policy and Research Division, Environment Department, The World Bank, Washington, DC.

Becker, H. (1990), 'Labour input decisions of subsistence farm households in southern Malawi', *Journal of Agricultural Economics*, **41** (2), 162–71.

Bishop, J.T. (1990), 'The cost of soil erosion in Malawi', Report to the Malawi Country Operations Dept., The World Bank, Washington, DC.

Bond, M. (1983) 'Agricultural responses to prices in sub-Saharan Africa', *IMF Staff Papers*, **30** (4), 703–26.

Carson, B. (1987), *A Comparison of Soil Conservation Strategies in Four Agroecological Zones in the Upland of East Java*, Melang, Indonesia: KEPAS.

Christiansen, R.E. and J. Kydd (1990), 'The political economy of agricultural policy formation in Malawi 1960–1987', Draft paper, The World Bank, Washington, DC.

Christiansen, R.E. and V.R. Southworth (1988), *Agricultural Pricing and Marketing Policy in Malawi: Implications for a Development Strategy*, MADIA Paper, Washington, DC: The World Bank.

Cocuzza, F. (1992), 'Supply responsiveness to prices of crops by Malawi's smallholders: an econometric analysis', MSc Thesis, Department of Economics, Birkbeck College, University of London.

Ehui, S.K. and T.W. Hertel (1989), 'Deforestation and agricultural productivity in the Côte d'Ivoire', *American Journal of Agricultural Economics*, **71** (August), 703–11.

Fones-Sundell, M. (1987), *Role of Price Policy in Stimulating Agricultural Production in Africa*, Issue Paper No. 2, Swedish University of Agricultural Science, Uppsala, Sweden.

Government of Malawi (GoM) (1987), 'Annual sample survey of agriculture 1986/87', unpublished data, Ministry of Agriculture.

Government of Malawi (GoM) (1990), *Economic Report 1990*, Office of the President, Zomba.

Hazell, P.B.R., M. Jaramillo and A. Williamson (1990), 'The relationship between world price instability and the prices farmers receive in developing countries', *Journal of Agricultural Economics*, **41** (2), 227–41.

Heady, E.O. (1955), 'The supply of US farm products under conditions of full employment', *American Economic Review*, **45** (2), 225–45.

Krishna, R. (1963), 'Farm supply response in India–Pakistan: a case study of the Punjab region', *Economic Journal*, **43** (291), 477–87.

Krishna, R. (1967), 'Agricultural price policy and economic development', in H.M. Southworth and B.F. Johnston (eds), *Agricultural Development and Economic Growth*, Ithaca, NY: Cornell University Press.

Kydd, J. (1989), 'Maize research in Malawi: lessons from failure', *Journal of International Development*, **1** (1), 112–44.

Lele, U. (1989), *Structural Adjustment, Agricultural Development, and the Poor: Some Lessons from the Malawian Experience*, MADIA Papers, The World Bank, Washington, DC.

Markandya, A. and D.W. Pearce (1988), *Environmental Considerations and the Choice of Discount Rate in Developing Countries*, Environment Department Working Paper No. 3, The World Bank, Washington, DC.

McConnell, K.E. (1983), 'An Economic Model of Soil Conservation', *American Journal of Agricultural Economics*, **65** (Feb.), 83–9.

Nerlove, M. (1956), 'Estimates of the elasticities of supply of selected agricultural commodities', *Journal of Farm Economics*, **38** (2), 496–509.

Ogbu, M. and E. Gbetibouo (1990), 'Agricultural supply response in sub-Saharan Africa: a critical review', *African Development Review*, **2** (2), 83–99.

Pearce, D.W., E.B. Barbier and A. Markandya (1990), *Sustainable Development: Economics and Environment in the Third World*, London: Edward Elgar and Earthscan Publications.

Repetto, R. (1988), *Economic Policy Reform for Natural Resource Conservation*, Environment Dept. Working Paper No. 4, The World Bank, Washington, DC.

Southgate, D. (1988), *The Economics of Land Degradation in the Third World*, Environment Dept. Working Paper No. 2, The World Bank, Washington, DC.

Southgate, D. (1990), 'The causes of land degradation along "spontaneously" expanding agricultural frontiers in the third world', *Land Economics*, **66** (3), 93–101.

Southgate, D. and Pearce, D.W. (1988), *Agricultural Colonization and Environmental Degradation in Frontier Developing Economies*, Environment Dept. Working Paper No. 9, The World Bank, Washington, DC.

Vousden, N. (1973), 'Basic theoretical issues of resource depletion', *Journal of Economic Theory*, **6**, 126–43.

Weaver, R.D. (1989), *An Integrated Model of Perennial and Annual Crop Production for Sub-Saharan Countries*, Washington, DC: International Economics Department, The World Bank.

World Bank (1989a), *Malawi – Agricultural Sector Adjustment Credit*, Washington, DC: World Bank.

World Bank (1989b), *Malawi – Food Security Report*, Washington, DC: World Bank.

13. The economics of soil erosion: theory, methodology and examples*

1. Introduction

Soil is an essential input to farming. This is especially true throughout Southeast Asia (SEA), where agricultural production is crucial to development, the livelihoods of the majority of the population depend on the primary sector, and non-labour inputs for the poorest farms are negligible. And yet agricultural land use in SEA countries often results in the degradation of natural soil fertility and reduced productivity. Soil degradation under farming also inflicts external or off-site costs, through the processes of erosion, sedimentation and leaching.

The impacts of land degradation and the depletion of soil resources have profound economic implications for low income countries. Environmental damage results in loss of current income and increased risk, and particularly affects the poor. Degradation of land resources also threatens prospects for economic growth and future human welfare.

In the developing countries, empirical research on the economic costs of land degradation is confined largely to analysis at the level of individual farms or watersheds. On-site impacts are most frequently studied, typically by analysis of the effect of soil loss on crop production. Limited data suggest that the impact of soil erosion on crops may be more dramatic in the tropics than under temperate conditions, due to the relative fragility of tropical soils, or more extreme climatic conditions (Lal, 1981, 1987; Stocking, 1987). The off-site impacts of land degradation are often much harder to evaluate, because the off-site benefits provided by land resources are not traded at all.

The available evidence indicates that the costs of land degradation, and thus the benefits of conservation, may be substantial in developing countries, despite relatively low average returns to agriculture. Estimates of the cost of land degradation in these countries vary from under 1 per cent to over 15 per cent of GNP (Barbier and Bishop, 1995). However, these calculations are often more illustrative than definitive, due to the paucity of empirical data and various methodological problems. Moreover, attempts to estimate the costs and benefits of soil conservation on a regional or national level confront serious methodological problems (Stocking, 1987).

The purpose of the following chapter is to provide an overview of an economic analysis of soil erosion, concentrating particularly on explaining the farm-level economics of soil erosion and discussing with examples the appropriate methodology for measuring on and off-site costs.

2. The farm-level economics of soil erosion

To understand fully why some farmers may decide to invest in soil conservation whereas others may not requires adopting an economic approach to soil erosion.

Soil is essentially a semi-renewable resource. Although one could argue that topsoil accretes, it does so at an extremely slow rate. In general, the rate at which topsoil is 'degraded' or 'eroded' through cultivation is generally faster than the rate at which it regenerates. Thus soil in agriculture is usually treated as a potentially depletable resource, and it is generally assumed that most farming practices will result in rates of erosion that will exceed the 'natural' or 'background' rate of soil erosion that would occur if no cultivation took place.

From an economic perspective, soil conservation implies 'saving' soil for future use. Alternatively, a farmer may choose to work the soil harder today, at the expense of more erosion and less soil available for the future. This suggests that, as with other natural resources, the terms conservation and depletion as applied to soil erosion have a particular economic meaning. That is, *conservation* essentially implies a redistribution of resource use rates into the future, whereas *depletion*, or in the case of soil, *erosion*, implies a redistribution of resource use rates towards the present. This terminology proves to be extremely important in thinking about a farmer's incentive to invest in more soil conservation.

For instance, this economic approach to soil erosion and conservation would suggest that the optimal rate of soil conservation should not be confused with eliminating soil erosion altogether, or even with reducing soil erosion to some 'background' or 'ideal' rate.[1] Rather, the optimal level of soil conservation is the level at which the marginal benefits of additional conservation just equal its costs. Since soil conservation is not costless, then clearly it is not optimal to reduce erosion to zero – even if it is physically possible to do so.

From the farmer's perspective, there are essentially two components to the *costs* of soil erosion:

- *direct costs* – the costs to the farmer of the effort (that is, labour), materials, equipment, physical structures, and so on, that are required to undertake soil conservation measures
- *foregone output* – any loss of current output that results from using 'less' soil today or less land.[2]

In comparison, the benefits that a farmer receives from soil conservation derives from soil being a potential income-yielding asset. The 'stock' of soil available to a farmer is essentially an economic asset that can be exploited through cultivation to yield a stream of present and future income. Thus to the farmer, the benefits of soil conservation are essentially the perceived gains in having more rather than less soil available currently and in the future. There are likely to be two types of such benefits of soil conservation:

- the *gains* in current and future production and thus income accruing to the farmer from having more soil available today and in the future.
- any additional future *resale* or *bequest* value that accrues to the farmer from having more soil and thus more potential land productivity at the time of the future bequest or sale.

Alternatively, we can turn this around and say that the economic costs of soil erosion are that the farmer must forego the above future productivity benefits. Hence the economics literature sometimes refer to these losses as the *user costs* of any soil erosion incurred today.

Consequently, from the perspective of the individual farmer, the optimal level of soil conservation (and thus soil erosion) can be determined in two ways:

- it is the level of erosion at which the additional user costs of soil erosion avoided just equal the additional costs of soil conservation, or
- it is the level at which the present value of the additional income (and resale/bequest value) derived from soil conservation just equal the additional costs of soil conservation.

In the Appendix to this chapter, a formal model of the farmer's decision to conserve or deplete soil is depicted.

3. Private versus social rates of erosion

If each farming household in Southeast Asia always eroded soil at an optimal rate, and if these optimal private rates of soil erosion were consistent with what all of society would wish erosion rates to be, then there would be no economic problem of soil erosion as such. Based on the marginal benefits and costs of additional conservation that it faced, each farming household would determine automatically its own private rate of soil erosion, and this rate would in turn automatically reflect the socially optimal rate of erosion.

However, it is much more likely that private rates of soil erosion diverge from social rates. Moreover, observed rates of soil erosion from cultivated land may not always even be privately optimal. There are several reasons for this.

First, at best farmers are concerned only with the *on-site* costs and benefits of soil erosion, whereas society must also be concerned with any *off-site* or external costs. Externalities are defined as costs or benefits arising in a process of production or consumption which are not reflected in market prices. A typical negative externality resulting from soil erosion on agricultural land is the sedimentation of downstream reservoirs, hydroelectric facilities or irrigation channels. The protection of watersheds provided by tree plantations, orchards and other perennial crops is an example of a positive externality. These off-site costs and benefits are not reflected in the prices of agricultural outputs, nor in farmer decision-making, but they are an integral part of the economic impacts of land degradation. Designing appropriate policies to correct such externalities is difficult. An efficient response may be to 'internalize' the off-site costs of land degradation through fiscal measures, for example, taxes on agricultural inputs or outputs, or through the development of legal mechanisms for the compensation of environmental externalities. However, the limited rural markets and weak institutions typical of many SEA countries reduce the appeal of such approaches. As a consequence, in regions where off-site costs are significant they would suggest that private rates of soil erosion diverge from social rates.

Imperfect land and capital markets may also play a significant role in affecting the farmer's decision to control soil erosion. The most reliable indicator that a farming household will have of the effects of soil erosion on future land productivity is through land prices. However, in many SEA countries, rural land markets are imperfect or distorted. Consequently, the user costs of soil erosion may not be reflected adequately or even bear any relation to land values. Similarly, the lack of effective rural credit markets may distort the farming household's decision as to whether it is worthwhile investing in protecting the soil because of its future productivity and income potential as opposed to exploiting it for immediate gain today. In other words, the 'opportunity cost' of conserving the soil may be extremely high. If the farmer has also to borrow in the short term to invest in conservation, then distorted or non-existent local capital markets may make the direct costs of conservation prohibitively expensive.

It is also likely that the farmer's private rate of discount – that is, the value attached to future as opposed to present income – will be higher than the social rate of discount. A farmer's discount rate may be affected by both *pure time preference*, reflecting the farmer's attitude to risk and uncertainty as well as the level of household poverty, and the marginal opportunity cost of capital, which represents the scarcity value of savings and returns to alternative investments. It was noted above how distorted land and capital markets may affect the marginal opportunity cost of capital faced by the farming household. However, even without these distortions, private individuals are also presumed to have a high degree of time preference, and thus employ higher discount rates, on average, than society as a whole. The rationale is that society can more effectively minimize risk by diversifying its investments; and of course society 'lives' forever while individuals do not. This divergence between public and private rates of time preference leads individuals to discount future benefits excessively and thus to consume assets that society as a whole would have them conserve. In other words, society will ascribe a higher value to future crop yields foregone due to soil exhaustion than will farmers. Society is also likely to be more concerned about long run stability, sustainability and equity in agriculture, all of which may depend in some measure on conservation efforts (Conway and Barbier, 1990). Hence a socially optimal level of soil depletion will usually be significantly below the level tolerated by farmers. The combination of widespread poverty and poorly developed land tenure institutions and rural capital markets in many SEA countries may also imply high rates of private time preference, and thus add to the significant divergence between public and private discount rates.

The farmer's decision to control soil erosion is clearly influenced by the future returns to a farming system, which in turn is affected by technological improvements. Technical innovation is largely devoted to devising substitutes for, or increasing the productivity of scarce factors. The depletion of a scarce natural resource poses a threat when it is considered essential to future economic opportunities, that is, if there is no apparent substitute for the resource, if degradation is for all practical purposes irreversible and/or if its future value is uncertain but believed to be high (Pearce, Barbier and Markandya, 1990). Fertile land clearly meets the definition of an essential resource, particularly in many low-income and lower middle-income economies which, despite development efforts over the past 25 years, still appear to be highly dependent on primary production from their resource base. In these countries subsistence agriculture accounts for a substantial proportion of national income and an overwhelming segment of the labour force. The prominent role of agriculture in national welfare in such countries justifies concern about the possible lack of substitutes for natural soil fertility, and the scarcity of alternative economic opportunities.

However, what holds for the economy as a whole may not hold for the individual farmer. From a private perspective, there are almost always substitutes for arable land, since individual farmers can often find alternative or supplementary occupations, and few people consider the value of their land in terms of national economic security. Hence farmers tend to treat soil fertility as just one income-producing asset among many, and as suggested already, there are many factors that may discourage them from maintaining soil fertility.

Finally, other market, policy and institutional failures, such as insecure tenure or ownership of the land, distorted market prices for inputs and outputs, imperfect competition, incomplete markets, and so on, can all affect the farmer's perception of the costs and benefits of controlling soil erosion. Throughout Southeast Asia, agricultural policies in particular have the most direct impact on the incentives for farmers to engage in soil conservation. In general, there are two ways in which agricultural policies affect these incentives.

First, polices that affect the prices of agricultural products do not automatically take into account the wider environmental costs of agricultural land use. As discussed already, markets fail to reflect the externalities arising from the off-site costs of soil erosion. In addition, imperfect capital and land markets may mean that farmers ignore the user costs of soil erosion, and thus over-produce for agricultural markets. In the absence of deliberate policies to internalize these costs, and without well-functioning markets for agricultural land, the market will tend to 'underprice' soil resources, leading to excessive land degradation from a social point of view.

In addition, agricultural policies can affect production decisions such that sub-optimal land management practices are encouraged, resulting in unnecessary land degradation. This can occur in several ways (Barbier and Burgess 1992):

- higher aggregate crop prices and lower agricultural input costs increase the profitability of crop production, thus encouraging an aggregate expansion of agricultural production onto marginal or more erodible land
- the impact of agricultural pricing on the relative returns to agricultural production can influence long-run decisions to invest in sustainable land management and conservation
- changes in the relative prices of crops (and crop inputs) can influence the substitution of more environmentally benign cropping and farm production systems for systems that are more environmentally damaging
- the variability of crop prices and crop price inputs can affect farmers' choice of crops and cultivation practices, and decisions to invest in sustainable land management, by affecting the risks associated with alternative agricultural investments and production systems.

In addition to agricultural policy, other economic policies can also have profound effects on land use. Virtually any policy which distorts the market prices of agricultural inputs and outputs can alter incentives for soil conservation. The impact of specific policies on farmer decision making and land degradation is often ambiguous, however, making generalization difficult. Impacts on households will vary to the extent that policies affect certain groups more than others.

Finally, soil conservation requires access to inputs: labour, capital (including land, equipment and materials, or the funds to obtain them) and information (technology). Poorer farmers – particularly female-headed households – often lack access to one or more of these inputs, preventing them from adopting conservation measures. Even when they know of appropriate technologies, farmers may lack access to sufficient labour to undertake soil conservation measures on their own, and may also suffer limited access to capital with which to hire additional manpower or purchase any tools required. For example, in many areas the best time to install or maintain soil conservation structures is at the beginning of the growing season, when soils are softened by rain and vegetation cover is light. But this is also the moment of peak labour demand for field preparation and planting. The true opportunity cost of soil conservation is thus often higher than at first appears, when considered in relation to other demands on farmers' resources.

To summarize, soil erosion is an economic problem if:

- farming households ignore all or some of the user costs of soil erosion
- any off-site, or external, costs are ignored.

Economic analysis of this problem requires:

- determining the farm-level incentives for soil conservation; that is, to what extent is the farmer ignoring the user cost of soil erosion, and if so, why?
- measuring the on-site and off-site costs of soil erosion
- determining the appropriate policies and investments to correct the problem.

The remaining sections will focus principally on the second of these issues, employing examples from Southeast Asia.

4. Measuring on-site costs: methodologies and examples

In measuring the on-site costs of soil erosion the main objective is usually to estimate the present value of net income lost through excessive (that is, sub-optimal) soil erosion. The methodologies for measuring these costs are generally straightforward, but they have to be used with care. As we shall see presently, a critical issue is determining what net income might be for the farming system 'without' erosion. The following section reviews briefly the various methodologies for measuring on-site costs, and illustrates them with some examples from Southeast Asia.

Methodologies

Figure 13.1 illustrates the basic methodology proposed in most empirical analyses for measuring the on-site cost of soil erosion on a plot of land.[3] The two curves depict for a farming household the present value of net revenues per hectare with and without erosion. The on-site cost of erosion would therefore be the difference between the two curves, or area *A*.

However, measuring *A* is not straightforward. The problem is that we observe the farm with erosion, and we do not necessarily know what land productivity and income would have been in the absence of erosion. Moreover, as discussed

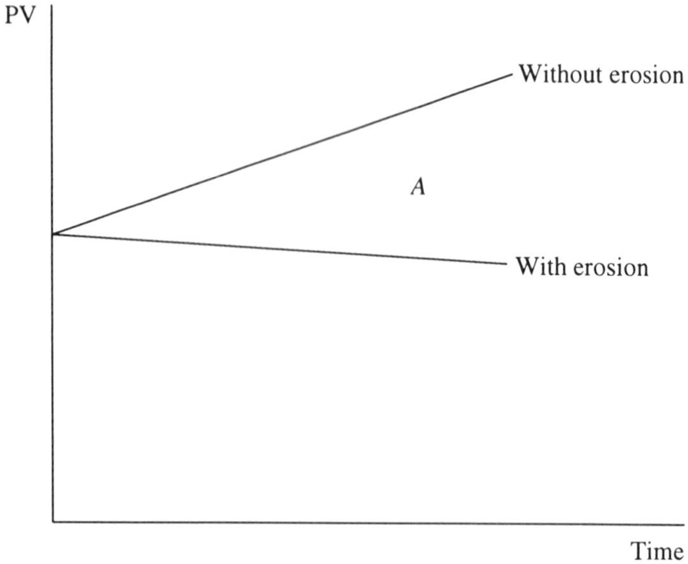

Note: PV = Present value of net revenues per hectare.

Figure 13.1 Measuring on-site costs of soil erosion

above, the optimal level of erosion on a farm will generally not be a 'zero level' of erosion.

Nevertheless, many studies of the on-site costs of soil erosion have attempted to estimate *A* in one of two different ways:

- *change in productivity approach* – the difference in crop yields with and without erosion, multiplied by the unit price of the crop, and less the costs of production
- *replacement cost approach* – as there often are nutrient and herbicide losses associated with erosion, on-site costs are sometimes measured in terms of the loss in marginal productivity of crop output from incremental changes in inputs, multiplied by the unit price of the crop, and less the costs of the foregone inputs.

Unfortunately, the application of both of these approaches to estimating the on-site cost of soil erosion is usually flawed and may lead to over-estimation of the on-site cost of soil erosion if not carefully applied. The problem again is that both approaches assume that the comparison is between a situation 'with' and 'without' erosion, as if it is possible to eliminate soil erosion altogether. This

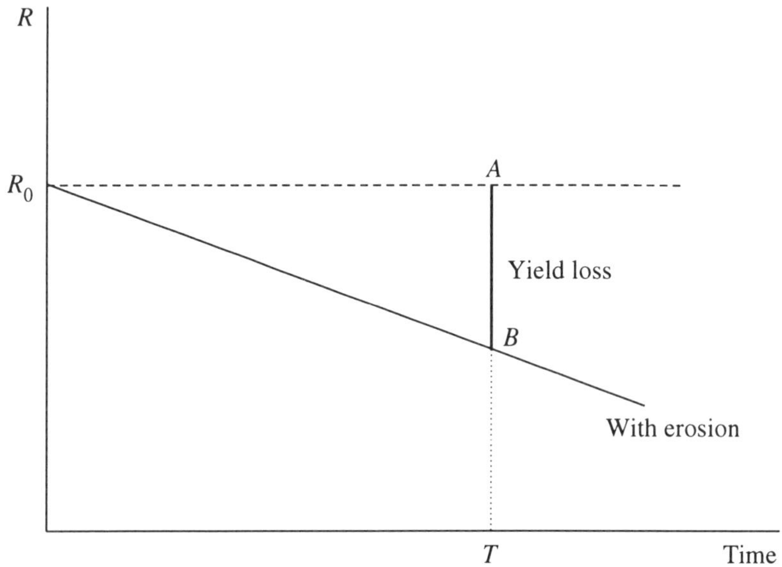

Note: R = Gross revenue per hectare.

Figure 13.2 Change in productivity approach to measuring on-site costs of soil erosion

is simply not the case. No feasible technology exists to produce crops without some degree of erosion. In addition, as discussed in Section 2, even if it is feasible to reduce erosion to negligible levels, this can only be accomplished by the farmer investing in conservation measures, which is not a costless exercise.

The change in productivity approach is illustrated in Figure 13.2. Assume for simplicity that soil erosion does not affect the costs of production but only revenues, through impacts on crop yields.[4] Let R_0 be the gross revenues per hectare of the farm if no soil loss occurred, which are also assumed to be the revenues at initial time T_0. However, soil erosion occurs over time so actual yields for any time $T > T_0$ will be less than R_0. The change in productivity approach assumes that for any particular time period, T, the (undiscounted) revenue impacts of yield losses from soil erosion in that period will be the distance AB between R_0 and the gross revenues per hectare with erosion.

However, this method is likely to over-estimate the on-site costs of soil erosion. The assumption that gross revenues could be maintained indefinitely at R_0 is not realistic. As argued previously, this is unlikely to be either feasible or optimal. Even if it is technically feasible to reduce soil erosion, the costs of investing in soil conservation on some plots of land may not be economically worthwhile. For other plots of land, it may be worthwhile reducing erosion and thus improving yields, but it may be too costly to restore yield and net income to the initial levels before erosion sets in. Thus measuring on-site costs in terms of all the net income losses associated with productivity changes before and after erosion on all cropland may be misleading.

The replacement cost approach is shown in Figure 13.3. Assume that the input (that is, fertilizer) is used optimally, at the point where its price equals its value marginal product. Thus X_1 is the actual level of use of fertilizer. However, soil erosion and runoff will cause some of the fertilizer to be washed away, and consequently only X_0 of the input is effectively applied to the crop. The loss of input is therefore $X_1 - X_0$, and the total input cost to the farmer of this loss is measured by area *B* in Figure 13.3, whereas the total loss in market value of changes in crop productivity is areas *A* and *B*. Thus the net loss to the farmer of soil erosion is really area *A*. However, as it is often difficult to obtain information on the value marginal product of inputs used in crop production, many analysts simply use the costs of 'replacing' the lost inputs $X_1 - X_0$, that is, area *B*, as an approximation of the net losses to the farmer, that is, area *A*. This is why this method has been referred to as the 'replacement cost' approach.

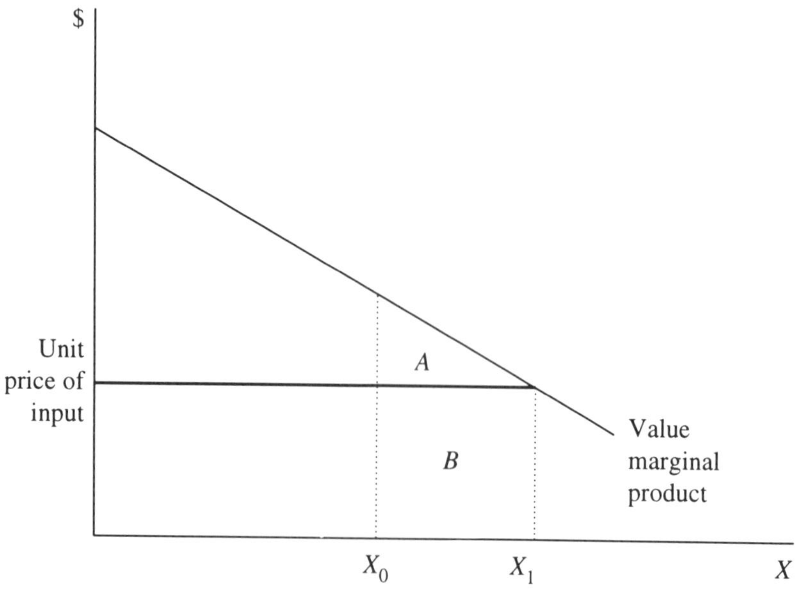

Note: X = Input use level.

Figure 13.3 Replacement cost approach to measuring on-site costs of soil erosion

Clearly, using the cost of replacing inputs to measure the market value of changes in crop output arising from losses in these inputs is a second-best approach. There is no reason to believe that area *B* will always be a good approximation of area *A*, and certainly such a 'replacement cost' estimate can only be an accurate reflection of on-site cost by chance. Moreover, it is doubtful in Figure 13.2 that area *A* would be an appropriate measure of on-site cost in the first instance. We simply do not know how to guarantee that all the purchased inputs applied, X_1, will reach the crop. Because it is generally infeasible – and often not optimal – to reduce soil erosion to zero, it is inevitable that some input runoff will occur. Thus to use the entire area *A* in Figure 13.3 to measure the on-site cost of soil erosion will generally overestimate this cost as well. To use the cost of 'replacing' the loss of $X_1 - X_0$ units of inputs as the 'proxy' measure of *A* compounds the estimation error further.

To understand the correct methodology for estimating the on-site cost of soil erosion, one must return to the basic theory outlined in Section 2. For the on-site cost of soil erosion to be an economic cost it must be an opportunity cost, which is defined as the value of a foregone alternative. In the case of soil erosion, the alternative for the farmer is to invest in soil conservation. However, soil conservation is not a costless activity, and in any case is likely to affect the net profitability of the farming system over time. Thus effectively, the on-site cost of soil erosion must be the loss in the long-run net profitability of the farming system from not investing in soil conservation, provided of course that such an investment is an economically worthwhile alternative. That is, the on-site cost of soil erosion is the difference between the (present value) net returns of the farming system with soil conservation and the (present value) net returns with erosion.

Figure 13.4 illustrates this approach for a typical case. The 'with erosion' curve shows the present value of net returns per hectare for a plot of cropland. Because of soil erosion, the net returns will eventually decline over time. The 'with conservation' curve shows the economic returns after the next best alternative, which is the investment in the most feasible conservation measures. As conservation usually involves upfront direct costs as well as possibly changes in cropping patterns and even loss of productive area, the present value net returns to the farming system with conservation will generally be lower than without conservation for some time initially. However, because conservation prevents topsoil from eroding so fast means that eventually at some future time *T* the present value net returns of the farming system with conservation will begin to exceed the returns without conservation, and will hopefully continue to do so indefinitely. Thus in the simple case shown in Figure 13.4, the on-site cost of soil erosion would be measured by the difference between the two curves, or areas *A* plus *B*.[5] Since in this example and in most typical cases area *A* is negative, then the on-site cost of soil erosion would translate into *B* – *A*.

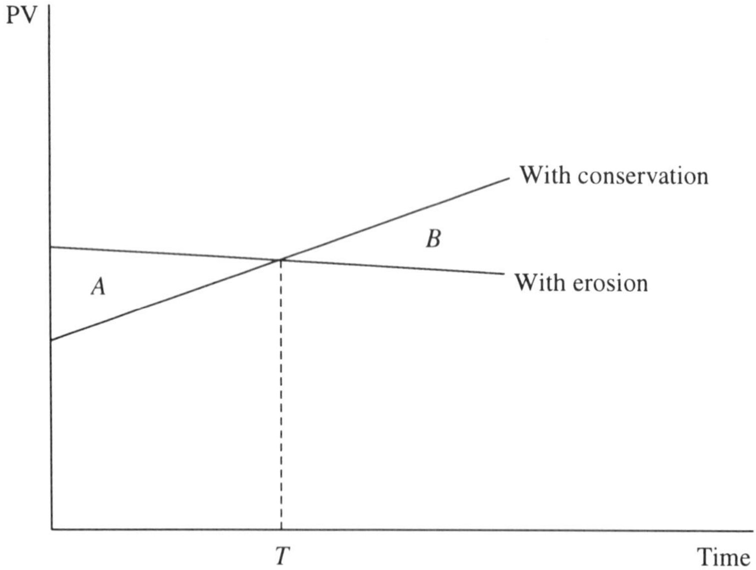

Note: PV = Present value of net revenues per hectare.

Figure 13.4 Correct approach to measuring on-site costs of soil erosion

A further point should also be emphasized here. Note that only if conservation is a viable economic alternative to continuing with current farming practices that lead to much greater erosion would there be any on-site cost to soil erosion. That is, in Figure 13.4 if area *A* turned out actually to be greater than area *B* than this would imply that the net present value of the farming system with conservation would be less than that with current erosive farming practices. In other words, there is no viable economic alternative to the present farming conditions that induce erosion, and so consequently the on-site cost of soil erosion is effectively zero – despite the fact that *physically* lots of erosion may be taking place. This is a very difficult point for non-economists to understand, but it is fundamental to understanding the correct economic methodology for assessing the on-site cost of soil erosion.[6]

Of course it does not follow from this that, because we may observe a farmer *not* investing in soil conservation, that it is always right to conclude that the on-site cost of soil erosion is zero. As discussed in Section 3, there are many factors that might distort the farmer's incentives to invest in soil conservation, and these distortions may mean that from the private perspective of an individual farmer the net present value of the farming system with conservation may appear to be much less than the present value of the existing system with severe erosion. In contrast, once the distortions to economic costs and benefits are taken fully into account, it may turn out that from a social (that is, economic) perspective the on-site cost of soil erosion in the farming system is significant. It is the task of the economic analyst to determine the true economic on-site cost of soil erosion of a farming system, regardless of whether or not the farmer is observed to be actually taking this cost into account in production decisions.

Although the methodology outlined above and in Figure 13.4 is the more sound approach to estimating the on-site cost of soil erosion, it has often proven to be very difficult to implement empirically. Determining an economically viable alternative conservation investment to current erosive practices is not easy, nor is projecting the likely current and future profitability of farming systems with this conservation investment and comparing it with the profitability of continuing with existing erosive farming practices. The data constraints are often formidable, whereas simplifying assumptions and generalizations may be misleading. This may particularly prove to be the case in developing regions such as Southeast Asia, where there are many diverse and heterogeneous small-scale farming systems scattered over extremely varied topological, climatic and soil conditions, and where differences in social, ethnic and household characteristics in rural areas can be important determinants of long-term investment and farm profitability. It is not surprising therefore that many analysts have ended up using the change in productivity and replacement methods as an alternative. These approaches may be less reliable or even second-best from an economic perspective, but they might be the only implementable choices.[7]

Example 1: On-site costs of soil erosion on Java, Indonesia

Magrath and Arens (1989) conducted an analysis of the on-site costs of soil erosion for mainly upland rainfed (*tegal*) cropping systems on Java, Indonesia. The results are also summarized in Repetto *et al.* (1989). The main method for estimating these costs was the change in productivity approach. The basic assumption was that yields and thus farm revenues would decline as erosion proceeds, and the available evidence suggested that costs that would tend to fall along with output account for a small share of production costs in Javanese rainfed agricultural systems. The result is that soil erosion was expected to lower net farm income, and might eventually lead to the adoption of less profitable crops. To account for possible adjustments in cropping systems, farm budgets for a variety of representative dryland cropping systems across Java were constructed, and then used to estimate the effects the yield losses from erosion on net farm incomes. This was done comprehensively for a single year (1985). Assuming that the one-year loss in net income recurs over each successive year, Magrath and Arens 'capitalize' this one-year cost of erosion to obtain a total present value of current and future losses. The latter figure is their estimate of the on-site costs of soil erosion on Java.

The method and results are illustrated in Table 13.1. As indicated in the table, the 1 per cent decline in productivity and the predicted average yield declines from soil erosion for dryland farming systems in each province of Java are applied to the total area of these cropping systems. This yields the single-year cost of soil erosion for 1985. This one-year loss is then capitalized to obtain the present value of losses in farm income in current and future years. For Java as a whole, this on-site cost of soil erosion in 1985 was estimated to be approximately Rp 539.6 million (US$327 million), which amounted to around 4 per cent of the total value of dryland crops on Java.[8]

Table 13.1 On-site costs of soil erosion on Java, 1985 (Indonesian Rupiah (Rp) 1650 = US$ 1)

	Dryland area ('000 ha)	Estimated current net farm income (Rp/ha)	Weighted production loss (%)	Annual cost of a 1% productivity decline (Rp/ha)	Single year cost (Rp million)	Capitalized cost (Rp million)	On-site cost as % of total dryland crop value
West Java	1440	95 039	4.4	3718	23 508	235 080	10
Central Java	1366	8196	4.1	859	4810	48 100	1
Jogyakarta	196	9531	4.7	1026	948	9480	1
East Java	1744	141 499	4.1	3453	24 690	246 900	4
All Java	4747	83 649	4.3	2686	53 956	539 560	4

Source: Magrath and Arens (1989); Repetto *et al.* (1989).

Despite the impressive and comprehensive effort that went into estimating of on-site erosion costs on Java, the analysis suffers from the standard limitations of the change in productivity approach to measuring these costs. Because Magrath and Arens do not take into account the costs and impacts of conservation in their measurement of the effects of yield losses from erosion on net incomes, their analysis essentially assumes that all these yield and net income losses represent the full economic costs of soil erosion. As discussed previously, this is unlikely to be the case. Thus their results probably overestimate the on-site costs of soil erosion on Java.

Example 2: On-site costs of soil erosion, Magat watershed, the Philippines
Due to data limitations, Cruz, Francisco and Conway (1988) employ the replacement cost method to estimate the on-site costs of soil erosion in the Magat watershed of the Philippines. The major upper watershed degradation problem was seen to be the conversion of primary and secondary forest to grasslands and other forms of land use. The average annual sheet erosion rate for grasslands was estimated to be around 88 tons per hectare compared to 28 tons for all other

land uses. The nutrient losses associated with this erosion on representative land unit areas for grasslands were translated into equivalent quantities of inorganic fertilizers – nitrogen (N), phosphorous (P) and potassium (K) – lost per ton of soil erosion. The cost of replacing these equivalent fertilizer losses were then valued in terms of both nominal and shadow fertilizer prices. The resulting estimate was considered to be the on-site cost of soil erosion from land conversion in the Magat watershed.[9]

The basic approach and results are shown in Table 13.2. The first column of the table indicates the weighted average of nutrients lost from erosion on grasslands in terms of their equivalents in kilograms of urea, solophos and muriate of potash. The second column shows the value of these fertilizer losses in terms of nominal, or actual, prices paid for these inputs by local farmers, and the third column shows the value in terms of shadow, or adjusted, prices that account for the full social cost of the fertilizer inputs. Thus the on-site cost of soil erosion is estimated to be around ₱1068 per ha (US$50.1/ha) in nominal prices and ₱2716 per ha (US$127.5/ha) in shadow prices.

Table 13.2 On-site costs of soil erosion, Magat watershed, the Philippines, 1988 (Philippine Peso (₱) 21.3 = US$ 1)

		Valuation with use of	
	Quantity (kg)	Nominal price (₱)	Shadow price (₱)
Urea			
– price		3.60/kg	9.86/kg
– amount lost/ton of soil eroded	3.08	11.09	30.37
– amount lost/ha of affected land	118.13	677.23	1854.96
Solophos (P_2O_5)			
– price		2.50/kg	6.20/kg
– amount lost/ton of soil eroded	0.79	1.98	4.90
– amount lost/ha of affected land	70.65	176.63	438.03
Muriate of Potash (K_2O)			
– price		4.20/kg	8.28/kg
– amount lost/ton of soil eroded	0.57	2.39	4.72
– amount lost/ha of affected land	51.07	214.49	422.86
All fertilizers			
– cost/ton of soil eroded		15.46	39.99
– cost/ha of affected land		1068.35	2715.85

Source: Cruz, Francisco and Conway (1988).

This use of the replacement cost approach to estimate the on-site costs of soil erosion clearly displays all the shortcomings of this method outlined above. More fundamentally, it is unclear whether soil erosion from grassland represents a true economic 'on-site' cost in the first place. It is true that erosion of grasslands results in loss of nutrients, but whether this loss translates into real economic costs in terms of foregone net income over time depends clearly on the economic activity utilizing the grasslands. It is not evident from the analysis what economic activity takes place on the grasslands, or whether these lands are utilized at all. Moreover, erosion rates on cultivated land may actually be higher than that on grasslands; for example, in the neighbouring Canili-Diayo and Pantabangan watersheds average rates of erosion on croplands are around 428.6 tons/ha annually as opposed to 197.8 tons/ha for grasslands (Cruz, Francisco and Conway, 1988). Erosion rates from grasslands are therefore not really representative of erosion on cultivated lands. Thus not only does the use of the replacement cost method of measuring the on-site costs of soil erosion on grasslands yield an unreliable estimate, it is doubtful whether erosion from these lands are actually an economic 'on-site' cost as such.

5. Measuring off-site costs: methodologies and examples

The main objective in measuring off-site costs is to estimate the present value of any external costs arising from sedimentation and other downstream impacts. The methodologies for measuring these costs are usually standard approaches of estimating environmental externalities, but again these estimation procedures have to be used with care. This section will overview briefly the methodologies for estimating off-site costs, and to illustrate them with examples relevant to Southeast Asia.

There are many possible downstream or off-site impacts of soil erosion that result from water-borne runoff and sedimentation. These impacts include: reservoir sedimentation; losses to navigation; irregular flow of irrigation; effects on agricultural, fishing and industrial production in lowlands and coastal regions; impacts on water supply and potability; and impacts on drought or flood cycles. The resulting economic costs of these impacts would normally be measured in terms of the present value of foregone net economic benefits from any loss of downstream economic activity, including loss or damage to property, or from any direct welfare effects.

However, the actual methodologies employed in estimating off-site costs are usually fairly specific to the type of downstream impacts and welfare losses encountered. In this short chapter, it is impossible to outline the approaches relevant to all the many possible downstream impacts of soil erosion. Instead, one particular off-site cost – sedimentation of dam reservoirs – will be examined in detail.

Sedimentation of dam reservoirs has been recognized throughout Southeast Asia as a major consequence of land degradation and erosion in upper watersheds. The potential economic costs in terms of losses in hydroelectric power, irregular or inadequate flow of irrigation water, reduced flood control and even impacts on water supply and potability have considered to be significant.

The basic methodology for estimating these costs is outlined in Figure 13.5. For simplicity's sake, assume that the purpose of the dam is to deliver water for irrigation. The curve *DD* represents the demand for irrigation water from the dam. Initially, without reservoir sedimentation, the dam is able to supply Q_0 amount of water at a price P_0 to satisfy this demand. However, sedimentation of the reservoir reduces its storage capacity and may affect the planned lifetime of the entire dam project. All of these impacts would effectively increase the marginal costs of the dam's delivery of irrigation water, or another way of looking at it, in order to supply the same quantity of irrigation water as planned before reservoir sedimentation, additional dredging costs or investments in sedimentation ponds would have to be incurred. In Figure 13.5, this can be represented by an increase in the marginal costs of delivering water, from $S = MC_0$ to $S = MC_1$. This results in a net loss in both consumer and producer surplus equal to area

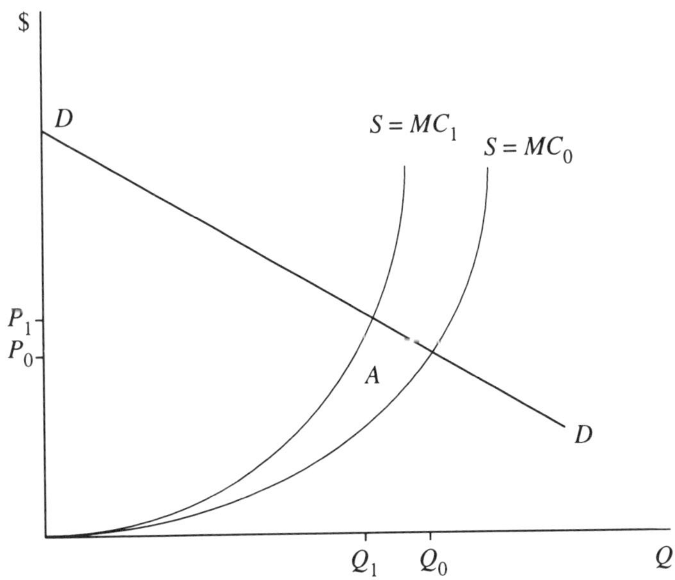

Note: Q = Quantity of water delivered.

Figure 13.5 Off-site costs of dam reservoir sedimentation

A. This net welfare impact is essentially the off-site cost associated with reservoir sedimentation.

This approach can be extended to estimating the off-site costs of reservoir sedimentation in terms of all other uses as well, such as hydroelectricity generation, flood control and domestic and industrial water supply. The most common method is to measure these impacts in terms of the present value of foregone net benefits from reductions in service life and storage of the reservoir caused by sedimentation. More specifically, the type of impacts that are usually measured and included as the costs of sedimentation are:

- *Reduction in service life* – As siltation of the reservoir means that the entire lifetime of the dam may be reduced, say from 50 to 35 years, then there will consequently be loss of future economic benefits (for example, hydroelectric power, flood control, irrigation) from this reduction in the service life of the dam.
- *Increase sedimentation of active storage* – Active or 'live' storage is the water in the reservoir that was assumed to be free of sedimentation and therefore available for use to deliver water for hydropower, irrigation, and so on. Sedimentation may reduce the live storage capacity of a reservoir with a consequent loss in economic benefits. This may particularly be the case where sedimentation that is supposed to be 'trapped' by sediment pools may actually find its way into the 'active' storage.
- *Increase sedimentation of dead storage (unplanned)* – The dead storage of a reservoir is the portion of total reservoir storage capacity that is allocated to 'storing' sediment. Usually, engineers plan for a certain amount of dead storage in a dam's reservoir based on existing sedimentation rates, with the remaining storage capacity assumed to be active. An 'unplanned' increase in sedimentation due to greater soil erosion upstream is assumed to increase the dead storage component of a reservoir. This in turn is assumed to mean that more active storage becomes 'inactive' and thus there is a consequent loss of water available for hydropower, irrigation and other economic benefits.
- *Increase sedimentation of dead storage (planned)* – Because of the presence of severe soil erosion and thus high sedimentation rates, engineers may have to plan for a larger amount of dead storage in the reservoir than if erosion and sedimentation rates were lower. This additional water could instead have been used for more active storage, if less sedimentation meant that less planned dead storage was required. The resulting foregone economic benefits are considered the cost of this increased in planned dead storage.

However, all these approaches need to be used with caution. There is always the danger of double counting if more than one of these approaches is applied simultaneously. Considerable information is also required on sedimentation delivery and deposition rates in the reservoir, and a clear understanding of the relationship between, dead storage, active storage and the service life of the dam needs to be formulated. To illustrate some of these issues, it is useful to look at two examples from Southeast Asia.

Example one: off-site costs of reservoir sedimentation on Java, Indonesia
Magrath and Arens (1989) examined the off-site costs of reservoir sedimentation in nine major dams on Java in terms of foregone hydroelectric and irrigation benefits. The basic assumption of the analysis was that the flow of these benefits were related to the remaining volume of storage in the reservoir. However, Magrath and Arens were unable to determine the precise relationship between active, dead and total reservoir capacity, and the effects of increased sedimentation on this relationship. Instead, they took as their upper and lower bounds the impact of sedimentation on loss of dead and total reservoir, assuming that these reductions would bracket the actual losses in active storage and thus hydroelectric and irrigation benefits.

The methods of calculation and results are shown in Table 13.3. Annual average sedimentation of around 24.8 million m^3 across the nine major reservoirs on Java reduce total reservoir capacity by around 0.5 per cent and dead storage capacity by 2.3 per cent. This results in an estimated annual loss of hydropower output of between 13.7 to 63 gigawatt hours (GWh) and 1.3 to 6.4 thousand ha respectively. Assuming an average price of electricity of around Rp 70/KWh, the annual loss in hydropower is valued at between Rp 958.4 and 4408.8 million (US$0.58 to 2.67 million). The reduction in irrigated cultivated area was valued by comparing the net returns to land with and without irrigation. That is, it was assumed that the formerly irrigated area would now be cultivated without irrigation water. The resulting difference in net returns amounted to Rp 1.2 million/ha. This suggests that the annual loss of reduced water for irrigation would be around Rp 1.73 to 7.94 billion (US$1.05 to 4.81 million). The total capitalized value of these combined annual hydropower and irrigation losses were estimated to be between Rp 26.9 and 123.5 billion (US$16.2 to 74.8 million). This range represents the estimate of the off-site costs of reservoir sedimentation.

By associating losses in hydropower and irrigation benefits with reductions in total and dead reservoir storage, Magrath and Arens obtain a fairly reliable range of estimates for the off-site costs of reservoir sedimentation. By capitalizing these annual losses, they are essentially assuming that the reductions in benefits are permanent. Given that loss of total storage is occurring at 0.5 per cent per year and dead storage at 2.3 per cent per year, it is likely that sedimentation may affect the active service life of the reservoirs and dams. Although Magrath and

Arens do indicate that the planned life of some of the major dams on Java may be affected, lack of data prevents them from calculating this additional cost of reservoir sedimentation. In any case, it is often difficult to determine how the active life of the dam is affected by such sedimentation.[10]

Table 13.3 Off-site costs from sedimentation of major reservoirs on Java, 1985

A. Storage Losses

	Initial capacity ('000 m^3)	Average sedim. rate ('000 m^3)	Annual total storage loss (%)	Initial dead storage ('000 m^3)	Annual dead storage loss (%)
Average all nine reservoirs, Java	5 297 500	24 801	0.47	1 074 500	2.31

B. *One-Year Hydropower and Irrigation Losses (Indonesian Rupiah (Rp) 1650 = US$ 1)*

	Hydropower	Irrigation	Total capitalized value (Rp '000)
Estimated output	2 738 412 Mwh	277 671 ha	
value (Rp/unit)	70/Kwh	1 244 000/ha	
Based on loss of total storage (0.5%)			
– Lost Output	13 692 Mwh	1388 ha	
– Annual Cost (Rp '000)	958 440	1 726 672	26 851 120
Based on loss of dead storage (2.3%)			
– Lost Output	62 984 Mwh	6386 ha	123 529 840
– Annual Cost (Rp '000)	4 408 800	7 944 184	

Source: Magrath and Arens (1989).

Example two: off-site costs of reservoir sedimentation in Magat and Pantabangan watersheds, the Philippines

Cruz, Francisco and Conway (1988) have also estimated the off-site costs of reservoir sedimentation of dams in the Magat and Pantabangan watersheds. Three components of these costs were measured: the reduction in service life of the dam; reduction in active storage for irrigation (Pantabangan only) and hydropower (Magat and Pantabangan); and the opportunity cost of dead storage for irrigation. Only annual and not capitalized costs were calculated. The results of the estimates are shown in Table 13.4.

Table 13.4 Off-site costs of sedimentation of Magat and Pantabangan reservoirs, the Philippines (Philippine Peso (₱) 21.3 = US$ 1)

	Annual Sedimentation cost (₱)[a]			
	Per hectare		per ton	
	Pantabangan	Magat	Pantabangan	Magat
Reduction in service life[b]	1.11	0.10	0.02	0.01
Reduction in active storage				
– for irrigation	12.99		1.19	
– for hydropower	2.91		0.15	
Opportunity cost of dead storage for irrigation	575.55	365.61	28.78	18.00
Total cost	592.56	365.71	30.14	18.01

Notes:
[a] The prices used for Patabangan are late 1970s prices; for Magat early 1980s prices are used.
[b] The Pantabangan estimates are based on the assumption that 75 per cent of sediments settle in dead storage and 25 per cent in active storage. For Magat, the assumption is that all sediments go to dead storage.

Source: Cruz, Francisco and Conway (1988).

The original service capacity of both the Magat and Pantabangan reservoirs was designed for an annual rate of sedimentation of 20 tons/ha per year. Thus their service lives were expected to be around 95 and 100 years respectively. However, actual sedimentation rates for Magat and Pantabangan are more likely to be 34.5 and 81 tons/ha/year respectively. Cruz, Francisco and Conway estimate that these changes in sedimentation rates will reduce the operational life of the Magat reservoir to 55 years and the Pantabangan reservoir to 61 years. Using a discount rate of 15 per cent, the present value of the net irrigation and hydropower benefits that are lost due to the reduced life of the two reservoirs were calculated and annualized. For the Magat reservoir the annual losses amount to ₱0.01 per ton of new sediment input per year, and for the Pantabangan reservoir ₱0.02 per ton.

For Pantabangan reservoir, it was assumed that 25 per cent of sediment deposition occurred in the active storage.[11] Cruz, Francisco and Conway suggest that the resulting displaced water could have been used for irrigation and hydropower generation. For example, an additional 70 ha could have been irrigated each year, and an 185 606 kWh of electricity generated. By employing with and without project estimates for irrigation, the yearly loss of irrigation benefits were estimated to be ₱3558/ha (US$167/ha). Assuming each year an additional 70 hectares were affected (that is, 70 ha in year one, 140 ha in year two, 210 ha in year three, and so on for the life of the dam), the present value of the stream of losses were calculated and annualized. The annualized loss totalled ₱1.19 per ton of sediment. Similarly, the annual loss of about ₱31 533 (US$1480) of power generation was expressed as a cumulative loss over the 61-year life of the reservoir, and the present value of this stream of losses was annualized. This amounted to₱0.15 per ton of sediment.

Finally, and most controversially, Cruz, Francisco and Conway argued that if the sediment, or dead storage, pools at Pantabangan and Magat had not been required to accumulate sediment, then the water stored in these pools could instead have been used for irrigation. They refer to this as the 'opportunity cost' of dead storage. The dead storage capacity of Magat reservoir is about 500 million m^3, and the sediment storage capacity of Pantabangan is around 225 million m^3. Using the same methods as described above for estimating lost irrigation benefits from displaced active storage, Cruz, Francisco and Conway calculate the opportunity costs of this water in terms of generating additional irrigation benefits to be ₱18 (US$0.84) and 28.78 (US$1.34) per ton of sediment for Magat and Pantabangan reservoirs respectively.

As can be seen from Table 13.4, by far the largest off-site costs of dam sedimentation are the opportunity costs of dead storage. Unfortunately, these latter costs are clearly overestimates. To assume that all the inactive storage of these reservoirs could be used instead to supply water for irrigation is tantamount to assuming that reservoir sedimentation could be reduced to zero. This is highly unlikely. All tropical watersheds are subject to some degree of 'natural' or 'background' erosion, which means that some degree of sedimentation storage in reservoirs must be planned for.[12] For example, as noted previously, the Pantabangan reservoir was designed for an annual rate of sedimentation of 20 tons/ha per year. With a sedimentation delivery rate of 30 per cent and a trap efficiency rate of 95 per cent, this amounts to a gross erosion rate in the upper watershed of around 70 t/ha per year. Given that over 45 per cent of the upper Pantabangan watershed is either grassland or cropland – which have an average gross erosion rate of 429 and 198 t/ha per year respectively – and that the average gross erosion rate across all land uses is 270 tons/ha per year, it is unrealistic to assume that the 'planned' dead storage of the reservoir could have been feasibly reduced below its present capacity. Thus there are really no 'opportunity costs' of the planned dead storage capacity of both the Magat and Pantabangan reservoirs, and these components of the off-site costs of sedimentation calculated by Cruz, Francisco and Conway should be ignored.

6. Conclusion

This chapter has explored several aspects of the economics of soil erosion, with reference to examples from Southeast Asia. Both the basic theory of the farm-level decisions to control soil erosion and the methodologies for estimating on-site and off-site costs of erosion have been explored.

Unfortunately, as the examples discussed here indicate, many popular approaches to estimating on-site costs may have yielded inaccurate results because these approaches have not fully taken on board some of the important points emphasized by the basic theory of the farm-level economics of soil erosion. Thus an important principle that this theory tells us is that the on-site cost of soil erosion must be the loss in the long-run net profitability of the farming system from not investing in soil conservation, provided of course that such an investment is an economically worthwhile alternative. That is, the on-site cost of soil erosion is the difference between the (present value) net returns of the farming system with soil conservation and the (present value) net returns with erosion. In the case of accounting for off-site costs, the main objective is to estimate the present value of any external costs arising from sedimentation and other downstream impacts. Although the methodologies for measuring these costs are usually standard approaches of estimating environmental externalities, mistakes can also be made if there is confusion over whether some physical downstream effects are true economic costs.

Finally, it is worth emphasizing that estimating the costs of soil erosion is only one dimension of improving economic approaches to the problem. In designing improved policies and investments to control erosion, a critical issue that must be addressed by policy makers and analysts alike is the farm-level incentives affecting a farming household's decisions to deplete or conserve topsoil. In Section 3, a whole host of factors influencing these incentives was explored briefly. Understanding why private and social rates of soil erosion might diverge gets to the heart of the economic problem of erosion, and deserves more treatment than is possible in this short chapter. Understanding how to design policies and investments to encourage farmers to 'move' towards more socially optimal rates of erosion is of course the greatest challenge of all, and certainly warrants more discussion than can be usefully covered here.

Appendix: a farm-level model of soil erosion

Barbier (1990) takes a formal model originally developed by McConnell (1983) and adapts it to describe the soil conservation decision of farmers in the upper watersheds in Java. For simplicity, it is assumed that the land holding is fixed and only one crop is produced, or if there are multiple crops, their combined production can be explained by a single crop production function.

The behaviour of the farming household in response to soil erosion is therefore determined by the impact of soil on profits. Thus the objective of the farming household is to maximize the following functional relationship of the net present value of income stream from farm land:

$$\text{Max}_{z_1,z_2}\text{PV} = \int_0^{T\to\infty} e^{-rt}\left[pf(z_1,x) - c_1 z_1 - c_2 z_2\right]\mathrm{d}t \quad (13.1)$$

subject to

$$\frac{\mathrm{d}x}{\mathrm{d}t} = \dot{x} = h(z_1, z_2),\ h_1 \leq 0,\ h_2 \geq 0,\ h_{22} \leq 0$$

$$x(0) = x_0,$$

where x = topsoil depth
z_1 = conventional crop production inputs
z_2 = conservation inputs
p = price of crops
$f(z_1, x)$ = crop production function, where $f_1 > 0, f_2 \geq 0$
r = farm household's private rate of discount
c_1 = costs of conventional inputs, and
c_2 = costs of conservation inputs.[13]

Allowing μ to represent the 'shadow' or 'implicit' price of soil, then the first-order conditions for maximizing (13.1) are:

$$pf_1 - c_1 + \mu h_1 = 0 \Rightarrow \frac{pf_1 - c_1}{-h_1} = \mu \quad (13.2)$$

$$-c_2 + \mu h_2 = 0 \Rightarrow \frac{c_2}{h_2} = \mu \quad (13.3)$$

$$\dot{\mu} = r\mu - pf_2 \Rightarrow \frac{\dot{\mu}}{\mu} + \frac{pf_2}{\mu} = r. \quad (13.4)$$

Condition (13.2) indicates that at any time t, for optimal use of conventional productive inputs, the value of the marginal product, pf_1, must be equal not only to the marginal costs of using these inputs, c_1, but also their additional costs in terms of worsening soil erosion, μh_1. Condition (13.3) shows that for optimal use of conservation inputs, the marginal costs of employing these inputs, c_2, must equal the additional value generated by controlling soil erosion, μh_2. Finally, condition (13.4) indicates that it is optimal to 'hold on' to soil up to the point where the 'capital gains' in terms of improved future value of the land from conserving soil, $d\mu/dt$, plus the contribution of soil to current profits, pf_2, must equal the opportunity costs of holding on to soil, $r\mu$. That is, the household could instead deplete the soil today and invest the proceeds elsewhere, obtaining a return $r\mu$. To see this, one can combine conditions (13.2) and (13.4) to obtain:

$$\dot{\mu} + pf_2 = r\mu = r\frac{(pf_1 - c_1)}{h_1}. \tag{13.5}$$

That is, it is worth conserving soil up to the point where the marginal gains from holding on to the soil as an asset must equal the marginal costs. The marginal gains are represented in condition (13.5) by the future and current value of having additional topsoil, $d\mu/dt + pf_2$, and the marginal costs are the foregone returns that could be earned from 'depleting' soil today and investing the proceeds elsewhere, $r[(pf_1 - c_1)/h_1]$. Note that in this model conservation requires the employment of inputs. Thus condition (13.3) must also still hold – that is, the marginal costs of employing these inputs, c_2, must equal the additional value generated by controlling soil erosion, μh_2. Consequently, conditions (13.3) and (13.5) together determine the overall costs and benefits to the farming household of controlling soil erosion and hence the 'optimal' level of erosion.

Note that the optimal conditions of this model assume that the farming household takes into account fully the 'shadow' price of the soil. That is, the household is aware that an increase in topsoil will lead to a marginal increase in the present value stream of income from the land, as represented by equation (13.1). As discussed in the text, for a variety of reasons the farming household may ignore or underestimate the shadow price of soil. Assume for example that the former is the case. In the above model, this is equivalent to assuming $\mu = 0$. Thus from (13.4) it follows that, to the household, the value of holding onto the soil will be

$$pf_2 = 0. \tag{13.6}$$

Soil will therefore be over-exploited because the household behaves as if there are no gains to conserving it. The result will clearly be excessive erosion.

Notes

* Paper based on a Presentation to the Fifth Biannual Workshop on Economy and Environment in Southeast Asia, Singapore, 28–30 November, 1995.

1. In fact, as will be argued in the next section, it is almost physically impossible to cultivate the soil continuously and simultaneously prevent any soil erosion from occurring.

2. For example, it is not uncommon for many physical conservation measures, such as bench terracing, bunds, gulley drains, and so on, to reduce the total land available for cultivation. On the other hand, on highly erodible soils, conservation can lead to improvements in productivity, particularly if the conservation measures are combined with changes in farming systems and crops that lead to better land management overall.
3. In what follows, Figures 13.1 to 13.3 are adapted from Dickson and Fox (1989).
4. This may not always be the case, as explained in Magrath and Arens (1989).
5. Another way of understanding this approach is to see the analogy with the standard 'with' and 'without project' method employed in cost–benefit analysis. That is, the farming system with soil erosion (that is, without conservation) is the 'without project' case, whereas the system with conservation is the 'with project' case. Therefore, the 'net loss' of choosing to continue eroding the soil must be the difference between the 'with' and 'without project' case.
6. Again, using the 'with' and 'without project' analogy, traditional cost–benefit analysis would suggest that if the net present value of the 'without project' case exceeds that of the 'with project' case, then the latter is essentially 'uneconomical' and the 'without project' case will always be preferred. Consequently, there would be no 'net loss' in economic terms of continuing with the 'without project' case.
7. Nevertheless, as Bishop (1995) has shown for Mali, it is possible to use limited data on conservation investments and costs to modify the change in productivity approach so as to produce estimates of on-site costs that more closely resemble the appropriate methodology for estimating these costs as outlined here. See also the original Mali results in Bishop and Allen (1989).
8. Given data limitations, Magrath and Arens (1989) were able to provide an estimation of on-site erosion costs for 1985 only. However, the results for 1985 were extrapolated for other years over the 1971–85 period by indexing physical erosion rates to the dryland cropping area in each year and indexing the costs of erosion to dryland crop prices in each year. The results are reported in Repetto *et al.* (1989).
9. Essentially the same replacement cost method was also applied to estimating the on-site cost of land degradation in the Pantabangan watershed. See Cruz, Francisco and Conway (1988) for further details.
10. As Magrath and Arens (1989) argue, it is unclear whether complete exhaustion of the planned dead storage of reservoirs is synonymous with the end of the economic life of a dam, as is often assumed.
11. The reservoir was designed to trap sediment in purpose-built sediment pools, but it was assumed that if excessive sedimentation occurred, some of it would find its way into the active water storage.
12. For example, Cruz, Francisco and Conway note that primary and secondary forest in the upper watershed has an average erosion rate of 2.15 tons/ha per year.
13. Where crop outputs or inputs are non-marketed, such as food produced for substitutes, in-kind inputs, labour exchange, and so on, p, c_1 and c_2 could represent the relative shadow prices respectively. Note also that including x in the production function assumes that there is an immediate productivity gain from soil conservation. In many situations, it may take some time before such a gain is realized.

References and suggested reading

Anderson, J.R. and J. Thampapillai (1990), 'Soil conservation in developing countries: project and policy intervention', *Policy and Research Series No. 8*, Washington, DC: The World Bank.

Barbier, E.B. (1989), 'Cash crops, food crops and sustainability: the case of Indonesia', *World Development*, **17** (6), 879–96.

Barbier, E.B. (1990) 'The farm-level economics of soil conservation: the uplands of Java', *Land Economics*, **66** (2), 199–211.

Barbier, E.B. and J.T. Bishop (1995), 'Economic values and incentives affecting soil and water conservation in developing countries', *Journal of Soil and Water Conservation*, (March–April), 133–7.

Barbier, E.B. and J.C. Burgess (1992), *Agricultural Pricing and Environmental Degradation*, Policy Research Working Papers, World Development Report, Washington, DC: The World Bank.

Bishop, J. (1995), 'The economics of soil degradation: an illustration of the change in productivity approach to valuation in Mali and Malawi', *LEEC Paper DP95–02*, Environmental Economics Programme, International Institute for Environment and Development, London.

Bishop, J. and J. Allen (1989), 'The on-site costs of soil erosion in Mali', Environment Dept. Working Paper No. 21, Washington, DC: The World Bank.

Bojö, J. (1991), 'Economics and land degradation', *AMBIO*, **22** (2), 75–9.

Conway, G.R. and E.B. Barbier (1990), *After the Green Revolution: Sustainable Agriculture for Development*, London: Earthscan.

Cruz, W., H.A. Francisco and Z.T. Conway (1988), 'The on-site and downstream costs of soil erosion in the Magat and Pantabangan watersheds', *Journal of Philippine Development*, **15** (26, 1), 85–111.

Dickson, E.J. and G. Fox (1989), *The Costs and Benefits of Erosion Control on Cropland in Southwestern Ontario*, Dept of Agricultural Economics and Business, Ontario Agricultural College, University of Guelph, Guelph, Ontario.

Feder, G. and T. Onchan (1987), 'Land ownership security and farm investments in Thailand', *American Journal of Agricultural Economics*, **69** (2), 311–20.

Kiker, C. and G. Lynne (1986), 'An economic model of soil conservation: comment', *American Journal of Agricultural Economics*, **68** (3), 739–42.

Lal, R. (1987) 'Effects of erosion on crop productivity', *Critical Reviews in Plant Sciences*, **5** (4), 303–67.

Lal, R. (1981), 'Soil erosion problems on Alfisols in Western Nigeria. VI Effects of erosion on experimental plots', *Geoderma*, **25**, 215.

Magrath, W. and P. Arens (1989), 'The costs of soil erosion on Java: a natural resource accounting approach', Environment Department Working Paper No. 18, Washington, DC: The World Bank.

McConnell, K.E. (1983), 'An economic model of soil conservation', *American Journal of Agricultural Economics*, **65** (1), 83–9.

McConnell, K.E. (1986), 'An economic model of soil conservation: a reply', *American Journal of Agricultural Economics*, **68** (3), 743–4.

Pearce, D.W., E.B. Barbier and A. Markandya (1990), *Sustainable Development: Economics and Environment in the Third World*, London: Earthscan.

Repetto, R. (1986), 'Soil loss and population pressure on Java', *AMBIO*, **15**, (1), 14–18.

Repetto, R., W. Magrath, M. Wells, C. Beer and F. Rossini (1989), *Wasting Assets: Natural Resources in the National Income Accounts*, Washington, DC: World Resources Institute.

Southgate, D. and R. Macke (1989), 'The downstream benefits of soil conservation in Third World hydroelectric watersheds', *Land Economics*, **65** (1), 38–48.

Stocking, M. (1987), 'Measuring land degradation', in P. Blaikie, and H. Brookfield (eds), *Land Degradation and Society*, London: Methuen, 49–63.

PART THREE

WETLANDS, WILDLANDS AND BIODIVERSITY

14. Economics for the wilds

Conservation and development: the role of economics

This chapter introduces some basic principles of economics that are relevant to wildlife and natural habitat preservation and management. The loss of the world's remaining natural areas and habitats for wild species is usually portrayed as a conflict between *development* and *preservation* options. Equally, the over-exploitation and extinction of key wildlife species is seen as the failure to preserve these species by controlling or limiting harvesting, hunting and extractive activities. Thus development is perceived as the principal threat to the continued survival of wildlife and wildlands, and 'stopping' development – at least for key species and select natural areas – is advocated as the best means for ensuring their preservation.

Portraying the alternative options as a 'polarized' choice between, at the one extreme, development, with the complete conversion or loss of natural areas and wildlife and, on the other, preservation, with no or extremely limited human use, is not always helpful. As previously noted, the vast majority of the world's remaining natural habitats are in the developing world, and only a modest fraction of this area is officially protected. For many developing countries, the option of 'preserving' all or most of their remaining areas of natural habitat as 'nature reserves' is unfeasible, given the social and economic pressures for increased economic development and poverty alleviation.

On the other hand, all societies must be made aware of the full costs of natural habitat conversion and loss. Too often, wildlands are treated as 'wastelands' and wildlife as 'free goods' to be exploited at little or no cost. Individuals undertaking the decision to exploit these resources face only the direct costs of converting natural habitats, extracting and harvesting natural products or hunting wildlife – and often these costs may be inadvertently or even deliberately subsidized through public policies. The wider social and environmental costs of habitat and wildlife loss – the 'external' costs imposed on others who benefited from the use of these resources, the disruptions to important ecological functions, the sacrifice of future income from depleting these assets today and the loss of unique species and natural areas that some may value merely for their existence – all these costs are rarely borne by the individual exploiters of wildlife and wildlands.

In sum, both the extreme development and preservation options for the remaining wildlife and natural areas of the world may have important and increasing social costs. Nevertheless, under certain conditions, the preservation option will be viewed as economically worthwhile – even in poorer developing countries – provided that the net benefits of creating a 'reserve' out of the natural area are perceived to be greater than any that development of the area could yield. Complete conversion of the natural area may also be justified if all the social and environmental costs of irreversible loss of this resource are properly accounted for and considered less than the gains from conversion.

Economics of sustainable management

In the majority of circumstances land and wildlife use options other than the conventional development and preservation extremes may be more attractive. There are a variety of conservation or sustainable management options that serve to maintain natural areas broadly in their original state and conserve wildlife species while at the same time allowing important human uses of these resources. Sustainable management regimes for these resources are extremely diverse, ranging from commercial wildlife ranching and harvesting to non-timber forest product extraction to community-based wildlife and wildlands development to tourism and recreation, and so on.

Because they appear to reconcile development and conservation objectives, sustainable management options for wildlife and natural areas are extremely attractive. However, just like any other option, a sustainable management regime will have a range of economic costs and benefits associated with it. These costs and benefits will, of course, vary considerably for different sustainable management options and for different locations and at different times. Thus it may be presumptuous to assume that a given sustainable management regime may always be economically worthwhile in all times and places. Box 14.1 illustrates this with the example of wildlife culling in Africa.

Careful economic assessment of the costs and benefits of a sustainable management option is required, both from the financial perspective of the individual or individuals undertaking the activity and from the economic perspective of society as a whole. The net benefits of sustainable management must also be compared to the net benefits of any other land and wildlife use options – perhaps a conventional development or preservation alternative – in order to determine which option is indeed the most economically worthwhile to pursue. Such an approach offers the best chance of encouraging efficient and sustainable use of our remaining, and rapidly dwindling, natural areas and wildlife resources.

Box 14.2 illustrates the usefulness of assessing the comparative returns to wildlife management options with an example from Botswana. The financial and economic returns indicate that, with the exception of game ranching, most wildlife management schemes are more profitable than cattle ranching for beef production, which is the main alternative use of rangelands in Botswana.

Total economic value

Unfortunately, it is rare that such an assessment as the one illustrated in Box 14.2 takes place. Moreover, even this example was only a partial analysis of comparative economic returns, to reflect accurately the costs and benefits of different land and wildlife use options, it is necessary to assess the total economic value (TEV), both marketed and non-marketed, that each option entails. TEV comprises direct and indirect use values, option values and

Box 14.1 Commercial wildlife cropping in Africa: successes and failures

Wildlife cropping or *culling* essentially implies the harvesting of wild animals to provide continuous, sustainable supplies of animal products – meat, hides, trophies, and so on. As distinct from traditional hunting practices for food and other subsistence needs and safari hunting for recreational sport, commercial cropping involves organized hunting operations to supply wildlife products to markets for financial gain. In some cases, control of wildlife populations is also an objective. More recently, cropping has been promoted as a viable sustainable management option for wildlife utilization and natural habitat conservation, and as a means to generate employment and revenues for local communities.

Since 1960, many commercial cropping schemes of elephants, hippos and smaller animals have been implemented with varying degrees of success in East, Central and Southern Africa. Although many projects have failed because they were unable to produce a safe, hygienic source of meat or had misjudged population densities, the vast majority were unsuccessful because the projects were simply financially unviable due to misjudgement of market demand, the costs of production and the constraints of rural subsistence economies. Very few commercial cropping schemes are ever subject to economic and financial analysis even to give a rough indication of their relative costs and benefits.

One exception is the analysis of the cropping scheme run by the Tanzanian Wildlife Corporation (TAWICO), which was appraised after four months of operation. The scheme essentially produced both skins (lion and zebra) and meat (zebra and wildebeest). The financial analysis indicated that after four months of operation the scheme returned a modest profit of about US$6650 (1988 prices). Other observed points were:

- neither the skins nor the meat alone led to a profit; profitability depended on both being taken;
- although the average costs of shooting and marketing products were high (around US$73 per animal), these costs were standard for commercial cropping schemes of this kind and do not indicate any inefficiencies;
- the type of operation would not benefit from economies of scale; on the contrary, any increase in yield must be achieved either by changing cropping methods or by increasing the number of shooting parties in the field.

A further analysis was conducted to see whether a large operation could increase foreign exchange earnings through selling wildebeest meat to external markets in Gulf states (zebra meat is not acceptable in these countries). The results are shown opposite.

Box 14.1 (continued)

Returns to exporting 1kg of culled wildebeest meat from Tanzania to Gulf markets (in US$)

Gross revenue	3.12
Major costs	2.72
of which:	
Freight and handling	2.10
Shooting	0.62
Net revenue	0.40
Additional (unquantified costs), for example:	
Transportation within Tanzania	
Chilling	
Butchering	
Packing	
Administrative overheads	
Contingencies	
Project net revenues	<0.0

The analysis shows that estimated net revenues of US$0.40 per kg are unlikely to meet the unquantified additional costs associated with this kind of operation. The conclusion reached was that the existing medium-scale cropping schemes run by TAWICO are close to optimal for the special conditions of Tanzania. Any attempt to expand the operations to export meat would probably undermine their profitability.

Source: I.S.C. Parker, 'Perspectives on Wildlife Cropping or Culling', Chapter 16 in R.H.V. Bell and E. McShane Caluzi (eds), *Conservation and Wildlife Management in Africa*, US Peace Corps, Washington, DC, 1984. Ministry of Lands, Natural Resources and Tourism, Tanzania, in collaboration with the International Trade Centre and IUCN, *Wildlife Utilisation in Tanzania*, IUCN, Gland, Switzerland, 1988.

existence values (see Box 14.3). Direct use values include wildlife and other harvested products (for example, skins, hides, tusks/horns, plants, resins) and direct use of natural areas for tourism and recreation. Indirect use values are essentially the ecological functions of species and natural areas (for example, protection, microclimatic and material cycling functions). All these values may have an 'option value' component if we are interested in preserving them for future use. Finally, existence value includes the values that people place on wildlife and natural areas 'in themselves' and is unrelated to any use.

Calculation of the above components of total economic value is important for assessing the costs and benefits of different wildlife and wildland use options. For example, if conversion of a natural area to agriculture entails the loss of natural habitat and environmental functions, we need to know exactly what

Box 14.2 Botswana – comparative returns to wildlife management options

The following table shows financial and economic rates of return in Botswana to different wildlife management options, in comparison to cattle ranching for beef production. With a cut-off rate of 10–12 per cent (that is, options exhibiting rates of return at this level or higher are acceptable, most wildlife management options should proceed. In comparison, beef production appears to be unprofitable. Moreover, the returns to cattle ranching do not take into account the subsidies for beef production in Botswana. Thus the subsidy is very uneconomic as it supports an industry that would not otherwise break even, displaces other more profitable wildlife management options and over the long term gives rise to land degradation. Surprisingly, game ranching also shows an unacceptable rate of turn, which underlies the need to assess carefully the costs and benefits of different wildlife management options before selecting the appropriate one to pursue.

Project	Internal rate of return (%)		Comment
	Financial	Economic	
Group small scale game harvesting	21	28	Biltong, skins, trophies, hunting
Ostrich farming	19	14	Skins, feathers, meat
Crocodile farming	18	14	Skins, tailmeat
Tourist lodge	18	35	
Safari hunting	16	45	<3% animal offtake, 12 bed lodge
Game ranching	6	7	Meat, hunting, live animals, 9000 ha
Cattle ranching	5	na	Beef, 6500 ha

Source: J. Barnes and D.W. Pearce, 'The Mixed Use of Habitat', mimeo, Centre for Social and Economic Research on the Global Environment, London, 1991.

economic values are being sacrificed by taking up this development option. However, care should be taken in adding up the various components of TEV, as there are inevitable trade-offs among them. Furthermore, a measure of TEV in itself does not tell us anything about the opportunity costs – the next best wildlife or wildland use option foregone – of a given development option. Only by carefully comparing the full costs and benefits of different options is it possible to determine which ones should take place. As noted above, even complete conversion of natural areas may be warranted if the benefits of this development option exceed the full economic and social costs of conservation.[1]

A major problem is that many of the components in total economic value have no market – especially subsistence use of wildlife and wildland products and the indirect use, option and existence values of natural areas. These values are often difficult to assess in developing countries, yet the few studies that have been made suggest that the various values of wildlife products and natural areas are considerable (see Table 14.1).

Box 14.3 Total economic value of wildlife and wildlands
The table indicates the many *use* and *non-use* values of wildlife and wildlands that may comprise their *total economic value* (TEV):

Classification of total economic value for wildlife and wildlands

Use values			Non-use values
(1) Direct value	(2) Indirect value	(3) Option value	Existence value
Sustainably harvested products (meat/fish, timber, plants, and so on)	Ecological functions/ roles	Future uses as per (1), (2)	Biodiversity
	Protection functions		Culture, heritage
Recreation	Waste assimilation		
Tourism			
Genetic material	Microclimatic functions		
Education	Carbon store		
Human habitat			
Other services (water transport/supply)			

Direct use values are the resources and 'services' provided directly by natural areas, or by directly harvesting and exploiting wildlife. *Indirect use values* comprise mainly the environmental functions of natural areas – ecological functions, such as nutrient cycling, protection functions, such as ground cover for key watersheds, waste assimilation functions, such as the retention or detoxification of pollution and wider functions such as microclimatic stabilization and carbon storage. These environmental functions all indirectly support economic activity and human welfare. However, wildlife species may also have important indirect use value through key ecological roles; for example, elephants are known to have an essential ecological role in African savannahs and forests through diversifying ecosystems, dispersing seeds, reducing bushlands, expanding grasslands and reducing tsetse fly, which is of value to livestock grazing (Western, 1989).

Option value relates to the amount that individuals would be willing to pay to conserve wildlife and wildlands, or at least some of their direct and indirect applications, for future use. Individuals are essentially valuing the guaranteed 'option' of future supply of these uses, the availability of which might otherwise be uncertain. *Existence value* relates to valuation of these resources as unique assets in themselves, with no connection to their use values. This would include the worth of wildlife species, natural areas and overall biodiversity as objects of intrinsic and 'stewardship' value and as unique cultural and heritage assets. As essentially an *attribute* of natural areas rather than a resource or function, biodiversity has a special value relationship (Aylward and Barbier, 1991). In addition to having existence value, the diversity of biological resources may contribute to the direct use value of a natural area for scientific research, education and as a source of genetic material. Biodiversity may also have additional indirect use value in protecting ecological stability and functions.

Table 14.1 Some recent wildlife and wildlands valuation estimates for developing countries (US$)

Direct use values	
Pre-ban ivory exports, Africa	$35–45 million/year
(Barbier *et al.*, 1990)	
Fruit and latex forest harvesting, Peru	$6330/ha
Sustainable timber harvesting, Peru	$490/ha
(Peters, Gentry and Mendelsohn, 1989)	
Buffalo range ranching, Zimbabwe	$3.5–4.5/ha
(Child, 1990)	
Wetlands fish and fuelwood, Nigeria	$38–59/ha
(Barbier, Adams and Kimmage, 1991)	
Viewing value of elephants, Kenya	$25 million/year
(Brown and Henry, 1989)	
Ecotourism, Costa Rica	$1250/ha
(Tobias and Mendelsohn, 1990)	
Tourism, Thailand	$385–860 000/year
Research/education, Thailand	$38–77 000/year
(Dixon and Sherman, 1990)	
Tourism, Cameroon	$19/ha
Genetic value, Cameroon	$7/ha
(Ruitenbeek, 1989)	
Indirect use values	
Watershed protection of fisheries, Cameroon	$54/ha
Control of flooding, Cameroon	$23/ha
Soil fertility maintenance, Cameroon	$8/ha
(Ruitenbeek, 1889)	
Carbon storage, tropical forests	$1300/ha/year
(Pearce, 1990)	
Option/Existence values	
Elephants and other species, Thailand	$4.7 million/year
(Dixon and Sherman, 1990)	
Amazonian forests	$3.2 billion
(Pearce, 1990)	

Unless valuation of these resources in developing countries is made specific, actual choice of natural land and habitat use is usually biased in favour of development and conversion options that do have marketed outputs, for example, ranching, timber exploitation, agriculture, mining, hydroelectricity. Alternatively, only marketed wildlife and wildland products, for example, game meat, hides/skins, horns/tusks, fruits/nuts, rattan/bamboos, are seen to have 'value', and these products are harvested or exploited exclusively for this purpose. The result is often too much conversion and over-exploitation, and too little sustainable management, of natural lands and products.[2]

Many of the studies indicated in Table 14.1 have shown that, when proper account is taken of the values of natural areas and products, sustainable management of these areas makes sound economic sense. Peters, Gentry and Mendelsohn (1989) have shown that the discounted financial returns from non-timber harvesting of fruit and latex plus selective cutting of timber from a rainforest in Peru easily exceed the returns from alternative options, such as clear-cutting timber, plantation harvesting and cattle ranching. Barbier, Adams and Kimmage (1991) demonstrated that the direct uses of the natural Hadejia-Jama'are floodplain in Northern Nigeria for fishing, fuelwood and recession agriculture appear to offer much higher economic returns than upstream irrigation developments that are diverting water away from the floodplain. The study by Ruitenbeek (1989) for the Korup Project, Cameroon, concluded that the economic benefits from preserving Korup National Park and from sustainable management of buffer zones were much greater than the direct costs of the project plus any foregone timber earnings and the lost production from resettling six villages. Similarly, Dixon and Sherman (1990) maintain that the various direct and indirect benefits of Khao Yai National Park place it in the socially beneficial category (that is, the net benefits to society at large are positive), thus deserving continued public support as a protected area.

Economic decision making over resource use

The failure to appreciate and assess the total economic value of wildlife and wildlands often results in a distortion in economic incentives. That is, excessive loss of natural areas and habitats is the outcome of their values not being fully recognized and integrated into decision-making processes by individuals in the market place and by government. If markets fail fully to reflect these values, then market failure is said to exist. Where government decisions or policies do not fully reflect the 'socially beneficial' values of natural areas, there is government or policy failure.

Throughout the developing world, the presence of environmental 'externalities', poorly defined property rights for resources, incomplete markets for labour and capital, endemic poverty and income constraints, imperfect competition, and high levels of uncertainty have limited the effectiveness of markets in reflecting the full social benefits of wildlife and wildlands. The existence of poorly formulated economic and regulatory policies has further exacerbated problems of natural resource management. By failing to make markets and private decision makers accountable for foregone values of natural areas, habitats and species, these policies may contribute to market failure. At worst, the direct private costs of resource-using and conversion activities are subsidized and/or distorted, thus encouraging the excessive loss of wildlife and wildlands.[3]

Appropriate incentive structures must be set against the context of management regimes – access and rights to land and other resources. Throughout the developing world, four types of resource management regimes exist – private ownership, common property ownership, state ownership and open access. In private ownership, resource rights and ownership are conferred on a private individual or group of individuals. For example, much farmland in developing countries is privately owned. In state or public ownership, resource ownership is vested in the government, which also tries to determine and control resource rights and ownership. Officially protected areas and many other natural resources – forests, mines, coastal seas, even wild animals – are often subject to state ownership in developing countries. However, the ability of these governments to control or regulate access to these resources is frequently undermined by high costs and lack of funds. Common property is the ownership and management of resources by a reasonably defined community. Often, communities will jointly own grazing land, forest, woodlots and even farmland.

A frequent misperception is that common property leads to overexploitation by individuals – the 'tragedy of the commons' – and should be replaced by state or private ownership of resources. However, many common property regimes traditionally have involved the sustainable use of resources, but may break down due to overpopulation, policy failures and the expropriation of resource ownership and rights. This often occurs in the case of wildlife and wildlands, where community management of these wild resources consists mainly of important social rules and rituals governing traditional 'rights of access' and harvesting. Such management systems are easily undermined by external forces of change.[4]

Open access exploitation increases the risks of rapid resource degradation of wildlife and wildlands. As exclusion (or control of access) of users is problematic, each individual has the incentive to exploit the resource as quickly as possible. Each individual will therefore ignore any user costs of exploitation; that is, the concern will be with maximizing returns today – before they are lost to somebody else – rather than with the loss of future income owing to resource depletion. Perversely, the presence of surplus profit, or economic rent, will also encourage overexploitation.[5] If large profits are available from resource exploitation but they accrue exclusively, say, to a single individual or to the government, then the single resource owner can sustain the income earned indefinitely by limiting overexploitation. However, if it is impossible to exclude others from exploiting the resource as well, then the existence of excess rents will be an incentive for many individuals to undertake this activity, or alternatively for the individuals already exploiting the resource to expand their activities. The result is that any profits will be quickly dissipated, as returns become rapidly dispersed over a growing number of individuals, none of whom will have any incentive to conserve the resource. In many developing countries, government policies – fiscal incentives, pricing policies, regulations and land titling – often exacerbate these tendencies by reducing or distorting the direct cost of rapid resource exploitation and conversion.[6]

Comparative returns and discounting

Another major problem affecting the incentives for managing natural areas and wildlife in developing economies is whether the returns realized in 'conserving' or 'holding on' to these resources is greater than the income earned from alternative sources. If wildlife and wildlands are considered a valuable asset, that is, a source of wealth that increases in value over time, then it may be worthwhile to maintain these resources into the future to take advantage of this increasing value. We have already seen how open access exploitation can undermine this incentive. In addition, there are other forms of wealth, or assets, that yield income. The comparable returns from these assets will determine the general rate of interest in the economy. Individuals therefore have the choice of harvesting or converting wild resources today and investing the returns in alternative economic assets, or 'holding on' to these resources to reap future income from them. Thus, the opportunity cost of conserving wildlife and other natural resources if the foregone earnings from alternative assets, as represented by the interest rate. Or another way of looking at it, in order to be economically worthwhile, the future income earned from maintaining wildlife and wildlands must be discounted at the rate of interest earned on other assets.

In addition, the rate at which we discount the future value of wildlife and natural areas is affected by individuals' time preference. That is, people may be reluctant to wait for future returns from maintaining wild resources because they are simply impatient for money now, because of uncertainty over the future (including a high risk of death) and because improving incomes mean that additional wealth in the future is less valuable today. In rural areas in developing countries, uncertainty of the future is compounded by threats of drought and other natural disasters, political instability and warfare, economic disruptions and policy changes and the cumulative impacts of widespread natural resource degradation. Finally, poverty itself may force individuals to have a high rate of time preference: under conditions of extreme poverty, a household's major concern is securing sufficient means for survival today.

Public policies also can affect the comparative returns to conserving wild resources by distorting capital markets and affecting individuals' perceptions of the future. For example, in many developing countries, scarce financial credit is often allocated through subsidies and tax inducements to certain economic activities, such as investments in large-scale commercial agriculture and industry, while the vast majority of rural households must rely on informal sources of credit with effective interest rates of 50 to 200 per cent or even higher. Thus, on the one hand, subsidized formal credit assists large-scale conversion of wildlands and natural habitat to 'income-earning' activities such as commercial ranching, agriculture and forestry. On the other, the lack of formal credit in many rural areas means that small farmers and pastoralists are discouraged from 'conserving' wild resources for future gain. They are also discouraged from borrowing to invest in land improvements and intensification that will contribute to future productivity. Instead, extending production into the remaining 'frontier' areas of natural habitat is the only means of guaranteeing subsistence and income.[7]

Sustainable development and resource management

So far we have argued that by affecting the relationships between prices, costs and the return on comparable investments – as reflected in the interest or discount rate – market and policy failures in developing countries distort the incentives for conservation of wild resources. Yet, paradoxically, excessive exploitation of wildlife and wildlands leads to the loss of important economic values. As these values are 'socially beneficial', appropriate public policies must be designed to ensure the protection and sustainable management of wild resources.

Wildlands and wildlife also have an important role to play in the sustainable development of developing countries. Sustainable development has been defined by the World Commission on Environment and Development (1987) as 'development that meets the needs of the present without compromising the ability of future generations to meet their own needs'. Underlying this concept is the notion of *intergenerational equity*; that is, future generations should enjoy at least the same, if not greater, economic opportunities as present generations. Since our economic opportunities are determined by our wealth, that is, by the value of the capital stock that we hold, then we can meet our obligations to the future by leaving them an inheritance of wealth no less than we inherited.

Now, if we are confident that our stock of man-made capital, skilled labour and environmental assets are totally interchangeable – that is, they can all perform the same functions and yield similar goods – then any irreversible loss of environmental assets would not matter as the environmental values foregone could be compensated for by greater man-made assets or labour. However, if future and current environmental values are unknown, particularly if there is uncertainty concerning cumulative environmental impacts, and if some of the ecological functions and goods provided by our 'natural' capital cannot easily be substituted for by man-made capital or labour, then irreversible loss of natural resources should be avoided.[8]

As argued in this chapter, much of the world's remaining wildlands and wildlife have substantial economic values that are not fully accounted for when decisions concerning their utilization are taken. Moreover, many of the environmental goods and services lost when natural resources such as wild species, wetlands, coral reefs, primary forest and so on are irreversibly degraded or depleted cannot be simply replaced by accumulation of more man-made capital or increasingly skilled labour. As the stock of natural capital declines, even in developing countries the increasing 'relative' scarcity of the economic values it provides will be felt in terms of diminishing economic welfare. Widespread environmental degradation and species loss can also push 'ecologically vulnerable' economic activities – fishing, pastoralism, fuelwood extraction, dryland farming – into the thresholds of carrying capacity, and ultimately environmental collapse.[9]

However, the emphasis of much of the sustainable development literature on the role of natural resources in securing the needs of future generations often obscures the important function of environmental assets in current development efforts. As argued by Barbier (1991b), there are several reasons why efficient and sustainable management of natural resources should be an important development goal, particularly for low income countries.

First, many of the low and lower-middle income economies of the world are currently dependent, and will continue to be dependent, on natural resource-based commodities for the largest share of their export-led development efforts– in terms of both economic growth and meeting debt repayments. Many of these economies rely on only one or two commodities for the majority of their export earnings. If these economies are to diversify their export base, their comparative advantage will most likely lie in the development of other natural resource-based products. Sustainable management of wildlife and wildlands will figure prominently in providing these products (Swanson, 1991).

Second, even if natural resource systems do not directly provide additional products for developing economies, they have important indirect use value in supporting and maintaining economic activity. As will be discussed in the following chapter, the role of natural systems and resources in protecting watersheds, maintain soil fertility, controlling flooding, preventing storm damage and mitigating pollution is often vital to human welfare and economic production in developing regions.

Finally, wildlands and wildlife are also important resources to the livelihood security of the poorest groups in developing countries. The vast majority of the rural 'core' poor live in ecologically fragile areas, cultivating marginal lands of low agricultural potential and directly dependent on natural resources for their livelihoods, that is, dependent on woody biomass and vegetation for livestock fodder, fuelwood and raw materials; wildlife meat and fish for protein; water supplies for domestic use; and so forth. Dependence on wild goods and resources by the rural poor increases when cultivated food and market supplies are scarce and during times of emergency brought on by drought, war and famine. Thus, more often than not, sustainability of the livelihoods of the poor is linked to the sustainability of natural resource systems and wildlife resources. Sustainable management of these assets may therefore be just as important for *intragenerational equity* – the need for the poor to gain better livelihoods – as it is for *intergenerational equity* – meeting the needs of future generations, or alternatively, the future needs of the present generation.

Conclusion

This brief chapter has introduced some of the important economic principles underlying management of the wilds in developing countries. The main message has been to emphasize that wildlife and wildland management decisions are essentially 'economic' choices that have important implications for the allocation of resources, and as a consequence, economics has an important role to play in determining appropriate management decisions for the wilds. Moreover, if wild resources are important to the economic development and welfare of developing countries, then more effort is required to ensure that proper economic analysis of this role is taking place.

Notes

1. For further discussion of the methodology for economic appraisal of different land use options for natural areas, for example, tropical forests and wetlands, and of environmental functions see Aylward and Barbier (1991), Barbier (1989a and 1991c) and Pearce (1990).
2. For a recent overview of the conversion versus conservation dilemma facing natural lands and wildlife, see Swanson (1991). There are also specific studies relevant to developing countries on the economic appraisal of land use options for protected areas (Dixon and Sherman, 1990); tropical wetlands (Barbier, 1989a; Barbier, Adams and Kimmage, 1991; Turner, 1991); tropical forests (Pearce, 1990; Ruitenbeek, 1989); and coastal systems (Hodgson and Dixon, 1988). Further studies are cited throughout this volume.
3. For an overview of market and policy failures and their impact on environmental degradation in developing countries, see Barbier (1991a, b); Pearce, Barbier and Markandya (1990) and Repetto (1988).
4. For example, Moorehead (1989) details the process of rapid breakdown in the common-property management systems that have developed over hundreds of years in the inland Niger delta of Mali. Richards (1985) describes a similar process for traditional harvesting and access rights to forest and forage resources in Sierra Leone. Marks (1983) argues how the displacement and abrogation of traditional hunting rights in the Luangwa Valley of Zambia encourages 'illegal hunting' of wildlife and the alienation of local communities from conservation efforts.
5. In economics, *rent* is the difference between the total value of selling a commodity and the costs of supplying it. Thus, rent can in principle be determined by deducting from the gross income earned the costs of labour, material and capital inputs (including the costs of paying a normal return, or profit, to capital). The existence of rent therefore implies more remuneration than is required to keep an activity in operation – hence the term *surplus profit*.
6. Barbier *et al.* (1990) analyse how inappropriate international and domestic management of the ivory trade has contributed to rent dispersion and dissipation, thus leading to over-harvesting of the African elephant and undermining conservation efforts (Pearce, 1990).
7. For further discussion of environmental problems in developing countries and discounting see Pearce, Barbier and Markandya (1990, ch. 2).
8. For further discussion of this particular economic interpretation of sustainable development and its implications for developing countries see Böjo, Mäler and Unemo (1990) and Pearce, Barbier and Markandya (1990).
9. On the role of pervasive environmental degradation in natural resource scarcity and development, see Barbier (1989b).

References

Aylward, B.A. and E.B. Barbier (1991), 'Valuing environmental functions in developing countries', in *Biodiversity and Conservation*, Vol. 1, 34–50.

Barbier, E.B. (1989a), *The Economic Value of Ecosystems: 1 – Tropical Wetlands*, LEEC Gatekeeper Series GK 89–02, London: London Environmental Economics Centre.

Barbier, E.B. (1989b), *Economics, Natural Resource Scarcity and Development: Conventional and Alternative Views*, London: Earthscan.

Barbier, E.B. (1991a), 'Environmental degradation in the third world', in D.W. Pearce *et al.* (eds), *Blueprint 2: Greening the World Economy*, London: Earthscan.

Barbier, E.B. (1991b), 'Environmental management and development in the south: prerequisites for sustainable development', Paper prepared for the UNCED Symposium *Sustainable Development: From Concept to Action*, The Hague.

Barbier, E.B. (1991c), *The Economic Value of Ecosystems: 2 – Tropical Forests*, LEEC Gatekeeper Series 91–01, London: London Environmental Economics Centre.

Barbier, E.B., W.M. Adams and K. Kimmage (1991), *Economic Valuation of Wetland Benefits: The Hadejia-Jama'are Floodplain, Nigeria*, LEEC Discussion Paper 91–02, London: London Environmental Economics Centre.

Barbier, E.B., J.C. Burgess, T.M. Swanson and D.W. Pearce (1990), *Elephants, Economics and Ivory*, London: Earthscan.

Böjo, J., K.-G. Mäler and L. Unemo (1990), *Environment and Development: An Economic Approach*, London: Kluwer.

Brown, G. Jr. and W. Henry (1989), *The Economic Value of Elephants*, LEEC Discussion Paper 89–12, London: London Environmental Economics Centre.

Child, B. (1990), 'Assessment of wildlife utilization as a land use option in the semi-arid rangeland of Southern Africa', in A. Kiss (ed.), *Living with Wildlife: Wildlife Resource Management with Local Participation in Africa*, Technical Paper No. 130, Washington, DC: World Bank.

Dixon, J.A. and P. Sherman (1990), *Economics of Protected Areas: A New Look at Benefits and Costs*, London: Earthscan.

Hodgson, G. and J.A. Dixon (1990), *Logging Versus Fisheries and Tourism in Palawan*, East–West Environment and Policy Institute Occasional Paper No. 7, Honolulu: East–West Center.

Marks, S.A. (1983), *The Imperial Lion: Human Dimensions of Wildlife Management in Central Africa*, Boulder, CO: Westview Press.

Moorehead, R. (1989), 'Changes taking place in common-property resource management in the inland Niger delta of Mali', in F. Birkes (ed.), *Common Property Resources: Ecology and Community-Based Sustainable Development*, London: Belhaven Press.

Pearce, D.W. (1990), *An Economic Approach to Saving the Tropical Forests*, LEEC Discussion Paper 90–05, London: London Environmental Economics Centre.

Pearce, D.W., E.B. Barbier and A. Markandya (1990), *Sustainable Development: Economics and Environment in the Third World*, London: Earthscan and Edward Elgar.

Peters, C., A. Gentry and R. Mendelsohn (1989), 'Valuation of an Amazonian rainforest', *Nature*, **339**, 655–6.

Repetto, R. (1988), *Economic Policy Reform for Natural Resource Conservation*, Environment Department Working Paper No. 4, Washington, DC: World Bank.

Richards, P. (1985), *Indigenous Agricultural Revolution*, London: Hutchinson.

Ruitenbeek, H.J. (1989), *Social Cost–Benefit Analysis of the Korup Project, Cameroon*, Report prepared for the World Wide Fund for Nature and the Republic of Cameroon, London.

Swanson, T.M. (1991), 'Conserving biological diversity', in D.W. Pearce *et al.* (eds), *Blueprint 2: Greening the World Economy*, London: Earthscan.

Tobias, D. and R. Mendelsohn (1990), 'Valuing ecotourism in a tropical rainforest reserve', *AMBIO*, **20** (2), 91–3.

Turner, R.K. (1991), 'Economics and wetland management', *AMBIO*, **20** (2), 59–63.

Western D. (1989), 'The ecological value of elephants, a keystone role in African ecosystems', in the ITRG Report, *The Ivory Trade and the Future of the African Elephant*, Prepared for the Second Meeting of the CITES African Elephant Working Group, Gabarone, Botswana, July.

World Commission on Environment and Development (1987), *Our Common Future*, Oxford: Oxford University Press.

15. An economic valuation of wetland benefits

with W.M. Adams and K. Kimmage

In northeast Nigeria, an extensive floodplain has been created where the Hadejia and Jama'are rivers combine to form the Komadugu Yobe river which drains into Lake Chad. The Hadejia-Jama'are floodplain wetlands stretch from the towns of Hadejia in the west, Nguru in the north and Gashua in the east. Although referred to as wetlands, much of the floodplain in dry for some or all of the year. In recent years, the maximum extent of flooding has ranged from 70 000 to 90 000 hectares. Since 1987, the floodplain has been the focus of the Hadejia-Nguru Wetlands Project, which is directly concerned with the conservation and sustainable management of the entire floodplain.

The Hadejia-Jama'are floodplain provides essential income and nutrition benefits in the form of agriculture, grazing resources, non-timber forest products, fuelwood and fishing for local populations. The wetlands also serve wider regional economic purposes, such as providing dry-season grazing for semi-nomadic pastoralists, agricultural surpluses for Kano and Borno states, groundwater recharge of the Chad Formation aquifer and 'insurance' resources in times of drought. In addition, the wetlands are a unique migratory habitat for many wildfowl and wader species from Palaearctic regions, and contain a number of forestry reserves. The region therefore has important tourism, educational and scientific potential.

In recent decades the wetlands have come under increasing pressure from drought, and upstream and downstream water developments. Upstream developments are affecting incoming water, either through dams altering the timing and size of flood flows or through diverting surface or groundwater for irrigation. Increased demand for water downstream for irrigated agriculture may lead to water being diverted past the wetlands through bypass channels. Intensified human use within the floodplain itself, notably wheat irrigation, is also putting pressure on the wetlands and fisheries resources are under some threat.

These developments are taking place without explicit consideration of their impacts on the floodplain or any subsequent loss of economic benefits that are currently provided by use of the floodplain. Water diverted to upstream and downstream uses clearly has an 'opportunity cost', or alternative use, in the form of the various wetland benefits provided by the floodplain.

The choices to be made in the use of the water in the Hadejia and Jama'are rivers are complex and difficult. There are trade-offs to be made between uses upstream, in the wetlands, or downstream. To a large extent, these uses are competitive for the limited amount of water available. Both users within the wetlands and those further downstream are threatened by consumptive use in headwater states. Irrigation at the top of the river basin threatens all downstream users. This is particularly serious since irrigation and hence water demand, is expanding in both the wetlands and downstream.

In the absence of a clear development plan for the basin, and lacking the data necessary to calibrate a full hydrological model, it is difficult to reach an entirely satisfactory solution. Nonetheless, it is clear that a great deal more needs to be known about the economics of each of the competing uses of water, and that information has to be placed within a clear decision- and policy-making structure. Otherwise the use of water will not only be economically inefficient, but also many people will suffer needlessly because of its maldistribution.

Economic appraisal methodology

Given the competing uses for water, any upstream or downstream development that diverts water that would otherwise reach the Hadejia-Nguru wetlands carries an additional cost. This cost is the loss in wetland benefits arising from any detrimental impacts on the floodplain. Thus, the net benefits of a development project cannot be appraised in terms of its direct benefits and costs alone. The foregone net benefits of disruption to the wetlands must also be included as part of the costs of diverting water away from the floodplain to development projects.

For example, assume that there is an upstream irrigation project on the Hadejia River that is providing water for agriculture. Given direct benefits (for example, irrigation water for farming), B^D, and direct costs (for example, costs of constructing the dam, irrigation channels, and so on), C^D, then the direct net benefits of the project are:

$$NB^D = B^D - C^D \tag{15.1}$$

It is assumed, of course, that all costs and benefits are discounted at some positive rate into present value terms. However, by diverting water that would otherwise flow into the downstream wetlands, the development project may result in losses to floodplain agriculture and other primary production activities, less groundwater recharge and other external impacts. Given these reductions in the net production and environmental benefits of the wetlands, NB^W, then the true net benefits of the development project (NB^P) are $NB^D - NB^W$. The development project can therefore only be acceptable if:

$$NB^P = NB^D - NB^W > 0 \qquad (15.2)$$

If the wetland benefits are as significant as they appear to be in the case of the Hadejia-Nguru wetlands then the failure to assess the loss of wetland benefits will clearly lead to an over-estimation of NB^P. This is tantamount to assuming that there is no opportunity cost of diverting floodwater from the wetlands.

Evidence from other countries suggests that in the case of large-scale water development projects this assumption may be misleading. For example, an ex-post analysis of the large-scale Ghezala irrigation project in Tunisia took into account disruptive hydrological and other environmental impacts on the neighbouring Ichkeul National Park and surrounding areas. The analysis revealed that these costs contribute to making the project economically inviable (Thomas, Ayache and Hollis, 1990). The floodplain of the Park provides important fishing and grazing uses for local communities, as well as tourism/educational benefits and essential environmental functions (de-salinization of the water table, sewage treatment, control of birds). These benefits are being threatened by the Ghezala and other upstream irrigation schemes. However, the net benefits of fishing and grazing alone easily exceed the returns to irrigation. From rule (15.2) above, it follows that diverting water to feed the Ghezala scheme is not beneficial.

A similar assessment of the benefits of the floodplain is required in order to determine the relative benefits of using water for upstream or downstream developments compared to its use when released into the floodplain. The basic methodology for assessing and valuing the economic benefits of wetlands is described by Barbier (1989a and 1989b) and shown in Figure 15.1.

It is useful to distinguish between direct use values, indirect use values and non-use values. Direct use of the wetlands would include, for example, grazing of floodplain pastures, fuelwood collection, floodplain agriculture and fishing. Recreation and tourism activities, such as bird-watching, would also involve direct use of the wetlands, as would navigation along water courses. However, various ecological functions of the wetlands may have indirect use values. Their values derive from supporting or protecting economic activities that have directly measurable values. The groundwater recharge by the floodplain replenishes the Chad Formation aquifer supplying village well water. Existence and bequest values are examples of values completely unrelated to use. Both are closely bound up with the uniqueness of natural environments. For example, some people might derive satisfaction just from knowing that a unique waterfowl habitat such as the wetlands exists and will be preserved. Similarly, some individuals may have no intention of using the floodplain, but value the fact that the wetlands will be preserved for future generations to enjoy. Finally, individuals may also express a preference for preserving the wetlands today as insurance against the risk of

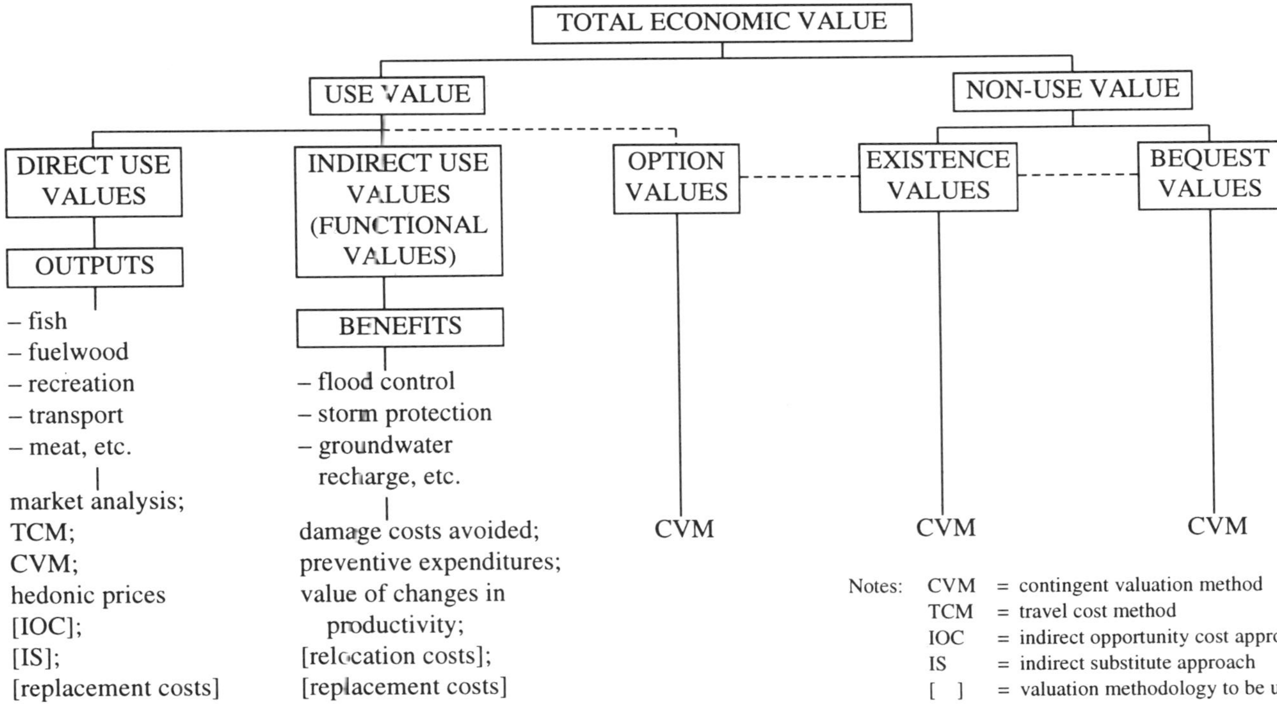

Notes:
CVM = contingent valuation method
TCM = travel cost method
IOC = indirect opportunity cost approach
IS = indirect substitute approach
[ ] = valuation methodology to be used with care

Source: Barbier (1989a).

Figure 15.1 Valuing wetland benefits: a methodology

losing any benefits which might prove valuable in the future. This option value is an extra 'premium' on the value of the wetlands, beyond its current use and non-use values, and will most likely be significant if individuals are averse to taking risks, if the future value of wetland benefits are expected to be high even if currently unknown, and if wetland loss is irreversible. Whilst the bequest, existence and option values of the wetlands are of importance in assessing the overall economic value of the wetlands, they are only significant in calculating the forgone values from wetland destruction if they can be captured by Nigeria, or if these values are held by Nigerians themselves.

Figure 15.1 indicates the various techniques appropriate to measuring each type of wetland benefit. Valuing the benefits derived from tropical wetland resources is relatively straightforward, usually involving the value of the production gained from directly exploiting these resources. For example, Kimmage and Adams' (1990a) study of the Hadejia-Nguru wetlands indicates that the total value of the annual production was Naira (N) 250–280 million for agriculture, N45 million for fishing and N14 million for fuelwood. However, measuring the indirect benefits of wetland environmental functions, such as groundwater recharge, or of any option, existence or bequest values, is more problematic. More sophisticated techniques of contingent valuation, travel cost method and hedonic pricing are now increasingly being used to value temperate wetlands in Europe and North America (Turner, 1990), but have yet to be applied to tropical wetlands.

Willingness to pay

Because the ultimate aim of all economic activity is to satisfy individuals' needs and wants, the objective of valuing the direct use, indirect use and non-use benefits is to measure society's willingness to pay (WTP) for these various benefits. In a competitive economy with no constraints on the movement of prices, one can assume that market prices reflect the WTP for goods and services. However, two complications arise in conjunction with wetland uses in developing countries.

First, in many developing countries, market prices may be distorted by deliberate interventions or imperfect competition such as the existence of exchange rate controls, price ceilings or supports, subsidies or taxes, monopoly conditions and so forth. Also, the significant size of the informal non-market sector may reduce the reliability of market prices as measures of value. In such instances, the use of shadow prices is often advocated. These are actual prices 'adjusted' to eliminate any distortions caused by policies or market imperfections so as to reflect true WTP. Since the ultimate concern is with the opportunity cost to society of allowing water to continue flowing into the floodplain compared to its diversion for other development uses, then actual prices should be adjusted to reflect economic values. However, there are limits to the indiscriminate use of shadow prices in place of market prices, which in certain cases may introduce larger discrepancies than the simple use of even imperfect, market prices (Gregersen *et al.*, 1987).

Second, many wetland values are not directly reflected in market prices at all. This is true for all the environmental functions, for resources harvested for own use by households, for most recreation and water transport services, and for all non-use values. In some cases, techniques such as travel cost methods, contingent valuation and hedonic pricing might be employed to estimate WTP directly. As noted above, however, these techniques are not easily applicable in remote and rural settings in developing countries. The alternative is second-best, and sometimes third-best, approaches to valuation, such as indirect substitute, indirect opportunity cost, relocation costs and damage costs avoided methods, which do not relate uniquely to WTP but may yield 'proxy' economic values.

A further consideration is whether current uses of a wetland are necessarily sustainable. Direct uses of a wetland area, including farming, fishing, grazing and harvest of fuelwood and timber, may over the long run lead to significant environmental degradation. Where it is apparent that current levels of exploitation undermine the sustainability of wetland resources and environmental functions, this must be taken into account in the analysis. As will be discussed below, in the Hadejia-Nguru wetlands concern is being raised over the sustainability of current levels of wheat production which has rapidly expanded throughout the area in recent years (Kimmage, 1990, 1991a). If current levels of wheat production are assumed to be sustained well into the future, whereas in fact production may dramatically collapse in a few years, then the analysis may be grossly overstating wetland benefits in terms of wheat production.

One approach to this problem would be to include an alternative sustainability scenario in the evaluation as part of a sensitivity analysis (Barbier, 1989a). For example, supposing that the sustainable yield of fuelwood from a wetland area is around 5 m^3/ha, which means that this amount of wood could be extracted over a long time horizon, say over 30 years, without disrupting any wetland ecological functions or endangering fuelwood supplies. But assume that current use is actually 10 m^3/ha, which current indications suggest may cause significant fuelwood depletion and environmental degradation from year 15 onwards. A sensitivity analysis could reflect this scenario by showing high current benefits from fuelwood extraction but at the expense of declining, and perhaps even zero, benefits from environmental functions over the long run.

A second approach would be to incorporate into the analysis the concept of an environmentally compensating project. As suggested by Barbier, Markandya and Pearce (1990), the methodology is to assume that within the project 'portfolio' there should be included at least one project that 'compensates' for the environmental degradation generated by other projects in the portfolio. This implies that the benefit of preserving sustainable use is at least equal to the cost of the compensating project. In the case of over-harvesting of fuelwood in a wetland area, the analysis would first have to calculate the costs of the environmental degradation caused by unsustainable fuelwood use. This amount would then provide the 'upper bound' for the costs of including an additional project, such as a reforestation scheme, that would offset the environmental impacts of excessive fuelwood extraction.

Economic valuation of the Hadejia-Nguru wetlands

Data limitations currently prevent a comprehensive analysis of the relative benefits of allocating water to upstream and downstream developments compared to allowing it to continue flowing into the floodplain. However, as indicated by rules (15.1) and (15.2) above, calculating the net benefits provided by the wetlands supplemented by other field surveys, NB^W, is the crucial component often missing from appraisal of development projects. To the extent that development projects threaten the floodplain, then the net economic benefits of the wetlands indicate the opportunity costs of diverting water to the development projects.

The main source of data for calculating these direct use benefits is from Kimmage and Adams (1990a), supplemented by field surveys undertaken by the two authors. Where appropriate, actual prices are adjusted to economic values using shadow prices. The terms financial and economic are used to express the values of commodities based on actual or market prices, and the values of commodities based on adjusted or shadow prices, respectively. Views on the sustainability of resource use, especially for wheat production are also discussed, and the implications incorporated through sensitivity analysis. To facilitate comparison with competing uses of water, values are expressed not only in per hectare terms, but also in terms of volume of river flow and seasonal water releases from upstream projects. Finally, other wetland benefits, such as important environmental functions, are briefly reviewed, and possible methods for valuing them indicated.

Estimating net benefits

Total cultivated area in the floodplain is estimated at about 230 000 ha, of which approximately 77 500 ha occurs in the dry season and 152 500 ha in the wet season. Of the latter, 112 000 ha is upland, mainly rain-fed cultivation (*tudu*) and 40 500 ha is floodplain *fadama* proper. However, these distinctions are somewhat artificial. An increase in the extent of flooding and in water depth can easily transform *tudu* land into *fadama*. Moreover, as farmers in the floodplain typically own both types of land, cultivation is inextricably linked. Any threat to the floodplain, therefore, would change *tudu* cultivation as well.

Table 15.1 indicates the current annual net benefits from fourteen agricultural crops grown in the floodplain. The crops are distinguished as tradeables and non-tradeables (Squire and van der Tak, 1975). Financial prices for all crops were estimated from surveys of prices and seasonal price changes in Nguru market in 1989 and 1990. These prices were converted to economic prices, using c.i.f. import prices at the official 1989 exchange rate, Naira (N) 7.5 = US$1, for the three tradeable crops (rice, wheat and soya beans) and using the standard conversion factor of 0.85 for Nigeria for the non-traceable crops. This factor is the rate recommended by the World Bank (Warner, pers. comm.).

Table 15.1 Agriculture – net benefits 1989–90 (N7.5 = US$1)

Crop	Average output (tons)	Financial price (N/ton)	Economic price (N/ton)	Financial benefits (N'000)	Economic benefits (N'000)	Net economic benefits (N'000)[d]
Tradeable[a]						
Rice	22 335	4 770.00	3 144.90	106 538	70 241	10 536
Wheat	43 350	4 010.00	1 382.88	173 834	59 948	8 992
Soya beans	6 000	3 310.00	2 137.50	19 860	12 825	1 924
Non-tradeable[b]						
Sorghum	50 315	720.00	612.00	36 227	30 793	4 619
Maize	15 705	842.00	715.70	13 224	11 240	1 686
Groundnuts	3 855	4 980.00	4 233.00	19 198	16 318	2 448
Millet	50 415	842.00	715.70	42 449	36 082	5 412
Cow-peas	25 035	3 310.00	2 813.50	82 866	70 436	10 565
Tomatoes	15 955	662.50	563.13	10 570	8 985	1 348
Onions	11 925	662.50	563.13	7 900	6 715	1 007
Peppers	32 400	1 336.00	1 135.60	43 286	36 793	5 519
Sweet potatoes	2 925	600.0	510.00	1 755	1 492	224
Aubergines	1 740	662.50	563.13	1 153	980	147
Pumpkins	1 414 500	3.00	2.55	4 244	3 607	541
TOTAL[c]	281 955			563 103	366 455	54 968
Total agricultural area (ha)			230 000			
Net economic benefits/ha (N/ha)			239[d]			

Notes:

a The economic prices of all tradeables are the c.i.f. import (border) prices converted at the official 1989 exchange rate of N7.5 = US$1.

b Non-tradeables are defined as crops whose prices exceed f.o.b. export prices but are less than c.i.f. import prices. The economic prices of non-tradeables are the financial prices adjusted by the standard conversion factor of 0.85.

c The total for average crop output excludes pumpkins.

d Anderson (1987) found the net economic benefit of crops in Kano State to be 15 per cent of gross economic benefits.

Source: Calculations based on Kimmage and Adams (1990) and field surveys undertaken by these authors; World Bank economic data; World Bank (1989) and Anderson (1987).

Calculation of the average annual output of each crop is based on low and high estimates of production from field surveys of farm households in the floodplain. Combining the price and output data results in annual gross economic benefits of N1578 per ha for agriculture in the floodplain. Using estimates by Anderson (1987) indicating that net economic benefits from agriculture in Kano State are generally 15 per cent of gross benefits, the net economic benefits of agriculture in the floodplain are N239 per ha per annum.

However, these net benefits may be an underestimate as they are for only fourteen crops grown in the floodplain. Six other crops okra, *yakuwa*, cucumber, cotton, guava and mango are also cultivated widely within the region, but no specific price or production data are available for these crops. Okra and *yakuwa* are grown by most households but usually in small amounts around field boundaries. Guava and mangoes are grown by perhaps 10 to 15 per cent of households. Anderson (1987) has demonstrated that fruit trees such as mangoes yield significant fruit, fuelwood and shelter belt benefits in Kano State.

Fishing takes place in approximately 100 000 ha of flooded land, with around 73 150 rural households in the floodplain participating in this activity throughout the year. Only 12 per cent of these households include 'full-time' fishermen. The rest comprise dry season fishing households (21 per cent), wet season fishing households (15 per cent) and households that only fish at fishing festivals (52 per cent). Moreover, of the 8750 'full-time' fishing households, only 980 may be sufficiently close to permanent water bodies to allow them to fish on an actual full-time basis.

Table 15.2 indicates the net annual benefits per ha from fishing in the wetlands based on data from six seasonal periods over the dry and rainy seasons. The pattern of fish catches varies throughout the year, as the seasonal variations in fishing intensity relate to differential access to *fadama* fishing sites and to the flooding period. In general, the highest catches are recorded during the 'fish-run' period of the falling flood; that is, at the end of the wet season and the beginning of the dry season when fish begin retreating from the *fadama*.

Estimates of fish prices were based on price data from Nguru market for the four most important species of fish caught for the period between the mid-dry season 1989 and the mid-dry season 1990. Economic prices for each season were calculated by employing the standard conversion factor (0.85). Survey data provided information on fishing intensity by season, that is, total fishing days per household per season, which when multiplied by the total number of fishing households, yields the total fishing days per season. Financial costs were calculated based on a rural cost of agricultural day labour of N7.79 per day, which were converted to economic costs by employing the standard conversion factor. The resulting estimate of annual net economic benefits from fishing in the floodplain comes to N179 per ha.

Table 15.2 Net benefits of fishing, 1989–90 (N7.5 = US$1)

Season	Total catch (tons)	Fin. price (N/kg)	Econ. price N/kg	Total fin. benefits (N'000)	Total econ. benefits (N'000)	Total fishing days	Total fin. costs (N'000)	Total econ. costs (N'000)	Net econ. benefits (N'000)
Dry – beginning	1 728	7.48	6.35	12 918	10 980	768 075	5 983	5 086	5 894
Dry – middle	931	9.75	8.29	9 079	7 717	621 044	4 838	4 112	3 605
Dry – end	313	5.35	4.55	1 674	1 423	313 082	2 439	2 073	–650
Wet – beginning	562	7.25	6.16	4 077	3 466	375 260	2 923	2 485	981
Wet – middle	717	6.35	5.40	4 555	3 872	478 401	3 727	3 168	704
Wet – end	2 012	6.50	5.53	13 077	11 116	569 839	4 439	3 773	7 342
Total	6 264			45 381	38 574	3 125 700	24 349	20 697	17 877
Average		7.11	6.05						
Total fishing area (ha)		100 000							
Net economic benefits/ha (N/ha)		179							

Notes:
Economic values are financial values adjusted by the standard conversion factor of 0.85.
Financial costs are based on rural cost of agricultural day labourer of N7.79/day. Total fishing days calculated on the average number of fishing days per household per season (73 150 fishing households total).

Source: Calculations based on Kimmage and Adams (1990) and field surveys undertaken by these authors; and World Bank data.

Net benefits from fuelwood production in the floodplain are calculated by distinguishing rural subsistence use from urban consumption (Table 15.3). With an estimated 86 000 rural households in the region and an average monthly fuelwood consumption per household of 50 kg, total rural fuelwood use is around 51 600 tonnes annually. Fuelwood collected from the floodplain is also consumed in local towns and urban centres, notably Gashua, Hadejia and Nguru. Applying the same monthly rate of 50 kg of fuelwood used per household to the 106 000 'non-rural' households yields a total urban consumption of fuelwood of 63 500 tonnes.

Table 15.3 Net benefits of fuelwood, 1989–90 (N7.5 = US$1)

Consumers	Total output (tons)	Fin. price N/kg	Econ. price N/kg	Total fin. benefits (N'000)	Total econ. benefits (N'000)	Total fin. costs (N'000)	Total econ. costs (N'000)	Net econ. benefits (N'000)
Rural	51 600	120	102	6 192	5 263	30	26	3 947
Non-rural	63 500	120	102	7 620	6 477	40	34	4 318
Total	115 100	120	102	13 812	11 740			8 265
Total fuelwood area (ha)				400 000				
Net economic benefits/ha (N/ha)				21				

Notes:
Economic values are financial values adjusted by the standard conversion factor of 0.85.
Financial costs are based on an initial felling/trimming cost of N18/t, cost of chopping down into bundles of N12/t and a transport cost to local urban centres of N10/t.

Source: Calculations based on Kimmage and Adams (1990) and field surveys undertaken by these authors; and World Bank data.

Financial prices of the rural and non-rural fuelwood uses were estimated at N120 per tonne, which reflected average retail price in the markets and by the roadside throughout the floodplain in 1989–90. The standard conversion factor of 0.85 gives an economic price of N102 per tonne. The financial costs of fuelwood supply for both rural and non-rural uses were calculated on the basis of initial felling and trimming costs of N18 per tonne and costs of chopping down into bundles of N12 per tonne. Non-rural supply incorporated an additional transport cost to local urban centres of N10 per tonne. With an estimated 400 000 ha of land in the floodplain yielding fuelwood, the net economic benefits of all fuelwood produced annually in the wetlands are N21 per ha.

Present value of net economic benefits

A cost–benefit analysis of the net economic benefits over time from agriculture, fishing and fuelwood in the floodplain was also conducted. The analysis assumes that the benefits provided by the floodplain do not arise just in a single year but that the wetlands, if properly managed, are capable of yielding a continuous stream of such benefits over a number of years. The sum of the stream of benefits discounted into present values indicates the present worth of the wetlands in terms of agriculture, fishing and fuelwood. As shown in equations (15.1) and (15.2), this estimate of the present worth of the wetlands, NB^W, is the benchmark for comparing the returns to development projects, NB^D, that may threaten the floodplain system.

The cost–benefit analysis comprises three parts:

1. a base case scenario, which assumes that the net economic benefits per ha for agriculture, fishing and fuelwood would be maintained at current levels for each year of the analysis;
2. an alternative sustainability scenario, which assumes that much of current wheat production in the wetlands cannot be sustained and will therefore decline rapidly over the next 4–5 years; and
3. a standard sensitivity analysis, which incorporates different assumptions concerning time horizons (30 and 50 years) and discount rates (8 per cent and 12 per cent) in both scenarios of the analysis.

The results of the analysis are displayed in Table 15.4. Depending on the discount rate and time horizon, the present value of total net benefits under the base case range from N895 to N1359 per ha. The net benefits from agriculture range between N607 and N921 per ha, from fishing between N197 and N300 per ha and from fuelwood between N91 and N139 per ha.

However, serious doubt has recently been expressed over the sustainability of wheat production in the floodplain. Kimmage (1991a, b) has argued that government efforts to subsidize domestic wheat production through generous subsidies and imposing a ban on wheat imports have led to rapid expansion of pump-irrigated wheat in the floodplain area. As a result of the subsidization of up to 50 per cent of all inputs and services for wheat cultivation and an increase in the domestic producer price of wheat by a factor of ten between 1986 and 1989, cultivated wheat area in the Hadejia-Jama'are region increased from around 200–300 ha prior to 1983 to almost 47 000 ha in the 1989–90 season. Much of the recent expansion has been through clearing and burning acacia scrubland, which generally has thin topsoils with low clay content and poor levels of organic carbon. Given the poor quality and structure of most of the soils, intensive cultivation of wheat in the floodplain region, especially on cleared scrubland, could lead to substantial land degradation within a few years. In scrubland areas, crop yields are likely to fall rapidly, with soil fertility irreversibly degraded within 4–5 years (Kimmage, 1991b).

Table 15.4 Present value net economic benefits per hectare (N/ha)[a] (N7.5 = US$1, 1989–90)

Base case	8%, 50 yrs	8%, 30 yrs	12%, 50 yrs	12%, 30 yrs
Agriculture	921	848	625	607
Fishing	300	276	203	197
Fuelwood	139	127	94	91
Total	1359	1251	923	895
Adjusted agriculture[b]	838	773	574	558
Adjusted total	1276	1176	872	846

Notes:

[a] Economic benefits averaged over total production area of 730 000 ha (400 000 ha for fuelwood, 230 000 ha for cropland and 100 000 ha for fishing).

[b] NPV of agriculture adjusted for sustainability of wheat production. Approximately 56 per cent of current wheat hectarage assumed unsustainable.

Source: Based on Tables 15.1 to 15.3.

Of total wheat cultivation in the floodplain, approximately 80 per cent of the recent large-scale clearances of acacia scrubland may be affected by severe degradation problems. As these clearances currently account for the majority of the area under wheat, the 'unsustainable' element in wheat cultivation is likely to be in the region of 26 100 ha. In the cost–benefit analysis, the alternative sustainability scenario was projected by 'adjusting' net benefits from agriculture over time. The basic assumption is that yields on the 26 100 ha of 'unsustainable' wheat cultivation fall by 20 per cent per year after the first year, eventually declining to zero by the sixth year. As shown in Table 15.4, adjusted agricultural net benefits are marginally lower, ranging from N558 to N838 per ha. Total net benefits are also adjusted lower to between N846 and N1276 per ha.

Expressing the discounted net economic benefits of the floodplain in 'per hectare' terms give one useful comparison with the present worth of upstream and downstream water development projects. However, given that these projects are essentially competing with the floodplain for the use of water, expressing net economic benefits in terms of 'water use' may provide a more useful comparison.

Two additional versions of the cost–benefit analysis were therefore conducted, with discounted net economic benefits re-calculated in terms of m^3 of water use by the floodplain. Both versions also contain a base case, a standard sensitivity analysis of time horizons and discount rates, and an 'adjusted' case to account for unsustainable wheat cultivation. The results are indicated in Tables 15.5 and 15.6.

Table 15.5 displays present value net economic benefits based on an average annual river inflow of 2549 $10^6 m^3$ into the floodplain over 1985–87. This volume of river inflow essentially corresponds to the 'maximum' amount of water input required by the floodplain to sustain agriculture, fuelwood harvesting and fishing. As Table 15.5 shows, total net economic benefits from the agriculture, fishing and fuelwood supported by the floodplain range from N256 to N389 per $10^3 m^3$ of river inflow. When adjusted for unsustainable wheat cultivation, the net economic benefits range from N242 to N366 per $10^3 m^3$ of river inflow.

Table 15.5 Present value net economic benefits per river inflow (N/000m^3)[a] *(N7.5 = US$1, 1989–90)*

Base case	8%, 50 yrs	8%, 30 yrs	12%, 50 yrs	12%, 30 yrs
Agriculture	264	243	179	174
Fishing	86	79	58	57
Fuelwood	40	37	27	26
Total	389	358	264	256
Adjusted agriculture[b]	240	221	164	160
Adjusted total	366	337	250	242

Notes:
a Based on average annual river flow into Hadejia-Nguru wetlands of 2549 $10^6 m^3$ over 1985–87.
b NPV of agriculture adjusted for unsustainability of wheat production. Approximately 56 per cent of current wheat hectarage assumed unsustainable.

Source: Based on Tables 15.1 to 15.3; Adams and Hollis (1988).

The hydrological simulation model determined the amount of water releases required from all existing and planned upstream development projects to avoid severe disruptions to the floodplain. The total release of regulated flooding amounts to 1848 $10^6 m^3$ per year. Although such a regime of controlled releases may be insufficient to maintain groundwater recharge at present levels, the regime would provide the 'minimum' amount of water input required to sustain floodplain agricultural, fishing and fuelwood benefits. As indicated in Table 15.6, these benefits total to between N396 and N602 per 10^3m^3 of controlled flood releases. Under the sustainability scenario, the adjusted total is between N375 and N565 per 10^3m^3 of controlled releases.

Table 15.6 Present value net economic benefits per controlled water release (N/000m³)[a] *(N7.5 = US$1, 1989–90)*

Base case	8%, 50 yrs	8%, 30 yrs	12%, 50 yrs	12%, 30 yrs
Agriculture	408	375	277	269
Fishing	133	122	90	87
Fuelwood	61	56	42	40
Total	602	554	409	396
Adjusted agriculture[b]	371	342	254	247
Adjusted total	565	521	386	375

Notes:

[a] Assumes a total controlled water release of 1648 10^6m^3 per annum from upstream water development projects on the Hadejia and Jama'are rivers.

[b] NPV of agriculture adjusted for unsustainability of wheat production. Approximately 56 per cent of current wheat hectarage assumed unsustainable.

Source: Based on Tables 15.1 to 15.3; Adams and Hollis (1988).

Comparison with development projects

Comprehensive cost–benefit analyses have not been carried out for existing and planned development projects along the Hadejia and Jama'are rivers to compare with the above analysis of floodplain benefits.

Although a complete cost–benefit analysis of the project has not been conducted, some information does exist on the costs and value of production when the project became fully operational over 1984–86. Calculations of the current net economic benefits of the project are indicated in Table 15.7. Although crop production and hectarage in the project are based on 1985–86 data, to facilitate comparison with the returns to the floodplain system, the same 1989–90 crop financial and economic prices from Table 15.1 are used. Similarly, the same assumption that net economic crop benefits are 15 per cent of gross benefits is employed.

Table 15.7 indicates that, once fully operational, net economic crop benefits per ha of the Kano River Project appear extremely high (N865/ha). They easily exceed the net economic benefits per ha of floodplain agriculture (N239/ha in Table 15.1), and are virtually double the total net benefits from floodplain

Table 15.7 Net economic benefits, Kano River Project Phase I (N7.5 = US$1)

Crop[a]	Output (tons)	Area planted ha	Yield t/ha	Fin. price (N/t)	Econ. price N/t)	Fin. benefits (N'000)	Econ. benefits (N'000)	Net econ. benefits (N'000[c])
Tradeable								
Rice	6 940	1 735	4.0	4 770.0	3144.9	33 104	21 826	3 274
Wheat	9 348	4 674	2.0	4 010.0	1382.9	27 829	9 597	1 440
Non-tradeable[b]								
Sorghum	2 767	2 306	1.2	720.0	612.0	4 997	4 247	637
Maize	8 212	4 131	2.0	842.0	715.7	5 843	4 967	745
Groundnuts	661	551	1.2	4 980.0	4233.0	34 561	29 377	4 407
Millet	3 078	3 078	1.0	842.0	715.7	5 843	4 967	745
Cow-peas	225	281	0.8	3 310.0	2813.5	22 971	19 526	2 929
Tomatoes	33 405	1 670	20.0	662.5	563.1	4 598	3 908	586
Peppers	302	20	15.1	1 135.6	1135.6	7 881	7 881	1 182
Others[b]	16 402	661	24.8	665.6	565.8	4 619	3 926	589
Total	81 340	19 107				152 248	110 222	16 533
Net economic crop benefits/ha (N/ha)				865[c]				
Less net operating costs/ha (N/ha)				846[d]				
Net economic project benefits/ha (N/ha)				19				
Net economic crop benefits per water input (N/000m^3)				1.10[e]				
Net economic project benefits per water input (N/000m^3)				0.02[e]				

Notes:

[a] Crop output based on 1985–86 production and hectarage; crop economic and financial prices as in Table 15.1.

[b] Mainly vegetables.

[c] See Table 15.1 for the calculation of net economic crop benefits.

[d] Net project operating costs include capital expenditure, capital works, recurrent costs and head office expenditure. The proportion of these costs to the total value of crop production in 1984 was 7.7 per cent, in 1985 21.1 per cent and in 1986 37 per cent. An average of these three figures was used to calculate net operating costs.

[e] Water input estimated at 15 000 m^3/ha/year.

agriculture, fishing and fuelwood (N438/ha summed from Tables 15.1–15.3). However, as in the case of most irrigation projects, the Kano River Project also has high net operating costs which include capital expenditure and works, recurrent costs and head office expenditure, minus any project income. Over 1984–86, these ranged from a low of 7.7 per cent to as much as 37 per cent of the total value of crop production. As shown in Table 15.7, when the net operating costs are deducted from net economic crop benefits, the resulting net economic project benefits are reduced to just N19/ha. Thus the current returns per ha to the fully operational Kano River Project do not compare favourably with those of floodplain agriculture, fishing and fuelwood.

Moreover, with an annual water requirement of 15 000 m^3 per ha, the Kano River Project is highly intensive in its water use. When expressed in terms of water input rather than in hectarage cultivated, current net economic benefits are extremely low around N1.10 per 10^3m^3 of water used (Table 15.7). Net project economic benefits are only N0.02 per 10^3m^3 of water input. In comparison, the flood-recession agriculture of the floodplain requires substantially less water. Thus, even when the 'maximum' annual water input into the floodplain of 2549 10^6m^3 is used, net floodplain agricultural benefits currently amount to N21.6 per 10^3m^3 of river water inflow. Total net economic benefits from agriculture, fishing and fuelwood amount to N31.8 per 10^3m^3 of river water inflow.

Table 15.8 Present value net economic benefits, Kano River Project Phase I. (N7.5 = US$1, 1989–90)

Per hectare[a]	8%, 50 yrs	8%, 30 yrs	12%, 50 yrs	12%, 30 yrs
Crop (N/ha)	10 586	9 741	7 186	6 970
Project (N/ha)	233	214	158	153
Per water use[b]				
Crop (N/10^3m^3)	13	12	9	9
Project (N/10^3m^3)	0.3	0.3	0.2	0.2

Notes:
[a] Based on total crop cultivated area of 19 107 ha in 1985–86.
[b] Assumes an annual water use of 15 000 m^3/ha.

Source: Based on Table 15.7; Adams and Hollis (1988).

Based on the current net crop and project benefits calculated in Table 15.7, a cost–benefit analysis was conducted for the Kano River Project Phase I. Adjustments to the time horizon and discount rate were included in a sensitivity analysis. The results are shown in Table 15.8. In comparison with the present value net benefits of the floodplain, it is clear that the present worth of the Kano

River Project is much lower. Only the present value of net crop benefits per ha are substantially higher for the project compared to the floodplain. As discussed above, however, to exclude current operating costs gives a misleading indication of the net economic returns to the project. In addition, the present value of net crop benefits per 10^3m^3 of water use for the project is substantially lower than for floodplain agriculture, let alone for total net floodplain benefits.

In sum, the returns to agriculture, fuelwood and fishing in the floodplain appear to exceed substantially that of the Kano River Project Phase I. This would suggest extreme caution in assuming that an irrigated agricultural project, such as the Kano River Project, is an economically better use of water. A straight comparison of the net economic returns to irrigated crop production and floodplain recession agriculture often gives such a misleading impression. The above analysis confirms the need for an economic analysis of a water development project not only to include net project operational costs as part of direct costs of the development but also to incorporate as opportunity costs the alternative uses of the water for downstream benefits, such as floodplain agricultural, fishery and fuelwood production.

Moreover, in the above analysis the estimation of the comparative returns to the Kano River Project may have been reduced further by a considerable amount if the following factors were also taken into account:

1. The economic analysis of the Kano River Project did not include sunk capital costs of around N180 million nor a 'gestation period' for crop production during the project start-up from 1981 to 1985–86. Rather, the analysis was based on current costs and benefits only and assumed the project to be fully operational in the initial year of the analysis. A full project appraisal that would take into account capital costs and a 'gestation period' would yield even lower, and perhaps even negative, present value returns.
2. No comparable 'sustainability' scenario was constructed for the analysis of crop benefits from the Kano River Project. It is likely that problems of land degradation, including waterlogging and salinization, may affect future yields in the project, especially for wheat.
3. The agricultural, fuelwood and fishing benefits are only some of the total economic benefits provided by the floodplain system. If full account is taken of other benefits, the opportunity costs of diverting water to development projects such as the Kano River Project may be even higher.

Other floodplain benefits

In addition to supporting agriculture, fuelwood use and fishing, the floodplain provides numerous other benefits that are less easy to value. Some of these benefits are extremely important, and collectively, they may even exceed the value of floodplain agriculture, fuelwood and fishing.

Livestock and grazing

The floodplain provides important grazing resources both for sedentary farmers (Hausa, Kanuri and Fulani) with livestock settled within the wetlands area and for nomadic Fulani herdsmen who use the floodplain for dry season pastures. Although it is clear that livestock production in the area is both high and increasing, there is currently little data available on livestock numbers, herd composition, in- and out-migration of herds, herd offtake or carcasses and livestock products, such as milk, yoghurt, and hides, delivered to market (Kimmage and Adams, 1990a). Additional data must be acquired on the productivity of different floodplain grazing resources, for example, pasture land, scrubland, marshes, forests. The role of livestock rearing in the community should also be assessed (Jimoh, 1991). If such data were available, then calculating the value of the average annual animal production attributable to floodplain grazing would be relatively straightforward. For example, Thomas, Ayache and Hollis (1990) used such an approach in valuing the grazing of the Ichkeul marshes in Tunisia.

Non-timber forest products

In addition to producing fuelwood, the forest reserves and bushland of the floodplain yield important non-timber forest products that are significant to the livelihoods and subsistence of local communities. Some are important marketed commodities that generate substantial income. These include leaves. Doum palm leaves are either processed into mats and other products or sold as raw material. The harvesting and processing of doum palm leaves is a dry season activity, and many people migrate to the wetlands even from Niger to harvest the palm. Mat-making from doum is also a specialized activity of many floodplain villages. Mats and other doum products, for example, rope and baskets, are sold locally or exported to other regions. *Baobab* leaves are used widely as an ingredient for soups and stews and are especially important as a 'drought food'. In local markets the *Baobab* leaves are sold for around N20 per sack. Honey produced by local beekeepers is a highly valued commodity. Local prices range from N10–20 per kg, with an annual production of 100–150 kg per hive being common.

Wildlife tourism, education and science

The wetlands are an important habitat for migratory wildfowl, with the number of birds sighted varying from 20 000 to 50 000, many of which are often Palaearctic species (Stowe and Coulthard, 1990).

The rich and highly concentrated bird populations of the wetlands suggest that they have potential value in terms of scientific, educational and tourism benefits.

Current uses of the wetlands for these purposes are, however, negligible. Poor tourist infrastructure and transportation in Northern Nigeria are major constraints on the development of any tourist potential. Nevertheless, some initial work is underway in these areas largely as a product of ongoing projects in the region.

Conservation of the wetlands as an important wildlife habitat therefore has important option values for future tourism, educational and scientific uses. The wetlands may also have an important non-use existence value, in that individuals who have no intention of visiting the wetlands may value the fact that it exists as an important wildlife habitat. Accounting for these values is extremely difficult, however, and may require sophisticated techniques of contingent valuation and travel-cost methods. These values also only have significance as opportunity costs if Nigeria can somehow 'capture' these values, for instance through receiving international financing for 'preserving' the wetlands or if these values are held by Nigerians themselves. Brown and Henry (1993) applied travel-cost methods to derive current and option values for viewing elephants in Kenya. A similar approach could be applied to bird-viewing in the wetlands.

Groundwater recharge

Perhaps the most important environmental function of the floodplain is its role in recharging the groundwater aquifer of the Chad Formation. Over 1964–71, when over 2000 km^2 were flooded almost every wet season and from 1975 to 1982 when inundation remained around 1000–2000 km^2, groundwater storage beneath the floodplain was largely stable. But during the drought years of 1973–74 and since 1983 when the extent of flooding dropped appreciably, groundwater recharge fell by an estimated aggregate amount of 5000 $10^9 m^3$. Continual loss of groundwater storage and recharging will have a significant impact on the numerous small villages throughout the wetlands and the wider region that depend on the aquifer for domestic use and agricultural activities. The apparent maintenance of groundwater levels in the area around the Marma Channel has already been ascribed to the sustained flows in that waterway.

Estimating the benefits of the wetlands' groundwater recharge function is a difficult, but not an insurmountable, problem. By combining hydrological information on the groundwater recharge supplied by the wetlands; the impacts on the water tables supplying village wells; and direct estimates of villagers willingness-to-pay (WTP) for water; it may be possible to value this recharge function. A recent study in Brazil demonstrates how surveys of actual and hypothetical water-use practices can provide estimates through contingent valuation methods of the WTP that vary according to household socio-economic characteristics, qualitative differences in water supply and delivery systems (Briscoe *et al.*, 1990).

In the absence of time and resources to apply such direct WTP estimation methods, it may be possible to estimate indirectly the benefits of the wetlands' groundwater recharge function. One approach is to measure the additional 'externality costs' of a depletion scenario based on continual loss of groundwater storage versus a conservation scenario whereby the recharging function is preserved. Munasinghe (1990) indicates how this approach provides a benchmark value for the damage costs of aquifer depletion in the Philippines. It may also be possible to value indirectly the recharge function by estimating the impact of losses in water supply from the village wells on agricultural production. The changes in agricultural productivity associated with the decline in water use could then be used to value the recharge function of the wetlands. However, more difficult to value through this approach would be the impact of groundwater recharge on domestic water use.

Conclusions

The economic analysis of the agricultural, fuelwood and fishing benefits provided by the floodplain indicates that these benefits are substantial on both a per hectare basis and in terms of the minimum and maximum amount of water required to sustain them. Not only are these wetland benefits currently important, but they can be expected to yield significant economic returns for some time provided that the floodplain system is properly managed and sustained. Even when taking into account the future unsustainability of much of the current wheat production in the floodplain, the economic analysis calculates the present worth of the aggregate stream of agricultural, fishing and fuelwood benefits to be around N850 to N1280 per ha. Or, given the 'maximum' and 'minimum' flood water inputs required to sustain the system, the benefits vary between N240–N370 per 10^3m^3 of water and N375–N565 per 10^3m^3 of water respectively.

When compared to the net economic benefits of an upstream water development project such as the Kano River Project Phase I, the economic returns to the floodplain appear much more favourable. This is particularly the case when the relative returns to the project in terms of water input use is compared to that of the floodplain system. This result should cause some concern, given that the existing and planned water developments along the river system, such as the Kano River Project, are currently and will continue diverting water from the floodplain. The failure to take into account the opportunity cost of this water diversion in terms of the forgone benefits of floodplain production may be leading to serious overestimation of the net economic returns to these development projects.

However, there are other significant economic benefits provided by the floodplain system than the ones estimated in the analysis. Livestock grazing and groundwater recharge are extremely important, although recreational, educational and scientific visits and control of bird pests may also prove substantial. The sum total of these additional benefits may actually exceed the estimated returns to floodplain agriculture, fishing and fuelwood.

The economic importance of the floodplain suggests that the benefits it provides cannot be excluded as an opportunity cost of any scheme that diverts water away from the floodplain system. Policy makers should be aware of this problem when designing water development projects in the river system. Further analysis is also required of the type of 'regulated flooding' regime, which could maintain much of the floodplain system intact while still allowing some upstream water developments. Further investigation of all the economic benefits provided by the wetlands is also needed, and the sustainability of production within the floodplain area should be more thoroughly examined.

References

Adams, W.M. and Hollis, G.E. (1988), *Hydrology and Sustainable Resource Development of a Sahelian Floodplain Wetland*, Report to the Hadejia-Nguru Wetland Conservation Project, London.

Anderson, D. (1987), *The Economics of Afforestation: A Case Study in Africa*, Washington, DC: John Hopkins University Press for the World Bank.

Barbier, E.B. (1989a), *Economic Evaluation of Tropical Wetland Resources: Applications in Central America*. London: London Economics Centre.

Barbier, E.B. (1989b), *The Economic Value of Ecosystems: 1 – Tropical Wetlands*. London: Gatekeeper 89–102, London Economics Centre.

Barbier, E.B., A. Markandya and D.W. Pearce (1990), 'Sustainable agricultural development and project appraisal', *European Review of Agricultural Economics*, **17**, 181–96.

Briscoe, J., P. Furtado de Castro, C. Griffin, J. North and O. Olsen (1990), 'Toward equitable and sustainable rural supplies: a contingent valuation study in Brazil', *The World Bank Economic Review*, **4** (2), 115–34.

Brown, G. Jr and W. Henry (1993), in E.B. Barbier (ed.), *Economics and Ecology: New Frontiers and Sustainable Development*, London: Chapman & Hall.

Farber, S. and R. Costanza, (1987), *The Value of Coastal Wetlands for Protection of Property against Hurricane Wind Damage*. Journal of Environmental Economics and Management **14**, 143–51.

Gregersen, H.M., K.N Brooks, J.A. Dixon and L.S. Hamilton (1987), *Guidelines for Economic Appraisal of Watershed Management Projects*, Rome: FAO.

HNWCP (1991), *Strategy for Phase II: 1991–94*, Nguru, Nigeria.

Jimoh, M.A. (1991), 'Pastoralists in the Hadejia Nguru floodplain: survey of two communities', HNWCP, Nigeria: Nguru.

Kimmage, K. (1989), 'The evolution of the wheat trap: the Nigerian wheat boom', mimeo, Dept., of Geography, Cambridge: University of Cambridge.

Kimmage, K. (1991), 'Small-scale irrigation initiatives: the problems of equity and sustainability', *Applied Geography*, **11**, 5–20.

Kimmage, K. and W.M. Adams (1990), *The Economic Value of Production in the Hadejia-Jama'are Floodplain, Nigeria*, Report to the Coordinator, Wetlands Programme, IUCN, Department of Geography, Cambridge: University of Cambridge.

Munasinghe, M. (1990), *Managing Water Resources to Avoid Environmental Degradation: Policy Analysis and Application*, Environment Working Paper No. 41, World Bank, Washington, DC.

Stowe, T.J. and N.D. Coulthard (1990), 'The conservation of a Nigerian wetland: the Hadejia-Nguru Wetland Conservation Project', *RSPB Conservation Review*, **3**, 80–85.

Thomas, D.H.L., F. Ayache and T. Hollis (1990), 'Use values and non-use values in the conservation of Ichkeul National Park, Tunisia', *Environmental Conservation*, **18** (2), 120–30.

Turner, R.K. (1990), 'A case study of wetlands', ch. 21 in D.W. Pearce and R.K. Turner, *Economics of Natural Resources and the Environment*, London: Wheatsheaf.

16. Valuing environmental functions: tropical wetlands*

Abstract
Recent studies have suggested that tropical wetland systems may have a crucial economic role to play in development. The following chapter provides an overview of these benefits, using the general framework of cost–benefit analysis as the methodological approach to assessing wetland values. An analysis of trade-offs between conserving or converting tropical wetlands demonstrates that taking into account the opportunity cost of wetland loss leads to a lower level of conversion than would otherwise be the case. Finally, the chapter discusses the extensions and limitations of the production function approach as applied to valuing nonmarketed wetland benefits (JEL Q20).

1. Introduction

Since 1900, over half of the world's wetlands may have disappeared. The United States alone has lost an estimated 54 per cent (87 million hectares) of its original wetlands, of which 87 per cent has been lost to agricultural development, 8 per cent to urban development and 5 per cent to other conversions (Maltby, 1986). The total area and status of tropical wetlands are still unknown, but the available evidence suggests that the pattern of wetland conversion in developing countries may be similar to that of the United States – and perhaps proceeding at even a faster rate in some regions.

Natural wetlands perform many important functions for humankind – prevention of storm damage, flood and water flow control, support of fisheries, nutrient and waste absorption and so forth. Wetlands can also be used for recreation and water transport, and their diverse resources can be directly exploited for fishing, agriculture, wildlife products, wood products and water supply. When properly measured, the total economic value of a wetland's ecological functions, its services and its resources may exceed the economic gains of coverting the area to an alternative use. Some economic studies have valued the benefits of *temperate* wetlands (see Turner, 1991; Turner and Jones, 1991; Farber and Costanza, 1987). But to date, little analysis of *tropical* wetland benefits has been undertaken. Yet recent studies across the developing regions of the world have suggested that tropical wetland systems – whether inland freshwater systems or coastal, mangrove systems – may have a crucial role to play in economic development (Barbier, 1993).

In particular, economic analysis of the environmental functions of tropical wetlands – the support and protection they provide for economic activity and property – is underdeveloped. A major problem is the lack of scientific data on ecological relationships and functions in developing countries. However, recent advances in the methodology for valuing nonmarketed environmental goods and services suggest that in many instances the data requirements for valuing environmental functions may not be too overwhelming. The production function approach to valuation may be especially promising as an approach to valuing certain environmental functions of tropical wetlands.

The following chapter discusses the valuation of environmental functions of tropical wetlands, focusing in particular on their *regulatory ecological functions* in support or protection of economic activities. The valuation problem is illustrated through the use of a basic model indicating the costs and benefits of converting or diverting wetland resources to an alternative use. The model indicates that failure to consider the foregone net benefits of *in situ* use of wetland resources can lead to an underestimation of the costs of alternative uses of these resources and their excessive appropriation from the wetlands. Given that many of the direct and indirect uses of wetland resources are nonmarketed, estimation of their value may be best approximated through the production function approach. Potential applications of this approach in the simple case of a single-use system are examined, along with the potential modifications and problems encountered. The full valuation problem of a multiple-use system presents further difficulties, which are also discussed. The paper concludes by highlighting the additional steps required to develop analytical techniques and applications which may have wider relevance to many valuation problems in developing countries.

2. Valuation approaches and methodology – an overview

'Valuing' a wetland essentially means valuing the characteristics of a system. Any system, whether natural or human-made, can be characterized by three concepts: stocks, flows, and the organization of these stocks and flows. These three system characteristics have parallel concepts in both ecology – structural component, environmental functions and diversity; and economics – assets, services and attributes. Table 16.1 summarizes the linkages between these basic system characteristics and their ecological and economic counterparts.

In ecology, a distinction is usually made between the regulatory environmental *functions* of an ecosystem (for example, nutrient cycles, microclimatic functions, energy flows, and so on) and its *structural components* (for example, biomass, abiotic matter, species of flora and fauna, and so on). This distinction is useful from an economic perspective, as it corresponds to the standard categories of resource *stocks* or *assets* (that is, the structural components) vs. environmental *flows* or *services* (that is, the ecological functions). In addition, ecosystems as

Table 16.1 General, ecological and economic system characteristics

General system characteristics	Ecological system characteristics	Economic system characteristics
Stocks	Structural components	Assets
Flows	Environmental functions	Services
Organization	Biological and cultural diversity	Attributes

Source: Adapted from Aylward and Barbier (1992).

a whole often have certain attributes (biological diversity, cultural uniqueness/heritage) that have economic value either because they induce certain economic uses or because they are valued in themselves.

It is therefore helpful to distinguish between:

1. *direct use* values (for example, the values derived from direct use or interaction with a wetland's resources and services);
2. *indirect use* values (the indirect support and protection provided to economic activity and property by the wetland's natural functions, or regulatory 'environmental' services); and
3. *nonuse* values (the values derived neither from current direct or indirect use of the wetland).[1]

Thus the total economic value of a tropical wetland system may comprise all three types of values – use (direct and indirect), option, and existence values. The standard techniques available for measuring the various economic values of wetlands are summarized in Figure 16.1.[2]

The use and nonuse values of temperate wetlands, which exist largely in developed countries, may differ significantly from those of tropical wetlands, which occur mainly in the developing world. For example, many tropical wetlands are being directly exploited, often through nonmarket, 'informal' economic activity, to support human livelihood, for example, through fishing, hunting, fuelwood extraction, and so on, whereas recreation/tourist use may often be limited. In contrast, direct exploitation to support livelihoods – except perhaps commercial fishing or forestry in some areas – may be small for most temperate wetlands, but their recreational value is often significant. Valuation of the non commercial direct use of wetlands by local populations is often critical in determining the economic value of tropical wetlands to developing countries. The failure to take this value into account is often a major factor behind policy decisions that lead to overexploitation or excessive degradation of tropical wetland systems.

Direct uses of the wetlands would therefore include both *consumptive* uses of its resources (for example, livestock grazing, fuelwood collection, forestry activities, agriculture, water use, hunting and fishing) and *nonconsumptive* uses of wetland 'services' (for example, recreation, tourism, *in situ* research and education, navigation along water courses).

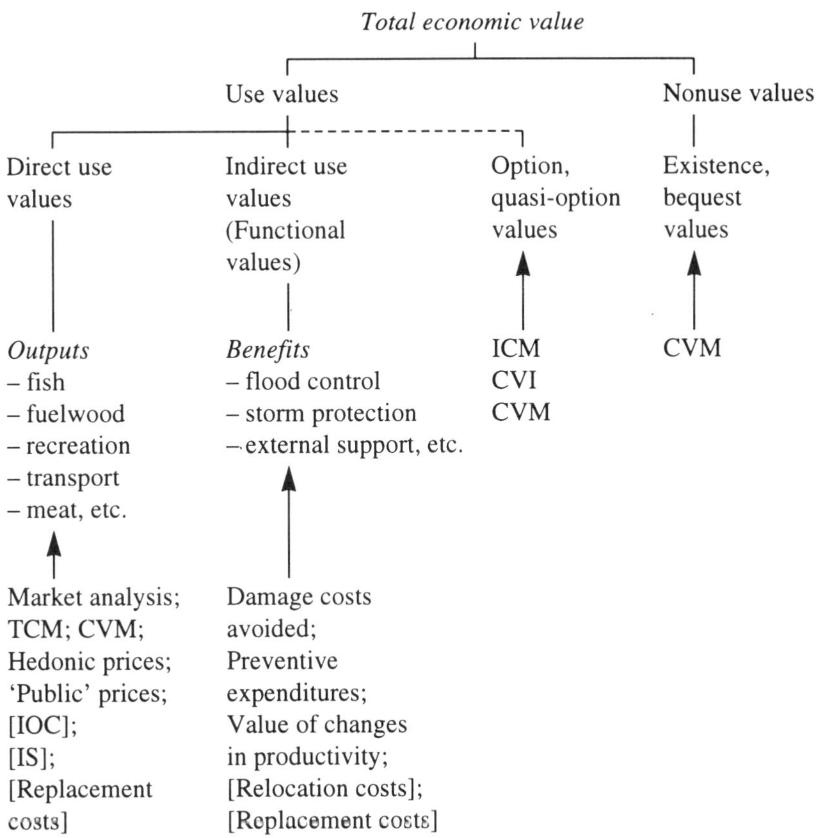

Notes:
ICM = individual choice models
CVI = conditional value of information
CVM = contingent valuation method
TCM = travel cost method
IOC = indirect opportunity cost approach
IS = indirect substitute approach
[ ] = valuation methodology to be used with care

Source: Adapted from Barbier (1989a).

Figure 16.1 Valuing wetland benefits

Direct uses of wetlands could involve both commercial and noncommerical activities, with some of the latter activities often being important for the subsistence needs of local populations. Commercial uses may be important for both domestic and international markets. In general, the value of marketed products (and services) of wetlands is easier to measure than the value of non-commercial and subsistence direct uses. As noted above, this is one reason why policymakers often fail to consider subsistence and informal uses of tropical wetlands in many development decisions.

Various regulatory ecological functions of tropical wetlands may also have important indirect use values. Their values derive from supporting or protecting economic activities that have directly measurable values. For example, the groundwater recharge function of floodplain wetlands may have indirect use value through its replenishment of aquifer systems that supply water for domestic use and agriculture. The storm prevention function of mangrove swamps may also have indirect use value through the protection afforded coastal property and economic activity. The biological diversity of a wetland ecosystem may also have an important role in maintaining regulatory functions, for example, changes in species diversity may affect how well support and protective services function, and in some cases, even their availability. The indirect use value of an environmental function is related to the change in the value of production or consumption of the activity or property that it is protecting or supporting. However, as this contribution is nonmarketed, financially unrewarded and only indirectly connected to economic activities, these indirect use values may be difficult to value (Aylward and Barbier, 1992). Although few valuation studies of key environmental functions in tropical wetlands have been conducted, the available evidence suggests that the economic value of regulatory environmental functions may be highly significant (Adams and Hollis, 1988; Barbier 1989a and 1993; Barbier, Adams and Kimmage 1991; Lal and Dixon 1990; Ruitenbeek 1992; Twilley 1991; Yañez-Arancibia and Day 1988).

Despite the range of benefits provided by tropical wetlands, they are currently under threat from a number of sources. In many cases, the loss of wetland resources, functions and even entire systems may be justified. To make consistent choices between wetland conservation, preservation and development options – or between a decision to halt, modify or continue with an activity that is inflicting damage on a wetland – requires the application of a consistent economic appraisal methodology for evaluating the alternative options. At the heart of the appraisal methodology is the determination of the various costs and benefits associated with each option. Critical to this assessment of costs and benefits is the choice of appropriate valuation techniques, as indicated in Figure 16.1 and discussed above.

Barbier (1993) suggests essentially three broad categories of assessment, with each category corresponding to each major type of policy decision concerning wetland use that generally needs evaluating:[3]

(a) *impact analysis* – an assessment of the damages inflicted on the wetland from a specific environmental impact (for example, oil spills);
(b) *partial valuation* – an assessment of alternative resource allocations or project options involving wetland systems or resources (for example, whether to divert water from the wetlands for other uses, or to convert/develop part of the wetlands at the expense of other uses); and,
(c) *total valuation* – an assessment of the total economic value of the wetland system (for example, for national income accounting or to determine its worth as a protected area).

Under the first approach, assessing a specific environmental impact involves valuing the changes in the wetland resulting from that impact. For example, assume that discharges of oil are regularly polluting an estuarine wetland, affecting both fish production and water quality in the wetlands. The costs of this activity are the losses in wetland values arising from damage to the ecosystem and its resources. These damages would amount to the losses in net production benefits (that is, the economic benefits of production less the costs) from the impacts of the oil spills on the fishery plus the losses in net environmental benefits in terms of poorer quality water supplies for wetland and neighbouring settlements, as well as for general ecosystem functioning. Thus, by assessing and valuing these losses, we would arrive at an estimate of the net production and environmental benefits of the wetlands, NB^w, that are affected by the oil spills. The total cost of this impact, C^I, in terms of damage to the wetland are these foregone net benefits:

$$C^I = NB^w. \tag{16.1}$$

Dixon and Hufschmidt (1986) and Dixon *et al.* (1988) provide case studies of applying this particular approach in the overall context of economic appraisal of environmental impacts. For example, in the analysis of the cost-effectiveness of various options for disposing of wastewater from a geothermal power plant on the island of Leyte in the Philippines, it was necessary to decide which means of wastewater disposal from the plant would protect the environment in the most cost-effective manner. For some of the options, the costs of the environmental impacts in terms of lost marine fishery and rice production were quantified. Other environmental costs, such as energy loss, lost riverine fishery production, human health effects and amenity impacts, were not possible to quantify. For example, the analysis showed that the quantifiable environmental costs of releasing untreated waste into the Bao River or into the Mahiao River were quite high, accounting for 41 per cent and 35 per cent of total measurable costs of these options, respectively. Both options may also seriously contaminate the marine ecosystem with unknown and unquantifiable effects.

An impact analysis was also conducted to examine the downstream effects of logging-induced sedimentation on the marine environment of Bacuit Bay, Palawan, the Philippines (Hodgson and Dixon, 1988).[4] The analysis indicated that continued logging of the Bacuit Bay watershed would result in a reduction in gross revenues of more than US$40 million from tourism and marine fisheries over a ten-year period. The present value of these lost earnings exceeded US$11 million. The major impact was on coral cover and diversity, which have an important indirect use value in supporting marine fisheries. Increased sedimentation of coastal waters reduces both coral cover and diversity, eventually causing a marked fall in fish biomass. Loss of pristine coral reefs and clear water also affects tourism, which is largely from an international clientele.

The second assessment approach, that is, partial valuation of wetland benefits, may be required when one or more development options may lead to alteration or conversion of wetland systems. That is, choices involving diversion, allocation or conversion of wetland resources should compare the opportunity costs of the proposed options in terms of the subsequent loss in wetland benefits. For example, assume that there is an upstream irrigation project on a river that is providing water for agriculture. If this project diverts water from a wetland downstream, then any resulting loss in wetland benefits must be included as part of the overall costs of the project. Given direct benefits (for example, irrigation water for farming), B^D, and direct costs (for example, costs of constructing the dam, irrigation channels, etc.), C^D, then the direct net benefits of the project are:

$$NB^D = B^D - C^D. \tag{16.2}$$

However, by diverting water that would otherwise flow into the downstream wetlands, the development project may result in losses to floodplain agriculture and other primary production activities, less groundwater recharge and other external impacts. Given these reductions in the net production and environmental benefits, NB^W, of the wetlands, then the true net benefits of the development project (NB^P) are $NB^D - NB^W$. The development project can therefore only be acceptable if:

$$NB^P = NB^D - NB^W > 0. \tag{16.3}$$

If the foregone wetland benefits are significant, then the failure to assess the loss of wetland benefits will clearly lead to an overestimation of NB^P. This is tantamount to assuming that there is no opportunity cost of diverting floodwater from the wetlands, which is rarely the case. Moreover, it may not be necessary to measure all affected wetland benefits – for example, if one or two impacts prove to be sufficiently large to render the development project uneconomical. In any case, it is not necessary to measure all wetland benefits but only those benefits which are affected by the development project – which is why this approach is called a 'partial valuation'.

A partial valuation was conducted to assess the economic importance of the Hadejia-Jama'are wetlands, and thus the opportunity cost to Nigeria of its loss, by estimating some of the key direct use values the floodplain provides to local populations through crop production, fuelwood and fishing (Barbier, Adams and Kimmage 1991).[5] The economic analysis indicates that these benefits are substantial on both a per hectare basis and a water input basis – that is, the minimum and maximum amount of floodwater required to sustain them. This proves to be the case even when the agricultural benefits were adjusted to take into account the unsustainability of much pump-irrigated wheat production within the wetlands. As indicated in Table 16.2, the present value of the aggregate stream of agricultural, fishing and fuelwood benefits were estimated to be around N850 to N1280 per ha, or around N240 to N370 per $10^3 m^3$ (with 'maximum' flood inputs).[6]

Table 16.2 Comparison of present value net economic benefits: Kano River Project Phase I and Hadejia-Jama'are floodplain, Nigeria

	(N7.5 = US$1, 1989–90)			
	(8%, 50 years)	(8%, 30 years)	(12%, 50 years)	(12%, 30 years)
Per hectare[a]				
HJF (N/ha)	1276	1176	872	846
KRP (N/ha)	233	214	158	153
Per water use[b]				
HJF ($N/10^3 m^3$)	366	337	250	242
KRP ($N10^3 m^3$)	0.3	0.3	0.2	0.2

Notes:

a Based on a total production area of 730 000 ha for Hadejia-Jama'are floodplain (HJF) and a total crop cultivated area of 19 107 ha in 1985/86 for the Kano River Project Phase I (KRP).

b Assumes an annual average river flow into Hadejia-Jama'are floodplain (HJF) of 2.549 Mm^3 and an annual water use of 15 000 m^3 per ha for the Kano River Project Phase I (KRP).

Source: Barbier, Adams and Kimmage (1991).

The economic importance of the wetlands suggest that the benefits it provides cannot be excluded as an opportunity cost of any scheme that diverts water away from the floodplain system. When compared to the net economic benefits of the Kano River Project, the economic returns to the floodplain appear much more favourable (see Table 16.2). This is particularly the case when the relative returns to the project in terms of water input use is compared to that of the floodplain system. The result should cause some concern, given that the existing and planned water developments along the Hadejia-Jama'are river system, such as the Kano River Project, will continue diverting water from the floodplain.

As the name implies, the final assessment approach involving total valuation of a wetland system requires an appraisal of all the net benefits of a wetland system. If the objective of the total valuation is to measure, say, the economic contribution of the wetlands to the welfare of society as part of a resource accounting exercise, then the objective should be to value as many of the net production and environmental benefits, NB^W, of the wetlands as possible. Another objective requiring total valuation would be the need to determine whether or not the wetlands should become a protected area with restricted or controlled use. The total net wetland benefits would therefore have to exceed the direct costs, C^P, of setting up the protected area (including any costs of relocating or compensating existing users) plus the net benefits foregone, NB^A, of alternative uses of the wetlands:

$$NB^W > C^P + NB^A. \tag{16.4}$$

Ruitenbeek (1989) has followed this approach in determining the economic value of Korup National Park in Cameroon, where the alternative use would be logging of the forest area.[7] Ruitenbeek (1992) uses a similar approach in evaluating the trade-offs between different forestry options in a mangrove system in Bintuni Bay, Irian Jaya, Indonesia – although in this example the comparison is between the total economic value of a wetlands preserved through a cutting ban and the total economic value generated by various forestry development options ranging from partial, selective cutting to clear-cutting.[8]

An important feature of the analysis is that it explicitly incorporates the linkages between mangrove conversion, offshore fishery productivity, traditional uses and the imputed benefits of erosion control and biodiversity maintenance functions. To the extent that these linkages exist, some of these direct and indirect uses become mutually exclusive with more intensive mangrove exploitation through forestry options. The 'optimal' forest management option will therefore depend on the strength of the environment linkages. The results indicate that the clear-cut option is optimal only if no environmental linkages exist – a highly unrealistic assumption. At the other extreme, a cutting ban is only optimal if the linkages are very strong, that is, mangrove alteration and conversion would lead to immediate and lineai impacts throughout the ecosystem. Even if weak interactions exist, an 80 per cent selective cutting policy with replanting is preferable to clear-cutting. However, given the considerable uncertainty over the dynamics of the mangrove ecosystem, and the fact that alteration and conversion may be irreversible and exhibit high economic costs, the analysis concludes that there is little economic advantage to cutting significant amounts (for example, more than 25 per cent) of the mangrove area.

3. The value of alternative tropical wetland uses – a more formal analysis[9]

A simple model can be invoked to indicate more formally the need for consistent choice in decisions to convert tropical wetlands, or to allocate their resources (for example, water) to other uses, when such decisions involve the loss of wetland benefits. As the previous sections indicate that many conflicts in tropical countries are over wetland resource use values – that is, whether to convert or exploit wetland resources to alternative productive uses or to maintain current direct and indirect uses of tropical wetlands – the following model will focus on this choice of alternative wetland use.

At any time, t, scarce tropical wetland resources can be represented as a stock, $S(t)$. Which resources are to be represented by S will of course depend on the allocation problem. For example, if a coastal mangrove is being converted to shrimp ponds or irrigated rice production, then S could represent the total stock of land area within the mangrove system. Alternatively, if the mangrove forest itself is valued, for example, for woodchip production, then S could be either the stock of mangrove biomass or forest area. Finally, in cases where the water flowing into the wetland is being reallocated, for example, floodplain water diverted by upstream developments for irrigation and industrial use, then S might represent the total volume of water stored in the wetlands.

Equally, the amount of wetland resources converted (or diverted) from the wetlands in any time period, $D(t)$, can also be defined dependent on the nature of the conversion (or diversion) activity.[10] To simplify matters, it is assumed that the conversion/diversion activity leads to an irreversible loss in the wetland resource, S, which is essentially nonrenewable:

$$\dot{S} = -D. \tag{16.5}$$

Thus, by virtue of (16.5), the analysis can focus on the costs and benefits of productive activities that lead to wetland loss.[11]

Two production activities are assumed to be competing for wetland resources. One activity combines resources extracted from the wetlands, D, with other inputs, Z, to produce a commodity, Y. The other activity either *directly* uses the remaining stock of resources, S, or is *indirectly* supported or protected by the wetland resources. The various direct and indirect use values of tropical wetlands were discussed in detail in previous sections and are outlined in Figure 16.1. The stock of wetland resources, S, can therefore be considered one input in the production function of the activity, which along with other inputs, X, produce a commodity Q.[12]

If the production functions for Q and Y are assumed to be increasing, strictly concave, twice differentiable and linearly homogeneous, and if their units are normalized so that X and Z are equal to 1, then:

$$Q = F(S, 1) = f(S), \quad f' > 0, \quad f'' < 0, \tag{16.6}$$

$$Y = G(D, 1) = g(D), \quad g' > 0, \quad g'' < 0. \tag{16.7}$$

Thus, the tropical wetlands country is assumed to maximize the present value of future welfare, W:

$$\underset{D}{\text{Max}}\, W = \int_0^\infty \{U(Q, Y) - C\} e^{-\delta t} \mathrm{d}t, \tag{16.8}$$

subject to (16.5), (16.6), and (16.7), and

$$C = c(D, S), \;\; c_D > 0, \;\; c_S > 0, \;\; c_{DD} \geq 0, \;\; c_{SS} \geq 0, \tag{16.9}$$

$$S(0) = S_0 \;\text{ and }\; \lim_{t \to \infty} S(t) \geq 0. \tag{16.10}$$

The control variable of the problem is D, and δ is the social rate of discount. The 'utility' function, U, essentially represents aggregate *gross consumer surplus*, and is assumed to have the standard properties with respect to its partial derivatives, $U'(\cdot) > 0$, $U''(\cdot) \leq 0$ and $U'(\cdot) \to \infty$ as $D, S \to 0$.[13] Equation (16.9) represents the aggregate *direct* costs to the country of producing Q and Y, using the (normalized) inputs of S and D.[14] Equation (16.10) contains the initial and terminal boundary conditions.

The current value Hamiltonian of the above optimal control problem is:

$$H = U(f(S), g(D)) - c(S, D) - \lambda D, \tag{16.11}$$

where λ is the costate variable of the shadow price of the 'unextracted' wetland resource.

Assuming an interior solution, the maximum principle yields the following conditions:

$$\lambda \geq U_Y g' - c_D, \quad (16.12)$$

$$\dot{\lambda} = \delta\lambda - (U_Q f' - c_S), \quad (16.13)$$

where $\partial U/\partial Q = U_Q$ and $\partial U/\partial Y = U_Y$. Equation (16.12) reflects the non-negativity constraint $D \geq 0$. If $D > 0$, then the shadow price of the 'unextracted' wetland resource must equal the difference between the value of the marginal product of the resource appropriated to produce Y and the marginal costs of this production. However, if λ exceeds the net value marginal product of the appropriated resource, then conversion of wetland resources is not worth it and $D = 0$.[15] Equation (16.13) indicates the optimal rate of increase in the value of the (unextracted) wetland resource. Assuming $D > 0$, (16.13) can be rewritten as:

$$\dot{\lambda}/\lambda = \delta - (U_Q f' - c_S)/\,(U_Y g' - c_D). \quad (16.13)$$

Thus, the rate of change in the shadow price of the tropical wetland, $\dot{\lambda}$, is determined not only by the social rate of discount, δ, as is the case in standard nonrenewable resource problems, but also by an additional factor indicating the relative social value of *in situ* wetland resources $(U_Q f' - c_S)/\,(U_Y g' - c_D)$. In other words, δ represents the opportunity cost of 'holding onto' wetland resources today – as opposed to appropriating them for current production of Y – whereas $(U_Q f' - c_S)/\,(U_Y g' - c_D)$ represents the social gains from 'holding onto' wetland resources in terms of their relative direct and/or indirect use values. Note that the right-hand side of (16.14) can be positive, negative or equal to zero. If $\dot{\lambda}/\lambda > 0$, then the optimal rate of extraction should increase over time; however, $\dot{\lambda}/\lambda > 0$ implies that $\dot{D} < 0$.[16]

Essentially, conditions (16.14) confirms the arguments in the previous section: if policymakers fail to take into account the 'opportunity' costs of wetland loss in terms of foregone direct and indirect use values, then they are misrepresenting the true social value of tropical wetlands. The failure to consider the foregone net benefits of *in situ* use of wetland resources can lead to an underestimation of the costs of alternative uses of these resources and their excessive extraction from the wetlands. The latter point will be illustrated explicitly in a moment. First consider the case where the net benefits of *in situ* wetland resource use are ignored.

If tropical wetlands are viewed only as a source of resources that essentially have no economic value unless they are converted or diverted to a 'productive' activity, then the planning problem as represented by (16.5)–(16.10) effectively reduces to the even simpler problem of nonrenewable resource extraction. As the previous sections of the chapter have indicated, this is precisely the view of tropical wetlands that is often taken in policy and investment decisions that determine the allocation of wetland resources. The Hamiltonian (16.11) therefore becomes:

$$H = U(g(D)) - c(D) - \lambda D. \tag{16.15}$$

Assuming $D > 0$ and $S > 0$ in finite time and an interior solution, the standard first-order conditions for optimal nonrenewable resource extraction result:

$$\lambda = U_Y g' - c_D, \tag{16.16}$$

$$\dot{\lambda} = \delta\lambda \text{ or } \lambda(t) = \lambda_0 e^{\delta t}, \tag{16.17}$$

where $\lambda_0 = \lambda(t)$. Condition (16.16) has the same interpretation as (16.12) for $D > 0$. Comparison of (16.17) and (16.14) confirm the difference between the standard nonrenewable extraction problem and the problem where the foregone net benefits of *in situ* wetland resources are an opportunity cost to appropriating these resources for an alternative productive use.

Following Dasgupta and Heal (1979), the extraction path $D(t)$ can be characterized as a demand for wetland resources that is inversely related to its price, $\lambda(t)$. Assuming this demand is isoelastic, then:

$$D(t) = \lambda(t)^{-1/\alpha}, \tag{16.18}$$

where $\alpha > 0$. Substituting (16.17) into (16.18) yields:

$$D(t) = \lambda_0^{-1/\alpha} e^{-\delta t/\alpha}. \tag{16.19}$$

However, the condition that D is essential to production of Y such that $D > 0$ over finite time also implies that:

$$\int_0^\infty D(t)dt = S_0 \quad or \quad (\alpha / \delta)\lambda_0^{-1/\alpha} = S_0. \tag{16.20}$$

Utilizing (16.17)–(16.20), optimal paths for D and λ can be determined:

$$D^*(t) = [\delta S_0/\alpha]e^{-\delta t/\alpha}, \tag{16.21}$$

$$\lambda^*(t) = [\delta S_0/\alpha]^{-\alpha} e^{\delta t}. \tag{16.22}$$

Thus, if the initial level of wetland resource appropriation is set at the optimal level $\delta S_0/\alpha$, $D(t)$ will decline thereafter at the rate δ/α. The value of 'unextracted' resources will begin at $[\delta S_0/\alpha]^{-\alpha}$ and rise at the rate δ.

Similar optimal paths can also be constructed for the original wetlands problem. To facilitate comparison with the paths just derived for the 'myopic' wetlands problem, assume that $\dot{\lambda} > 0$ in the first-order conditions of the original model. Returning to (16.13) and integrating yields:

$$\lambda(t) = \lambda_0 e^{\delta t} - \int (U_Q f_s - c_S)\mathrm{d}t. \tag{16.23}$$

The second term on the right-hand side of (16.23) represents the cumulative stream of net benefits from *in situ* wetland resources over time. Effectively, this term is the undiscounted asset value of 'conserved', or 'unappropriated', wetland resources at time t. Defining $\phi(t) = \int (U_Q f_S - c_S)\mathrm{d}_t$ and substituting (16.23) into (16.18) yields:

$$D(t) = \lambda_0^{-1\alpha} e^{-\delta t/\alpha} - \phi^{-1/\alpha}. \tag{16.24}$$

Letting $\phi(t) = \phi_0 e^{\beta t}$, where $\beta > 0$,[17] then

$$\int_0^\infty D(t)\mathrm{d}t = (\alpha/\delta)\lambda_0^{-1/\alpha} + (\alpha/\beta)\phi_0^{-1/\alpha}. \tag{16.25}$$

It is possible for expression (16.25) to be greater than or equal to S_0. Assuming first that the entire stock of wetland resources is appropriated in the long run, then (16.25) suggests that:

$$\lambda_0^{**} = [\delta S_0/\alpha]^{-\alpha} - (\alpha/\beta)\,\phi_0 < \lambda_0^{*}\,. \tag{16.26}$$

From (16.23) and (16.24), the optimal paths for D and λ can therefore be determined as:

$$D(t)^{**} = [(\delta S_0/\alpha) - ((\alpha/\beta)\,\phi_0)^{-1/\alpha}]e^{-\beta t/\alpha} - \phi^{-1/\alpha} < D(t)^{*}, \tag{16.27}$$

$$\lambda(t)^{**} = [(\delta S_0/\alpha)^{-\alpha} - (\alpha/\beta)\,\phi_0]e^{\delta t} - \phi < \lambda(t)^{*}. \tag{16.28}$$

Taking into account the asset value of 'unappropriated' wetland resources has the effect of shifting down both the optimal path of resource extraction, $D(t)$, and that of the shadow price, $\lambda(t)$. The difference in the two extraction paths (16.24) and (16.25) is:

$$\Delta(t) = D(t)^* - D(t)^{**} = ((\alpha/\beta)\,\phi_0)^{-1/\alpha} e^{-\beta t/\alpha} + \phi^{-1/\alpha}, \qquad (16.29)$$

where $d\Delta/dt < 0$. Thus as shown in Figure 16.2, the two paths eventually will converge in the long run.

In the second case, where some of the stock of wetland resources remain even in the long run, then:

$$\int_0^\infty D(t)dt + R = S_0, \qquad (16.30)$$

Where R is the remaining long-run stock of wetland resources. Defining $\hat{D}(t)$ as the new extraction path for wetland resources, it follows that:

$$\hat{D} = [(\delta/\alpha)\,(S_0 - R)) - ((\alpha/\beta)\,\phi_0)^{-1/\alpha}]e^{-\beta t/\alpha} - \phi^{-1/\alpha} < D(t)^{**} < D(t)^*. \qquad (16.31)$$

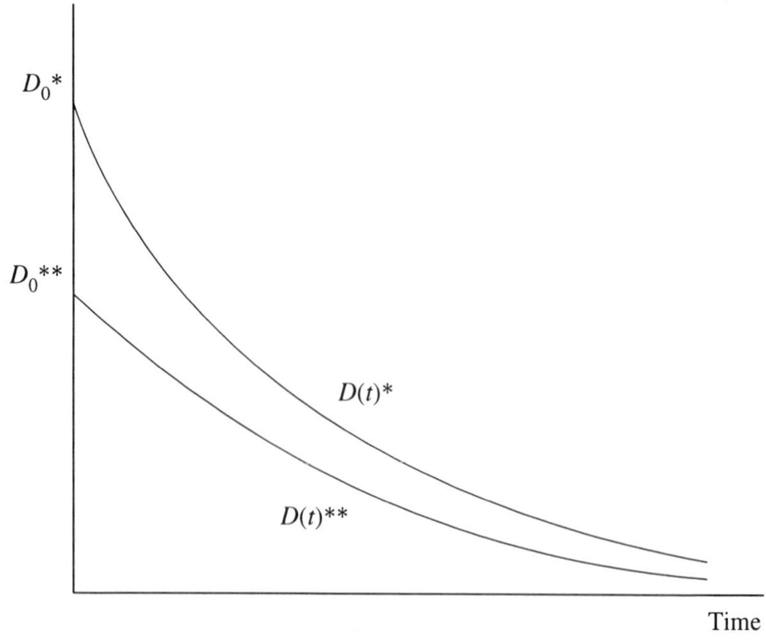

Figure 16.2 Optimal extraction paths for wetland resources

In sum, the above analysis has demonstrated formally that, when the loss of wetland benefits is taken into account in decisions to convert tropical wetlands, a lower level of wetland conversion will result than would be the case if these wetland benefits are ignored. In other words, policymakers should be absolutely certain that the opportunity cost of wetland resource conversion and appropriation is zero before embarking on investment and policy decisions that are based on this assumption and lead to irreversible wetland loss.

If the opportunity cost of wetland loss is not zero, then the wetland benefits foregone must be explicitly accounted for in development decisions. This again raises the issue as to what is the best method for valuing these benefits, given that the economic contribution of wetland resources – particularly their environmental functions – is often nonmarketed.

4. Valuation of wetland environmental functions: the production function approach

The preceding analysis noted the importance of wetland resources for production by including them explicitly in the production function for Q. The assumption was that wetland resources were being either *directly used* in production as inputs or *indirectly used* in the sense that the environmental functions of wetland resources were supporting or protecting economic activity. Earlier sections have noted the important economic contribution of many wetland indirect use values, such as support of fisheries, groundwater recharge, flood and water flow control, prevention of storm damage, and so forth. The results of the previous analysis would suggest that decisions concerning wetland conversion and resource use do require proper valuation of the environmental functions of tropical wetlands where these functions are instrumental in supporting or protecting economic activity.

One promising method is to employ the production function approach,[18] as implied by equation (16.6) above, to capture the indirect use value of regulatory ecological functions:

$$Q = F(X_i \ldots X_k, S), \tag{16.32}$$

where $F_S > 0$, $F_{SS} < 0$. For example, a common ecological function of mangroves is support of offshore fisheries by serving as both a spawning ground and a nursery for fry (see, for example, Yañez-Arancibia and Day, 1988). The area of mangroves in a coastal region, S, may therefore have a direct influence on the catch of mangrove-dependent species, Q, which is independent from the standard inputs of a commercial fishery, $X_i \ldots X_k$. Including mangrove area as a determinant of fish catch may therefore 'capture' some element of the economic contribution of this important ecological support function.

Applying the production function approach to the various indirect use values of tropical wetlands may prove a useful method of estimating these nonmarketed – but often significant – economic values. However, it is extremely important that the relationship between the environmental regulatory function of the tropical wetlands and the economic activity it protects or supports is well understood.

Mäler (1991) distinguishes between applications of the production function approach. When production, Q, is measurable, and either there is a market price for this output or one can be imputed, then determining the marginal value of the resource is relatively straightforward. If Q cannot be measured directly, then either a marketed substitute has to be found, or possible complementarity or substitutability between S and one or more of the other (marketed) inputs, $X_i \ldots X_k$, has to be specified explicitly. Although all these applications require detailed knowledge of the physical effects on production of changes in the wetland resource, S, and its environmental functions, applications that assume complementarity or substitutability between the resource and other inputs are particularly stringent on the information required on physical relationships in production. Clearly, cooperation is required between economists, ecologists and other researchers to determine the precise nature of these relationships.

Applications of the production function approach may be most straightforward in the case of *single use systems* – that is, wetland systems in which the predominant economic value is a single regulatory function or a group of ecological functions providing support or protection for an economic activity in concert. For example, Ellis and Fisher (1987) use this approach to model explicitly the environmental function of Gulf Coast wetlands in support of the commercial blue crab fishery. Taking the sum of consumers' and producers' surpluses as the measure of economic value, they hypothesize that an increase in wetland area increases the abundance of crabs and thus lowers the cost of catch. The value of the wetlands' support for the fishery – which in this case is equivalent to the value of increments to wetland area – can then be imputed from the resulting changes in consumers' and producers' surplus.

In the Ellis and Fisher model, equation (16.32) above assumes the specific Cobb–Douglas form:

$$Q = AX^a S^b, \tag{16.33}$$

where Q is the quantity of crab catch in pounds, X is catch effort measured by traps set and S is area of wetlands. The corresponding cost functions is:

$$C = WA^{-1/a} S^{-b/a} Q^{1/a}, \tag{16.34}$$

where W is the unit cost of effort and S is determined exogenously. Assuming an isoelastic demand for crabs and either private ownership or optimal public management (that is, price equals marginal cost in both cases), Ellis and Fisher solve the two-equation model for the incremental value of the wetland's support function.

However, using the Ellis and Fisher model for the blue crab fishery, Freeman (1991) has made the important additional point that the values imputed to the wetlands are influenced by the market conditions and regulatory policies that determine the conditions of access and rate of utilization of the fishery. For example, under open access, rents in the fishery would be dissipated, and price would be equated to average and not marginal costs. As a consequence, producer surplus is zero and only consumer surplus determines the value of increased wetland area. When the demand for crabs is inelastic, the social value of an increase in area is higher under open access than under optimal regulation, whereas the wetlands are more valuable under optimal regulation when demand is elastic. This result stems from the role of price changes in allocating welfare gains between producers and consumers: in the case of optimal regulations, part of the consumers' gain is a transfer from producer surplus, whereas under open access and zero producer surplus, any reduction in the price of fish associated with the average cost curve shifting down (in response to an increase in wetland area) results in a gain in consumer surplus and increases wetland value.[19] These different impacts of market conditions and regulatory policies for the production function approach to valuing wetlands are an important consideration in the application of this approach to tropical wetlands in many developing regions, where open access and imperfect markets for resources are common.

In the case of *multiple use systems* – that is, wetland systems in which a regulatory function may support or protect many different economic activities, or which may have more than one regulatory ecological function of important economic value – applications of the production function approach may be slightly more problematic. In particular, assumptions concerning the ecological relationships among these various multiple uses must be carefully constructed.

For example, an important feature of the analysis of the mangrove wetlands of Bintuni Bay, Irian Jaya, Indonesia was that it attempted to incorporate explicitly the possible ecological linkages between indirect and direct use values (Ruitenbeek, 1992). Specifically, the mangroves may support many economic activities within the wetlands, such as commercial shrimp fishing, commercial sago production and traditional household production from hunting, fishing, gathering and cottage industry; they may also have indirect use value through controlling erosion and sedimentation, which protects agricultural production in the region; and they have an indirect role in supporting biodiversity. To the extent that the ecological linkages in terms of support or protection of these activities are strong, then the opportunity cost of forestry options that lead to the depletion or degradation of the mangroves will be high. Thus, as discussed above, the 'optimal' forest management option – whether clear-cutting, selective cutting or complete preservation – depends critically on the strength of the ecological linkages.

In the absence of any ecological data on these linkages, Ruitenbeek developed several different scenarios based on different linkage assumptions. This essentially amounted to specifying more precisely the relationship between Q and S in the production function (16.32) for each productive activity at time t, Q_{it}:

$$Q_{it}/Q_{i0} = (S_{t-\tau}/S_0)^{\alpha}, \tag{16.35}$$

where S_t is the area of remaining undisturbed mangroves at time t, α and τ are impact intensity and delay parameters respectively, $Q_{i0} = Qi_t\ (t = 0)$ and $S_0 = S_t\ (t = 0)$. For example, for fishery–mangrove linkages, a moderate linkage of $\alpha = 0.5$ and $\tau = 5$ would imply that shrimp output varies with the square root of mangrove area (for example, a 50 per cent reduction in mangrove area would result in a 30 per cent fall in shrimp production), and there would be a delay of five years before the impact takes effect. If no ecological linkages are present, that is, there is no indirect use value of mangroves in terms of supporting shrimp fishing, then $\alpha = 0$. At the other extreme, very strong linkages imply that the impacts of mangrove removal are linear and immediate, that is, $\alpha = 1$ and $\tau = 0$. As discussed above, the analysis concluded that the assumption of no environmental linkages is unrealistic for most economic activities in the wetlands. Moreover, given the uncertainty over these linkages and the high costs associated with irreversible loss if environmental linkages prove to be significant, then only modest selective cutting (for example, 25 per cent or less) of the mangrove area was recommended.

Two major difficulties in specifying ecological–economic relationships for the application of the production function approach to estimating indirect use values in multiple use tropical wetland systems are the problems of 'double-counting' and 'trade-offs' between various direct and indirect use values (Aylward and Barbier, 1992). The problem arises when analysts attempt to 'aggregate' the total economic value (TEV) of the wetlands from the different use value subcomponents.

Aylward and Barbier provide an example of both on-site and off-site double-counting in terms of the nutrient retention function of a coastal wetland. Coastal wetlands often absorb organic nutrients from sewage and other waste emitted into water-ways further upstream. Suppose that the nutrients held by the wetland are indirectly supporting both shrimp production within the wetland area and the growth of fish fry that supply an offshore fishery. If the full value of the shrimp production is already accounted for as a direct use value of the wetland's resources, adding in the share of the nutrient retention service as an indirect value and aggregating to obtain TEV would double-count this indirect use. In other words, the value of shrimp production already 'captures' the value-added contribution of nutrient retention. If instead one wanted to explicitly account for the value-added contribution to shrimp production of the nutrient retention function, then the direct value of the shrimp must be decreased to account for the return in value now attached to the nutrient retention service.

Similarly, if the fish fry supported through nutrients retained in the wetland eventually migrate to an offshore fishery, then the indirect contribution during the fry's stay in the wetland is included as an off-site component of the service's value. That is, the nutrient retention function of the wetland produces an 'external' benefit in terms of supporting an offshore fishery. Again, care must be taken to adjust the value of harvested fish in any companion analysis of the adjoining fishery to avoid misrepresenting the total economic value of the wetland and the fishery taken together.

Trade-offs between two or more indirect use values of a given ecosystem may also occur. For example, as discussed above, the Hadejia-Jama'are floodplain in Northern Nigeria supports a number of important agricultural, forestry and fishing activities within the wetland area. The floodplain also contributes to the recharge of groundwater, which is in turn drawn off by numerous small village wells throughout the region for domestic use and agricultural activities. However, concerns have recently been expressed about the excessive water use of pump-irrigated wheat production within the floodplain (Barbier, Adams and Kimmage, 1991). Increasing use of the floodplain water to support this activity may mean less water available for natural groundwater recharge – and thus for village wells outside the floodplain. If there are trade-offs between the two environmental support functions, then adding the full value of the wetland's contribution to pump-irrigated wheat production within the floodplain to the full value of groundwater recharge of wells in neighbouring regions would overestimate the total benefit of these two environmental functions.

In sum, the problems posed by double-counting and possible trade-offs need to be sorted out in any measurement of the indirect use values of environmental regulatory functions in multiple use tropical wetland systems. While it is necessary to disaggregate the goods, services and attributes of an ecosystem for valuation purposes, any complementarity and substitutability of these services must be accounted for in arriving at either total indirect use or total use values. Otherwise these values may be grossly overstated.

Finally, a major difficulty that any interdisciplinary effort to improve economic valuation of ecological functions must overcome is reconciling the different 'world views' of economics and ecology. Despite the apparent unifying methodology over system concepts implied by Table 16.1, fundamental disagreements do arise between economists and ecologists over what these concepts actually entail and how they relate to the ecosystem as a whole, especially in a dynamic context of ecological change. For example, Common and Perrings (1992) have argued that disagreements over the interpretation of economic and ecological 'sustainability' have hindered cooperation between the two disciplines on the decision rules concerning economic use of ecosystem goods and services. Bridging these conceptual differences is fundamental to progress in economic valuation of ecological functions, which is best accomplished through more applied interdisciplinary research on such problems.

5. Conclusions

Increasingly, tropical wetlands are seen to perform many important ecological regulatory functions that protect or support economic activity. Valuing this indirect use value may be important to decisions concerning wetland conversion and the diversion of wetland resources to other uses. When the economic value of environmental functions are significant, less 'extraction' of wetland resources appears to be more optimal than in the case where the opportunity cost of extraction is zero.

Consistent choice in the allocation of wetland resources therefore requires careful analysis of the economic values provided by tropical wetlands, in particular the indirect use values of environmental regulatory functions. Because the economic services of these functions are generally nonmarketed, special valuation techniques may need to be employed to assess their economic contribution. Although the production function approach is promising, care must be taken to specify correctly the ecological–economic relationships determining the role of wetland environmental functions in production, the regulatory policies and market conditions that influence the value of this production and the problems of double-counting and possible trade-offs encountered when the indirect use values of multiple use systems are analysed.

However, there are certain ecosystem valuation issues that are problematic for a cost–benefit framework to address without adequate guidance from policymakers.[20] One is the possibility that human activities can lead to changes in ecosystems with uncertain and irreversible consequences. As discussed previously, economic concepts such as option and quasi-option value can be incorporated into the cost–benefit analysis to allow for certain contingencies arising from environmental losses. However, economists have increasingly recognized that valuation of whole-scale ecosystem changes must explicitly or implicitly make judgements involving intergenerational equity, with implications for the choice of discount rate and/or the valuation methodologies chosen.[21] When these changes may potentially endanger key species, or even whole ecosystems, then some recent economic thinking has advocated the more precautionary approach of respect for 'safe minimum standards' and 'ecological threshold effects', particularly where there is reason to believe that the social costs of species loss or system collapse may be high.[22] It is conceivable that a cost–benefit framework involving marginal valuations is only relevant when development decisions influencing environmental losses operate within the bounds established by 'safe minimum standard' and 'ecological threshold' criteria. Nevertheless, any approach that puts the requirements of an ecological–economic system above those of the individual again requires an ethical judgement about the role and rights of present and future generations – a judgement that is beyond the scope of the analyst alone to make.

Addressing such major issues requires not only guidance from policymakers, but also close cooperation between economists and ecologists to determine the policy-relevant analytical framework and the decision choices open to society. There is clearly a strong case to be made for more interdisciplinary research to bridge the gap between ecological and economic views of the world. As this chapter has sought to demonstrate, such cooperation has already begun to make a worthwhile contribution to developing a more complete cost–benefit analysis, particularly with regard to valuation of important ecological regulatory functions that protect or support economic activity.

Notes

* This chapter was taken from a paper presented to the Biodiversity Programme Workshop, The Beijer Institute for Ecological Economics of the Swedish Royal Academy of Sciences, Stockholm, 29–31 July 1992. The author is grateful to Carl Folke, Karl-Göran Mäler, and Charles Perrings and to the comments provided by two anonymous referees. All errors and omissions are, of course, solely those of the author.

1. A special category of value is *option value*, which arises because an individual may be uncertain about his or her future demand for a resource and/or its availability as a wetland in the future. There is a general consensus in the economics literature that option values are not a separate form of value but represent a difference between *ex ante* and *ex post* valuation (Smith, 1983; Freeman, 1984). If an individual is uncertain about the future value of a wetland but believes it may be high or that current exploitation and conversion may be irreversible, then there may be *quasi-option value* derived from delaying the development activities. Quasi-option value is simply the expected value of the information derived from delaying exploitation and conversion of the wetland today. Again, there is a consensus that quasi-option value is not a separate component of benefit but involves the analyst properly accounting for the implications of gaining additional information (Fisher and Hanemann, 1987). In contrast, however, there are individuals who do not currently make use of tropical wetlands but nevertheless wish to see them preserved 'in their own right'. Such an 'intrinsic' value is often referred to as *existence value*. It is a form of nonuse value that is extremely difficult to measure, as existence values involve subjective valuations by individuals unrelated to either their own or others' use, whether current or future. An important subset of nonuse or preservation values is *bequest value*, which results from individuals placing a high value on the conservation of tropical wetlands for future generations to use. Bequest values may be particularly high among the local populations currently using a wetland, in that they would like to see the wetland and their way of life that has evolved in conjunction with it passed on to their heirs and future generations in general.
2. Note that in Figure 16.1, option and quasi-option values are indicated with a dotted line, since these values are not strictly a separate component of total economic value in the sense that direct and indirect use values can be separated from existence value. Moreover, in most cases, the preferred approach for incorporating option values in the cost–benefit analysis would be

to develop well-specified models of individual choice, through reasoning about how marginal utilities of income differ in the various contingency states (Freeman, 1984). Similarly, quasi-option value can be calculated by an analysis of the conditional value of information in the decision problem (Fisher and Hanemann, 1987). Such approaches are particularly valid in the case of uncertainty surrounding 'decrements' in natural environments, for example, the losses in value that might occur if a tropical wetland is converted to an alternative use. In contrast, Brookshire, Eubanks and Randall (1983) have argued that in cases of 'supply-side uncertainty' surrounding 'increments' in natural environments, for example, a project to protect wetlands might provide additional future values such as recreation, contingent valuation methods (CVM) might be employed. However, Freeman (1985) has argued that this scenario is only one of four possible patterns of supply uncertainty, and has cautioned against the use of CVM in cases where either the project can only reduce but not eliminate supply uncertainty or where there is a positive probability of supply even without the project.

3. In what follows, it is assumed that all costs and benefits are discounted at some positive rate into present value terms.
4. See Aylward and Barbier (1992) for a critical review.
5. See Barbier, Adams and Kimmage (1991) for further details on the analytical approach of the study, including the difficulties encountered, and Barbier (1993) for a retrospective view. Both papers also discuss possible alternative approaches to valuing the groundwater recharge function of the floodplain.
6. In 1989–90 prices, 7.5 Nigerian Naira (N) = US$1.
7. See Aylward and Barbier (1992) for a critical review.
8. The 'production function' methodology of the Bintuni Bay case study is discussed in more detail later in the chapter. For a critical review, see Barbier (1993).
9. The analysis of the following section benefited greatly from discussions held with Karl-Göran Mäler and Carl Folke at the Beijer Institute of Ecological Economies, Royal Swedish Academy of Sciences, in preparation of a project proposal on mangrove valuation. Based on these discussions, Mäler (1992) has also extended a production function model to incorporate mangrove valuation.
10. In what follows, notation is simplified by omitting the argument of time-dependent variables, by representing a derivative of a function by a prime, by employing numbered subscripts to indicate partial derivatives of a function, and by denoting the time derivative of a variable by a dot.
11. This is an obvious simplification in some problems of wetland resource conversion or diversion. For example, mangroves and other wetland forests do regenerate, and even the total land area of some wetland systems has been known to grow in size as more sediment (and water) is 'trapped' by the system. Thus for some wetland resource allocation problems, a more realistic formulation of equation (16.1) would be:

$$\dot{S} = g(S) - D, \tag{16.1'}$$

where g represents the rate of natural growth, or accumulation, of the wetland resource, with $g_S > 0$ and $g_{SS} < 0$. Alternatively, as noted in the previous section, wetland systems and resources may be indirectly affected by the environmental impacts of neighbouring activities, such as oil spills and other forms of pollution. Equation (16.1) could therefore be written in the form of a damage function:

$$\dot{S} = -h(D), \tag{16.1''}$$

where $h_D > 0$ and $h_{DD} < 0$.
12. See, for example, the following section and Mäler (1991) for a discussion as to why this formulation may be appropriate for capturing the major use values of wetland resources. As the next section will discuss, including the stock of resources, S, explicitly as an argument in the production function for Q is particularly appropriate for the indirect use values of wetland environmental regulatory functions.
13. For example, it is conceivable the U takes the form:

$$U(Q,Y) = \int_0^Q B_1(Q)\mathrm{d}Q + \int_0^Y B_2(Y)\mathrm{d}Y\mathrm{d}Y$$

where $B_1(Q) = p_1 = d_1^{-1}(Q)$ and $B_2(Y) = p_2 = d_2^{-1}(Y)$ are the inverse demand functions for Q and Y determining their prices p_1 and p_2, respectively, if $d'_1(Q)$ and $d'_2(Q) < 0$. It follows that $U'(Q) = p_1 > 0$ and $U'(Y) = p_2 > 0$. Note that the objective function (16.8) would also result if U is a quasi-linear utility function, that is, if it is linear in some good m (for example, 'money') which serves as the numeraire and is assigned the price 1, such that $U = U(Q, Y) + m$. For proof, see Varian (1984).

14. For example, C may take the form $c(D, S) = c(D) + c(S)$. It is conceivable that $c(D) = w_1 D$, where w_1 is the average cost of 'extracting' or 'converting' a unit of wetland resource D to produce commodity Y. It is also possible that $c(S) = w_2 S$ is the costs of 'maintaining' or 'utilizing' the remaining stock of wetland resource, S for activity $f(S)$. However, if this latter activity only indirectly uses the resource S, then there may be no direct costs of utilization or maintenance and $c(S)$ is effectively zero. In either instance, as the next section discusses, the correct approach to valuing the net welfare contribution of S is through the production function approach applied to the (non-normalized) production of $Q = F(X, S)$.
15. However, it follows from the standard economic theory of exhaustible resources that Y can still be produced if D is not essential to its production (Dasgupta and Heal, 1974, 1979). Note also that conditions (16.12) and (16.13) depend on the assumption that $S(t) > 0$ in finite time. This assumption can be revoked in cases where D is not essential to producing Y, and either S is not essential to producing Q or Q can be perfectly substituted by another commodity (for example, Y) in social utility, W.
16. If it is assumed as before that $U(Q, Y)$ is additively separable, and additionally that $Y = g(D)$ is constant over all periods, then totally differentiating (16.12) with respect to time yields $\dot{\lambda} = (U_{YY}(g')^2 + U_Y g'' - c_{DD})\dot{D}$. Thus when $\dot{\lambda}$ is negative in expressions (16.13) and (16.14) then $\dot{D} > 0$. If positive, then $\dot{D} < 0$. However, note that $\dot{D} > 0$ is infeasible over an infinite time horizon as wetland resources are fixed and must eventually be exhausted. Nevertheless, $D(t)$ is not necessarily monotonic over the planning horizon; for example, depletion could conceivably increase in earlier and decrease in later periods.
17. This expression assumes that the (undiscounted) asset value of wetland resources through production activity $Q = f(S)$ will increase with time over its initial period value. The presumption is that $U_Q f_S - c_S > 0$ over time, which is a reasonable assumption provided that the activity, Q, is 'sustainable' – that is, it does not itself lead to degradation of the wetland resource base, S. For instance, some direct uses of wetland resources, such as harvesting for fuelwood and timber or certain farming systems, may prove to be 'unsustainable' with time. As discussed by Barbier (1989a, 1993), it is important that any calculation of the future stream of net benefits from these activities takes into account their 'unsustainability'; otherwise, the asset value of wetland resources as reflected in the economic value of these activities will be overestimated. For example, the analysis of agricultural benefits in the Hadejia-Jama'are floodplain of Nigeria took into account the impact on land degradation of pump-irrigated wheat production within the wetlands that could arise within three to four years (Barbier, Adams and Kimmage, 1991).
18. Another term for this method is the *household production function* approach, which is a more appropriate term for applications based on the derived demand by households for environmental quality (Smith, 1991). In such applications, F can be thought of as a 'household' production function that appears directly in the household utility function:

$$U = U(F(X_i \ldots X_k, S), Y),$$

where Y is a vector of other goods and services for which both prices and quantities are known. Thus by explicitly incorporating nonmarketed environmental functions in the modelling of individuals' preferences, household expenditures on private goods can be related to the derived demand for environmental functions. Some well-known techniques in applied environmental economics – such as travel cost, recreation demand and averting behaviour models – are based on this approach. However, applications at the household level in developing countries may be limited given the detailed data requirements for household patterns of expenditures, time allocations, commodity prices and wage rates, along with measures of levels of environmental quality experienced by the same households (Smith, 1991).

19. Freeman (1991) also calculates the social value of the marginal product of wetland area, which is given by:

$$VMP_S = bPQ/S,$$

where P is the price of crabs. As optimal regulation should lead to a higher price than open access, an inelastic demand means that VMP_S is higher under optimal regulation.

20. There is always the danger, however, that this guidance may be dominated by special-interest groups. For an interesting review of how the methodology of appraisal of natural resource projects can become a public 'bargaining' process, and not always for the worse, see Henry (1989).
21. For the general issues involved in economic appraisal, see Krutilla and Fisher (1985) and Porter (1982). For issues related to the specific concerns of developing countries, see Markandya and Pearce (1988).
22. On 'safe minimum standards' and endangered species, see Bishop (1978), Ready and Bishop (1991), and Tisdell (1990). On the implication of ecological threshold effects for economic development, see Barbier (1989b) and Perrings and Pearce (1992).

References

Adams, William M. and G.E. Hollis (1988), 'Hydrology and sustainable resource development of a Sahelian floodplain wetland', Report prepared for the Hadejia–Jama'are Wetlands Conservation Project, Nguru, Nigeria.

Aylward, Bruce A. and Edward B. Barbier (1992), 'Valuing environmental functions in developing countries', *Biodiversity and Conservation*, **1**, 34–50.

Barbier, Edward B. (1989a), *The Economic Value of Ecosystems: 1 – Tropical Wetlands*, LEEC Gatekeeper 89–02, London: London Environmental Economics Centre.

Barbier, Edward B. (1989b), *Economics, Natural Resource Scarcity and Development: Conventional and Alternative Views*, London: Earthscan.

Barbier, Edward B. (1993), 'Valuing tropical wetland benefits: economic methodologies and applications', *Geographical Journal*, **59** (1) (March), 22–32.

Barbier, Edward B., William M. Adams and Kevin Kimmage (1991), *Economic Valuation of Wetland Benefits: The Hadejia-Jama'are Floodplain, Nigeria*, LEEC Discussion Paper Dp 91–02, London: London Environmental Economics Centre.

Bishop, Richard C. (1978), 'Endangered species and uncertainty: the economics of a safe minimum standard', *American Journal of Agricultural Economics*, **57**, 10–18.

Brookshire, David S., Larry S. Eubanks and Alan Randall (1983), 'Estimating option prices and existence values for wildlife resources', *Land Economics*, **59** (February), 1–15.

Common, Michael S. and Charles Perrings (1992), 'Towards and ecological economics of sustainability', *Ecological Economics*, **6**, 7–34.

Dasgupta, Partha S. and Geoffrey R. Heal (1974), 'The optimal depletion of exhaustible resources', *Review of Economic Studies, Symposium on the Economics of Exhaustible Resources*, **41**, 3–28.

Dasgupta, Partha S. and Geoffrey R. Heal (1979), *Economic Theory and Exhaustible Resources*, Cambridge: Cambridge University Press.

Dixon, John A., Richard A. Carpenter, Louise A. Fallon, Paul B. Sherman and Supachit Manopimoke (1988), *Economic Analysis of the Environmental Impacts of Development Projects*, London: Earthscan Publications in association with the Asian Development Bank.

Dixon, John A. and Maynard M. Hufschmidt (eds) (1986), *Economic Valuation Techniques for the Environment: A Case Study Workbook*, Baltimore, MD: John Hopkins University Press.

Ellis, Gregory M. and Anthony C. Fisher (1987), 'Valuing the environment as input', *Journal of Environmental Management*, **25**, 149–56.

Farber, Stephen J. and Robert Costanza (1987), 'The economic value of wetland systems', *Journal of Environmental Management*, **24**, 41–51.
Fisher, Anthony C. and Michael W. Hanemann (1987), 'Quasi-option value: some misconceptions dispelled', *Journal of Environmental Economics and Management*, **14**, 183–90.
Freeman, A. Myrick III (1984), 'The sign and size of option value', *Land Economics*, **60** (February), 1–13.
Freeman, A. Myrick III (1985), 'Supply uncertainty, option price, and option value', *Land Economics*, **61** (May), 176–81.
Freeman, A. Myrick III (1991), 'Valuing environmental resources under alternative management regimes', *Ecological Economics*, **3**, 247–56.
Henry, Claude (1989), 'Investment projects and natural resources: economic rationality in Janus' role', *Ecological Economics*, **1**, 117–35.
Hodgson, Gregor and John A. Dixon (1988), 'Logging versus fisheries and tourism in Palawan', East–West Environmental Policy Institute Occasional Paper No. 7. Honolulu: East–West Center.
Krutilla, John V. and Anthony C. Fisher (1985), *The Economics of Natural Environments: Studies in the Valuation of Commodity and Amenity Resources*, Washington, DC: Resources for the Future.
Lal, Padma M. and John A. Dixon (1990), 'The management of coastal wetlands: economic analysis of combined ecologic–economic systems', Australian Bureau of Agricultural and Resource Economics, Canberra, Mimeo.
Mäler, Karl-Göran (1991), 'Measuring environmental damage – the production function approach', in J.R. Vincent, E.W. Crawford and J.P. Hoehn (eds), *Valuing Environmental Benefits in Developing Countries*. Special Report 29, East Lansing: Michigan State University.
Mäler, Karl-Göran (1992), 'Multiple use of environmental resources: a household production function approach to valuing resources', Paper presented at the International Society of Ecological Economics Meeting on Investing in Natural Capital: A Prerequisite for Sustainability, 3–6 August, Stockholm.
Maltby, Edward (1986), *Waterlogged Wealth: Why Waste the World's Wet Places?*, London: Earthscan Publications.
Markandya, Anil and David W. Pearce (1988), 'Environmental considerations and the choice of discount rate', Environment Department Working Paper No. 3, Washington, DC: The World Bank.
Perrings, Charles and David W. Pearce (1992), 'Biodiversity conservation and economic development', Paper presented at the Economics and Ecology of Biodiversity Loss, 29–31 July, Beijer Institute for Ecological Economics, Stockholm.
Porter, Richard C. (1982), 'The new approach to wilderness preservation through benefit–cost analysis', *Journal of Environmental Economics and Management*, **9**, 59–80.
Ready, Richard C. and Richard C. Bishop (1991), 'Endangered species and the safe minimum standard', *American Journal of Agricultural Economics*, **70**, 309–12.
Ruitenbeek, H.J. (1989), 'Social cost–benefit analysis of the Korup Project, Cameroon'. Report prepared for the World Wide Fund for Nature and the Republic of Cameroon, London.
Ruitenbeek, H.J. (1992), *Mangrove Management: An Economic Analysis of Management of Options with a Focus on Bintuni Bay, Irian Jaya*, Jakarta and Halifax: Environmental Management Development in Indonesia Project.
Smith, V. Kerry (1983), 'Option value: a conceptual overview', *Southern Economic Journal*, **50**, 654–68.
Smith, V. Kerry (1991), 'Household production functions and environmental benefit estimation', in J.B. Braden and C.D. Kolstad (eds), *Measuring the Demand for Environmental Quality*, Amsterdam: North-Holland.
Tisdell, Clem (1990), 'Economics and the debate about preservation of species, crop varieties and genetic diversity', *Ecological Economics*, **2**, 77–90.
Turner, R. Kerry (1991), 'Economics and Wetland Management', *AMBIO*, **20** (2), 59–63.
Turner, R. Kerry and Tom Jones (1991), *Wetlands: Market and Intervention Failures*, London: Earthscan Publications.
Twilley, Robert R. (1991), 'Properties of mangrove ecosystems related to the energy signature of coastal environments', Department of Biology, University of Southwestern Louisiana, Lafayette. Mimeo.
Varian, Hal R. (1984), *Microeconomic Analysis*, 2nd edn, New York: W.W. Norton.
Yañez-Arancibia, Alejandro and John W. Day (eds) (1988), *Ecology of Coastal Ecosystems in the Southern Gulf of Mexico: The Terminos Lagoon Region*, Mexico: UNAM Press.

17. Capturing the pharmaceutical value of biodiversity in a developing country

with B.A. Aylward[*]

Abstract
The conservation of biodiversity is increasingly being defined as a process made up of three components- saving, studying and sustainably using biodiversity. If the conservation of process is expanded to incorporate the need for both the protection of biodiversity – either *in situ* or *ex situ* – and the generation of valuable information about biodiversity, an important issue is the correct balance of investment in these two types of activities. This chapter explores this issue by focusing on efforts in a developing country to capture the pharmaceutical potential of biodiversity and species information. A model of biodiversity investment choice is developed, and an analysis of royalty returns to effort in biodiversity protection, taxonomic information and the collection of biotic samples is conducted based on data from Costa Rica. The results suggest that although a country can be adequately compensated for its investment in the generation of taxonomic information, it is unlikely that pharmaceutical prospecting alone will cover the high opportunity costs of biodiversity protection.

Introduction[1]

There is currently a resurgence of interest in the use of biodiversity as a source of novel chemical compounds for the development of new pharmaceuticals. A growing number of pharmaceutical companies are initiating or upgrading research programmes that screen microbial sources, higher plants and other taxonomic groups for useful activity against disease targets. On the supply side developing country governments, development agencies and non-governmental organizations are increasingly interested in assisting developing country institutions to capture the 'pharmaceutical value' of biodiversity.

However, there are some potential misunderstandings in the view that pharmaceutical prospecting can serve as a mechanism by developing countries to extract compensation for conservation of their biodiversity. In an effort to clarify the pharmaceutical value of biodiversity and species information, this chapter investigates the economic relationships involved in pharmaceutical prospecting.[2] It argues that too much emphasis is placed on how developing countries can earn royalties from pharmaceutical prospecting rather than focusing on whether the economic returns from prospecting are sufficient to warrant investment in the generation of biochemical information.

Our analysis of the economic returns from pharmaceutical prospecting suggests that, under certain contractual arrangements, it is feasible for the social investment in information-generating effort by developing countries, such as the collection and identification of biotic samples as well as basic pharmaceutical R&D, to be economically worthwhile. Nevertheless, it does not necessarily follow that pharmaceutical prospecting by itself can finance biodiversity conservation. Our results indicate that although royalties from the pharmaceutical value-added process can contribute to the financing of conservation, the full social costs of biodiversity protection are simply too high to be compensated through prospecting on its own. That is, it is unreasonable to expect that pharmaceutical prospecting alone should be able to bear the full cots of biodiversity protection in developing countries.

Misperceptions concerning thc economic potential of biochemical prospecting usually stem from a failure to draw a clear distinction between biodiversity as the 'raw material' in the production process and information about biodiversity – the 'intellectual property' that drives innovation. As a raw material, biodiversity is typically treated as a *free good*. As a consequence, pharmaceutical prospecting provides little in the way of financial incentives for a developing country to invest in biodiversity protection. On the other hand, the ability to patent novel chemical compounds does provide an incentive to generate information about species that is useful in producing new and marketable drugs. The economic link between biodiversity and pharmaceuticals is the development of information about species and their chemical constituents.

This chapter suggests that in order to capture a greater share of the pharmaceutical value of biological diversity, developing countries may consider investing in three activities: the protection of biodiversity, the collection and identification of biotic samples, and conducting pharmaceutical research into and development (R&D) of the pharmaceutical properties of natural products. The last two activities consist of investments that add value to the resource itself, and thus such investments enable the country to appropriate a larger share of value added to the drug development process.

To illustrate some of these issues, the chapter develops a theoretical model of the investment choices that face a developing country seeking to engage in pharmaceutical prospecting of its biological diversity. The model distinguishes between the investment, or 'effort', devoted to the *in situ* protection of biodiversity and the 'effort' involved in generating information through expending effort on species classification and conducting research into the pharmaceutical properties of natural products. Thus the developing country faces two investment choices: (i) investing in protection of biodiversity and (ii) expanding the capacity to produce species information. By indicating the likely relative returns to these two types of 'effort' the model demonstrates that investments in protection and information generation are complementary activities and should be considered in tandem if a country is to achieve an optimal mix of the human and biological resources at its disposal.

These points are further illustrated by drawing on an example of pharmaceutical prospecting in Costa Rica. Using data collected from the international pharmaceutical industry, the National Biodiversity Institute (INBio) of Costa Rica, and Guanacaste National Park in Costa Rica, a royalty model for pharmaceutical prospecting is developed and used to determine the net returns to effort invested in biodiversity protection, taxonomic information and the collection of biotic samples. As noted above, our main results suggest that although a country can be adequately compensated for its investment in the generation of taxonomic information, it is unlikely that pharmaceutical prospecting alone will cover the high opportunity costs of biodiversity protection. Our chapter therefore touches on an important paradox: investment in biodiversity protection is a *necessary* complement to investment in the biodiversity information activities that may allow a developing country to capture a substantial share of the returns from pharmaceutical prospecting; however, the economic returns from pharmaceutical prospecting 'captured' by a developing country are by themselves unlikely to pay fully for the required investments in biodiversity protection.

Pharmaceutical prospecting as an economic activity

In the past few years, new technological developments – including advances in receptor and mechanism-based screening technology – have rekindled the interest of pharmaceutical companies in the exploration of plants, marine organisms, microbial sources and insects for novel chemical compounds.[3] Farnsworth and Morris (1976) point out that although 'guesstimates' can be made about the untapped potential of biodiversity, it is practically impossible to determine actually when a particular species has been fully investigated for its pharmaceutical properties. For example, Douros and Suffness (1980) report that in the first natural products screening programme by the National Cancer Institute (NCI), 35 000 species of plants were screened for anti-cancer activity. In other words, in the most extensive pharmacological investigation of plants ever recorded, only a fraction of the total number of plant species were evaluated for a single type of activity (Farnsworth and Morris, 1976). In addition, these plants were only tested against a particular set of cancer screens. In its new programme initiated in 1986, NCI is testing natural products against a revised set of disease-oriented screens (Suffness *et al.*, 1989). Hence, it is possible to conclude that due to improvements in NCI's screening technology the original 35 000 species of plants are once again 'uninvestigated' sources of anticancer compounds.

Improvements in screening technology and the development of new screens clearly 'extend' the potential applications of the chemical diversity resident in natural products. Thus the sheer scale of the resource – on the order of 10 to 100 million species – and the continuing evolution of screens, screening technologies and disease targets implies that biodiversity will never be fully explored or exploited for its pharmaceutical potential. This suggests that the chemical properties of biodiversity represent effectively a reusable resource 'pool' for use in the development of new pharmaceuticals. The real threat to this resource is not its potential physical exhaustion but from competing uses of land and natural habitat, as well as the failure to protect areas rich in biodiversity, particularly in the developing world.[4]

However, simply because a resource can potentially generate economic rents for a pharmaceutical industry does not imply that it is economically worth exploiting; the returns from prospecting must be sufficient to cover the full costs of investment in this activity. 'Pharmaceutical prospecting' – the process of generating new pharmaceuticals from natural products – begins with biodiversity and ends with the production of a marketable drug. There are a number of activities in this process, including:

- the protection of biodiversity,
- the collection and identification of biotic samples,
- the extraction and screening of biotic samples,
- the isolation and structural determination of lead compounds,
- additional pre-clinical research laboratory and animal testing,
- clinical research, and
- development of mass-production techniques for marketable compounds.

Pharmaceutical prospecting does not necessarily proceed in a linear, stepwise fashion as outlined above. However, the process generally involves adding information to the 'raw material' of biodiversity and its subsequent forms.

In economic terms pharmaceutical prospecting activities can be segregated according to three major types of investment:

- investment in protection of biodiversity,
- investment in collection and identification of biotic samples, and
- investment in pharmaceutical R&D.

The economic outputs of these investments are:

- the 'raw material' for pharmaceutical prospecting – biodiversity,
- species information and the 'processed product' – biotic samples, and

- information about a species' pharmaceutical properties and the 'final product' – a marketable compound.

Understanding the main economic activities and related outputs associated with the process of 'capturing' the pharmaceutical value of biodiversity is an important prerequisite for assessing a developing country's potential for engaging successfully in pharmaceutical prospecting, that is, determining whether it is worthwhile investing in exploiting the pharmaceutical potential of its biodiversity as opposed to engaging in other activities, including competing uses of land and natural habitat. Before developing our economic analysis of pharmaceutical prospecting further, we outline briefly the three main types of investments required for prospecting.

The protection of biodiversity

The protection, or maintenance, of biodiversity must be included in an economic analysis of pharmaceutical prospecting because the supply of this 'raw material' input involves a significant social cost. The social costs of protecting biodiversity are the direct costs of protection and the opportunity cost of allocating land to the 'production' of biodiversity. As economically profitable alternative land uses may exist for lands currently functioning as reservoirs of tropical biodiversity, it is important that the production of biodiversity be capable of generating real economic benefits Otherwise, there is little economic incentive for society to protect biodiversity.

The use of the 'raw material' input in pharmaceutical prospecting may involve three different interventions at the level of the biological resource itself:

- initial collection for identification to the species level,
- further collection for further research and development, and
- 'mass' collection or cultivation if a marketable drug results.[5]

Depending on the case, only the first or second collections may be required or all three interventions may be necessary. Collection of microbial species in the form of a single environmental sample typically yields enough 'starter' material for researchers to develop methods for culturing species that show promise in the early screens. Prospecting with plants, on the other hand, will usually involve all three interventions.

Non-intensive collection of biotic samples from public wildlands in developing countries is generally not subject to much in the way of government restriction or control. Collecting permits are required in some countries; fees payable to public authorities expressly for the privilege of collection are virtually unheard of. The difficulty and cost of asserting *exclusivity* to biological resources in some regions has left public authorities with little effective control over access to biodiversity. In these situations biodiversity is a *non-exclusive*, as well as *non-rival*, resource and fits the definition of a public good.[6] As a result, biodiversity is effectively left in a state of open access and is freely collected by all comers – biodiversity is treated as a 'free good' by collectors. Under such conditions, pharmaceutical prospecting provides no incentive for continued investment in the protection of biodiversity, alternative land uses appear more favourable, and land will be taken out of the production of biodiversity.

Establishing exclusive rights to the biodiversity contained in protected areas must therefore be a prerequisite for a developing country seeking to capture the pharmaceutical value of its own biodiversity. Such exclusion might involve some combination of the institution and enforcement of legal property rights over species found in public wildlands, or effective managerial control over these wildlands. If it is possible to exclude potential consumers from access to biodiversity – or some subset of species – effective control over the benefits of the resource may be assured through the institution of a system for charging potential collectors for access to the resource.[7] The potential stumbling block to this approach is the existence of pan-tropical species. Since many species are not endemic to a single country, a country may be able to exclude a collector from access to a particular species (known or unknown) that is found within its borders but of course cannot stop the collector from obtaining access to that species elsewhere in the tropics.

A second method for capturing some of the value of pharmaceutical prospecting for biodiversity protection is the establishment of contracts with local or foreign collectors for a share of any future returns from marketable uses of a species' chemical compound or semi-synthetic derivatives of the compound. The initiation of either exclusion mechanism or contractual arrangements begin to address the incentives problem with regard to biodiversity protection because they implicitly insert the costs of biodiversity protection into the pharmaceutical prospecting process. Currently, these costs are not reflected in pharmaceutical prospecting as collectors are typically not required to purchase specimens or access rights.

Species information: collection and identification of biotic samples

In producing biotic samples for use in pharmaceutical R&D, a number of different types of information about species may be generated. This information often guides the selection of species for screening and includes:

- collection information (date, location, site conditions, and so on),
- taxonomic classification of the organism,[8]
- ecological data indicating biochemical activity,

- ethnobotanical information about traditional medicinal uses of plants, and
- reports of biochemical activity for a given species, genus or family.

In this chapter we focus mainly on the task of generating species information in *collection and taxonomic identification activities*, which are essential inputs in pharmaceutical prospecting.

Access to species information – the taxonomic classification and details regarding the collecting – and the physical specimen itself, is typically kept confidential by the collector and the buyer of biotic samples. Collectors of biotic materials are competing for 'market share' and are unlikely to share species information with other collectors. In addition, pharmaceutical companies may request or require that collectors keep descriptions of collected species confidential. Collectors of biotic samples are, therefore, certain to exert exclusivity over the species information and physical specimens they collect. Pharmaceutical companies are also likely to restrict access to biotic samples and their associated information, thus making it practically impossible for competing collectors to gain access to this taxonomic information or biotic samples.

However, commercial collectors also rely on existing natural history museums or botanic gardens for a number of 'taxonomic' services – services often received free of charge. These taxonomic inputs are often an important element in the production of biotic samples. In the case of known species, commercial collectors may utilize existing reference collections in order to gather data on collection sites, or to confirm the identification of a specimen already collected. In the case of species that are not held in local collections or are outside the area of expertise of a collector, the collector may actually submit a sample to one of the large public institutions in the North (or South) that has the taxonomic expertise necessary to make an identification.

In developing countries the taxonomic services provided to commercial collectors by local institutions are largely uncompensated. Consequently, the investment of such institutions in developing the expertise of their staff, the physical collections and the information contained in collections and databases, generally receive little financial returns from pharmaceutical prospecting activities. Whether this unpaid social cost is interpreted as an external factor of production or as an implicit government subsidy (since most collection facilities are publicly funded) is probably less important than recognizing that the carrying out of such services for free is a drain on already scarce taxonomic resources in a developing country.

An obvious solution to this problem would be for taxonomists to begin charging fees for their services. These fees should reflect not only the costs of generating biotic samples, but also the costs of identification (Townes, 1992). This would mean that species classification work necessary to pharmaceutical prospecting that is 'farmed out' to other specialists would no longer be free but charged to third parties who purchase biotic samples, such as pharmaceutical companies. Charging fees would still permit the circulation of information; however, the generation of such information would be priced in an open and competitive market. Clearly, such an innovation might take time to implement given current attitudes and methods of 'doing business' in the systematics profession.

Collectors of biotic samples may also enter directly into contracts that access future monopoly profits successful products or provide non-monetary benefits. Laird (1992) provides a detailed description of a number of emerging contractual arrangements between pharmaceutical companies and the suppliers of biotic samples. As these contracts are negotiated directly with pharmaceutical companies the ability of a developing country to invest in the development of the human resources necessary for collection and identification of species will allow a country to gain a large share of the returns from pharmaceutical prospecting. As noted by Aylward *et al.* (1993), two key features that have made Costa Rica's INBio initiative an attractive contracting partner to pharmaceutical companies are the development by INBio of well-trained local para-taxonomists who undertake initial collecting and identifying of species and biotic samples from protected areas and the coordination of these taxonomic efforts with existing scientific institutions in Costa Rica that are undertaking basic taxonomic activities.

Species information: pharmaceutical R&D

The objective of pharmaceutical R&D into natural products is the generation of the requisite amount of knowledge about a species and its chemical constituents to ascertain if any of these compounds has potential as a marketable drug. As with species information generated during the collection stage, this information is *non-rival*. In general, those engaging in pharmaceutical R&D guard the information they generate very closely. Despite the assertion of *exclusivity* over this information, other potential consumers of this knowledge are, in theory, still able 'reinvent the wheel' or 'reverse engineer' the information through access to the original raw material or the final product.[9]

In order to resolve the incentives problem posed by the *non-rivalness* of information produced in pharmaceutical R&D, most developed countries have legislated intellectual property rights that provide patent protection for novel compounds.[10] In obtaining a patent, a company gives up its *exclusivity* over the information it has generated in return for a legal guarantee of *exclusive* rights (over a set time period) to sell the product itself. Thus a company will reap monopoly profits from its investment in R&D should any of its lead compounds prove to be of commercial value.

Practical difficulties in 'reinventing the wheel' and 'reverse engineering' information derived from biological sources reduce the extent of the incentives problem encountered in pharmaceutical prospecting relative to that found in the case of R&D based on compounds fabricated in the laboratory. Patenting, therefore, might be less important in the case of pharmaceutical prospecting. It is unlikely that this situation would, however, justify a separate policy approach for natural product derived pharmaceuticals – particularly as advances in basic science and technology may render natural product compounds more amenable to commercial synthesis.

A developing country seeking to develop its R&D capacity for pharmaceutical prospecting of natural products generally faces two additional challenges. First, the pharmaceutical industry in most developing countries is at best in a nascent stage and in many countries non-existent. Consequently, the capacity for generating in-country R&D for pharmaceutical prospecting may be limited. In addition, protection of the information generated by pharmaceutical prospecting may be incomplete because of the inadequate development of intellectual property rights and patenting laws in a developing country, which may be compounded by the lack of international agreements and guidelines governing the protection of the intellectual property rights of the genetic information derived from biotic sources.

Faced with these constraints, the most cost-effective avenue open to a developing country for fostering an in-country R&D capacity for pharmaceutical prospecting may be through contractual arrangements or vertically integrated operations in which the initial stages of pharmaceutical R&D are performed in-country (Aylward *et al.*, 1993; Sedjo, 1992; Simpson, 1992). However, such investments are not completely costless for a developing country and usually require a parallel commitment of public and private resources to complementary human, technological and commercial infrastructure. Developing countries wishing to capture a larger share of the value generated by pharmaceutical prospecting must continue to make the latter investments in order to attract additional external investment by multi-national pharmaceutical companies. Ultimately, once an 'infant' pharmaceutical industry is established, public and private resources may be invested more directly in developing and expanding internal R&D capabilities for pharmaceutical prospecting of biodiversity.

Finally, there may be synergies between efforts made at different stages in the pharmaceutical prospecting process. The ability on the part of a developing country to control access to its biodiversity might also serve to limit any problem posed by the *non-rivalness* of species information generated during collection and identification. Collectors that are guaranteed exclusive access to particular species are in a much better contractual negotiating position. It may also be the case that by investing in the generation of species information and striking contracts with pharmaceutical companies, a developing country may be able to capture the value attributable to its biodiversity without the need to engage in developing potentially costly mechanisms of exclusion.

In sum, there may be a number of ways that a developing country can try to capture the value of pharmaceutical prospecting, beyond even the steps that some countries are already taking. Drawing the distinction between the three stages in pharmaceutical prospecting suggests that the value of *conservation* does not lie simply in protecting, or 'saving,' biodiversity. Throughout the entire process of pharmaceutical prospecting, information – and consequently value – is being added to the species under investigation. If a developing country wants to appropriate a large share of the value-added from pharmaceutical prospecting it must invest – or encourage outsiders to invest – in the generation of species information within the country. While public funding of biodiversity protection and the generation of species information has a long tradition, both budgetary limitations and the increasing commercialization of biodiversity suggest that methods for 'privatizing' these activities are worth exploring.[11]

Recognition of the distinction between biodiversity and species information suggests that the processes of getting to 'know' and 'sustainably use' biodiversity are rewarding endeavours of economic merit in their own right. Indeed, as the model of the next section indicates, investments in biodiversity protection and species information are likely to be complementary activities. Thus, if conservation of biodiversity is to be a meaningful concept, and sustainable over the longer term, it must be understood as a process involving the complementary steps of 'saving, knowing and sustainably using' biodiversity (Janzen, 1990; WRI, 1992).

A model of biodiversity investment choice

So far we have discussed the various economic activities, or investments, that comprise the overall process which we call 'capturing' the pharmaceutical value of biodiversity, as well as some possible strategies available to a developing country that could make such investments feasible. However, simply because such investments are feasible does not necessarily imply that they are worthwhile pursuing. There are two questions related to this issue: (i) what is the 'optimal' level of investment by a developing country in pharmaceutical prospecting of biodiversity, in particular the optimal 'mix' of investments in the various economic activities comprising prospecting; and (ii) are the economic returns to these investments sufficient for a developing country to engage in pharmaceutical prospecting of biodiversity? In this section, we explore the first question using a theoretical model of biodiversity choice. In the next section, we use empirical analysis of returns to pharmaceutical products and prospecting activities in Costa Rica to examine the potential economic returns to biodiversity.

We have described investment in pharmaceutical prospecting of biodiversity as essentially involving three activities: biodiversity protection, generating species information and pharmaceutical R&D. The decision between, on the one hand, protecting the stock of *in situ* biodiversity, and on the other, generating species information through taxonomic work and pharmaceutical R&D that 'adds value' to this stock is captured below in an analytical model of biodiversity investment choice. The model is therefore useful for examining the conditions determining the optimal allocation of resources between the different activities associated with capturing the pharmaceutical value of biodiversity, as well as the conditions that are likely to affect optimal investments in these activities.

We assume that 'information-generating effort' is distinct from the effort that is involved in protecting the *in situ* biodiversity stock. 'Protection effort' consists of protected area management, maintenance and monitoring efforts, and so on – all of which are essential to production of the biochemical 'raw material' input but do not by themselves 'add value' to this input. As argued in previous sections, pharmaceutical value can only be added to the 'raw material' input through increased in-country information-generating effort in taxonomic and pharmaceutical research and development (R&D) processes.

To make the problem interesting, we assume that scarce resources in the developing country mean that the total 'effort' that can be allocated to protection as opposed to information generation activities is fixed, thus imposing an opportunity cost on the country's decision to invest more effort in the latter activities. To simplify the analysis, we also assume that the final pharmaceutical product must compete with similar products on the international market, and thus faces a competitive price.

The process of pharmaceutical production from natural products can therefore be characterized by a production function, in which the final pharmaceutical commodity, Q, results from the extracted input of biochemical 'raw material', R, from the protected biodiversity stock and the accumulated 'knowledge', K, generated by the taxonomic and R&D effort. As in standard renewable resource (for example, fishery) models, *effort* will be used in this model as some combination or index of the vector inputs required for either protection or information-generation activities, for example, labour, materials, capital, and so on.

However, it is important to note that, unlike in standard renewable resource models, there is not necessarily a biological limit on the supply of biochemical 'raw material', R, into the pharmaceutical production process. As discussed in the previous section, the continuing evolution of screens, screening technologies and disease targets implies that the chemical properties of biodiversity may represent a potentially limitless source of biochemical raw material to pharmaceutical prospecting.

Thus in the following model, although the supply of R is dependent on allocating effort to protecting biodiversity, a potentially 'limitless' supply of biochemical raw material may be obtained from the stock of biological resources contained in protected areas.

It is assumed that the production function for Q has the following properties

$$Q = f(R, K), \tag{17.1}$$

where $f_R > 0, f_{RR} < 0, f_K > 0, f_{KK} < 0.$[12]

As noted above, R and K are products of 'protection effort', E_2, and 'information-generating effort', E_1, respectively and are determined by

$$R = h(E_2), \tag{17.2}$$

$$\text{where } h' > 0,\ h'' < 0,$$

$$\dot{K} = g(E_1) - wK,\ K(0) = K_0 \geq 0, \tag{17.3}$$

where $g' >, g'' < 0$ and w can be considered the 'rate of depreciation' of useful accumulated knowledge in the pharmaceutical value-added process. Equation (17.2) suggests that the supply of biochemical raw material for pharmaceutical production is a function of protection effort, and subject to diminishing returns. Equation (17.3) indicates that the knowledge accumulated through additional taxonomic and R&D activities is a function of the effort devoted to these information-generating activities in connection with pharmaceutical value-added. However, this knowledge can quickly become 'obsolete', so K is assumed to decay at the rate w. To simplify matters, we have not included any 'direct' costs of using effort; rather, we impose a total limit, $\bar{E}$, on the availability of effort such that

$$\bar{E} = E_1 + E_2,\ E_1 \geq 0,\ E_2 \geq 0. \tag{17.4}$$

If p is the competitive price for the pharmaceutical product, i is the opportunity cost of accumulated capital (knowledge) and c is the cost of supplying raw biochemical material inputs to the process, including the full opportunity costs of biodiversity protection (see next section), then the discounted economic returns to the developing country of investing in pharmaceutical value added are

$$\int_0^\infty e^{-\delta t}\{pQ - iK - cR\}\mathrm{d}t, \tag{17.5}$$

where δ is the social rate of discount, which also represents the returns from alternative assets in the economy.[13] We assume that the country wants to maximize (17.5) subject to (17.1)–(17.4) through allocating 'effort' between protection and information generation. The Hamiltonian function of the above problem becomes

$$H = pf(h(E_2), K) - iK - ch(E_2) + \lambda[g(\bar{E} - E_2) - wK], \qquad (17.6)$$

where λ is the costate variable or the shadow price of accumulated knowledge gained from information-generating activities in the pharmaceutical value-added process. In the above control problem, K is a state variable and E_2 is the control variable. Assuming an interior solution, the maximum principle yields the following conditions

$$g'\lambda = (pf_R - c)h', \qquad (17.7)$$

$$\dot{\lambda} = (\delta + w)\lambda + i - pf_K. \qquad (17.8)$$

Equation (17.7) determines the optimal allocation of effort along the optimal path. It states that the marginal value to allocating effort to protection must equal the marginal value of allocating effort to information-generating activities. Equation (17.8) governs the change in value of knowledge gained through the latter activities. We can interpret it as stating that the net 'profit' to accumulating such knowledge is determined by the current value marginal product of that knowledge, pf_K, plus any capital gains, $\dot{\lambda}$, *less* the total opportunity costs of accumulating K, $(\delta + w)\lambda + i$.

By differentiating equation (17.7) we obtain

$$[pf_{RR}(h')^2 + pf_R h'' - ch'' + \lambda g'']\dot{E}_2 = \dot{\lambda}g'. \qquad (17.9)$$

The long-run equilibrium can be solved by utilizing equations (17.3), (17.7), (17.8) and (17.9), and assuming that it occurs when protection effort, accumulated knowledge and the value of that knowledge are all constant. Through substitutions, the equilibrium can be characterized by the following system of equations

$$(\delta + w)(Pf_R - c)h' + g'i = pf_K g', \quad \text{for } \dot{E}_2 = \dot{\lambda} = 0, \qquad (17.10)$$

$$g(\bar{E} - E_2) - wK = 0, \quad \text{for } \dot{K} = 0. \qquad (17.11)$$

Equation (17.10) indicates that in the long run, the net returns in terms of pharmaceutical value added from effort allocated to protection, $(pf_R - c)h'$, must be equated with the (discounted) net returns from information-generating effort that leads to accumulated knowledge, $(pf_K - i)g'/(\delta + w)$. Equation (17.11) suggests that in the long run sufficient effort must be allocated to information-generating activities in order to replace knowledge about the pharmaceutical process that has become 'obsolete'.

From equation (17.10) and (17.11), the slopes of the curves $\dot{E}_2 = \dot{\lambda} = 0$ and $\dot{K} = 0$ can be determined in (E_2, K) space as

$$\left.\frac{dE_2}{dK}\right|_{\dot{K}=0} = -\frac{w}{g'} < 0, \qquad (17.12)$$

$$\left.\frac{dE_2}{dK}\right|_{\dot{E}_2=0} = \frac{g'\, pf_{KK}}{\alpha} > 0, \qquad (17.13)$$

where $\alpha = (\delta + w)[pf_{RR}(h')^2 + pf_R h'' - ch''] + [pf_K - i]g'' < 0$.[14]

Thus the curve $\dot{K} = 0$ is negatively sloped, whereas the curve $\dot{E}_2 = \dot{\lambda} = 0$ is positively sloped. As shown in Figure 17.1, the resulting equilibrium is a saddle point, and the saddle path is positively sloped.

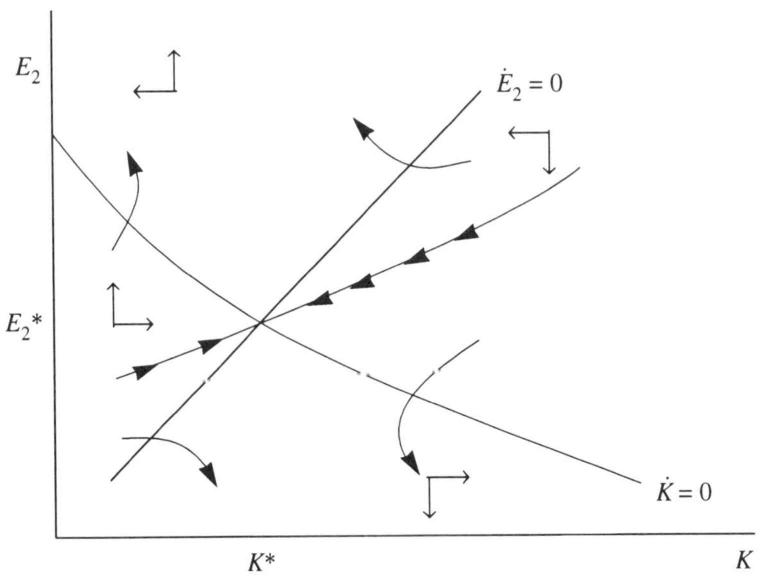

Figure 17.1 Optimal allocation of conservation and information-generating effort

The equilibrium (E_2^*, K^*) shows the optimal allocation of effort between protection of biodiversity *in situ* and 'building' up knowledge about the valuable biochemical properties of species in order to capture the long-run returns to pharmaceutical value added. Not surprisingly, effort has to be allocated to both activities if the full 'value added' is to be gained; that is, the two types of activities are *complements* in the long run. If the initial level of accumulated knowledge is low ($K_0 < K^*$) in the developing country, then the optimal path indicates that both protection effort, E_2, and information-generating effort, E_1, must be increased. However, Figure 17.1 also indicates that if the initial K is low and the country allocated too much effort to protection, then the resulting path will be inefficient. Similarly, if the initial K is high ($K_0 > K^*$), then the initial protection effort must also be high, and both accumulated knowledge and E_2 must be scaled down over time. If the initial K is high in the country, but too little effort is allocated to biodiversity protection, then the resulting path is sub-optimal with regard to the long-run returns to pharmaceutical value added.

Comparative static analysis of the long-run equilibrium can be employed to indicate the impacts of changes in the price of the final pharmaceutical product, p, the discount rate, δ, the rate of obsolescence on accumulated knowledge, w, the 'interest payments' associated with this knowledge, i, the costs of using biochemical raw material, c, and total effort, $\bar{E}$. Here, we show explicitly only the effects of changes in the product price and discount rate, although we briefly indicate the results of the other comparative statics.

A change in p has the following impacts on the long-run equilibrium

$$\frac{\mathrm{d}K^*}{\mathrm{d}p} = \frac{g'\left(f_K g' - f_R h'\right)}{D} \quad \begin{matrix} \geq 0 \text{ if } f_K g' \geq f_R h' \\ \leq 0 \text{ if } f_K g' \leq f_R h', \end{matrix} \tag{17.14}$$

$$\frac{\mathrm{d}E_2^*}{\mathrm{d}p} = \frac{-w\left(f_K g' - f_R h'\right)}{D} \quad \begin{matrix} \geq 0 \text{ if } f_R h' \geq f_K g' \\ \leq 0 \text{ if } f_R h' \leq f_K g', \end{matrix} \tag{17.15}$$

where D is the determinant of the Jacobian matrix for the comparative static solution of the long-run system (17.10) and (17.11), with $D = \alpha w - (g')^2 p f_{KK} > 0$.

Clearly, the relative marginal productivity of protection as opposed to information-generating effort in terms of pharmaceutical value added will determine which input is increased if the product price rises. If the marginal productivity of E_1 is relatively higher, then in response to the price rise more effort should go into this activity, and thus the accumulation of knowledge, and less into protection of *in situ* biodiversity. If the marginal productivity of E_2 is relatively higher, the opposite is the case.

An increase in the discount rate, δ, has the following impacts on the long-run equilibrium

$$\frac{\mathrm{d}K^*}{\mathrm{d}\delta} = \frac{-g'\left(pf_R - c\right)h'}{D} < 0 \tag{17.16}$$

$$\frac{\mathrm{d}E_2^*}{\mathrm{d}\delta} = \frac{w\left(pf_R - c\right)h'}{D} < 0. \tag{17.17}$$

A rise in δ will lead to an increase in the equilibrium level of protection effort and a fall in K^*. Effectively, this implies that the developing country finds the long-run returns to the pharmaceutical value-added process to be a less attractive economic proposition, and is less willing to 'tie up' as many economic resources in accumulating knowledge for use in this process over the long term.

The comparative static effects of increases in the 'interest' cost associated with K and the costs of the input R are fairly straightforward. An increase in i causes a reallocation of effort in the long run away from information generation, and thus knowledge accumulation, and to more *in situ* protection; whereas an increase in c leads to the opposite result. Increases in w and in $\bar{E}$ both result in a fall in equilibrium K, but the effect on E_2 is less certain.

Expected returns to biodiversity investment

Our theoretical model has indicated that investment in both protection of biodiversity and generating information about its biochemical properties is necessary if a developing country is to capture any long-term returns from pharmaceutical value added. However, the question still remains that, if a developing country does decide to undertake these investments, can it capture sufficient returns from pharmaceutical prospecting to justify these investments?

In this section, the results of a royalty model are used to estimate the net returns to effort invested in biodiversity protection, the collection of biotic samples and taxonomic information by a biodiversity-rich developing country conducting pharmaceutical prospecting. The royalty model is presented in the annex to this paper, and the results are presented in Table 17.1. Full details can be found in Aylward (1993), which used data from surveys of the international pharmaceutical industry, Costa Rica's National Biodiversity Institute (INBio) and Costa Rica's system of protected areas to derive the parameters and calculations indicated in Table 17.1.[15]

The estimates of the expected mean royalty per biotic sample and the number of samples per species screened are derived and explained in the annex. The private cost of producing a biotic sample is set at US$50 per sample based on interviews with collectors involved in commercial collection in developing countries. The per sample collecting fee of US$63 is based on similar sources, indicating that collectors receive an additional 25 per cent mark-up on the cost of procuring a biotic sample. The full social costs of generating two plant samples from the same species will include the private costs of producing the two biotic samples and the social costs of developing taxonomic information for each species screened. An analysis of INBio operations reveals that the latter cost, which is essentially the additional social investment to obtain, curate and positively identify a specimen of a species that is not already held by the local reference collection, is approximately US$100 per species screened (Aylward *et al.*, 1993).

Lewin *et al.* (1992) point out that the opportunity costs of park land is reflected by the discounted net returns of neighbouring agricultural land, US$200 per hectare in the case of Costa Rica's Guanacaste National Park. An alternative estimate is the price of private land bought out in the formation of the Park. Based on these estimates, and assuming that most of the 500000 species presumed to reside in Costa Rica lie in that country's fully protected area of 600000 ha, the annual per species cost of biodiversity protection is around US$50 (see Table 17.1).

A review of recent activity in the market for biotic samples suggests that the number of samples that a single biodiversity-rich country is likely to produce annually for screening would be around 2000 or 1000 species screened per year (Aylward, 1993).[16] This is much less than the 20 000 samples required on average for a 'hit' (that is, the development of a successful pharmaceutical product), which is the basis of the estimated US$233 royalty paid per sample supplied (see the Appendix). Using this royalty rate, the amount of total royalties earned on the 2000 samples supplied then becomes a revenue figure received each and every year by the developing country. In Table 17.1, we assume that this screening process continues for 40 years. However, this in turn implies that all 500000 species must also remain fully protected over this period, that is, the 600000 ha of protected area is established at the beginning of the period and remains in place throughout.

Based on these assumptions and employing a discount rate of 10 per cent, the present value net returns to effort invested in biodiversity protection, taxonomic information and collection of biotic samples are calculated in Table 17.1. Net private returns, *NPR*, and net social returns, *NSR*, are respectively

$$NPR = TRY + F - CC^P, \tag{17.18}$$

$$NSR = TRY + F - CC^P - CT^S - CP^S, \tag{17.19}$$

where *TRY* is total royalty payments, *F* is sample fees, CC^P the private costs of collection, CT^S the social costs of taxonomic information and CP^S the opportunity costs of biodiversity protection.

Table 17.1 Analysis of royalty returns from pharmaceutical prospecting (US$ 1990)

	Units	Amounts		
General parameters				
Expected royalty paid per sample[a]	$/sample	233		
Number of samples per species[a]		2		
Per sample collecting fee	$/sample	63		
Private costs of collection	$/sample	50		
Costs of taxonomic information	$/species	100		
Discount rate		10%		
Number of prospecting years		40		
Country parameters (Costa Rica)				
Annual cost of biodiversity protection	$/species	50		
Total protected area	ha	600 000		
Number of species for screening		500 000		
Annual supply of samples for screening		2 000		
Total benefits and costs (present value)				
Royalty payments (*RYP*)	$ million	4.56		
Sample fees (*F*)	$ million	1.23		
Costs of collection (CC^P)	$ million	0.98		
Costs of taxonomic information (CT^S)	$ million	0.98		
Costs of biodiversity protection (CP^S)	$ million	244.48		
Net returns				
Net private returns (*NPR*)	$ million	4.81		
Net social returns (*NSR*)	$ million	240.64		
Distribution of net social returns		100-0-0[b]	50-25-25[b]	25-25-50[c]
Developed country				
Collector/broker	$ million	4.81	2.28	
Taxonomic institutions	$ million	–0.98		
Developing country				
Collector/broker	$ million		1.39	1.27
Taxonomic institutions	$ million		–0.98	–0.16
Biodiversity protection	$ million	–244.48	–243.34	–242.07

Notes:

a See Appendix.

b First share goes to the developed country collector/broker, second share to the developing country collector/broker and final share to biodiversity protection.

c First share goes to the developing country collector/broker, second share to the local taxonomic institution and final share to biodiversity protection. In addition, 10 per cent of the sample payment goes to biodiversity protection.

In Table 17.1, the expected royalty returns from screening 2000 samples every year for forty years come to US$4.6 million, or US$7.60 per hectare. The private costs of procuring biotic samples are around US$1 million and the value of fees paid for samples is US$1.2 million. Thus the net private returns to pharmaceutical prospecting are significantly positive but not necessarily substantial, around US$4.8 million in total. Hence the recent interest of the private sector in pharmaceutical prospecting of biodiversity is supported by our calculations, which suggest that there are good chances of a reasonable financial gain from private investment in these efforts.[17]

However, the net social returns from pharmaceutical prospecting must also take into account the social costs of taxonomic information and biodiversity protection. As indicated in Table 17.1, the social costs of investing in developing taxonomic knowledge for the species screened comes to an additional US$1 million. The more substantial burden is the total social costs of biodiversity protection for all 500 000 species. These costs amount to almost US$250 million, which means that net social returns are hugely negative – a loss of around US$240 million.

The large negative returns for net social returns indicates that current demand for biotic samples from the developing world cannot cover the full opportunity costs of biodiversity protection, which as we have demonstrated in previous sections is an important and necessary precondition to generating information about the biochemical properties of species. Even if our estimates of total royalty payments and sample fee understate the full economic value of the contributions of biodiversity to the development of new drugs, a deficit of US$240 million is simply too large.[18] In other words, the potential economic returns from pharmaceutical prospecting of biodiversity are on their own insufficient justification for the establishment of protected areas in developing countries.

Actual returns to developing countries from pharmaceutical prospecting will also be affected somewhat by the type of contractual arrangements, including distribution of royalties, involved in the pharmaceutical prospecting process. In Table 17.1, we indicate three possible scenarios. The first distributional arrangement describes the case of a private collector from a developed country who incurs all collecting costs as well as the taxonomic costs, but then also appropriates all royalty payments. The developing country is left with the full social costs of biodiversity protection. The second arrangement involves a developed country institution – such as a botanic garden or a private company – acting as a broker for a developing country collector. The local collector is, in turn, assumed to rely on a local institution as the source of taxonomic information. Under this arrangement the broker captures 50 per cent of the royalties, with the remainder going to the local collector who then apportions half again (that is, 25 per cent of the total) to biodiversity protection activities. Although both the developed and developing country agents make a net financial gain, the full costs of taxonomic information is now borne by the developing country. There is some return to biodiversity protection, but the net deficit is reduced only slightly. The third case is based on the current contractual arrangements favoured by Costa Rica's INBio, in which a developing country institution replaces the developed country broker. In this arrangement the developing country broker (INBio) pays 50 and 25 per cent of royalties, respectively, to biodiversity protection and the local taxonomic institution, as well as an additional 10 per cent contribution to biodiversity protection out of fees received for samples. The result is a net return to the developing country broker and taxonomic institutions; however, despite additional compensation the net deficit for biodiversity conservation is still substantial.

The distributional analysis indicates that different contractual arrangements for pharmaceutical prospecting will not increase significantly the contribution to biodiversity protection – even under the third scenario where 50 per cent of the royalties and an additional 10 per cent surcharge on sample fees are refunded to protection. The full costs of protection over the prospecting period – US$250 million – are simply too high.[19] However, our analysis does show that contractual arrangements are extremely important for the incentives for developing country investments in taxonomic information, that is, the 'information-generating effort' that comprises collection and identification of biotic samples as well as basic pharmaceutical R&D. For example, if the collecting and taxonomic activities are vertically integrated, then both the second and third contractual arrangement will lead to positive returns on these combined activities. This is an important observation, given the crucial role of information-generating effort in the pharmaceutical prospecting process, the high opportunity costs that many developing countries face in allocating scarce resources to the taxonomic sector and the current lack of support by the donor community for this effort.

Finally, it must be pointed out that the distribution of costs and benefits over time is a key factor working against the overall net social returns to developing countries from pharmaceutical prospecting. Even if a developing country is able to secure upfront royalties for samples supplied and favourable contractual arrangements initially, it may not be in a position to capture such financial returns in the future if it is unable to provide the quality and quantity of samples demanded or if it is simply unlucky in recording a 'hit'. Thus, a large degree of risk is assumed by a country that enters into pharmaceutical prospecting with the aim of generating future revenues, given the costs of taxonomic information must be paid up front and the costs of biodiversity are incurred from year one. Our analysis suggests that the risk may be worth taking in some instances, provided the country is realistic about the prospects of capturing the pharmaceutical value of biodiversity, including the returns to the different investments involved and the necessary contractual arrangements.

Conclusion

Should a developing country invest more in taxonomic and R&D effort in order to accumulate more knowledge about the use of natural products in developing new pharmaceuticals, or should greater effort by allocated to protection of the *in situ* biodiversity stock that is the source of the biological 'raw material' in the first instance?

In this chapter, we have suggested that an important issue that needs to be addressed *a priori* to this allocation decision is the ability of a developing country to find solutions to the incentives problem posed by the non-rival and non-exclusive characteristics of biodiversity and species information. Fundamental to any such solution is recognition of the distinction between biodiversity and species information. That is, simply 'saving' or protecting a country's stock of biodiversity is not in itself sufficient for 'capturing' pharmaceutical value. Throughout the entire process of pharmaceutical prospecting information – and consequently value – is being added to the species under investigation. If a developing country wants to appropriate a large share of the value-added from pharmaceutical prospecting it must invest – or encourage outsiders to invest – in the generation of species information within the country.

Given this problem, then the issue of how best to allocate effort between biodiversity protection and information-generating activities becomes crucial. The model of this paper has confirmed that both activities are complementary to the pharmaceutical value-added process, but there is always a danger of combining 'too much' protection effort with 'too little' taxonomic and R&D effort, and *vice versa*. The crucial determinant of the optimal allocation of effort between these activities is their relative marginal productivity in the pharmaceutical prospecting process over the long term, particularly in the fact of changes in the pharmaceutical product price, the discount rate and other parameters. In order for developing countries to maximize the potential returns from capturing the pharmaceutical value of their *in situ* biodiversity it is important to distinguish between the value added of the 'information' input and that of the 'raw material' input.

However, before investing in the pharmaceutical value added process, the country must determine whether there is a potential economic return to be made from allocating *any* resources to this process. Resources are scarce in developing countries, and it is not at all obvious that the returns from capturing the full pharmaceutical value of biodiversity is worth the costs of this enterprise for all countries. Our analysis of the economic returns from pharmaceutical prospecting suggests that there are potentially sufficient net returns to make investments financially attractive. However, a much more important result is that under certain contractual arrangements it is feasible for the social investment in information-generating effort, such as the collection and identification of biotic samples as well as basic pharmaceutical R&D, to be economically worthwhile.

What is unreasonable is to expect that pharmaceutical prospecting alone should be able to bear the full costs of biodiversity protection in developing countries. Although seemingly substantial royalties from the pharmaceutical value-added process can be 'earmarked' for financing protection, the full social costs of biodiversity protection are simply too high to be compensated through prospecting on its own. Other economic benefits of establishing protected natural areas – from ecotourism to watershed protection – must make up the difference if the full costs of biodiversity protection are to be justified. This suggests that pharmaceutical prospecting is just one of the economic benefits that should be considered in the establishment of protected areas for biodiversity conservation. Alternatively, if a developing country has already established protected areas because other economic and environmental benefits justify the costs, then the additional returns from investing in pharmaceutical prospecting of the biodiversity in these areas may be worthwhile.

The general results of our study are supported by related findings that attempt to estimate the maximum willingness to pay by a pharmaceutical company to conserve a marginal hectare of biodiversity with pharmaceutical prospecting value (Simpson *et al.*, 1996). The authors calculate that the maximum possible pharmaceutical value of the marginal species is US$9431. However, when this figure is applied to the eighteen critical biodiversity 'hot spots' identified as potential protected areas in developing countries, the greatest willingness to pay for conservation of this pharmaceutical value amounts to US$20 per hectare. In other areas with even less genetic diversity the willingness to pay could be considerably lower, possibly even a dollar per hectare or less. Thus the authors conclude that given that these relatively negligible values derived from genetic prospecting 'considerable caution and scepticism should be employed when considering the potential for genetic prospecting as a conservation tool'.

Nevertheless, despite every indication that pharmaceutical prospecting cannot sustain biodiversity protection by itself, and despite the apparent risks involved, our results do suggest that prospecting activities remain a potentially profitable commercial activity for developing countries. Although difficult to quantify, the development of taxonomic information through prospecting may also yield other economic benefits to society, ranging from improvement in human and technical skills to environmental education to 'scientific tourism'.[20] In addition, investments in higher value-added activities such as chemical extraction, primary screening, and chemical fractionation and isolation may be important stepping stones in developing scientific and technological capacity. Given the potential returns to pharmaceutical prospecting of biodiversity and the possibility of wider benefits, investment in prospecting activities must be carefully considered by a country rich in biodiversity, particularly if it is already protected for sound economic reasons.

As indicated in the empirical analysis of this paper, one useful approach for conservation planning would be to investigate the extent to which the social viability of prospecting in protected areas varies according to royalty values and preservation costs. If conducted across different regions rich in biodiversity, then this approach could be developed as a method for defining zones of prospecting potential based on returns from prospecting and preservation. However, it is worth repeating once again that our results suggest that it is unlikely that the returns from biodiversity prospecting alone will be sufficient to cover the full costs of establishing protected areas.

Appendix: A royalty model of pharmaceutical prospecting

The calculation of expected royalties paid per biotic sample in Table 17.1 is derived from a model of the estimated royalties generated through the development of a new pharmaceutical product from a biotic source. The assumptions underlying this royalty model are outlined in the following appendix. Full details can be found in Aylward (1993).

As royalties on new pharmaceutical products are not generally paid on sales occurring after patent expiration, *PE*, the present value of the gross revenues generated by sale of a new drug, *GR*, during the patent period can be defined as

$$GR = \sum_{t=0}^{t=PE} S_t / (1+r)^t, \quad \text{with} \quad S_t = S_0(1+\alpha)^t, \qquad (17A.1)$$

where S_t is the expected real value of sales in year t, S_0 is the expected value of sales in the initial year $t = 0$, α is the annual real rate of growth in the price of the pharmaceutical product and r is the rate of discount. Aylward *et al.* (1993) derive an estimate of US\$69 million (1990 prices) for average annual drug sales, S_t, based on an industry analysis by Grabowski and Vernon (1990) and assuming an average patent life of 18 years and a real price trend in pharmaceuticals of 5 per cent per year.[21] Using a discount rate of 10 per cent in formula (17A.1), the present value of gross revenues, *GR*, is on average US\$245 million for a new drug over an eighteen-year patent period.

In the pharmaceutical industry product royalties are paid on net revenues, which typically involve adjusting gross revenues for distribution costs from the point of production. As distribution costs, δ, are generally expressed as a percentage of gross returns, then net revenues, *NR*, can be defined

$$NR = (1 - \delta)GR, \qquad 0 < \delta < 1. \qquad (17A.2)$$

Total royalty payments on a successful drug as received by the producer of biotic samples, RY^{BS}, then depend on the expected rate of royalty, λ, and the level of net revenues for a drug

$$RY^{BS} = \lambda NR = \lambda(1 - \delta)GR. \tag{17A.3}$$

Industry sources suggest a royalty rate of around 1–3 per cent and distribution costs of 5 per cent are typical for pharmaceuticals (Aylward, 1993). Assuming λ is 2 per cent in Equation (17A.3), total royalty payments, RY^{BS}, are on average US$4.66 million for a successful new drug.

Given expectations regarding the success rate for species entering the screening process, $P(i)$, and the number of samples screened per species, η, the expected gross royalty earned per sample, k, can be defined as

$$RY_k^{BS} = P(i)\lambda NS/\eta \tag{17A.4}$$

Assuming $P(i)$ is 0.0001 and an average of 2 samples collected per species, Aylward (1993) estimates an average royalty payment per biotic sample, RY_k^{BS}, of US$233, which is the figure used in Table 17.1.[22]

Notes

* Environmental Economics Programme, International Institute for Environment and Development, London WC1H 0DD, UK.

1. This paper is based on research undertaken for the London Environmental Economics Centre (LEEC) on 'The economic value of species information and its role in biodiversity conservation: case studies of Costa Rica's National Biodiversity Institute and Pharmaceutical Prospecting' (Aylward *et al.*, 1993). The study was supported by the Swedish International Development Authority and conducted in cooperation with Costa Rica's National Biodiversity Institute and the Tropical Science Center. We are grateful to these institutions as well as for comments by Josh Bishop, Jo Burgess, Richard O'Doherty, Roger Sedjo, David Simpson and two anonymous reviewers on previous versions. However, we alone remain responsible for any errors or faults. A version of this paper was presented at the European Association of Environmental and Resource Economists (EARE) Fifth Annual Conference, University College, Dublin, 22–24 June 1994.
2. 'Pharmaceutical prospecting' is defined as the process of deriving marketable pharmaceuticals from natural products.
3. See Findeisen and Laird (1991), and Mallincrodt and Laird (1992) for an update on pharmaceutical companies engaged in prospecting. Also, note that the industry has shown a sustained interest in microbial diversity as a source of new leads.
4. See Barbier *et al.* (1994) for an overview of the potential role of biodiversity in economic development and the factors contributing to the loss of biodiversity.
5. This is necessary if commercial synthesis of the compound is not feasible. Balandrin *et al.* (1985) suggest that since most natural product leads are secondary metabolites from a technical perspective they will be difficult – and therefore costly – to synthesize.
6. See Aylward (1992) for further discussion of the public good aspects of biodiversity.
7. A recent law passed in Costa Rica requires collectors to submit an application for a collection licence that details their collection plans. If approved, non-resident foreigners are required to purchase a $30 collecting licence that is valid for six months. All collectors must deposit voucher

samples with the national collections and send copies of related publications to the national library.

8. Environmental samples are an exception. They are usually put through at least an initial screen before they are classified (Garrity, pers. comm., 1992).
9. In the case of drugs derived from natural products the practical difficulty of generating identical information leading to the development of the same drug should not be understated. For pharmaceutical prospecting, 'reinventing the wheel' involves retracing a number of complex steps including collection of the same species and development of comparable screens that search for the same disease target. It is unclear how such a process would generate a significant cost advantage for a potential competitor. 'Reverse engineering' involves working backwards from the marketed drug to the structural determination of the chemical compound. However, naturally produced compounds are often difficult to commercially synthesize. If this is the case, then 'reverse engineering' would require a company to work backward from a chemical compound to the original and *unknown* species. The ability to exclude others from the taxonomic and collection information generated earlier in the prospecting process would make this a difficult feat – akin to looking for a needle in a haystack.
10. Tyler (1979) points out that as an unfortunate consequence of the current system of intellectual property rights maintained in countries such as the US and the United Kingdom, disincentives are established for research into other potentially useful areas of natural products such as multi-source drugs and compound-based drugs with a long history of use.
11. See Sedjo (1992) and Simpson (1992) for theoretical overviews of contracting and property rights issues. Both authors suggest that the seemingly gradual move towards property rights over wild genetic resources in the form of legal and administrative control is driven by technological change. Improvements in biotechnologies may make the benefits of biological resources more apparent, while growing ability to identify species might lower the costs of enforcing exclusivity.
12. In this model we will follow conventional notation by omitting the argument of the time-dependent variables, by representing a derivative of a function by a prime, by employing lettered subscripts to indicate partial derivatives of a function, and by denoting the time derivative of a variable by a superscript dot.
13. The distinction between i and δ needs to be clarified somewhat. Although K is considered accumulated 'knowledge' about the pharmaceutical potential of extracted biodiversity, it clearly has to be 'stored' somewhere, for example, in laboratories, computers, researchers, and so on. It will obviously cost something to maintain this research infrastructure for storing knowledge, and i represents the 'interest payment' associated with this direct cost. On the other hand, δ is the social rate of discount, which is determined both by the pure rate of social time preference and the marginal opportunity cost of capital in the economy. Effectively, it represents the economic opportunity cost for the whole pharmaceutical value-added process, in that the stream of income gained from investing in this process must be weighed against other economic opportunities available to the developing country.
14. Note that $[pf_K - i]$ must be greater than zero if $\dot{\lambda} = 0$ in condition (17.8) for the long-run equilibrium.
15. Grabowski and Vernon (1990) and DiMasi *et al.* (1991) provide important baseline data on pharmaceutical sales and R&D costs respectively which were also used in the development of the model.
16. For example, the US National Cancer Institute (NCI) has a total annual screening capacity of 20 000 biotic samples for cancer and 30 000–40 000 for AIDS (Cragg *et al.*, 1993). NCI has a number of different contractors supplying natural products. Three five-year agreements are currently in place with the major US botanical gardens, each of which is responsible for assembling over 1000 samples a year. Actual collection is often undertaken by collaborators in the developing world. As a result, NCI's supply of plant material comes from approximately 25 different countries. In the private sector, Biotics Ltd provides samples for major pharmaceutical companies. In the past few years Biotics has provided over 3000 samples from more than eight countries to a number of industry screening programmes. Recent reviews suggest that such programmes have relatively smaller capacities relative to NCI's ranging from a few hundred samples to 15 000 (Mallincrodt and Laird 1992; Reid *et al.*, 1993). The majority of the

samples screened are from microbial sources rather than from plant, marine or other natural products. Thus the actual demand for biotic samples supplied annually from a biodiversity-rich developing country is more likely to be around 2000, much less than the then 20000 samples (10000 species screened) needed for a 'hit' as estimated in the royalty model of the annex.

17. These returns assume that any successful pharmaceutical product developed from biotic sources is an 'average earner' in the market. Based on estimates from Aylward *et al.* (1993), the returns are more than four times higher if the product turns out to be a 'big seller'.
18. We also have not allowed for any increase in the opportunity costs of holding on to land in protected areas that may occur as the country develops economically or its population grows.
19. For example, in order for royalty revenues over the period to cover the US$250 million costs of protection, sensitivity analysis indicates that it would be necessary to screen 110 000 species per year, which is clearly infeasible. Moreover, even under the third distributional arrangement, only US$125 million of royalties would be allocated to biodiversity protection.
20. Aylward *et al.* (1993) discuss many such 'additional' benefits for Costa Rica provided through INBio's taxonomic information and biodiversity prospecting activities. Only one benefit – the improved 'human capital' skills resulting from the training of 38 parataxonomists – could be quantified. The total value of the productivity benefits amounted to just over US$14000 (1990 prices), or approximately US$375 per parataxonomist trained. The total cost of the training programme was around US$10000.
21. According to a recent United Nations Industrial Development Organization study, patent life, PE, in OECD countries varies between 15 and 60 years (Ballance *et al.*, 1992). The figure of 5 per cent for the real price trend in pharmaceuticals was obtained by adjusting nominal price rises in US pharmaceuticals over the period 1980–91 by the US consumer price index. See Aylward (1993) for further details.
22. The species 'hit' rate, $P(i)$, is extremely difficult to estimate. It reflects the risk and uncertainty surrounding pharmaceutical prospecting, which can be affected by such diverse factors as the 'quality' of the biodiversity, the skills and equipment of the prospectors and the organizing of the prospecting activities. Various studies suggest figures for $P(i)$ in biodiversity-rich countries ranging from 1 in 125 to 1 in 40000, with the 'best guess' being the midpoint of 1 in 10000 used in our calculation (Aylward, 1993). In equation (17A.4) we have based the hit rate on the number of species, not samples, as there is no empirical evidence suggesting that the 'hit' rate will improve if more samples are collected from a single species. On the other hand, the costs of pharmaceutical prospecting are affected by the number of samples collected from each species. Thus prospectors generally avoid collecting multiple samples per species, which is why our calculation assumes that on average only two samples are collected per species.

References

Aylward, B.A. (1992), 'Appropriating the value of wildlife and wildlands', in T.M. Swanson and E.B. Barbier (eds), *Economics for the Wilds*, London: Earthscan Publications.

Aylward, B.A. (1993), 'The economic value of pharmaceutical prospecting and its role in biodiversity conservation', *LEEC Paper DP 93-05*, London: London Environmental Economics Centre.

Aylward, B.A., J. Echeverría, L. Fendt and E.B. Barbier (1993), 'The economic value of species information and its role in biodiversity conservation: Costa Rica's National Biodiversity Institute', *LEEC Paper 93-06*, London: London Environmental Economics Centre.

Balandrin, M., Klocke, E. Wurtele and W. Bollinger (1995), 'Natural plant chemicals: sources of industrial and medicinal material', *Science*, **288**, 1154.

Ballance, R., J. Pogány and H. Forstner (1992), *The World's Pharmaceutical industries: An International Perspective on Innovation, Competition and Policy*, Aldershot, UK: Edward Elgar.

Barbier, E.B., J.C. Burgess and C. Folke (1994), *Paradise Lost? The Ecological Economics of Biodiversity*, London: Earthscan Publications.

Cragg, G.M., M.R. Boyd, J.H. Cardellina III, M.R. Grever, S.A. Shepartz, and K.M. Snader (1993), 'The role of plants in the drug discovery program of the United States Cancer Institute', in D.R. Buxton *et al.* (eds), *International Crop Science 1*, Wisconsin: Crop Science Society of America.

DiMasi, .J.A., R.W. Hansen, H.G. Grabowske and L. Lasagna (1991), 'Cost of innovation in the pharmaceutical industry', *Journal of Health Economics*, **10**, 107–42.

Douros, J. and M. Suffness (1980), 'The National Cancer Institute's Natural Products Antineoplastic Development Program', in S.K. Carter and Y. Sakurai (eds), *Recent Results in Cancer Research*, **70**, pp. 21–44, Berlin: Springer-Verlag.

Farnsworth, N. and R. Morris (1976), 'Higher plants – the sleeping giant of drug development', *American Journal of Pharmacy*, **148** (2), 46–52.

Findeisen, C. and S. Laird (1991), *Natural Products Research and the Potential Role of the Pharmaceutical Industry in Tropical Forest Conservation*, Report prepared by The Periwinkle Project of the Rainforest Alliance, New York.

Garrity, George (1992), Senior Research Fellow, Microbial Resources, Merck & Co. Personal communication.

Grabowski, H. and Vernon, J. (1990), 'A new look at the returns and risks to pharmaceutical R&D', *Management Science*, **36** (July), 804–21.

Janzen, D. (1990), *A North–South Perspective on Science in the Management, Use, and Economic Development of Biodiversity*, Paper prepared for the International Conference on Conservation of Genetic Resources for Sustainable Development, Roros, Norway, 10–14 September.

Laird, S. (1992), *The Commercialization of Biological Samples: Contracts for the Prospecting of Biodiversity*, Draft paper, Periwinkle Project, Rainforest Alliance, New York.

Lewin, A., J. van Door, M. Flint and R. Solóranzo (1992), *Biodiversity Conservation in Costa Rica*, An evaluation of the Guanacaste and INBio projects prepared for SIDA and MIRENEM, Swedish International Development Authority, Stockholm.

Mallincrodt, E. and S. Laird (1992), *Update of Pharmaceutical Industry Involvement in Natural Products Research*, Paper prepared by the Periwinkle Project of the Rainforest Alliance, New York.

Reid, W.V., S.A. Laird, R. Gomez, A. Sittenfield, D.H. Janzen, M. Gollin and C. Juma (1993), 'A new lease on life', in W.V. Reid *et al.* (eds), *Biodiversity Prospecting: Using Genetic Resources for Sustainable Development*, Baltimore: WRI Publications, Chapter 1, pp. 1–52.

Sedjo, R.A. (1992), 'Property rights, genetic resources, and biotechnological change', *The Journal of Law & Economics*, **35** (1), 199–213.

Simpson, R.D. (1992) *Transactional Arrangements and the Commercialization of Tropical Biodiversity*, ENR Discussion Paper 92-11, Resources for the Future, Washington, DC.

Simpson, R.D., R.A. Sedjo and J.W. Reid (1996), 'Valuing biodiversity for use in pharmaceutical research', *Journal of Political Economy*, **104**, 163–85.

Suffness, M., D.J. Newman and K. Snader (1989), 'Discovery and development of antineoplastic agents from natural sources', in *Bioorganic Marine Chemistry, Volume 3*, pp. 131–68, Berlin: Springer-Verlag.

Townes, H.K. (1992), 'Charging fees for taxonomic services', *Association of Systematics Collections Newsletter*, **20** (4), 129–31.

Tyler, V. (1979), 'Plight of plant-drug research in the United States today', *Economic Botany*, **33** (4), 377–83.

PART FOUR

TRADE AND ENVIRONMENT

18. Elephant ivory and tropical timber: the role of trade interventions in sustainable management

Trade interventions have been increasingly advocated in recent years as a means to influence the incentives for sustainable resource management in developing countries. The commonly held view is that, for a few key resources, international trade has been a contributing factor to over-exploitation and depletion. As a consequence, curtailing this trade has been advocated as a major part of the solution to the problem. In the case of African elephant ivory, a trade ban has been imposed through the Convention on International Trade in Endangered Species. For tropical timber, there are moves to restrict trade to only sustainably produced timber. This chapter argues that, at least in these two cases, restrictive interventions may at best be ineffective and at worst counterproductive. Instead, alternative trade and other international mechanisms ought to be developed to encourage trade-related incentives for sustainable management.

Introduction

Many natural resources in developing countries are currently being exploited, or could potentially be exploited, to yield important tradable resource products. Trade in oil and natural gas products, mineral ores, agricultural commodities, fish and tropical timber, earns substantial export revenues for many developing countries. With these commodities, the role of international trade in providing incentives for sustainable management of the resource base – oil and natural gas reserves, production forests, fisheries, mineral reserves and the stock of arable and grazing land – has been an important topic for a number of years. Yet, even with these major tradable resource products, the emphasis has been more on the economic potential of sustaining export earnings, rather than on sustaining the resource base upon which these products depend.

Developing countries also export a range of minor tradable resource products. These include wildlife products, nontimber forest products (for example, gums, resins, rattan, plant medicines, cosmetics, and so on) and other products harvested directly from natural areas. The international trade in these products is generally not well documented, partly because the volume of trade for many of these products is low compared to domestic and local trade and subsistence use, and partly because of the generally insignificant amount of foreign currency earned. Our understanding of the production potential of the resource base that sustains these products and the impact of harvesting on yields is also limited. Thus, to date, we can say very little about the role of international trade in providing incentives for sustained management of many minor tradable resources.

Growing concern over the state of tropical forests and other natural areas, the extinction of key species and the loss of biodiversity, and the extent of land degradation in developing countries has sparked a movement towards the sustainable use of natural resources. Both developing countries and the international community are now expressing a strong interest in the development of sound domestic and international policies for management of key tradable resources. Economic studies of the trade in resource products have an important role to play in these policy developments by:

- analysing in detail the exact nature of the resource product trade flow between countries and its implication for supply and demand;
- evaluating policies in both exporting and importing countries that affect the trade flow and the incentives for sustainable resource management – including both border policies such as tariff and nontariff barriers and domestic policies such as domestic taxes and subsidies, policies on value-added processing, and so on; and,
- determining the trade and complementary domestic policy options, including international regulations and agreements, that could improve incentives for sustainable resource management.

Economic trade studies of this kind, for either major or minor tradable resource products of interest to developing countries, have only recently begun to appear. In 1990 and 1994, two analyses have been conducted for the trade in elephant ivory and in tropical timber.[1] The rest of this chapter summarizes some of the findings of these two studies to illustrate how economic analysis can contribute to the evaluation of alternative policies for international control and regulation of key tradable resources.

Case study of the ivory trade and elephant conservation

In the 1980s, the population of elephants in Africa fell from 1.2 million to just over 600 000. Elephant populations are stabilizing or rising only in South Africa, Botswana, Zimbabwe and Namibia. The dramatic decline in elephant numbers in most of Africa has been largely attributable to illegal harvesting, that is, poaching, of elephants for ivory. That is, the ivory has been harvested and traded internationally without the appropriate national or international authorization.

The incentives for illegal harvesting and export of elephant ivory stem from a number of important factors:

- Historically, ivory has always been a highly valued commodity as a precious raw material for sculpture, jewellery and other ornamental uses. Over the past four decades, strong consumer demand has existed in hard currency countries experiencing rapid income growth: Europe, the United States and, more recently, Japan. Ivory products have also been 'culturally demanded' in Asia for many centuries.
- Despite ivory's high value, very little of this value accrues to Africans. Surveys have revealed that prices for raw ivory in Africa are typically only 10–30 per cent of the value for the same ivory imported into Asia. Most of the value added goes to international traders.
- For individual harvesters, receiving a relatively insignificant proportion of value added contributes to the uncertainty and risk of postponing harvesting today. Given the slow growth in elephant populations, the returns from holding on to the current 'ivory crop – that is, the standing stock of elephants – is less attractive as compared to harvesting the ivory today and reinvesting in other higher-yield assets. Moreover, as the individuals hired to do the illegal hunting are often very poor and are paid rates just marginally higher than the prevailing rates, current profits can be high.
- For African governments, with the possible exceptions of Zimbabwe and South Africa, the failure to capture sufficient returns from the ivory trade has led to inadequate investments in elephant management and protection. Only 1.5 per cent of the elephants' total range of 5.9 million square kilometres lies within strictly warded and adequately protected areas, which have actually shrunk by 20 per cent (from 7.5 million square kilometres) during the 1980s.

If the only value of the elephant lay in its tusks, then the recent declines in its populations might be socially acceptable to some range states. However, the wider social values of elephants are not reflected in ivory prices. These values may include ecological and tourist values and the loss of existence value to people who simply want elephants to be conserved.[2] Some of these values may be significant and reflect a large willingness to pay for conservation. For example, a travel-cost study recently estimated the value of viewing elephants in Kenya to be US$25 million per year – as much as ten times the value of its (poached) ivory exports.[3] The existence value of elephants may also be very important, judging by the successful public campaigns in both Africa and the West to save the elephant.

The role of the ivory trade

The economic incentives for either controlling or accelerating the decline in Africa's elephant population clearly originate within the ivory trade. Perceptions of this link recently led to pressure for a ban of the international ivory trade, enacted in October 1989. A comprehensive analysis of the impact of the ivory trade on elephant populations and the incentives for sustainable management is necessary in order to clarify whether a ban on the trade is the appropriate policy response.

Between 1979 and 1988, the price of raw ivory increased dramatically, from around $60 to $150 per kilogram. In early 1989, before the international ban, the price rose to nearly $300 per kilogram. Thus, the ivory trade has been highly lucrative.

Total exports of unworked ivory leaving Africa have risen from between 200 to 400 tons per annum in the 1950s to around 1000 tons in 1980. This represents a greater than 400 per cent increase in the trade over 40 years, or a 10 per cent increase in each year of the past four decades. Up to 1986, records indicate that between 700 and 1000 tons of raw ivory were traded internationally each year (see Table 18.1). The sum total of ivory exported between 1979 and 1988 amounted to between 7625 and 7955 tons. Although average tusk weights have changed over time, an average pair of tusks weighs between nine and ten kilograms. It can therefore be estimated that during this period, between 700 000 and 800000 elephants were killed for their ivory.

The decline in tonnage since the mid 1980s looks encouraging, but the statistics hide the real impact of the ivory trade on the elephant population. In 1979, a ton of ivory represented approximately 54 dead elephants. These were mainly the bull elephants, valued for their bigger tusks, with an average tusk weight per elephant of 9.3 kilograms. By 1987, most of the mature bull elephants had been shot, leaving cows and calves to support the demand for ivory. They have a much lower average tusk size of 4.7 kilograms, such that one ton of ivory now directly represents about 113 dead elephants. In addition, the high female ratio of the harvested population leads to the death of an additional 55 calves who are orphaned or die of starvation. As a consequence, almost the same number of elephants were harvested in 1987 as in 1979 to support the demand for ivory, but from a much reduced and more fragile population.

Table 18.1 lists the main African ivory exporters. The exporters are not necessarily the elephant-producing countries, however. Several African countries have acted as entrepots for neighbouring countries. These include Sudan, Burundi, the Central African Republic (CAR), and Congo, each of which exported more than 900 tons of ivory between 1979 and 1988. The annual value of ivory exports from Africa in the 1980s is estimated to be $50–$60 million. Because this amount includes c.i.f. costs and marketing margins in international trade, $35–$45 million is probably a more realistic value for African ivory exports. This amount is a tiny fraction of all African export earnings, and although significant for a few individual countries, the loss of these ivory revenues would not severely impair African development. Moreover, as noted above, other values of the African elephant, such as its importance to tourism in some countries such as Kenya, may be considerably more significant in terms of foreign exchange earnings.

Table 18.1 Raw ivory exports by major African exporters, 1979–88 (tons)

	'79	'80	'81	'82	'83	'84	'85	'86*	'87*	'88*
Botswana	13	5	9	5	6	4	17	0.4	0.4	0.1
Burundi	139	126	61	46	124	184	215	138	50	9
CAR	181	183	107	202	204	122	117	19	2	0.3
Chad	27	4	13	28	34	4	0.03	0	2	0
Congo	93	175	237	102	53	95	72	17	86	19
Gabon	4	1	1	0.2	0.9	0.2	0.4	0.5	4	14
Kenya	46	31	6	12	4	13	19	2	0.1	0
South Africa	42	35	33	28	46	36	50	41	18	8
Sudan	124	206	269	278	337	68	22	78	70	0
Tanzania	33	45	27	18	15	45	114	302	56	43
Uganda	25	19	45	12	13	100	206	3	0	0.2
Zaire	160	84	45	78	157	90	22	23	12	11
Zambia	16	22	28	34	18	2	14	11	4	2
Zimbabwe	3	2	1	14	14	21	23	8	8	7
All Africa Min. total	944	952	905	890	1032	798	912	719	331	142
All Africa Max. total	950	1164	912	900	1040	798	912	805	331	142

Note: These are the 'best estimates' of African exports, disaggregated by country of export, using import and export data from customs sources and CITES data. Both *legal* and *illegal* exports are likely to be included. For starred years (*), because of the adoption of the management quota system by CITES, there may have been an incentive to evade both customs and CITES systems in some countries.

Source: Barbier *et al.* (1990), *Elephants, Economics and Ivory*, Table 1.2.

As stated above, the flow of ivory in international trade has generally been toward the hard currency consumers – the United States, Europe, and, more recently, Japan. These three consumers have acquired about 75 per cent of all ivory worked in Hong Kong and Japan this decade. The remainder of the ivory in international trade has gone to carving industries within various developing countries, for example, India and China, and then been re-exported or sold to tourists for hard currency. The same is true for much of African worked ivory.

Therefore, it is very likely that nearly all the ivory in international trade has ultimately found its way to the United States, Europe or Japan.

The primary cause of the growth in the ivory trade may be traced to ivory's character as a precious material, used in sculpture and jewellery. Ivory has been a culturally demanded substance in Asia for several centuries. In Japan, the ivory is especially prized for making *hankos*, personal seals traditionally used in place of a signature. The major demand for raw and worked ivory since 1979 has been in East Asia.[4]

An economic analysis of demand for raw ivory in Japan indicates that raw ivory is a luxury good; that is, as real income grew in the past, Japanese consumption of raw ivory grew even faster. Hong Kong is also a major importer of raw ivory.[5] However, unlike Japan, Hong Kong is less of a final end-use consumer than a major entrepot in the world ivory trade. The vast majority of its imports are re-exported to other countries as worked ivory, principally to Japan, Europe and the United States. A demand analysis of Hong Kong's import market indicates that, as its economy grows, Hong Kong will expand its re-export market in raw ivory and perhaps allow its carving industry to disperse to newly industrializing countries that are developing this capacity.

It is clear from the high income elasticity in the analysis of Japan and Hong Kong that one of the consequences of economic development in Asia has been a substantial demand for elephant ivory. It is apparent that this latent demand for ivory exists in a number of other Asian states, such as Korea and Taiwan, where demand has increased by 1000 per cent in the past decade, and that demand pressures will remain high so long as rapid economic growth continues in this region. Other rapidly developing countries, such as Singapore, Thailand, Dubai and Macau, have also been playing an increasingly important role in the movement of ivory stocks and in their processing and carving. This fluidity represents one of the characteristics of both the legal and illegal trade: whenever one channel has been blocked, another has opened up almost immediately. The entrance of new countries into the ivory trade and the fluidity of the ivory trade are important issues to be tackled by any regime of international regulation.

The CITES ban

At the Seventh Conference of the Parties to the Convention on International Trade in Endangered Species (CITES) in 1989, the African elephant was transferred from an Appendix II listing (which allows some trade, with permits, in elephant ivory and skin) to Appendix I. This effectively bans all trade in elephant products. However, in the future, individual countries with healthy elephant populations, an effective elephant conservation and management programme, and effective ivory trade controls will be able to apply to a technical committee (Panel of Experts) to have their elephant populations transferred back to Appendix II listing. It was also agreed that the international trade ban should apply to all existing ivory stocks, with no special exemptions for countries holding large ivory stockpiles, for example, Hong Kong and Burundi. Elephant trophy imports into the United States from countries taking a reservation would also be prohibited.

The CITES ban received support from the majority of the African nations and consuming countries, some of which had already banned ivory trading domestically; for example, Kenya, the United States and Europe. However, some countries voiced dissatisfaction at the proposal, with Zimbabwe, Botswana, South Africa, Malawi and Zambia refusing to agree to the CITES resolution. China and Hong Kong also declared reservations against the ban and have continued trading in African elephant ivory. India intended to enter a reservation, but failed to do so due to an administrative oversight.[6] Hence, there appears to be substantial support for an ongoing ivory trade amongst some African producers and processors of ivory.

At the Eighth Conference of the Parties to CITES in 1992, Botswana, Malawi, Namibia and Zimbabwe submitted a proposal requesting resumption of trade in nonivory elephant products on the grounds that such trade would support conservation efforts to manage their elephant populations sustainably. The Panel of Experts Report to CITES subsequently concluded that Botswana and Zimbabwe had met the conditions for a transfer of their elephant populations to Appendix II. South Africa also submitted a proposal, again supported by the Panel of Experts, that its elephant population be transferred to Appendix II. However, due to opposition from a large number of delegations to CITES, including many from other African countries, both proposals were withdrawn. In reaction to this rebuttal at the conference, Botswana, Malawi, Namibia and Zimbabwe have stated their intention to resume their ivory trade unilaterally, although 'every effort will be made so that controls will prevent any poached ivory being laundered through the system'.[7]

Despite these problems, initial reports have claimed success for the ban in halting the ivory trade. A survey of Asian consuming countries found major declines in the ivory carving industries of India, Hong Kong and China, with less than a third of carvers still processing ivory.[8] Other influential observers, such as Richard Leakey, former Director of Kenya's Wildlife Service, have strongly supported the ban for being essential to antipoaching policies.[9] In 1990, 46 elephants were killed in Kenya, while in the previous year 300 elephants were killed. Before the ban, ivory earned the poachers only US$2–$3 per kilogram. After the ban, the poachers were to earn upwards of US$40–$50 per kilogram of ivory.[10]

Other sources suggest that poaching activity is still high in a number of range states. In Malawi, the rate of elephant poaching in 1990 was comparable to the average rate of 30 animals poached over the past three years. At the end of 1990, 27 elephants were killed in the Korup Forest of Cameroon. The fall in the price of ivory in Central Africa from US$200 a kilogram to US$20 may have actually increased demand within Africa, because the commodity became more affordable for ceremonial and decorative purposes.[11]

Since the CITES ban in October 1989, price movements have also become less clear. Immediately after the ban the uncertainty surrounding the future of the ivory brace appears to have affected the price of raw ivory in most importing countries, but only marginally.[12] The major initial impact seems to have been the reduction of the price of raw ivory in Africa, as many African countries have found themselves with major stockpiles of ivory that could not be traded on the international market. A survey of ten Asian countries confirms that little if any reduction in raw ivory prices has occurred in major Asian importing and consumer countries.[13] The price of ivory in Japan, the largest consumer country, rose to US$700–$800 per kilogram in early 1990, but then fell to around US$500 per kilogram for an average tusk. However, the latter price for raw ivory in Japan still exceeded early 1989 average prices, before they began rising in response to international pressure for a ban. In smaller Asian importers, such as Laos and Vietnam, the price of good quality tusks doubled to US$200 per kilogram from 1988 to 1990.[14]

There are indications that the gradual depletion of raw ivory stocks in consumer countries will continue to put upward pressure on prices.[15] The price differential, with African countries holding large stockpiles, could provide an incentive for illegal trade. Although the amount traded may initially be small, it could be sufficient to cause prices to rise in Africa, thereby stimulating more poaching. Furthermore, countries with substantial carving industries, including Japan, that are adversely affected by the ban may become increasingly frustrated by the lack of legal supplies.

If a sufficient number of both ivory producing and consuming countries defy the CITES ban, then it may prove ineffective in protecting elephant populations. The problem is that, as the trade has always consisted of both a legal and an illegal component, banning the trade may provide the incentives for expanding its illegal component. Countries also could establish trading arrangements outside CITES regulations, as evidenced by the reactions of Southern African range states to the outcome of the Eighth Conference. Continuation with the CITES ban will only have an impact on the illegal component of the ivory trade if the costs of relocating the illegal trade are very high. However, as discussed above, historically the ivory trade has proven to be very fluid. The only way to increase the costs to an illegal trade would be to ensure maximum compliance with the ban, that is, with virtually no existing or potential consumers and producers continuing to trade. If the ban is defied, then eventually the illegal trade, consisting of former legal trade which would be more difficult to monitor and control, would increase.

Figure 18.1 illustrates this situation. The effect of the ban is to cause initial demand, D_0, to decrease. This is the result of the exit from the market of the primary consumers: the United States, the European Economic Community and Japan. The initial impact could be a fall in price – as is currently occurring in Africa – until demand adjusts by the entrance of new consumers (for example, the rapidly developing Asian economies and/or nonmembers of CITES) or the demand by existing consumers picks up again. However, while overall demand will fall, the illegal component of demand, D_i, could actually increase. Similarly, the effect of the ban may cause initial supply, S_0, to decrease somewhat, but it

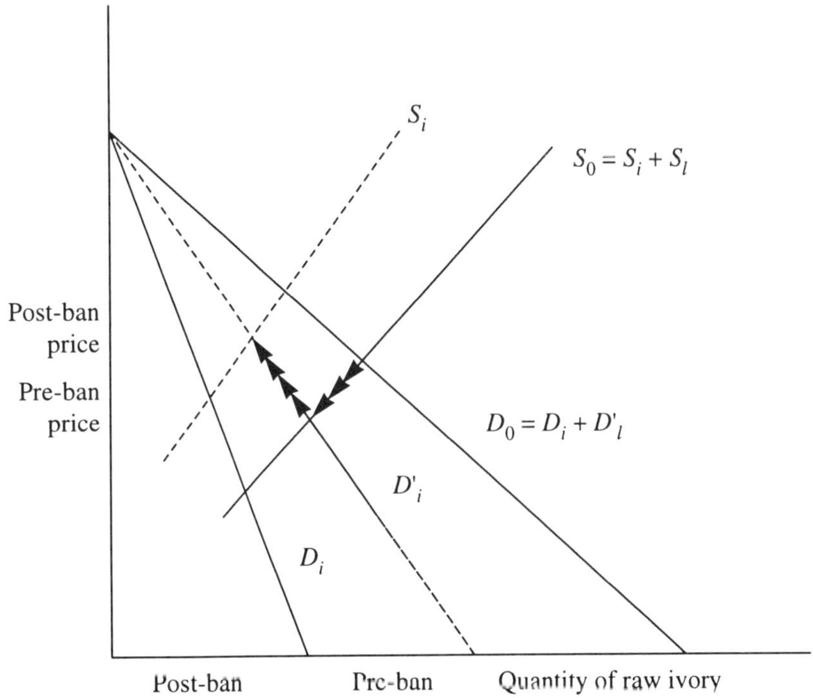

Notes:
S_0 = Supply curve before ban, illegal and legal supply ($S_i + S_l$).
S_i = Supply curve after ban, illegal supply only.
D_0 = Demand curve before ban, illegal and legal demand ($D_i + D_l$).
D_i = Demand curve before ban, illegal demand only.
Di' = Demand curve after ban, illegal demand only.

Source: E. Barbier, J. Burgess, T. Swanson and D. Pearce (1989), *Elephants Economics and Ivory*, London: Earthscan Publications.

Figure 18.1 The long-term effects of an ivory ban

would comprise a large proportion of 'illegal' supplies, S_i, and would also include supplies by African states that have decided to defy the CITES ban. The eventual effect could be a price rise, increasing the incentives of poachers and the illegal trade to supply this market. As ivory demand is highly responsive to income growth, these price rises could be sustained if a sufficient number of consumer countries and range states defy the ban.

An alternative policy option[16]

An ineffective, indefinite ban may therefore be worse for the survival of the African elephant over the medium and long term than a policy aiming to establish a controlled trade based on a sustainable yield of ivory, however small. There are several reasons for this:

- A modest production of ivory – say a sustainable yield of 50 tons – offers an incentive to consuming nations to accept a controlled legal trade and to enforce it, whereas they lose all benefits from a banned trade.
- Allowing a sustainable yield of ivory would enable selection of those producer countries to participate in the sanctioned trade under precise rules, such as the demonstration of healthy and sustainably managed elephant populations.
- A properly constructed trade mechanism could allow for a larger share of the revenues from ivory sales to be retained in the producer states, which could be reinvested in sustainable management of elephant populations.

One means for controlling a sustainable-yield ivory trade would be through the establishment of an ivory exchange. The essential principles of the exchange would be to encourage exclusive agreements by consumer countries to purchase all ivory through the exchange, and to restrict the number of suppliers to those producers who conform with some sustainability criterion, as suggested above. The critical consuming countries would be existing and potential end-users of worked ivory, as unworked ivory is simply an intermediate product. In return, these purchasers of ivory would be assured access to long-term supplies. The producers, guaranteed a stable and secure demand, would have an incentive for conforming to the rules of the exchange.

To work effectively, the exchange must also set ceilings on the sale of confiscated ivory; agree on ivory production limits and a policy on price floors; certify public auctions and purchasing agents; establish a revolving fund for ploughing back revenues into elephant management and antipoaching activities; and develop appropriate certification and monitoring of exchange ivory. The establishment and funding of such an exchange would be a formidable undertaking. It may require additional external funding through taxes on wildlife tourism, import duties by consumer countries and possibly export taxes.

Whether future regulatory mechanisms for the ivory trade involve either an ivory exchange or the maintenance of an indefinite ban, international compensation will play a critical role. For example, the incentives for producer countries to invest in the maintenance of elephant populations are slight under a ban unless some compensation is offered for their lost export earnings and other costs imposed. Compensation could take the form of cash transfers to Africa to help enforce any ban. The money could be used to assist in the costs of anti-poaching activities; in the diversification of rural carving industries to other products; in the improvement and expansion of tourist facilities and reserved lands; and in the investment in community-based wildlife conservation projects. Similar compensation would be required to assist producing countries to conform to the sustainable management rules of an ivory exchange. This would enhance the transition to sustainable management of elephant populations for long term. The gains would be more evenly distributed, as opposed to the current practice of over-exploiting the dwindling populations for short-run gains.

Although necessary, international compensation is not sufficient without improving the incentives for local communities to participate in the conservation of elephant and wildlife resources.[17] Protection of elephant populations, as well as their habitats and migration routes, may involve the loss of local community access to traditional hunting and resource rights. These losses must be compensated for through gains from conservation. Such gains could include ownership of any tourism facilities and/or a share in tourist revenues; the allocation of sufficient hunting quotas of nonendangered species in protected areas to local communities for meat, hides and other products; the employment of the local population in protection activities, surveys and even culling operations; and full representation and participation of local communities in decisions affecting the allocation of land uses and resource rights. The international community together with African governments must ensure that the efforts to protect and conserve elephant populations include projects and programmes that enhance the cooperation of local communities.

Case study of the timber trade and tropical forest conservation

In recent years, concern about the destruction of tropical forests has led to increased interest in the role of the international timber trade in promoting deforestation in the tropics. It has also led to interest in ways to restrict or reform the trade as a means to protect and preserve tropical forests. For example, recent estimates from the United Nations Food and Agriculture Organization (FAO) suggest that the annual rate of tropical deforestation from 1980–90 was around 0.9 per cent and has increased substantially in recent years.

However, the linkages between the trade in tropical timber products and tropical deforestation suggest that the trade is not the major source of the problem. Not only is conversion of forests to other uses, such as agriculture, a more significant factor, but an increasing proportion of tropical timber harvested in producer countries is for domestic consumption and does not even enter international trade. For example, current trends in the tropical timber trade suggest that:

- Only 17 per cent of tropical nonconiferous wood is used for industrial purposes; the remainder is used for fuelwood and other nonindustrial uses. With the exception of wood-based panels, exports of industrial roundwood logs and tropical timber products continue to be a small proportion of total production (see Table 18.2).
- In addition, tropical timber plays a minor role in the global timber market. Tropical countries account for approximately 15 per cent of the total volume of global timber production, and 11 per cent of the value of global exports.[18] However, for a few countries (for example, the Central African Republic, Ghana, Indonesia, Malaysia and Papua New Guinea), timber export earnings account for over 10 per cent of total export earnings (see Table 18.3).
- Tropical Asia and Oceania are the most important regions in terms of volume of timber produced (over 50 per cent of tropical production) and exported (over 85 per cent of tropical exports). The regions also dominate the processing of timber products. Higher-valued timber products account for an increasing proportion of their exports.[19]
- Domestic timber consumption in tropical countries will continue to increase due to population and income growth. Many tropical timber producers are already, or are rapidly becoming, net timber importers. The level of South–South trade is expected to expand over the next few years.
- Demand for industrial timber is expected to increase until the year 2000. Although developing countries will account for an increasing share of this growth, developed countries will continue to dominate the global timber market.
- Over the long term, declining tropical timber inventory, combined with demand growth in producer countries, will push up log prices in these countries and decrease their log exports. Expanding temperate resources will generally prevent commensurate increases in the prices of hardwood products. Processors of tropical logs will see their profits squeezed, leading to declining demand by importing countries.

Although a small and declining proportion of harvested tropical timber enters international trade, the industrial forest sector and timber trade may be

Table 18.2 The volume of world and tropical timber production and trade 1990

	Production	Exports	Tropical production as a % of world production	Tropical exports as a % of world exports
Total roundwood (million m^3)				
World	3450.4	120.5		
Tropical	1397.0	30.0	40.49	24.90
Industrial roundwood (million m^3)				
World	1654.2	118.2		
Tropical	275.0	29.1	16.62	24.62
Sawnwood and sleepers (million m^3)				
World	485.9	88.9		
Tropical	59.0	9.0	12.14	10.12
Wood based panels (million m^3)				
World	124.9	31.2		
Tropical	19.4	13.0	15.53	41.67
Wood pulp (million tons)				
World	154.4	25.0		
Tropical	7.2	0.7	4.66	2.80
Paper and paper board (million tons)				
World	238.2	55.2		
Tropical	15.5	2.2	6.51	3.99

Note: Tropical countries are all developing countries excluding China, Chile, Argentina, Turkey and South Korea.

important to tropical countries for a number of reasons. First, the industrial forest sector makes a direct contribution to the economy of producer countries. In 1989, for example, the industrial forest sector accounted for 3–6 per cent of total gross domestic product (GDP) in Malaysia and Indonesia, and 2–3 per cent of total GDP in the Ivory Coast, Gabon, Ghana, Brazil and Costa Rica. In most other tropical timber producing countries, however, the industrial forest sector represented less than 2 per cent of total GDP in 1989.[20] Second, wood-related industries are an important source of employment in the manufacturing sector of many developing countries, although the level of employment in wood-related industries is modest compared to the size of economically active populations in developing countries. Third, although across the tropics as a whole exports of forest products do not generate substantial foreign exchange earnings compared to total export earnings (Table 18.3), they are an important source of

Table 18.3 Forest products trade balance and percentage of total trade in tropical countries, 1990

	Forest product imports US$'000	Forest product exports US$'000	Forest product net exports US$'000	Total imports US$ million	Total exports US$ million	Forest products imports as a % of total imports	Forest products exports as a % of total exports
Tropical Africa							
Cameroon	35 412	99 833	64 421	1 300	1 200	2.7	8.3
CAR	468	29 994	29 526	170	130	0.3	23.1
Congo	4 500	106 087	101 587	570	1 130	0.8	9.4
Côte d'Ivoire	27 200	236 147	208 947	2 100	2 600	1.3	9.1
Gabon	3 655	136 774	133 119	760	2 471	0.5	5.5
Ghana	5 129	76 526	71 397	1 199	739	0.4	10.4
Kenya	23 594	4 054	(19 540)	2 124	1 033	1.1	0.4
Madagascar	8 546	534	(8 012)	480	335	1.8	0.2
Malawi	8 058	1 993	(6 065)	576	412	1.4	0.5
Nigeria	33 083	1 680	(31 403)	5 688	13 671	0.6	0.0
Sierra Leone	1 028	146	(882)	146	138	0.7	0.1
Tanzania	15 700	1 539	(14 161)	935	300	1.7	0.5
Zaire	3 666	17 032	13 366	888	999	0.4	1.7
Zimbabwe	5 765	4 169	(1 596)	NA	NA	NA	NA
Tropical Central and South America							
Costa Rica	40 020	21 895	(18 125)	2 026	1 457	2.0	1.5
El Salvador	21 800	2 725	(19 075)	1 200	550	1.8	0.5
Guatemala	69 410	18 326	(51 084)	1 626	1 211	4.3	1.5
Honduras	137 921	31 061	(106 860)	1 028	916	13.4	3.4
Mexico	403 605	13 884	(389 721)	28 063	26 714	1.4	0.1
Nicaragua	10 566	2 569	(7 997)	750	379	1.4	0.7
Panama	76 979	3 988	(72 991)	1 539	321	5.0	1.2

Table 18.3 Continued

Trinidad & Tobago	54 396	458	(53 938)	1 262	2 080	4.3	0.0
Bolivia	4 060	22 160	18 100	716	923	0.6	2.4
Brazil	299 402	1 750 981	1 451 579	22 459	31 243	1.3	5.6
Colombia	104 056	20 060	(83 996)	5 590	6 766	1.9	0.3
Ecuador	157 834	24 373	(133 461)	1 862	2 714	8.5	0.9
Paraguay	13 055	24 971	11 916	1 113	959	1.2	2.6
Peru	104 914	2 558	(102 356)	3 230	3 277	3.2	0.1
Tropical Asia and Oceania							
Hong Kong	1 752 273	705 535	(1 046 738)	82 495	29 002	2.1	2.4
India	290 967	16 337	(274 630)	23 692	17 967	1.2	0.1
Indonesia	330 157	3 069 199	2 739 042	21 837	25 553	1.5	12.0
Malaysia	483 372	3 040 884	2 557 512	29 251	29 409	1.7	10.3
Philippines	173 662	123 119	(50 543)	13 080	8 681	1.3	1.4
Singapore	747 548	663 302	(84 246)	60 647	52 627	1.2	1.3
Sri Lanka	28 771	600	(28 171)	2 689	1 984	1.1	0.0
Thailand	1 002 371	101 551	(900 820)	33 129	23 002	3.0	0.4
Papua New Guinea	5 504	115 500	109 996	1 288	1 140	0.4	10.1

Source: Barbier *et al.* (1994.)

foreign exchange. Finally, there are numerous wider economic and social benefits associated with timber production and trade that are also important for tropical developing countries, such as rural infrastructure development and the provision of other social amenities.

In addition, although the long-term trends suggest that tropical timber products may lose ground to temperate products and nontimber substitutes, recent evidence suggests that the demand for tropical timber products is still buoyant. Empirical studies indicate that demand for tropical timber products is relatively price insensitive and that substitution between tropical and temperate timber products in importing markets has not been very significant.[21] However, in response to export log bans by tropical producers, some importers are increasingly diversifying the source of their supply. While substitution of nonwood products for timber may be occurring, the evidence is largely anecdotal. Substitution between tropical timber products originating from different countries or regions does appear to be very high, particularly for plywood. This would suggest not only that importers can substitute between sources of origin with relative ease, but also that tropical exporters can easily capture market share through price competition. That is, although individual exporters are highly competitive, producers, as a group, may enjoy significant market power. As a consequence, coordinated price increases by all tropical producers would not lead to a significant decline in total demand. On the other hand, there are potential short-term gains for individual producers, especially for producers of value-added products who undercut rivals and increase their market share.

Trade policy measures and sustainable forest management

The evidence presented on the linkages between the trade in tropical timber products and tropical deforestation suggests that the trade is not the major source of the problem.[22] In fact, the main linkage may be the other way around: the impact of increasing scarcity of tropical timber resources, and thus tropical hardwood logs, on production and export. Moreover, there is little evidence that tropical timber products are currently being squeezed out of consumer markets by nontropical products or through price discrimination. If anything, tropical timber producers appear to be competing among themselves for dominant shares of a strong market.

Nevertheless, there is a genuine cause for concern over the excessive exploitation and rapid depletion of tropical production forests in many regions, including the indirect impacts of unsustainable harvesting practices on the loss of nontimber forest values and the incentives to convert forest land to other uses (for example, agriculture). A particularly significant impact may be the role of unsustainable timber production in opening up forest areas to subsequent agricultural encroachment and conversion. However, these effects do not in themselves warrant major interventions in the timber trade in order to improve sustainable forest management. To the contrary, they suggest that the proper focus for policy intervention ought to be at the concession and forest level.

Timber trade can lead to greater net returns for forestry investments and sustainable management of production forests, making this option more attractive than alternative uses of forest land such as agriculture. Unfortunately, in many producer countries the widespread prevalence of market and policy failures has distorted the incentives for sustainable management and has had a major influence on the conversion of forest land to agriculture and other uses.[23] Failures in concession and pricing systems have produced counterproductive incentives that lead to the 'mining' of production forests.

Thus the key factor in reducing timber-related tropical deforestation is ensuring proper economic incentives for efficient and sustainable management of tropical production forests. Appropriate forest management policies and regulations within producer countries ought to provide these incentives so that the long run income-generating potential of harvesting timber is maximized, and any significant external environmental costs associated with timber harvesting are internalized. The starting point for sustainable production forest management is therefore to tackle the problem at its source by enabling producer countries to improve forest sector policies.

In particular, royalty, contract and concessional arrangements are key incentive mechanisms determining levels of trespass, high-grading and loss of some nontimber values.[24] Lack of proper forest management regulations and controls on encroachment can also exacerbate forest degradation problems. In addition, the failure of stumpage prices (that is, the prices of harvested logs at the stand) to take into account the additional social costs associated with the loss of nontimber values (for example, watershed protection, carbon storage, nontimber forest products) can generate excessive net returns, or economic rents, from timber harvesting. This leads to socially inefficient harvesting levels.[25] Finally, over the long term, if stumpage values are underpriced, they will also fail to reflect increasing scarcity as old-growth forests are depleted. As a result, efficient development of forest industries will be undermined, particularly the transition from dependence on old-growth to secondary-growth forests and the coordination of processing capacity with timber stocks.[26]

Timber trade policy in producer and consumer countries has, if anything, magnified the problems created by poor forestry policy and regulations in tropical forest countries. Although log export restrictions in producer countries have stimulated growth and employment in domestic processing, they may have led to serious problems of processing over-capacity and inefficiency. To the extent that this is the case, log prices are artificially depressed and recovery rates fall, thus increasing pressure on timber resources. For larger exporters, such as Indonesia and Malaysia, the expansion in processing capacity from export restrictions has contributed to their ability to capture a large share of international markets. This has proved more difficult for smaller exporting countries. Nevertheless, the economic costs for all countries are extremely high. When export restrictions lead to over-capacity and inefficiencies in processing, logging pressure on the tropical forest resource may actually increase over the medium and long terms.[27]

Although import tariffs on tropical forest products are generally low and declining in major developed consumer markets, nontariff barriers may be significant and increasing.[28] Tariff barriers in the smaller developing country markets generally remain much higher, although these also appear to be declining. In some cases, the increase in nontariff barriers in major importing markets may reflect backsliding on previous commitments to reduce tariffs in order to maintain some degree of protection for domestic industry – particularly plywood processing. In many developed countries, however, these trends also appear to reflect growing pressure from media and advocacy groups to reduce consumption of tropical timber which, rightly or wrongly, is perceived to be an environmentally unsound product.

Restrictions on imports depress the global demand for tropical timber products and can reduce stumpage values in producer countries, thereby discouraging the incentives for more efficient processing and better forest management. Moreover, producer countries will continue to argue that they need to compensate their domestic processing through subsidies and export restrictions. The potential impact of any new environmental initiatives to reduce tropical timber imports is similar to that of traditional import barriers. Total trade with the largest and most profitable markets would be reduced, forcing producers to cut back production and look for alternative markets. In the short term the rate of tropical deforestation might be reduced, but the long-term effects could be perverse. If new markets cannot be developed at home or abroad, the income received by tropical timber exporters would presumably fall, along with the economic incentive to invest in forest management. The influence of developed country consumers over tropical forest management would also be reduced by their actions, as the relative importance of these markets declines.

Tropical timber trade bans and quantitative restrictions

Pressures from environmental groups and consumer-led boycotts in developed market economies are leading to serious consideration of a complete ban on the import of all tropical timber products, or at least a selective ban on those products that are not sustainably produced. However, despite their popular appeal, the use of such bans would not be appropriate for encouraging sustainable management in tropical timber exporting countries and may even be counter-productive. There are several reasons for this.

- Diversion of trade to other markets (domestic, export markets without bans, and so on). If these markets are for lower-value products, producer countries may need to supply higher volumes of tropical timber to generate substantial earnings, thus leading to more pressure on timber resources.

- Lower political leverage of importing countries to influence forestry policies in producer countries.
- Little positive reinforcement of the incentives for sustainable management. Selective bans would have an immediate impact on a country's ability to derive value from timber production, and would act as a disincentive for medium- and long-term maintenance of tropical forests for timber production, as opposed to conversion to agriculture and other uses.
- Incentives to circumvent the ban. Given that there is high elasticity of substitution for tropical timber products from different sources of origin, particularly for higher-valued products such as plywood, producer countries would gain significantly if they could pass off their unsustainably produced timber as sustainably produced.

The effects of a total import ban on a major tropical timber producer, Indonesia, were recently simulated.[29] According to the results of the analysis, an import ban would have a devastating impact on Indonesia's forest industry in the short term (see Table 18.4). Although there would be significant diversion of plywood and sawnwood exports to domestic consumption, this would be insufficient to compensate for the loss of exports. Net production in both processing industries would fall. Given its export orientation, the plywood industry would be particularly hurt, with its output reduced by over 40 per cent. Net production losses in the sawnwood industry would be closer to 10 per cent. The overall effect is to lower domestic log demand in the short term by around 25–30 per cent.

This policy scenario assumes that the import ban is 100 per cent effective. It is unlikely that all importers of Indonesia's tropical timber products – many of them are also newly industrializing or producer countries with processing capacities – would go along with a Western-imposed ban. In any case, one would expect that over the longer term there would be some diversion of Indonesian plywood and sawnwood exports to either new import markets or existing markets that prove to be less stringent in applying the ban.

The long-term implications of an import ban on tropical deforestation are also not encouraging. Even if the ban is 100 per cent effective in the short term, any reduction in tropical deforestation resulting from lower levels of timber harvesting is likely to be shortlived. A total import ban would cause a major diversion of Indonesian timber products to meet domestic demand. Although in the short term net production of wood products, and thus log demand, would fall, this situation would not necessarily be sustained over the long run. Even if this is not the case, the ban may be ineffective in permanently reducing tropical deforestation because: (1) timber production is not the main source of deforestation in Indonesia; and, (2) as the value of holding on to the forest for timber production decreases the incentives to convert more of the resource to alternative uses such as agriculture would increase.[30]

Table 18.4 Indonesia: timber trade and tropical deforestation simulation model. Policy scenario: import ban and revenue raising taxes (% change over base case)

Key variables	Total import ban[a]	1% Revenue raising import tax[b]	5% Revenue raising import tax[d]
1. *Prices (Rp/m³)*			
Log border-equivalent price (unit value)	–	–0.17	–0.82
Sawnwood export price (unit value)	–	–0.11	–0.54
Plywood export price (unit value)	–	–0.21	–1.03
2. *Quantities ('000 m³)*			
Log production	–28.33	–0.04	–0.19
Log domestic consumption	–27.37	–0.04	–0.18
Sawnwood production	–10.64	–0.03	–0.14
Sawnwood exports	–100.00	–0.23	–0.14
Sawnwood domestic consumption	30.01	0.06	0.30
Plywood production	–43.84	–0.04	–0.22
Plywood exports	–100.00	–0.10	–0.51
Plywood domestic consumption	214.51	0.23	1.12
3. *Deforestation (km²)*			
Total forest area	–	0.00[c]	0.01
Annual rate of deforestation	–	–0.41	–0.72

Notes:

a. Large price changes were used deliberately to constrain sawnwood and plywood exports to zero in this simulation and therefore are no longer endogenously generated by the model. Also, the functional form of the deforestation equation and its estimation using regional panel data imply that the large changes in log production associated with the import ban scenario cannot be used to predict reliably the effects on forest cover and deforestation. Thus both price and deforestation effects are eliminated from this policy scenario simulation.

b A total of US$23.1 million (1980 prices) in revenue would be raised, with US$5.8 million and US$17.3 million from Indonesian sawnwood and plywood exports respectively.

c A negligible increase over the base case forest cover of 53 km².

d A total of US$113.9 million (1980 prices) in revenue would be raised, with US$28.5 million and US$85.4 million from Indonesian sawnwood and plywood exports respectively.

Source: Barbier *et al.* (1993), *The Timber Trade and Tropical Deforestation in Indonesia.*

Similar problems exist for the application of quantitative restrictions, such as quotas or bans, on timber products derived from endangered tree species and quotas conditional on the level of sustainable offtake of specific species. Appendix I and II listings for several tropical timber species are increasingly being proposed at recent CITES meetings, despite frequent opposition by affected producer countries. Problems of monitoring and enforcement are exacerbated when the producer countries affected either oppose this approach or do not receive adequate incentive (that is, compensation) to participate. For example, at the eighth CITES Conference, Ghana and Cameroon opposed the proposed Appendix II listing of aformosia, and subsequently informed the conference that the timber trade was outside the scope of their countries' CITES managing authorities.[31] Such lack of compliance by producer countries undermines the effectiveness of such policy options.

Problems of incentives for management, enforcement and monitoring will occur for any import quotas based on the level of sustainable offtake of specific species that are imposed without the cooperation of tropical timber-producing countries. For such a policy to be workable from the outset, cooperation from producer countries, in determining the scientific and trade data necessary for establishing quotas for sustainable offtake and exports, will be essential.

It might be possible to establish a more comprehensive trade mechanism that establishes sustainable offtake export quotas for those species that are endangered, thus offering an incentive to both consumers and producers not only to accept a controlled legal trade, but also to enforce it. A properly constructed trade mechanism for each endangered species, using economic instruments such as taxes and subsidies to manage trade where appropriate, could be designed to enable sufficient profits from the trade to be channeled back into producer states. These profits could be used to encourage management efforts and to support improved monitoring of harvesting and export activities.[32] However, full acceptance of and adherence to any such mechanism by affected producer countries are essential to its success, in terms of compliance with export regulations and cooperation between exporters and regulating agencies.

Trade taxes

An international trade tax has been promoted as a means of increasing the costs associated with trading tropical timber products. However, a tax suffers from the same sort of problems of implementation and effectiveness faced by trade bans and quantitative restrictions.

First, it is unlikely that tropical timber exporting countries would endorse an international tax that would discriminate against tropical timber products. As noted, these countries have employed their own export taxes on selected products (for example, log exports, and more recently sawnwood exports). However, the main purpose of such policies has not been to reduce the overall trade in tropical timber products, or for that matter timber-related tropical deforestation. The main purpose has been to change the pattern of their tropical timber exports to higher-valued products, thereby stimulating wood-based processing industries.

Second, a tropical timber trade tax would probably be ineffective in reducing timber-related tropical deforestation – for the same reasons outlined above in the discussion of trade bans. In the short run, producer countries may increase their volumes of exports to maintain their level of foreign exchange earnings. An overall trade tax would probably reduce the incentives for sustainable timber management, because the tax would lower the net returns from production and trade. As a result, the tax may actually prove to be counterproductive – encouraging the conversion of permanent production forests and any remaining virgin forest areas to alternative uses in the long run.

It is often argued that some problems associated with an indiscriminately applied tax on all tropical timber products could be avoided by a tax imposed selectively on unsustainably produced tropical timber products. For example, selective import duties on tropical timber products could be applied, while sustainably produced timber would be duty free. However, as argued in the case of selective bans and quantitative restrictions, there are obvious problems of certification, monitoring and enforcement that need to be sorted out – along with the political feasibility of such an approach.

The economic impact of an import tax on tropical timber was analysed recently in a policy simulation.[33] The policy scenario simulates the tax by assuming a 10 per cent increase in the transfer cost of products reaching destination countries. The results suggest that:

- Some product exports are expected to be driven out by competition with domestic supplies.
- Log prices in consumer countries rise, but fall in producer countries. As a consequence, most consumer countries reduce their imports of tropical timber logs.
- With such a large impact on log imports for their processing industries, consuming country demand for processed products results in a small increase in tropical plywood exports, at least initially. However, as this import demand slackens and as log scarcity in producer countries becomes binding, tropical plywood exports fall significantly after 1995.
- All tropical hardwood suppliers suffer a decline in production, at least initially. Indonesian production declines up to 2 million m^3 compared to base case projections. However, the declines are not permanent in all regions. For example, Malaysia East (including Sabah and Sarawak) experiences an initial decline of 4 million m^3, but its log production generally exceeds the base case scenario after 1995.

- The net effect of log production declines in producing countries, distortions in trade patterns and falling producer prices for tropical timber harvesting will be less motivation to manage production forests sustainably and reduced revenue to finance these investments.

The timber trade model of Indonesia also employed the effects of import taxes on a major exporter (Table 18.4). The results suggest that tax rates beyond 1–5 per cent would begin introducing major distortionary effects. Moreover, the low levels of tax would clearly have little impact on reducing deforestation in Indonesia. Their only purpose would be to raise revenue that could be transferred to Indonesia and other tropical forest countries for forest conservation and sustainable management initiatives.[34] It would probably be more effective if Indonesia raised the money itself for sustainable management programmes by imposing revenue-raising export surcharges. As discussed below, the main issues are whether the funds raised would be adequate and whether they should be raised from sources outside of the trade.

In sum, a trade tax on tropical timber products would not be an effective means of encouraging sustainable production forest management, and may even be a disincentive for sustainable management. A smaller surcharge imposed by exporting countries on their own trade may be more appropriate, but may not raise sufficient funds. In any case, as will be discussed next, the rationale for raising more substantial funds for international transfers may be more compelling – although politically difficult.

International transfers

The main rationale for providing financial assistance for tropical forest countries moving towards sustainable forest management is that there is an important principle of international compensation at stake. There are essentially three reasons for this argument:

- It is often claimed that timber-exporting countries receive an insufficient share of the returns from tropical timber product exports – at least to incur the additional harvesting costs and other economic impacts of sustainable timber management.
- Implementation of the forestry policies and regulations required to ensure the proper enforcement and monitoring of sustainable management of production forests will impose substantial additional costs on producer countries.
- To the extent that all nations benefit from the global external benefits resulting from sustainable management of large tracts of tropical forest lands, the international community should compensate producing nations

for the loss of potential income that they would incur by reducing tropical deforestation, timber sales and conversion of forest land to other uses.

The first point is difficult to substantiate. The issue may have less to do with whether the unequal distribution of revenues along the chain of trade reduces the incentives for sustainable management of the forest level, but whether any excess revenues along the chain can be tapped for additional funds to assist sustainable management of tropical production forests. The second and third points are much more relevant to the argument for international compensation. It is now generally accepted, as well as enshrined in the Forest Principles of the 1992 UN Conference on Environment and Development (UNCED), that compensating tropical forest countries for their role in maintaining a resource that has value on a global level is a fundamental basis for multilateral policy action. However, this would suggest that compensation is needed for tropical timber-producing countries for the income they may forgo in protecting their forests and for the additional costs incurred in implementing sustainable management practices for their production forests. This has to be demonstrated empirically.

A policy simulation was recently conducted to evaluate the additional economic impacts on tropical forest countries from setting aside some of their forest resource base.[35] Essentially, this was simulated by a reduced timber supply scenario where the inventory of commercial tropical hardwood resources is reduced by 10 per cent, which is equivalent to land being taken out of product forests and permanently protected. The result is that severe shortages in log production and higher sawlog prices are experienced in tropical forest regions, notably in Malaysia and Indonesia. The model indicates that such reductions in supply would result in a loss of wealth for tropical timber-producing countries. Over the long run, permanent set-asides would mean that the remaining production forest inventory could not support as high a level of sustainable harvest as under base case projections.

There are also indications that the additional costs required to implement sustainable forestry management policies and regulations are significant. Drawing on the work by Poore *et al.* (1989), a rough assessment of the resources needed by producer countries to attain sustainability by the year 2000 was conducted on behalf of the International Tropical Timber Council (ITTO) [36] The estimates are shown in Table 18.5. Although preliminary and very approximate, they show that an additional US$330.1 million is required each year in order to assist producer countries of ITTO in attaining the Year 2000 target. At best, the estimates are an indication of the minimum financing required.

Sizeable though this figure may seem, it is less than the estimated amount required for sustainable management of all tropical forest resources. For example, Agenda 21 of the UNCED has estimated that international financing of over US$1.5 billion annually will be required by tropical forest countries to reduce deforestation.[37] Using these two estimates as broad bounds for the type of financing required, the LEEC study suggests that additional funds required by producer countries to implement sustainable management of their tropical forest resource to be in the range of US$0.3 to US$1.5 billion annually.[38]

Table 18.5 Estimates of the resources needed by producer countries to attain sustainability by the year 2000

Policy actions needed	Resources needed (US$ million/year)		
	Existing*	Additional	Total
Securing the permanent forest estate	60.2	191.3	251.5
Mapping	0.0	6.0	6.0
Inventories	7.3	28.2	36.5
Production and consumption	2.1	5.0	7.1
Land use planning	0.8	19.3	20.2
Policy and legislation	50.0	132.8	182.1
Implementing sustainable forest management	84.0	108.5	192.5
Demonstration forests	4.0	26.0	30.0
Implementation (mid-range)	80.0	82.5	162.5
Improving resource utilization	1.0	13.0	14.0
Trials and missions	1.0	13.0	14.0
Improving the social and political environment	0.0	8.1	8.1
Social sciences	0.0	4.4	4.4
Political and consumer awareness	0.0	3.7	3.7
Strategy plans and progress reports	4.0	9.2	13.2
Total	149.2	330.1	479.3

Note: * Existing resources are estimates of producer country expenditures based on the current status of activities undertaken, including those using external funding.

Source: ITTC (1992a), based on Ferguson and Muñoz-Reyes Navarro, 'Working Document for ITTO Expert Panel', 1992.

There is a strong rationale for additional funds for sustainable forest management to be made available to producer countries from sources outside of the tropical timber trade. Comprehensive international agreements, targeted financial aid flows and compensation mechanisms to deal with the overall problem of tropical deforestation may ultimately eliminate the need to consider intervention in the timber trade. Given that commercial logging is not the primary cause of tropical deforestation, such approaches would avoid unnecessary, and possibly inappropriate, discrimination against the timber trade. On the other hand, a comprehensive tropical forest agreement seems much more difficult to negotiate and raises its own problems of workability and effectiveness.[39]

Given the rapidly diminishing aid budgets of the developed economies, it is unlikely that a concerted international effort to increase substantially bilateral or multilateral aid flows for sustainable production forest management will be forthcoming. However, optimists who point to the mounting public concern for tropical forests in advanced industrialized countries would argue otherwise. Nevertheless, there still remains the possibility of designing new sources of financial assistance that are separate from existing developing country aid budgets. The Forestry Principles are effectively a step in that direction. International commitments through the Tropical Forestry Action Plan and Global Environmental Facility continue to reinforce the global interest in forestry and biodiversity protection. The case could be made for more comprehensive international agreements to raise revenues for sustainable management of tropical forests, including production forests. The main focal points of such agreements should be the development of alternative revenue-raising mechanisms other than trade interventions or reliance on existing aid budgets.

For example, Amelung and Diehl argue the case for the establishment of an international rain forest fund, as proposed initially by the United Nations Environment Programme, in order to avoid freeriding among nontropical countries.[40] Similar arguments are put forward by Sedjo, Bowes and Wiseman, although their preference is for the establishment of a global system of marketable forest protection and management obligations. Over the long term, international negotiations leading towards an agreement for new revenue-raising mechanisms for sustainable management of tropical forests, including production forests, could be the most effective and equitable means for reducing global tropical deforestation. Although such negotiations are difficult and arduous, they may be the best hope of ensuring a global commitment to control tropical deforestation, as well as the sustainable management of production forests.

Trade incentives for sustainable tropical forest management

The overall conclusion must be that trade interventions are not the best means for achieving these objectives. However, there is a role for additional tropical timber trade policies in fostering trade-related incentives for sustainable management. Trade policies will be the most effective if:

- they are employed in conjunction with and complement improved domestic policies and regulations for sustainable forest management within producer countries;
- they improve rather than restrict access to markets for tropical timber products, ensuring maximum value added for sustainably produced tropical timber exports;
- they assist producer countries in obtaining the additional financial resources required to implement comprehensive national plans for sustainable management of tropical production forests.

The first set of policies would require producer countries to undertake substantial reviews of their forest sector policies to determine the implications of their existing domestic forestry policies and regulations on timber-related deforestation and the extent to which their timber export policies may also be affecting deforestation, either directly or through exacerbating problems caused by poor domestic forestry policies and regulations. Producer countries ought to correct those policy distortions that work against sustainable timber production objectives, as such distortions seriously undermine efficient and sustainable forest sector development and worsen deforestation.

The second set of policies is aimed at removing any remaining barriers to tropical timber imports into consumer markets, particularly for those producer countries that demonstrate a commitment to forest sector policy reform. For example, the removal of specific tariff and nontariff barriers on imports could take place on a case-by-case basis, depending on demonstrable progress by each exporting country. This could occur through normal bilateral trade negotiations or through multilateral agreements and organizations. In addition, consumer countries should actively promote, through information and market intelligence campaigns, the use of tropical timber imports from exporting countries that are implementing sustainable management policies.

The final set of policies, additional financial assistance, is not straightforward. As discussed above, this option raises complicated issues concerning the need for international compensation, the scale of resource transfers required and the possible mechanisms for implementation. Nevertheless, tropical forest countries may need additional financial assistance in implementing sustainable management. To avoid distortionary impacts, the additional funds should come from sources external to the trade. However, in the current global economic climate more official development aid for this purpose is unlikely. The use of a tax or revenue transfer scheme to redistribute the existing revenue from the trade back to producer countries is the most promising and immediate option. If necessary, it could be supplemented by a revenue-raising trade surcharge of less than 5 per cent – but this approach should be used cautiously to avoid any distortionary or discriminatory effects.[41] However, over the long run, the global community should look toward the establishment of more innovative mechanisms, such as a tropical forest fund or a global system of marketable forest protection and management obligations, as the best means to combating the overall problem of tropical deforestation.

Conclusion

This chapter has examined two case studies to indicate the scope of trade policy interventions in promoting the sustainable management of critical natural resources. In both examples, interventions to restrict the trade can be counter-productive.

In the case of the ivory trade, the ivory trade ban may prove effective in the short run, but less so over the long term as incentives to defy the ban increase. A more realistic approach would be to use the period during which the general ban is in force to set up an ivory exchange to manage trade on a strict sustainability criterion. In the case of the tropical timber trade, restrictions on trade will have little impact on the overall problem of tropical deforestation, and may prove counterproductive in controlling timber-related deforestation. Again, however, both producer and consumer countries could cooperate to develop additional tropical timber trade policies that foster trade-related incentives for sustainable management.

Over-exploitation of African elephants and timber-related tropical deforestation are both serious problems that need to be addressed urgently. Although both have an important trade aspect, particularly in terms of the impact of the ivory trade on elephant poaching, designing appropriate policies should begin with correcting distortions in incentives closest to the problem. In the case of illegal ivory harvesting, this involves improving the incentives of local communities to participate in the conservation of elephant and wildlife resources. The key factor in reducing timber-related tropical deforestation is ensuring proper economic incentives for efficient and sustainable management of tropical production forests, starting with appropriate forest sector policies and regulations at the concession and forest stand level. If trade policies are to help mitigate the decline in elephant populations in Africa and timber-related deforestation, they must reinforce rather than contradict the appropriate economic incentives on the ground.

Notes

1. Edward B. Barbier, Joanne C. Burgess, Timothy M. Swanson and David W. Pearce, *Elephants, Economics and Ivory*, London: Earthscan Publications, 1990. See also Edward B. Barbier, Joanne C. Burgess, B.A. Aylward, J.T. Bishop and C. Bann, *The Economics of the Tropical Timber Trade*, London: Earthscan Publications, 1994.
2. For many areas in Africa, these wider benefits might be offset by elephant damage costs, such as crop damages, woodland destruction and even occasional loss of life.

3. Gardner Brown and Wes Henry, 'The economic value of elephants', in *Economics and Ecology: New Frontiers and Sustainable Development*, Edward B. Barbier (ed.), London: Chapman and Hall, 1993.
4. For more information on this topic, please refer to Barbier *et al.*, *Elephants*, Tables 1.3 and 1.4.
5. Edward B. Barbier, 'Managing trade and environment: the demand for ivory in Japan and Hong Kong', *World Economy*, December 1991, pp. 407–30.
6. However, since 1990, India has been a more enthusiastic supporter of the ban. In April 1992, the government of India banned the import and domestic sale of all African elephant ivory products, primarily to reduce the potential for Asian elephant ivory to be laundered as African elephant ivory. 'India reinforces ivory trade ban', *Traffic Bulletin*, Vol. 13, No. 1, 1992, pp. 3–17.
7 Ibid.
8. E.B. Martin, 'Ivory Billiard Balls', BBC Wildlife, September 1990, pp. 622–3.
9. Richard Leakey has suggested that it is reasonable to sell ivory from elephants culled for conservation reasons, which is the policy pursued by Zimbabwe and by some other southern African states. However, his main concern has been that 'the trade is unable to distinguish legal shipments from illegal ones'. Quoted in C. Trudge, 'British policy boosts ivory poaching', *New Scientist*, 3 March 1990, p. 22.
10. Richard Leakey, quoted in 'The ivory paradox', *The Economist*, 2 March 1991, p. 18.
11. 'Elephants: Poachers' Pause', *The Economist*, 2 March 1991, p. 64.
12. J.R. Caldwell and R.A. Lawrence, 'Recent changes in world ivory trade', *Traffic Bulletin*, Vol. 11. No. 4, 1990, pp. 50–8.
13 Martin, *Ivory Billiard Balls*, pp. 622–3.
14. Please refer to E.B. Martin, 'Observations on wildlife trade in Vietnam', *Traffic Bulletin*, Vol. 13, No. 2, 1992, pp. 61–7, or E.B. Martin, 'The trade and uses of wildlife products in Laos,' *Traffic Bulletin*, Vol. 13, No. 1, 1992, pp. 22–8.
15. Caldwell and Lawrence, *Recent Changes*, pp. 50–8. Significantly, in Laos, the rise in raw ivory prices is attributed to increased demand by foreign buyers, particularly Thais. One consequence is heavy poaching of Asian elephants in Southern Laos – one alarming side effect of the ban on trade in African elephant ivory. See Martin, 'Wildlife products', pp. 22–8.
16. I am particularly grateful for the ideas and input of Tim Swanson on policy options for international regulation of the ivory trade. Interested readers are referred to Barbier *et al.*, *Elephants*, Chapters 5 and 6, and Timothy M. Swanson, *International Regulation of Ivory Trade* (LEEC Discussion Paper DP89-04), London: London Environmental Economics Centre, 1989.
17. For more on these issues, see Timothy M. Swanson and Edward B. Barbier (eds), *Economics for the Wilds: Wildlife, Wildlands, Diversity and Development*, Washington, DC: Island Press, 1992.
18. Barbier *et al.*, *Tropical Timber Trade*.
19. Ibid.
20. World Bank, *World Tables*, Washington, DC: The World Bank, 1992.
21. For a review of this evidence, see Barbier *et al.*, *Tropical Timber Trade*.
22. See, for example, Barbier *et al.*, *Tropical Timber Trade*, C.S. Binkley and J.R. Vincent, *Forest Based Industrialization. A Dynamic Perspective* (HIID Development Discussion Paper No. 389), Cambridge, MA: Harvard University, 1991; and William F. Hyde, David H. Newman and Roger A. Sedjo, *Forest Economics and Policy Analysis: An Overview* (World Bank Discussion Paper), Washington, DC: The World Bank, 1991.
23. For examples, additional references and discussion, see Ibid. and Robert Repetto, 'Deforestation in The Tropics', *Scientific American*, Vol. 262, No. 4, 1990, pp. 36–45.
24. For further discussion see Hyde *et al.*, *Forest Economics*, 1991. *Trespass* is a forestry term that refers to losses due to logging theft, which could also be extended to include losses due to graft. *High-grading* refers to the removal of high-valued timber and leaving a degraded stand. Both trespass and high-grading usually indicate the failure of policy to internalize the private costs of long-run forest management, leading to a short-run privately inefficient harvest level.
25. The question of to whom this rent is allocated is not strictly an economic issue. Hyde *et al.*, *Forest Economics*, strongly suggest that the allocation of rent is merely a matter of distributive

preference. Each country must make its own judgment over the equitable distribution of the nation's natural wealth. Such concerns over equitable distribution are, however, likely to be influenced by expectations concerning the ensuing productive use of such economic surplus. More importantly, if a government leaves all the profits to the concessionaires without seeking to appropriate a reasonable return as the owner of the resource, the government leaves a powerful incentive in place for concessionaires to 'mine' the forests. This is particularly true in cases where – as mentioned above – concessions policy and regulation are not strictly controlled and enforced.

26. Binkley and Vincent, *A Dynamic Perspective*.
27. For examples, additional references and discussion, see Barbier *et al.*, *Tropical Timber Trade*.
28. See I.J. Bourke, *Trade in Tropical Forest Products: A Study of the Barriers Faced by the Developing Countries* (FAO Forestry Paper 83), Rome: Food and Agricultural Organization of the United Nations, 1988.
29. Edward B. Barbier, N. Bockstael, Joanne C. Burgess and I. Strand, *The Timber Trade and Tropical Deforestation in Indonesia* (LEEC Discussion Paper DP93-01), London: London Environmental Economics Centre, 1993.
30. See ibid. for further discussion.
31. International Tropical Timber Council, *Report on the Eighth Committee of Parties to the Convention on International Trade in Endangered Species*, Kyoto, 1–13 March, 1992.
32. Joanne C. Burgess, 'The Environmental Effects of Trade in Endangered Species', *The Environmental Effects of Trade*, Paris: Organization of Economic Cooperation and Development, 1994.
33. John M. Perez-Garcia and Bruce R. Lippke, *The Timber Trade and Tropical Forests: Modeling the Impacts of Supply Constraints and Trade Liberalization* (LEEC Discussion Paper DP89-04), London: London Environmental Economics Centre, 1993.
34. See also Joseph Buongiorno and T. Manuring, 'Predicted effects of an import tax in the European community on the international trade of tropical timbers' (draft document, Department of Forestry), Madison, WI: University of Wisconsin, Madison, 1992.
35. Perez-Garcia and Lippke, *Timber Trade and Tropical Forests*, 1993.
36. Duncan Poore, *No Timber Without Trees*, London: Earthscan Publications, 1989, and I.S. Ferguson and J. Munez-Reyes Navarro, 'Working document for ITTO expert panel on resources needed by producer countries to achieve sustainable management by the year 200', Yokohama: International Tropical Timber Council, 1992.
37. The proposed international financing is specifically for sustaining the multiple roles and functions of all types of forests, forest lands and woodlands (US$860 million per year) enhancement of the protection, sustainable management and conservation of all forests the greening of degraded areas through forest rehabilitation, afforestation, reforestation and other rehabilitation measures (US$460 million per year); and promoting efficient utilization and assessment to recover the full valuation of the goods and services provided by forests, forest lands and woodlands (US$230 million per year). Please refer to the International Tropical Timber Council, *Report on Preparations for the 1992 United Nations Conference on Environment and Development, Tenth Session*, Yaunde, Cameroon, 6–14 May 1992.
38. Barbier *et al.*, *The Timber Trade*.
39. See Scott Barrett, 'The Problem of Global Environmental Protection', *Oxford Review of Economic Policy*, Vol. 6, No. 1, 1990, pp. 68–79, for a general discussion of the difficulties involved in securing international environmental agreements.
40. Torsten Amelung and Markus Diehl, *Deforestation of Tropical Rainforests: Economic Causes and Impact on Development*, Kieler Studien 241, Tübingen: J.C.B. Mohr, 1991.
41. For further details on these schemes, see Barbier *et al.*, *Tropical Timber Trade*, 1994.

19. Trade, tropical deforestation and policy interventions*

with M. Rauscher

Abstract
Trade interventions are increasingly advocated as a means for controlling timber-related tropical deforestation. This paper analyses the impact on deforestation of such policy instruments in a dynamic framework. The forest is modelled as a potentially renewable resource, and timber is extracted for purposes of export and domestic consumption. Optimality conditions for a variety of model specifications are derived, and the impacts of changes in the terms of trade and market structure on long-run deforestation are analysed. The results of this analysis suggest that trade interventions that seek to affect the terms of trade against the export of tropical timber products are in the long run a second-best policy option for influencing the deforestation process.

1. Introduction

Concerns about tropical deforestation have led to an increased focus on the role of the timber trade in promoting forest depletion and degradation. Recent reports suggest a marked increase in tropical deforestation in the 1980s, with the overall rate doubling from 0.6 per cent in 1980 to 1.2 per cent in 1990 (Dembner, 1991). However, the deforestation rate varies across regions, with an estimated annual rate for Latin America of only 0.9 per cent compared with 1.7 per cent for Africa and 1.4 per cent for Asia.

Despite concern over the state of tropical deforestation and its implications for global welfare, several recent studies have indicated that the tropical timber trade is not the major *direct* cause of the problem – perhaps less than 10 per cent of total deforestation – whereas conversion of forests for agriculture is much more significant (Amelung and Diehl, 1992; Barbier *et al.*, 1993; Binkley and Vincent, 1991; Hyde *et al.*, 1991). Nevertheless, it is clear that current levels of timber extraction in tropical forests – both open and closed – exceed the rate of reforestation (WRI, 1992). Less than one million hectares, out of an estimated total global area of 828 million hectares of productive tropical forest in 1985, was under sustained-yield management for timber production (Poore *et al.*, 1989). Moreover, timber extraction has a major *indirect* role in promoting tropical deforestation by opening up previously unexploited forest, which then allows other economic uses of the forests such as agricultural conversion to take place (Amelung and Diehl, 1992; Barbier *et al.*, 1991). For example, in many African producer countries, around half of the area that is initially logged is subsequently deforested, while there is little, if any, deforestation of previously unlogged forested land (Barbier *et al.*, 1993).

Some of the environmental values lost through timber exploitation and depletion, such as watershed protection, non-timber forest products, recreational values, and so on, may affect only populations in the countries producing the timber. Concerned domestic policymakers in tropical forest countries should therefore determine whether the benefits of incorporating these environmental values into decisions affecting timber exploitation balance the costs of reduced timber production and trade, as well as the cost of implementing such policies. The socially 'optimal' level of timber exploitation and trade is one where the additional domestic environmental costs of logging the forests are 'internalized' in production decisions, where feasible. Designing policies to control excessive forest degradation is clearly complex and requires careful attention to harvesting incentives. As recent reviews suggest, many domestic policies do not even begin to approximate the appropriate incentives required to achieve a socially optimal level of timber harvesting. More often than not, pricing, investment and institutional policies for forestry actually work to create the conditions for short-term harvesting by private concessionaires, and in some instances, even subsidize private harvesting at inefficient levels.[1] Over the long term, incentive distortions that understate stumpage values and fail to reflect increasing scarcity as old growth forests are depleted can undermine the transition of the forestry sector from dependence on old growth to secondary forests and the coordination of processing capacity with timber stocks (Binkley and Vincent, 1991).

Increasingly the world's tropical forests, including their remaining timber reserves, are also considered to provide important 'global' values, such as a major 'store' of carbon and as a depository of a large share of the world's biological diversity (Pearce, 1990; Reid and Miller, 1989). Similarly, even some 'regional' environmental functions of tropical forests, such as protection of major watersheds, may have transboundary 'spillover' effects into more than one country. But precisely because such transboundary and global environmental benefits accrue to individuals outside of the countries exploiting forests for timber, it is unlikely that such countries will have the incentive to incur the additional costs of incorporating the more 'global' environmental values in forest management decisions. Not surprisingly, sanctions and other interventions in the timber trade are one means by which other countries may seek to coerce timber producing countries into reducing forest exploitation and the subsequent loss of environmental values. In addition, trade measures are increasingly being explored as part of multilateral negotiations and agreements to control excessive forest depletion, to encourage 'sustainable' timber management and to raise compensatory financing for timber producing countries that lose substantial revenues and incur additional costs in changing their forest policy.

However well-intentioned they may be, both domestic and international environmental regulations and policies that attempt to 'correct' forest management decisions may have high economic, and even 'second order' environmental, costs associated with them (Barbier *et al.*, 1993). There is increasing concern that the potential trade impacts of environmental policies that affect forest and forest-based industries may increase inefficiencies and reduce international competitiveness. Moreover, the trade impacts of domestic environmental regulations may affect industries in other countries and lead to substantial distortions in the international timber trade. The overall effect on the profitability and efficiency of forest industries may be to encourage forest management practices that are far from 'sustainable'. Careful analysis of both domestic and international environmental policies affecting forest sector production and trade is therefore necessary to determine what the full economic and environmental effects of such policies might be.

The following model has been developed to facilitate analysis of the impact of policy interventions, market structure and transfers on a timber exporting tropical forest country. The main focus of the analysis is on how these impacts relate to the country's decisions to produce timber, or processed goods that are based on timber extraction, and thus the rate of tropical deforestation. The model is similar to the one developed by Rauscher (1990), but it differs in two important respects. First, timber products can either be exported or consumed domestically, and the export earnings are used to import domestic consumption goods from abroad. This facilitates analysis of the *trade diversion* effect to domestic consumption of a policy intervention in the international timber market. Second, it is assumed that the tropical forest has positive *stock externalities* in the form of watershed protection, genetic diversity, microclimatic functions, and so on which directly affect the overall welfare of the country. The analytical results derived from the model are clearly affected by this assumption that the forest stock has some direct social value in addition to its use as a timber resource.

The model is simplified in some important respects. Domestic capital accumulation and any tropical reafforestation efforts are not modelled, and no other production or trade sectors are included, as this would complicate the analysis without providing deeper insights into the role of timber trade policy interventions in tropical deforestation. Initially, it is assumed that the country is a price taker in the international timber market and that trade is balanced. Later in the analysis we relax these assumptions to allow for market power and foreign asset accumulation (or debt).

2. The basic model

For the basic model, the following variables, parameters and functions are defined:

$N(t)$	tropical forest stock
$q(t)$	tropical timber logs extracted or commodities produced (log equivalents)[2]

$x(t)$	tropical timber logs/products exported (log-equivalents)
$q(t) - x(t)$	domestic consumption of logs/products
$c(t)$	consumption of imported goods
$g(N(t))$	regeneration function of tropical forests
a	deforestation rate, per unit of (log-equivalent) timber extracted
p	terms of trade, p_x/p_c
δ	social rate of discount

Notation is simplified by omitting the argument of time-dependent variables, by representing a derivative of a function by a prime, by employing numbered subscripts to indicate partial derivatives of a function, and by denoting the time derivative and growth rates of a variable by a dot and hat, respectively.

The tropical forest country is assumed to maximize the present value of future welfare, W

$$\underset{q,x,c}{\text{Max}}\ W = \int_0^{\infty} U(q - x, c, N)e^{-\delta t}\mathrm{d}t \tag{19.1}$$

subject to

$$px = c, \tag{19.2}$$

$$\dot{N} = g(N) - aq, \tag{19.3}$$

$$N(0) = N_0 \ \text{ and } \ \lim_{t\to\infty} N(t) \geq 0, \tag{19.4}$$

$$N^{\max} > N^{\min} > 0,\ g(N^{\min}) = g(N^{\max}) = 0, \text{ and } g''(N) < 0. \tag{19.5}$$

The control variables of the model are q, x and c. The additively separable utility function, U, is assumed to have the standard properties with respect to its partial derivatives, $U_i > 0$, $U_{ii} < 0$ $(i = 1, 2, 3)$. Equation (19.2) is the initial trade balance assumption. Equations (19.3) to (19.5) are the standard renewable resource constraint, which suggest that any deforestation due to timber extraction net of regeneration will lead to a decline in the tropical forest stock.

3. Optimality conditions

The Hamiltonian of the above optimal control problem is

$$H = U(q - x, px, N) + \lambda\,[g(N) - aq], \tag{19.6}$$

where λ is the costate variable or the shadow price of the tropical forest. Assuming an interior solution, the maximum principle yields the following conditions

$$U_1 = \lambda a, \tag{19.7}$$

$$U_1 = pU_2, \tag{19.8}$$

$$\dot{\lambda} = (\delta - g')\lambda - U_3, \tag{19.9}$$

where $U_1 = \partial U/\partial(q - x)$, $U_2 = \partial U/\partial c$ and $U_3 = \partial U/\partial N$. Equation (19.7) indicates that, along the optimal trajectory, the marginal value of extracting one unit of timber (in terms of domestic consumption), U_1, must equal its marginal depletion cost, λa. Since extraction costs are zero in the model, the latter costs are *user costs*, the future stream of timber income foregone from extracting a unit today. Equation (19.8) indicates that, if international terms of trade are given, the relative marginal value of domestic timber to imported good consumption must be equated with the terms of trade, p. Finally, equation (19.9) yields a standard renewable resource dynamic condition for denoting the change in the value of the tropical forest stock when that stock also has direct value, as represented by U_3. As this condition is important for the analytical results of our model, we state its interpretation formally as

PROPOSITION 1. *The rate of change in the shadow price of the tropical forest, $\dot{\lambda}$, equals the difference between the opportunity cost of holding on to a unit of the forest, $(\delta - g')\lambda$, and the marginal social value of that unit, U_3.*

Since the Hamiltonian is concave in (q, x, c, N), the above conditions are also sufficient for an optimum. By combining equations (19.7) and (19.9) one obtains

$$\frac{\dot{q} - \dot{x}}{q - x} = 1/\eta_1\left(\delta - g' - aU_3/U_1\right), \tag{19.10}$$

where η_1 is the elasticity of marginal utility, U_1. Utilizing (19.10) and conditions (19.3), (19.4), (19.5), (19.7) and (19.8), one can solve for an optimal saddle path and the long run equilibrium. As the system is in equilibrium when the user costs, the felling rate, domestic and imported consumption and the forest stock are constant, the equilibrium can be characterized by the following system of equations

$$U_1 - pU_2 = 0, \tag{19.11}$$

$$(\delta - g')U_1 - aU_3 = 0 \text{ for } \dot{q} = \dot{x} = 0, \tag{19.12}$$

$$g(N^*) - aq^* = 0, \text{ for } \dot{N} = 0, \tag{19.13}$$

where the equilibrium values of N and q are denoted by asterisks. Total differentiation of the system of equations (19.11)–(19.13) with respect to (q, x, N) can lead to characterization of the equilibrium state and trajectories leading to that state. It can be demonstrated that the determinant D of the Hessian matrix of above system must be negative in order for there to be a unique equilibrium in (q, N) space; that is, the requirement for the curve $\dot{q} = 0$ to be positively sloped and to cut the curve $\dot{N} = 0$ from below is that $D < 0$ (see Appendix). This implies that the equilibrium is a saddle point, and the saddle path is positively sloped. Using these results, the optimal solution is represented graphically in Figure 19.1. The solution suggests

PROPOSITION 2. *The equilibrium forest stock,* N^*, *is determined by equating the social discount rate,* δ, *and the rate of return from holding on to the forest stock,* $g'(N^*) + aU_3/U_1$. *The equilibrium will occur to the left of the maximum*

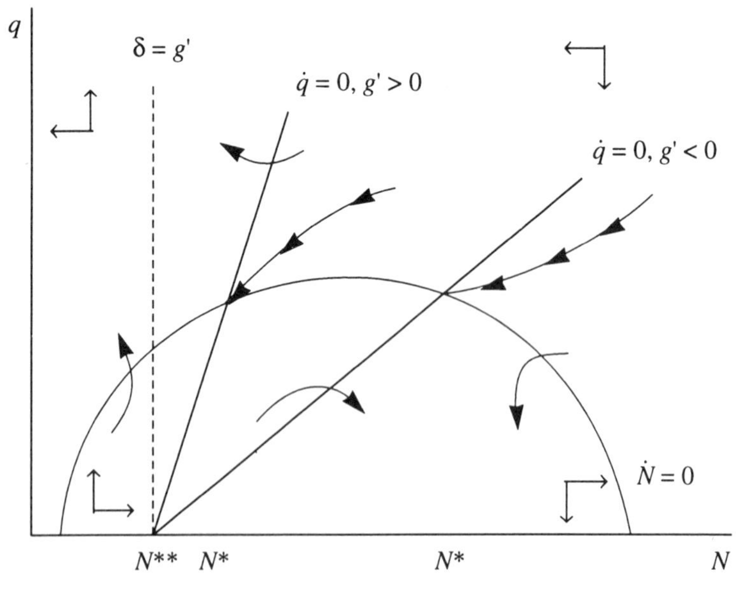

Figure 19.1 The long-run equilibrium of the tropical forest economy

*sustainable yield (*MSY*) if* g'(N*)$ > 0$*, and it will occur to the right of the* MSY *if* g'(N*)$ < 0$.

Thus, as depicted in Figure 19.1, if the initial level of the forest stock is high (that is, $N_0 > N^*$), then the economy will deforest some of this stock through timber extraction.

Moreover, equations (19.11)–(19.13) also imply

PROPOSITION 2a. *If* U_3 *were* $= 0$*, then the equilibrium forest stock,* N***, would occur at* $\delta = g' > 0$.

As shown in Figure 19.1, it must follow that $N^{**} < N^*$. That is, if the economy values only tropical timber then it will tolerate a lower level of tropical forest in the long run than if it also considers the other values provided by the forest.

4. Comparative static analysis: trade interventions vs. transfers

Comparative static analysis of the long run equilibrium can be employed to indicate what impacts that reductions in the terms of trade for tropical timber and forest products, either through import bans, tariffs or other controls, may have on the tropical forest country's decision to deforest. As noted, the model already suggests that the tropical forest has positive *domestic* externalities in the form of watershed protection, genetic diversity, microclimatic functions, and so on which directly affect the overall welfare of the country. However, the *international* externalities, such as the role of the forests as a 'store' of biodiversity and carbon and their 'macro' climatic functions, are essentially ignored by domestic policymakers. Thus it can be assumed that intervention in the global timber market is motivated by the international community – notably tropical timber importers – attempting to force the country to 'internalize' the global values ascribed to its tropical forest that are lost through the depletion arising from timber production.

A ban on tropical timber imports or the imposition of import taxes that discriminate against trade in tropical timber reduces the terms of trade. In the model, a reduction in the terms of trade, p, has the following impacts on the long run equilibrium forest stock of the timber exporting country

$$\frac{dN^*}{dp} = \frac{[1+\eta_2]U_2[-a(\delta - g')U_{11}]}{D}, \tag{19.14}$$

where η_2 is the elasticity of marginal utility, U_2, with respect to imported consumption goods. If the absolute value of η_2 is large, then marginal welfare in the economy is highly responsive to a change in imported consumption goods, c. We characterize this condition as 'import dependency'. The following proposition therefore results from (19.14)

	$\lvert\eta_2\rvert > 1$	$\lvert\eta_2\rvert < 1$
$g' > 0$	$dq^*/dp > 0$ dx^*/dp ?	$dq^*/dp < 0$ dx^*/dp ?
$g' < 0$	$dq^*/dp < 0$ $dx^*/dp < 0$	$dq^*/dp > 0$ $dx^*/dp > 0$

If trade interventions by importing countries do not always achieve the desired effect of encouraging timber exporting nations to reduce exploitation of their tropical forest stock, then an alternative policy may be the provision of an 'international transfer' of funds to encourage exporting countries to forego the income earned from forest exploitation. Essentially, the rest of the world is 'subsidizing' tropical forest countries to conserve rather than cut down their trees. For example, Agenda 21 of the UN Conference on Environment and Development has estimated that international financing of over US$1.5 billion annually will be required by tropical forest countries to reduce deforestation (ITTC, 1992).[3]

A large transfer of international funds to tropical forest countries to assist with sustainable forest management and forest conservation has the effect of 'freeing up' domestic financial resources for other purposes. In our model, an international transfer or subsidy can be represented by an increase in foreign exchange available for consumption of imported goods; that is, it supplements timber export earnings. Thus (19.2) now becomes

$$px + s = c, \tag{19.2'}$$

where s is the amount of the international transfer, or subsidy. The comparative statics of equation (19.11) in the system (19.11) to (19.13) becomes

$$U_{11}\,dq + [-U_{11} - p^2 U_{22}]\,d_x = pU_{22}\,ds. \tag{19.17}$$

Thus an increase in international transfers, s, has the following impact on the long-run equilibrium forest stock, N^*

$$\frac{dN^*}{ds} = \frac{pU_{22}\left[-a(\delta - g')U_{11}\right]}{D} > 0. \tag{19.18}$$

The following proposition therefore holds

PROPOSITION 4. *A direct international transfer,* s, *will increase the long run equilibrium forest stock,* N^*, *unambiguously.*

In comparing Propositions 3 and 4, it is clear that the comparative statics of the long run equilibrium clearly favour international transfers as the preferred method of inducing tropical timber exporting countries to conserve their tropical forests.

5. The large country exporter

The above model has assumed that the timber exporting country is a pricetaker in the international market; that is, as one of many tropical timber exporters, the country is unable to affect the world price of traded tropical timber products through changing its own level of production and export of timber products.

However, currently some tropical timber exporters, particularly the major South East Asian producers (for example, Malaysia and Indonesia), dominate the international markets in certain tropical timber products. Other countries (for example, Brazil, Zaire and Papua New Guinea) have the potential also to become large-scale producers and exporters (Barbier *et al.*, 1993). The ability of these large-country exporters to use their apparent market power to influence global prices for their timber products depends to a large extent on the availability of alternative supplies, for example, from both other tropical and temperate forest regions, and on end-use substitution between tropical timber products from different sources, between tropical and temperate timber products and between timber and non-timber substitutes (for example, aluminium, concrete, plastics, ceramics, and so on). Some analysts suggest that global supplies of timber are more than adequate even in the long run, and that the shift in production from 'old growth' to secondary forests could rule out the possibility of even large tropical timber producers of asserting any market power (Sedjo and Lyon, 1990). Others have indicated that, while there is always scope for greater substitutability between tropical timber and other products in the long run, substitution for some tropical timber products in major importing markets may be more problematic in the short run (Buongiorno and Manarung, 1992; Vincent, Brooks and Gandapur, 1991). Finally, Rauscher (1990) has shown that, at least theoretically, the 'cartelization' of a group of tropical timber exporters could lead to significant market power and greater conservation of their tropical forests.

As the possibility of a large country exporter (or group of exporters) of tropical timber products influencing international prices cannot be definitely ruled out, it is worth exploring the potential impacts further.

In our model, if a large country exporter is able to influence prices then

$$x = x(p), \text{ with } x'(p) < 0 \text{ and } x''(p) > 0. \quad (19.19)$$

(19.11) now becomes

$$U_2 p(1 + 1/\varepsilon) = U_1, \text{ where } \varepsilon = x'(p)p/x. \quad (19.11')$$

The Appendix indicates that the determinant D of the Hessian matrix of the modified simultaneous system (19.11'), (19.12) and (19.13) is less than zero, which is again a necessary condition for a unique equilibrium. If this is the case then

$$\frac{dN^*}{d(1/\varepsilon)} = \frac{pU_2[-a(\delta - g')U_{11}x'(p)]}{D} > 0. \quad (19.20)$$

PROPOSITION 5. *An increase in market power, 1/ε, of the large country exporter(s) will increase the long run equilibrium forest stock,* N^*, *unambiguously.*

To the extent that large country exporters can increase their market power and influence international timber prices, then they can afford to conserve more of their tropical forests in the long run. Increased monopolistic power or cartelisation of tropical timber supply appears to have a resource-conserving effect.[4]

Will increased international transfers to a large country exporter also enhance forest conservation? The effects of an increased international subsidy, s, has the following impact on the long run equilibrium forest stock

$$\frac{dN^*}{ds} = \frac{p(1 + 1/\varepsilon)U_{22}[-a(\delta - g')U_{11}x'(p)]}{D} > 0. \quad (19.21)$$

Assuming $|\varepsilon| < 1$, an international transfer to a large country exporter will increase its forest stock in the long run. Thus Proposition 4 also holds for the large country exporter.

6. Foreign assets and debt

An initial assumption of the model was that the trade of the tropical timber exporting country is balanced. We now relax this assumption to analyse qualitatively the effects of foreign asset (or debt) accumulation. The inclusion of a foreign capital market results in an additional condition in the model

$$\dot{A} = px - c + rA, \tag{19.22}$$

where $A > 0$ implies accumulated foreign assets, $A < 0$ accumulated foreign debts, and r is the interest earned (or owed). In what follows, we assumed that $A > 0$.

The Hamiltonian (19.6) is modified to

$$H = U(q - x, c, N) + \lambda[g(N) - aq] + \mu[px - c + rA], \tag{19.23}$$

with μ as the costate variable representing the shadow value of foreign asset accumulation. Assuming an interior solution, the maximum principle yields the following conditions

$$U_1 = \lambda a, \tag{19.24}$$

$$\mu = U_2 = U_1/p, \tag{19.25}$$

$$\dot{\lambda} = (\delta - g')\lambda - U_3, \tag{19.26}$$

$$\dot{\mu} = (\delta - r)\mu. \tag{19.27}$$

Conditions (19.24) and (19.26) have the same interpretation as (19.7) and (19.9) before. Equation (19.25) is similar to (19.8), although now the relative marginal value of domestic timber to imported good consumption must be equated not only with the terms of trade, p, but with the implicit value of accumulated foreign assets, μ. Condition (19.27) governs the rate of appreciation in the value of foreign assets, which is determined by the opportunity cost of holding on to a unit of these assets, $(\delta - r)$.

Conditions (19.24)–(19.27) also imply that the growth rates of the variables U_1, U_2, λ and μ are equal along the optimal path, which lead to the following relationships

$$(r - g') = aU_3/U_1 > 0, \text{ and} \tag{19.28}$$

$$\dot{N} = \frac{(r - g')(\delta - r)}{(aU_{33}/U_1) + g''}. \tag{19.29}$$

Equation (19.28) can be interpreted as an efficiency condition. It suggests that in order for foreign assets to be an optimal form of wealth for the timber exporting country, the rate of return on these assets, r, must equal the rate of return from 'holding on' to its tropical forests, $g' + aU_3/U_1$. Otherwise, there is no point in the country extracting and exporting timber as a means to accumulating foreign assets.

Condition (19.29) governs the growth (or depletion) path of the tropical forest along the optimal trajectory for the economy. If the opportunity cost of holding onto foreign assets is negative, that is, $\delta - r < 0$, then the forest stock will be allowed to expand, that is, $\dot{N} > 0$. Moreover, the social value of accumulating foreign assets is falling, that is, $\dot{\mu} < 0$. Effectively, the interest rate r is so large (relative to the return on other assets in the economy as represented by δ) that the economy is better off becoming a net lender of its foreign assets and reducing its timber exploitation to hold on to more forests. However, if the opportunity costs of holding assets is positive, that is, $\delta - r > 0$, then the country will continue to exploit its tropical forests for timber and $\dot{N} < 0$.

Moreover, due to equations (19.25) and (19.27), U_1 grows at a rate $(\delta - r)$, and this implies that the right hand side of (19.28) goes to zero for small discount rates and to infinity for large values of this parameter. Therefore, the very long run solution is $N = N^{\max}$ in the first case, and $g' = r$ in the latter. If the discount rate is small, then the economy will save and consumption is increasing over time. The marginal utility of consumption is reduced such that the value of the tropical forest in terms of the consumption good rises. The opposite argument applies if δ is large. Then the marginal utility of consumption is increased along the optimal path, and the relative value of the forest resource declines until the pure arbitage condition $g' = r$ holds.[5]

Thus assuming in equilibrium that $\delta = r$ and that condition (19.28) will also be valid in the long run, so long as $U_3/U_1 > 0$, then the following proposition holds

PROPOSITION 6. *With a foreign capital market and positive stock externalities* ($U_3 > 0$)*, the forest resource will never be exhausted. Equilibrium forest stock* N^* *will be determined by* $\delta = r = g' + aU_3/U_1$*, which will always be greater than the equilibrium* N^{**}*, as determined by* $\delta = g' > 0$ *in Figure 19.1.*

The system of equations determining the equilibrium now correspond to (19.11)–(19.13) with r inserted for δ. But the second argument of the utility function is no longer px as before but $px + rA$. Unfortunately A is not determined. It can be computed from the starting values of A and N, which implies

$$A_0 + pN_0 = A + pN \text{ or } A = A_0 + pN_0 - pN. \qquad (19.30)$$

Using this in the comparative statics, it follows that the first-row third-column element of the first matrix in the Appendix has to be rp^2U_{22}. Thus the sign of the determinant of the Hessian matrix D remains negative as before. Thus we obtain

PROPOSITION 7. *The comparative static effects on the long-run equilibrium forest stock,* N^*, *have the same signs in the borrowing-and-lending and the previous model of the timber exporting country. The magnitude of the effects may differ.*

7. Conclusion

This paper has examined several aspects of the links between the trade in tropical timber and deforestation from the perspective of an exporting country. The various versions of the model developed here have highlighted a number of important features of this linkage.

First, if the producer country values its tropical forests solely as a source of timber export earnings then it will aim for a smaller forest stock in the long run than if it also considers the other values provided by the forest. Understanding the full range of benefits accruing from their tropical forests, for example, watershed protection, genetic diversity, tourism, microclimatic functions, and so on, is important to determining the direct social value of forest conservation.

Second, if importing nations want the exporting countries to conserve more of their forests, trade interventions appear to be a second-best way of achieving this result. Under certain conditions, they may even prove to be counterproductive. In contrast, international transfers, which in our model simply reduce the dependency of the producer country on the exploitation of the forest for export earnings, are more effective in promoting conservation of the forest stock.

Third, increased market power by a large country exporter or group of exporters may actually lead to greater forest conservation. The greater the market power, the higher the returns per unit of output and the less need to exploit tropical forests more heavily. Nevertheless, even in the monopoly case, an international subsidy to reduce dependence on tropical timber exploitation will incite greater forest conservation.

Finally, the existence of a foreign capital market may further ensure that the tropical timber country may conserve its forest stock in the long run. If the rate of return on foreign assets is very high, the economy may switch into becoming a net lender and prefer even to increase its forest stock. However, even when interest rates are low and consequently the opportunity cost of holding on to foreign assets is high, the economy will not completely exhaust its forests.

Several recent reviews of global forest sector policies have discussed implications similar to those analysed theoretically in our model (Barbier *et al.*, 1993; Binkley and Vincent, 1991; Hyde *et al.*, 1991). Generally, these studies have also concluded that trade intervention is a 'second best' option for controlling tropical deforestation. Nonetheless, the use of bans, tariffs and other trade measures to discourage 'unsustainable' tropical timber exploitation continue to be advocated. As our paper has attempted to show, sometimes the more simple solutions lead neither to a straightforward, nor to the desired, results.

Appendix

Comparative static solution of the simultaneous equation system (19.11), (19.12) and (19.13) can be represented by

$$\begin{vmatrix} U_{11} & -U_{11}-p^2U_{22} & 0 \\ (\delta-g')U_{11} & -(\delta-g')U_{11} & -g''U_1-aU_{33} \\ -a & 0 & g' \end{vmatrix}\begin{vmatrix} dq \\ dx \\ dN \end{vmatrix} = \begin{vmatrix} U_2+pxU_{22} & 0 \\ 0 & U_3 \\ 0 & q \end{vmatrix}\begin{vmatrix} dp \\ da \end{vmatrix}.$$

Solution can be derived through the application of Cramer's rule. However, the key issue is the sign of the determinant of the Hessian matrix of the above system. We therefore derive this result. Having signed the determinant, the comparative static results are fairly straightforward.

The determinant D of the Hessian matrix is

$$D = g'\,p^2\,U_{11}U_{22}(\delta - g') - a(U_{11} + p^2U_{22})\,(g''U_1 + aU_{33}).$$

The right-hand side is negative but the left-hand side is ambiguous as g' is unsigned. However, it can be shown that $D < 0$ is a requirement for the curve $\dot{q}$ to be positively sloped and to cut the curve $\dot{N}$ from below, which is a necessary (but not sufficient) condition for there to be a unique equilibrium in (q, N) space.

The implicit function rule applied to the above simultaneous equation system (19.11), (19.12) and (19.13) yields

$$U_{11}\,dq = (U_{11} + p^2U_{22})\,dx$$

$$(\delta - g')\,U_{11}\,dq - (\delta - g')\,U_{11}\,dx = (g''\,U_1 + aU_{33})\,dN$$

$$-\,a\,dq = -\,g'\,dN.$$

Substituting for dx yields

$$\left.\frac{dq}{dN}\right|_{\dot{q}=0} = \frac{(g''U_1 + aU_{33})(U_{11} + p^2U_{22})}{(\delta - g')p^2U_{22}U_{11}} > 0.$$

$$\left.\frac{dq}{dN}\right|_{\dot{N}=0} = \frac{g'}{a}.$$

It follows that

$$\left.\frac{\mathrm{d}q}{\mathrm{d}N}\right|_{\dot{N}=0} < \left.\frac{dq}{dN}\right|_{\dot{q}=0}$$

also implies that $a(U_{11} + p^2U_{22})\,(g''U_1 + aU_{33}) > g'p^2U_{11}U_{22}(\delta - g')$, and thus $D < 0$.

In the monopoly case, comparative static solution of the simultaneous equation system (19.11), (19.12) and (19.13) can be represented by

$$\begin{vmatrix} U_{11} & \phi & 0 \\ (\delta - g')U_{11} & -(\delta - g')U_{11}x' & -g''U_1 - aU_{33} \\ -a & 0 & g' \end{vmatrix} \begin{vmatrix} \mathrm{d}q \\ \mathrm{d}p \\ \mathrm{d}N \end{vmatrix}$$

$$= \begin{vmatrix} U_2p & 0 \\ 0 & U_3 \\ 0 & q \end{vmatrix} \begin{vmatrix} \mathrm{d}1/\varepsilon \\ \mathrm{d}a \\ \; \end{vmatrix}.$$

The determinant D of the Hessian matrix of the above system is

$$D = a[g''U_1 + aU_{33}]\phi - g'(\delta - g')U_{11}[U_{11}x'(p) + \phi],$$

where

$$\phi = -U_{11}x'(p) - p^2U_{22}(1 + 1/\varepsilon)^2 - U_2(1 + 1/\varepsilon) + U_2p(\varepsilon'(p)/\varepsilon^2) < 0.$$

It follows that the condition

$$\left.\frac{\mathrm{d}q}{\mathrm{d}N}\right|_{\dot{N}=0} > \left.\frac{dq}{dN}\right|_{\dot{q}=0}$$

also implies that $a(g''U_1 + aU_{33})\phi < g'(\delta - g')U_{11}[\phi + U_{11}x'(p)]$, and thus $D < 0$.

Notes

* We would like to thank Joanne Burgess for contributing to discussions that resulted in this paper, which were held at the Beijer Institute of Ecological Economics of the Royal Swedish Academy of Sciences. We acknowledge the financial support given by the Beijer Institute and the hospitality of its staff, and in particular we are grateful to Prof. Karl-Göran Mäler for inviting us to use the facilities at Beijer and to Charles Perrings, Director of the Biodiversity Programme.

Additional support for Edward Barbier's participation in the research was also provided by the International Tropical Timber Organization, under contract no. PCM(XI)/4, 'Economic Linkages Between the International Trade in Tropical Timber and the Sustainable Management of Tropical Forests'. We are grateful to comments provided by two anonymous referees; however, the usual disclaimer applies.

1. For example. see Barbier *et al.* (1991); Gillis (1990); Hyde *et al.* (1991); Pearce (1990); and Repetto (1990).
2. Processed timber products are assumed to be converted to log-equivalents.
3. The proposed international financing is for, specifically, sustaining the multiple roles and functions of all types of forests, forest lands and woodlands (US$860 million per annum); enhancement of the protection, sustainable management and conservation of all forests, the greening of degraded areas through forest rehabilitation, afforestation, reforestation and other rehabilitation measures (US$460 million p.a.); and promoting efficient utilization and assessment to recover the full valuation of the goods and services provided by forests, forest lands and woodlands (US$230 million p.a.).
4. According to Solow (1974, p. 8), 'the monopolist is the conservationist's friend'. Usually this holds along an adjustment path towards a steady state, which is independent of market structure. In our model, in contrast, the long run equilibrium is also affected.
5. Note that Equation (19.28) also implies that there is a relocation of assets at $t = 0$ such that (19.28) holds forever after. Thus, there is a jump in N corresponding to a jump in the opposite direction in A. The extraction rate is plus or minus infinity in this point of time. However, the long-run equilibrium remains unaffected.

References

Amelung, T. and M. Diehl (1991), *Deforestation of Tropical Rainforests: Economic Causes and Impact on Development*, Kielen Studien 241, Tubingen, Mohr, Germany.

Barbier, E.B., J.C. Burgess and A. Markandya (1991), 'The economics of tropical deforestation', *AMBIO*, **20** (2), 55–8.

Barbier, E.B., J.C. Burgess, B.A. Aylward, J.T. Bishop and C. Bann (1993), *The Economic Linkages Between the Trade in Tropical Timber and the Sustainable Management of Tropical Forests*, Final Report: ITTO Activity PCM(XI)/4, International Tropical Timber Organization, Yokohoma.

Binkley, C.S. and J.R. Vincent (1991), *Forest Based Industrialization: A Dynamic Perspective*, HIID Development Discussion Paper No. 389, Harvard University, Cambridge, Massachusetts.

Buongiorno, J. and T. Manurung (1992), 'Predicted effects of an import tax in the European Community on the international trade of tropical timbers', Draft paper, Department of Forestry, University of Wisconsin, Madison.

Dembner, S. (1991), 'Provisional data from the forest resources assessment 1990 project', *UNASYLVA*, **42** (164), 40–44.

Gillis, M. (1990), Forest Incentive Policies', Paper prepared for the World Bank Forest Policy Paper, The World Bank, Washington, DC.

Hyde, W.F., D.H. Newman and R.A. Sedjo (1991), *Forest Economics and Policy Analysis: An Overview*, World Bank Discussion Paper No. 134, The World Bank, Washington, DC.

International Tropical Timber Council (ITTC) (1992), *Report on Preparations for the 1992 United Nations Conference on Environment and Development*, ITTC(XII)/8, 12th Session, 6–14 May 1992, Yaoundé, Cameroon.

Pearce, D.W. (1990), *An Economic Approach to Saving the Tropical Forests*, LEEC Discussion Paper 90–06, London Environmental Economics Centre, UK.

Poore, D., P. Burgess, J. Palmer, S. Rietbergen and T. Synnott (1989), *No Timber Without Trees: Sustainability in the Tropical Forest*, London: Earthscan Publications Ltd.

Rauscher, M. (1990), 'Can cartelization solve the problem of tropical deforestation', *Weltwirtschartliches Archiv*, 380–87.

Reid, W.V. and K.R. Millier (1989), *Keeping Options Alive: The Scientific Basis for Conserving Biodiversity*, Washington, DC: World Resource Institute.

Repetto, R. (1990), 'Deforestation in the tropics', *Scientific American*, **262** (4), 36–45.
Sedjo, R.A. and K.S. Lyon (1990), *The Long-Term Adequacy of World Timber Supply*, Washington, DC: Resources for the Future.
Solow, R.M. (1974), 'Richard T. Ely Lecture: The Economics of Resources or the Resources of Economics', *American Economic Review*, **64**, 1–14.
Vincent, J.R., D.J. Brooks and A.K. Gandapur (1991), 'Substitution between tropical and temperate sawlogs', *Forest Science*, **37** (5), 1484–91.
World Resources Institute (WRI) (1992), *World Resources 1992–93*, London: Oxford University Press.

20. The linkages between the timber trade and tropical deforestation – Indonesia

with N. Bockstael, J.C. Burgess and I. Strand

1. Introduction

The following chapter examines the links between the trade in tropical timber products and deforestation in Indonesia. We briefly review some of the evidence suggesting that timber production is a factor in tropical deforestation, and the role of timber trade policy in Indonesia in influencing this process by affecting forest-based industrialisation. These issues are of particular concern to Indonesia, as the country has recently prohibitively taxed the export of sawnwood exports to encourage further rapid development of plywood processing.

We develop a partial equilibrium timber trade model of Indonesia to analyse the effects of various policy interventions on the trade and tropical deforestation. The basic timber trade model is developed as a *simultaneous equation* system determining supply and demand in the logging, sawnwood and plywood sectors of Indonesia. The system is linked to a *recursive* relationship determining tropical deforestation, which is estimated separately. We use the model to simulate several policy options, including the impacts of sawnwood export taxes/effective bans. import bans imposed by consumer countries, revenue-raising import taxes, and increased harvesting costs associated with 'sustainable management'.

The chapter concludes by summarizing the results of the policy analysis, and discusses the policy options open to the Government of Indonesia (GoI) and importing countries.

2. The timber trade and tropical deforestation in Indonesia

South East Asia currently accounts for around 20 per cent of the world's tropical moist forest (TMF). Indonesia alone has over 50 per cent of the region's TMF and over 10 per cent of the world's total (see Table 20.1). The rate of deforestation in South East Asia, measured in terms of hectares (ha) lost per year, is also fairly high – approximately two million ha annually – and the total area deforested is much higher than in Amazonia and Central Africa. Close to 85 per cent of South East Asia's annual deforestation occurs in Indonesia.

The major 'cause' of tropical deforestation in South East Asia and in Indonesia in particular is generally thought to be the conversion of forests to agricultural

Table 20.1 Tropical deforestation in Southeast Asia and other regions[a]

	Total forest area (mn ha)	Undisturbed operable forest (mn ha)	Annual deforestation ('000 ha)	Total TMF area deforested (mn ha)
SE Asia Insular	167.3	72	1707	117
Indonesia	108.6		1315	
Papua New Guinea	33.5		22	
Malaysia[b]	18.4		255	
Philippines	6.5		110	
Brunei	0.3		5	
Other SE Asia[c]	39.3	18	346	na
Myanmar	31.2		102	
Thailand	8.1		244	
Total SE Asia	206.6	90	2053	>117
Amazonia	613.6	453	4129	100
Central Africa	167.1	107	325	30
Other Regions	58.4	<10	1900	177[d]
World Total	1045.7	652	8480	424

Notes:

[a] Unless indicated, 1990 estimates based on Schmidt (1990). Note that *tropical moist forests* are defined as broadleaf high closed tropical forests, including wetland and mangrove forests but excluding the deciduous dry forests of South Asia, sub-Saharan Africa and sub-tropical South America. In 1988, the FAO estimated the total area of all *tropical closed forests* (including deciduous dry forests) to be 1269.6 million ha.

[b] Includes forests from Peninsular Malaysia.

[c] End of 1980 revised estimated based on Forest Resources Division, Forestry Department, *An Interim Report on the State of Forest Resources in the Developing Countries*, FAO, Rome (1988).

[d] May include estimates for Thailand and Myanmar.

land. Tropical timber production, although significant in large areas of 'production' forests, is considered to be a less significant factor in overall tropical deforestation More recently, however, attention has focused on the indirect role of timber production in 'opening up' inaccessible forest areas, which then encourages other economic uses of the forest resources, such as agricultural cultivation, that lead to deforestation on a wider scale. For example, Amelung and Diehl (1992) identify the major shifts in land use changes and the causes of deforestation in tropical countries, including Indonesia. As indicated in Table 20.2A. the direct impact of forest activities on deforestation appears to be minimal (that is, less than ten per cent of total deforestation), as compared to agriculture. For Indonesia, this is partly because timber is harvested predominately by selective logging, which does not meet the 'strong' definition of deforestation that is commonly used. In contrast, the forestry sector in Indonesia is almost completely responsible for converting virgin forests into productive closed forests or other forms of land use through *forest modification*, and has a much more significant role in *biomass reduction* (see Table 20.2B). In short, there are some indications that timber extraction is largely responsible for opening up previously unexploited forest, leading to further forest degradation and outright deforestation.

Table 20.2A Sources of deforestation in tropical countries, 1981–88[a]

	Brazil	Indonesia[b]	Cameroon	All major tropical forest countries
Forestry	2[d]	9	0	2
				(10)[e]
Agriculture	89	80	100	(83)[f]
shifting cultivators[c]	13	59	92	na
	(23)	(67)	(95)	(47)
permanent agriculture:	76	21	8	36
– pastures	40	9	0	17
– permanent crops	4	2	5	3
– arable land	32	19	3	16
Mining and related industries	<3	<0.3	0	na
Hydroelectric production	4[b]	0	0	2[b]
Residual[g]	2	11	0	(13)[h]

Notes:
[a] Percentage shares in deforestation refer to averages for the respective period.
[b] Data refer to the 1980–90 period.
[c] Figures in parentheses show the results of the FAO for 1980. These data include also market oriented farmers who produce cash and export crops and engage only partly in shifting cultivation.
[d] Deforestation due to logging is due to charcoal production.
[e] The figure in parentheses refers to the estimation of Enquete-Kommission zum Schutz der Drdatmosphäre, *Schutz der tropichen Wälder*, Deutscher Bundestag 11, Wahlperiode, Drucksache 11/7220, 24.05.1990, Bonn, 1990. The calculation includes only Indonesia and Brazil, since these countries account for the largest share in clear cutting by the forestry sector.
[f] This percentage rate is based on the assumption that the percentage share calculated for shifting cultivators can be taken as an average for the 1981–88 period.
[g] This includes other industries, housing, infrastructure services and fire loss.
[h] The residual has been calculated from the data in this column which includes data from different periods.

Table 20.2B Sectoral share in forest degradation and forest modification, 1981–85[a]

Sector	Percentage share in biomass reduction (degradation)				Percentage share in forest modification			
	Brazil	Indonesia	Cameroon	Total[b]	Brazil	Indonesia	Cameroon	Total[b]
Forestry	6	44	10	10	(100)[c]	(100)[c]	98	71
Agriculture[d]	85	49	90	76	0	0	2	26
Others[d]	9	7	0	13	0	0	0	4

Notes:

[a] For the definition of modification and biomass reduction (degradation) see FAO, *Tropical Forest Resources*, FAO Forestry Paper 30, Rome (1982).

[b] Total refers to all major rain forest countries.

[c] Following FAO statistics, deforestation in virgin forests is 0, since clearing by agriculture and other sectors concentrates on disturbed forests. Even though some clearing occurs in virgin forests, there is reason to assume that the bulk of deforestation is due to forests that have been logged over prior to the clearing of the respective areas.

[d] These figures have been derived from Table 20.2A and reflect averages for the 1981–88 period or, in the case of Indonesia, the 1980–88 period.

Source: Amelung and Diehl (1992).

Other studies indicate the possible acceleration of this process, given the trends in timber production in Indonesia (Burgess, 1989). With the exception of Sabah and probably Papua New Guinea, Indonesia has one of the last remaining reserves of virgin forest in South East Asia, yet well over one third of the country's tropical forests have been allocated to conversion or permanent production forest (Table 20.3A). As a very large part of the production in Indonesia in the past has come from the conversion forests, which are essentially clear cut and turned over to agriculture, future supplies must depend on the permanent production forests (and any remaining virgin forest reserves allocated to them) – provided that these supplies can be maintained on a sustained basis.

Although Table 20.3B suggests that Indonesia's permanent production forests are not being 'mined' to the extent of those in other South East Asian countries, there is concern that Indonesia has over-estimated the extent of its production forest, under-reported current timber extraction (for example, there is substantial illegal felling), or both (Burgess, 1989). Moreover, several analysts predict a decline in South East Asia's (and Indonesia's) share of world production and trade, and some deterioration in the quality of hardwood timber produced from forests in the region (Arnold, 1991; Burgess, 1989; and Sedjo and Lyon, 1990). Thus, it is unlikely that Indonesia will be able to maintain its current dominance of world production and trade of timber products, as indicated in Table 20.3C, without further and extensive exploitation of its remaining old growth reserves.

Table 20.3A Forest areas in major Southeast Asian tropical timber countries (sq km)[a]

	Total land area	Total forest area	Permanent protection forest	Permanent production forest	Conversion production forest	Total production forest	Remaining virgin forest
Thailand	513 115	142 958	na	na	na	na	na
Malaysia							
Peninsular	131 596	63 532	10 679	29 984	4 080	34 064	7 815
Sabah	73 711	44 869	6 000	29 984	4 080	34 064	7 815
Sarawak	123 253	94 384	24 200	32 400	37 784	70 184	50 387
Philippines	300 000	63 830	16 800	44 030	9	44 030	10 420
Papua New Guinea	468 860	359 900	na	na	na	na	na
Indonesia	1 930 270	1 439 700	490 410	338 666	305 370	644 036	524 000
Total	3 540 805	2 209 173	548 089	479 587	356 334	835 921	602 222

Note: Based on Burgess (1989).

Table 20.3B *Production and yield potential in major Southeast Asian tropical timber countries*[a]

	Permanent production forest (million ha)	Sustained yield at 1.5 m^3 per year	Sustained yield at 2.0 m^3 per year	Annual timber harvest (m^3)
Malaysia				
Peninsular	2.85[b]	4 275 000	5 700 000	7 914 328
Sabah	3.00	4 500 000	6 000 000	11 739 262
Sarawak	3.24	4 860 000	6 480 000	11 470 000
Philippines	4.40	6 600 000	8 800 000	3 433 774
Indonesia	33.87	50 805 000	67 740 000	28 500 000
Total	47.36	71 040 000	94 720 000	63 057 364

Notes:
[a] Based on Burgess (1989).
[b] The author does not explain the discrepancy between Tables 20.3A and 20.3B over the size of the permanent production forest in Peninsular Malaysia.

Table 20.3C *Production and trade of wood products in major Southeast Asian tropical timber countries*[a]

	Products	Production	Imports	Exports	ACD[b]
Indonesia	logs	23 684.0	0.0	0.0	23 684.0
	sawnwood	10 546.0	0.0	2 692.0	7 854.0
	plywood	8 500.0	0.0	8 040.0	460.0
	veneer	53.9	0.0	29.0	24.9
Malaysia	logs	38 900.0	10.0	21 100.0	17 810.0
	sawnwood	7 660.0	197.0	5 134.0	2 723.0
	plywood	1 001.0	15.0	915.0	101.0
	veneer	445.0	5.3	248.7	201.6
Papua New Guinea	logs	1 700.0	0.0	1 260.0	440.0
	sawnwood	118.0	0.0	3.0	115.0
	plywood	18.0	0.0	0.0	18.0
	veneer	0.0	0.0	0.0	0.0
Philippines	logs	2 773.0	393.5	6.0	3 160.0
	sawnwood	975.0	12.0	438.1	548.9
	plywood	341.0	3.0	130.9	213.1
	veneer	75.0	0.0	53.1	21.9

Table 20.3C continued

	Products	Production	Imports	Exports	ACD[b]
Thailand	logs	1 770.0	1 135.0	0.0	2 905.0
	sawnwood	1 160.0	744.0	30.0	1 874.0
	plywood	185.0	4.0	35.0	154.0
	veneer	60.0	2.0	5.0	57.0
Total SE Asia producers	logs	68 827.0	1 538.5	22 366.0	47 999.5
	sawnwood	20 459.0	953.0	8 297.1	13 114.9
	plywood	10 045.0	22.0	9 120.9	946.1
	veneer	633.9	7.3	335.8	305.4
Total ITTO producers[c]	logs	126 967.0	2 536.7	25 749.2	103 754.5
	sawnwood	48 846.0	1 083.5	9 518.1	40 411.4
	plywood	12 115.6	59.2	9 565.2	2 609.6
	veneer	1 705.7	42.5	555.5	1 192.7
Total world producers[d]	logs	1 677 454	130 230	124 846	1 682 838
	sawnwood	500 685	100 231	99 088	501 828
	wood panels[e]	129 108	28 692	28 443	129 357

Notes:

a Based on International Tropical Timber Council, *Elements for the 1990 Annual Review and Assessment of the World Tropical Timber Situation*, Tenth Session, Quito, Ecuador (29 May–6 June, 1991).

b ADC = Apparent domestic consumption.

c ITTO = International Tropical Timber Organisation.

d All tropical and temperate timber producers, derived from FAO, *Forest Products Yearbook 1989* (Rome, 1991).

e Includes veneer sheets, plywood, particle board and fibreboard (compressed and non-compressed).

3. Indonesian timber trade policies

The tropical timber trade has been subject to severe distortions by export restrictions imposed by log producing countries, including Indonesia. One justification often cited for these policies is that they compensate exporters for the import barriers in developed economy markets by making the price of raw logs higher to the processors in the importing country while reducing the cost disadvantage faced by domestic processors within the timber producing countries. This strategy usually has as its primary aim the creation of more export revenues and employment for the forestry sector, with a secondary objective of reducing harvesting pressure on the forests by increasing value added per log extracted.

Several authors have recently reviewed the role of export taxes and bans in encouraging forest-based industrialization and sustainable timber management in tropical forest countries (Barbier *et al.*, 1994; Gillis, 1990; Vincent and Binkley, 1991; and Vincent, 1992b). Initially, the preference seems to have been for export taxes, through employing escalating rates. For most countries, export tax rates on logs generally ranged between 10 and 20 per cent. Export taxes on sawn timber, veneer and plywood have been negligible. Where sawn timber exports were taxed, rates were typically half that of logs. More recently, the use of export tax structures to promote forest-based industrialization has become largely replaced by export bans in tropical forest countries, although export taxes are still being used in certain regions and for specific timber products (see Table 20.4).

Table 20.4 Export taxes and bans on tropical timber – Southeast Asia

Country	Tax rate/Export policy	Remarks
Indonesia	Log export taxes, ranging from US\$500 to US\$4800 per m^3 depending on species	Log export ban since 1985 was replaced by export taxes in May 1992, which is effectively perpetuating the ban
	Specific export taxes on sawn timber, ranging from US\$250–2400 per m^3	Specific export taxes on sawn timber introduced in 1989; plywood exempt from all export taxes
	Specific export taxes on wet and dry veneer of US\$250 per m^3	Imposed in May 1992
Malaysia:		
Peninsular	Log export ban since 1971	
Sabah	No specific export tax or ban but see remarks	The Sabah timber royalty has a strong export tax feature: the royalty rate for log exports is almost 10 times the rate for logs used domestically
Sarawak	15 per cent *ad valorem* of f.o.b. log values	Tax applies to one hardwood species only
Papua New Guinea	10 per cent of f.o.b. log values	Tax reported to have been widely evaded through transfer pricing. Log export ban proposed
Philippines	Log exports restricted to 25 per cent of annual allowable cut since 1979	Ostensibly to control deforestation

Source: Gillis (1990), updated with FAO data.

Tropical timber export taxes and bans have proved only moderately successful in achieving the desired results in South East Asia. For example, although expanded processing capacity was established in Malaysia, the Philippines and Indonesia, it was achieved at high economic costs, both in terms of the direct costs of subsidisation as well as the additional costs of wasteful and inefficient processing operations (Barbier, 1987; Gillis, 1988 and 1990; Vincent and Binkley, 1991; and Vincent 1992a and 1992b).

In addition, as a long-term forest industrialization strategy, ensuring export sales of processed products through denying processors in other countries access to logs may prove difficult to sustain (Bourke, 1988). Importers of South East Asian logs, such as Japan, have been known to substitute other raw materials (for example, cement, steel, plastics, fiberboard, and so on) for timber, and alternative sources of supply, such as sawlogs from temperate and other developing regions (Bourke, 1988: and Vincent, Gandapur and Brooks, 1990).

As Indonesia, the *ad valorem* export tax on logs was doubled from 10 to 20 per cent 1978, while most sawnwood and all plywood were exempted. Beginning in 1980 controls on the export of logs were progressively enforced, until an outright ban was introduced in 1985 (Gillis, 1988). The export tax structure created effective rates of protection of 222 per cent for plywood manufacture, and the drop in export revenue to the government from diverting log exports was not compensated by any gain in value-added in sawmilling, resulting in a loss of US$15 per m^3 at world prices. The consequence has been the creation of inefficient processing operations and expanded capacity, with consequences for the rate of timber extraction and forest management. Gillis (1988) has estimated that over 1979–82, due to the inefficient processing operations resulting from this policy, over US$545 million in potential rents was lost to the Indonesian economy, or an average cost of US$136 million annually. Moreover, as the switch from log to processed exports occurred at a time when forest product prices were falling sharply in real terms, the cost to the economy in export earnings was high. Over 1981–84, the net loss in export earnings amounted to US$2.9–3.4 billion, or approximately US$725–850 million annually. Additional losses were also incurred through selling plywood below production cost, which amounted to US$956 million in 1981–84, or US$239 million annually (Fitzgerald, 1986).

Although the switch to value-added processing of timber initially slowed down the rate of timber extraction, the inefficiencies and rapidly expanding capacity of domestic processing may have actually increased the rate of deforestation over the medium and long term.[1] For example, by the early 1980s, the major operational inefficiencies in domestic processing due to high rates of effective protection in Indonesia led to the lowest conversion rates in Asia. As a result, for every cubic metre of Indonesian plywood produced, 15 per cent more trees had to be cut relative to plymills elsewhere in Asia that would have processed Indonesia log exports (Gillis, 1988). Thus the protection given to Indonesian mills not only increased rather than reduced total log demand, but the gross operational inefficiencies also ensured that millions more logs may have been harvested than if a more efficient policy to boost domestic processing capabilities than forced industrialization through export taxes and bans had been implemented.

More recent analysis of the impacts of the log export ban in Indonesia on the efficiency of timber processing industries confirms that the policy did not increase wood recoveries and thus reduced log consumption compared to pre-ban levels (Constantino, 1990). By depressing prices, the log export ban led to the substitution of wood for other factor inputs, with substantial wood recovery losses in sawmilling and a slower growth in wood recovery than other factor productivities in plymilling. In both industries, wood consumption was the main source of output growth over the 1975 to 1987 period, with efficiency gains contributing very little. However, the log export ban did not affect efficiency in the plywood industry so seriously, which could be explained by the much newer capital vintages in plywood milling, its export orientation that requires higher production standards, and possibly its access to better quality logs.

Despite the problems with the export restriction policy, it is still being aggressively promoted by the Government of Indonesia (GOI) to encourage forest-based industrialization. In May 1992, under pressure from the United States through GATT, the export log ban was largely replaced by restrictively high taxation on exports of raw logs, which has effectively perpetuated the ban (see Table 20.4).[2] More importantly, in October 1989 export taxes on sawn timber were also increased substantially to prohibit exports and shift processing activities to plywood. A secondary objective has been to eliminate the marginal saw mills leaving only the competitive ones operational, thus improving overall industrial efficiency. The implications of the policy for wood recovery, log demand and thus tropical deforestation in Indonesia is less clear.

In this chapter we develop a timber trade model for Indonesia, linked to impacts on deforestation through log demand, in order to compare the sawnwood export ban with other possible trade policy options. Through the various policy option simulations, we explore the relative merits of the different policy interventions in terms of production, prices, trade and deforestation in Indonesia. However, we first briefly review other models applied to the tropical timber trade in South East Asia.

4. Other Southeast Asian timber trade models

Various partial equilibrium models of forest product markets and timber supply have been developed for countries in South East Asia to examine the implications of policies that restrict log exports.

Vincent (1989) employed a simulation model of the timber trade of Malaysia, other South East Asian producers and the major importers from the region to determine the optimal tariffs on intermediate and final goods for log, sawnwood and plywood products. The results of the model indicated that the large export tariffs imposed by Malaysia and other South East Asian exporters reduced domestic prices in those countries, leading to losses in producer surplus. More recently, Vincent (1992a) constructed an economic model of sawlog and sawnwood production, consumption and trade in Peninsular Malaysia during 1973–89 to examine in more detail how the log-export restrictions imposed in 1985 affected the forests products industry in Peninsular Malaysia, and whether the restrictions generated net economic benefits. Although the export restrictions seemed to stimulate growth in the processing industries and employment, the economic costs were high. On an average annual basis, Peninsular Malaysia lost US$6100 in economic value-added, US$16 600 in export earnings, and US$34 300 in stumpage value for every sawnmill job created by the log-export restrictions. No attempt was made in either of the above models to link the impacts of timber trade interventions on timber harvesting levels and tropical deforestation.

As part of the forest sector policy review of Indonesia conducted by the United Nations Food and Agricultural Organisation (FAO) and the GOI, a domestic and international trade model of timber products centred on Indonesia was developed (Constantino, 1988a, b; and Constantino and Ingram, 1990). The simulation model had as its main purpose the determination of supply and demand projections for the Indonesian forestry sector, but it was also used to run policy scenarios on different trade interventions, including the implications of Indonesia's log export restrictions. The impacts of different government harvesting policies were simulated through scenario assumptions concerning the elasticity of the supply of forest land in Indonesia. For example, a small elasticity of supply was interpreted as a deliberate government policy to impose sustained yield constraints; whereas large elasticities reflected the GOI allowing expansion of forest land harvested. Using these different elasticity assumptions, the analysis could then focus on whether in response to each policy scenario the GOI should expand the area of forest land harvested, at the risk of greater tropical timber depletion and deforestation, or whether Indonesia would be better off limiting supply through greater harvest restrictions. Detailed results are provided in Constantino (1988a), which are summarized here:

1. If international competitors follow conservative harvesting practices, then Indonesia should do the same in order to take advantage of greater employment, foreign exchange earnings and rent capture. On the other hand, if competing countries follow expansionary policies, it is not clear what Indonesia ought to do. Harvest restrictions will lead to a loss in international market share and to declines in employment – but also increases government revenues.

2. Export restrictions on sawnwood and plywood result in a loss in international market share for Indonesia, lower foreign exchange earnings, employment, labour income, royalty revenues for logging and economic rent to forest land. On the other hand, the restrictions lead to lower domestic prices thus benefiting Indonesian consumers, to higher profits in the processing industries and to less forest land harvested. Imposing harvest restrictions as well would improve matters, as employment would decline less, even less forest land would be harvested and economic rent to forest land would increase more, thus leading to more revenues if the GOI increased rent capture.
3. A ten per cent currency devaluation by the GOI coupled with restrictive harvesting policies will lead to the conservation of the resource and greater economic rent from forest land, but at the expense of higher domestic prices and less employment, value added, foreign exchange earnings and royalty revenues. This would suggest that some increase in forest land harvested in conjunction with a currency devaluation would be preferred.
4. The impacts of a ten per cent US import tariff on tropical plywood is dissipated somewhat if it is imposed on all exporters and not just Indonesia, and if there is limited substitution between tropical and temperate plywood. For Indonesia, the overall effects are a decline in total plywood exports, a smaller increase in sawnwood exports, and increased domestic consumption and trade diversion to other regions for both products. If harvesting restrictions are imposed, consumer prices will fall more, but employment, capital, foreign exchange earnings and value added will decline.

The following simulation model is an additional attempt to examine the relationship between policy interventions, tropical timber product trade and deforestation in Indonesia.

5. Timber trade and deforestation model of Indonesia

The simulation model employed to examine timber trade and tropical deforestation in Indonesia is a static (single-period), partial equilibrium model of the production, consumption and trade of forest products that is related to the impact of log harvesting on forested area. The model is comprised of two components: a *simultaneous equation system* determining supply and demand in the logging, sawnwood and plywood sectors of Indonesia, and a *recursive relationship* determining tropical deforestation. Each component was estimated separately over the period 1968–88, before the 1989 tax rises on Indonesia sawnwood exports. The resulting estimated relationships were linked together in the simulation model using 1988 data.[3] The model was then used to examine the varying impacts on Indonesia's timber markets and tropical forests of the 1989 sawnwood export tax policy and other policy interventions.

Table 20.5 Indonesia – timber trade simultaneous equation system and deforestation equation

1. *Roundwood Market*	
QLI = 30868.4 + 0.172*(RPXLI-XTLI-ROYLI) – 0.433* CSTLI (2.43) (2.59) (– 1.1)	t = 1968–84 SE = 5534.3 DW = 0.76
XLI = – 165246.2 – 34562.3*(RPXLI/(PLTENC*EXR)) – 4.74*YPCML. + 1.397*POPML (–2.64) (–2.03) (–1.51) (2.83)	t = 1968–84 SE = 6131.6 DW = 0.89
CONLI = 2513.5 + 2.09*QSWI + 1.43*QPWI (0.96) (2.08) (1.43)	t = 1968–88 SE = 3679.5 DW = 0.86
2. *Sawnwood Market*	
QSWI = 776.3 + 0.011*RPXSWI + 10.427*CAPSWI – 0.021*(CSTSWI + RPXLI – XTLI) (1.32) (2.00) (3.94) (–1.41)	t = 1968–88 SE = 702.8 DW = 1.53
XSWI = – 2149.3 – 0.029*(JEXR*RPXSWI) + 68.27*JAPIND – 0.201*YPCMSW (–2.24) (–1.96) (5.66) (–0.98)	t = 1974–88 SE = 315.5 DW = 2.13
CONSWI = – 5914.5 – 0.106*RPXSWI + 0.000077*POPI + 34.6*GDFI – 0.209*INDVA (–0.89) (–2.43) (1.19) (2.90) (–1.82)	t = 1968–88 SE = 452.8 DW = 1.63
3. *Plywood Market*	
QPWI = 537.8 + 0.0042*(RPXPWI) + 0.706*(CAPPWI) – 0.008*(CSTPWI + RPXLI – XTLI) (0.73) (1.41) (5.45) (–1.48)	t = 1975–88 SE = 371.3 DW = 1.75
XPWI = – 43846.4 – 1537.9*(RPXPWI/(PHIPW*EXR)) + 0.943*YPCMPW + 0.148*POPMPW – 104.2*MFXUV (–9.45) (–2.34) (4.71) (8.33) (–6.65)	t = 1975–88 SE = 370.9 DW = 1.97
CONPWI = – 7014.6 – 0.0033*RPXPWI + 0.000055*POPI (–3.06) (–2.59) (4.16)	t = 1975–88 SE = 219.7 DW = 1.75

Deforestation Equation

$$LN(F/A) - LN(1 - FA) = \underset{(4.45)}{0.875} - \underset{(-1.98)}{5.695^{*}LOGA} - \underset{(-5.82)}{0.013^{*}POPD} + \underset{(2.84)}{0.0037^{*}GDPA} + \underset{(4.40)}{0.997^{*}D88}$$

$R^2 = 0.51$
SE = 0.82
DW = 1.57

Dependent Variables

QLI	Industrial roundwood production ('000 m^3)
XLI	Industrial roundwood exports ('000 m^3)
CONLI	Apparent domestic log consumption ('000 m^3)
QSWI	Sawnwood and sleeper production ('000 m^3)
XSWI	Sawnwood and sleeper exports ('000 m^3)
CONSWI	Apparent domestic sawnwood and sleeper consumption ('000 m^3)
QPWI	Plywood production ('000 m^3)
XPWI	Plywood exports ('000 m^3)
CONPWI	Apparent domestic plywood production ('000 m^3)
F/A	Forest area (F) per total land area (A), km^2

Independent Variables

RPXLI	Log export prices (unit values) in domestic currency (Rp/m^3)
XTLI	Log export taxes (Rp/m^3)
ROYLI	Log royalties and other taxes (Rp/m^3)
CSTLI	Logging and log transport costs (Rp/m^3)
PLTENC	Average world price of temperate non-coniferous logs (US$/$m^3$)
EXR	Exchange rate, Indonesian Rupiah (Rp)/US$
YPCML	Average GNP per capita of Indonesian log importers (US$)
POPLM	Average population of Indonesian log importers
RPXSWI	Sawnwood and sleeper export prices (unit values) in domestic currency (Rp/m^3)
CAPSWI	Sawmill capacity ('000m^3)
CSTSWI	Total input sawmill costs (Rp/m^3)
JEXR	Exchange rate, Japanese yen (Y)/Rp
JAPIND	Japan – industrial production index 1985 = 100
YPCMSW	Average GNP per capita of Indonesian sawnwood importers (US$)
POPI	Indonesia – population
GDFI	Indonesia – GDP deflator index 1980 = 100
INDVA	Indonesia – industrial value added, Rp billion
RPXPWI	Plywood export prices (unit values) in domestic currency (Rp/m^3)
CAPPWI	Plymill capacity ('000m^3)
CSTPWI	Total input plymill costs (Rp/m^3)
PHIPW	Export wholesale Tokyo spot price of Philippine (luan) plywood (US$/$m^3$)
YPCMPW	Average GNP per capita of Indonesian plywood importers (US$)
POPMPW	Average population of Indonesia plywood importers
MEXUV	Average world manufacturers export unit values index 1980 = 100
LOGA	Roundwood production per total area ('000m^3/km^2)
POPD	Population density (per km^2)
GDPA	GDP per capita ('000 Rp/km^2)
D88	Dummy variable for 1988

Statistical Data

t	Time period of the regression
SE	Standard error of the regression
DW	Durbin–Watson statistic
R^2	*R*-squared statistic

Notes: All values are in constant (1980) prices; *t*-statistics are indicated in parentheses under the relevant coefficients.

The simultaneous equation system of the supply and demand for Indonesia's roundwood (log), sawnwood and plywood markets was estimated using two-stage least squares employing linear functional relationships (see Table 20.5). As Indonesia essentially prohibits competing foreign timber product imports, supply comes solely from domestic production. In all three markets, demand is assumed to consist of both domestic consumption and foreign demand for Indonesian exports. Separate relationships for domestic production, consumption and import demand for each of the three products were then estimated. All values were based on 1980 real prices.

In the case of the log market. domestic consumption was assumed to be determined by the level of sawnwood and plywood production, multiplied by the respective wood recovery rates. Log export demand was considered to be influenced by log export unit values relative to the price of substitutes in world markets and by macro-economic factors affecting final demand in those countries importing Indonesian logs.[4] Due to insufficient data on domestic log prices, roundwood production (harvesting) was related to log export unit values, net of log royalties and export taxes, and the costs of harvesting. Domestic plus foreign log demand was therefore assumed to equal total log production. However, because the log export ban in 1985 effectively reduced Indonesian export volumes and unit values to zero, estimation of the log supply and foreign log demand relationships was only possible for the period 1968–84. As a check on the recovery rates used as coefficients in the domestic log consumption equation employed in the simulation model (see below), a regression representing this demand was run for the entire 1968–88 period.

In the sawnwood and plywood markets, domestic consumption was assumed to be a final demand, determined by the respective product prices and Indonesian macro-economic factors. Again, as domestic price and taxation time series data were scarce, plywood and sawnwood export unit values were used as proxies for domestic prices for these products.[5] Plywood export demand was considered to be influenced by its export unit value relative to the international price of a substitute (that is, Philippine luan) but in the case of sawnwood export demand, only the export unit value alone proved significant. Both plywood and sawnwood exports were influenced by macroeconomic factors affecting final demand in the main importing countries for each product.[6] Sawnwood and plywood production in Indonesia were determined by their respective prices (as represented by export unit values), processing capacity and costs – including the price of logs.[7] In the sawnwood market, domestic production and consumption was estimated for the entire 1968–88 period; however, as sawnwood was not exported significantly until after 1973, foreign demand could be estimated only for the 1974–88 period. As plywood production did not take off in Indonesia until after 1974, the demand and supply relationships for this market were estimated over 1975–88 only.

The separate recursive relationship linking tropical deforestation to log production (harvesting) was estimated using a logit equation for panelled cross-sectional and time series data across the principal tropical hardwood forest provinces of Indonesia.[8] The relationship estimated the probability of forested relative to non-forested area as a function of log production per square kilometre (km^2), population density and GNP per capita for each province and time period. A dummy variable for 1988 was also employed, as the inventory methods for provincial forestry statistics were modified in this year leading to revisions in the estimates for total forest area.

The results of the estimation of the simultaneous equation system for the three timber product markets and of the deforestation equation are presented in Table 20.5. The twelve endogenous variables of the timber trade supply and demand system are the prices (export unit values), production levels, domestic consumption levels and export levels for roundwood, sawnwood and plywood respectively. The remaining variables used to estimate the supply and demand equations are exogenous, which were also employed along with the respective constant terms as instrumental variables in the two-stage regressions.[9] In Table 20.5, *t*-statistics are displayed in parenthesis under each coefficient, and other regression statistics are placed to the right of each estimated equation.

The deforestation regression indicates that increases in population density have a more significant impact than log production in terms of changes in forested area in Indonesia's forested provinces. For every cubic metre (m^3) of timber extracted per km^2, the proportionate change in forested to non-forested area is –0.6 per cent. For every additional person per km^2, the proportionate fall in forest area is –1.3 per cent. In contrast, a rise in incomes of Indonesian Rupiah (Rp) 10 000 per person, approximately US$6.00 in 1988, would counteract deforestation at a rate of 0.4 per cent.[10]

However, the deforestation equation in Table 20.5 may overestimate the contribution of log extraction alone to regional changes in forest area in Indonesia. First, there is the usual problem of reliability and accuracy of data. More importantly, however, is that data limitations prevent distinguishing in the regression between log production from permanent production forests as opposed to conversion forests. If log production is mainly from conversion forests, then timber extraction is essentially a precursor or by-product to agricultural conversion, which is the principal factor in the resulting deforestation. As indicated in Table 20.3A, close to 50 per cent of Indonesia's total production forests consist of conversion forests, and anecdotal evidence suggests that a good deal of the log production during the period 1973–88 came from the latter forests (Burgess, 1989). To the extent that this is the case, then the deforestation equation may be reflecting mainly the impact of agricultural conversion, rather than the initial logging operations' on changes in forested area. This is supported somewhat by the evidence presented in Table 20.2, which shows logging much more responsible for 'opening up' the forest rather than outright forest conversion.

On the other hand, in the 1980s Indonesia's permanent production forest began contributing an increasingly larger share to overall log production – and is expected to be the main source of tropical hardwood logs in the future. Although forest regulations for this permanent forest estate are increasingly requiring concessions to harvest timber on a sustained production basis, clear cutting is allowed under certain conditions. Moreover, problems of implementing these regulations and policy failures in forestry management also contribute to over-harvesting and clear-cutting of permanent production forests, as well as illegal felling of non-production forests (Barbier, 1987; Burgess, 1989; Gray and Hadi, 1990; Sedjo, 1987; and World Bank, 1989). Evidence for the 1980–90 period suggest that logging damages alone contributed *directly* to just under ten per cent of the annual average rate of deforestation in the Outer Islands of Indonesia (Pearce, Barbier and Markandya, 1990, ch. 5). Moreover, if timber operations in Indonesia are also 'opening up' permanent production and virgin forests to subsequent encroachment and deforestation, then logging may have a major role in *indirectly* furthering the deforestation process of these forested areas.

In short, it is difficult to determine the extent to which the deforestation equation in Table 20.5 overestimates, if at all, the impact of log production on tropical deforestation in Indonesia. The available evidence would suggest that, at the very least, the equation is correct in indicating that this impact is significantly greater than zero and positive.

The key relationships in the simultaneous equation system of the three main timber markets of Indonesia are for price and quantity. Table 20.6 compares the price elasticity estimates for each of the supply and demand equations of the model with other recent estimates for the Southeast Asian region. In general, the elasticity estimates compare favourably. According to our estimates, the supply of timber products in Indonesia appears to be fairly price inelastic. In the case of the processed products, this may reflect the Indonesian policy of expanding sawnwood and plywood capacity over the 1968–88 period. In our regressions, export demand for sawnwood seems slightly more elastic than domestic demand, whereas for plywood the opposite seems to be the case. A similar result was obtained by Vincent (1983) for all Southeast Asian exporters.

The simultaneous equation system and the deforestation regression are combined to form a simulation model of timber trade-deforestation linkages, using data for 1988. The results are displayed in Table 20.7. Given the Indonesian policy of banning log exports, the export log demand equation from Table 20.5 was not included in the model. It is assumed the total log production in Indonesia supplies domestic log demand. The latter is again related to sawnwood and plywood production, although in the simulation model actual recovery rates for the mid-1980s were used as coefficients rather than those generated by the regression for the entire 1968–88 period.[11]

Table 20.7 compares the results of the base case scenario with the actual values of key price, quantity and deforestation variables for Indonesia in 1988. The model appears to be a reasonably good simulation of these variables. The impacts of Indonesia's forest industries and log production on the tropical forest are indicated by effects on forest cover and the annual rate of deforestation. The latter indicator was not simulated by the base case scenario; instead, the most recent FAO estimate of annual deforestation in Indonesia was used.

The following sections compare different policy scenarios to the base case, focusing particularly on the sawnwood export tax intervention, the imposition of an import ban, the use of revenue-raising import surcharges and the implementation of improved sustainable timber management practices. There are, of course, a number of important limitations on the use of the simulation model for these policy scenarios.

First, as discussed above, the linkages of the impacts of log production on tropical deforestation do not take into account changes in the type of forests being exploited (that is, permanent production forests, conversion forests or new forest areas) or in the production management regime (that is, selective cutting or clear cutting). The deforestation equation also cannot distinguish between the direct versus indirect impacts of logging on the forest.

Second, although the model is well suited to examining the effects of a particular policy intervention on the *internal diversion* of timber product flows in Indonesia, that is, between export and domestic markets for sawnwood and plywood, the model does not explicitly indicate the effects of an intervention in terms of *external diversion* of timber products, i.e. between different import markets for sawnwood and plywood. That is, elasticities of substitution by product or by sources of origin in existing importing markets are not explicitly modelled, and the possibility of new import markets opening up as a result of the intervention is not taken into account. In addition, 'leakages', or the ability to avoid any restrictions imposed by an intervention, are also not shown.

Finally, the model is capable of only showing 'static', or one-period, partial equilibrium effects of a policy intervention. Many of the impacts may have economy-wide, or general equilibrium, impacts that feedback to effect the timber product markets and deforestation. In addition, the impacts may have lag, or dynamic, effects that manifest themselves over a medium or long term horizon. Some of the policy interventions themselves, such as the implementation of sustainable management practices, would realistically involve a longer process of implementation than a single period (that is, one year).

Keeping these obvious limitations in mind, it is nevertheless useful to use the simulation model to obtain an approximate indication of the relative impacts of different trade and forest sector policy interventions on Indonesia's timber product markets and forest resource base.

Table 20.6 Comparative price elasticity estimates for Southeast Asian tropical timber

	Time period	Short run	Long run
1. *This Study*			
Indonesia – log supply	1968–84		0.20
Indonesia – log export demand[a]	1968–84		–1.51
Indonesia – sawnwood supply	1968–88		0.27
Indonesia – sawnwood domestic demand	1968–88		–0.36
Indonesia – sawnwood export demand	1974–88		–0.68
Indonesia – plywood supply	1975–88		0.31
Indonesia – plywood domestic demand	1975–88		–0.91
Indonesia – plywood export demand[b]	1975–88		–0.46
2. *Constantino (1988)*[c]			
Indonesia – sawnwood export demand[d]	See note	–0.08	–0.21
Indonesia – plywood export demand	1975–85	–0.26	–0.58
Importers – elasticity of subst.. tropical and temperature sawnwood	1975–85	1.30	2.11
Importers – elasticity of subst., tropical and temperature plywood	1975–85	0.75	1.23
World – elasticity of substitution, source of origin, sawnwood	1979–85	2.50	4.39
World – elasticity of substitution, source of origin, plywood	1979–85	4.56	12.30
3. *Vincent (1992)*[e]			
Peninsular Malaysia – log supply	1973–89		1.10
Peninsular Malaysia – sawnwood supply	1973–89		1.70
Peninsular Malaysia – sawnwood domestic demand	1973–89		–0.55
Other tropical exporters – log export supply	1973–89		2.70
Other tropical exporters – sawnwood export supply	1973–89		0.70
Importers – tropical log demand	1973–89		–1.59
Importers – tropical sawnwood demand	1973–89		–5.67
4. *Vincent (1989)*[f]			
Malaysia – log, supply	1960–85		0.64
Malaysia – sawnwood supply	1960–85		1.00
Malaysia – plywood supply	1960–85		1.00
Malaysia – sawnwood domestic demand	1960–85		–0.27
Malaysia – plywood domestic demand	1960–85		–0.94
Other SE Asia exporters – log supply	1960–85		0.46
Other SE Asia exporters – sawnwood supply	1960–85		1.00
Other SE Asia exporters – plywood supply	1960–85		1.00
Other SE Asia exporters – sawnwood domestic demand	1960–86		–0.53
Other SE Asia exporters – plywood domestic demand	1960–85		–0.85
Importers – SE Asian and Malaysian sawnwood demand	1960–85		–1.22
Importers – SE Asian and Malaysian plywood demand	1960–85		–0.46

Table 20.6 continued

Notes:

[a] Export price of Indonesian logs relative to average world price of temperate non-coniferous logs.

[b] Export price of Indonesian plywood relative to export wholesale spot price of Philippine (luan) plywood.

[c] Elasticity of substitution between sources of origin is defined as the percentage reduction in the ratio of imports from two different countries if the ratio of import prices of the two countries increases by one per cent.

[d] Based on Buongiorno (1979) for coniferous sawnwood.

[e] Elasticities based on Cardellichio *et al.* (1989). Note that in the latter study, Indonesian sawnwood and plywood supply are both estimated to have elasticities of 0.7, and Indonesian sawnwood and plywood domestic demand have own-price elasticities of –0.92 and –1.55 respectively.

[f] Elasticities for sawnwood and plywood supply were assigned a value of one in the analysis.

Table 20.7 Indonesia – timber trade and tropical deforestation simulation model

Key variables	Base case 1988 values	Actual 1988 values
1. *Prices (Rp/m³)*		
Log border-equivalent price (unit value)	36 714	na
Sawnwood export price (unit value)	333 930	262 013
Plywood export price (unit value)	458 179	464 124
2. *Quantities ('000 m³)*		
Log production	28 766	29 819
Log domestic consumption	28 480	28 887
Sawnwood production	9 351	10 290
Sawnwood exports	2 923	3 083
Sawnwood domestic consumption	6 427	7 207
Plywood production	7 770	7 733
Plywood exports	6 383	6 372
Plywood domestic consumption	1 387	1 361
3. *Deforestation (km²)*		
Total forest area	1 401 163	1 401 144
Annual rate of deforestation[a]	13 150	13 150

Notes:

[a] No data available.

[b] Not calculated in simulation model but based on Schmidt (1990). See Table 20.1.

6. Sawnwood export taxes

As indicated in Table 20.4 and discussed above, in 1989 Indonesia imposed substantial taxes on sawnwood exports in an effort to shift processing activities to plywood. A secondary objective of the policy is to improve competitiveness and overall efficiency of sawmills. However, the implications of the policy for wood recovery, log demand and thus tropical deforestation in Indonesia is less clear.

Table 20.8 displays the results of imposing varying levels of sawnwood export taxes in the simulation model of Indonesia's forest sector. The results compare the changes in key price, quantity and deforestation variables to the 1988 base case scenario.

Table 20.8 Indonesia – timber trade and tropical deforestation simulation model policy scenario – sawnwood export tax (per cent change over base case)

Key variables	10 per cent tax %	50 per cent tax %	100 per cent tax %	250 per cent tax %	700 per cent tax %
1. *Prices (Rp/m³)*					
Log border-equivalent price (unit value)	–0.70	–3.35	–6.39	–14.07	–29.03
Sawnwood export price (unit value)	–0.98	–4.72	–9.01	–19.84	–40.93
Plywood export price (unit value)	0.05	–0.23	–0.44	–0.97	–2.00
2. *Quantities ('000 m³)*					
Log production	–0.16	–0.77	–1.47	–3.23	–6.66
Log domestic consumption	–0.15	–0.74	–1.42	–3.12	–6.44
Sawnwood production	–0.33	–1.58	–3.01	–6.64	–13.69
Sawnwood exports	–2.26	–10.89	–20.79	–45.79	–94.47
Sawnwood domestic consumption	0.55	2.66	5.07	11.17	23.06
Plywood production	0.01	0.07	0.13	0.29	0.60
Plywood exports	0.01	0.03	0.06	0.13	0.26
Plywood domestic consumption	0.05	0.25	0.48	1.06	2.18
3. *Deforestation (km²)*					
Total forest area	0.00[a]	0.02	0.03	0.06	0.13
Annual rate of deforestation	–0.3	–1.60	–3.06	–6.73	–13.88

Note: [a] A negligible increase over the base case forest cover of 44 sq km.

In the model, the sawnwood export taxes appear to have the effect of reducing export demand for Indonesian sawnwood, thus lowering the export price received and the quantity exported. The price effects appear to be outweighed by the quantity effects. Although some sawnwood production falls. The impacts on Indonesia's sawnwood markets are more severe the greater the tax. As indicated in the model, a tax rate of 700 per cent imposed in 1988 would effectively choke off sawnwood export demand. With proposed taxes of US$250–$4000 per m^3, actual government policy would be represented by the higher range of sawnwood export taxes shown in Table 20.8.

Significantly, the imposition of a tax on sawnwood exports does not appear to instigate a major shift of processing capacity to plywood – at least not in the one-period duration of the simulation model. Only at extremely high rates of taxation does this occur even slightly, and it appears that increased domestic plywood consumption is the most noticeable effect. Evidence would suggest that there are several structural factors limiting diversion of production between Indonesia's sawnwood and plywood industry in the short term, such as the much newer vintages of capital in plywood milling, and its export orientation that requires higher production and possibly access to better quality logs (Constantino, 1990). The simulation model therefore confirms that, if a sawnwood export tax is to shift Indonesian processing capacity towards greater plywood expansion, then it will be a long-term process. Unfortunately, the economic costs of reduced sawnwood exports and production appear to be severe from the outset.

Only at high rates of taxation does the sawnwood export tax have a modest impact on deforestation. The inability of the policy to increase plywood output in the short term means that the net reduction in sawnwood production translates into less log extraction. At higher rates of taxation, the fall in log production is much larger, thus resulting in a lower rate of deforestation. However, as noted, the economic costs particularly in terms of lost exchange earnings of a prohibitive sawnwood export tax are severe. Moreover, if the policy is successful over the long run in shifting processing to plywood production, then one would expect log demand, and thus deforestation rates, also to be revived.

In sum, a prohibitive sawnwood export tax in Indonesia appears to be a high cost strategy for shifting processing capacity to plywood production and export, which may only be successful – if at all – over the long term. In addition, the policy does not appear to be an effective approach for reducing timber-related deforestation in Indonesia. Only modest reductions in deforestation may occur, and these will be short-lived if plywood production begins replacing the lost sawnwood output.

7. Import ban

Some environmental pressure groups in Western tropical timber importing countries have been urging their governments to ban the import of tropical timber. or at least imports of timber that is 'unsustainably' produced. Consumer-led boycotts against tropical timber products have also been instigated. The presumption is that an import ban is the most effective way of ending timber-related deforestation in tropical forest countries. Despite the various economic and legal implications of such a move, as well as questions about its effectiveness, an import ban on tropical timber is a realistic possibility in the near future.[12]

The first column of Table 20.9 indicates the effects of a total import ban, compared to the base case scenario, in the timber trade-deforestation model of Indonesia. In order to simulate an import ban in the model, large price changes were used deliberately to constrain sawnwood and plywood exports to zero. Timber product prices are therefore no longer endogenously generated by the model, and as a result, are not shown in Table 20.9. Also, the functional form of the deforestation equation and its estimation using regional panel data imply that the large changes in log production associated with the import ban scenario cannot be used to predict reliably the effects on forest cover and deforestation. Thus the impacts on deforestation are also not reported for this policy scenario simulation.

As shown in Table 20.9, an import ban would have a devastating impact on Indonesia's forest industry in the short term. Although there would be significant diversion of plywood and sawnwood exports to domestic consumption, this would be insufficient to compensate for the loss of exports. Net production in both processing industries would fall. Given its export orientation, the plywood industry would be particularly hurt – reducing its output by over 40 per cent. Net production losses in the sawnwood industry would be closer to 10 per cent. The overall effect is to lower domestic log demand in the short term by around 25–30 per cent.

The policy scenario is of course assuming that the import ban is 100 per cent effective. It is unlikely that all importers of Indonesia's tropical timber products – many of which are also newly industrialising or producer countries with processing capacities – would go along with a Western-imposed ban. In any case, one would expect that over the longer term there would be some diversion of Indonesian plywood and sawnwood exports to either new import markets or existing markets that prove to be less stringent in applying the ban. As discussed above, these effects cannot be captured in our model.

In addition, the long-term implications of an import ban on tropical deforestation are also uncertain. Even if the ban is 100 per cent effective in the short term, any resulting reduction in tropical deforestation is likely to be short-lived. There are several reasons for this.

First, as indicated in the model, diversion of timber products to satisfy domestic demand is likely to continue as Indonesian population and economic activity expands (see Table 20.5). Thus one can expect the wood processing industries to recover somewhat through re-orientation to meet local consumption of timber products. Moreover, past evidence suggests that domestic-oriented processing in Indonesia is less efficient than export-oriented processing, implying poorer wood recovery rates and greater log demand (Constantino, 1990).

Pressure on the tropical hardwood forests may therefore increase after the initial 'shock' of a ban.

Table 20.9 Indonesia – timber trade and tropical deforestation simulation model policy scenario – import ban and revenue raising taxes (per cent change over base case)

Key variables	Total import ban[a] %	One per cent raising import tax[b] %	Five per cent raising import tax[d] %
1. *Prices (Rp/m³)*			
Log border-equivalent price (unit value)	–	–0.17	–0.82
Sawnwood export price (unit value)	–	–0.11	–0.54
Plywood export price (unit value)	–	–0.21	–1.03
2. *Quantities ('000 m³)*			
Log production	–28.33	–0.44	–0.19
Log domestic consumption	–27.37	–0.04	–0.18
Sawnwood production	–10.64	–0.03	–0.14
Sawnwood exports	–100.00	–0.23	–1.12
Sawnwood domestic consumption	30.01	0.06	0.30
Plywood production	–43.84	–0.04	–0.22
Plywood exports	–100.00	–0.10	–0.51
Plywood domestic consumption	214.51	0.23	1.12
3. *Deforestation (km²)*			
Total forest area	–	0.00[c]	0.01
Annual rate of deforestation	–	–0.41	–0.72

Notes:

[a] Large price changes were used deliberately to constrain sawnwood and plywood exports to zero in this simulation and therefore are no longer endogenously generated by the model. Also, the functional form of the deforestation equation and its estimation using regional panel data imply that the large changes in log production associated with the import ban scenario cannot be used to predict reliably the effects on forest cover and deforestation. Thus both price and deforestation effects are eliminated from this policy scenario simulation.

[b] A total of US$23.1 million (1980 prices) in revenue would be raised, with US$5.8 million and US$17.3 million from Indonesian sawnwood and plywood exports respectively.

[c] A negligible increase over the base case forest cover of 53 sq km.

[d] A total of US$113.9 million (1980 prices) in revenue would be raised, with US$28.5 million and US$85.4 million from Indonesian sawnwood and plywood exports respectively.

However, it is unlikely that the domestic market in Indonesia will generate the same demand for higher valued timber products as the international market. Instead, domestic demand is likely to be strongest for high-volume but lower valued wood products. As a consequence, it may be difficult for Indonesia to justify holding as large a proportion of its tropical forests as permanent production forests if the expected economic returns from sustainable management decline as a result of the ban. More of the resource may be shifted to conversion forests, and timber production will become residual to satisfying the growing demand for agricultural land. In short, without the timber trade providing increased value added in the form of external demand for higher valued products, there may be less reason for Indonesia 'holding on' to these forests as opposed to converting them to an alternative use, such as agriculture (Barbier, 1993; and Vincent, 1990).

To summarize, a total import ban would cause a major diversion of Indonesian timber products to meet domestic demand. Although in the short term net production of wood products, and thus log demand, would fall, this situation would not necessarily be sustained over the long run. Even if this is not the case, the ban may be ineffective in permanently reducing tropical deforestation because, in the first place, timber production is not the main source of deforestation in Indonesia, and secondly, as the value of holding on to the forest for timber production decreases the incentives to convert more of the resource to agriculture will increase.

8. Revenue-raising import tax

International cooperation and compensation to assist developing countries in achieving sustainable management of timber production forests have also been discussed in recent years. For example, the International Tropical Timber Council (ITTC) unanimously adopted a 'Year 2000 Target' that encourages 'ITTO members to progress towards achieving sustainable management of tropical forests and trade in tropical forest timber from sustainably managed sources by the year 2000' (Decision 3(X) ITTC, 1992). One suggestion for raising additional funds for this strategy is for importing countries to impose a small import surcharge on tropical timber, which is then directed to tropical forest countries that have shown 'demonstrable progress' towards achieving the Year 2000 Target.

A recent study has indicated that a 1–3 per cent surcharge on the tropical timber imports (excluding plywood and based on 1986 trade levels) of the EEC, Japan and USA would raise approximately US$312.4 to 94.1 million with little additional distortionary effects (NEI, 1989). Buongiorno and Manurung (1992) also examine the scope for a five per cent revenue-raising import levy on tropical timber by the Union pour le Commerce des Bois Tropicaux (UCBT) of the EEC.[13] The results indicate that tropical timber exporters would lose around US$44.8 million in trade earnings – with Indonesia and Malaysia suffering the worst – but importing countries would earn US$87.7 million in additional revenues. Thus if the funds raised by the tax were rebated to exporting countries, they could be made better off by over US$40 million.

The final two columns of Table 20.9 show the impacts of a one and five per cent revenue-raising import tax on Indonesian tropical timber exports in the simulation model. In the case of a one per cent surcharge, a total of US$23.1 million (1980 prices) in revenue would be raised, with US$5.8 million and US$17.3 million from Indonesian sawnwood and plywood exports respectively. For the five per cent surcharge, a total of US$113.9 million (1980 prices) in revenue would be raised, with US$28.5 million and US$85.4 million from Indonesian sawnwood and plywood exports respectively. When compared to the revenue estimates from the NEI (1989) study, the above figures would suggest that, in the case of Indonesia, applying the import surcharge to plywood would significantly raise the total amount of financing appropriated.

The results shown in Table 20.9 confirm that a small import surcharge would have very little distortionary effect on Indonesia's timber product flows and prices. There would also be a negligible direct impact on deforestation. However, around the five per cent level, the impacts of the surcharge on exports in particular would become more noticeable. Thus from the standpoint of minimizing additional distortionary effects, the policy scenario confirms that an import surcharge of less than five per cent would be optimal.

A more pertinent issue is whether it is worth imposing an import surcharge to raise revenue for sustainable management of tropical forests. In the simulation model, the same result, and thus the same amount of revenue, could be achieved if Indonesia raised the money for its own 'sustainable management' initiatives by imposing a revenue-raising export surcharge of one to five per cent. The NEI study argues that the imposition of an export levy by producing countries themselves has the advantage of directly addressing the forest management systems of these countries, as well as avoiding the transaction costs involved in international transfers, but prevents obvious problems of monitoring and evaluating success in achieving sustainable management. The counter-argument is that an import surcharge not only has problems of transaction costs and administration, but that it is also possibly discriminatory if it is limited only to the *tropical* timber trade. Moreover, the import surcharge-cum-international transfer mechanism would still require the cooperation of producer countries, as well as raise similar problems of monitoring and evaluation of progress towards sustainable management and expenditures. Finally, there is the issue of whether the amount of funds raised through any trade surcharge would be adequate for the task, and whether it would be a more appropriate avenue for raising additional large-scale funding *outside* the timber trade altogether (Barbier *et al.*, 1994).[14]

In sum, it is possible to raise revenue through an import surcharge of less than five per cent with minimal distortionary effects on Indonesia's timber trade and production. The key issue is whether this is the most efficient and appropriate means of raising financing for improved sustainable management of production forests.

9. Sustainable timber management

An alternative to the above trade interventions would be a more direct policy initiative by Indonesia to improve 'sustainable' management of its remaining production forests. As discussed above, several studies have pointed to considerable problems of policy failures in Indonesian forestry management that are contributing to over-harvesting and clear-cutting of permanent production forests, as well as illegal felling of non-production forests (Barbier, 1987; Burgess, 1989; Gray and Hadi, 1990; Sedjo, 1987; and World Bank, 1989). Correcting these policy failures would improve sustainable management of Indonesia's remaining tropical forests, and thus reduce timber-related deforestation, but would also mean higher harvesting costs per m^3 of wood extracted.

Table 20.10 indicates the most likely effects of such a 'sustainable' management policy scenario, which it represented by an increase in harvesting costs. As there is insufficient data to determine the extent to which costs would rise if such a policy were to be implemented in Indonesia, we have arbitrarily chosen a 25 and 50 per cent harvest cost increase for comparison.

A surprising feature of the scenario is that although log prices are affected significantly by the increased harvest costs, any resulting impacts on the rest of Indonesia's forestry sector seem to be somewhat dissipated. There appears to be several factors at work. First, the price-elasticity of log supply for Indonesia is very inelastic in our model (see Tables 20.5 and 20.6). This is not surprising given that Indonesian policy has been to devote log production solely to supplying domestic processing capacity, which of course has expanded considerably over the 1968–88 period. Second, increased log costs are only one component of the total factor costs of Indonesia's processing industries, and have increasingly become the least important component in recent years (Constantino, 1990). Finally, Indonesia's sawnwood and plywood exports seem to be the least affected by the increased harvest costs, which would suggest that external demand factors exert an important counter-acting influence.

There is reason to believe that the impacts of the sustainable management scenario on reducing timber-related deforestation may be underestimated in Table 20.10. As discussed above, the deforestation equation in the model can only record changes in forest cover due to changes in overall log production rates. It cannot distinguish between *qualitative* changes in the management of log production that may also affect timber-related deforestation more indirectly, such as controlling residual stand damage, improved replanting and reforestation, reduced high-grading of stands, limiting trespass, improving the incentives to control stand abandonment and encroachment, and so forth.[15] These latter factors may be more important in timber-related deforestation than log extraction alone. In addition, some sustainable management techniques, such as utilising lesser known species and improved harvesting techniques, may actually increase the amount of logs produced from a given timber stand, thus simultaneously limiting harvest costs and reducing the pressure to exploit the remaining tropical forest.

Table 20.10 *Indonesia – timber trade and tropical deforestation simulation model policy scenario – sustainable timber management (per cent change over base case)*

Key variables	25 per cent rise in harvest costs %	50 per cent rise in harvest costs %
1. *Prices (Rp/m³)*		
Log border-equivalent price (unit value)	41.59	83.06
Sawnwood export price (unit value)	4.04	8.09
Plywood export price (unit value)	2.86	5.72
2. *Quantities ('000 m³)*		
Log production	–0.94	–1.87
Log domestic consumption	–1.37	–2.73
Sawnwood production	–1.89	–3.77
Sawnwood exports	–1.03	–2.05
Sawnwood domestic consumption	–2.28	–4.55
Plywood production	–0.87	–1.73
Plywood exports	–0.38	–0.75
Plywood domestic consumption	–3.12	–6.24
3. *Deforestation (km²)*		
Total forest area	0.02	0.04
Annual rate of deforestation	–2.28	–4.23

Finally, it is unlikely that the implementation of any sustainable management techniques would occur in a single year, as implied by the simulation scenario. A longer lead time for implementation would mean more time for the Indonesian forest industries to absorb the increased costs, but it would also imply a longer period before the effects on reducing deforestation would be fully felt.

In sum, Indonesia's timber industries may not be badly affected by the higher harvest costs associated with implementing sustainable forestry management policies. Although there would be some reduction in tropical deforestation due to reduced log production, this direct effect may be less significant than the improvement in forest management and protection resulting from qualitative changes in timber stand management and ownership.

10. Conclusion

The simulation model developed to examine the relationship between Indonesia's timber trade and tropical deforestation has provided some important insights into this linkage as well as the scope for the use of trade policy instruments to limit deforestation. As discussed throughout, there are obvious constraints on the use of such a model to examine such dynamic, complex and pervasive effects. Nevertheless, the model and the policy simulations would suggest extreme caution in the use of broad trade policy interventions as a means to affect timber-related deforestation in Indonesia, and in some cases even as an economic tool to develop further Indonesia's timber processing capacity.

First, it is clear that timber production is not the major cause of tropical deforestation in Indonesia. Even where timber production is a factor in deforestation, most timber-related deforestation, including subsequent deforestation by agricultural encroachment, may have more to do with the management and regulation of the timber stand than with the amount of logs extracted from the stand *per se*.

Second, extreme trade interventions, such as the current GOI policy of prohibitive sawnwood export taxes and a total ban by consumer countries on the imports of tropical timber products, may have an initial 'shock' impact on tropical deforestation in Indonesia. However, this may be short-lived as dynamic factors in the economy – notably the shifting of processing capacity or the transfer of permanent production forests to conversion forests – may take hold. Both forms of trade intervention clearly impose high economic costs on Indonesia's forestry industries. Surprisingly, a high sawnwood export tax would appear to make little headway in the short run in achieving its stated objective of spurring development of Indonesia's plywood sector.

Third, an import surcharge on tropical timber imports would have minimal distortionary impacts on Indonesia's timber trade – provided that it was imposed at a level of less than five per cent. A more pertinent issue is whether this policy is the correct means for raising funds for sustainable management of production forests, and whether the financing raised would be sufficient for the task.

Finally, improvements in sustainable timber forest management and regulation by Indonesia could raise log harvesting costs, but there may not be such significant impacts on Indonesia's processed products and trade. The reduction in timber-related deforestation in Indonesia resulting from the policy may not be fully captured by the model.

In sum, there seems little scope for the use of trade policy interventions as a means to reducing tropical deforestation in Indonesia. If there is concern over timber-related deforestation, a more appropriate approach may be to deal more directly with the problem by improving sustainable production forest management and regulation at the timber stand level. However, a key factor is whether the GOI has sufficient incentive to ensure that better forest management policies are implemented and enforced. By ensuring access of sustainably managed timber to import markets and by providing financial assistance for Indonesian policy efforts, the major tropical timber consumer countries could go a long way towards encouraging the appropriate incentives for action by the Indonesian government.

Focusing on a single country has allowed us to examine specific linkages between trade policy interventions and tropical deforestation. At the same time, international trade by definition involves economic linkages across more than one country. In the case of tropical timber, trade interventions affecting one country's exports can have important implications for substitution between alternative suppliers and the resulting impacts on regional deforestation. Thus examining trade policy changes and the geographical pattern of production across competing tropical timber product exporters, such as the South East Asian countries, remains an important area for further research.

Notes

1. Barbier (1987) points out that much of the reported decline in log production over the initial period 1979–82 can be attributed to depressed world prices for all timber products, and therefore, was not necessarily attributable to less exploitation because of increased processing activities. Moreover, there has always been a discrepancy between officially reported harvesting levels and rates based on processing industry output. For example, official logging statistics suggested that total log production peaked, before the ban in 1985, at around 25.3 million m^3 per year and decline initially with the ban. In contrast. estimates of log demand based on processing industry output, capacity and conversion rates indicate that log demand reached 27.3 million m^3 per annum soon after the ban, and of course continues to increase as capacity and output expands.
2. Specific export taxes on wet and dry veneer of US$250 per m^3 were also imposed. However, from Table 20.3C it is clear that Indonesia does not produce or export substantial amounts of veneer.
3. The time series and cross-sectional data used in estimating these relationships and constructing the model came from a variety of sources, including World Bank, FAO, IMF and GOI publications, and previous studies on the Indonesia forestry sector cited in this paper.
4. The main importers of Indonesian logs over 1968–84 were China. Hong Kong, Japan, Korea and Singapore.
5. Given that Indonesian sawnwood and plywood are tradeables, the assumption that domestic and export prices of these products are highly correlated over time seems reasonable. This is confirmed by the limited time series data available on both export and domestic prices.
6. The main importers of Indonesian plywood over 1975–88 were China. Hong Kong, Japan. Singapore and USA. The main importers of Indonesian sawnwood over 1974–88 were China. Hong Kong, Italy, Japan. Korea. Malaysia. the Netherlands, Singapore, Thailand and UK. Given

the predominance of Japan and its main South East Asian newly industrializing competitors among these importers. the Japanese/Indonesian exchange rate and Japanese industrial activity proved to have strong explanatory power in the demand for Indonesian sawnwood exports (see Table 20.5).

7. However, because the price of logs was represented by log export unit values, it is only included in the estimation for the period before the ban. 1968–84.
8. Twenty provinces selected, spread over the Indonesian islands of Sumatra, Kalimantan, Sulawesi, Maluku, Irian Jaya and Nusa Tenggara. Data were available for the years 1973, 1979, 1981, 1982, 1984 and 1988.
9. As some of the instrumental variables were highly correlated, the list of instruments included in each two-stage regression was sometimes modified.
10. Indonesia's real GNP per capita in 1988 (1980 prices) was approximately US$230.
11. In the simulation model, the log domestic demand equation is therefore CONLI = 77.95 1.5*QSWI 1.85*QPWI. A comparison with the regression for CONLI of Table 20.5 indicates that, by the mid-1980s, recovery rates for sawmills in Indonesia had improved slightly, whereas they had deteriorated somewhat for plymills. This seems reasonable intuitively, given that by the 1980s the expansion in sawmill capacity as the GOI attempted to improve efficiency and quality, whereas plymill capacity was deliberately encouraged to expand.
12. For a review of the arguments, see Barbier *et al.* (1994).
13. The UCBT countries are Belgium, Denmark, France, Germany, Luxembourg, the Netherlands and the United Kingdom.
14. One problem is that the scale of financing required may be well beyond what can be raised from either an import or export surcharge levied on the trade. For example, Agenda 21 of the UN Conference on Environment and Development has estimated that international aid of over US$I.5 billion annually will be required by tropical forest countries to reduce deforestation (ITTC, 1992).
15. *Trespass* is a forestry term that refers to losses due to logging theft, which could also be extended to include losses due to graft. *High-grading* refers to the removal of high-valued timber and leaving a degraded timber stand.

References

Amelung, T. and M. Diehl (1992), *Deforestation of Tropical Rain Forests: Economic Causes and Impact on Development*, Mohn, Germany: Tubingen.

Arnold, M. (1991), 'Forestry expansion: a study of technical, economic and ecological factors', Oxford: Oxford Forestry Institute Paper No. 3.

Barbier, E.B. (1987), 'Natural resources policy and economic framework', Annex 1 in J. Tarrant *et al.* (eds), *Natural Resources and Environmental Management in Indonesia*, Jakarta: USAID.

Barbier, E.B. (1993), 'Economic aspects of tropical deforestation in South East Asia', in *Global Ecology and Biogeography Letters*, **3**, 215–34.

Barbier, E.B., J.C. Burgess, J.T. Bishop and B.A. Aylward (1994), *The Economics of the Tropical Timber Trade*, London: Earthscan Publications.

Bourke, I.J. (1988), *Trade in Forest Products: A Study of the Barriers Faced by the Developing Countries*, FAO Forestry Paper 83, Rome: FAO.

Buongiorno, J. (1979), 'Income and price elasticities for sawnwood and wood-based panels: a pooled cross-section and time series analysis', *Forest Science*, **9**, 141–8.

Buongiorno, J. and T. Manurung (1992), 'Predicted effects of an import tax in the European Community on the international trade in tropical timbers', mimeo, Department of Forestry, University of Wisconsin, Madison.

Burgess, P.F. (1989), 'Asia', in D. Poore *et al.* (eds), *No Timber Without Trees: Sustainability in the Tropical Forest*, Chapter 5, London: Earthscan Publications Ltd.

Cardellichio, P.A., Y.C. Youn, D.M. Adams, R.W. Joo and J.T. Chmelik (1989), *A Preliminary Analysis of Timber and Timber Products Production, Consumption, Trade, and Prices in the Pacific Rim Until 2000*, CINTRAFOR Working Paper 22, Center for International Trade in Forest Products, University of Washington, Seattle.

Constantino, L.F. (1988a), 'Analysis of the international and domestic demand for Indonesian wood products', mimeo, Report for the FAO, Dept. of Rural Economy, University of Alberta, Edmonton, Alberta.

Constantino, L.F. (1988b), 'Demand, supply and development issues in the Indonesian forest sector', mimeo, Report for the FAO, Dept. of Rural Economy, University of Alberta, Edmonton, Alberta.

Constantino, L.F. (1990), *On the Efficiency of Indonesia's Sawmilling and Plymilling Industries*, D.G. of Forest Utilization, Ministry of Forestry, Jakarta: Government of Indonesia and FAO.

Constantino. L.F. and D. Ingram (1990), *Supply-Demand Projections for the Indonesian Forest Sector*, D.G. of Forest Utilization, Ministry of Forestry, Jakarta: Government of Indonesia and FAO.

Fitzgerald, B. (1986), *An Analysis of Indonesian Trade Policies: Countertrade, Downstream Processing, Import Restrictions and the Deletion Program*, CPD Discussion Paper 1986–22, Washington, DC: World Bank.

Gillis, M. (1988), 'Indonesia: public policies, resource management, and the tropical forest', in R. Repetto and M. Gillis (eds), *Public Policies and the Misuse of Forest Resources*, Cambridge: Cambridge University Press.

Gillis, M. (1990), 'Forest incentive policies', Paper prepared for the World Bank Forest Policy Paper, Washington, DC: The World Bank.

Gray, J.A. and S. Hadi (1990), *Fiscal Policies and Pricing in Indonesian Forestry*, D.G. of Forest Utilization, Ministry of Forestry, Jakarta: Government of Indonesia and FAO.

International Tropical Timber Council (ITTC) (1992), *Report on Preparations for the 1992 United Nations Conference on Environment and Development*, ITTC(XII)/8, 12th Session, 6–14 May, Cameroon: Yaoundé.

Netherlands Economic Institute (NEI) (1989), *An Import Surcharge on the Import of Tropical Timber in the European Community: An Evaluation*, Rotterdam: NEI.

Pearce, D.W., E.B. Barbier and A. Markandya (1990), *Sustainable Development: Economics and Environment in the Third World*, London: Edward Elgar and Earthscan.

Schmidt, R. (1990), 'Sustainable management of tropical moist forests', Presentation for ASEAN Sub-Regional Seminar, Indonesia, Forest Resources Division, Forestry Department, Rome: FAO.

Sedjo, R.A. (1987), 'Incentives and distortions in Indonesian forest policy', mimeo, Washington, DC: Resources for the Future.

Sedjo, R.A. and K.S. Lyon (1990), *The Long-Term Adequacy of World Timber Supply*, Washington, DC: Resources for the Future.

Vincent, J.R. (1989), 'Optimal tariffs on intermediate and final goods: the case of tropical forest products', *Forest Science*, **5**, 720–31.

Vincent, J.R. (1990), 'Don't boycott tropical timber', *Journal of Forestry*, **8**, 56.

Vincent, J.R. (1992a), 'A simple, nonspatial modelling approach for analyzing a country's forest-products trade policies', in R. Haynes, P. Harou and J. Mikowski (eds), *Forestry Sector Analysis for Developing Countries*, Proceedings of Working Groups, Integrated Land Use and Forest Policy and Forest Sector Analysis Meetings, 10th Forestry World Congress, Paris.

Vincent, J.R. (1992b), 'The tropical timber trade and sustainable development', *Science*, **56**, 1651–5.

Vincent, J.R. and C.S. Binkley (1991), *Forest Based Industrialization: A Dynamic Perspective*, Development Discussion Paper No. 389, Harvard Institute for International Development (HIID), Cambridge, Massachusetts.

Vincent, J.R., A.K. Gandapur and D.J. Brooks (1990), 'Species substitution and tropical log imports by Japan', *Forest Science*, **6**, 657–64.

World Bank (1989), *Indonesia – Forest Land and Water: Issues in Sustainable Development*, Washington, DC: The World Bank.

21. Trade in timber-based forest products and the implications of the Uruguay Round

This chapter examines the implications of the recently signed Uruguay Round Agreement of the General Agreement on Tariffs and Trade (GATT) for trade in forest products. An estimate is provided of the likely trade impacts on selected forest products of the reduction in tariff rates in key importing markets. The article also discusses the potential contributions of the Uruguay Round to reducing some important non-tariff barriers to forest products trade. Despite the progress achieved in the Uruguay Round, a number of 'new' trade barriers are emerging in the forest products trade that could undermine this progress and pose problems for the GATT/World Trade Organization.

Trade in forest products is highly regionalized within three important trading blocs – the Pacific rim, North America and Western Europe (see Table 21.1). Within each trading bloc the major importers are mainly industrialized countries. More than one-half of global forest products imports by value are accounted for by Europe, and over 25 per cent of the remaining imports are to Canada, Japan and the United States (FAO, 1994). Canada and the United States are the major world exporters of industrial roundwood, sawnwood and wood pulp; European countries are the major world exporters of paper products.

In recent years, developing countries, particularly in Asia, have continually increased their share of global imports, mainly logs and semi-finished wood products as raw materials for export-oriented processing industries. Indonesia and Malaysia have emerged as dominant world exporters of non-coniferous wood-based panels, logs and sawnwood, and Brazil, Chile and the newly industrializing countries of Asia are becoming major exporters of wood pulp and paper products. In general, the trade in forest products has shifted towards value-added processed products, with the fastest expansion in processing capacity occurring in Asia, and short- and long-term projections of the forest products trade confirm the increasing importance of developing countries as both exporters and importers of value-added forest products (Barbier *et al.*, 1994).

Trends in pre-Uruguay Round trade barriers to forest products

Trade in forest products has generally benefited from successive postwar GATT agreements. Tariff barriers to forest products trade have continued to decrease in recent years, particularly in the post-Tokyo Round era (Bourke in FAO, 1988). The extent of tariff reductions differs according to the market and the product. With few exceptions, tariff rates in developed country markets had fallen to very low levels even before the Uruguay Round schedules were agreed (see Table 21.2).

However, tariff escalation – the extent to which tariff levels rise with the level of value-added processing of a forest product – has continued in most developed countries, with specific processed products such as wood-based panels, builder's joinery, coated and corrugated paper, craft and furniture generally receiving relatively higher rates. In comparison with developed country markets, tariff rates have been consistently higher – often substantially – in developing country markets. Although tariff escalation is also a feature in most developing country markets, some countries have preferred a high uniform rate applied across all forest products.

One important impact of the decline in tariff rates for forest products in developed country markets is that the tariff differential between most favoured nation (MFN) and generalized system of preferences (GSP) rates has been reduced significantly (Bourke in FAO, 1988). Most tariff reductions have led to a general decline in the MFN rate, while the GSP rate (often zero) has been left largely unchanged. This suggests that, for certain forest products, exporters facing the full MFN rates may have gained more from falling tariff rates than developing countries that had previously benefited from the GSP and other preferential schemes.

The most common non-tariff measures applied to forest products trade have been quantitative restrictions and/or quality controls directed at specific products, wood species and even individual exporters. However, a variety of non-tariff measures have been employed, and their use has been both prominent and increasing for some products in the period leading up to the conclusion of the Uruguay Round.

Implications of the Uruguay Round for the forest products trade

The Uruguay Round Agreement signed in Marrakesh, Morocco, in April 1994, has a number of important implications for trade in forest products. Tariff elimination for pulp and paper items was agreed by Canada, the European Union, Japan and the United States, and several other major importers, including Finland, the Republic of Korea and New Zealand. Using the 1986 level of tariffs as the base rate, these countries will halve tariffs by the year 2000 and phase them out completely by 2004. Most of the other countries that have not agreed to complete tariff elimination for pulp and paper products will also be reducing their tariffs, but to a lesser extent.

The major developed country importers arc also committed to reducing tariffs by 50 per cent for solid wood products on an average trade-weighted basis over a five-year period starting in 1995. In the case of furniture, some major importers such as the European Union, Japan and the United States have agreed

Table 21.1 Forest products direction of trade, 1992 (US$ million)[a]

Major importers \ Major exporters	Canada	United States	Sweden	Finland	Germany	France	Indonesia	Austria
United States	11 863		92	336	196	95	402	32
Germany	591	702	2 116	1 553		1 179	58	921
Japan	1 964	3 802	43	100	37	16	1 006	3
United Kingdom	804	580	1 594	1 372	739	476	106	141
Italy	365	639	533	322	729	656	63	1 052
France	248	318	664	750	1 152		54	187
Netherlands	157	399	624	588	820	285	151	112
China	306	769	87	69	79	13	949	28
Belgium-Luxembourg	255	278	351	255	507	431	158	69
Spain	58	277	262	408	267	474	2	46
Republic of Korea	236	835	14	30	12	7	340	5
Canada		2 053	8	27	36	25	14	4
Hong Kong	41	256	20	55	26	22	210	4
Austria	34	16	1 53	1 23	689	59	1	
Denmark	3	40	604	306	196	37	16	14
Switzerland	37	15	173	178	396	155	0	195
Australia	117	229	29	127	89	30	35	11
Thailand	48	62	35	19	21	11	21	1
Mexico	45	1 025	23	15	9	6	18	10
Sweden	31	32		220	164	27	2	14
Singapore	34	66	45	37	19	12	157	7
Norway	4	7	365	108	40	5	6	4
Portugal	12	12	46	45	38	47	0	4
Egypt	26	75	109	78	21	16	48	11
Finland	22	10	103		54	13	1	1
Other developed	307	893	373	415	560	0	6	251
Other developing	561	1 657	542	624	397	0	152	217
Total	18 167	14 947	9 008	8 160	7 293	4 097	3 976	3 344

Table 21.1 Continued

Malaysia	Belgium-Luxembourg	Netherlands	United Kingdom	Former USSR	Italy	Japan	Other developed	Other developing	Total
131	62	46	88	4	56	192	188	902	14 685
141	553	680	293	151	554	31	1 608	419	11 548
1 091	7	4	9	489	5		787	1 876	11 239
137	261	279		164	128	28	1 019	559	8 387
41	89	47	83	186		7	1 147	578	6 537
83	487	337	257	88	318	19	633	507	6 082
82	431		190	50	64	17	426	203	4 599
349	5	22	22	27	9	332	155	652	3 873
74		403	176	47	72	7	204	128	3 415
7	45	57	69	26	116	5	396	274	2 787
507	2	9	10	29	4	91	141	311	2 583
4	3	7	27	1	14	20	7	41	2 291
107	2	13	30	0	9	381	76	615	1 867
5	26	20	19	30	53	2	415	22	1 667
4	21	23	48	11	7	1	189	35	1 555
1	20	25	21	0	50	4	80	24	1 374
103	13	14	28	0	48	70	337	79	1 359
417	2	14	11	11	4	67	100	410	1 254
0	3	2	1	0	2	4	18	42	1 223
2	15	19	40	55	4	7	386	40	1058
306	3	10	25	0	3	99	91	110	1 024
2	4	18	14	8	2	1	54	42	684
1	16	66	22	1	11	1	173	170	665
9	5	2	7	5	11	4	148	69	644
0	5	4	26	151	4	6	148	93	641
5	0	251	131	65	136	47	408	100	3 948
95	36	131	200	92	142	190	514	896	6 346
3 704	2 116	2 503	1 847	1 671	1 826	1 633	9 846	9 197	103 334

Note: [a] Contains estimated and unofficial figures.

Source: FAO (1994)

Table 21.2 Uruguay Round tariff reductions in developed countries by major industrial product group[a]

Product category	Imports from all sources				Imports from developing countries			
	Import value[b] (US$ billlon)	Tariff pre-UR (%)	Tariff post-UR (%)	Reduction (%)	Import value[b] (US$ billion)	Tariff pre-UR (%)	Tariff post-UR (%)	Reduction (%)
Fish and fish products	18.5	6.1	4.5	26	10.6	6.6	4.8	27
Forest products[c]	40.6	3.5	1.1	69	11.5	4.6	1.7	63
Textiles and clothing	66.4	15.5	12.1	22	33.2	14.6	11.3	23
Leather, rubber, footwear and travel goods	31.7	8.9	7.3	18	12.2	8.1	6.6	19
Metals	69.4	3.7	1.4	62	24.4	2.7	0.9	67
Chemicals and photographic supplies	61.0	6.7	3.7	45	8.2	7.2	3.8	47
Transport equipment	96.3	7.5	5.8	23	7.6	3.8	3.1	18
Non-electrical machinery	118.1	4.8	1.9	60	9.8	4.7	1.6	66
Electrical machinery	86.0	6.6	3.5	47	19.2	6.3	3.3	48
Mineral products and precious stones/metals	72.9	2.3	1.1	52	22.2	2.6	0.8	69
Manufactured articles NES	76.1	5.5	2.4	56	10.9	6.5	3.1	52
Industrial tropical products	32.8	4.2	2.0	52	14.4	4.2	1.9	55
Natural resource products	80.2	3.2	2.1	34	33.4	4.0	2.7	33
All industrial products	736.9	6.3	3.8	40	169.7	6.8	4.3	37

Notes:
UR = Uruguay Round; NES = not elsewhere specified.
Tariffs are based on weighted averages on imports from all sources
[a] Excluding petroleum products.
[b] Import data from 1990 or latest available year, and for all developed country participants in the Uruguay Round, excluding imports from free trade area partners (e.g. intra-European Union trade) and from contractual preferential arrangements.
[c] Wood, pulp, paper and furniture.

Source: GATT (1994).

Table 21.3 Uruguay Round tariff reduction profile by major industrial product groups: developed countries[a]

Product category	Import value[b] (US$ billion)	Duty free Pre-UR	Duty free Post-UR	0.1–5% Pre-UR	0.1–5% Post-UR	5.1–10% Pre-UR	5.1–10% Post-UR	10.1–15% Pre-UR	10.1–15% Post-UR	15.1–35% Pre-UR	15.1–35% Post-UR	Over 35% Pre-UR	Over 35% Post-UR
		Percentage of imports											
Fish and fish products	18.5	21	24	42	44	18	21	12	8	7	3	0	0
Forest products[c]	40.6	50	85	24	6	20	7	2	2	4	0	1	0
Textiles and clothing	66.4	2	4	6	14	27	29	30	25	33	27	2	1
Leather, rubber, footwear and travel goods	31.7	16	19	17	29	47	37	7	4	11	9	3	2
Metals	69.4	36	70	36	21	23	7	3	1	2	1	10	
Chemicals and photographic supplies	61.0	13	34	31	30	40	34	10	2	5	1	1	0
Transport equipment	96.3	16	21	52	51	21	19	2	2	5	4	4	3
Non-electrical machinery	118.1	11	52	74	38	10	7	2	1	2	2	1	0
Electrical machinery	86.0	5	30	54	55	26	6	11	7	3	2	1	0
Mineral products and precious stones/metals	72.9	59	81	28	9	10	8	3	1	2	1	0	0
Manufactured articles NES	76.1	15	49	38	37	40	10	5	3	2	1	0	0
All industrial products	736.9	20	44	41	32	24	15	7	5	6	4	1	1

Notes:
UR = Uruguay Round; NES = not elsewhere specified.
Tariffs are based on weighted averages on imports from all sources.

[a] Excluding petroleum products.

[b] Import data from 1990 or latest available year, and for all developed country participants in the Uruguay Round, excluding imports from free trade area partners (e.g. intra-European Union trade) and from contractual preferential arrangements.

[c] Wood, pulp, paper and furniture.

Source: GATT (1994).

to eliminate tariffs completely over the next eight to ten years. Most of the other countries have agreed to reduce tariffs for solid wood products and furniture, or at least to declare bound rates.

Although tariffs were not eliminated for all forest products, the average rate of Uruguay Round tariff reductions for these products in developed country import markets compares favourably with that of other industrial goods (Table 21.2). Pre-Uruguay Round tariff rates for forest products were the lowest of all major industrial products groups – about 45 per cent lower than the average rate across all products. Nevertheless, the absolute decrease in average trade-weighted tariff rates for forest products was the same as the decrease in rates for all industrial goods.

As a result of the Uruguay Round Agreement, on a trade-weighted basis forest products have the highest percentage of all imports (85 per cent) without duty in developed country import markets – almost double the proportion of imports of all industrial goods that have zero tariffs (Table 21.3). This again reflects the fact that the Agreement has meant that already low developed country tariff rates for forest products have been reduced further.

Table 21.4 Uruguay Round change in tariff escalation of selected products in developed countries

Product category by stage of processing	Weighted average			Change in tariff escalation
	Pre-UR (%)	Post-UR (%)	Reduction (%)	
Hides, skins and leather				
Raw	0.1	0.1	0	NA
Semi-manufactures	4.6	3.6	22	–22
Finished products	8.7	7.0	20	–20
Total	5.2	4.1	21	NA
Rubber				
Raw		0.1	0.0	100
Semi-manufactures	5.5	3.3	40	–39
Finished products	5.1	3.6	30	–67
Total	3.4	2.3	32	NA
Wood				
Wood in the rough (logs)	0.0	0.0	0	NA
Wood-based panels	9.4	6.5	31	–30
Semi-manufactures	0.9	0.4	50	–50
Wood articles	4.7	1.6	67	–67
Total	2.0	1.1	43	NA

Table 21.4 continued

Product category by stage of processing	Weighted average			Change in tariff escalation
	Pre-UR (%)	Post-UR (%)	Reduction (%)	
Paper				
Pulp and waste	0	0	0	NA
Paper and paper board	5.3	0	100	–100
Printed matter	1.7	0.3	83	–83
Paper articles	7.3	0	100	–100
Total	3.5	0	99	NA
Jute				
Fibres	0	0	0	NA
Yams	5.4	0.1	98	–98
Fabrics	5.7	3.2	43	–43
Total	5.1	1.8	64	NA
Copper				
Unwrought	0.9	0.7	30	NA
Semi-manufactures	4.3	3.1	28	–28
Total	1.7	1.2	29	NA
Nickel				
Unwrought	0.5	0.3	40	NA
Semi-manufactures	2.6	1.0	63	–68
Total	0.7	0.4	48	NA
Aluminium				
Unwrought	2.1	1.6	23	NA
Semi-manufactures	5.9	4.8	17	NA
Total	3.0	2.4	20	NA
Lead				
Unwrought	2.4	1.3	45	NA
Semi-manufactures	4.5	2.8	37	–29
Total	2.4	1.4	44	NA
Tobacco				
Unmanufactured	14.7	11.5	22	NA
Manufactured	22.1	9.2	58	–131
Total	17.3	10.7	38	NA

Notes:
UR = Uruguay Round; NA = not applicable.
Tariffs are based on weighted averages on imports from all sources.
Tariff escalation is defined as the tariff wedge between the processed and unprocessed or raw product.

Source: GATT (1994).

Table 21.5 Estimated trade effects on selected forest products of Uruguay Round tariff changes in key developed and developing country markets: 1991 trade levels (US$'000)

Importer	Developing country imports					
	Trade creation		Trade diversion		Total effect	
	A	B	A	B	A	B
Australia	2 042	5 073	(256)	0	1 786	5 073
Canada	19	689	(77)	0	(58)	689
European Union	0	65 746	(201 756)	0	(201 756)	65 746
Japan	36 701	74 759	(16 383)	0	20 318	74 759
New Zealand	0	128	(3)	0	(3)	128
South Africa[a]	36	36	0	0	36	36
United States	0	24 472	(604)	0	(604)	24 472
All developed countries	38 798	170 902	(219 079)	0	(180 281)	170 902
China	4 402	4 402	0	0	4 402	4 402
India	303	303	0	0	303	303
Republic of Korea	1 402	1 402	0	0	1 402	1 402
Malaysia	569	569	0	0	569	569
Thailand	5 337	5 337	0	0	5 337	5 337
All developing countries	12 013	12 013	0	0	12 013	12 013
All countries	50 811	182 915	(219 079)	0	(168 268)	182 915

Developed country imports						Total change			
								Percentage of forest products imports	
Trade creation		Trade diversion		Total effect					
A	B	A	B	A	B	A	B	A	B
10 871	10 871	256	0	11 127	10 871	12 913	15 944	1.1	1.3
3 596	3 596	77	0	3 673	3 596	3 615	4 285	0.2	0.2
198 591	198 591	201 756	0	400 346	198 591	198 591	264 336	0.4	0.6
37 783	37 783	16 383	0	54 166	37 783	74484	112543	0.6	0.9
560	560	3	0	563	560	560	689	0.3	0.4
30	30	0	0	30	30	66	66	0.0	0.0
24 317	24 317	604	0	24 921	24 317	24 317	48 788	0.2	0.4
275 748	275 748	219 079	0	494 827	275 748	314 546	446 650	0.4	0.5
3 570	3 570	0	0	3 570	3 570	7 972	7 972	0.2	0.2
651	651	0	0	651	651	954	954	0.2	0.2
8 486	8 486	0	0	8 486	8 486	9 889	9 889	0.4	0.4
146	146	0	0	146	146	715	715	0.1	0.1
827	827	0	0	827	827	6 164	6 164	0.5	0.5
13 682	13 682	0	0	13 682	13 682	25 694	25 694	0.3	0.3
289 430	289 430	219 079	0	508 509	289 430	340 240	472 345	0.4	0.4

Notes:
Scenario A assumes a medium elasticity of demand for forest product imports; pre-Uruguay Round tariffs on imports in developing country markets are at MFN rates; and pre-Uruguay Round tariffs on imports in developed country markets are at GSP rates for developing country imports and MFN rates for developed country imports. Scenario B assumes a medium elasticity of demand for forest product imports, and pre-Uruguay Round tariffs on imports in all markets are at MFN rates.
[a] No GSP rates for developing country imports in pre-Uruguay Round tariffs.

Source: Barbier (1995).

A major contribution of the Uruguay Round has been to reduce the degree of tariff escalation faced by forest products in developed country markets (Table 21.4). For solid wood products, tariff escalation for wood-based panels has been reduced by 30 per cent, semi-manufactures 50 per cent and wood articles 67 per cent. The phasing out of tariffs on pulp and paper products will also eliminate tariff escalation completely for paper and paper board and paper products and reduce escalation by 83 per cent for printed matter. Of the forest products listed in Table 21.4, only wood-based panels have significantly higher tariff rates than their unprocessed equivalent (that is, logs).

The implications of the Uruguay Round for non-tariff barriers faced by forest products is less clear. However, two special agreements – the Agreement on the Application of Sanitary and Phytosanitary (SPS) Measures and the Agreement on Technical Barriers to Trade (TBT) – do provide the basis for tackling certain non-tariff measures that have been used as trade barriers against forest products. The SPS agreement could reduce the use of inspection, quarantine and treatment of imported forest products as prohibitive measures beyond what is necessary to protect domestic human, animal and plant populations from pests or diseases. The TBT agreement could limit the use of technical regulations on forest products as non-tariff restrictions rather than for legitimate purposes of protecting human health and safety, preventing environmental degradation and ensuring adequate product quality and design standards.

Other provisions of the Uruguay Round that may also help to reduce barriers to the forest products trade include limitations and clarifications on the use of anti-dumping and countervailing duties, customs valuation and licensing procedures and market access restrictions.

A possible indirect impact of the Uruguay Round is that it may have prompted other longstanding non-tariff barriers in individual markets to be lessened. For example, the European Union has recently proposed eliminating for 1995–96 its plywood tariff/quota scheme for GSP beneficiaries.

A recent estimate has been made of the likely impacts of the Uruguay Round tariff reductions on trade in forest products for selected products and markets (Barbier, 1995). As indicated in Table 21.5, these impacts consist of two effects:

- *Trade creation*. The reduction in the tariff on a forest product will cause its import price to fall, thus stimulating additional demand for imports of the product; the extent of this trade creation effect will depend on the original level of imports of the product as well as the responsiveness of import demand to changes in price (that is, the price elasticity of demand).
- *Trade diversion*. If tariff changes are not uniform across all imports – for example, in developed country markets the fall in MFN rates will generally

be more than that of GSP rates (often zero) – the resulting changes in import prices could lead to diversion, or substitution, between developing and developed country imports; the extent of this trade diversion effect will depend on the relative change in tariff rates on developed and developing country imports as well as the substitution response of domestic output and both sources of inputs to changes in the relative price of imports.

The results of the analysis indicate the total trade effects of the Uruguay Round tariff changes for selected forest products may range from US$340 million to $472 million in key developed and developing country markets (Table 21.5). However, these impacts amount to only 0.4 per cent of total 1991 forest products imports in the markets analysed, which had an aggregate value of $85 600 million. This suggests that, although the real trade gains from the tariff changes are positive and significant, they may not have a substantial impact on global forest products trade. One factor limiting the gains from the Uruguay Round for forest products is that the pre-Uruguay Round tariff rates for most of these products in major importing markets were already very low.

Perhaps more important than the estimated gains in trade for forest products is that the Uruguay Round will have succeeded in reducing forest product tariff rates in major markets to even lower levels than before, and for some forest products and markets tariffs will be phased out completely. In addition, the new and often lower rates in developed country markets will be bound, as will an increasing proportion of tariffs in developing country markets. Binding a tariff means that a country has agreed officially to a ceiling on the tariff rate.

Finally, as post-Uruguay Round tariffs for forest products in most major markets will be at very low rates, any further reductions in forest products tariff rates that may be agreed in subsequent GATT/World Trade Organization rounds should no longer have a trade diversion effect, as both developing and developed countries should be facing a single tariff rate in most importing markets. As indicated in Table 21.2, given that tariff rates on forest products in major markets are on average only 1.1 per cent, the trade creation gains from additional tariff reductions may be significant but not substantial.

New barriers to forest products trade

In recent years there has been a proliferation of additional policies and regulations that have the potential of becoming ‘new’ barriers to the forest products trade. These barriers include:

- export restrictions by developing countries to encourage domestic processing of tropical timber for export;
- environmental and trade restrictions on production and exports in developed countries that affect international trade patterns;

- quantitative restrictions on imports of 'unsustainably produced' timber products;
- the use of ecolabelling and 'green' certification as import barriers.

Although only the last two measures could be strictly defined as new, all of these trade measures have been increasingly employed in recent years and have the potential to affect forest product trade flows significantly.

For example, developing countries are continuing to use export restrictions on wood in rough and semi-processed products to support domestic processing industries and improve export prospects for higher-valued forest products (Barbier *et al.*, 1994). Although an expanded processing capacity was established in Malaysia, the Philippines and Indonesia, it was achieved at high economic costs, both in terms of the direct costs of subsidization as well as the additional costs of wasteful and inefficient processing operations. A recent simulation analysis of the prohibitive sawnwood export tax in Indonesia indicates that the policy not only may fail to encourage higher-valued processing for export but also may have little significant impact on timber-related deforestation (Barbier *et al.*, 1995). Despite the losses in terms of economic inefficiencies and the implications for the management of their forest resource base, developing countries are unlikely to end such policies in the near future but may instead employ them more extensively.

Developed countries are also beginning to employ a variety of environmental regulations in their forest industries – both alone and in conjunction with export restrictions – that may have significant trade implications (Barbier, 1994). Whether or not such regulations are used specifically for this purpose, they may lead to trade distortions and discrimination. For example, Perez-Garcia (1991) found that trade and environmental restrictions on logging in the Pacific Northwest of the United States combined to have significant domestic and global impacts, including increases in global sawlog prices and regional shifts in production with related effects in major sawnwood and plywood markets.

Many developed countries are also under pressure to adopt quantitative restrictions to limit the import of 'unsustainably' produced forest products or to impose countervailing duties on imported products that benefit from an 'environmental' export subsidy – unsustainable forest management that leads to lower harvesting costs and thus lower export product prices. This may result in an attempt to amend GATT/WTO rules to allow exceptions for quantitative restrictions and countervailing duties on these environmental grounds. For example, Arden-Clarke (1991) has argued that the General Agreement on Tariffs and Trade should be amended to allow contracting parties to:

- discriminate between like products that vary in the degree to which the environmental and resource costs of their production are incorporated in their price;
- protect domestic industries that internalize more of their costs than foreign competitors, with import tariffs or export subsidies; and
- provide subsidies to maintain the competitiveness in international markets of exported products with greater cost internalization than competing products.

Such an approach would clearly allow nations to invoke the full range of policy measures available to them for intervention in the timber trade. For example, as noted above, the United States has already imposed environmental restrictions on its own Pacific Northwest logging operations. Given this policy, and under amended GATT/WTO rules, the United States Government would be able to limit timber imports from other countries that did not maintain similar environmental standards for their timber operations. Alternatively, the United States could choose to subsidize plywood and sawnwood mills in the region and elsewhere in the country for their loss of 'international competitiveness' as a result of the environmental restrictions.

Moreover, under the amended GATT/WTO rules, any importing country or trading bloc could impose trade sanctions on producer countries that appeared to be producing timber or timber products 'unsustainably'. To the extent that unsustainable management leads to lower harvesting costs and thus lower export product prices, importing countries would have the right to impose tariffs as a means of correcting this environmental export subsidy. If such a broadening of the GATT/WTO rules is achieved, then the use of quantitative restrictions and even countervailing duties by importing countries – to restrict imports of timber products that are not sustainably produced or to counter perceived environmental export subsidies – will increasingly become a feature of the forest products trade.

Finally, the number of ecolabelling and certification initiatives applied to the forest products trade has increased rapidly in recent years although few schemes have been put into practice so far. Generally, the aim of these initiatives is to distinguish sustainably produced forest products or to ensure that forest product imports conform to domestic environmental standards and regulations. Provided that such regulations and schemes are non-discriminatory, transparent and justified, are agreed mutually between trading partners or through multilateral negotiations, comply with GATT rules and conform with internationally recognized guidelines, then their potential use as trade barriers will be drastically reduced.

Although there are legitimate uses of all the above policy measures, the rate at which they are being implemented and the frequency with which they have led to trade distortion and discrimination suggests that their use must be examined carefully. International agreements and rules governing their use should also be negotiated. Indiscriminate and widespread application of these trade measures as new barriers to the forest products trade could easily override the gains resulting from the recently concluded Uruguay Round.

Conclusion

The Uruguay Round Agreement has continued the substantial progress made during recent decades in reducing barriers to the trade in forest products. In fact, because tariff rates for most forest products in importing markets were already somewhat low, estimates of the gains in trade from the additional reductions achieved in the Uruguay Round suggest that net impacts on trade may not be substantial compared with the overall volume of trade. However, further gains to the trade may occur through reducing uncertainty by the binding of tariffs in major importing markets and the continuing improvement in the degree of tariff escalation. In addition, some progress was made in curtailing some important non-tariff and other barriers that have affected the trade in forest products in the past. However, all of these potential benefits of the Uruguay Round to the trade in forest products may be overshadowed by the new trade barriers to forest products identified in this chapter. Tackling these barriers could be an important task for the World Trade Organization as well as subsequent rounds of GATT negotiations.

Bibliography

Arden-Clarke, C. (1991), *The General Agreement on Tariffs and Trade, environmental protection and sustainable development*, A World Wide Fund for Nature discussion paper, Geneva, WWF International.

Barbier, E.B. (1994), 'The environmental effects of the trade in the forestry sector', in *The environmental effects of trade*, Paris: OECD.

Barbier, E.B. (1995), Assessment of the effects of the Uruguay Round Agreement on the international trade in forest products. Draft report prepared for the Forest Products Division, FAO, Rome.

Barbier, E.B., J.C. Burgess, J.T. Bishop and B.A. Aylward (1994), *The Economics of the Tropical Timber Trade*, London: Earthscan Publications.

Barbier, E.B., N. Bockstael, J.C. Burgess and I. Strand (1995), 'The linkages between the timber trade and tropical deforestation – Indonesia', *The World Economy*, **18** (3), 411–41.

FAO (1988), *Trade in forest products: a study of the barriers faced by developing countries*, FAO Forestry Paper No. 83, Rome.

FAO (1994), *FAO Yearbook of Forest Products 1981–1992*, Rome.

GATT (1994), *The results of the Uruguay Round of multilateral trade negotiations. Market access for goods and services: overview of the results*, Geneva.

Perez-Garcia, J.M. (1991), *An assessment of the impacts of recent environmental and trade restrictions on timber harvests and exports*, Working Paper No. 33, Seattle, WA, Center for International Trade in Forest Products, University of Washington.

22. Wildlife, biodiversity and trade

with C.-E. Schulz

Abstract

The following chapter develops a model of wild resource exploitation that includes both the standard bioeconomic properties of growth and harvesting as well as a species-area relationship linked to habitat conversion. The model is developed for both a closed and open economy. In the closed economy model the characteristics of the long-run equilibrium are analysed in three versions of the model: the basic bioeconomic model, the inclusion of habitat conversion and finally the addition of biodiversity value. In the case of the open economy model, we also examine the potential effects of trade interventions on the optimal exploitation of species and habitat conversion in the long run. The results confirm that the inclusion of habitat conversion as well as biodiversity value in a model of wild resource exploitation yields significantly different outcomes than a basic bioeconomic model.

Summary

The conservation of wild resources in developing countries is often portrayed as being in conflict with development activities such as agriculture, forestry and infrastructure investments that lead to the conversion of natural habitats. However, economic models of optimal exploitation of wild resources generally ignore this land use allocation aspect of the problem and instead apply standard bioeconomic models of population dynamics and harvesting. Moreover, the role of wild resource exploitation in international trade and the potential use of trade sanctions to enforce sustainable management of resources have been largely neglected, even though the threat of such sanctions for conservation purposes is on the increase. Finally, many of the wild species and resources contained in the natural areas of developing countries may have significant non-consumptive use and ecological values that may make an important contribution to overall welfare. Although generally non-marketed, these 'biodiversity' or 'stock externality' values are often significant and should be taken into account in allocation decisions affecting wild resources.

This chapter attempts to address some of these issues by developing a theoretical model of wild resource exploitation that includes both the standard bioeconomic properties of growth and harvesting as well as a species–area relationship linked to habitat conversion. We also assume that the standing 'stock' of biological resources generates important ecological and non-consumptive use values. Defining $S(t)$ as the total stock or 'inventory' of biological resources (species), we suggest that changes in this stock are not only determined by the aggregate biological growth rate across these species but also affected by the expansion in the number of species as the size of the natural area or habitat changes. As in a standard bioeconomic model, these changes in the total species stock, $S(t)$, must be net of any harvesting offtake. Finally, we account for any ecological or non-consumptive values by assuming that the stock $S(t)$ also affects welfare directly.

We explore the implications of this model for the long-run optimal stock of species held by the developing country. We do this first in the context of a closed economy (without trade) model. The results are depicted in Figure 22.1, which have two important outcomes.

First, modifying the standard bioeconomic model to account for the costs of habitat conversion leads to a decrease in the equilibrium level of total species stock, that is, $S_2^* < S_1^*$ as shown in Figure 22.1. In the modified model changes in the total stock of biological resources are dependent not only on the natural biological regeneration but also on the total habitat area. However, holding land as natural habitat also implies an opportunity cost, which is represented by foregone consumption from development activities that use converted habitat land. Because conventional bioeconomic models do not take into account explicitly the opportunity cost of maintaining 'wild' lands as habitat for species, the equilibrium level of species stock – and thus implicitly habitat area – is higher than if the opportunity cost of maintaining habitat were included.

Second, we extend our closed economy model further to include the 'stock externality' or 'biodiversity' value of $S(t)$. If it turns out that this value in the long run is extremely high, then the equilibrium total species stock level may even exceed that of the standard bioeconomic model, that is, $S^* > S_1^*$. However, whether S^* is less than, equals or exceeds the equilibrium species stock of the bioeconomic model, S_1^*, will depend crucially on whether the marginal value of biodiversity, U_S, is less than, equals or exceeds the marginal opportunity cost of maintaining natural habitat, $-U_c f'$. In Figure 22.1 we depict an equilibrium where $U_S < -U_c f'$ and thus $S^* < S_1^*$.

In the second half of the chapter, we develop our model to allow for trade. The basic assumption in this open economy model is that some wildlife products are exported, which in turn allow the import of consumption goods that can substitute for domestic production from converted habitat land. One potential optimal solution is depicted in Figure 22.2. However, it is unclear whether the long-run equilibrium species stock under an open economy will be less than, equal to or greater than that under a closed economy. This ambiguous outcome derives from two counteracting influences of trade: exports of wildlife products means more harvesting of wild resources, but imports reduce the reliance on domestic consumption from habitat conversion activities.

We also employ the open economy model to examine the relative effectiveness of employing trade interventions as opposed to international transfers as means to inducing a developing country to conserve more of its total species stock in the long run. Under certain conditions, trade interventions may be unambiguously counterproductive, whereas the alternative policy of an international transfer of funds would lead to greater long-run conservation of species and habitat. Although in our model it is possible for trade interventions (trade bans, tariffs or trade subsidies) to have the desired effect of increasing long-run equilibrium species stock and habitat area, we need to know the specific conditions underlying both the bioeconomic, habitat conversion and trade sectors of the model in order to determine the precise influence of trade policy interventions.

Hence, we conclude that trade in wildlife products may not necessarily lead to greater species and habitat conservation in a developing country, but once an open economy is established, trade intervention by the global community is a second-best approach for inducing the country to achieve further biodiversity conservation.

1. Introduction[1]

Many of the world's remaining natural areas and habitats for wild species are believed to be located mainly in the developing regions of the world. However, the demand for resources and land to meet the needs of growing populations and developing economies has meant that much of these wild resources and wildlands are under threat. At the same time, it is also economically feasible and worthwhile to maintain some natural areas broadly in their original state and conserve wildlife species while at the same time allowing important human uses of these resources (Swanson and Barbier, 1992). Sustainable management regimes can be extremely diverse, ranging from commercial wildlife ranching and harvesting to non timber forest product extraction to community-based wildlife and wildlands development to tourism and recreation and so on. They may take the form of traditional uses of wild resources by local communities (IIED, 1994). Alternatively, they may be deliberate attempts to reconcile conservation and development aspirations through integrated community-based development projects (Wells and Brandon, 1992), or through major international aid programmes such as biodiversity reserves funded by the Global Environmental Facility (Munasinghe, 1993).

Economics clearly has an important role to play in the assessment of the 'sustainable' exploitation and management of wildlife and wildlands. However, it is important to recognize that there are two important facets to the economic analysis of optimal exploitation of wildlife species.

First, there is the familiar bioeconomic problem of determining the long run optimal harvest or use rate, given certain characteristics of the population dynamics of wild species such as their growth or regeneration rates. This approach does not include any cost for land (or sea) used as habitat and is particularly appropriate in the analysis of intertemporal allocation of marine resources for which it was originally developed (Clark, 1976). It is less applicable to allocation decisions involving terrestrial wildlife resources, which require determining not only the optimal stock and harvesting rate of species biomass but also simultaneously the optimal size or area of the natural habitat that maintains the species (Swanson, 1994).

Thus a second important facet to the economics of wildlife use or exploitation is the optimal allocation of natural habitat. Correctly determining the optimal size or area of habitat requires comparing the benefits of maintaining habitat with its opportunity costs – which are none other than the foregone economic activities dependent on the conversion of natural habitat to other uses (Barrett, 1993; Swanson and Barbier, 1992). However, determining the optimal area to be preserved as natural habitat alone is again only half the story; it tells us nothing about the optimal rate of exploitation of those species found within the preserves. Thus if we are interested in the possibility of sustainable utilization of species beyond either their complete preservation in a biosphere reserve or only their non-consumptive uses such as for tourist viewing, then we must consider the problem of optimal habitat provision and species exploitation together.

There are two additional dimensions to the problem that may be worth considering: the role of trade interventions to promote sustainablement management and the wider social values of biodiversity as a public good for humankind.

Although many wild resources are used locally, some products of natural areas are important traded goods, for example, wildlife products (skins, horns, ivory and even the animals themselves), timber logs and products (tropical hardwoods) and non-timber products (rattan, honey, resins, and so on).

In recent years, trade interventions imposed either unilaterally or through multilateral agreements have been proposed to control overexploitation of the traded products derived from wild resources and thus to encourage their sustainable management within developing countries (Barbier *et al.*, 1990; Burgess, 1994). Environmental pressure groups in major importing countries are also advocating sanctions and interventions in the tropical timber trade as a means to coercing producer countries into reducing tropical deforestation and the subsequent loss of environmental values (Barbier *et al.*, 1994).

However, in addition to their direct use or exploitation, the wild species and resources contained in the natural areas of developing countries are also considered to have wider social values that are usually linked to the stock size and not to the harvesting rate. These values are considerably diverse, and could include non-consumptive uses of species (for example, for tourism, recreation and scientific study); their ecological functional role that may indirectly support or protect economic activity (control of pests, genetic diversity, improving productivity); their potential future use values (option and quasi-option values); and their non-use or pure 'existence' value. Various studies indicate that non-consumptive use and ecological values of wild species and resources can be significant and, if potentially capturable by a developing country, may make an important contribution to overall welfare (see Table 22.1). Some of these values are attributed to a single species, but in many cases it is the entire stock of species in a wild area and its inherent diversity, or biodiversity, that are the source of value. Moreover, many important social values of biodiversity may be currently underestimated, as there is a lot we still do not know about the potential ecological role of species and biodiversity in supporting ecosystem functioning and 'resilience' (Holling *et al.*, 1995).

Table 22.1 Various valuation estimates for non-consumptive uses of wild resources in developing countries (US$)

Activity	Estimated net present value
Viewing value of elephants, Kenya (Brown and Henry, 1993)	$25 million/year
Ecotourism, Costa Rica (Tobias and Mendelsohn, 1990)	$1250/ha
Tourism, Thailand	$385–860 000/year
Research/education, Thailand (Dixon and Sherman, 1990)	$38–77 000/year
Tourism, Cameroon	$19/ha
Genetic value, Cameroon (Ruitenbeek, 1989)	$7/ha
Ecotourism, Madagascar (Kramer, 1993)	$0.8 to 2.16 million
Net private return to pharmaceutical prospecting, Costa Rica (Barbier and Aylward, 1996)	$4.81 million/product
Impact on crop productivity of pest control by Anolis lizard, Greater and Lesser Antilles (Narain and Fisher, 1994)	$670 000/year in lost output per 1 % decline in population

Sources: See references.

The following chapter attempts to integrate some of these concerns by developing a model of wild or natural species exploitation that extends the traditional bioeconomic model for renewable resources to include conversion of habitat and the wider social value of biodiversity. The model is developed for both a closed and open economy. In the case of the closed economy we demonstrate how extending the bioeconomic model of species exploitation to account explicitly for the opportunity costs of habitat conservation plus any non-consumptive biodiversity values produces a different optimal extraction rate for wild species than if only the harvesting problem alone were considered. The case of the open economy model is an extension of this model, which is used to examine the potential effects of trade interventions on the optimal exploitation of species and habitat conversion in the long run as a means of determining whether such interventions can encourage less exploitation of wild resources.

2. The basic model of species exploitation and habitat conversion

In the following model we assume that the key allocation problem is determining the optimal stock and rate of exploitation of wild species or resources given that this total resource stock is a function of a natural rate of population growth or regeneration, harvesting and the total area of natural habitat or 'wildlands'. To do this, we combine a standard bioeconomic model of species exploitation with an approach developed by Barrett (1993), which was used principally to determine the optimal allocation of habitat between preservation and conversion to other economic uses.[2] Our approach requires setting up the problem so that both the biological growth of populations and changes in habitat area affect the aggregate stock of species.

For example, let $S(t)$ be the total stock of species (wild resources) comprising the various populations or species found in a given area, aggregated in some appropriate way.[3] This aggregate stock will consist of many animal and plant populations with the capacity for reproduction and growth. As these populations regenerate and grow, so must the aggregate stock of these populations, $S(t)$. However, the size of $S(t)$ will also be affected by the total number of species comprising this aggregate stock, and as research from island biogeography indicates, the total number of species should be related to the total area of habitat available to these species. For our model, this implies that changes in habitat area will affect the total number of species, and hence determine changes in the total species stock, $S(t)$. We therefore introduce an important modification to the standard bioeconomic model: changes in the total species stock are not only determined by the aggregate biological growth rate across these species but also affected by the expansion in the number of species as the size of the natural area or habitat changes. Finally, we assume that changes in the total species stock, $S(t)$, must be net of any such harvesting offtake.

Thus defining $A(t)$ as the total area of natural habitat or wildlands, and $y(t)$ as the aggregate rate of harvest of species or 'wild' resources, then the change in total species stock, $dS(t)/dt$, can be depicted as

$$\frac{dS(t)}{dt} = \dot{S} = G(S(t), A(t)) - y(t) = G_1(S(t)) + G_2(A(t)) - y(t). \quad (22.1)$$

That is, change in the total species stock is determined by a growth function, G, which is in turn a function of the size of the stock, $S(t)$, and the total habitat area, $A(t)$, as well as the total offtake, $y(t)$. We assume that the growth function G is additively separable into subcomponents G_1 and G_2. This separability condition facilitates our ability to depict our results graphically in a two-dimensional (S, y) space. However, assuming separability is not essential to our main results. In Appendix 2 we illustrate this with an alternative formulation of the allocation problem that includes a non-separable version of the growth function, G.

In equation (22.1) $G_1(S(t))$ can be defined as the aggregate growth or regeneration function of the total species stock.[4] This function is assumed to display the standard bioeconomic properties; that is, G_1 is defined over the interval $S(t) \geq 0$, and there exists values $\underline{S} < S_{max}$ such that $G_1(\underline{S}) = G_1(S_{max}) = 0$ and $d^2G_1(S(t))/dS(t)^2 < 0$.

However, $G_2(A(t))$ is an additional component to the standard bioeconomic properties of a renewable resource growth function. G_2 represents the growth in the total species stock that is attributable to an expansion in the number of species based on a species-area relationship. The basic premise behind this relationship is that the total number of species found in a given habitat will increase with the size or area of the habitat. Originally developed through the study of island biogeography, species-area relationships were initially employed to estimate the unknown number of species in biologically diverse habitats such as tropical deforests. Now, however, such curves are being used to forecast the extent of species loss associated with current trends in tropical deforestation. As noted by Barrett (1993), a typical species-area relationship employed by ecologists is

$$S(t) = \alpha A(t)^{\beta} \text{ or } \quad A(t) = \alpha^{-1/\beta} S(t)^{1/\beta}, \quad 0 < \beta < 1. \quad (22.2)$$

The parameter α may depend on the type of species, its population density and the biogeographic region. The parameter β determines the shape of the species-area curve, and for most regions of the world it has been estimated to range between 0.16 and 0.39 (Lugo, Parotta and Brown, 1993). Although β has been observed to increase as habitat area becomes smaller, in the following model we assume it to be fixed.[5] As shown in equation (22.2), by inverting the species–area relationship one can also determine the habitat area required to maintain a given number of species.

Ignoring G_1 in equation (22.1) for the moment, following Barrett's approach we can determine from (22.2) the growth in the total species stock that is attributable to the effect of a change in habitat area on the species–area relationship

$$\begin{aligned} G_2(A(t)) &= \beta\alpha A(t)^{\beta-1} r(t), \quad \text{where } r(t) = \mathrm{d}A(t)/\mathrm{d}t = \dot{A} \\ &= \beta\alpha^{1/\beta} S(t)^{(\beta-1)/\beta} r(t) \\ &= aS(t)^{-b} r(t), \quad \text{where } a = \beta\alpha^{1/\beta} \text{ and } b = (1-\beta)/\beta > 0. \end{aligned} \tag{22.3}$$

Thus equation (22.3) suggests that the growth in the total species stock attributed to the species–area relationship can be expressed in terms of the rate of change in habitat area, $r(t)$, and the size of the total stock, $S(t)$. It therefore follows that (22.1) can be rewritten as

$$\dot{S} = G(S(t), A(t)) - y(t) = G_1(S(t)) + aS(t)^{-b} r(t) - y(t). \tag{22.1'}$$

Equation (22.1') is the basic equation of motion of our model, which links changes in the total stock of species, or wild resources, to biological growth, habitat area, and harvesting offtake.

As noted in the previous section, in developing countries the main threat to natural habitat is conversion to other economic activities. Again, following Barrett (1993) this can be incorporated in our model. Let $D(t)$ be defined as the total developed area arising from conversion of natural habitat, then

$$D(t) = D_0 + \int_0^t r(\tau)\mathrm{d}\tau = D_0 + A_0 - A(t), \tag{22.4}$$

if the total land area is fixed and $r(t) \leq 0$. That is, natural habitat is converted into land used for other activities at the rate $r(t)$ over time. This implies that $r(t)$ is non-positive in equation (22.1'). Conversion of habitat occurs because the resulting economic activities produce goods and services for consumption, which in turn contributes to economic welfare.[6] Let $F(D(t))$ be the aggregate production function for economic activities dependent on converted land, which is assumed to have the normal properties $\mathrm{d}F(D(t))/\mathrm{d}D(t) > 0$ and $\mathrm{d}^2F/\mathrm{d}D(t)^2 < 0$. It therefore follows from (22.2) and (22.4)

$$F(D(t)) = F(D_0 + A_0 - \alpha^{-1/\beta} S(t)^{1/\beta}) = f(S(t)), \tag{22.5}$$

with $df/dS(t) < 0$ and $d^2f/dS(t)^2 < 0$ for $0 < \beta < 1$. That is, an increase in the total species stock due to an expansion in the number of species has an increasingly negative impact on aggregate production of output from converted habitat land. This is not surprising, given that the species–area relationship suggests that the number of species can increase only if there is more habitat area, which of course implies less converted land and a corresponding fall in aggregate output from this land.

Finally, if we assume that all output is consumed and that total consumption, $c(t)$, can be defined as $c(t) = F(D(t)) = f(S(t))$, then we can take into account explicitly in the social utility function of the country the trade-off between, on the one hand, the harvesting or utilization of wild species from their conserved natural habitat, and on the other, the conversion of habitat land to produce other commodities. This trade-off can be further elaborated if we assume also that any positive stock externalities, or biodiversity values, associated with $S(t)$ enter directly into our utility function. Defining the latter as U, then

$$U = U(y(t), c(t), S(t)), \qquad (22.6)$$

which is assumed to be additively separable and to have the standard properties with respect to its partial derivatives, $\partial U/\partial i > 0$, $\partial^2 U/\partial i^2 < 0$ and $\lim_{i\to 0} \partial U/\partial i \to \infty$, $i = y(t), c(t), S(t)$. It is clear from all the above relationships (22.1) to (22.6) that an increase in consumption and its consequent social benefits must occur at the expense of the gains from additional harvesting of wild species and biodiversity values.

Equations (22.1) to (22.6) represent the basic relationships of the model. In the next two sections we analyse formally the intertemporal allocation problem assuming closed and open economy conditions respectively. In the following optimal control problems, notation is simplified by omitting the argument of time-dependent variables, by representing a derivative of a function by its prime, by employing numbered subscripts to indicate partial derivatives of a function, and by denoting the time derivatives of a variable by a dot.

3. Closed economy model

We initially assume a closed economy model. This may be a realistic representation of the problem if all consumption from converted land and harvesting of wild species are non-tradeable commodities. We relax this assumption in the next section. Our principle aim in developing the closed economy model is to demonstrate explicitly how including the opportunity costs of habitat conversion plus any non-consumptive value of biodiversity in a bioeconomic model of species exploitation affects the equilibrium stock and thus the optimal harvesting path.

The developing country is assumed to maximize the present value of future welfare, W

$$\mathrm{Max}_y W = \int_0^{\infty} \left[U(y,c,S) - w(S)y\right] e^{-\delta t} \mathrm{d}t \qquad (22.7)$$

subject to (22.1') and (22.5). Let $w(S)$ be defined as the unit social cost of harvesting, with $w' \leq 0$ and $w'' \geq 0$, and $\delta > 0$ be the social discount rate. For simplicity, we assume that the rate of land conversion, $r(t) \leq 0$, is a constant which we define as $-r$. Finally, the initial and terminal boundaries of the state variable, S, are respectively $S(0) = S_0$ and $\lim_{t\to\infty} S(t) \geq 0$. We exclude the situation with total conversion of the habitat.[7]

The current value Hamiltonian of the above problem is

$$H = U(y, f(S), S) - w(S)y + \lambda[G_1(S) - aS^{-b}r - y], \qquad (22.8)$$

where the costate variable λ can be interpreted as the shadow price of the total species stock, S. Assuming an interior solution, the first-order conditions of the control problem are

$$\mathrm{d}H/\mathrm{d}y = U_y - w(S) - \lambda = 0 \quad \text{or} \quad U_y = w(S) + \lambda \qquad (22.9)$$

$$-\mathrm{d}H/\mathrm{d}S = \dot{\lambda} - \delta\lambda \text{ or } \dot{\lambda} = (\delta - G_1' - baS^{-(b+1)}r)\lambda + yw' - U_c f' - U_S \qquad (22.10)$$

$$\mathrm{d}H/\mathrm{d}\lambda = \dot{S} = G_1(S) - aS^{-b}r - y. \qquad (22.11)$$

Condition (22.9) indicates that, along the optimal trajectory, the marginal benefit of harvesting or utilizing wild species for domestic consumption, U_y, must equal its marginal cost, which consists of marginal harvesting costs, $w(S)$, as well as the marginal costs of stock depletion, λ. Condition (22.11) simply recovers equation (22.1') for determining the change in the total species stock, which we have discussed above. Finally, condition (22.10) resembles the standard renewable resource dynamic condition for denoting the change in the value of the stock of wild resources, S, but it includes not only the standard (net) marginal bioeconomic costs for retaining species, $(\delta - G_1')\lambda + yw'$, but also the net marginal benefits of 'holding on' to land as habitat, $-baS^{-(b+1)}r\lambda - U_c f'$, and the marginal social value of an additional unit of the total species stock, U_S. As this condition is important for the analytical results of our model, we state its interpretation formally as

PROPOSITION 1. *Along the optimal path the rate of change in the shadow price of the total species stock, dλ/dt, equals the difference between the marginal 'bioeconomic' costs of holding on to an additional unit of the total species stock,* $(\delta - G_1')\lambda + yw'$, *less both the marginal net benefits of holding on to natural habitat for that additional unit of total stock,* $-baS^{-(b+1)}r\lambda - U_c f'$, *and the marginal social value of that additional unit,* U_S.

The long-run equilibrium for the closed economy can be determined by assuming that in the steady-state the shadow price of the stock of wild resources, the rates of harvesting and land conversion, and the total species stock are constant, that is, $d\lambda/dt = dy/dt = r = dS/dt = 0$. From the first-order conditions, the long-run equilibrium can be characterized as

$$\delta - G_1' + \frac{\left[-yw' + U_c f' + U_s\right]}{\left[U_y - w(S)\right]} \quad \text{for} \quad \dot{\lambda} = \dot{y} = r = \dot{S} = 0 \qquad (22.12)$$

$$y = G_1(S) \quad \text{for} \quad \dot{S} = r = 0. \qquad (22.13)$$

Equation (22.12) is the standard long-run equilibrium for holding on to renewable resources, but in this case with some important modifications. This is best seen by interpreting the different components on the right-hand side of (22.12). Let

$$R_1(S, y) \equiv G_1' + \frac{-yw'}{\left[U_y - w(S)\right]} > 0 \qquad (22.14)$$

$$R_2(S, y) \equiv \frac{U_c f'}{\left[U_y - w(S)\right]} < 0 \qquad (22.15)$$

$$R_3(S, y) \equiv \frac{U_S}{\left[U_y - w(S)\right]} > 0 \qquad (22.16)$$

Then it follows that R_1 is the standard marginal net 'bioeconomic' return for holding on to species, R_2 is the (relative) marginal opportunity cost of holding on to land as natural habitat for wild species and R_3 is the (relative) marginal non-consumptive value of biodiversity. If a solution exists for the long-run equilibrium,, then it suggests

PROPOSITION 2. *In a closed economy, the equilibrium total species stock, S^*, is determined by equating the social discount rate, δ, and bioeconomic returns net of the opportunity cost of natural habitat plus the non consumptive value of biodiversity, $R_1 + R_2 + R_3$.*

Verifying Proposition 2 requires determining whether an optimal saddle path and solution exist for the long-run equilibrium characterized by equations (22.12) and (22.13). For our purposes, it is useful to conduct this analysis of the long-run equilibrium in stages using three versions of the model: the basic bioeconomic model, the inclusion of habitat conversion and finally the addition of biodiversity value. As will become evident, each version has different implications for the optimal long-run stock of wildlife species and harvesting rates in the closed economy. The derivation of these results is shown in Appendix 1, which are summarized below.

Case 1. Bioeconomic model ($\delta = R_1$)

We begin with the basic bioeconomic model with no costs of holding onto land as habitat and no positive stock externalities associated with biodiversity, that is, $R_2 = R_3 = 0$. As indicated in Appendix 1, the result is a standard modification

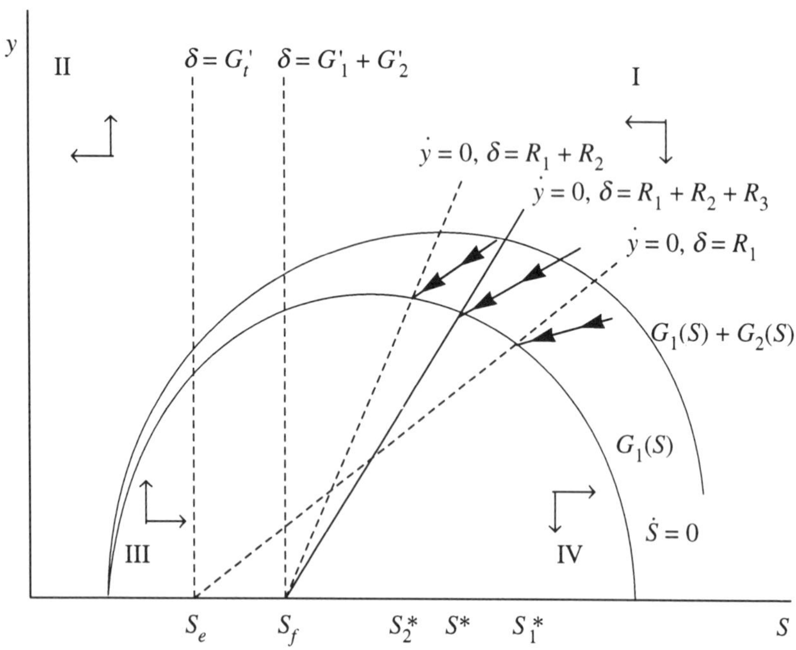

Figure 22.1 The long-run equilibrium of the closed economy

of the conventional bioeconomic harvesting model, where the optimal steady-state species stock is determined by equating the social discount rate and bioeconomic returns net of harvesting costs that vary with stock size.

The locally stable equilibrium (S_1^*, y_1^*) for Case 1 is depicted in Figure 20.1. An optimal trajectory is represented graphically assuming $G_1' < 0$ and $S_0 > S_1^*$. Note that for any $y_1^* > 0$ it follows that $S_1^* > S_e$, that is, the equilibrium level of wild species stock in Case 1 must lie to the right of the vertical $\delta = G_1'$ curve in Figure 22.1. This result is caused by the decreasing unit costs as the stock increases. We therefore note that if in our closed economy model there is no opportunity cost of holding on to land as natural habitat and if there is no non-consumptive value of biodiversity, then we obtain

PROPOSITION 2.1. *In a closed economy if* $R_2 = R_3 = 0$, *there exists an equilibrium harvesting rate* $y_1^* > 0$ *such that equilibrium total species biomass stock occurs to the right of* $\delta = G_1' > 0$, *that is,* $S_1^* > S_e$.

Case 2. Habitat conversion model ($\delta = R_1 + R_2$)

In this version the basic bioeconomic model is extended to include the costs of habitat conversion, that is, R_2 of equation (22.15). As shown in Figure 22.1 and demonstrated in Appendix 1, S_2^* and y_2^* are the new equilibrium levels of total species biomass and harvesting respectively. Corresponding to these values must be an equilibrium level of natural habitat area, A_2^*. Appendix l indicates that the equilibrium of Case 2 is a saddle point for an upward-sloping $dy/dt = 0$ curve. In Figure 22.1, the optimal trajectory assuming $G_1' < 0$ and $S_0 > S_2^*$ is shown.

In Appendix 1 the respective equilibriums of Cases 1 and 2 are compared, and the result suggests that $S_1^* > S_2^* > Sf > S_e$, that is, the equilibrium level of wild species stock in Case 2 must be less than the equilibrium level derived in Case 1. Intuitively, the reasoning is fairly straightforward: now that there is an opportunity cost for holding onto land as natural habitat, in the long run a smaller total stock of species will be maintained.

This result is an important modification of the standard bioeconomic model of renewable resource utilization. We have suggested that the growth in the total species stock is dependent not only on the natural biological regeneration rate of species but also on the total number of species contained in a given habitat area. However, holding land as natural habitat also implies an opportunity cost, which in our Case 2 version of the model is represented by foregone consumption from development activities that use converted habitat land. Because conventional bioeconomic models do not take into account explicitly the opportunity cost of maintaining 'wild' lands as habitat for species, the equilibrium level of species stock – and thus implicitly habitat area – is higher than if the opportunity cost of maintaining habitat were included. Consequently, this outcome can be stated more formally as

PROPOSITION 2.2. *In a closed economy if* $R_3 = 0$, *there exists an equilibrium harvesting rate* $y_2^* > 0$ *such that equilibrium total species stock occurs to the right of* $\delta = G_1' + G_2' > 0$ *but is less than the equilibrium stock of the bioeconomic model, that is,* $S_1^* > S_2^* > S_f > S_e$.

Case 3. Inclusion of biodiversity value ($\delta = R_1 + R_2 + R_3$)
Finally, we extend the model to include $S(t)$ in the social utility function to represent the stock externalities associated with non-consumptive biodiversity values, thus arriving at the original optimal control problem and corresponding first-order conditions (22.9), (22.10) and (22.11). As shown in Figure 22.1 and demonstrated in Appendix 1, S^* and y^* are the new equilibrium levels of total species stock and harvesting respectively, which in turn imply a new equilibrium level of natural habitat area, A^*. Appendix 1 confirms that the equilibrium of the full version of the model (Case 3) is a saddle point for an upward-sloping $dy/dt = 0$ curve, thus verifying Proposition 2. The optimal trajectory is depicted in Figure 1 assuming $G_1' < 0$, $S_0 > S^*$ and $S_1^* > S^* > S_2^*$.

As indicated in Appendix 1, comparison of the results of Case 3 with that of Cases 1 and 2 yields two interesting conclusions. First, comparing Cases 2 and 3, the inclusion of non-consumptive biodiversity values in the model will tend to offset the opportunity costs of holding on to habitat, resulting in a higher long-run equilibrium level of species stock and habitat area. That is, in the full version of the model with biodiversity values included (Case 3), the equilibrium wildlife stock and habitat area will always exceed that of Case 2 which excludes these values. Second, comparing Cases 1 and 3, it is not clear whether the equilibrium level of species stock (and habitat area) in the full model will be less or greater than the equilibrium stock determined by the simple bioeconomic model. The outcome will depend on whether in the long run the marginal value of biodiversity, U_S, compensates sufficiently for the marginal opportunity cost of maintaining habitat, $-U_c f'$. Only under special conditions will the bioeconomic model (Case 1) actually be able to predict the long-run equilibrium of the full model (Case 3), that is, when $U_S = -U_c f'$.

It is worth summarizing these results with a further addition to Proposition 2

PROPOSITION 2.3. *In a closed economy if the* $\dot{y} = 0$ *curve is defined by* $\delta = R_1 + R_2 + R_3$, *there exists an equilibrium harvesting rate* $y^* > 0$ *such that equilibrium total species biomass stock occurs to the right of* $\delta = G_1' + G_2' > 0$ *and exceeds the equilibrium stock of the habitat conversion model, that is,* $S^* > S_2^* > S_f > S_e$; *however, whether* S^* *is less than, equals or exceeds the equilibrium species stock of the bioeconomic model,* S_1^*, *will depend on whether* U_S *is less than, equals or exceeds* $-U_c f'$.

4. Open economy model

In this section we develop the model to allow for trade. The basic assumption is that some wildlife products are exported, which in turn allow the import of consumption goods in addition to domestic production from converted habitat land. As noted in the introduction, if wildlife or natural products enter international markets then the possibility exists that trade interventions may be used to influence the optimal level of harvesting and species biomass stocks. The likely scenario is that importing nations may use such interventions to control exploitation of wildlife stocks and conversion of habitat land. Following the approach of Barbier and Rauscher (1994), we extend the full version of our model to examine the likely implications of such trade interventions, and compare them to the impacts of an alternative policy, such as an international transfer.

We assume the following additional relationships for the open economy model

$x(t)$	exports of wildlife or natural resource products (in terms of biomass)
$m(t)$	consumption of imported goods
$y(t) - x(t)$	domestic consumption of wildlife or natural resource products
P	terms of trade, p_x/p_m.

As before two outputs are produced domestically, $f(S(t))$ from converted habitat land and $y(t)$ from harvesting wildlife resources. By assumption habitat land is a net exporter of resource products, that is, $x(t) > 0$. All domestic products and imports are assumed to be homogeneous. Consequently, the open economy model includes a trade balance equation and a new definition of total domestic consumption, c

$$px(t) = m(t) \tag{22.17}$$

$$c(t) = f(S(t)) + m(t) \tag{22.18}$$

From substituting (22.17) and (22.18) into (22.7) the open economy welfare maximizing problem for the developing country is now

$$\text{Max}_{y,x} W = \int_0^\infty \left[U\left(y - x, f(S) + px, S\right) - w(S)y\right]e^{-\delta t}\,dt \tag{22.19}$$

subject to (22.1') and (22.5) and the initial and terminal conditions as defined before. Thus the open economy problem contains an additional dimension to the social decision to trade-off wildlife utilization with habitat conversion: on the one hand, holding on to natural habitat implies an opportunity cost of foregone consumption from less habitat conversion; on the other, trade in wildlife and natural resource products allows consumption of imported goods which can substitute for commodities produced from converted habitat.

The current value Hamiltonian of the problem is

$$H = U(y - x, f(S) + px, S) - w(S)y + \lambda[G_1(S) - aS^{-b}r - y], \quad (22.20)$$

which yields the following first order conditions, assuming an interior solution

$$dH/dy = U_1 - w(S) - \lambda = 0 \text{ or } U_1 = w(S) + \lambda \quad (22.21)$$

$$dH/dx = -U_1 + pU_2 = 0 \quad \text{or} \quad U_1 = pU_2 \quad (22.22)$$

$$-dH/dS = \dot{\lambda} - \delta\lambda \quad \text{or} \quad \dot{\lambda} = (\delta - G_1' - baS^{-(b+1)}r)\lambda + yw' - U_2f' - U_3 \quad (22.23)$$

$$dH/d\lambda = \dot{S} = G_1(S) - aS^{-b}r - y. \quad (22.11)$$

where $U_1 = \partial U/\partial(y - x) > 0$, $U_2 = \partial U/\partial(c + m) > 0$ and $U_3 = \partial U/\partial S > 0$. We assume as before that these marginal utilities are subject to diminishing returns, and will tend to infinity as their arguments approach zero.

Condition (22.21) indicates that, along the optimal trajectory, the marginal benefit of harvesting or utilizing wild species for domestic consumption, U_1, must equal its marginal cost, which consists of marginal harvesting costs, $w(S)$, as well as the marginal costs of stock depletion, λ. However, the only difference with condition (22.9) of the closed economy is that domestic consumption is now defined as harvested output net of exports, $y - x$. Condition (22.22) is entirely new, and it indicates that, if the developing country is a price-taker in international trade, then the relative marginal value of domestic consumption of wildlife and natural resource products to imported good consumption must be equated with the terms of trade, p. Finally condition (22.23) is almost identical with the renewable resource dynamic condition (22.10) for denoting the change in the value of the total species stock in the closed economy, and it includes not only the standard (net) marginal bioeconomic costs for holding on to species, $(\delta - G_1')\lambda + yw'$, but also the net marginal benefits of 'holding on' to land as habitat, $-baS^{-(b+1)}r\lambda - U_2f'$, and the marginal social value of an additional unit of biodiversity, U_3.

By combining (22.21) and (22.23) we obtain

$$\dot{y} - \dot{x} = \frac{\left[\left(\delta - G_1' + baS^{-(b+1)}r\right)\left(U_1 - w(S)\right) + w'\left(G_1(S) - aS^{-b}r\right) - U_2 f' - U_3\right]}{U_{11}}$$

(22.24)

Utilizing (22.24) and the first order conditions (22.21), (22.22), (22.23) and (22.11) one can solve for the following system of equations describing an equilibrium where $dy/dt = dx/dt = dS/dt = r = 0$

$$U_1(y^\dagger, x^\dagger) = pU_2(S^\dagger, x^\dagger) \qquad (22.25)$$

$$\delta - G_1'\left(S^\dagger\right) = \frac{-y^\dagger w'\left(S^\dagger\right) + U_2\left(S^\dagger, x^\dagger\right) f'\left(S^\dagger\right) + U_3\left(S^\dagger\right)}{\left(U_1\left(y^\dagger\right) - w\left(S^\dagger\right)\right)} > 0, \quad \dot{y} = \dot{x} = \dot{S} = r = 0$$

(22.26)

or

$$\delta = V_1(S^\dagger, y^\dagger, x^\dagger) + V_2(S^\dagger, y^\dagger, x^\dagger) + V_3(S^\dagger, y^\dagger, x^\dagger)$$

$$G_1(S^\dagger) = y^\dagger, \quad \dot{S} = r = 0, \qquad (22.27)$$

where the equilibrium values of y, x and S are denoted by daggers (†), and $V_1 = G_1'(S^\dagger) - y^\dagger w'(S^\dagger)/[U_1(y^\dagger, x^\dagger) - w(S^\dagger)]$, $V_2 = U_2(S^\dagger, x^\dagger)f'(S^\dagger)/[U_1(y^\dagger, x^\dagger) - w(S^\dagger)]$ and $V_3 = U_3(S^\dagger)/[U_1(y^\dagger, x^\dagger) - w(S^\dagger)]$.

Total differentiation of the system of equations (22.25) – (22.27) can lead to characterization of the equilibrium state and trajectories leading to the equilibrium. As shown in Appendix 1, the equilibrium is a saddle point and the saddle path is positively sloped. Using these results, the optimal solution is represented graphically in Figure 22.2 for $S_0 > S^\dagger$ and $G_1' < 0$. This solution suggests

PROPOSITION 3. *In an open economy if the dy/dt = dx/dt = 0 curve is defined by $\delta = V_1 + V_2 + V_3$, there exists an equilibrium harvesting rate $y^\dagger > 0$ such that equilibrium total species stock, $S^\dagger$, occurs to the right of $\delta = G_1' + G_2' > 0$.*

It is useful to compare the equilibrium (S^*, y^*) of the full (Case 3) version of the closed economy model with the new equilibrium $(S^\dagger\ y^\dagger)$ obtained in the open economy. If we assume that the marginal utilities of consumption and biodiversity values are the same in the two models, then $x = 0$ implies that $U_2(f(S^\dagger)) = U_c$

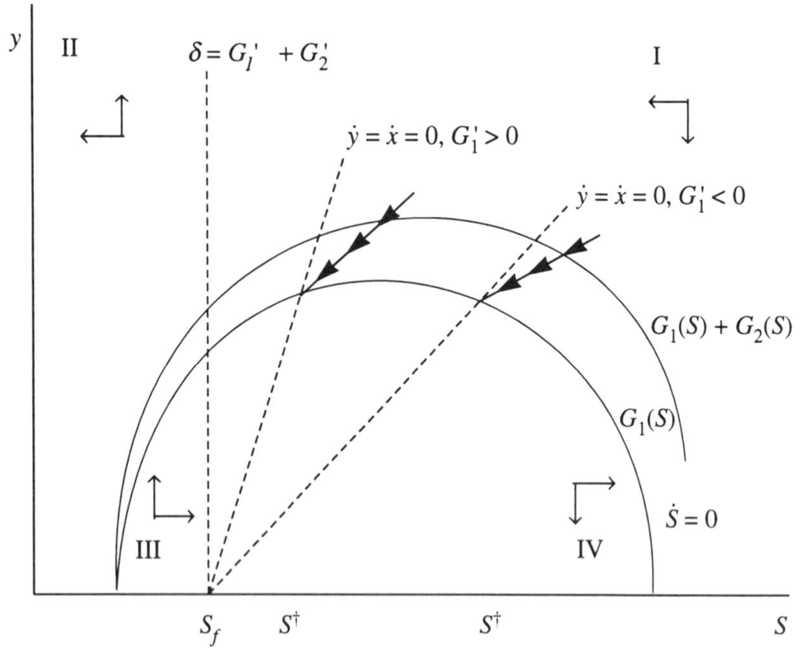

Figure 22.2 The long-run equilibrium of the open economy

$(f(S^*))$, $U_1\ (y^\dagger) = U_y\ (y^*)$ and $U_3\ (S^\dagger) = U_S\ (S^*)$. Consequently, equilibrium in the closed and open economy will be the same, that is, $S^\dagger = S^*$ and $y^\dagger = y^*$. However, for any $x > 0$ then $U_2(f(S^*) + x) < U_2(f(S^*))$ and $U_1\ (y^* - x) > U_1(y^*)$. From inspection of equation (22.26), it is unclear in which direction S must change in order to maintain the equilibrium condition. This is because, on the one hand, exports of wildlife products reduce the need for domestic consumption from habitat conversion activities, but on the other, increased wildlife exports mean less domestic consumption of these products. If the marginal utility of the latter effect outweighs that of the former, then the right-hand side of (22.26) may increase, and S must therefore also increase to keep the equilibrium condition. However, if the increase in U_1 is the more powerful effect, then the right-hand side of (22.26) could decrease and S would have to rise correspondingly. Thus it is unclear whether the open economy equilibrium for $x^\dagger > 0$ will yield a long-run equilibrium species stock, $S^\dagger$, that will be less than, equal to or greater than the equilibrium, S^* under the closed economy.

There is also an intuitive explanation of this ambiguous result. For the economy to begin trading in wildlife products, p must rise sufficiently high to make exports worthwhile. Starting from autarky this has two effects. First, the development of an external market means that it is more profitable to harvest from wildlife resources, as the external terms of trade with respect to consumption goods is now higher than the domestic terms of trade. This may increase exploitation of the resource base to produce wildlife exports. On the other hand, as noted above, there is less pressure for conversion of land to other uses, as it is now relatively less expensive to obtain consumption goods from world markets. We shall evaluate these effects in the next section.

5. Global biodiversity values: trade interventions vs transfers

Comparative static analysis of the long-run equilibrium can be employed to determine the impacts of trade interventions in influencing the developing country's decision as to how much wildlife species to maintain. Our model already includes positive *domestic* biodiversity values, such as the non-consumptive values that the developing country may capture from maintaining species and natural habitat. However, it is unlikely that the developing country will take into account any positive *global* biodiversity values associated with wildlife and habitat conservation, for example the values that the rest of the world attaches to 'conserving' genetic material for future unknown uses, the global educational and scientific research value of biodiversity, and the 'existence' value of living creatures and natural systems.[8] If the global values of biodiversity are being ignored by domestic policy makers, then it is likely that the international community would want the developing country to conserve more species and habitat in the long run than the country would do on its own.

There are essentially two broad approaches that the international community could take to achieve this objective. First, as described in the introduction, the international community could, through trade interventions such as import bans, tariffs or other controls on wildlife and natural resource products trade, try to influence the developing country's decision to 'hold on' to species and habitat. Second, an alternative policy would be to encourage the developing country to 'internalize' any global biodiversity values through an international transfer of funds to reduce the need to exploit and convert wild lands. The effects of both approaches can be characterized through comparative static analysis of our open economy model.

Following Barbier and Rauscher (1994), we assume that imports bans, controls and restrictions have the effect reducing the terms of trade to the wildlife trade of the developing country. In our open economy model, a change in the terms of trade, p, has the following impacts on the long run equilibrium of total species biomass stock

$$\frac{dS^{\dagger}}{dp} = -\frac{\left[\psi(1+\eta_2)U_2 - f' \, U_{22}x\left(U_{11} + p^2U_{22}\right)\right]}{\Delta} \qquad (22.28)$$

where $\eta_2 < 0$ is the elasticity of marginal utility, U_2, with respect to imported consumption goods, m and $\psi = (\delta - G_1')\,U_{11} + f'U_{22}p$. If the absolute value of η_2 is large, that is, $|\eta_2| > 1$, then marginal welfare in the developing country is highly responsive to a change in imported commodities. The situation with $|\eta_2| > 1$ occurs only when the export supply curve of the developing country is backward bending. Hence $|\eta_2| < 1$ is the normal case in the trade sector of the model.

From (22.28) it follows that

$$\frac{dS^\dagger}{dp} < 0 \;\text{ when }\; |\eta_2| < 1 \;\text{ and }\; \psi < \frac{f'\,U_{22}x\left(U_{11} + p^2U_{22}\right)}{(1+\eta_2)U_2} < 0, \;\text{ or}$$

$$\frac{dS^\dagger}{dp} < 0 \;\text{ when }\; |\eta_2| > 1 \;\text{ and }\; \psi > \frac{f'\,U_{22}x\left(U_{11} + p^2U_{22}\right)}{(1+\eta_2)U_2} > 0.$$

These conditions are not necessarily fulfilled. For example, if $\psi(1 + \eta_2)U_2 > f'\,U_{22}x(U_{11} + p^2U_{22})$, we get $dS/dp > 0$, quite contrary to the results of standard bioeconomic models (Clark, 1976). A situation with $dS/dp > 0$ will always occur for a positive ψ when $|\eta_2| < 1$, and for a negative ψ when $|\eta_2| > 1$. Under these latter conditions, trade interventions are counterproductive to conserving species and habitat, and therefore are the wrong strategy for coercing the developing country to 'internalize' global biodiversity values. Thus without further information on the value of η_2 or the sign of ψ it is impossible to determine whether trade interventions that reduce the terms of trade, p, will increase or decrease the equilibrium value of species stock, $S^\dagger$. The ambiguous stock effects make trade interventions a poor policy instrument for securing biodiversity conservation.

A large transfer of international funds to the developing country, perhaps through provisions of the international Convention of Biodiversity or the Global Environmental Facility (GEF), could assist the country in wildlife and habitat conservation. For example, the GEF has the mandate to fund biodiversity conservation projects in developing countries that yield global values but not sufficient domestic net benefits to be funded by these countries. Such international transfers have the effect of 'freeing up' domestic financial resources for other purposes. The developing country is essentially receiving a subsidy by the rest of the world to 'internalize' global biodiversity values. In our model, these transfers can be represented by an increase in foreign exchange available for consumption of imported goods. This has a double benefit in terms of species and habitat conservation; it not only supplements wildlife export earnings but it also reduces consumption from habitat conversion activities. Thus from (22.17) and (22.18) consumption now becomes

$$c = f(S) + px + i, \tag{22.29}$$

where i is the amount of international transfer. An increase in the subsidy has the following effect on the long-run equilibrium of total species biomass stock

$$\frac{\mathrm{d}S^{\dagger}}{\mathrm{d}i} = -\frac{\left[\psi p U_{22} - f' U_{22}\left(U_{22} + p^2 U_{22}\right)\right]}{\Delta} \tag{22.30}$$

A transfer of funds will increase the long run stock, $\mathrm{d}S^{\dagger}/\mathrm{d}i > 0$, if $(\delta - G_1') > f'/p$. This is always the case if the equilibrium is to the right of $\delta = G_1'$ as shown in Figure 22.2, and assuming no impact of the transfer on p. The effect of the international transfer is therefore to make the receiving country better off, with increased income to import from abroad. The subsidy not only replaces wildlife exports as a means to importing consumption goods but also puts less pressure on the species stock through increased harvesting for domestic consumption. Consequently, an increased international transfer leads to a greater long run equilibrium total species stock.[9]

From the discussion of the effects of trade interventions and a direct international transfer it is worth stating that

PROPOSITION 4. *In an open economy, if* $(\delta - G_1') > f'/p$ *then a direct international transfer,* i*, will increase the long-run equilibrium total species stock,* $S^{\dagger}$*, unambiguously; however, the effect of a trade intervention is ambiguous.*

6. Conclusion

We have attempted to explore two issues in the analysis of this chapter. First, by developing several versions of a closed economy model of optimal species utilization, we have examined the extent to which the long-run equilibrium of the basic bioeconomic model is affected by the inclusion of habitat conversion and then additionally biodiversity value as a positive externality. Second, by developing an open economy version of the full model, we were able to compare the likely impacts of trade interventions as opposed to international transfers on the developing country's long-run decision to conserve wildlife species and habitat. Several important results emerged from this analysis.

The inclusion of habitat conversion proves to be an important modification of the standard bioeconomic model of renewable resource utilization. We have suggested that the growth in the total species stock is dependent not only on the natural biological regeneration rate of species but also on the total number of species contained in a given habitat area. However, holding land as natural habitat also implies an opportunity cost, which is represented by foregone consumption from development activities that use convert habitat land. Because conventional bioeconomic models do not take into account explicitly the opportunity cost of maintaining 'wild' lands as habitat for species, the equilibrium level of species stock – and thus implicitly habitat area – is higher than if the opportunity cost of maintaining habitat were included. Consequently, when applied to wildlife utilization problems, conventional bioeconomic models may overestimate the optimal long-run levels of wildlife species and habitat.

Our analysis shows that the additional inclusion of biodiversity values as a positive stock externality will counteract, to some extent, the effects of the opportunity cost of maintaining habitat for species. If the marginal value of biodiversity is sufficiently high, then despite the marginal opportunity cost of maintaining habitat, the optimal equilibrium levels of species and habitat can equal or even exceed the levels determined by the conventional bioeconomic model.

These results for the closed economy model highlight the importance of extending the conventional bioeconomic model for wild species and resource utilization to include both the opportunity costs for maintaining species habitat and positive biodiversity values if these costs and values are considered to be significant. If they are instead excluded, the conventional bioeconomic model will predict the 'correct' long-run equilibrium level of species stock (and habitat area) only under very special conditions.

The open economy model provides an additional dimension to the social decision to trade-off wildlife utilization with development benefits from converted habitat land: on the one hand, holding on to natural habitat implies an opportunity cost of foregone consumption from less habitat conversion; on the other, trade in wildlife and natural resource products allows consumption of imported goods which can substitute for commodities produced from converted habitat. However, it is unclear when compared to the closed economy equilibrium whether the open economy leads to a higher long-run optimal level of species and habitat conservation. Exports of wildlife products appear to reduce the need for domestic consumption from habitat conversion activities, but exports also mean less domestic consumption of these products.

Comparative static analysis of the long-run equilibrium of the open economy model suggests caution in the use of trade interventions as an international policy for coercing a developing country to internalize global externality values of biodiversity. Under certain conditions, trade interventions may be unambiguously counterproductive, whereas the alternative policy of an international transfer of funds would lead to greater long-run conservation of species and habitat.

Although in our model it is possible for trade interventions (trade bans, tariffs or trade subsidies) to have the desired effect of increasing long-run equilibrium species stock and habitat area, we need to know the specific conditions underlying both the bioeconomic, habitat conversion and trade sectors of the model in order to determine the precise influence of trade policy interventions. Hence, we conclude that trade intervention is a second-best approach for global biodiversity conservation.

Finally, it is worth commenting that the results of the open economy model may be affected if it were extended to reflect other aspects of trade–environment dimensions to resource exploitation problems in developing countries. For example, Chichilnisky (1994) examines the interactions of ill-defined property rights regimes and international trade in resource products from developing countries; Barbier and Rauscher (1994) expand their basic model of trade and tropical deforestation to allow for market power and foreign asset accumulation (or debt); and Schulz (1994) examines the effects of trade on wildlife utilization in developing countries by explicitly accounting for species interactions, such as predator–prey relationships. Extensions to our model along these lines may further increase its applicability to resource utilization problems in developing countries.

Appendix 1. Solutions of the closed and open economy models

The following appendix derives the long run equilibrium solutions and stability conditions for the various versions of the model developed in this paper.

Case 1. Bioeconomic model ($\delta = R_1$)

We begin with the basic bioeconomic model of the closed economy with no costs of holding onto land as habitat and no positive stock externalities associated with biodiversity, that is, $R_2 = R_3 = 0$. Thus the following equations of motion can be derived from the first-order conditions (22.9), (22.10) and (22.11)

$$\dot{y} = \frac{\left[(\delta - G_1')\left(U_y - w(S)\right) + yw' + w'\dot{S}\right]}{U_{yy}}$$

$$= \frac{(\delta - G_1')\left(U_y - w(S)\right) + w' G_1(S)}{U_{yy}}$$

$$\dot{S} = G_1(S) - y,$$

which yield the following long-run equilibrium condition for dy/dt = dS/dt = 0

$$\delta - G_1'\left(S_1^*\right) = \frac{-y_1^* w'\left(S_1^*\right)}{\left(U_y\left(y_1^*\right) - w\left(S_1^*\right)\right)} > 0, \quad \dot{y} = \dot{S} = 0$$

$$G_1(S_1^*) = y_1^*, \quad \dot{S} = 0,$$

where S_1^* and y_1^* are the equilibrium levels of the total species stock and harvesting respectively. This equilibrium for Case 1 is depicted in Figure 22.1. Note that from the above equations that $y_1^* = 0$ results in $\delta = G_1'$, which means that the origin of the d*y*/d*t* = 0 curve for Case 1 in Figure 22.1 is $(S_e, 0)$. Therefore, for any $y_1^* > 0$ it follows that $S_1^* > S_e$, that is, the equilibrium level of wild species stock in Case 1 must lie to the right of the vertical $\delta = G_1'$ curve in Figure 22.1. This result is caused by the decreasing unit costs as the stock increases.

Through linearizing the above two equations of motion and evaluating the resulting matrix of coefficients at the equilibrium (S_1^*, y_1^*), it can be shown that the equilibrium is a saddle point if the determinant of the matrix is negative, and the curve d*y*/d*t* = 0 is positively sloped and cuts the curve d*S*/d*t* = 0 from below. Through linearizing we obtain

$$\dot{S} = G_1'(S - S_1^*) - (y - y_1^*)$$

$$\dot{y} = \frac{X\left(S - S_1^*\right) + Z\left(y - y_1^*\right)}{U_{yy}},$$

where $X = -(\delta - G_1')w' - (U_y - w(S))G'' + G_1'w'' > 0$, $Z = (\delta - G_1')U_{yy} + w' < 0$ and U_{yy} is assumed to be constant.[10] The determinant Δ of the matrix of coefficients of the above equations is

$$\Delta = \frac{G_1' Z + X}{U_{yy}}$$

It follows that $\Delta < 0$ if $G_1' < 0$ or if $G_1' > 0$ and $-X/U_{yy} > Z/U_{yy}$. However, if these conditions hold then comparing the d*y*/d*t* = 0 and d*S*/d*t* = 0 curves shows that

$$\left.\frac{dy}{dS}\right|_{\dot{y}=0} = -\frac{X}{Z} > G_1' = \left.\frac{dy}{dS}\right|_{\dot{S}=0}.$$

Consequently, the requirement that dy/dt = 0 is upward sloping and cuts the dS/dt = 0 curve from below is a necessary condition for $\Delta < 0$. The equilibrium (S_1^*, y_1^*) is therefore locally stable (a saddle point). Thus as shown in Figure 22.1, for Case 1 isosectors I and II are convergent and contain optimal trajectories to the locally stable equilibrium (S_1^*, y_1^*). An optimal trajectory is represented graphically assuming $G_1' < 0$ and $S_0 > S_1^*$.

Case 2. Habitat conversion model ($\delta = R_1 + R_2$)
In this version the basic bioeconomic model is extended to include the costs of habitat conversion, that is, R_2 of equation (22.15). The equations of motion for the closed economy are now modified to

$$\dot{y} = \frac{\left[\left(\delta - G_1' - G_2'\right)\left(U_y - w(S)\right) + yw' + w'\dot{S} - U_c f'\right]}{U_{yy}}$$

$$= \frac{\left[\left(\delta - G_1' + baS^{-(b+1)}\right)\left(U_y - w(S)\right) + w'\left(G_1(S) - aS^{-b}r\right) - U_c f'\right]}{U_{yy}}$$

$$\dot{S} = G_1(S) + G_2(S) = G_1(S) - aS^{-b}r - y.$$

This leads to the following long-run equilibrium conditions for dy/dt = dS/dt = r = 0

$$\delta - G_1'\left(S_2^*\right) = \frac{-y_2^* w'\left(S_2^*\right) + U_c f'\left(S_2^*\right)}{\left(U_y\left(y_2^*\right) - w\left(S_2^*\right)\right)} > 0, \quad \dot{y} = \dot{S} = r = 0$$

$$G_1(S_2^*) = y_2^*, \quad \dot{S} = r = 0,$$

where S_2^* and y_2^* are the new equilibrium levels of the total species stock and harvesting respectively, as depicted for Case 2 in Figure 22.2. From equation (22.2) in the text it is clear that corresponding to these values must be an equilibrium level of natural habitat area, A_2^*. Since we have added $G_2(S)$ to the growth function, we must change the origin ($y_2^* = 0$) of the dy/dt = 0 curve to S_f, such that $\delta = G_1'(S_f) + G_2'(S_f)$ and $S_f > S_e$. Therefore as shown for Case 2 in Figure 22.1, if the dy/dt = 0 curve is upward sloping, then for any $y_2^* > 0$ it follows that $S_2^* > S_f$; that is, the equilibrium level of wild species stock will be to the right of the point S_f.

By linearizing the above equations of motion and evaluating them at the equilibrium point (S_2^*, y_2^*) it is possible to prove that the above condition holds for Case 2. Given that at this equilibrium $r = 0$, we obtain through linearizing

$$\dot{S} = G_1' \,(S - S_2^*) - (y - y_2^*)$$

$$\dot{y} = \frac{\left[X - U_{cc}(f')^2 - U_c f''\right]\left(S - S_2^*\right) + Z\left(y - y_2^*\right)}{U_{yy}},$$

where $X > 0$ and $Z < 0$ as before and $-U_{cc}(f')^2 - U_c f'' > 0$. The determinant Δ of the matrix of coefficients of the above linearized equations is

$$\Delta = \frac{G_1' Z + \left(X - U_{cc}(f')^2 - U_c f''\right)}{U_{yy}}.$$

It follows that $\Delta < 0$ for $G_1' > 0$. If $G_1' > 0$, then $\Delta < 0$ requires $-(X - U_{cc}(f')^2$ $U_c f'')/Z > G_1'$. The result of such conditions is

$$\left.\frac{\mathrm{d}y}{\mathrm{d}S}\right|_{\dot{y}=0} = \frac{-\left(X - U_{cc}(f')^2 - U_c f''\right)}{Z} > G_1' = \left.\frac{\mathrm{d}y}{\mathrm{d}S}\right|_{\dot{S}=0}.$$

Thus for Case 2 the requirement that $\mathrm{d}y/\mathrm{d}t = 0$ is upward sloping and cuts the $\mathrm{d}S/\mathrm{d}t = 0$ curve from below is a necessary condition for $\Delta < 0$. The equilibrium (S_2^*, y_2^*) is therefore locally stable (a saddle point). In Figure 22.1, the optimal trajectory assuming $G_1' < 0$ and $S_0 > S_2^*$ is shown.

In comparing the respective equilibriums of Cases 1 and 2, note that in Case 2 if in equilibrium $-w'G_1(S) > -U_c f'$, then $(\delta - G_1') > 0$ and the $\mathrm{d}y/\mathrm{d}t = 0$ curve is upward sloping. This result suggests that $S_1^* > S_2^* > S_f > S_e$, that is, the equilibrium level of wild species stock in Case 2 must be less than the equilibrium level derived in Case 1.[11] That is, because in Case 2 there is an opportunity cost for holding onto land as natural habitat, in the long run a smaller total stock of species and habitat will be maintained.

Case 3. Inclusion of biodiversity value ($\delta = R_1 + R_2 + R_3$)

Incorporating $S(t)$ in the social utility function to represent the stock externalities associated with non-consumptive biodiversity values yields the original optimal control problem and corresponding first-order conditions (22.9), (22.10) and

(22.11). The equation of motion for optimal harvesting derived in Case 2 now becomes

$$\dot{y} = \frac{\left[\left(\delta - G_1' - G_2'\right)\left(U_y - w(S)\right) + yw' + w'\dot{S} - U_c f' - U_S\right]}{U_{yy}}$$

and the long-run equilibrium conditions for $dy/dt = dS/dt = r = 0$ are the same as (22.12) and (22.13) in the text

$$\delta - G_1'\left(S^*\right) = \frac{-y^* w'\left(S^*\right) + U_c f'\left(S^*\right) + U_S\left(S^*\right)}{\left(U_y\left(y^*\right) - w\left(S^*\right)\right)} > 0, \quad \dot{y} = \dot{S} = r = 0$$

$$\text{or} \quad \delta = R_1(S^*, y^*) + R_2(S^*, y^*) + R_3(S^*, y^*)$$

$$G_1(S^*) = y^*, \quad \dot{S} = r = 0,$$

where S^* and y^* are the new equilibrium levels of total species stock and harvesting respectively, which in turn imply an equilibrium level of natural habitat area, A^*. Note that once again $y^* = 0$ results in $\delta = G_1'(S_f) + G_2'(S_f)$; that is, as shown in Figure 22.1 for Case 3 the $dy/dt = 0$ curve originates at S_f and the equilibrium level of wild species stock will lie to the right of this point.

The stability condition for this case is similar to that of Case 2. That is, the inclusion of biodiversity value means that the determinant Δ of the matrix of coefficients of the linearized equations of motion evaluated at the equilibrium (S^*, y^*) is

$$\Delta = \frac{G_1' Z + \left(X - U_{cc}(f')^2 - U_c f'' - U_{SS}\right)}{U_{yy}}.$$

It follows that $\Delta < 0$ for $G_1' < 0$. If $G_1' > 0$, then $\Delta < 0$ requires $-(X - U_{cc}(f')^2 - U_c f'' - U_{SS})/Z > G_1'$. The result of such conditions is

$$\left.\frac{dy}{dS}\right|_{\dot{y}=0} = \frac{-\left(X - U_{cc}(f')^2 - U_c f'' - U_{SS}\right)}{Z} > G_1' = \left.\frac{dy}{dS}\right|_{\dot{S}=0}.$$

Thus for Case 3, the requirement that $dy/dt = 0$ is upward sloping and cuts the $dS/dt = 0$ curve from below is a necessary condition for $\Delta < 0$. The equilibrium (S^*, y^*) is therefore locally stable (a saddle point). In Figure 22.1, the optimal trajectory assuming $G_1' < 0$ and $S_0 > S^*$ is shown.

It is useful to compare the equilibrium species stock derived in Case 3 to that resulting from Cases 1 and 2. In Case 3 if $-w'G_1(S) + U_S > -U_c f'$, then $(\delta - G_1')$ > 0 and the $dy/dt = 0$ curve is upward sloping.[12] An immediate result of this condition must be that $G_1'(S_2^*) > G_1'(S^*)$, which in turn implies $S^* > S_2^*$. That is, in the full version of the model with biodiversity values included (Case 3), the equilibrium wildlife stock exceeds that of Case 2 which excludes biodiversity values. However, the relationship between S^* and S_1^* is more ambiguous and is governed by the following condition

$$\text{if } U_S \lesseqqgtr -U_c f' \text{ then } S^* \lesseqqgtr S_1^*.$$

That is, if the marginal value of biodiversity is sufficiently high relative to the marginal opportunity cost of maintaining natural habitat, then the optimal equilibrium level of species, S^*, can equal or even exceed the equilibrium level of the bioeconomic model. In Figure 22.1, the optimal trajectory assumes that $S^* < S_1^*$ which implies $U_S < -U_c f'$.

The open economy model

The stability conditions for the open economy model can be derived in the following manner. Total differentiation of the simultaneous equation system (22.25)–(22.27) characterizing the equilibrium $(S^\dagger, y^\dagger, x^\dagger)$ yields

$$U_{11}dy - (U_{11} + p^2U_{22})dx - (pU_{22}f')dS - (U_2 + pU_{22}x)dp = 0$$

$$[(\delta - G_1')\,U_{11} + w']dy - \psi dx + \phi dS - f'U_{22}x dp = 0$$

$$-\,dy + G_1'/dS = 0,$$

where $\psi = (\delta - G_1')U_{11} + f'U_{22}p$ and $\phi = -(U_1 - w(S))G_1'' - (\delta - G_1')w' + yw''$ $- U_{22}(f')^2 - U_2 f'' - U_{33} > 0$. The determinant of the Hessian matrix of coefficients for dy, dx and dS in the above system of equations is

$$\Delta = G_1'[((\delta - G_1')U_{11} + w')(U_{11} + p^2U_{22}) - \psi U_{11}] + [\psi p U_{22} f' + \phi(U_{11} + p^2U_{22})].$$

Signing Δ again requires comparing the slopes of the $dy/dt = dx/dt = 0$ and dS/dt $= 0$ curves. Substituting for dx in the above system of equations yields

$$\left.\frac{\mathrm{d}y}{\mathrm{d}S}\right|_{\dot{S}=0} = G_1'$$

$$\left.\frac{\mathrm{d}y}{\mathrm{d}S}\right|_{\dot{y}=\dot{x}=0} = -\frac{\psi p U_{22} f' + \phi\left(U_{11} + p^2 U_{22}\right)}{\left(\left(\delta - G_1'\right)U_{11} + w'\right)\left(U_{11} + p^2 U_{22}\right) - \psi U_{11}}.$$

It follows that if $G_1' < 0$ and the dy/dt = dx/dt = 0 curve is upward sloping then $\Delta < 0$. However, if $G_1' > 0$ then not only must the dy/dt = dx/dt = 0 curve be upward sloping but also the slope of this curve must exceed the slope of the dS/dt = 0 curve.[13] If these conditions are met, then the equilibrium ($S^\dagger$, $y^\dagger$, $x^\dagger$) is locally stable (a saddle point). Finally, from equation (22.26) in the text it is clear that $y^\dagger = 0$ implies that the dy/dt = dx/dt = 0 curve originates at S_f, which was derived for Case 2 of the closed economy model. Using all these results, the optimal solution is depicted graphically in Figure 22.2 for $S_0 > S^\dagger$ and $G_1' < 0$.

Appendix 2. An alternative formulation of the allocation problem

Equation (22.1) in the text specifies a growth function for the total species stock, S, which is additively separable into sub-components, $G_1(S)$ and $G_2(A)$, that indicate the influence respectively of stock size and total habitat area, A, on growth. The following appendix demonstrates that it is possible to specify a non-separable version of the growth function, $G(S, A)$, and an alternative formulation of the biodiversity and habitat allocation problem without affecting significantly the main results of this chapter.[14]

For example, following more conventional bioeconomic models, if total habitat area, A, is effectively interpreted as the maximum carrying capacity of the total stock of species, S, then (22.1) could reasonably be specified as a non-separable logistic function, that is,

$$\frac{\mathrm{d}S(t)}{\mathrm{d}t} = \dot{S} = G\left(S(t), A(t)\right) - y(t) = \alpha S(t)\left(A(t) - S(t)\right) - y(t).$$

Similarly, if it is assumed that land is still allocated through conversion, r, from habitat area and developed land, D, used to produce consumption goods, c, then the optimal allocation problem for the closed economy can be re-specified as

$$\mathrm{Max}_{y,r}\, W = \int_0^\infty \left[U(y, c, S) - w(S)y\right]e^{-\delta t}\mathrm{d}t$$

$$\text{subject to } \dot{S} = \alpha S(t)(A(t) - S(t)) - y(t),\ S(0) = S_0,\ \lim_{t\to\infty} S(t) \geq 0$$

$$\dot{A} = -r,\ A(0) = A_0$$

$$\dot{D} = r,\ D(0) = D_0$$

$$c = F(D),\ F' > 0,\ F'' < 0,$$

where r is now a control variable in the problem. Specifying μ and ξ as the costate variables for habitat area and developed land respectively, the following current value Hamiltonian and first order conditions result

$$H = U(y, F(D), S) - w(S)y + \lambda[\alpha S(A - S) - y] - \mu r + \xi r$$

$$\mathrm{d}H/\mathrm{d}y = U_y - w(S) - \lambda = 0 \text{ or } U_y = w(S) + \lambda$$

$$-\mathrm{d}H/\mathrm{d}S = \dot{\lambda} - \delta\lambda \text{ or } \dot{\lambda} = (\delta + 2\alpha S)\lambda - U_S + w'y$$

$$\mathrm{d}H/\mathrm{d}r = \xi - \mu = 0 \text{ or } \xi = \mu$$

$$-\mathrm{d}H/\mathrm{d}A = \dot{\mu} - \delta\mu \text{ or } \dot{\mu} = \delta\mu - \lambda\alpha S$$

$$-\mathrm{d}H/\mathrm{d}D = \dot{\xi} - \delta\xi, \text{ or } \dot{\xi} = \delta\xi - U_c F'.$$

The last three conditions can be combined with the first to derive $\lambda = U_y - w(S) = U_c\ F'/\alpha S$, that is, along the optimal trajectory, the marginal net benefits of harvesting an additional unit of the species stock must equal the net marginal costs of maintaining that unit. Utilizing this relationship and the remaining first order conditions, the equations of motion for the system are

$$\dot{y} = \frac{\delta\left(U_y - w(S)\right) + 2U_c F' + w'\left(\alpha S(A - S) - U_S\right)}{U_{yy}}$$

$$\dot{S} = \alpha S\ (A - S) - y$$

$$\dot{A} = -\dot{D} = -r.$$

Assuming as before that in equilibrium $\mathrm{d}y/\mathrm{d}t = \mathrm{d}S/\mathrm{d}t = r = 0$, the long run steady-state conditions are

$$\delta = \frac{-y^* w'\left(S^*\right) - 2U_c F'\left(D^*\right) + U_S\left(S^*\right)}{U_y\left(y^*\right) - w\left(S^*\right)} \quad \text{for } \dot{y} = \dot{S} = r = 0$$

$$G(S^*, A^*) = \alpha S^* (A^* - S^*) = y^* \text{ for } \dot{S} = r = 0.$$

Comparison with the equilibrium conditions (22.12) and (22.13) derived for the version of the model presented in the text indicates the similarity between the two sets of conditions. That is, Proposition 2 also holds for the above steady state; that is, in the closed economy the equilibrium total species stock, S^*, is determined by equating the social discount rate, δ, and bioeconomic returns net of the opportunity cost of habitat plus the non-consumptive value of biodiversity. Although not shown here, it is possible to demonstrate that the above equilibrium is locally stable in (S, y) space, and that a necessary requirement for stability is that the $\mathrm{d}y/\mathrm{d}t = 0$ curve is upward sloping and cuts the $\mathrm{d}S/\mathrm{d}t = 0$ from below. Similarly, it is also fairly straightforward to extend the above version of the model to verify Propositions 3 and 4 derived for the open economy model, although this is not attempted here.[15]

Notes

1. Chapter prepared for the European Association for Environmental and Resource Economics Sixth Annual Conference, Umeå, Sweden, 17–20 June 1995. We are grateful to comments provided by Rögnvaldur Hannesson, Charles Perrings and three anonymous referees; however, the usual disclaimer applies.
2. Barrett (1993) does not include the bioeconomic growth of the species stock or harvesting from this stock in his habits allocation model.
3. For example, the stock of species could be aggregated by the number of individuals in each distinct population or species. Alternatively, the total 'biomass' of each population or species could be aggregated across all species. Some form of 'weighted average' combination of the two approaches could also be employed.
4. It is possible that G_1 is aggregated from individual species' growth rates in some meaningful way, such as taking the weighted average of growth rates across all the species comprising the total species stock at time t. Alternatively, G_1 could be simply the observed aggregate growth rate of the total species stock at time t.
5. Precise estimation of the species–area curve has become an important – and controversial – issue in ecology, given the tendency to use such curves to predict species extinction associated with tropical deforestation. In particular, the value of β can have a significant impact on such estimates. For example, if β is assumed to be low (< 20 per cent), then the relationship predicts that more than 50 per cent of the land area can be deforested before additional deforestation results in rising rates of extinction. Conversely, at high values for β (> 60 per cent), extinction rates are almost proportional to deforestation rates. For further discussion see Lugo, Parotta and Brown (1993).
6. We ignore any windfall gain from the conversion.
7. Equation (22.7) includes the opportunity cost of land in the developed sector, and additionally, the assumption that the unit cost function, $w(S)$, represents the contribution of harvest to costs.
8. See WCMC (1992) for further discussion and summary of such global values.

9. Note that if $\psi < 0$ and $|\eta_2| < 1$ then (22.30) and (22.32) suggest that an international subsidy will still be preferred to a trade intervention so long as $pU_{22} > -(1 + \eta_2)U_2$. However, it is not necessary for ψ to be negative in order for a subsidy to be preferred to a trade intervention. For example, letting $\omega = f' U_{22}(-U_{11} - p^2U_{22})$, if $\psi > 0$ and $|\eta_2| > 1$ then a subsidy is still preferred if $\omega \geq \psi(1 + \eta_2)U_2$ and $\omega > \psi pU_{22}$. Similarly, if $\psi > 0$ and $|\eta_2| < 1$ then a subsidy is preferred if $\omega > \psi pU_{22}$.
10. We take advantage of the fact that at the equilibrium $G_1' dS_1^* = dy_1^*$.
11. It is fairly easy to show why this equilibrium condition for Case 2 is necessary to yield an upward-sloping $dy/dt = 0$ curve. In Case 2 if $-w'G_1(S) = -U_c f'$ then $\delta = G_1'$. It follows that $y_2^* = y_f = G_1(Sf)$. Alternatively, if $-w_1'(S) < -U_c f'$, then $\delta < G_1'$ and $S_2^* < S_f$ and $y_2^* < Y_f$. However, the result would be $-U_c f' \to \infty$, $S_2^* \to \underline{S}$ and $G_1(\underline{S}) = y = 0$. That is, there is complete conversion of habitat in the initial time period $t = 0$. Thus a necessary condition for an upward-sloping $dy/dt = 0$ curve is $-w'G_1(S) > -U_c f'$.
12. As in the previous note, for Case 3 if $-w'G_1(S) + U_S = -U_c f'$, then $\delta = G_1'$, and $y^* = y_f = G_1(Sf)$. Similarly, if $-w'G_1(S) + U_S < -U_c f'$, then $\delta < G_1'$, $S^* < S_f$ and $y^* < y_f$. However, as $-U_c f' \to \infty$, $S^* \to \underline{S}$ and $G_1(\underline{S}) = y = 0$, which again suggests complete conversion in the initial time period $t = 0$. Thus for Case 3 a necessary condition for an upward-sloping $dy/dt = 0$ curve is $-w'G_l(S) + U_S > -U_c f'$.
13. However, an additional restriction in both cases is that the numerator of the slope of the $dy/dt = dx/dt = 0$ curve must be negative and the denominator positive.
14. We are grateful to an anonymous referee for suggesting the following logistic function as an alternative non-separable version of the growth function $G(S, A)$. This referee raised doubts about the empirical relevance of the original specification of equation (22.1) in the text as a separable function, but also noted that 'this assumption does not materially affect the subsequent results'. We hope that the appendix goes some way towards illustrating this latter point.
15. For example, it is clear that the open economy model would simply add an additional equilibrium condition, $U_1(y^*, x^*) = pU_2(D^*, x^*)$ to those already derived in this appendix. The similarity with equilibrium conditions (22.25)–(22.27) is readily apparent.

References

Barbier, E.B. and B.A. Aylward (1996), 'Capturing the pharmaceutical value of biodiversity in a developing country', *Environmental and Resource Economics*, **8**, 157–81.

Barbier, E.B. and M. Rauscher (1994), 'Trade, tropical deforestation and policy interventions', *Environmental and Resource Economics*, **4**, 75–90.

Barbier, E.B., J.C. Burgess, J.T. Bishop and B.A. Aylward (1994), *The Economics of the Tropical Timber Trade*, London: Earthscan Publications.

Barbier, E.B., J.C. Burgess, T.M. Swanson and D.W. Pearce (1990), *Elephants, Economics and Ivory*, London: Earthscan Publications.

Barrett, S. (1993), 'Optimal economic growth and the conservation of biological diversity', in E.B. Barbier (ed.), *Economics and Ecology: New Frontiers and Sustainable Development*, London: Chapman & Hall.

Brown, G. and W. Henry (1993), 'The viewing value of elephants', in E.B. Barbier (ed.), *Economics and Ecology: New Frontiers and Sustainable Development*, London: Chapman & Hall.

Burgess, J.C. (1994), 'The environmental effects of trade in endangered species', *The Environmental Effects of Trade*, Paris: OECD.

Chichilnisky, G. (1994), 'North–South trade and the global environment', *American Economic Review*, **84**, 851–74.

Clark, C. (1976), *Mathematical Bioeconomics: The Optimal Management of Renewable Resources*, New York: John Wiley.

Dixon, J.A. and P. Sherman (1990), *Economics of Protected Areas: A New Look at Benefits and Costs*, London: Earthscan.

Holling, C.S., D.W. Schindler, B.W. Walker and J. Roughgarden (1995), 'Biodiversity in the functioning of ecosystems: an ecological primer and synthesis', in C. Perrings, K.-G. Mäler,

C. Folke, C.S. Holling and B.-O. Jansson (eds), *Biodiversity Loss: Ecological and Economic Issues*, Cambridge: Cambridge University Press.

International Institute for Environment and Development (IIED) (1994), *Whose Eden? An Overview of Community Approaches to Wildlife Management*, A Report to the UK Overseas Development Administration, London: IIED.

Kramer, R.A. (1993), 'Tropical forest protection in Madagascar', Paper prepared for Northeast Universities Development Consortium, Williams College, Massachusetts, October 15–16.

Lugo, A.E., J.A. Parrotta and S. Brown (1993), 'Loss of species caused by tropical deforestation and their recovery through management', *AMBIO*, **22** (2–3), 106–9.

Munasinghe, M. (1993), 'Environmental economics and biodiversity management in developing countries', *AMBIO*, **22** (2–3), 126–35.

Narain, U. and A.C. Fisher (1994), 'Modelling the value of biodiversity using a production function approach', in C. Perrings, K.-G. Mäler, C. Folke, B.-O. Jansson and C.S. Holling (eds), *Biodiversity Conservation: Policy Issues and Options*, Dordrecht: Kluwer Academic Publishers.

Ruitenbeek, H.J. (1989), *Social Cost–Benefit Analysis of the Korup Project, Cameroon*, Report prepared for the World Wide Fund for Nature and the Republic of Cameroon, London: WWF.

Schulz, C.-E. (1994), 'Trade policy and ecology', mimeo., Department of Economics, NFH, University of Tromsø, Norway.

Swanson, T.M. (1994), 'The economics of extinction revisited and revised: a generalized framework for the analysis of the problems of endangered species and biodiversity losses', *Oxford Economic Papers*, **46**, 800–21.

Swanson, T.M. and E.B. Barbier (eds) (1992), *Economics for the Wilds: Wildlife, Wildlands, Diversity and Development*, London: Earthscan Publications.

Tobias, D. and R. Mendelsohn (1990) 'Valuing ecotourism in a tropical rain-forest reserve', *AMBIO*, **20** (2), 91–3.

Wells, M.P. and K.E. Brandon (1992), *People and Parks: Linking Protected Area Management with Local Communities*, Washington, DC: The World Bank.

World Conservation Monitoring Centre (WCMC) (1992), *Global Biodiversity: Status of the Earth's Living Resources*, London: Chapman & Hall.

Index